BORN TO
NEW ZEALAND

BORN TO NEW ZEALAND

A Biography of Jane Maria Atkinson

FRANCES PORTER

Allen & Unwin/
Port Nicholson Press

*Published with the
assistance of the
Alexander Turnbull
Library Endowment
Trust*

First published in 1989 by Allen & Unwin New Zealand Limited in
association with the Port Nicholson Press, Private Bag,
Wellington, New Zealand.

Allen & Unwin Australia Pty Ltd, NCR House, 8 Napier St, North Sydney,
NSW 2059, Australia.

Unwin Hyman Ltd, Broadwick House, 15–17 Broadwick St, Soho, London W1,
England.

Allen & Unwin Inc., 8 Winchester Place, Winchester, Massachusetts 01890,
USA.

ISBN 0 4614 008 5

Cover design by Neysa Moss
Typeset by Saba Graphics Ltd, New Zealand
Printed by Southwood Press, Australia

CONTENTS

Acknowledgements

I am indebted first of all to members of the Atkinson clan at York Bay for their friendliness and helpfulness towards an interloper who wished to embark on a biography of one of their ancestors and, in doing so, to explore the network of relationships within the Richmond, Atkinson and Hursthouse families who settled here last century. The late Alison Atkinson's memory reached back to the second generation of 'the mob'; Jinny Atkinson, Tudor Atkinson and Ann Paterson freely made available their collections of manuscript, photos, paintings and drawings. They read much typescript and were always encouraging. Elsie Crompton-Smith allowed me to use her collection of Stephenson Smith, S. Percy Smith and Hursthouse papers.

Ron Lambert, Director of the Taranaki Museum, and Ian Matheson, Parliamentary Librarian, gave me permission to reproduce J.C. Richmond drawings held in their respective libraries. Dawn Smith, Librarian of the Nelson Provincial Museum, responded with alacrity to all my requests. My good friends Nan Taylor and Ilse Jacoby patiently read and advised.

The bulk of the primary sources are housed in the collections of the Alexander Turnbull Library, Wellington, and most of my research took place when that library was in the process of moving from one building to another. Nothing, however, disrupted the competent and courteous service provided by its staff. I can only acknowledge and endorse the Turnbull Library's reputation for nurturing scholarship.

Frances Porter
Wellington 1989

THE MOB

Richmonds

Maria (*Lely*) Richmond née Wilson (1791–1872), mother of:
Christopher *William* (1821–95), married Emily Elizabeth Atkinson (1829–1906)

       Children Mary Elizabeth (1853)
                  Anna Wilson (1855)
                  Margaret (1857)
                  Christopher Francis (*Kit*) (1859)
                  Alfred (1862)
                  Alice (1863)
                  Robert Richardson (1865)
                  Edward Thomas (1867)
                  Emily (1869)

James Crowe (1822–98), married Mary Smith (1834–65)

       Children Ann Elizabeth (*Alla*) (1858)
                  Maurice Wilson (1860)
                  Dorothy Kate (*Dolla*) (1861)
                  Richard Hutton (1863)
                  James Wilson (*Wilsie*) (1865)

Jane *Maria* (1824–1914), married Arthur Samuel Atkinson (1833–1902)

       Children Margaret (1856; died at birth)
                  Edith Emily (*Edie*) (1858)
                  Ruth (1861)
                  Arthur Richmond (1863)
                  Alice *Mabel* (1864)

Henry Robert (1829–90), married Mary *Blanche* Hursthouse (1840–64)

       Children Helen (1859; died in infancy)
                  Robert (1861; died in infancy)
                  Francis William (1863)
                  Maria *Blanche* (1864)
                      married Emma Jane Parris (1845–1921)
       Children Beatrice Jane (*Busy Bee*) (1873)
                  Rachel Mary (1876)
                  Howard Parris (1878)

Atkinsons

William Smith (1826–74), married Eliza Ronalds (1840–1915)
> Children William Edmund (*Willie*, later *Billa*) (1860)
> Janet (1863; died in infancy)
> Esther (1864)
> John (1865; died in infancy)
> Beatrix (*Trix*) (1872)
> Philip Basil (*Buff*) (1873)
> Kenneth Walter (1874)
> Baby (1876; died in infancy)

Emily Elizabeth (1829–1906), married C.W. Richmond *qv*

Harry Albert (1831–92), married Amelia *Jane* Skinner (1831–65)
> Children Harry *Dunstan* (1857)
> Edmund *Tudor* (1859)
> Frances Elizabeth (*Fanny*) (1861)
> Alfred Charles (1863)
> > married Annie Smith (1838–1919), sister

of Mary (married to J.C. Richmond) *qv*
> Children Theodora (1870; died in infancy)
> Samuel *Arnold* (1874)
> Alice *Lucy* (1876)
> Harry Temple (1880)

Arthur Samuel (1833–1902), married Jane *Maria* Richmond *qv*

Decimus (1836–84), married Marion (*Polly*) Ronalds (1829–90)
> Children Hugh *Ronald* (1863)
> Frank Wilson (1864; died in infancy)
> Arnold *Hugh* (1863)
> Harry Albert (1867)
> John Staines (1869)
> Edmund Greg (*Ned*) (1873)

Alice (1840–63)

Hursthouses

Helen Hursthouse née Wilson (1803–95), sister of *Lely* Richmond
qv, married John Hursthouse (1811–60)
> Children Helen Maria (*Nellie*) (1838)
> Mary *Blanche* (1839) (m. H.R. Richmond *qv*)
> Charles *Wilson* (1841)
> Kate Emma (1843)
> Richmond (1845)

Flinders (1848)
(Charles Hursthouse (1781–1854), father-in-law of Helen, and
Mary Hursthouse, a younger daughter (1822–1898), came to New
Plymouth with the Stephenson Smith party in 1849. Charles
Flinders Hursthouse, brother of John, was not a member of the
mob.)

Wilsons

Maria (*Lely*) Richmond and Helen Hursthouse were the daughters
of William and Jane Maria Wilson, and aunts of Calvert and
Charlie Wilson.

Ronalds

Frank, Hugh, and James Ronalds, who emigrated to Taranaki in
1853, established Denby Farm adjacent to Hurworth. Their sisters,
Eliza and Marion (Polly), who came out in 1856, married W.S.
Atkinson *qv* and Decimus Atkinson respectively.

Stephenson Smiths

Hannah Hursthouse (1813–1891), married John Stephenson Smith
(1811–1874)

Children Stephenson Percy (1840)
Norah Mary (1842)
Ida Ann (1844)
Frank (1846)
Harry (1848)
Nina (1851)
Ella Maria (1853?)
Dora Isabel (1859)

Fells

Charles Yates (1844–1918), married Edith Atkinson
Walter (1855–1932), married Margaret Richmond

Non-family members

William Crow, James Brind, Edward (*Teddo*) Patten, Robert
Pitcairn

CHAPTER ONE

A Modest Competence

London and the Hautes Pyrenees, 1840-43

Argelès, France, 12 June 1842

BURN THIS AT ONCE

You will be surprised to learn that you are likely to see Mamma and Maria almost immediately as circumstances have occurred here which render such a step most advisable, nay absolutely necessary. Mr Dupré has become most strongly attached to Maria & has proposed for her. Her sense of duty has led her to refuse him, but it is a sacrifice which has cost her much & Argellez wo^d seem a wilderness to her now & she must have a change of scene. Just at the crisis a letter from Aunt Helen arrived which informed us of the delay in her departure [for New Zealand]. This was a strong additional reason for Mamma's wishing to quit Argellez – *it must go for the sole reason with our friends.* (C.W. Richmond to his brother, J.C. Richmond[1])

An *affaire de coeur* when she was eighteen has to serve as an introduction to Jane Maria Richmond.[2] It does at least set the scene of offended Victorian proprieties – the man was French and therefore viewed with suspicion as an adventurer, and Maria, following in the best tradition of Victorian womanhood, was prepared to sacrifice the ardour of an attachment for filial duty. William was equally prepared to shield his sister from taunts or whisperings from Yorkshire aunts and uncles who had already expressed doubts about the wisdom of living, even temporarily, in France. Let into the secret, however, was Marcella Nugent, a schooldays' friend of Maria, now a governess. Marcella's reply to Maria's mother, Lely, is marvellously expressive of the predicament in which girls of Maria's class could find themselves when delicacy of feeling and innocence of motive (or at least what was interpreted as such) became entwined in the toil of male passion:

To think that my own dear sensible strong minded Maria should fall a victim to that misery-giving passion; to think that she who used to be so happy so innocent & pure should be made to swell the number of the unhappy, was more than I could ever have been prepared for. Yes, you were right to confide in me . . . and all that a friend can do, situated as I am, shall not be left untried & unthought of. My first desire is to discuss how to screen Maria from the comments & cruel remarks of others. In the first place let your confidence go no further than myself at present, at least I mean in England. I cannot bear to think of the noble minded Maria becoming an object of pity and private discussion among her acquaintances whether among the Squad [northern relatives] or elsewhere . . . My opinion of the French as friends is great . . . my opinion of them in the more intimate relations of life such as Lovers, Husbands or Wives is not worth having it is so low . . . It is seldom I ever speak so openly where my opinions are concerned – but there they are!! Pouf!![3]

It is a spirited letter. Reading it, it is difficult to believe that Maria had not actually been compromised but had simply been proposed for in a perfectly proper way – through an approach to Lely – by the respected doctor of a small town in the Pyrenees. Furthermore, why, if Maria was 'sensible' and 'strong minded', 'happy and innocent', should there have been so much fuss? The Victorian code for relations with the opposite sex put a young girl of refinement in an awkward position. As a contributor to *A Chaplet for Charlotte Yonge* stated:

In the first place modesty forbade her to set her heart on anyone who had not first made clear his preference, but in the second place it was considered mercenary of her to marry for anything but love; and yet if she saw enough of the young man to find out if she loved him or not, she was probably regarded as having encouraged his advances. The girl was supposed to be innocent and ignorant of the whole business until the young man proposed, or his attentions at least became marked, and after that she must leap to it, and do some very decisive thinking indeed.[4]

The upshot was that Maria and Lely did not return to London forthwith but remained in Argelès with William until the beginning of 1843. Monsieur Dupré continued to be friendly, within the bounds of propriety, and continued to write to Lely hoping Maria was not 'entirely indifferent'. Doing her duty apparently cast a shadow over Maria, who was generally described as despondent.

The episode is important. Not only does it provide a cameo of some aspects of Victorian manners but it is also the first glimpse, albeit as a passive character, of Maria Richmond. There are no earlier surviving letters from her and indeed there are few family

letters before the Richmonds' sojourn in France. The extant sources
for the early years are mainly in brief notes compiled by the family
when a biography of Sir Harry Atkinson was contemplated towards
the end of the century (these deal more with Atkinsons than
Richmonds) and even more modest notes in 'Family Letters of the
Richmonds and Atkinsons 1824–62', compiled and edited about 1930
by Mary and Emily Richmond, daughters of C.W. Richmond. From
these sources and possibly from personal recollections to which
Dr Guy Scholefield had access in his editing of the *Richmond–Atkinson
Papers* (1960) come the following few facts.

Jane *Maria* Richmond, named after her grandmother, Jane Maria
Wilson of Norton near Stockton-on-Tees, was born on 15 September
1824. Her father, Christopher Richmond, was a barrister of the
Middle Temple, London, who had married, on 14 October 1819,
Maria Wilson (known as Lely within her family), daughter of
William, a merchant of Stockton-on-Tees, and Jane Maria Wilson.
Some years later, on 24 January 1837, Lely's younger sister, Helen,
who had been governess to the children of Charles and Mary
Hursthouse, married John, their eldest son. This union was the
first of subsequent intermarriages between Richmonds, Hursthouses,
and Atkinsons which begat 'the mob' who settled in and about
New Plymouth during the 1840s and 1850s.

Lely's husband died in 1832, leaving his widow, aged forty-one,
with a modest competence derived mainly from property rents,
and four young children: William (10), James (9), Maria (7), and
Henry (2). Two other children, including a daughter, Fanny, had
died in infancy. It was an unenviable position. Lely was not poverty
stricken – she was able to afford a general servant – but with
four children to educate, in the boys' case for the professions, she
now belonged to what Edward Gibbon Wakefield called the 'anxious
classes'. The economic condition of England during the 1830s and
1840s was not encouraging. By the mid-thirties the trade boom
of a decade before had broken, but the population boom had not.
Unemployment was rife, particularly among the professional and
trading classes. Lely, moreover, had an additional problem. William
was a delicate child who suffered severely from asthma, as did
Lely herself. However, far from agreeing with Mrs Sarah Stickney
Ellis, whose books *Women of England, Daughters of England, Wives
of England*, and *Mothers of England* were found on the bookshelves
of most middle-class households and held that in unpropitious
circumstances a woman's highest duty was 'to suffer and be still',
Lely managed her slender resources both to ensure her children's

adequate schooling and to enable her family to have frequent changes of air for the sake of William's health. Arranging for one such 'change', she wrote to Charles Hursthouse, father-in-law of her sister, Helen, for his help in finding a house to rent in Norwich: 'Economy is the order of the day,' she stated firmly.[5] She was not without family advisers. Her husband's brother, Thomas Richmond, administered the estate; James Crowe, a great-uncle and a solicitor of Stockton-on-Tees, became guardian of the family and paid for William's legal education; her brother-in-law, H.R.E. Wright, and her numerous Wilson relatives from Stockton, Witton-le-Wear, Norton, Norwich, and Durham admonished and cautioned as relatives in such situations generally do.

Fortunately, Lely was a woman of more than ordinary intellectual stature and stamina. Widely read, she encouraged her children to be so, and to keep abreast of contemporary thought in religion, art, and politics. While William was in France awaiting the arrival of Lely and Maria, he asked his mother to bring a selection of poetry books. But then, discarding his suggested list, he exclaimed: 'Bring me what you please. I can't recommend you books, you duck, that have read The Deserted Village & "passing rich with £40 a year" & all the poetry in the world.'[6] The evening circle for family reading and discussion became the accepted custom in the Richmond household, and visiting friends and cousins were always drawn in. There was an easy familiarity within the family; Lely was seldom referred to as 'mother', nor was her manner towards her children that of a *materfamilias*. She and William shared the headship of the family companionably. Still in her forties when the children were growing up, she was not without suitors, and her refusal shows a certain independence of spirit in an age when marriage was seen as the only guarantee of a woman's status. One such suitor was R.T. Maxon, a financial adviser who also acted as Lely's rent collector. After his wife's death he made a preliminary advance. 'So poor Mr Maxon is a widower at last,' wrote Helen to her sister, 'but don't have him honey, he is so fat and dirty.'[7]

Bolstering independence of spirit and stimulating independence of mind was the family's religious belief – although 'way of thinking' rather than 'belief' might better express it. The Richmonds, the Wilsons, the Hursthouses, and Maria's great friend, Margaret Taylor, were Unitarians. In an age of religious revivals ranging from the godly fervour and often mawkish sentimentality of the Evangelicals to the spiritual ardour and ceremonial piety of the Tractarians, Unitarians were people with feet firmly planted on this earth. As the name indicates, Unitarians rejected the divinity of Christ, seeing him only as the perfect man, and believed that in nature and in scripture there is evidence of but one uncompounded God. Rejecting also the orthodox view of humanity's essential depravity, Unitarians firmly proclaimed that religion was not to do with revelation but with morality. It was not on credal statements or on arcane rituals that Unitarians took their stand, but on the moral consciousness of humankind:

> It is essential to our faith that it should be rational, developing no inherent inconsistencies and asking no refuge in mystery; that it should be moral, giving emphasis to duty in man and attributing even-handed justice to the administration of God; that it should be enlightened, able to bear itself creditably in the presence of our foremost knowledge.[8]

Lely, when she thought some Unitarian 'big-wigs' were too hesitant in their support of certain gifted individuals among their younger brethren, showed her own unequivocal stand: 'I confess myself wholly fearless as to the results of the most perfect freedom of enquiry.'[9]

As a way of thinking, Unitarianism was demanding; as a religion it was tough. There was little room for the solace of trust and resignation. Truth was to be searched for; morality and duty were to be discerned in every human situation. Sometimes in the letters of Maria and her brothers one can see that the demands of morality and duty exacted a price, but for an educated family living in some financial stress and with an uncertain future, they were stars to steer by.

Suitable openings for gentleborn sons of the mid-nineteenth century tended to be restricted to the church or to the bar, and the Unitarian ministry held a strong attraction for William, Lely's eldest. But although Lely was later to write, 'William has never quite abandoned all thoughts of the ministry',[10] there were strong reasons for his turning instead to the legal profession. His lawyer great-uncle was willing to pay for his education, and, following in his father's footsteps, William could hope to retain some of his clients. He would, however, have perfectly understood and sympathised with one of Charlotte Yonge's characters who complained of having to go to the bar: 'It somehow always gave him a thwarted injured feeling of working against the grain.'[11] Throughout his life William sought opportunities to retreat from both law and politics so that he could wander at will where his interests really lay – in the field of metaphysics.

William had not come well through the winter of 1840. His asthma attacks had increased and Lely decided that a reading–walking–sketching holiday in the French Pyrenees would be beneficial. By April 1841 William was living as a recluse in the fashionable winter health resort of Pau. He was prepared to enjoy living frugally but as the weeks went by asceticism, for a man of twenty, began to seem dull. He made little attempt to find congenial company, rather despising the 'watering place acquaintances' and the 'rich English in their carriages doing a deal in the dressing and staring way'.[12] Wrapped in his noticeably English but badly cut overcoat, he felt by turns 'excessively poetical and excessively misanthropical'.[13] He was homesick; he was seldom without a cold; he was not eating enough. In London, Lely became increasingly worried, and determined, although it meant leaving James, to take Maria and Henry with her and join William. By September 1841 they were all in lodgings at Argelès, a small town south-west of Pau in the Hautes Pyrenees. With their London house let and the cost of living much less in France, there were obvious financial advantages in the move, but 'the squad' (Marcella Nugent's term for the northern relatives) was dubious. What of Henry's morals, and would not 'our own sweet simple-minded honest-hearted English Maria become Frenchified?'[14] To the former objection William replied that Henry would be more exposed to vice at London University College School than in France. And he was, too, prepared to further his brother's and sister's education. Maria was apparently letting her imagination run riot in 'vines & snow covered mountains & rushing torrents & sylvan retreats & all manner of lusciousness'.[15] This William tempered with arithmetic and French. With Henry, aged twelve, he read Cicero, Euclid, and Seneca.

Of all the Richmonds at this time, Henry appears as the most unperturbable. He also seems to have borne with equanimity the nickname of 'The Childe' bestowed on him by his family. In addition to the solid reading which William prescribed, he spent his time botanising, collecting specimens, and bird watching. Maria later described him as 'a curious creature. He is not formed for enjoying life very greatly, at any rate in youth, he is more reserved about his feelings than any of us.'[16] Reserve was probably a natural defence for the youngest member of a talented but mercurial family. For the time being and particularly during the Dupré affair, Henry's staid presence was a positive asset.

Anxiety about William's health and the financial advantages to be derived from living in France were possibly not the only reasons for Lely's decision to quit London. At eighteen Maria was a personable young woman, and suitors were beginning to gather. Sam Clegg, one of James's engineering friends, 'fell in love with Maria's nose', wrote Marcella Nugent, who also acted as go-between for a 'poor Mr Johnson'. She thought him generous and kind and was sure he would get on in the world, but he was also a diminutive man and this, he thought, might have damaged his chances – 'was he the object for the finger of mockery and the titter of young ladies?',[17] he inquired of Marcella. She assured him that Maria and Lely were 'too high minded to consider his size'. Lely (and one feels sure William would concur) wished to keep Maria free for the time being. Again there is no response from Maria.

The Richmonds' *pension* at Argelès was comfortable and the society, less dashing than at Pau, was more agreeable. There were the five Miss Shannons, émigrées from Ireland, and there was, at the beginning at least, the companionship of the local doctor – 'our dear friend Monsieur Dupré'. Marcella Nugent, fretting under the restraints and boredom of governessing, hoped to join them, but on her terms:

> Do you suppose . . . that I am going to stay for a few weeks in the Pyrenees and sit down all the time as meekly and quietly to eat my breakfast and dinner as your monotonous gentry of Argellez? Not a bit of it – I shall get me a mule and a long skirt and . . . I shall cross the Pyrenees . . . It will be something new & something exciting & do Maria good. I wish you all to sit down gravely and study the history of Spain – particularly the North – that we may lose nothing.[18]

Unfortunately this expedition did not eventuate and the even tenor of reading, walking, 'calling', and attending *soirées* was disturbed only by the sacrifices implicit in unrequited love, and by letters from James.

Still in England, and most gloomily so, was Lely's second son, James Crowe Richmond. J.C. Richmond is now remembered as a watercolour painter, and it was an artist's career that he wanted when, in 1839, at the age of seventeen, he left the school attached to London University College. But an artist's life needed an assured private income, and that he did not have. Instead James apprenticed himself as a designer to the well-known civil engineer, Samuel Clegg. This should have been the beginning of a successful career, for if opportunity was lacking in the 'gentlemanly professions', technical advances made possible by the burgeoning economic power of coal and iron meant that there were exciting prospects for bright young engineers, especially if they were, like James, interested in railway design. However, Samuel Clegg, in association with Jacob Samuda, was chiefly involved with an abortive, if ingenious, method of propelling railway trains by atmospheric pressure alone. James Richmond was an enthusiast, and he was prepared to give himself without stint to the design of railway engines – 'O that I had regular and useful employment & how I do love my profession and how hard I would work in it,'[19] he wrote. But hope constantly deferred over the atmospheric railway's prospects, and growing dissatisfaction with the spasmodic tuition he was getting from Samuel Clegg, induced a sort of frenzied melancholy. He sang madrigals; he joined in the Anti Corn Law demonstrations; he became a Chartist and a member of the Young Men's Antimonopoly Society; he painted and sold a watercolour at an Anti Corn Law bazaar. Even in the smoky murk of St Pancras where he lived and of the Isle of Dogs where he worked, he saw beauty with a painter's eye: 'Yesterday was one of the clearest days I ever saw. The air was as if regenerated . . . The purity was the point, it was in fact quite Italian. I don't know what you see in Argélès but I could hardly stand anything more lovely.'[20] Nothing, however, dispelled his low spirits. 'Oh that cursed Atmospheric,' William wrote from France, 'it will be the death of James.'[21]

James was frequently in love but not adept in women's company. Margaret Clegg, Ann Shaen, Marcella Nugent, and a young cousin, Ann Richmond, all excited his admiration. 'Upon my word it's very dreary to have such creatures as she [Ann Shaen] flash across your eyes making you conscious of the darkness surrounding you without stopping long enough to do anything towards dispelling it,' he lamented.[22] Marcella Nugent noted, 'I saw James two evenings – he fell over a chair & tore his coat in hurried service of Miss Clegg and then talked of cutting his throat.'[23] On another occasion when he was alone with Marcella she commented, 'He only looked volumes – you know what folios and quartos he can look.'[24] His Norwich relatives couldn't make him out at all. Uncle Wright thought him rash and lacking any interest in his profession. Aunt Helen Hursthouse, more easily pleased, wrote to Lely, 'Dear James – I like him very much but how odd he is.'[25]

James badly missed his family. His letters to his mother are as unrestrained and voluble as if written to a contemporary. After walking about in the pouring rain all day without a coat because he was convinced he was dying, he wrote to Lely, 'What would

you have said if one letter having informed you of my perfect
health, another had brought intelligence that my body was in the
ground?'[26] Lely was used to her self-dramatising son, but as each
succeeding letter intimated that James was becoming 'queerer and
queerer', and as William's cousin, Robert Richmond, had joined
William and Henry on a walking tour of the Pyrenees, Lely resolved
to return to England with Maria. She suggested to James that he
come to Paris to meet them.

During February and March 1843, Lely and Maria stayed at a
Paris *pension* in company with people of varying nationalities. James
enjoyed hugely the time he spent there with them, and, sporting
whiskers, was even more extravagantly mannered than in England.
He spoke French all the time to Maria and Lely, and attended
the opera, *soirées*, and a masked ball. At the ball he wore his normal
clothes and 'supported his character so well that as soon as he
made his appearance there were loud vociferations of L'Anglais
L'Anglais on all sides'.[27] Lely was much admired by a Russian general
and Maria by a pleasant young Norwegian who wished to call
on them in London: 'what will he think of our obscure nutshell,'
Lely commented. Maria accompanied James on a round of
sightseeing and found it tiring: 'Pleasure hunting is very hard work
& too great a responsibility for my taste but I suppose we shall
enjoy the remembrance when we are peaceably at home . . . [I
am] haunted with the fear of not seeing half that should be seen.'[28]

Then, rather devastatingly, Monsieur Dupré turned up in Paris.
He and William had both farewelled Lely and Maria from Argelès
but, possibly tormented by the thought that Maria was about to
leave France, Dupré came on in pursuit. He was still very much
in love – as it would seem Maria was with him – but, wrote
Lely, 'she sees his faults, knows his sanguine nature & can understand
how he might deceive himself.'[29] Dupré called at the *pension* but
Lely was not at home to him.

By 15 April 1843, Lely, Maria, and James were back at 56 Burton
Street, St Pancras, London. 'How lovely the valley must have
looked,' Maria wrote to William, who was still at Argelès, 'how
lovely Burton St didn't.'[30] After the pure air of the Pyrenees (Paris
seems to have made no lasting impression), London's smoke and
dinginess were deadly to their lungs and spirits and they yearned
for that 'loveliest and most romantic of valleys'. But as Lely
philosophically wrote:

> streams, rocks, trees and mountains are not all that we mortals
> require to make us happy . . . Employment and the stir of the

world are necessary for young people, and our first object being accomplished in the improved health of my son William, I shall be glad to see my children pursuing their occupations at home again.[31]

CHAPTER
TWO

'Uncertainties & scheming'

London, 1842–50

It was the imminent departure of Lely's sister, Helen Hursthouse, for New Zealand in 1842 which was to have provided the excuse for the return of Lely and Maria from France. Helen's husband, John Hursthouse, was employed in the Norwich corn and timber trade. It was a family business managed by his uncles in which he took little interest and did not see his future. One of the firm's branches was at Beccles, a short distance from Norwich, where John's brother-in-law, John Stephenson Smith,[1] was employed. In 1836 John Hursthouse's younger brother, Charles Flinders, sailed to North America to test out the possibilities of either Canada or the United States for a family settlement. Five years later his future brother-in-law, Dr William Stanger,[2] went as doctor and geologist with the African Civilisation Society's expedition which penetrated 320 miles up the Niger River and attempted to establish a farm settlement. Stanger, who survived the fever which took a heavy toll amongst the expedition, returned to England in January 1842, and became adviser to the kin group on all practical matters related to the outfitting of emigrants. Charles Flinders Hursthouse also returned. He rejoined his brother in Norwich but could find no regular or suitable employment there.

Both he and John Hursthouse were attracted to Edward Gibbon Wakefield's scheme of 'systematic colonisation'. Wakefield saw the gentry, to whom the Hursthouses – although in reduced circumstances – belonged, as a most valuable class of emigrants. Nor was he in doubt about their material prospects:

> They may become landowners in the colony, or owners of capital lent at interest, or farmers of their own land, merchants, clergymen, lawyers or doctors, so that they may be respectable people in the sense of being honourable, of cultivated mind, and gifted with the

right sort, and right proportion of self respect.[3]

Mrs Micawber put the position of aspiring colonial gentry more firmly:

> 'I wish Mr Micawber to stand upon that vessel's prow and say, "Enough of delay: enough of disappointment: enough of limited means. That was in the old country. This is the new. Produce your reparation. Bring it forward." '[4]

There was something of Micawber in John Hursthouse's character. A legacy from his grandfather towards the end of 1841 provided the means to emigrate, and from that time on he thought of little else. He was quite confident that he would supplement his income from farming by surveying, although in neither of these occupations had he any experience. He spent the early part of 1842 making sea chests and building a row boat. Nor was he apprehensive about the sea voyage to the Antipodes, the longest and most arduous of all the emigration routes. Like Micawber he was willing to see it as 'merely crossing'. 'John Hursthouse,' James Richmond reported in 1841, 'is agog about New Zealand.'

His wife, Helen, was not so sure. 'I cannot tell you how I feel at the approaching *awful step* of my life,'[5] she wrote to Lely. And she was not consoled by her husband's brimming confidence, believing him *'almost too happy at the prospect of emancipation. I wish I could be more sure he is not too sanguine.'*[6] But as her lot was cast so she was determined to see it through in the best spirit possible. 'Poor darling Helen' was the expressed reaction of her relatives; 'as she had brewed so must she bake,' wrote her brother.[7]

The Hursthouse party of John, Helen, Charles Flinders, three young children, and a Norwich friend, John Newbegin, left Gravesend in the *Thomas Sparks* on 1 August 1842. Lely was still in France, so James Richmond was at the docks to see his aunt and her family off: 'Aunt Helen kept up very well to the last,' he wrote.[8] Her younger sister, Catherine Wilson, advised Lely:

> Our darling lost Helen sailed on the 1st. Blanche & Baby were *both* poorly – she had engaged a servant & was tolerably pleased with her – much pleased with the Capt – but horrid to relate the ship, tho' beautiful, was discovered to be swarming with bugs. She left in tolerable spirits.[9]

That word 'tolerable' carried many Victorian women through domestic drudgery, through pregnancy and infant mortality, and through changes of fortune over which they had little control. Fortitude and resilience shine through it, but the word also expresses a kind of resignation to the vicissitudes of womanhood.

The voyage out was eventful. On entering Table Bay, Cape Town, the ship struck a rock and was nearly wrecked. For two months the passengers had to stay in Cape Town while it was repaired. When the voyage resumed, the gales of the Roaring Forties were fearful, especially to Helen, and even John Hursthouse observed that 'if the weather we have experienced since leaving the Cape be a fair specimen of mid-summer in 40 South then winter must be cruel indeed'.[10] Nor was the captain as congenial or as confidence-inspiring as they had first thought. He was, Helen wrote home, 'a bullying ill-tempered man, occasionally *getting tipsy* & when tipsy almost mad.'[11] She and John advised any who might follow them to be more careful about selecting a captain than a vessel. When at last the *Thomas Sparks* entered Port Nicholson heads on 31 January 1843, it was then accidentally rammed by a following brig. This time the ship suffered no major damage and 'we went up to Wellington in grand style with colors and Ensign flying'.[12]

John Hursthouse had intended to buy land at Wellington but a 'glowing' account of Taranaki, combined with the fact that his friend, John Wicksteed, had been appointed New Zealand Company agent at New Plymouth, persuaded him to settle his family there. On 7 April 1843 the Hursthouses landed from a coastal schooner at New Plymouth to be met by the Wicksteeds. Within a fortnight Hursthouse had rented a temporary house for six shillings a week – 'rather crowded but will do well' – and bought a Company section near the town with a good road to it. His brother bought a smaller section nearby. Helen's chief joy was that her piano 'proved to our great surprise to be nearly in the same trim as when we left England'.

In one of Maria Richmond's early Taranaki letters she qualifies her enthusiasm for colonial life by adding:

> But imagine a delicate woman coming out, unable to get a servant to stay with her, half killed with work & unable to tear thro' the bush as I do, what an utterly different feeling she wd. have; there wd. be no poetry for her in N.Z. all wd. be wearisome horrible prose.[13]

During her early life in New Plymouth, Helen Hursthouse was possibly such a one. She made no complaint, and she was not delicate – 'never been fatter', wrote her somewhat unperceptive and less than industrious husband. But the coarseness, the isolation, the monotony of domestic toil took a toll. Unlike Maria she took no satisfaction in baking bread or making butter. James and Henry

Richmond described their aunt as haggard and careworn when they arrived at New Plymouth at the end of March 1851. In their early years her family was nearly destitute. John Hursthouse, like many others, planted wheat on his cleared land. It grew well the first year but there was no market for surplus, subsequent yields declined, and he became less and less interested in farming. 'I have wept, yes often, when my children cried out for bread,'[14] Helen wrote to her father-in-law. Grazing sheep and raising pigs turned out to be more profitable, but it was not until John Hursthouse took out an auctioneer's licence that the family's fortunes improved. This meant, however, that he spent most of his time in New Plymouth township where he was a popular figure, particularly in the town's taverns, while Helen and the children ran the farm.[15] S. Percy Smith in his *Reminiscences* describes his first meeting with his cousins at the end of 1849:

> As Aunt Helen and I went up the Carrington Road we met a girl dressed in dungaree who turned out to be my cousin Helen Hursthouse . . . I thought 'How poor these people must be to dress like that.' When we got to the house I met my other cousins, Blanche, Wilson, Richmond & Kate, then a baby, all dressed in dungaree.[16]

Blanche was her mother's mainstay. Helen regretted that although she could ill afford to lose her from the house, she was unable, even eight years after their arrival, to find the six guineas per year which would have enabled Blanche to have a 'plain English education': 'It seems hard after so many years of fag not to be able to spare so small a sum'.[17]

In contrast to Maria's long, exuberant letters from New Plymouth, Helen's more meagre correspondence describes her life as taxing, monotonous, and stultifying. 'I can scarcely find anything to say in a letter and have almost forgotten how to write,' she said. Helen's different circumstances – young children, a marriage that gave 'little peace of mind and much anxiety', financial worry, even the fact that she was ten years older than Maria, probably imposed too great a burden. Perhaps it was simply a difference in readiness and response, the one seeing only mud, rough dwellings, fire-blackened tree stumps, the different and the indifferent; the other, while aware of the mud and the stumps, able to appreciate the fern-clad banks of the Te Henui, the immensity of the bush, the soaring majesty of Mt Taranaki, and, above all, the opportunities for living a different sort of life. Maria discovered New Zealand to be 'home'; for Helen it was a hard, demanding, and perhaps always an alien land.

In 1846 Lely left the smoke and bustle of 56 Burton Street and took a long lease of 'Springholm', at Merton, on the outskirts of Wimbledon. Surrounded by garden, fruit trees, and adjacent meadows, with the nearest neighbour almost a mile away, it was effectively in the country, although the family was still able to travel by horse-drawn omnibus to the Carter Lane Unitarian chapel,[18] Ludgate Hill, where the minister was their close friend, Dr Joseph Hutton. The only drawback Maria saw in such a relatively large house was the necessity for servants. Under the reign of Eliza Moss, the cook-general, the house became 'frightfully disorderly'. Eliza also had 'callers'. 'She has been receiving male visits several times a week, & what is worse, has told lies frequently to conceal that the youth was her friend.'[19] In this instance at least Maria conformed completely with the mores of her time.

It was not the servant question, however, but concern for 'the boys'' prospects in England which became an almost obsessive worry to Maria. In her now numerous letters she seemed always prepared to subdue her own quest for self-fulfilment provided that William, James, and Henry were usefully and happily employed. At the top of her list was James, and James was no great help to himself. He had left Clegg and Samuda's service about 1845 and joined the staff of the famous Victorian engineer, Isambard Kingdom Brunel. Brunel, too, was interested in the atmospheric railway and was using it on the South Devon line based at Dawlish. The stuttering career of the atmospheric came to a stormy end in September 1848 when irate shareholders forced Brunel to abandon it. 'I wake every morning,' Maria wrote that same month, when she and Lely were staying near Dawlish, 'fearing to hear a nasty puffing screaming locomotive tearing along the quiet beach.'[20] The shareholders' decision made no great difference to James, who had already determined to quit.

One of the attractions New Zealand was to hold for James was its potential for varied pursuits: 'The dearth of men to fill the multitude of our offices here makes great fun at times.'[21] But there was no fun in England, and having James alternately 'merry and foolish', almost too merry and foolish for William's taste, and 'sinking into a torpor of soul' was tiresome.[22] Apart from his abiding interest in painting, at which he was always willing to work, unemployment simply increased his inclination to be indolent. He toyed briefly with the idea of farming, if Henry would join him, arguing that they would lose money more slowly in farming than in engine designing. William and the northern uncles were not encouraging, and Maria expressed the family sentiment that James would find it as difficult to get out of his 'pottering habits' when a small farmer as when a half-employed engineer. The farming scheme died a natural death near the beginning of 1849.

It was succeeded by the pottery scheme. The northern uncles, to Maria's astonishment, took this venture more seriously, although it was they who would have to put up the capital. Uncle Charles Wilson, who was prepared to introduce James to an acquaintance who owned a pottery, was dismayed by James's total lack of business acumen. He was also dismayed by the interest his daughter Hetty and James were taking in each other. 'James is not "flirty",' wrote Maria, rushing to her brother's defence, but even she feared James's susceptibility to the opposite sex and his 'almost *wilful* blindness' in not seeing the strong attraction he held for his young cousin. It was decided that if the pottery scheme went ahead, Hetty would have to be sequestered with Lely and Maria at Wimbledon while James was at Middlesbrough. The shuttling of Hetty, William's firm opposition, and James's own vacillation combined to induce him to abandon potting. There remained only painting. Basil Holmes, the nineteenth-century landscape artist, was encouraging, and so too was William, who considered it 'not too sanguine to believe that Jas may make as much by art as he would in trade with his small capital and artist-like temperament.'[23] On the strength of some money owed to him by Sam Clegg (senior), he entered a London drawing academy, 'quite determined to make a vigorous push in Art'. 'He considers he has only half used his powers in this direction yet,' Maria wrote, 'he considers it quite uncertain what his success will be but he is going to exert all his energies before falling back on emigration.'[24]

William, meanwhile, seemed embedded in the legal profession but was not fattened by it. He had, by 1847, his own conveyancing practice and for a time lived – 'drudging' was how Maria described it – in Chancery Lane. He had little remunerative work, most of his father's clients had died, and although he was sufficiently interested in the law of inheritance to intend writing a book about it, Maria was convinced that a 'great deal of *hard* head work' was more than his body could stand. The quandary for Lely and Maria was whether by living with James and supplying at least some of his wants they might not be withdrawing from William and thus producing 'a counter balancing evil'. In a moment of unusual candour, Lely remarked that 'Wm took the opportunity of her absence to be poorly.' For William's comfort, Maria was even prepared to coax her friend Margaret Taylor 'to warm her heart towards him', but here Lely, writing to Margaret 'on the sly' when Maria was shopping, took a hand:

He will never act on the adage 'Faint heart never won fair lady'. He thinks it might not be impossible for him to win a sort of regard from you, that you might even deceive yourself into the notion that your affection for him was sufficient to warrant your acceptance of him. He is sure if you did so your good and high principles would enable you to perform well all your duties towards him, but he says it would be 'a galvanic affection' & he does not believe that you would be happy with anyone from whom your love was not spontaneous.[25]

This communication bemused rather than enlightened Margaret Taylor, and much of the subsequent correspondence between her and Maria over William's ambivalent intentions was of the does-he-or-doesn't-he, could-I-or-should-I variety.

Maria's younger brother, the normally imperturbable Henry, was also affected by the uncertainty around him. He had been briefly caught up in the heady prospect of going farming with James but had since returned to London University College, where his main interest was in chemistry and electricity. Maria considered 'The Childe' one of the more satisfactory members of the household, even though 'wild with some electrical theory he is continually in the stable when at home trying experiments and can neither eat nor sleep from excitement'.[26] His friends recommended that he stay at university and complete his degree, but Henry was quite against another three years of student life. Maria agreed with him; she thought Henry 'did not look as well as he ought' and that the 'chemical atmosphere' in which he spent his days could not be wholesome; 'besides he is much too much a hermit by nature, & such a long course of study would confirm his isolation. He will be better for activity and being forced among his fellow creatures.'[27]

Of her own life, Maria wrote at the beginning of 1850, 'I am tired out of uncertainties and scheming.'[28] It was a heartfelt cry, for in addition to her concern for her brothers and her involvement in their mostly abortive plans, she had problems of her own. Whether it was for the shape of her nose or for her mind, suitors were still attracted, and for one of them she felt an equal attraction. In the opinion of her family and friends he was a most unsuitable match. Jane Eyre's cry, 'Women feel just as men feel', which so shocked many of Charlotte Brontë's early readers, is echoed in the letters which Maria wrote to Margaret Taylor about her ambivalent feelings for Charles Hargrove.[29] It was to Margaret alone that Maria felt she could unburden herself. Difficulties in interpreting male approaches and intentions, and often a very real exclusion from the world of men, frequently built up a compensatory affection between women; it was part of the manners of the time. For Margaret and Maria, living far apart, the correspondence was a source of mutual sustenance.

Born on 20 January 1823, Margaret was a little older than Maria. They had become close friends at Mrs Lailor's school in Highgate, and the friendship continued during the years that Margaret Taylor and her sister Kate, thirteen years her senior, ran a school for poor children at Stoke Ferry. Then in January 1843 Margaret left England for Germany. Initially she stayed with friends at Wiesbaden, but when Kate married James Whittle, Margaret lived with them, first at Cassel and later at Dresden. She occasionally visited England, but it was the musical and intellectual society of Cassel and Dresden which captivated her. At the former she took singing lessons from and became a close friend of the composer Ludwig Spohr. Soon, according to a slightly envious Maria, she was able 'to compose elegant & lengthy German epistles' and to 'converse fluently on literature, art & politics with the leading men of Germany'.[30] Margaret Taylor also kept at least the bulk of Maria's letters. It is now a one-way conversation, for few of Margaret's own letters survived the continual packing and tidying up of Maria's remaining years in England and the cramped quarters of her early life in Taranaki.

For all the turmoil that he caused, Charles Hargrove remains a shadowy figure. William, Lely, and James were steadfastly opposed to him, the latter even refusing an offer of financial help from him. His 'defects of character' repelled and alarmed William, and even Maria, in whose love was also an element of charity, wrote that he fell 'far short of my idea of what is noble in man' – although she added, 'considering the immense inferiority of his opportunities . . . I feel in moral worth he is my equal'.[31] Moral worth could, however, slip from the balance:

> Margaret dear, until you have tasted the exquisite delight of being all in all to one person for weeks & months, of knowing yourself 'to be the ocean to the river of his thoughts', the mainspring of every action, the beginning & end of every wish & hope, of being in short, his past, his present, his future, his *all*, you cannot tell the exact nature of the grief I feel.[32]

Maria toyed briefly with the idea that perhaps the love of a 'good woman' might work miracles with Charles's 'deficiencies', but she was honest enough to admit that in her pride and self-sufficiency there was not enough warmth to keep alive such an aim. So she was prepared to accept Charles for what he was, writing, 'I should, I am nearly sure, have been quite content & happy as his wife.'[33]

But grief came when her overriding sense of duty to her family was added to her niggling doubt about life with Charles. William's words and feelings were the first thing to turn her aside. A possible estrangement from her close family circle –' 'that curious entanglement of duties'[34] – was not something she could long abide. She broke off the engagement and became resolute: 'I must not blush for a love (even tho' it be in most eyes wasted) over which I have control, & which has not blinded me to duty.'[35] Unfortunately, her family, seeing only that Maria's good sense had prevailed, were blind to the fact that a sacrifice had been made. 'Nowhere,' she wrote despondently, 'can I meet *one* spark of sympathy.'[36]

In an attempt to alleviate the langour which followed from her broken engagement, Maria herself proposed a change of scene. In 1848 James was still at Dawlish on the Devon coast and Lely and Maria went to join him. There was also a financial advantage in the move in that Springholm could be let for £50 for twelve weeks. In spite of this, Maria rather begrudged others living there:

> At this moment a party of abominable Knills are roaming over the house & garden . . . I am so reasonable as quite to dislike these people just because they are coming to take possession of our very nice old home in the prime part of the year.[37]

Except that it was away from London, Maria was not particularly drawn towards Dawlish society and the 'dull calls & dull tea-drinkings we shall probably have to pass through'.[38] In the event they did not have to; they found lodging in the seclusion of Berry Lodge, home of the Duke of Somerset's woodman. It was nearer to Totnes than Dawlish but James could walk over every day. For Maria, Berry Lodge was a rural retreat and restorative. 'In my wildest dreams I never fancied anything more to my taste than this life,' she told Margaret Taylor. In the first place there was the 'complete release from servants'. Then there were the Duke's extensive woodlands where James and Maria made evening scrambles and enacted the sentimental but appropriate *Paul et Virginie* 'most romantically' several times. The labyrinthian Devonshire lanes were perfect to wander in and there was also the Duke's castle to which their landlady held the key and in which Lely, James,

and Maria spent hours whenever they chose, reading, writing, and
sketching:

> I have not told you anything of my *mental* food. Whilst you are
> corrupting your innocent mind with George Sand, I am poring
> over Bishop Butler & Wordsworth. I delight in the Excursion more
> & more. Whenever it is fine enough I go to the entrance tower
> of the castle to the top of the most inacessible turret & there huddled
> against the ivy read it. James has been sketching a view from there
> & I read aloud to him.[39]

Following Wordsworth even more dangerously, Maria and James
experienced a 'most glorious storm' one night on the Dawlish coast.

> The wind had raised the sea a good deal & it came rolling in in
> long white breakers; we walked cautiously down the breakwater
> & stood in the very midst of the gleaming surf watching the lightning.
> The night was pitchy dark, & the foam seemed to glow like sheets
> of white flame through it & every now & then the whole heavens
> became one mass of lurid fire . . . We very nearly had a soaking
> in return for our love of the sublime.[40]

Maria made no attempt to confine her intellectual curiosity within
the conventional middle-class channels of household duties, visiting,
light reading, and fancywork, although embroidery was a favourite
pastime. William's frugality did not extend to the purchase of books,
and Dr Hutton, the Richmonds' pastor, also made his library freely
available. What William read (apart from his law books) was also
read by Maria. Included during 1848–50 were J.S. Mill, Ruskin
(she and James thought the latter's 'work' ethic sounded like
drudgery), and the Newman brothers. Cardinal Newman, whom
she heard lecture, was her *beau idéal* of a Catholic priest, although
she was most uncertain of his theology; F.H. Newman's *The Soul*
she enjoyed as an antidote to R.H. Froude's *The Nemesis of Faith*.
She also read sermons of James Martineau and Joseph Butler; the
Christian socialist writers, F.D. Maurice, J.M. Ludlow, and Charles
Kingsley; Carylyle, Milton, Wordsworth, Bunyan, Machiavelli, and
Macaulay. The first volume of Macaulay's *History of England* (1848)
Maria enjoyed greatly – 'It is certainly the lightest history I have
ever read' – but of his *Essays* she wrote, 'He dins things into one's
ears too much for my taste & wears his subject quite threadbare
before he will let it drop.'[41] It is doubtful if William read novels,
but *Vanity Fair, Pendennis, Dombey and Son*, and *David Copperfield* were
part of Maria's lighter reading. Elizabeth Gaskell's *Mary Barton,
a Tale of Manchester Life* (1848) she thought a 'very good tale indeed'.
Her favourite was *Jane Eyre*, 'wickedly devoured in bed' during

one of Margaret Taylor's visits. *Shirley*, Maria felt, was a 'falling off'. The intriguing question about both novels was, who was Currer Bell? Maria was certain that only a woman's insight and feelings were at work in them, and she went on to relate an account, from one of the Huttons, of Currer Bell's visit to the Richard Martineaus in order to meet Harriet Martineau:

> They all watched with much interest scarcely knowing whether a man or woman was to appear . . . At the appointed time a very small lady, very much like Jane Eyre in appearance arrived . . . It seems she does not communicate her real name, but said her father was a clergyman . . . that he did not know she had written 'Jane Eyre' . . . she lives a very retired life & knows very few people.[42]

'I only hope she will keep herself snug & retired,' Maria added, 'your lioness authoresses are abominations.'[43] Maria was obviously thinking of 'lioness' Harriet Martineau. With their shared intellectual Unitarian background, the Richmonds were on friendly terms with the Martineau family. It is thus surprising that there is no reference to Harriet in Maria's letters, nor does a book of hers appear to have been read. But Maria would have deplored the breach which Harriet's views occasioned between herself and her brother Joseph, the Unitarian minister, for it would have offended Maria's strong sense of the paramount importance of family. The following comment to Margaret Taylor is likely to have been an oblique reference to the fame or, as some would have it, the infamy of Harriet Martineau: 'I am inclined to grow bigoted on the subject, & to object to women writing books or doing *anything* which can draw or claim the attention of a larger circle than can really *love* & appreciate their private characters.'[44]

Maria was also determined to keep up with Margaret in German literature. Scorning a translation, she battled with *Wilhelm Meister*, but if she recognised Goethe's genius she also thought him 'disgustingly cool & unimpulsive'.[45] Neither did she have much time for the prolific but jejune work of the minor women novelists of the age. Of one of them she wrote: 'I should say . . . she had fed on sponge cake & walked on lawns at least half her life (I mean mental sponge cake & moral lawns) . . . There was such a want of health & vigour in the book.'[46]

Vigorous in reading, Maria was also vigorous out-of-doors, an energetic scrambler, often out of breath and déshabillée. The 'tearing about' she was to do through the Taranaki bush and her climbing of Mt Taranaki itself were simply part of a natural exuberance.

She was always ready to declare herself totally lacking in refinement, and for Margaret Taylor, more hemmed in by proprieties, she had some concern: 'What shall you do for exercise at Cassel? Surely there must be some German ladies who have the use of their legs?'[47]

Nevertheless, Maria had come to Berry Lodge wretched and distracted, with something of her physical elasticity and mental buoyancy diminished. She was soothed by the quiet beauty of the Devonshire countryside and by being at one with her family again. When the three-month retreat was over, in September 1848, instead of returning to Merton with Lely and James, she journeyed north by rail to act as a temporary governess to her Uncle Charles Wilson's three young children at Witton-le-Wear in Durham. 'I had,' she wrote, 'a very calm unadventurous day . . . as you know I am like you, a cool collected traveller. I get into no fusses or troubles about luggage or anything.'[48] For several months Maria lived comfortably in the village, the monotony of governessing and village life occasionally enlivened by visits to the neighbouring county town of Sunderland. Other excitement was provided by Margaret Taylor's letters about the revolutionary upheavals in Europe. It was the liberty of women rather than that of Italy which became an issue between the two friends. Margaret wanted to augment her income and her independence in her brother-in-law's house by teaching German and English; James Whittle disapproved. It was not genteel for a lady to be so engaged. Margaret accepted his censure, but Maria was not mollified:

> I wonder why *translating* German is so much more genteel than *teaching* it. I don't attempt to deny that this is so . . . but I should like to know *why*. Perhaps it is one of those mysteries which one must submit to never fully comprehending, that a woman should earn money or do anything for her own independence is [thought] extremely *low* and *vulgar*; as an aristocratic lady of our acquaintance once declared to Lely, 'The moment a woman does anything to maintain herself, that moment she ceases to be a gentlewoman.'[49]

The uselessness of 'delicate feminine dependence' was one of Maria's crusading themes and it flowed over into a concern for the more adequate education of women. Apparently Margaret must have thought her friend too vehement, for Maria replied:

> All I want to express is that there is a trimming & topping off in female education here that seems to me more likely to do harm than good . . . A great deal that people talk of as self respect & high principle is mere false shame & regard to appearances. I think the French are not far wrong in thinking that an English woman's

terror of public opinion is often the cause of her propriety of conduct. A more complete *distortion* of a human being than a boarding school young lady in this country, the world cannot produce.[50]

By the beginning of March 1849 Maria was back at Springholm, and writing: 'Oh Margie dear, home is home after all, there is nothing like it & one's own family, & I intend to look to nothing but the pleasantness of being once more settled here, all united under one roof.'[51] But Lely was not well and Maria was soon enmeshed in household chores and the everlasting servant problem. Eliza had been replaced, and the new maid, originally thought of as 'such a treasure', had 'gone off dreadfully', gossiping at the gate morning and evening. 'I long to rush away & live in a nutshell,' Maria wrote, 'where I can do all we want & have no one to mistrust.'[52] In an effort to put the house to rights herself, she went through every box, drawer, closet and corner, cleaning, mending, weeding out and rearranging. Added to the domestic irritations was her continuing concern about James's future. He was now living at home, unemployed. Household expenses were also a worry. Maria toyed with the idea of boarding 'some quiet old bachelor', preferring a man to a woman because 'a lady unless very agreeable would be almost sure to give Mamma & me more of her society than we should desire'.[53]

To keep her mind active she considered taking classes at Queen's College, London, which had opened in 1848 for the higher education of women. Its trustees had governesses largely in mind, but the establishment was also open to ladies who might wish better to prepare themselves for their traditional roles as wives and mothers. Maria thought of taking a course of German lessons and possibly 'a guinea's worth of English Literature or History'. In the event she decided not to go; the solitary journeys, the expense, and then, 'after spending such a mint of money to find I was no wiser, how provoking!'[54]

The uncertainty which hung over her brothers' futures extended also to the family's tenure of Springholm. Maria wrote that she would be sorry to leave the house, but if it was for the boys' good then she would not repine. 'However, I should like to know whether we are to do so because it is easier to make up one's mind to the worst than to live in suspense, & if we may keep this as our home for many years I should like to be able to enjoy it with a quiet mind.'[55] In the terrible cholera epidemic which afflicted London in the late summer and autumn of 1849, in which between 200 and 400 people died each day, Merton with its green fields, fresh air, and uncontaminated water was an oasis. Even so, Maria was bored – 'I do nothing useful, think of nothing pleasant & yet am quite well.'[56]

William solved the problem temporarily by looking so ill – he had little paying business and was harassed by the mismanagement of the family property trust by his father's agent, Thomas Maxon – that, in spite of expense, a change of climate was immediately thought necessary and he and Maria went to Le Havre for a few weeks. Walking in the bracing Normandie air restored William's appetite, and Maria reported that within a few days he was looking quite strong again. This reinforced her conviction that if William was to lead a less sedentary life and was more in the open air, his health would improve. On their return to Merton they found that uncertainty and scheming still prevailed. James was tossing up between farming in England or engineering in India. He applied for a job with the Great Peninsula of India Railway Company, was considered, but was not chosen. Thrown back for employment onto gardening in a desultory fashion at Springholm, he was moody and difficult to deal with. A semi-invalided, elderly aunt descended upon them, outstayed her welcome, and continued to be demanding, morbid, and impossible to please. Lely also was poorly. The refreshment of Normandie dissipated, and household cares and anxieties once again closed around: 'I am quite out of heart about everybody & everything & should enjoy sitting down to a good cry,'[57] wrote Maria.

Into this confused household walked yet another supplicant male. He was Henry Dix Hutton, son of Maria's pastor and mentor Dr Joseph Hutton. Henry ('the Dix') was a lawyer, well bred, well connected and considered likely to get on at the bar. His father approved of the suit but Maria did not: 'If he were an angel I could not marry him as long as C.J.H. [Charles Hargrove] is alive and single, indeed unless I meet some one who could move my nature more strongly than it has ever yet been moved I can never marry now.'[58] That the affair made little progress was due largely to the ministrations (what Maria called the 'kindness') of William and Lely. Maria herself 'cruelly and unconsciously' fostered Henry Hutton's sentiment by continuing to read the books he always brought – until Isabella Boult informed her that 'he built strong hopes for success' on this fragile foundation. (This information was passed on to Margaret Taylor many years later when Henry was making approaches to Margaret.) At the time, Lely thought it unpleasant for William to have to do all the 'damping business of the family, so she wrote to 'the Dix' advising him that he was mistaken over Maria's affections. On his next visit, Maria was particularly careful in her manner, and presumably declined his literary offering. The following day William received a note thanking him and Lely for their frank and friendly behaviour and saying that 'the gentleman saw it would be [unwise] to visit Merton again during his present stay in England'.[59] 'So that affair is satisfactorily finished off,' Maria commented, although in retrospect she dismissed the luckless suitor as 'a very worthy being, [who] would have been a good husband to anyone who *could* have fancied [him].'[60]

About this time Maria also learned that her erstwhile lover, M. Dupré, had married a Mexican heiress. 'My French Mr Rochester', as she now referred to him, 'was very good-for-nothing & interesting . . . & led us all a dreadful life . . . I dare say he has married for money as all Frenchmen do.'[61] James, she knew, was currently playing with his cousin Hetty's affections and William was pondering on the propriety of rekindling his for Margaret Taylor; Maria wrote to her friend:

> Do you not wish there were nothing but women in the world? I am sure all things considered men are more bother than they are worth; for a month's enjoyment they make us pay a year's pain – if we could but confine them to one hemisphere whilst we single females took possession of the other. Of course the poor deluded females who are wives may go with the male part of creation.[62]

Remembering her engagement to Charles, she wrote that it now seemed 'inexpressibly hurtful & sad'.

Always at the back of the family mind during these perplexing times was emigration. At first Lely and Maria treated the prospect with some dread, not wishing to lose James and Henry, who seemed the most likely emigrants. As the decade progressed two more kin groups set out. On 2 June 1845, William Hursthouse (younger brother of John and Charles) and his sister, Ann, left with William and Sarah Stanger (née Hursthouse) for South Africa, where William Stanger was to take the appointment of surveyor-general at Natal. In May 1848, Charles Flinders Hursthouse left New Plymouth, where he had become New Zealand Company agent, and returned to England. His object was to publicise the merits of Taranaki for settlement by writing a 'cheap pamphlet . . . in a plain style for circulation amongst rural populations of the Western Counties'.[63]

An Account of the Settlement of New Plymouth was published in London
in 1849. C.F. Hursthouse's first recruit was his brother-in-law, John
Stephenson Smith, of Beccles. With the Stephenson Smiths – John,
Hannah, and five children – went Mary Hursthouse, another of
John's sisters, and her father. Helen had been pressing Charles
Hursthouse to join them at New Plymouth: 'it would be an
inexpressible comfort to me,' she wrote, 'for with John now an
auctioneer and much from home the family devolves upon me &
I am not fitted for a farmer.'[64] She was also hopeful that her father-
in-law, a keen gardener with an eye for landscaping, could 'beautify
us with arbours, verandahs, etc, etc . . . [our place] would become
quite a bijou'.[65] When the Stephenson Smith party arrived in London
to begin the process of embarking, Maria offered to mind the five
young children. It was an arduous undertaking:

> I took them to town & passed the day at the Smith's lodgings
> in Thavies Inn in the midst of indescribable chaos . . . William
> joined the party in the afternoon & we accompanied them to
> Gravesend where their ship the Pekin lay. It was a fine vessel,
> & . . . I was more aggreeably impressed than I expected with their
> prospects for the voyage. All the females were hoisted on board
> in an armchair wrapped in the ship's colours, a most new & exciting
> method of travelling to me.[66]

Maria was impressed with 'old Mr Hursthouse', sixty-eight when
he emigrated, 'a more delightful specimen of an upright true-hearted
Englishman I never beheld'.[67] Before the vessel sailed from
Gravesend on 9 August 1849, he took Maria aside and told her
that he had just received news from Natal that William, his youngest
son and a consumptive who had gone to South Africa with the
Stangers, had died there. His father thought it right to conceal
the news from his fellow emigrants.

C.F. Hursthouse had also talked to James about emigrating to
New Plymouth. At that stage, Maria could not bring herself to
think that he might leave them, but after the Stephenson Smiths'
departure she was more ready to accept the idea of a family
emigration: 'I have really wanted the whole family to pack up
& away to New Zealand but neither Lely nor William will listen
to such a project.'[68] By November, with cholera raging in London,
with Henry's prospects dim and a hiatus in James's affairs, William
and Lely were more willing to discuss the possibility. Maria wrote
to Margaret:

> We seem to have travelled in imagination over half the habitable
> globe . . . accompanying James to all the colonies in turn. The

emigration scheme has been more particularly discussed during the
last three weeks than it has ever been before.[69]
Then James's pottery scheme came to light, and that, combined
with his renewed inclination towards art, kept emigration thoughts
at bay until the following year, when the fact that Henry was
as much at a loose end as James, reopened the whole question.
Their friends, the Huttons, were considering Ireland, but the poor
rates and the peasantry alarmed William: 'he does not wish to
establish the family in the midst of mud deluges as Carlyle called
them'.[70] Three weeks later Maria was writing: 'it seems settled,
so far as any of our affairs in this world are settled, that James
& Henry sail for New Zealand in August'[71] – essentially to
reconnoitre:

> Should they be disappointed in the Colony or find its social and
> moral state prevents their desiring that Mamma Wm & I should
> join them I little fear but that both will return to recommence
> the struggle in the crowded old country, but if they find Taranaki
> *is* rich as we are led to believe it to be, we shall all follow them
> in '52 if no unfortunate obstacle occurs to prevent it.[72]

Maria was astonished to discover the rate at which emigration
was proceeding among the middle classes and, in particular, among
educated single women. The rate of increase of women over men
during the population explosion in Britain made governessing and
spinsterhood the likely lot of 'redundant women'. Maria, however,
would not have been beguiled by the prospect of escape from the
'greatest and saddest convent that the world has ever seen',[73] which
Wakefield held out to women of her class. It was not the increased
likelihood of marriage which drew her to emigration but the
opportunity it offered for stretching her mind and limbs in what
seemed to be the less constricted colonial environment. Charlotte
Brontë, writing to her sister Emily about the decision of her friend
Mary Taylor to emigrate to New Zealand, was at a loss to decide
whether the contemplated action was based on 'rational enterprise'
or 'absolute madness' – although she did acknowledge the constraints
put upon female usefulness in England:

> Mary has made up her mind she can not and will not be a governess,
> a teacher, a milliner, a bonnet-maker nor housemaid. She sees no
> means of obtaining employment she would like in England, so she
> is leaving it.[74]

Maria was under no compulsion to earn her living, but when
Margaret Taylor, in some financial difficulty, considered returning
to England to seek a post as a governess, Maria cried: 'I had sooner

turn washerwoman in the Colonies with hut of my own for a house than make such an attempt.'[75] She was quite prepared to live in a 'rougher plainer style than we do here', and saw in emigration a new freedom from financial harassment, the opportunities of a new lifestyle, and the likelihood that her brothers would have abundant employment and become influential men. 'They do not go to make a fortune but to found a home where they can have abundant employment & where we may all live at health & at ease.'[76]

Lely, who had not long before been in tears at the prospect of emigration, now accepted James's and Henry's departure with equanimity:

> I receive consoling letters and people come to see me, full of kindness and sympathy, doubtless expecting to find me either drowned in tears, or wearing a woe-begone countenance. Lo and behold they find me as tranquil and placid as a lake in calm weather. It must be that throughout I have entertained the belief almost unconsciously, that this separation is not to be permanent.[77]

As the departure date drew closer, Maria's one fear was that something might upset this scheme as others had been upset before: 'I shall not feel they are certain to go till their ship has positively sailed,' she told Margaret Taylor. On 3 October 1850 the barque *Victory* sailed from Gravesend for New Zealand with James and Henry on board.

By the end of the decade, 'the mob' (Maria's name for her emigrant kin group) was assembling in Taranaki. The Hursthouses and Stephenson Smiths were already at New Plymouth; James and Henry were on their way, with Lely, Maria, and William likely to follow. There remained one important family group who were to have the strongest links with the Richmonds – the Atkinsons of Frindsbury in Kent.

CHAPTER
THREE

'Meetings & partings'

London and Frindsbury, 1848–May 1853

In the mid-1840s, while James Richmond was working on the South
Devon atmospheric railway, he struck up a friendship with another
of Brunel's engineers, John Staines Atkinson. During February
1848 a visit by John Atkinson's younger sister, Emily Elizabeth,
coincided with one by Maria and Margaret Taylor to see James.
Although Emily was five years younger, the three girls became
friendly. When exchanges of visits between the two families had
become quite frequent, Maria reminded Margaret of their first
meeting:

> Emily Atkinson often enquires about you, she appears to be
> perpetually referring to her Dawlish journal & recalled to me the
> day of her first introduction to you & of our first walk with you
> to Langstone. I think that time was as pleasant to her as to you
> & me.[1]

Arthur Atkinson's diary for 1847 and 1848 records several visits
paid by 'Mr James' and 'Mr Henry' to Frindsbury, and, in 1848,
by Emily to Merton. The age difference – on average the Atkinsons
were several years younger than the Richmonds – is apparent in
Maria's slightly condescending remark to Margaret: 'A fortnight
ago we had Emily Atkinson spending four days here; she appears
to have such thorough enjoyment of her visit, it was really quite
pleasant to have her. She amused Mamma & Het [cousin Hetty
Wilson] with her droll ways & remarks.'[2] One of the things which
must have impressed Emily was the relative orderliness of
Springholm, for the Atkinson household at Frindsbury was, as Maria
often remarked, 'quite chaotic'. She told Margaret:

> My visits to Frindsbury are of a very indescribable character –
> I don't doubt if in all your experience you have ever been in a
> household at all resembling the Atkinsons' & whether you would
> find it possible to get over ten days of it. One certainly gains some
> experience in human nature amongst these good folks which is not
> uninstructive.[3]

Going to Frindsbury was far from going slumming, but the
background and upbringing of the two families were different.

Like the Richmonds, the Atkinsons had their roots in the north
of England. Traditionally weavers, they had been hard hit by the
industrial revolution. John Atkinson (1762–1827) became a
stonemason and left for London. There he joined his uncle, William
Staines, later to become Lord Mayor, and together they built up
a very successful partnership as stonemasons and building
contractors. John Atkinson also acquired property in London and
on his death left his wife, Elizabeth (née Goadby), a substantial
income. Elizabeth Atkinson lived into her eighties, a formidable
if eccentric woman of strong religious convictions, well remembered
by two of her grandchildren, Emily and Harry Atkinson.

John Atkinson, second son of John and Elizabeth, was born at
Islington, on 19 November 1798. He was trained as an architect
and inherited his father's contracting business. In 1821 he married
Elizabeth Smith, daughter of a wealthy London businessman with
Calvinistic beliefs. Although the Atkinsons were comfortably off,
London's rapid building expansion was over by the 1830s, and in
the succeeding depressed times John Atkinson sought building
contracts further afield. He took his wife and young children with
him on these expeditions, the family living in nearby farmhouses
while he added wings and towers to the country seats and castles
of the nobility. Finally John Atkinson gave the building profession
away and retired with his ever-growing family – John, William,
Emily, Harry, and Arthur – to Frindsbury[4] in Kent, there to live
on the rents from the London houses he had inherited from his
father. From scattered references in Arthur Atkinson's diaries it
would seem that he also had a small farm. On one of his rent-
collecting trips he stayed with the Richmonds at Merton, and Maria,
for all that she declared her own lack of refinement, found him
definitely uncouth: 'Old Mr Atkinson did not much please the
inhabitants of Springholm as his scruffy habits & Yankee manners
are anything but prepossessing.'[5]

Dr Guy Scholefield in his introductory chapter to *The Richmond–
Atkinson Papers* writes that by his early retirement John Atkinson
had time to attend to his family's schooling: 'he drew up for the
home school a curriculum that was essentially modern. He had
many books of reference, current literature and periodicals, and
bought the works of standard novelists as they appeared.'[6] This
description implies a more orderly regimen than that which actually
took place. In 1847 (the year from which Arthur began keeping

a diary), Harry (16) and Arthur (14) still spasmodically attended
Blackheath school where the curriculum seems to have been more
devoted to cricket than to higher learning. At home it would appear
that they did as they liked when they liked, with scarcely a reference
to their father who was, ironically, called 'the Governor'. Sometimes
Arthur stayed in bed all day, ranging in his reading from Alison's
twenty-volume *History of Europe* and Adam Smith's *Wealth of Nations*,
to *The Times, Spectator*, and *Atheneum*. Shakespeare, Byron, Milton
(which he and Harry read aloud to each other), Thackeray, Dickens,
Scott, and Tennyson were dipped into. Calculus appears from time
to time in his diary entries, as do brief forays into French, Latin,
and Greek. Other days he spent bird collecting for his aviary (his
family nicknamed him 'Birdie') or gardening, working at the
carpentry bench, walking, shooting or playing cricket – a lifelong
passion for both brothers. Harry appears to have been more
influenced at this stage by his mother's Calvinistic views; he read
his Bible every day, was a regular (Anglican) church attender,
and worried about his religious convictions. He read, perhaps not
so avidly as his younger brother, from the same range of books,
indulged in the same pursuits, and was keen about keeping hens.
Occasionally 'the Governor' suggested some additional practical
ploy such as boot-making, and when Harry and Arthur determined
to emigrate they spent a great deal of time building, at their father's
suggestion, a 'New Zealand house' on their lawn. Otherwise John
Atkinson seems to have played a small part in their lives. There
is an element of disrespect in the diaries and Harry, as he grew
older, frequently quarrelled with him. Maria recorded one such
incident, revealing too the extent to which the Richmond friendship
was already an influence in the brothers' lives:

> Harry's hasty temper has led him to disagree with his father so
> that he has some idea of setting off at once to NZ if his mother
> can raise the money for his passage & outfit. [She had inherited
> £15,000 under her grandfather's will.] He has written to Wm as
> the only friend whose judgement he can trust, & Wm has of course
> counselled him to reconcile himself to his father as soon as possible.[7]

Harry and Arthur's mother, Elizabeth Atkinson, appears even
less in the diaries than her husband. Her numerous pregnancies
and the burden of child raising would have left her little time
to become the kind of companion Lely was to her older children.
Between the ages of eighteen and forty-three she bore thirteen
children, of whom four died in infancy. Emily, Harry, and Arthur,
with whom the Richmonds were mostly involved, were respectively

her sixth, seventh, and eighth born. In reminiscences given to Maurice Richmond (son of J.C. Richmond), Elizabeth Atkinson is remembered with affection. Emily, who could not get on with her mother in life, described her as 'impulsive, warm-hearted and very loveable': 'If she met a poor under-clothed woman when out walking, she would step into a cottage, take off her own petticoats and give them to her. She often brought dirty and neglected children whom she found playing in the streets, into her own house, to wash and re-clothe them.'[8] All agreed, however, that the marriage did not work. John and Elizabeth Atkinson were 'originals' and should have interested each other, but there were always difficulties about money. 'He sat still and smoked [he was also overfond of brandy] and talked very cleverly but did nothing to support the family.'[9]

Maria thought Elizabeth Atkinson a very odd woman and was obviously as intrigued by her as by Emily. When the Stephenson Smith party sailed for New Zealand in 1849, Mrs Atkinson came on board the *Pekin* to interest the emigrants in her sailor son, William, who had left for New Zealand in June of that year. Maria commented:

> It was very amusing to see the easy manner in which she made herself useful & at home with all on board. We had a curious tea party in the cabin [Mrs Atkinson presiding] at which basins & small mugs, dolls' spoons & carving knives figured prominently.[10]

The demands of household management impinge upon the boys' diaries not at all; meals were presumably cooked and eaten, probably on the same self-help principle that governed the children's education. There is no mention of servants, although it would be unusual in such a large household if none was kept. A governess was employed for the younger children and Harry and Arthur occasionally helped out by teaching them arithmetic. Nevertheless, 'chaotic' as the household always appeared to Maria, there must have been a degree of bonhomie between its members – Maria wrote of the 'merry Atkinsons' – as they went their separate and absorbing ways. It is no wonder that Harry and Arthur Atkinson were to take so easily to colonial life. Frindsbury had prepared them well.

The two families complemented each other. The Richmonds were well-educated, high-principled intellectuals, inclined to be reserved in company other than their own, and, in spite of reduced circumstances and an inclination to poke fun at some of the rigid proprieties of their milieu, upper middle class in manners and upbringing. The Atkinsons were altogether less inhibited; theirs was a rumbustious household, whose members' ages ranged downwards from the early twenties at two-year intervals. They were less cultivated, and less intellectually disciplined, but apart from the flair Maria was to show in Taranaki, Harry and Arthur were far more practically minded than any of the Richmonds. Duty, particularly towards the family, which sat so heavily on Lely's, William's, and Maria's shoulders, bothered the Atkinsons far less. On the other hand, Harry and Arthur saw in William a father figure, turning to him for advice and relishing a conversation with him: 'There is no one talks to me as he does,' Arthur wrote in his diary. William once suggested that if Harry and Arthur wanted employment they should improve their handwriting, and both boys immediately and assiduously practised.

It was the unpretentious and unreserved friendliness of Emily and Arthur in particular that William and Maria found so engaging. When 'sadly fagged', as he often was, William enjoyed going to Frindsbury 'to get a little Kent air to freshen him'. It is very likely that Maria saw that Emily, or 'Em' as she rapidly became, was by her very zest and lack of artifice just the sort of woman to appeal to William's somewhat introverted, care-burdened nature. Both William and Emily later described her as the author and finisher of their marriage.

In Taranaki, the mob was to thrust up two leaders, mutually complementary and acceptable: C.W. Richmond and Harry Atkinson.

As if in confirmation of the family's intention to come together again in Taranaki, Lely put the lease of Springholm on the market soon after the *Victory* sailed. Within a few weeks it was sold. The Richmonds were, as they frequently pointed out to each other, 'a rootless family'. After her husband's death in 1832 and before her comparatively long lease of Springholm, Lely changed houses four times within the London area; before they left for New Zealand at the end of 1852 they were to face four more shifts. Lely remarked that she could never understand an attachment to place independent of people, but to Maria, Springholm had become 'this dear old home'. She wrote to Margaret, 'I am astonished that I can leave . . . so tranquilly.'[11] From Merton, Lely and she went to lodge with Unitarian friends, the Boults, of Ridgeway Terrace, Wimbledon. William was living in his chambers at 54 Chancery Lane.

During the autumn of 1850 Margaret Taylor visited friends in England, and at Lely's insistence (although she required no urging), it was planned for Maria to return to Germany with her. Maria's excitement is immediately apparent: 'what garments are best procured in England besides flannels? warm stockings? boots & shoes? or can the latter be bought as good & cheap in Germany? I care little where we are this winter so that I am with you, old wretch.'[12] For comfort during the journey she invested eight shillings in 'a capital warm railway wrapper' to serve them both. The Whittles, with whom Margaret lived, had moved to Dresden but they frequently went to Eichenberg, a small town near Cassel, and Maria, who stayed with them until the beginning of June 1851, joined them at both places. One unfortunate consequence of her being *with* Margaret is that her letters dry up completely, although two letters to her from Lely survive. From them it is clear that by April 1851 Maria was penniless; her mother, a little reluctantly, enclosed £10 in one letter, adding, 'we don't seem to be saving as much in our present mode of life as might have been hoped'.[13] ('We are as poor as church rats,' Maria commented when she was back in England.)

Dresden had much to offer. Emil Devrient, a member of the famous acting family and attached to the Dresden court theatre, lived close by. Eduard Bendemann, the romantic painter with a penchant for portraits of beautiful women, was a professor at the Dresden Academy. He had a commission to decorate the throne room of the King of Saxony's palace at Dresden, and in the frieze depicting the evolution of culture he painted Maria as a sibyl in a blue gown.[14] 'Of course I expect particular account of my Bendemann,' Maria wrote to Margaret after her return to London in June 1851:

> if I had the Arabian piece of carpet would not I come and worship his eyes & sit for him a month if he liked. I am sure the King of Saxony (and all the future Kings, I may say) not to speak of the court, are deeply to be pitied if that unlucky little sitting was too short, and they are to be robbed of my phiz and bumps in consequence.[15]

It is also certain, from later letters written from Taranaki, that she met Ludwig Spohr and listened to some of his quartets. She asked Margaret to send her the music of 'that Waltz we heard so often at the Casino' to remind her of the Dresden days and so that she might have it to play 'in the Bush'. The quieter days at Eichenberg, too, she remembered as 'a real solid valuable *possession* that nothing can rob me of & when I tell Great Aunt's histories of Europe to young colonists I shall have a great deal to say of Eichenberg'.[16] But for all the excitement of Dresden life, it was, Maria recalled, 'too full': 'I cannot describe to you how oppressive & painful even enjoyments become to me when they are crowded together so as to leave me no breathing space in which to look around me & into myself.'[17]

Meanwhile, William's conveyancing business was again in the doldrums. His interest was now taken up with Christian socialism and with reading and listening to its leading protagonist, F.D. Maurice. Lely worried about him:

I feel that his unquiet mind is wearing him out . . . he sees, and cannot see calmly great and crying evils of which he seems utterly powerless to attempt the remedy. Whether he could find his place in a new country is a problem only to be solved by experiment.[18]

Some solace came from his now frequent visits to Frindsbury, where he walked and discussed philosophy, religion, and politics with 'the boys' and the 'old Governor'. He was also becoming less staid with Emily: 'Paid Em Atk 6d for letting a cockchafer walk up her face.'[19]

In the middle of May 1851, letters from James and Henry arrived. Commenting on James's shipboard journal Maria wrote, 'he seems to have been schoolmaster, policeman & guardian angel . . . his description of the voyage in the intermediate cabin is certainly not tempting'.[20] The captain had been harsh in his treatment of both passengers and crew, and the intermediate passengers had included some dissolute and drunkenly aggressive men and women whom James, with difficulty, attempted to keep apart. He had also been in charge of a mess[21] and had conducted a school for the children. Henry, less demanding than his older brother, made prodigious puddings. Both, however, were disgusted by the habits of other passengers who, bored with shipboard life, shot at whales and sea birds for amusement.

The *Victory* arrived at Auckland on 7 February 1851. James and Henry's first impressions were not favourable; they wrote of wooden houses 'rather cockney in appearance' and of boorish settlers with 'Yankee manners'. Then, accompanied by four fellow passengers, Maori guides, and carriers, they set off on a twenty-five-day walk to New Plymouth.

There, James and Henry lived at first with John and Helen Hursthouse, and were appalled both by Aunt Helen's appearance – fatigue had taken its toll and she had lost all her front teeth

– and by their house, 'nothing but a pigstye'. The brothers were
more pleased with the nearby seventeen acres, including a cottage
and barn, which they bought for 100 guineas.[22] The cleared land
had been planted in wheat and potatoes but they intended grassing
it and dairy farming. 'The country is by no means romantically
beautiful, that is without the mountain,' Henry wrote, 'but when
he is visible I can hardly take my eyes off him, he is so very
beautiful.'[23] Henry had no firm advice to give.

> I cannot bear the idea of condemning you to this; you know that
> I myself am contented with a very material existence and if you
> would all marry nice colonial young men and women it would
> be all very well. Of course there are advantages to the thing: the
> delight of having a place of one's own is by no means an imaginary
> one . . . the climate is beautiful & so is the mountain, . . . but
> if you come you must bring more people with you.[24]

He added that they both thought the Atkinson lads would do well
in Taranaki, provided that they were able to keep clear of their
elder brother, William Smith Atkinson, who was currently in Otago
and was reported 'not to conduct himself very respectably'.[25]

The knowledge that the boys had arrived in Taranaki and were
safely settled was welcome indeed, but to Lely, William, and Maria,
anxious about their own plans, the first letters gave no clear
guidelines: 'there is nothing in the letters to fix *our* future,' Maria
complained.[26] Neither were they too surprised that Henry appeared
to have settled down: 'The Childe' was likely to be contented
anywhere. But what about James? Apart from voyage journals,
the first long letter had been from Henry, writing whilst James
was in Wellington in pursuit of the *Victory* which had failed to
call at New Plymouth and still had the bulk of their luggage on
board. If James found nothing to satisfy him or, even worse (Henry's
note about marriage prospects would not have gone unnoticed by
Maria), were to throw himself into some unsuitable union, then
the whole project would be disastrous.

There were also shifting sands at Wimbledon. The Boults were
now thinking of moving to Manchester. Lely was again suffering
from asthma, and like Maria found 'the constant waiting for
something to fix our future, very trying'.[27] Living in somebody
else's house, with their possessions in boxes around them, Maria
felt uncomfortably useless. 'Really,' Lely wrote, 'Maria is too
vigorous for civilized life – she has not half enough to employ
her energies in an old country.'[28] Two events interrupted the
monotony; one was seeing again 'the magnificent Emil' (Devrient)

in Goethe's *Egmont*; the other was a visit to the Royal Academy's summer exhibition, where Maria was much impressed by the 'peculiar vigour & truth' of the Pre-Raphaelite school.

Towards the end of August, with all their belongings packed for removal if the Boults moved before their return, Lely, William, and Maria went north. Lely was going to stay with her aged mother at Norton, and William and Maria were to visit the Charles Wilsons at Witton-le-Wear. They were all to come together at Redcar, a small watering place on the Yorkshire coast. 'I cannot tell you,' Maria wrote to Margaret,

> how I am reckoning on the sea breezes & the complete quietness which I trust we shall have here for a few weeks . . . I have no comfort or satisfaction in any thing or any body lately . . . It seems almost impossible to know what to do with all our property as we cannot settle even where next winter will be spent.[29]

Lely and Maria enjoyed the broad sands of Redcar, walking for miles without the least fatigue, while William, joined by his cousin Robert Richmond, went on a walking tour of the Lake District. He returned to Redcar at the end of September refreshed and delighted by the natural scenery but incensed at the concessions made to 'vulgar-minded tourists'. Maria echoed his feelings:

> All the charm is taken away from a waterfall when one must *pay* for seeing it and rocks lose a good deal certainly when comfortable *steps* are provided for ascending them. He seems to have felt a savage joy at the thought of one day perhaps 'being out of genteel humanity's reach', and where people need not tread upon each other's heels in search of the picturesque.[30]

From the bracing air of Redcar, Lely and Maria went to Stockton-on-Tees and to the same invalid aunt who had stayed with them at Springholm. Much as she tried to sympathise, Maria felt 'bottled up' by her aunt's obsessive concern for domesticity – her 'foolish twaddling about trifles', as she described it. By the end of 1851 they were back in London and found that the Boults had indeed gone to Manchester. Lely, however, was able to find another house in the same street, cheerfully and comfortably furnished and with spare rooms for visitors and space for all their boxes. Christmas was celebrated with the Joseph Huttons at Twickenham, and on Christmas eve they received 'the pleasantest of Xmas boxes – the Doctor's dear voice at our bedroom door, calling, "Letters from the lads, letters from the lads" '.[31]

James and Henry had been 'allowed' six months from their arrival

in which to make up their minds about staying in Taranaki. Their
Christmas letters showed them to be hard at work at 'New Merton'
and finding the 'process of converting rank forest into green pastures
. . . a very satisfactory one'.[32] They were also seeing something
of New Plymouth's polite society. 'A little note with a silver wafer'
informed the Messrs Richmond that 'Mr & Mrs Charles Brown
would be at home on the 8th, 9th & 10th'; Mr and Mrs King
and the Misses King[33] invited them to a ball in their schoolroom
but, misinterpreting the invitation, the brothers went in their boots
and were unable to dance. They were also taking the education
of the Hursthouse children in hand, and James was determined
to become proficient at making cheese. They were, however, still
unwilling to decide a course of action for the others, writing first
on one side then on the other, urging caution, suggesting Ireland,
but finding it impossible to pronounce the final sentence. 'This
is a crude country,' James wrote,

> crude forms of hills, crude changes of weather, rain beginning and
> ending as abruptly as if regulated by a valve like a shower bath,
> and this peculiarity the shingle roof lets one know distinctly enough.[34]

The Huttons were not keen to lose their friends to Taranaki.
Nor was Margaret Taylor. In reply to a letter from her on the
subject, Maria wrote:

> I cannot help trying to slur over all you say in dread & dislike
> of our emigration . . . & were we all females not to be endured
> or thought of for a moment. But . . . our boys must have
> employments & scope they can never possibly find here.[35]

She was also prepared to be critical of her friend's somewhat aimless
way of life:

> Even for you as a woman & not a chooser therefore of your own
> path, it seems to me there are evils in your present way . . . I
> think it not safe & wholesome to be without *roots*, to float along
> where chance or fancy takes one, to have no natural social relations
> such as spring up round a real home.[36]

At Frindsbury plans were going forward. Harry Atkinson, now
twenty, was determined to emigrate in spite of his father's
disapproval. The only question in his mind was whether he should
take Arthur, two years younger. (Neither Harry nor Arthur
considered seeking employment in England. Kent's prosperity had
steadily declined since the Napoleonic wars, and by 1822 it was
described as the most depressed county in England. Its population
had increased, there was not enough work, and its young men
were encouraged to emigrate.) However, both Harry and Arthur

decided to wait, for at the beginning of April 1852 very cheerful and decisive letters arrived from Taranaki which were to put in motion another set of plans. James, of whose ability to cope with bush life his family had been doubtful, now wrote:

> Henry and I are getting much more able-bodied from dealing with logs instead of spirit lamps & squares . . . I fancy myself rather a dab hand at a rough fence, digging post holes & milking cows all of which accomplishments baffled me much at first. We shall have a smooth bit of land before any old faces from England look at us again. The more I see of this country the more beautiful I find it . . . the purity of the sky is such as I never saw in blessed old England.[37]

A few weeks later, all caution and vacillation tossed aside, he wrote: 'how I want you all, come my own diamonds – bring as many good creatures as you can'.[38] Henry wrote more cautiously, 'The only way to have anything like society here is, as we always thought, to form a little nucleus of one's own.'[39]

James and Henry's advice reinforced an earlier suggestion made to William by C.F. Hursthouse, for whom the Richmonds did not otherwise care,[40] 'that you would do well all to go together'.[41] It was decided that the emigration would be in two stages. William, to the delight of Harry and Arthur, proposed that if they would only wait until later in the year, he would go with them. Then, with a new home ready and waiting, Lely and Maria would join them the following year. At the end of April 1852, William left his legal practice and sold his office furniture for £8. 'Free of London's legal shackles,' he wrote in his diary, 'beginning to have a reckless colonial feeling about appearances.'[42] He wore a wideawake (a broad-brimmed felt hat) instead of his customary top hat, and at Frindsbury was mistaken for an Atkinson. Maria told Margaret that it was 'quite settled that we should follow the boys.' For this reason she was conscious of looking at England's beauty as if for the last time. Of a walk in Richmond Park she wrote: 'I never saw the place look lovelier, it was a sunny afternoon, the furze in its full golden glory smelling so lusciously, & the park enchanting with the hundred softly varied tender greens of Spring – never to be seen in NZ.'[43]

Before William's projected departure, the Richmonds faced yet another move. The Joseph Huttons were leaving Twickenham and Carter Lane chapel for Derby, where the doctor was to take up an appointment at the Unitarian chapel. It was agreed that the Richmonds should have their Twickenham house. As Maria sorted

and packed, William described her 'sitting in the yard all day like
an apple woman without any apples'.[44] On 30 April a farewell
for the Huttons was held at Carter Lane; three days later, with
William 'wretched and suicidal' and Maria 'wearied out', the
Richmonds moved into the Huttons' former home. Cobby, the dog,
and puss, probably grown accustomed to shifting about, made
themselves at home, but for Lely it was all too much: 'When will
all this turmoil end?' she wrote in her diary, 'my heart sickens
of it.'[45] Maria, also weary, was further disconcerted by a letter
from Margaret (one of the few to have survived) in which she
revealed that she still had a deep attachment to William:

> I cannot get out of me the feeling of what he once was to me,
> of the trusting loving friendship I had for him, the delight in his
> society, the confidence in him, the longing to be with him . . .
> the life long affection (as it seemed) I had for him.[46]

She asked Maria to send her a daguerreotype of William and not
to tell anyone. The letter was written in the past tense, but Maria
could not but feel annoyed 'at the muddle you & William have
made of your likings. If you had only had a real love . . . then
you ought both to have been very happy & useful together'.[47]

It seemed time for Maria and William to make a refreshing
trip to Frindsbury. Getting there was easy: a boat trip down the
Thames to Gravesend and then by omnibus to Strood or, taking
a short cut at Gravesend, by boat or towpath along the canal to
Frindsbury. Maria was fond of Kent 'altho' there is *really* no romantic
beauty' (it was scarcely Wordsworth country), but there was
'something so thoroughly English in its character'.[48] At Frindsbury
they went for walks with Harry, Arthur and Emily; one in particular
Maria described as a 'real treat' – nineteen miles in the wet along
the old Canterbury pilgrims' road, wading through muddy pools
and slipping about in muddy lanes. In the evenings, with 'the
Governor putting in his oar & disapproving of most modes of
proceeding', they discussed plans for emigration and drew up lists.
'Nails bother me,' William wrote, 'they want me to take a ton.'[49]
In preparation for colonial life Harry and Arthur had both
apprenticed themselves to the local blacksmith. They intended to
follow this with a course from a cooper, but at £2 considered it
too expensive. Much time was spent perfecting their New Zealand
house and they tried, unsuccessfully, to acquaint William with the
skill of dovetailing. The post, too, brought the good news that
an elderly Smith uncle had given Harry and Arthur £150 each for
their passage. It was a time of excitement and preparation for

adventure, and Maria captured the spirit in a letter to Margaret:

> The Atkinson lads are so intoxicated with happiness at their NZ
> prospects that much as their mother & Emily dread losing them
> they cannot resist the infection of their high spirits. All the family
> (except the father) enter with immense zest into all the preparations
> of the emigrants, & the most noisy & jovial rehearsals of hats,
> serge shirts, 'jumpers', jerseys, fustian, velveteen, corduroy, canvas,
> & in short every imaginable species of colonial garment continually
> comes forward. The whole party was much delighted by Harry's
> appearing in cord shorts, or knee breeches one morning at breakfast.
> He looked exactly like one of those very clean Opera peasants
> who advance to the footlights & sing in praise of 'Porter-bier' or
> some such national beverage. His appearance was considered so
> highly effective that Arthur immediately ordered himself a pair,
> but altho' Wm quite approved of the garments for *them* they could
> not persuade him to array his spindle shanks in similar style.[50] The
> advantage of the dress with stout leather gaiters will be great in
> the bush or among the stumps, & also on the bad roads in the
> rainy season.[51]

A female fashion, somewhat similar to knickerbockers but too risqué
for Maria, was soon to arrive in England from America. Maria
asked her friend, who inclined to the masculine in garments, whether
she would be taking to bloomers:

> Do rumours of the Bloomer excitement reach you? There are
> positively *anti*-Bloomer lectures already tho' no solitary instance
> of public Bloomerism has been seen . . . Ladies are beginning at
> the wrong end by wearing jackets & waistcoats with something
> resembling a shirt front.[52]

Refreshed by the interlude, Maria and William returned to
Twickenham and into the thick of packing for William's departure:

> I shall be from 9 till 4 I dare say every day for at least a month
> in a large workshop with Wm packing immense cases amidst a
> chaos of straw, hay, chips, shavings, rags, waste paper, horse hair,
> tape, string, crockery, iron mongery – in short every sort of 'ery',
> tool, utensil, odd or end necessary for a colonial establishment,
> & a good many unnecessaries & elegancies besides. The whole place
> at present looking in the most awful confusion you can imagine.[53]

By the beginning of July 1852, William, Harry and Arthur were
ready to go, only to find that there was no chance of a ship sailing
for New Plymouth before September at the earliest. The gold rushes
to New South Wales and Victoria had effectively diverted
emigration and shipping. In the midst of 'disagreeable London' –
the weather was very hot and the atmosphere stagnant – Maria

had one treat. With William and John Staines Atkinson she went to Covent Garden to see Spohr's opera, *Faust*. She loved the music but thought the libretto, which was not based on Goethe, 'stupid'. Faust was 'nothing but a milk & water Don Juan'. William, to Maria's surprise, 'did a great deal of clapping & shouting – an uncommon thing on his part'.[54]

London's July weather soon took a toll on Lely's asthma, and another sojourn to Frindsbury, Lely's first, was proposed. It was to be eventful.

William was sent on ahead to find lodgings, Maria thinking that 'chaotic' Frindsbury would scarcely suit Lely. He found them in the village of Wainscot, across the Medway from Frindsbury. The weather was splendid and Lely's wheeziness diminished. Backwards and forwards went Richmonds and Atkinsons three or four times a day. Together they went boating on the Medway – 'very sweet reading Uncle Tom as we let ourselves drift on the tide through the reaches'[55] – walking, picnicking, sketching, reading Ruskin aloud in the shade of the walnut trees in the orchard. All things seemed propitious for 'faint-hearted' William to at last make a move. But, cautious as ever, he first consulted Arthur Atkinson, only to find that Emily had been doing the same. The following diary extracts explain the strategy:

C.W.R. 12 Aug. [1852] I told Bird [Arthur] what I am thinking of. Em had been consulting him & he advised me to speak today. I dined at Frindsbury & Bird at Wainscot. I wrote a letter at Frindsbury. After dinner Em, Hal & I walked down to Wainscot . . . I gave Em the letter, she bid me goodnight at the door.

A.S.A. 12 Aug. I have had deep cause to thank God for what has happened today, and I do it heartily.

C.W.R. 13 August. This morning on my way to Frindsbury met Bird who brought me the answer.[56]

Emily had said 'yes'; Mrs Atkinson, 'with some good kisses', had also agreed, and even the Governor consented to the engagement. At first he wanted to do nothing at all by way of marriage settlement, Emily having inherited property under the will of her grandfather Atkinson. William persuaded him to make Emily an allowance of £25 a year. In the general goodwill which followed the engagement, William wrote in his diary: 'I often think we are not kind enough to him.'[57] For Emily there was unreserved praise. Lely wrote to Margaret Taylor, to whom the news must have had a bitter-sweet flavour:

As you know Emily is anything but a model young lady. I may

confess to you that she interests me more than half the girls of
my acquaintance who have been shaped in the approved form –
there is a raciness and originality about her quite refreshing, and
a more frank generous nature I never saw. I have little doubt that
William & she will improve each other.[58]
John Holt Hutton wrote to William, remarking Emily's moral
earnestness and charming spontaneity of character: 'she is not I
fancy, plagued with that 19th century self consciousness for which
you have such a great dislike'.[59] His brother, Richard, described
her as 'the Child of Nature'. Both William and Emily were to
acknowledge Maria's guiding hand, but at the time of their
engagement there is no recorded comment from her. Something
unexpected eventuated which caused her to leave Frindsbury at
once for Germany and Margaret Taylor.

Margaret was spending some weeks at Boppard, a town on the
Rhine south of Coblenz. It was not as far away as Dresden, and
Margaret had written earlier that she hoped Maria might join her
there after William's departure. The unexpected intelligence which
had reached Frindsbury, however, was that James had proposed
to Margaret from Taranaki. What probably happened (the Richmonds seeming to need intermediaries for proposals) was that James
wrote to his sister as well as to Margaret, asking Maria to intercede
on his behalf. Maria's letter telling her friend she was coming to
Boppard divulges nothing but impatience to be together:

> We should not reckon for certain on more than a clear week together.
> I feel that all I have to say dearest Margaret will take three months
> at least of the week. I am almost bursting with impatience to be
> with you; how I shall bear the dull Rhine and remain sane I don't
> know.[60]

What James had written, what Maria said to Margaret and Margaret
to Maria is not known; the only clue comes from a letter from
Maria to Emily:

> Much as I should delight in having dear M. of our family in NZ,
> I think all the circumstances of the case considered she cannot rightly
> accept James's offer. In a similar position to hers, after talking
> it all over with her, I feel that I should myself decide as she is
> doing.[61]

Margaret had declined the offer. One might surmise that affection
for William could not be easily transferred; in fact, such was the
friendship between Margaret and the Richmond family that her
feelings, deep as they were for both brothers, were more those
of a sister. She also felt, as Maria frequently chided her, beholden

to her delicate sister and was not at this time in very good health herself. And, from frequent exchanges in previous letters, it is clear that Maria doubted whether Margaret, who so enjoyed the cultivated society of Germany, could ever find satisfaction in colonial life. In a letter written just before she sailed, Maria contrasted their natures:

> Apart from my own wishes I cannot but feel very grave doubts as to your chances of happiness in the life I am going to. I certainly have . . . much more flexibility of nature. I can turn & bend into a new position & enjoy myself amongst people & things that would never lose their repulsiveness to you.[62]

The problem of suitable partners for colonial sons was similar to that faced by prospective missionaries among the empire's heathen, captured so succinctly by Charlotte Brontë in *Jane Eyre*: 'Rosalind a sufferer, a labourer, a female apostle? Rosalind a missionary's wife? No.' Not every woman, as Maria later expressed it, 'was born to a bullock cart'.

On Maria's return to Wainscot, Lely wrote Margaret a letter more in good sense than in sorrow. In tone it was not too dissimilar to the one she had written on William's behalf:

> Dear Margaret I cannot but grieve that you should have been exposed to such hard trials through your intimacy with my family. Does it not seem strange that much as we love each other, suited as we appear to be to live together . . . Providence should have decreed our paths to lie so widely apart? I cannot but acquiesce in the good sense and conscientious feeling which have brought you to decide against a measure that would have contributed so largely to the happiness of me and mine.[63]

Lely concluded that if Henry, who had also expressed to his mother his love and admiration of Margaret, should invite her to 'share his cabin', then Lely would take no denial.

Now, however, it was James's future which seemed to Maria to be anything but secure. With news of Margaret's rejection and of William's happy state reaching him in the same bundle of letters, Maria feared that he would either sink into gloom and apathy or, 'what would be *infinitely worse*, throw himself away on some foolish girl who might persuade him that she loved him whilst she neither appreciated him nor could be a companion to him'.[64] She had Mary Hursthouse in mind. In order to bolster up James, Maria was now intent upon reaching Taranaki as soon as possible. Fortunately, with marriage between William and Emily imminent, plans were once more changed: Lely and Maria would travel with

William and Emily, Harry and Arthur. In all the bustle that followed, Maria spared many thoughts for 'dearest Margie', who had been going through some emotional upheaval through her involvement with the family. 'Come to my conclusion,' urged Maria, 'that all these meetings & partings have nothing to do with ourselves & you will get thro' better. I am longing to hear from you darling.'[65]

Wedding preparations now involved Maria completely. Mrs Atkinson was determined on 'a bit of a splash', and with Maria one of the seven bridesmaids[66] she was caught up, rather reluctantly, in a host of deliberations over bonnets and mantles. Emily's outfit was to be on a very noble scale – 'upwards of 200 yards of linen & calico have been torn up', 'about 20 flannel petticoats are lying on the kitchen table', 'four French merino dresses are bought & they consist of from 12 to 14 yards each, *I* call them 8 dresses'.[67] By dint of a most vigorous effort on her part, Maria got the Atkinson house into something like order, 'at least in all parts visible to visitors' eyes'. The Governor, Harry, and Arthur were hard at work on the New Zealand house in which the wedding breakfast was to be held, flooring it and constructing a large square table to seat six on each side. The night before the wedding they decorated the house with ferns, hops, and clematis. The wedding was on 15 September, to coincide with Maria's birthday, and went off in a very satisfactory style. At the breakfast there was a good deal of laughing, kissing and crying – Dr Joseph Hutton who proposed the toast to the bride and groom was 'visibly affected'. The only objectionable part for Maria was that 'horrid old Mr A. would kiss me although I eluded the ceremony by clever dodging for about an hour after the other bride's maids suffered'.[68] Of one thing she was certain: the complete suitability of Emily for William:

> I really believe you could not help liking her if you saw her now, she is so loving, womanly & true . . . There is something particularly sweet to me in her ways with Wm, so frank & modest, in fact I find her a dear loveable creature tho' I do not wear Cupid's spectacles.[69]

After the wedding, William and Emily went to the Lake District and the Yorkshire Dales. Lely went to stay with the Cleggs in London, and Maria went to a dairy farm at Broxton, near Cheshire, to learn cheese making. After a fortnight she considered herself 'quite au fait' with the art and hoped to get an insight into brewing and candle making before she left.

From the cheese farm Maria made a final round of visits to relatives, some of whom were relieved to find that Maria and

Lely were not now to undertake the journey alone, while others felt they were wrong to be leaving at all. Maria found that the latters' lack of sympathy made it virtually impossible to speak of future prospects and she felt under an 'unpleasant restraint' during the three weeks she spent among them. Lely was also 'suffering' at Norton, where she had gone for a last visit to her mother – although her mother's mind was so troubled with trifles, large events were of no great worry. One uniting factor was Emily, who was 'wonderfully' liked by all parties:

> Her great frankness & naturalness of manner together with her cheerful happy looks take most people by storm & she had just the way of meeting Stockton coldness without offending anyone. Everyone said she had the merit of originality for they never saw anybody in the least like her before.[70]

Emily, however, had not been groomed, as a housewife. 'Apples and plums stewed for dinner today', is one of Williams diary entries. 'What we should do if it were not for my housekeeping abilities I do not know.'[71]

Before returning to London and Frindsbury, Maria, Emily, and William spent three nights with the Joseph Huttons at Derby. Cobby, the Richmonds' dog, was left with them. On Sunday they went to the Unitarian chapel, 'a good old Presbyterian structure' where Hutton preached his opening – 'to us his farewell' – sermon. 'They have Martineau's hymn book & we had some exquisitely beautiful hymns of Wesley's,'[72] recalled William.

Harry Atkinson, to whom the Richmonds had entrusted shipping arrangements, now told them there was no likelihood of a ship to Auckland and New Plymouth until December. When William got back to London at the end of October, he went to St Katherine Dock to view the vessel, the *Sir Edward Paget*. He thought it uninviting – 'cockroachy, dark and dirty' – but it was filling fast and seemed a sound enough vessel, so he booked the only two poop cabins left. For the final packing during November, Lely rented a house for herself and Maria in Holloway Road. Now there was total bustle and confusion about what to take. Would a piano be more useful or more delightful than a dog cart? Parcels arrived from Germany and farewell presents were exchanged, among them an exquisite honiton lace scarf – 'it is far too good & expensive for the colonies & as I am not likely to be a bride over there I am afraid I can never wear it'.[73] Everybody gave daguerreotypes to everybody else: 'we have a ton in the house'. Maria was not happy with the 'Dag' of Margaret Taylor: 'you managed to get up such a regular daguerreotype expression, you villain,' she admonished. By good luck, through another family's cancellation, Lely and Maria were able to get one of the stern cabins and William and Emily the adjoining one at a greatly reduced rate. Maria described theirs, ten feet by eleven with two large windows, as 'quite a little parlour'; each cabin had its own 'WCs' and both had oil cloth from the passage at Springholm on the floor. 'The Governor could not go out more luxuriously . . . it seems to me like a haven of rest.'[74]

'The boys', who were travelling Intermediate, now numbered six. The nucleus was expanding. In addition to Harry and Arthur were Maria's two cousins, Charles and Calvert Wilson; the Atkinsons' friend from Frindsbury, Edward (Teddo) Patten; and James Brind, a boy of sixteen who joined the party at his father's[75] request, but of whom the others knew very little. Arthur had 'probed him as to his literary tastes,' Maria wrote, and the answer was Dickens. 'When Ar asked him what he liked (meaning pursuits), answer, Smoking!!!'[76] Maria was sure that Harry and Arthur, the latter 'such a dear kind boy & Lely quite spoils him he is such a pet of hers', would be the master spirits among 'the lads' and 'would give their tone to their companions'.[77]

On 6 December 1852 the *Sir Edward Paget* left St Katherine Dock, but the Richmond–Atkinson party did not join it until 8 December from Gravesend. They were having a last gathering at Frindsbury – '20 at table' and 'in some unaccountable manner accommodated in the Atkinson household or in beds in the village'.[78] The final levee on board was 'a curious scene, such a mixture of pleasure, pain, laughing & crying'. Through all this Maria kept herself in good spirits. Excitement, bustle, sheer hard work, and the thought of seeing 'the boys' again kept more gloomy sentiments at bay. She had written to Margaret that she would think of her once every twenty-four hours; 'nobody can ever estimate & care for me as you have done'. Both had exchanged lockets and Maria had sent her a copy of *The Wide Wide World* (recommended as suitable voyage reading by James Martineau)[79] so that they would both be reading the same book, at least for a time. In the accepted fashion she had told Margaret that they would meet again 'when earthly troubles are over'. As the departure grew closer, she was more practical and hopeful of meeting in this world:

Margie dear I hope you will keep a good heart. You must & shall see me again before long . . . we intend to grow rich people so that a pleasure trip to England may be quite possible some day. But really this new route (by Panama)[80] will bring us much nearer

in the matter of letters . . . Our household will be a curious jumble
at first, & whether the chaotic elements will come forth into anything
like *external* cultivation I can't say. I shall make it my constant
effort to establish a certain rustic refinement amongst us & you
shall hear how far I succeed. My letters from Taranaki will be
very interesting.[81]

Towards the end of her life Margaret wrote to James Richmond:
'It is altogether a life by itself that is made of all my NZ letters.
It is very like fairy tales where people go into the caves of the
earth . . .'[82]

Leaving English waters proved to be difficult. The *Sir Edward
Paget* sailed from Gravesend on 9 December 1852, but because of
storms and contrary winds did not quit the Isle of Wight until
nearly five weeks later. During this time the party made expeditions
ashore which were 'all very unreal', except for one that nearly
swept the ship's boat out to sea. Mrs Atkinson also made a sortie
to the vessel and when the *Paget* dropped anchor at Cowes, William,
Emily, Lely, and Maria took lodgings with her for eight days.
Finally the *Paget* and an armada of waiting ships were off, and
the rest of the voyage passed in what was becoming the familiar
way: an insufferable captain who quarrelled violently with Harry
Atkinson and in numerous petty ways made life as unpleasant as
possible for others in the party; rations ran low; many of the crew
became ill with scurvy and passengers helped work the ship, and
there was the usual boredom and bickering amongst the other
passengers. The Richmond–Atkinson party passed the time reading,
sketching, discussing, and producing *The Cuddy Times and Intermediate
Observer*. William conducted a class in Greek history.

There was also, as is legendary on long voyages, a shipboard
romance, although this one was unexpected, private (apart from
the one inevitable confidence), and long-lived. Maria and Arthur
Atkinson fell in love.

Falling in love with a view to matrimony was not often an option
for nineteenth-century women. Generally, women sought marriage
for economic security and social status, and men for legitimate
procreation and domestic convenience. Charlotte Brontë, writing
always 'something real, cool and solid', provides an illustration
in *Shirley*. Caroline and Shirley are discussing Eve, the primordial
woman:

'Milton tried to see the first woman, but Cary he saw her not.'

'You are bold to say so, Shirley.'

'Not more bold than faithful. It was his cook that he saw; or

it was Mrs Gill . . . preparing a cold collation for the rector.'[83]
There were also, as E.M. Forster later pointed out in *Howards End*,
Property, Propriety and Pride to be assured, assuaged and tidied
up. Love was fortunate to be involved and luckier still to survive.
Yet, one says again, firmly, Maria fell in love.

Of course she had to an extent done this before; in spite of
her Unitarian upbringing and sense of duty, she was romantically
inclined. She had been prepared to love Charles, in spite of various
defects, and then to leave him, almost as if the loving and the
leaving were an affair of the will. At twenty-eight, she was quite
resigned to being an 'old maid' or, as she more constructively put
it, to being an aunt or even great-aunt:

> I quite agree with you that it is a matter to be regretted that
> you should never marry [Margaret had refused a German]; in my
> own case I think it even more unlikely, but tho' always *bad* it is
> not so very sad for me as for you, as a hundred duties must obviously
> present themselves to me without that unnatural *seeking* for them
> which many single women are driven to . . . Lely & I do not intend
> to reside with any of the young Mrs Richmonds whoever they
> may be, so we shall always have a little roof of our own to welcome
> you to.[84]

As this letter reinforces, Maria favoured independence for women,
but not at the expense of close relationships. She thought life without
marriage was 'bad' for a woman (in this, her counterpart in
contemporary literature was Jane Eyre rather than Shirley Keeldar)
and she disliked stridency in women as much as flippery. In Margaret
she had her one intimate companion, and she had even flippantly
suggested that Margaret might come to New Zealand and they
might marry each other.

So, Maria was in full possession of her senses and experience,
and yet she was in love with, as she had previously called him,
'a lad' of nineteen. It was a mutual attraction: Maria and Arthur
thoroughly enjoyed each other's company, and Arthur's initial
respect and admiration had grown into liking and loving. Probably
the affection he and Lely had shown for each other bolstered his
confidence with Maria. His raciness, his zest for living, his curiosity
about things, his ready wit, intelligence and willingness – the phrase
is not a felicitous one – to improve himself, had all appealed to
Maria, as Emily's 'originality' had appealed to William. In neither
Atkinson was there any of the self-conscious affectation which was
anathema to both Richmonds.

But the unescapable fact remained: he was nineteen, she was

twenty-eight. If the positions had been reversed, as in the case of William and Emily, there would have been no embarrassment to either. The letter Maria wrote to Margaret about the relationship is for once a little awkward, even self-conscious; she had after all been so resigned, even didactic, on the unlikelihood of either of them marrying.

> There is one thing I should be dishonest to you not to mention tho' I do it with reluctance knowing it will give you pain; to me I admit it is like inward sunshine after a dark troubled time. Now you will be a little prepared for the blow perhaps . . . You were right in concluding that one young Atkinson would fall in love with his grandmother, but perhaps you did not expect my second childhood & dotage would commence at 8 & twenty – that I should have to admit, there being no objection, to marrying my grandson when he shall reach man's estate! Margie dear, I did not *wish* to be an old fool (not that it is being foolish to love the purest, noblest soul that happens to suit your peculiarities in every particular) but I could not help it. I am not engaged however & if Arthur has the sense to see the error of his ways in preferring old age to youth hereafter, he is free to choose again.[85]

On 25 May 1853, the *Paget* sailed up the Waitemata Harbour. The special relationship between Maria and Arthur was, as it were, treasured and put away. Maria's journal or 'general letter no.1' makes no mention of their feelings towards each other, and is full of the pleasure of landfall and landing: 'I cannot tell you the delight of sniffing the air smelling of earth & plants after so many months of sea, & the pleasure of putting one's feet in cool grass.'[86] She was also pleasantly surprised to see 'the dear old gorse so completely at home'. The *Paget* was to be two months at Auckland before sailing for New Plymouth; to Maria it seemed an insufferably long time, even though she found everything around her 'so vigorous & promising'. Then Harry Atkinson found that a small schooner, *The Sisters*, was leaving Manukau for New Plymouth within a few weeks, and he, Arthur, and James Brind decided to take passage in it. When Maria heard that there was accommodation for one more lady she determined to go with them, and a letter was sent to inform James and Henry.[87] After a twenty-four-hour run, *The Sisters* anchored off the New Plymouth beach on 18 June. James was there to meet them; Henry was putting their cottage in order. It was pouring with rain, the mountain would not have been visible, but James and Maria rushed away from the crowd on the beach and took a footpath to New Merton. It was a sort of homecoming.

CHAPTER
FOUR

Settling In

New Plymouth, June 1853–Dec. 1854.

Early European visitors were enthusiastic about New Plymouth. A visit in 1842 had led Bishop Selwyn to recall his favourite verse: 'Thy lot is fallen unto me in a fair ground'; Lieutenant-Governor Hobson, in a remark which came to be repeated again and again, described the settlement as 'the garden of New Zealand'; Edward Jerningham Wakefield in 1843 found the town 'a dull place' but was much taken with the small farms springing up on its outskirts; and the Reverend Richard Taylor, who came tramping around the coast from Wanganui on a pastoral visit in 1844, thought the town had 'quite an English village look about it'. Helen Hursthouse would have disputed this last remark, for as late as 1851 she wrote to her sister of 'the queer little houses that most people have. I have not the least doubt that my cottage is greatly inferior to any of your back premises.'[1] Naturally, Mount Taranaki[2] came in for its share of praise. J.C. Richmond noted, probably with Charles Heaphy's watercolour in mind, that

> all drawings you have seen are very wide of the mark. Those which exaggerate the least make it too steep. Then the exquisite lines of the spur that runs off towards the West are utterly blurred out. Great flanges of cliff, or gullies if you prefer, run up & down the cone casting fine shadows & redeeming it from formality.[3]

The first six ships of the Plymouth Company,[4] which arrived at New Plymouth between March 1841 and January 1843, brought just under 1,000 settlers, mostly from Devon and Cornwall. By the end of the decade the European population of both town and country districts had risen to about 1,400. Small farm agriculture predominated. There were a few men of substance such as Henry King of Brooklands, but for the most part settlers had little capital and relied solely on their own industry. George Jupp, who landed from the *Simlah* in October 1851 and found work as a gardener, described New Plymouth as a 'beautiful home for the labouring man, who if he is industrious may soon live under his own vine and fig tree'.[5] Before the vine or fig tree – actually wheat, grass, and rhubarb – could be established, dense standing bush had to be cleared, for by the end of the decade houses and sections about the town or within a mile of it were dear and scarce.

Here was one of the settlement's problems. The greater part of Taranaki,[6] far more than in any other province, was in deep bush. The town site was clear and the coastal belt fern-clad, but the bush began about a mile inland. Few settlers had enough money to bring the 'back bush' into production on any substantial scale, and lack of capital forced many of those who actually possessed bush land to become, in the words of one of them, 'half labourers and half farmers'. Clearing was laborious, slow, and often dangerous, and if a wind change caused a fire to burn out of control it was potentially devastating. In the hierarchy of the workforce, bullock drivers and sawyers were at the top and earned the most money. For some time James and Henry had living with them a young man named Worsley who had a bullock team and was carting stone for their chimney. 'He is a son of a Church of England clergyman, a tall young man of a cut very frequently observable with short young ladies at polka parties, but he takes to a blue serge shirt and "Way! Woap!" with bullocks in a manner not to be enough commended.'[7] New Plymouth's 'Sawyer King', as James Richmond described him, was also their neighbour. James had hoped for some sheltering bush to be left where his land abutted theirs: ' "No", said friend Broadmore, "I was sent here to cut down the bush and I shall go on as long as I live – them that come after me may plant." '[8]

Although Maria was to find amusement in the 'snobocracy' of the little settlement, there was among the scattered bush farmers the camaraderie of frontier democracy. James, Hugh, and Frank Ronalds, relatives of the Martineaus and friends of the Huttons, were typical of those among the 'gentle class' who came out with high hopes of bush farming in Taranaki. Arriving on the *Cashmere* in July 1853, they had little money, and when that ran out,

> Frank and I [Hugh] started on the tramp and went many miles into the bush and stopped at every bushman's house and asked if they wanted help. I daresay you will laugh when you think of us going to a house touching our hats . . . but I can assure you it is quite different here. We go to a house, walk in, wish them good morning and in a very independent way tell them we will come and work for them.[9]

The payment, if they were hired, was very often only board and lodging.

Passing visitors may have admired New Plymouth; settlers, especially during the forties, had to accept that access both to and from the settlement was difficult. Ships, other than coastal cutters and schooners, were infrequent; there was no natural harbour and there was a lee shore. Ernst Dieffenbach, naturalist for the New Zealand Company, had recommended Waitara for the Plymouth settlement, but F.A. Carrington, chief surveyor for the Plymouth Company, excluded it because of the constant surf on the river bar and centred the town of New Plymouth at the mouth of the Huatoki River.[10] Instead of a harbour for overseas vessels, New Plymouth would have an open roadstead with a surf-boat service to the Huatoki. By the time James and Henry arrived in New Plymouth, large vessels were still enough of a rarity to cause general excitement and the cessation of all business in the town when they were sighted. The lighter service, under the efficient management of John Watson, beachmaster, functioned so well that Henry noted that when the *Victory* eventually appeared its cargo was landed with speed and efficiency. He contrasted this with the delays experienced at Auckland. But New Plymouth's reputation as a difficult anchorage lived on, much to the chagrin of its citizens. During 1853 the *Simlah* and *Cashmere* spent weeks in the crowded port of Auckland before sailing to New Plymouth, while the *Sir Edward Paget*, with most of the Richmond–Atkinson party on board, spent nearly three months there. This habitual delay in Auckland, so different from the speedy unloading and despatch of vessels at New Plymouth, caused the *Taranaki Herald* to exclaim: 'It is well known that New Plymouth cannot yet boast a harbour; but it is equally well known that as an open roadstead few better can be found.'[11]

By the beginning of the 1850s, New Plymouth contained the scatter of houses and open fields, shops and small industries, a police barracks and gaol (in which Europeans mostly on charges of drunkenness outnumbered Maori) characteristic of small colonial towns. It could also boast a stone church designed by Frederick Thatcher in association with Bishop Selwyn, and a handsome colonial hospital designed by Thatcher and patronised more by Maori than European. Dissent was strong and evidenced by small unpretentious chapels. Communication with Auckland and Wellington was assured by a weekly overland mail service, carried by Maori. A book club had become a public library in 1847 and there was also a Mechanics Institute and a horticultural society. Overseas newspapers were still the most sought-after reading

matter, until the *Taranaki Herald* began publishing in August 1852.
There was a high level of illiteracy – about 25 per cent – among
the settlers. Owing to the earlier avid desire of Maori for 'the
book' – the taonga or treasure of missionaries – returning Ati Awa
at this time were more likely to be able to read and write in
their own language. The one government-endowed school, the Grey
Institute, was run by Wesleyan missionaries for the 'training' of
Maori boys and girls. Horse racing was the most popular recreation
for both Maori and settler.

Exports were mainly potatoes and grain crops, although settlers
were turning more to cattle and sheep grazing, with smaller amounts
of pork, bacon, beer, and butter. The last was often used by farmers,
whose wives were also dairymaids, in barter with local storekeepers
for goods. The Maori, who earlier had been door-to-door traders,
were by the end of the 1840s exporting their own potatoes and
wheat from the Waitara. European mechanics constructed two flour
mills for them in 1847, for which the payment (about £350) was
in pigs. Agriculture was the principal occupation and most of the
thirty or so professional men in New Plymouth who practised as
lawyers, doctors or ministers could also be described as part-time
farmers. As was customary in frontier society, males outnumbered
females. Parties involving the bush farmers were few – farms were
too scattered – but those which were held were regarded as social
occasions of moment, and so was the gossip which followed: 'It
is most laughable the reports that are circulated here. I have been
to three parties since I have been here and I have heard about
a week after each I am to be married to a different young lady.
I wonder who the next will be.'[12]

Into this society James and Henry had fitted reasonably well.
Henry lectured on chemistry and astronomy at the Mechanics
Institute, and James, considered one of the cleverest men in the
settlement, was invited to stand for the district of Taranaki in
the abortive assembly of New Ulster. He was defeated, but his
friend, Charles Brown, was elected unopposed for the town.

On his return to England in 1850, C.F. Hursthouse had painted
an idyllic picture of Taranaki for the intending Richmond emigrants:

> On landing in New Plymouth you would rent a cottage near John
> and Helen as a temporary abiding place; then whilst the ladies
> were unpacking the household gods, revelling in a succession of
> tea parties and picnics . . . you three, staff in hand and wallet on
> shoulder, accompanied by John or some other man cunning in land,

would stroll through the district and choose your hundred acres. This done, you would build your house, lay out your orchard, move on to the property and take possession.[13]

The Richmonds, who never put too much faith in anything C.F. Hursthouse said or wrote, would no doubt have considered his description too fulsome. But neither they nor their fellow emigrants ever doubted that in the North Island of New Zealand were thousands upon thousands of acres of unoccupied, untilled land simply awaiting the axe, the plough, and European occupancy. Nor did they question their right to convert this 'waste' land into private property. Engrained in English political philosophy since promulgated by John Locke in the seventeenth century and usefully spelt out again by Thomas Arnold in the nineteenth, was an implicit belief in the labour-value right to private property: 'Men were to subdue the earth . . . and with the labour so bestowed upon it came the right of property in it.'[14] C.F. Hursthouse embellished his argument on his 1848 lecture tour of the western counties by adding that this task of being fruitful and multiplying, of subduing the earth and replenishing it 'would seem indeed to have been peculiarly inherited by the British people'. Carried into the service of colonial politics, this meant that 'From the moment that British dominion was proclaimed in New Zealand, all lands not actually occupied . . . ought to be considered as the property of the Crown in its capacity as Trustee for the whole Community.'[15]

Of what significance then was the Treaty of Waitangi, which guaranteed that native land rights were inalienable unless land was ceded voluntarily to the Crown? The treaty was, in the decade following its signing, invoked by Maori, attacked by settlers, and defended by missionaries, but it was never actually an instrument of policy. In the view of a Select Committee of the House of Commons reporting on New Zealand in 1844, the terms of the treaty were 'ambiguous' and 'highly inconvenient' and had given natives 'notions' of their having a proprietary title to land which they did not actually occupy.[16] This 'notion' was, presumably, the traditional Maori view of land as an indivisible communal heritance. Within the tribal boundaries there was no 'waste' land; it was all known and used in the shifting seasonal way for the berries, birds, eels, fish, kumara which different localities produced; it was named and cherished.

James Richmond had no doubt about the validity of the settlers' claims:

I imagine that a day will come not long hence, when the preposterous

Waitangi treaty will be overruled . . . and the ridiculous claims of the natives to thousands upon thousands of acres of untrodden bush & fern will be no longer able to damp the ardour & cramp the energies of the industrious white man.[17]

He was also contemptuous of 'all nauseous maudlin maori fancying stuff' propagated by missionaries in order to keep their 'happy valleys' free from the consequences of colonisation. His opinions, shared by the mob, now seem arrogant, arbitrary, and mischievous, yet they arose out of the colonising situation. Emigrants came to Taranaki and to other New Zealand settlements hungry for the opportunity to better themselves. Maori tribal rights to unoccupied land seemed to be at best tenuous and, if they impeded settlement, downright dog-in-the-manger. It is easy enough to deplore James's sentiments, but one can only warm to the delight and enthusiasm with which Maria responded to her new country, forgetting that her words also imply the same intrinsic right to private ownership:

Everything that you can see is your very own, the absolute possession of land gives a sort of certainty that with common industry and care, you are in what may be your *home* till death . . . the feeling of coming home as it were to a country *wanting* you, asking for people to enjoy and use it, with a climate to suit you, a beauty to satisfy and delight, and with such capabilities and possibilities for the future . . . is enough to make the most sluggish nature 'feel spirited'. Sometimes I am in such a state that I feel convinced nothing short of going up Mt Egmont can properly relieve me and let off the steam; at present I only explode in the baking o ten loaves or in making up a dozen pounds of butter and an occasiona scramble down a gully tearing my clothes nearly to pieces.[18]

And one can respond equally well to the sentiments expressed b Wiremu Kingi Te Rangitake and other Te Ati Awa chiefs in letter addressed to Governor FitzRoy about the possible purchas of the fruitful land of Waitara, the apple of the settlers' eyes:

Listen to us respecting this land, respecting Waitara. Our hearts ar dark by reason of Mr Spain's award. Indeed, the Europeans are wron in striving for the land which was never sold by its owners, th men of Ngatiawa . . . This . . . is the determination of our peopl Waitara shall not be given up . . . Friend Governor, do you no love your land – England – the land of your fathers? as we als love our land at Waitara. Friend let your thoughts be good to u We desire not to strive with the Europeans, but, at the same tim we do not wish to have our land settled by them; rather let the be returned to the places which have been paid for by them, le a root of quarrel remains between us and the Europeans.[19]

Both 'voices' are part of our heritage; we cannot, with integrity, choose to listen to one and ignore the other.

Looking back with understanding on the conflict of interests between Maori and Pakeha in Taranaki it seems obvious that warfare would occur. It did not seem obvious at the time. Missionaries, so it was believed, had pacified the warring tribes, who were now caught up in the excitement of Christianity, literacy, and the trading opportunities which European settlement presented. The civilising influence of Europe, if not yet fully acclimatised, was at hand. Maori were to be both 'saved' and 'changed'. There had been one or two small alarms in the New Plymouth settlement during the 1840s, notably in 1843 when about 250 special constables were sworn in to face a possible threat from Waikato which did not eventuate. Two years later, in March 1845, special constables were again sworn in when both local Maori and settlers feared that Hone Heke's attack on Kororareka might presage an attack by Ngapuhi on the settlement. Again fears were groundless. Fighting which broke out in Wanganui in 1847 remained a local issue, and in fact the Maori grievance there was not so much against land sales and settlement, as against the military presence. It had no repercussions on New Plymouth except that some Wanganui settlers, including S.P. King, Dr Peter Wilson and their families, moved from Wanganui to New Plymouth. At no time did Maori in Taranaki, or elsewhere in New Zealand, present a completely united front against European land purchase. So strong was settler demand that there was always a chief or tribal faction willing to sell. This was particularly the case in north Taranaki, where the disarray of Te Ati Awa tribal organisation excited the insatiable settler appetite and finally provoked open warfare.

About 1827 part of Te Ati Awa from Waitara migrated to the Waikanae area to trade with European whalers in the Cook Strait–Kapiti region. Then, in the 1830s, Waitara and the land to the south was overrun by war parties from Waikato, who did not occupy the land but who took slaves and forced many Ati Awa survivors to flee to their Waikanae kin. When the New Zealand Company and the Plymouth Company negotiated for 60,000 acres in Taranaki during 1839 and 1840, they thus dealt with only a handful of Ati Awa, either exiles or the few still living in the settlement area. This 60,000-acre purchase, which included the Waitara, was upheld by Commissioner Spain in 1844, but Ati Awa who were already beginning to return to their homeland, protested the award to Lieutenant-Governor FitzRoy and he, sympathetic towards their

grievance – and to the fury of the New Plymouth settlers – abrogated
Spain's award and confined the settlement to a repurchased 3,500-
acre block in the immediate vicinity of the town. The settlers hoped
for better things from his successor – 'a man come to judge the
most vital questions between the Settler and the Savage'.[20]

Lieutenant-Governor Grey, who had already been instructed by
Earl Grey, Secretary of State, 'to avoid . . . any further surrender
of the property of the Crown',[21] authorised Donald McLean to
repurchase at no more than one shilling and sixpence per acre
(never did the government purchase price approach this figure)
as much of the 60,000 acres as the Maori could be persuaded to
relinquish, and to compensate settlers for land which Maori wished
to retain by making an equivalent purchase outside the 60,000 acres.
As a result, in 1847 two blocks of land, Omata and Tataraimaka,
totalling 16,000 acres, were purchased south of New Plymouth,
together with the Grey block of about 10,000 acres adjacent to
the town. In the bush-clad Grey block, thrown open to selection
in 1848 at ten shillings per acre, were New Merton, where James
and Henry lived, and the mob's future home, Hurworth.

Most coveted by settlers was that 'splendid tract of land covered
with luxuriant fern', the Waitara, and its purchase was beset with
future complications by the return to their Waitara homeland during
1848 of approximately 600 Ati Awa under Wiremu Kingi Te
Rangitake. Great was the rejoicing among the settlers when in
November 1848 F.D. Bell, New Zealand Company agent, purchased
with Grey's permission, 1,400 acres from a portion of the Puketapu
hapu of Ati Awa on the approach to Waitara.[22] The land was
offered by Rawiri Waiaua, a Puketapu chief and native assessor.
His offer was violently opposed by another Puketapu chief, Waitere
Katatore, who was supported by Wiremu Kingi. The New Plymouth
settlers were theoretically not involved in the 'native feud', as it
came to be called, and were advised by Colonel R.H. Wynyard
Adminstrator in the interregnum between Governors Grey and Gore
Browne, to stay clear of it. But simply because land was the
argument, the settlers felt themselves to be committed, and pressed
to commit the government to the 'selling' party. Among the most
vociferous of these was Maria:

> We feel clear that this place *must* go to the dogs, if Government
> will not interfere with a high hand in the Native feud . . . We
> (or most of us do) love the place with a sort of family affection
> which will make us cling on to the last, and we are quite justified
> in screaming for help let who will be in power.[23]

It was not until 1860 that fighting between Maori and settler broke out in Taranaki, but although C.F. Hursthouse could advise the Richmonds in 1850 that 'the land question, and its host of attendant ills is satisfactorily set at rest . . . and the Colony fast rising in favour',[24] the seeds of the conflict which was to destroy lives, livelihoods, and morale of both Maori and Pakeha in Taranaki had already been planted.

'Setting to rights' engaged Maria's immediate attention after her arrival at New Plymouth. Henry had earlier written that 'the poor ladies here are doomed to wood fires and prodigious iron pots',[25] but such was Maria's relief at finding James unwed and her delight at being reunited with 'the boys', she was in no way cast down by 'the sea of employment' which awaited her: 'I thank God I am here and that those dear boys' loneliness is over.'[26]

A month later, following a daily round of cooking over an open fire, making bread and butter, washing and mending an accumulation of clothes, and everlastingly sweeping out mud, she was still enthusiastic, even though she had little time for reading, writing or needlework other than darning socks. James was relieved to find no servant had accompanied her, and 'the boys' – Harry and Arthur Atkinson, James Brind, and Henry and James Richmond – took it in turns to stop indoors and help. Harry was the best riser; with the first streak of daylight he was up and had the fire lit, the floor swept and the water on for breakfast by the time Maria was dressed. The question uppermost in mind was, when would the *Paget* arrive from Auckland? Maria was particularly worried about Emily, who had become pregnant during the voyage and whose confinement was imminent. Henry, Arthur, and William Crow had begun work on a house in the town primarily intended for William and Emily. Built of stone – the work of a local mason – and lined in rimu, Beach Cottage was to become one of the most elegant of the town's houses. It was also on a fine site in St Aubyn Street overlooking the sea.[27] There was, however, an initial delay in getting shingles for the roof, and later in the year the energies of the mob were directed elsewhere. It was not until shortly before November 1854 that William, Emily, and the baby moved in.

On 16 August 1853, two months after Maria and the first party had landed from *The Sisters*, and eight months after it had left Gravesend (a normal voyage could have been made to England and back in the same time), the *Paget* was sighted in the roadstead with 'all our dear people on board in good health and great spirits

at finding themselves at last here'.[28] A spell of fine weather enabled
the carting from the beach and the unpacking of goods to be done
in favourable circumstances, but the house which had held six in
reasonable comfort was now stretched to accommodate twelve.
At New Merton (generally referred to as Merton) were Maria,
Lely, William, Emily, James, Henry, Harry, Arthur, Teddo Patten,
Charlie and Calvert Wilson, and James Brind. Within a fortnight
there were three more – Dr W.R. Bridges, surgeon on the *Paget*,
who had been unable to find accommodation in the town and who
was on hand for Emily's confinement; a nurse, and Mary Elizabeth
Richmond, born on 30 August. The baby arrived ahead of the nurse
and was given into Maria's care:

> I washed and dressed it with a boldness quite unexampled considering
> I never touched a baby so young . . . It is very nice to see the
> four uncles so pleased with their niece . . . Old Wm is at the summit
> of human satisfaction.[29]

Merton now consisted of sixty-seven acres, Henry and James
having bought an adjoining fifty acres before the others arrived.
It was about one and a half miles from town, near the present
junction of Carrington Street with Brooklands and Tarahua Roads,
and half a mile from the Hursthouses. The original seventeen acres
were mostly cleared of standing bush and planted in grass or mangel
wurzel interspersed with large blackened stumps. Henry and James
had run three cows (now increased to five) and let the rest of
the cleared land for grazing. Fences which were at first simply
branches of trees piled on top of each other were replaced with
post and rail – chasing after wandering cattle and pigs had been
an irritating and daily occurrence. The house, thirty feet by fifteen
was divided into kitchen, sitting room, and two bedrooms, one
on the ground floor, the other, which James and Henry had added
built under the roof. A barn served also as sleeping quarters for
five of the household. The original cob chimney had collapsed and
had been replaced by a stone one, the expense and solidity of which
effectively put paid to any plans for rebuilding. The new fifty
acres through which the Henui flowed was still bush-clad. Harry
Teddo, and Arthur set to work to make a clearing for another
mangel wurzel crop and for a small cottage for some of their number

But even when Merton was finally transformed into farmland
it would not support more than two people. In September 1852
William and Henry purchased 200 acres, at ten shillings per acre
further back in the Grey block along the as yet uncut line of the
Carrington Road. So delighted were the others with the land that

after their first exploratory expedition Harry and Arthur Atkinson bought an adjoining 200 acres. This was the beginning of Hurworth.

In the burst of activity which followed the bush purchases, Beach Cottage was rather neglected. However, there was some relief to the overcrowding at Merton when James, Arthur, Harry, Teddo, and James Brind, who were all at work clearing the new bush land, built a fern-post whare there and lived in it during the week, returning to Merton on Sunday. Back at Merton, Lely and Maria shared the downstairs bedroom; Henry, Calvert, and Charlie slept in what Maria called 'the tent room' above, and William, Emily, and the baby used the sitting room as a bedroom. When they came in from the bush, Harry and Arthur slept in the newly built Orchard Cottage alongside. One of the items which arrived from the *Paget* was a cooking stove which James and Charlie fixed in brick and housed in a lean-to added to the existing kitchen. 'Be it known,' wrote Maria,

> we call the new part [the roof bedroom of the house] the Giraffe House . . . the new kitchen over the cooking stove has v. deep eaves and reminds me of a certain Persian goat house . . . Orchard Cottage . . . looks well adapted for buffalos, bisons or elks. Altogether our premises have a v. zoological aspect.[30]

As the major-domo of this bustling establishment, Maria was in her element. Gone was the introspection which clouded so many of her English letters; the longing to be usefully employed was more than satisfied. If Lely often despaired, Maria was relishing the monumental task of settling in: 'there are 10 times as many clothes as there are drawers or chests to contain them, 10 times as many books as shelves and cupboards, etc etc, so that boxes bags sacks cases hampers and bundles embarrass you at every turn'.[31] Her piano, which had taken precedence over a dog cart, was unpacked and much used, but her 'beloved German songs' had not yet surfaced. The outside barn now served as a dairy, 'a rough affair but it is roomy and sweet'. She was, however, rather relieved when James joined the bush party. Henry, who remained at Merton, was much less 'crotchety and a better *finisher* of things. He has not so many *bigotries* as Js.; he is more disposed to listen to feminine plans for indoor improvements.'[32]

Maria had never taken kindly to servants. Now with none, and the task of providing for eight during the week and thirteen on Sunday, she exulted in her independence and looked back to the easier circumstances of England without regret:

> I consider myself a much more respectable character than I was

when . . . a fine lady, did nothing for anybody but made a gt many people do things for me. The worst part of the life for me is that it makes me fearfully conceited. I am so proud at finding how easy it is to be independent. Lely talks about not being able to bear my being a slave, but I really feel myself less a slave now that I can see I can do everything for myself, than I ever did before. When my pantry shelves are scrubbed, and it contains as it will tomorrow afternoon (Saturday) a round of boiled beef, a roast leg of pork, a rhubarb pie, 15 large loaves and 8 pounds of fresh butter ready for Sunday and the bush party, I feel as self-satisfied and proud as mortal can. A little while since I shd have thought it necessary to have somebody to prepare all these things for me, now I can do it all for myself.[33]

Maria then launched into a spirited attack on the 'gt servant plague in England'. It would have been too much for Margaret Taylor, and probably confirmed her view that life in Taranaki was too singular to be tempting.

I am quite certain that the gt servant plague in England must go on increasing till people learn that they are much better and happier in body and mind for not having a separate class to do everything for them they are too stupid lazy or refined to do for themselves. I don't mean to say that I think there is to be no division of labour or distinction of class (the total want of the former here leads to a terrible waste of time), but that things in England are going too far, that there is an unnatural division between the served and the servers, wh. is I believe wicked and unchristian. Nine tenth of the women who are so much waited on make no use of the time gained to them . . . Of course for those who do make a noble use of it it is a gain to all the world that they shd. be waited on; but I must say I have nothing but contempt for dozens of niminy piminy little dolls of women who do nothing but go about the world *shopping* and looking smart, and get another maid for every baby that comes to them. I wish the cooks and housemaids an nursemaids of such wd. strike and leave the mistresses let ther be ever so rich, to cook the dinners, clean the rooms, and nurs the children themselves. I daresay that you will think that I ar a cross democratic old colonist and that I had better go to be than write such rubbish, so good night.

NB. If anyone can show me that it is right, wholesome and Xtia that one set of human beings shd. do everything commonly calle dirty or disagreeable for the sake of keeping the hands of anothe set white and their heads full of frippery, I will retract all I hav said.[34]

Maria was not unique in finding independence and satisfaction in this rough-and-ready domesticity. A.J. Hammerton, in *Emigrant Gentlewomen*, has stated that once out of Britain middle-class women were 'remarkably adaptive': 'women showed a willingness to risk their gentility by undertaking work which would have been unthinkable at home'.[35] Some, like Charlotte Godley and Sarah Selwyn, brought a personal maid along with them; others like 'Lady Barker' seemed helpless without a cook. Mrs Monro bemoaned the scarcity of 'good' servants in Nelson, and her husband was mortified to see his wife 'do many things which ladies in civilized countries are commonly supposed to be spared'.[36] But Sarah Greenwood wrote that she had never been happier or better in her life than as 'a complete maid of all work',[37] and Mary Taylor, who opened a draper's shop in Wellington and did her own domestic chores, wrote, 'I had much rather be tired than ennuyée.'[38]

Nevertheless, Maria was also sensible of what had, for the time being, gone from her life:

Everything that is good, that gives elegance and beauty to life is wanting here . . . everything that makes life *wholesome* for mind and body our life possesses. If it were possible to combine this wholesomeness and that beauty I suppose earthly existence would be too perfect and there would be no chance of anyone's wishing for a heaven.[39]

One of her joys from the moment she set foot in Taranaki was the Te Henui stream:

It is considered rather a disadvantage to have your land divided by a stream like the Henui, but . . . not being as yet a *practical* farmer I felt great delight in scrambling down to the beautiful stream and feeling that a piece of it was our very own having our estate on both sides.[40]

If some of her fellow settlers missed the orderly landscape of England, Maria saw Taranaki's beauty in the luxuriance of the ferns on the banks of Te Henui, on the trunks of trees and on the bush floor, so profuse, so different from the 'patches' of greenery grown under steamy glass in England. She saw beauty, too, in the mountain, 'so grand and solemn, rising with such a beautiful dazzling summit' and, when the sun set behind it, lighting up the snow like 'a glimpse of fairy land or dream land, the wide space of lonely unexamined forest before you makes the feeling of mystery and unattainableness as strong as that of admiration'.[41] She also saw the other side:

But I cd. also tell you of an afternoon when walking from Aunt's house to ours, the scene was ugly, quite ghastly in ugliness; a drizzling rain was falling . . . hiding all that was more than a hundred yards off; the wide rough road full of deep ruts and with here and there an old giant stump sticking up in it, the clumsy looking fences on each side of the road, and beyond, the fields full of stumps of all sizes and shapes that seem in dim twylight more like neglected churchyards than fields, were the only things I cd. see, except here and there a tall blasted tree killed 10 years ago by the fires made in clearing these fields. Nothing more dreary looking cd. be imagined. Yet the same features seen as foreground to the beauties beyond, never struck me before as *being* ugly.[42]

Bush walking or 'scrambling', sitting on a rock in Te Henui reading Wordsworth or Spenser to James while he sketched, the 'delicious practice' of bathing in the river alone or with Emily or the Hursthouse girls provided Maria's recreation. She occasionally went visiting to Aunt Helen Hursthouse or to the Stephenson Smiths who lived about two to three miles from Merton. There were also the S.P. Kings – 'simple, friendly, sensible people' – the Charles Browns, and the Blacketts[43] whom she found congenial company. Maria did not expect to find many with whom she could share ideas, but her own large and harmonious party – 'such a good set as would be difficult to equal'[44] – made it impossible to be dull. Nor were they without expectations: 'We feel ourselves to be members of an infant state which will every day become more important.'[45]

One of the members of the infant state who seemed, in Maria's eyes, to have arrived 'in the very nick of time', was William 'He is wanted,' she wrote, 'and seems to enjoy watching the progress of the baby constitution.'[46] William had wanted to see a constitution granting representative government to New Zealand before he committed his future to the colony. On 30 June 1852, Parliament at Westminster passed 'An Act to grant a Representative Constitution to the Colony of New Zealand'. The country was divided into six provinces, each with an elected provincial council and superintendent. There was also provision for a 'General Assembly' consisting of an elected House of Representatives and a Legislative Council, to which members were nominated for life by the governor. The property qualification was low, but except in a few instances it disqualified Maori from the all-male franchise as their land was not held by individual title. The election for superintendent of the Taranaki Provincial Council took place shortly after Maria landed. Every Saturday at the Seven Stars Inn James

chaired the committee to promote Charles Brown; the William
Halse party attended the Omata Inn and the Ship Hotel. James
also wrote anonymous 'squibs and satires' for Brown, and these
were considered 'too clever to be written by anybody in the
settlement but one of the Mr Richmonds'.[47]

> We have come into quite a new world of gossip and politics on
> a very small scale . . . The ridiculous part of the business seems
> that at present there are no vital questions on wh. the people can
> differ so as to arrange them into parties.[48]

Charles Brown was elected superintendent, and in the subsequent
provincial council establishment the posts of clerk of the council
and attorney of the province were given to C.W. Richmond at
a combined yearly salary of £150. 'A fine little income here,' Maria
commented, 'and the post will make him the chief lawyer in N.
Plymouth. I think Wm is *sure* to prosper and be happy here.'[49]
Henry too looked flourishing and was a '*solid* treasure', but James,
in a manner that was all too reminiscent, was alternately 'languid
and unsatisfactory' and then disconcertingly 'merry for an evening'.

In October 1853 Maria confided to Margaret Taylor that she
found James 'very trying' and that 'it would have needed a great
deal, a perfect mountain of love to make you happy as his wife'.[50]
Five months later James was on his way back to England, ostensibly
to renew his suit for Margaret's hand. As always happened when
James appeared at risk or vulnerable – an impression no doubt
reinforced by his giving his shocked family only twenty-four hours'
notice of his departure – Maria flew to his aid. All previous irritation
forgotten, she begged her friend:

> Margie dearest, deal trustfully, lovingly with him; if you *can*, be
> his help mate thro' life; never did creature need a faithful wife
> as he does, all his excellences, all his weaknesses make him restless,
> uncomfortable, almost useless in life till he is anchored and supported
> as he can be by you. The claims and advice of others *must not*
> be allowed to turn the balance against him if your own heart does
> not.[51]

Maria's rationality appears to have deserted her whenever she was
anxious about James's well being. In a flight of fancy she saw
James and Margie being wed on her birthday, as were William
and Emily, 'giving me too a dearer sister than before'. Failing
that, she hoped that the day she herself married Arthur – they
were thinking of marrying early in 1855 – would be brightened
by the belief that 'you are then my sister in fact as well as in
love, and on the seas bringing us back dear old Jas'.[52]

It was not to work out like that. James's real need, and it remained so for most of his life, was respite from New Zealand. As he wrote later to his future wife:

> I feel intensely the outlandishness of New Zealand, the wind does not sound like the English wind, the rain is fiercer, the sea is wilder at least to the imagination. These weigh more in my mind than the rough living.[53]

Letters crossed and recrossed. Margaret Taylor was in some confusion of mind, but held fast to her previous refusal. A sense of duty to her sister, Kate, weighed with her – though Maria insisted that it was a mistaken one: 'she [Kate] seems so utterly incapable of understanding James . . . that it is really painful to read her letter'. And Margaret was still disinclined to give up Dresden for Taranaki, although she conceded to William that 'everything I hear of it does but give it new charm . . . for a man'.[54] Maria persevered, but little survives from Margaret and nothing from James about his intention to woo her. By February 1855, however, Maria was calm enough to think Margaret 'ought *not* to marry James for *his* sake . . . and I dread hearing under the painful agitation of your meeting, either of you should be hurried into an unwise decision.'[55]

Maria's own engagement had meantime been proceeding most satisfactorily. Prior to James's departure, Arthur, Maria, and James took themselves off to the Te Henui on Sundays. There Arthur joined in the make-believe games that so delighted the other two: 'We went through a great deal of jungle in which we felt exactly like tigers and I was as fierce as a lion . . .'[56] Maria often gave Arthur presents – carved ivory foxheads, diamond pins and, on his twentieth birthday, 'a chain curiously and beautifully worked'. If there was a gaiety and a playfulness in their relationship which delighted them both, it did not preclude reverence. 'I pray God she may always be holy to me,' wrote Arthur,[57] who frequently comments in his diary: 'I can so sweetly rest in her.'

By October 1853 it was agreed among the mob that Arthur was indeed walking out with Maria. James ceased chaperoning (i that had in fact been his role), and Maria and Arthur went to the Te Henui alone, sometimes to bathe – Arthur always retired to another part of the stream – and sometimes to read. They also went 'calling' together, mostly to the Hursthouses and once, 'i gorgeous array', to tea with the S.P. Kings.

'Every month,' Maria wrote to Mary Hutton, 'has drawn m more strongly to him, and now not one doubt or scruple remain as to the rightness of my course in accepting him.'[58] To Maria relief, Margie had responded favourably to her first intimation of love for Arthur:

> Your kind and loving trustfulness dear Margie are comforting to me. I do hope you will learn to know and love Arthur, meantime it is sweet that you try and believe in him for my sake. All that you may not like in him you would see or find out in a week's acquaintance, all there is to love and respect you would not have discovered in a year.[59]

William had also written to Margaret to appraise her of the engagement, fearing that it would upset her and that what he was unwise enough to call her 'bigotry' would estrange her from Maria. He was smartly told that 'Maria was true enough to our love for each other to tell me what was coming and wrote to me so beautifully so *truly* that I felt she would be making no mistake.'[60] Apparently Margaret had always been fearful that it would be the eldest Atkinson, John Staines, who would fall for Maria, and for him she had no time. Neither had Maria: 'of dreadful Dawlish memory' was how she remembered him. Margaret concluded that Arthur must be a very different man, though she could 'never fancy anyone good enough for her on this earth'.[61]

The mob was continuing to grow both in numbers and possessions. During 1854 and early in 1855, William, Harry, and Arthur bought more land, so that by June 1855 they owned between them 1,070 acres of 'the back bush (henceforward to be known as Hurworth)'.[62] Frank and Hugh Ronalds, now reconciled to the Richmonds (they had at first found James and Maria rather stiff and off-putting) and in fact dependent on William for raising a mortgage, bought 200 acres next to the Richmond holding. William told them that nothing would please him so much as having them as neighbours. The Ronalds thus came within the orbit of Hurworth and consolidated their place within the mob when their two sisters, Marion (Polly) and Eliza, who joined their brothers in October 1856, later married Decimus and William Atkinson respectively. William Smith Atkinson, who was the first of the family to live in New Zealand and had acquired something of a disreputable character on the Otago goldfields, suddenly turned up at Merton on 20 January 1854. He had walked there from Wellington. 'Old Bill' elected to throw in his lot with his brothers but Harry and Arthur, aware of his record, let him have 100 acres of their land only after he had proved himself a willing and steady worker. Hurworth was about seven miles from New Plymouth and about five from Merton (which became a convenient staging-post on the journey from town to the back bush), and making a road to Hurworth was one of the first jobs of 1854. Henry and Charlie Wilson worked from the Merton end; Teddo Patten and Bill Atkinson assisted by Frank and Hugh Ronalds worked from the bush end. A small government subsidy was of some assistance, but the main cost was born by the landowners along the road who contributed one shilling per acre to the wages of the working parties. The Carrington Road to Hurworth was completed as a useable track for bullocks, horses, and people by mid-1855.

The remainder of the bush party worked at making clearings for future houses and for the fifty or so cattle which they ran; some were their own, others were taken on at one shilling per head per week. In making a clearing, the undergrowth was first cut with a bill-hook, then the smaller trees and 'the pines' (generally a reference to rimu), with their branches lopped off, were felled, so that the whole lay 'snug and compact'. After drying for four or five months, the heaps were fired in a strong wind. A 'good burn' destroyed all the small stuff and burnt the surface of the ground well. Clearing up, the worst job of all, with everything black and dirty, involved stacking the residue against the axed giants and reburning. Grass seed or mangel wurzel was then sown. This was the theory; if the wind changed during a burn then all property was in danger. After the long hot summer of 1853–4, the fallen bush round Merton was tinder dry. Maria recalled:

> Just as several people had lighted their clearings a strong gale from the south east, what is called here 'the mountain wind', sprang up. In a few hours all the dead trees and stumps in the neighbourhood were on fire . . . Nothing grander at night can be imagined and if the stream of fire did not run in the direction of any human habitation there would be unmixed pleasure in watching it.[63]

But the fire did run close to property, and there were some hasty removals.

> Richard Lethbridge removed all his furniture and took out his doors and windows and carted his wheatstack into John Hursthouse's grass field . . . However, the active exertions of some 20 people who came to Lethbridge's assistance saved the house . . . Broadmore's premises were not in as perilous a position but he watched on his stack all night and all the family were slaving to and fro with pails of water to extinguish the nearest fires in logs or stumps all day.[64]

Another burn, out of control, put Orchard Cottage in danger. Fo two days and nights everyone laboured with buckets of water until the wind lulled.

Fatigue and excitement notwithstanding, Maria continued to enjoy her life. At Merton they were almost self-sufficient with cheese, milk, and butter from the dairy, vegetables from the garden, eggs from their poultry (also Maria's preserve), and honey – between fifty and sixty pounds – from the orchard bees. 'I love Taranaki more every day,' she wrote in June 1854 to Margaret:

> I suppose I was born to live here, certainly it fits me well, tho' I feel doubtful as to any woman without my peculiar crotchets being happy here. Your Dresden life is the more interesting in a thousand ways but it has no root, it is like a beautiful nosegay of rare flowers, whilst my life is an ugly little stick of a rosebush with plenty of prickles but . . . in good soil it will give me a few sweet smelling blossoms for years.[65]

The first member of the kin group to die in Taranaki was 'old Mr Hursthouse'. Thanks to his unremitting exertions – 'the old gentleman works from morning till night in the garden' – Okoare, the Stephenson Smith's home, had a very finished and civilised air, so Maria thought when she visited in July 1853. She found Charles Hursthouse 'a good deal shrunk and aged, but as energetic and cheerful as ever'.[66] He died on 21 June 1854 and was buried under a simple gravestone in Te Henui cemetery. The garden on which he had laboured was later destroyed in the Taranaki Wars. His true memorial was in the trees he planted in his home parish of Tydd St Mary's in the county of Lincolnshire, as a parting gesture to show his respect for the parish.

In the late summer of 1854, Maria and most of the mob made a picnic excursion to the Waitara by bullock waggon. They passed through the open fern country of Bell block and came to the Waitara River. There they walked by the cultivated fields of the Maori who were at work bringing in their harvest. 'When the English possess and cultivate the Waitera plains,' Maria wrote in her journal, 'it will assume a more English aspect than any tract I have yet seen in NZ.'[67] Possession of the Waitara and other Taranaki land seemed simply a matter of course.

Early in March 1854, Land Purchase Commissioner Donald McLean met with 2,000 Maori gathered in New Plymouth to talk over the sale of land to the government. The town presented 'a busy and picturesque appearance from the numerous encampments of natives', and although 'like a fair during the whole time, all

passed off without the slightest disturbance'.[68] Purchase of the Hua
and Waiwakaiho blocks, upwards of 30,000 acres, seemed settled.
Maria wrote that

> the grand Maori meeting . . . terminated most satisfactorily for
> Taranaki by the acquisition of a splendid tract as large as the whole
> of the land before in possession of Europeans . . . Let no one hesitate
> coming now from fear of a want of land. Everyone is in great
> spirits at the purchase and I am more than ever glad that we did
> not stop at Auckland.[69]

A public dinner was given in McLean's honour and among the
laudatory speeches were those given by the native assessors. No
one seemed concerned at the absence of Wiremu Kingi of Waitara,
who had also been invited. Caught up in the euphoria of the moment,
the editor of the *Taranaki Herald* launched into a paean to the land
of promise, Taranaki:

> The only cause of hesitation heretofore has been the want of Land;
> that difficulty is now removed, and thousands of acres of this
> favoured district, as emphatically as truly termed the GARDEN OF
> NEW ZEALAND, await those who yearn for the delights of a purely
> pastoral existence, protected by institutions which every Englishman
> has been educated to reverence and appreciate; and enjoying an
> immunity from crime and violence, the parallel of which, is not
> to be found in the world elsewhere.[70]

There was nothing at all in the *Taranaki Herald* about a subsequent
meeting which, in significance, outrivalled the loudly acclaimed
one in New Plymouth. Early in May 1854 at Whareroa, near present-
day Hawera, more than 1,000 delegates from West Coast tribes
met in the huge meeting house, Taiporohenui, especially built by
Ngati Ruanui for the occasion, and pledged themselves to stop
all further land sales to the government.

At the beginning of August 1854, while Superintendent Charles
Brown was attending the first session of the General Assembly
at Auckland and C.W. Richmond, as acting provincial secretary,
was effectively at the helm of Taranaki, an incident occurred which,
although not shattering to the tranquillity of the province at the
time, was to have far-reaching consequences. Rawiri Waiaua, native
assessor, Puketapu chief, and an advocate of the 'selling party' was
killed along with others of his party by Watere Katatore and
followers who were also of the Puketapu hapu of Te Ati Awa
The dispute had tribal origins but what gave it its cutting edge
was the fact that Rawiri had offered a block of land to the
government, and while he and his party were marking the boundaries

– an act understood by Maori to be 'not merely a description of the land but also a considerable proof of title to dispose of it'[71] – they were attacked, after being warned by Katatore and his supporters, and, in Richmond's words, 'shot like dogs'. Four were killed on the spot; Rawiri's brother died the following morning, and Rawiri, mortally wounded, was taken to the Colonial Hospital.[72] Rawiri's people immediately sent into New Plymouth for arms and ammunition and went down to Katatore's pa, firing some hundreds of rounds into it without causing casualties. 'For us,' William commented, 'there seems nothing to do but to keep clear of the row if possible.'[73] The *Taranaki Herald* gave greater coverage to the Crimean War; it did caution settlers against visiting the scene of the dispute.

There was no direct threat to the settlement, but C.W. Richmond worried about its defenceless state. He suggested to Brown that some expedient should be thought of whereby the town might acquire a new gaol. 'It should have loopholed walls and a substantial blockhouse in the centre – something like the Auckland barracks on a small scale. At present we are absolutely without refuge'.[74] He was not anxious for troops. 'What we should best like would be that a ship of war should look in on us and see how matters are going on. That would be less likely to alarm the natives than soldiers.'[75]

Such faintheartedness on William's part – or so it was interpreted – did not appeal to the mob. Some of the young men were eager to storm Katatore's pa, Kaipakopako, and either shoot Katatore or 'drag him to justice'. Harry Atkinson intimated that 'if a man of vigour like the Superintendent had been at the head of affairs, it would have been done. I believe,' wrote William, 'he considered it my duty as having control of the police, to head the storming party.'[76] Maria's rhetoric was even more aggressive:

> These men [Rawiri and his followers] are neither more nor less murdered in cold blood and yet it seems thought that our law cannot touch the murderers, as we have not force enough to compel the natives to give up the culprits. I must say it makes my blood boil to think of standing quietly by and permitting such outrages as these, but the settlers are I feel a mean-spirited set, thanks in part to wretched misgovernment which has discouraged a manly independent spirit amongst them. I am afraid 'moral force is moral humbug' when addressed to savages.[77]

Fortunately for harmonious relationships, tree felling, road making, housekeeping, bush scrambling, and wedding preparations

absorbed the mob's more bellicose energy. The marriage of Maria
and Arthur was intended to take place in the approaching summer.
Maria thought January or February; Emily was determined on
November, and in the event it was celebrated on 30 December
1854. Always opposed to anything that invaded family privacy,
Maria saw a church wedding as likely to be 'very public and
disagreeable in a little gossiping place like this where anything
that can be made into an event *is*'.[78] Marriage by special licence
at the Beach Cottage was thought too expensive a luxury, and
a civil marriage which could also have been quietly performed
was rejected because neither Maria nor Arthur wanted only a secular
ceremony. William, *in loco parentis*, determined that Maria should
have after marriage the same full power over her share of the
inherited Richmond income as she presently enjoyed: 'That seems
to me the right thing when as in her case there is no doubt about
the prudence of the lady and her ability to manage her own affairs.
There will in fact be no settlement at all.'[79] William was here
ahead of his time and was relying on a similar gesture of liberality
on Arthur's part.

James's absence cast a shadow. Maria still thought him to be
tossing his way to England in discomfort and ill health. On the
day before the wedding a budget of letters arrived and Maria,
who had worked herself up to bear bad news about 'our dear Jas',
was 'intoxicated' to find him safe in England and in wonderfully
good health – 'his mind too had resumed its right tone'.

The day itself was gloriously fine. The wedding took place at
St Mary's Church at 8.30 in the morning, so as to avoid heat and
spectators:

> I went down to the Beach cottage on the 28th and on the 30th
> the bridesmaids who were Mary Hursthouse and the three young
> cousins[80] came early and dressed there. All the young men wished
> to attend so they appeared from the bush about 8.15 leaving Arthur
> and Cal [Calvert Wilson] in ambush near the church. The procession
> was not a formal one, the party dropped off in twos and threes,
> Wm and I being the last couple. The short walk to the church
> gave me a most singular feeling – the lovely morning, the pleasant
> friendly party, Wm's elegant little home nestled down by the sea
> looking . . . as tho' part of a picture. I tried to follow back the
> stream of circumstances that had assembled such a party in that
> spot. I couldn't feel the present to be a reality but looking back
> only made it more strange and wonderful. I believe no strangers
> were in the church which looked very pretty as all the Xmas

decorations were still fresh. Mr Govett read I should think all the church service which does not appeal to my feelings or suit one's taste, but most certainly as he is a sincere good man I forgive him. The signing of names and universal kissing was done in the school house near the church, there being no vestry. Then Arthur and I walked home to Merton by the same path along which James took us on the day we landed in the pouring rain. We talked of that day and of him and you, and were enchanted with the loveliness of everything around.[81]

After the ceremony the party returned to Beach Cottage, where they were later rejoined by Maria and Arthur. From there they all proceeded in bullock carts and on foot to the Sugar Loaves for a picnic dinner. The numbers now included the S.P. Kings and the young Hursthouse male cousins. In her letter to Margaret Taylor, Maria enclosed a scrap of her wedding dress and added, 'Antediluvian as I am [she was 30] I wore the same bonnet as that I had on at Wm and Em's wedding and a beautiful *honiton* lace scarf given me by kind Mrs Vowler before I left England.'[82]

For three weeks Maria and Arthur had Merton to themselves. Their 'old bustling ways recommenced on Sunday 25 January 1855 when the bush and beach parties reassembled round the social board.'[83] With all the familiar faces around her, Maria wondered about 'the change' made by her married state:

Does it not seem absurd to think of me as Mrs? I cannot believe I am not Maria Richmond, the change has come so quickly and I fill so nearly the same position as there to fore that it is difficult to believe that people are addressing me when they talk of Mrs Atkinson or Mrs Arthur.[84]

'Bird's Nest' at Merton

New Plymouth, Jan. 1855–Dec. 1856

'It has been such a gay busy exciting summer,' Maria wrote to
Margaret in February 1855. Visiting began soon after the wedding
and the highlight was the 'entertainment' the S.P. Kings gave the
newly-weds:

> Everything was beautifully managed, they all have so much neatness,
> cleverness & taste that I have often been at parties where a pastry
> cook & a dozen assistants have been employed which might be
> called clumsy or vulgar in comparison with this colonial & servantless
> entertainment. We went to an early tea that we might enjoy the
> lovely evening in their beautiful garden, the latter was in finer
> order than I have ever yet seen it, glowing with choice flowers.
> Miss King[1] is a wonderful woman; besides doing all the cooking
> & household management & assisting in the school[2] three days a
> week she has found time to make a wilderness at the extremity
> of their garden blossom like the rose . . . clearing away all the
> ugly undergrowth from a number of beautiful fern trees, draining
> a little swamp . . . & then making terraced paths & beds on the
> steep side of the gully from which you can look down on the spreading
> fern trees & get glimpses of the flower garden, thatched cottage
> & sea beyond.[3]

After sunset, all forty present assembled in the schoolroom where
music and dancing kept up until one o'clock. The Hurworth bushmen
thought the evening broke up too soon for they were enthusiastic
dancers:

> After a hard day's felling they will come a six miles rough walk
> [and] metamorphose themselves from wild men of the woods into
> smart patent leather booted young gentlemen, some of them
> demanding white pt. handkerchiefs & scent, for the sake of dancing
> till two or three o'clock.[4]

A week later the Charles Browns gave a party which Maria

acknowledged as very pleasant but she thought the Kings' schoolroom was much more suited to dancing than the drawing room of Egmont House, the superintendent's town residence. On 1 February Aunt Helen Hursthouse, rising above the despondency induced by her husband's alcoholism and her fears for the future, gave a 'tea champetre'. The sixty-five guests amused themselves in playing *les graces* (a fashionable French game played with pairs of light sticks and a wicker ring), battledore, and shuttlecock, or in simply strolling about the garden and field. Aunt Helen and Aunt Hannah Stephenson Smith dispensed tea and coffee at a long table under peach and mimosa trees. 'When sunset & moonlight were mingling' the whole party adjourned to Merton to dance.

An 'entertainment' of a different sort occurred on 23 January.

The week has been made much more bustling & exciting by the . . . longest & strongest earthquake shock that has been experienced in this settlement . . . suddenly the room began to creak & roll precisely as a steamer does when moving away from the side of a wharf. The feeling was so wonderful & astounding we could only look awe-struck in each other's faces.[5]

Merton's inhabitants thought it prudent to slip through the French windows on to the grass as the chimney had already been cracked by a previous earthquake. Outside trees swayed as though drunk, dead branches came crashing down, and at some distance to the south they heard explosions like the discharge of heavy artillery.[6] The rolling, tumbling motion which lasted upwards of two minutes Maria thought 'an awful thrilling sensation, not altogether without a species of enjoyment in it'.[7] The bush party who arrived in haste took down the top half of the chimney. Otherwise the earthquake, which resulted in considerable damage and loss of life in Wellington, caused only minor damage – cracked chimneys, smashed crockery, and a good deal of spilt milk and cream – in New Plymouth. Not a stone or a piece of mortar moved in Beach Cottage. For several nights after the major quake there were smaller shocks, and one night a just-perceptible movement felt 'as tho' we were lying on the back of some huge creature breathing regularly & gently'.[8]

More thrilling still was Maria's ascent of Mt Taranaki at the end of the summer of 1855 – 'the celebrated Mountain expedition on which alone my hopes of fame rest!'[9] Apparently she found writing about it more of a daunting task than the climb itself. 'The ascent of Mount Egmont I have attempted to describe, but it is a most difficult subject & if I covered quires of paper I should still fail in giving you a notion of it . . . On the 7th March we stood on his snowy head.' Maria was the first reported European woman to climb to the summit. The climbing party consisted of Arthur and Maria, Harry Atkinson, Henry Richmond, Teddo Patten, and Calvert and Charlie Wilson. The only surviving account is a reminiscence given to the *Taranaki Daily News* on 20 October 1909 by Charlie Wilson.[10] They left the Hurworth clearings in good weather at the end of February. The method of attack was for the men to cut a line through the bush, leaving their swags with Maria at each overnight bivouac. Late in the afternoon they returned to eat the meal Maria had prepared and then the whole party moved forward about one and a half to two miles along the cut line. Their last camp before the summit was opposite the site of the former North Egmont hostel.

Shortly after Maria's and Arthur's marriage, Broadmore's bullocks and 'a whole army of assistants under the guidance of the great Broadmore' dragged Orchard House, which Harry and Arthur had built, up the slope to within a few yards of Merton. Renamed 'Bird's Nest' (from Arthur's nickname) by Lely and repapered and decorated by Maria, it became her and Arthur's new home. Although no bigger than a one-roomed cottage it enabled them to have a small place apart, and Maria wrote enthusiastically to Margaret: 'I suppose to your palatial eyes it would look very scrubby and insignificant . . . though to colonial eyes its pale green paper, bright furniture and scarlet [tablecloth] make it seem very gay indeed.'[11]

Arthur rented the small Merton farm from Lely, and that summer and autumn hacked out the ever-encroaching thistles, planted furze (gorse) hedges, worked on the road to Hurworth, milked his cows, and, almost as frequently, hunted for strays in the bush – 'a drift of cows' was one of his apt descriptions: 'Only think what milch cows are fetching. We can get £20 for Blackbird, who is just about calving, or has calved, that is if we fetch her out of the bush; £18 if the purchaser has to find her.'[12] One of Arthur's diary entries shows how time consuming was this lack of adequate fencing: 'Took Daisy to neighbours for mating. Then went over Henui to fetch bull. Brought bull back by which time Daisy had disappeared. Found Daisy but bull had gone home.'[13] Wandering stock were the bane of bush farmers and the cause of much trespass litigation. Fortunately the animals themselves were not blind to the advantages of a home paddock in emergencies: 'This afternoon "Croaker" appeared, after being absent about six weeks,' Maria reported to Margaret, 'this is very lucky as she is to calve very soon.' Sometimes a human agency was involved. Martha King, on looking out of her schoolroom window, happened to see Emery Edmonds cutting the rope which tethered a cow. Her gasp drew the attention of all in the room and Emery made off. The Edmonds threatened Martha with legal proceedings if she spoke of what she had seen. The upshot was that the Kings 'cut the little villain remorselessly and Mrs Edmonds, a model of conjugal tenderness',[14] cut them. The *Cashmere* which brought Jane Skinner and Decimus to New Plymouth at the end of November 1855 also carried five Leicester sheep including a ram. The sheep arrived in splendid condition and were apparently regarded with some envy, for the ram disappeared. It was later found, but Arthur suspected it had been purposely taken.

At Merton, Maria, Arthur, and Lely now had their own circle of friends which, as well as the S.P. Kings, included the Curtises and Cromptons of Omata, the Blacketts, the Thomas Kings and Hindes (brother and sister) of Mangorei, the Chilmans, the Charles Browns, the Ronalds brothers, and the kin group. Arthur's diary frequently records 'a great concourse of people' at Merton, often as many as twenty in the weekend. Maria and Lely appear at first to have enjoyed the company, but Arthur, unless he could find a crony with whom to play chess, was bored with social chatter. On a particularly crowded Sunday Lely noted in her diary, 'Arthur remained in his shell all day creeping out towards night when he found the coast clear.'[15]

'The Richmond hotel', as Lely called Merton, was a convenient stopping place for parties going between Hurworth and the town, and even Maria began to tire of the incessant interruptions and wished that

> more of our Mob [could] have decent homes of their own & this place ceased to be the rendezvous or rallying point for half a dozen bachelors besides the natural household . . . We can never reckon on two quiet days and evenings running, consequently it is next to impossible to establish any regular system of reading, or any regular plans of any sort.[16]

Arthur did most of the butter churning and often helped with the housework but it was Maria who continued to be the housekeeper and the provider for the mob during the weekends. She still wrote loftily to Margaret that her colonial life was preferable to being 'a dillitante, do-nothing, aesthetically elegant-minded man or woman with plenty to live on and the freedom of seeking health improvement or amusement all the world over'.[17] At times the realities of making and mending pressed hard, particularly when

most provokingly our right hand, Miss White, who used to come
at least two days every fortnight, has chosen to open a small store,
and now only takes in a little sewing. You cannot imagine what
a loss she is to us. I never can enjoy either reading or writing
in the evenings for the heaps of mending screaming to be done.[18]

That winter of 1855, Maria was unable to throw off a cold which
persisted for seven weeks. She was also struggling to look after
both Arthur, who had a badly infected throat, and Lely, recovering
from shingles. Lely confided to James that Maria felt a change
would do her good and had 'expressed a wish the other day that
some strong-minded & able-bodied lady would offer to take her
place & bid her throw aside household cares & labours'.[19]
Occasionally Maria went to Beach Cottage, but now that William
and Emily had two young children – Anna Wilson Richmond was
born on 4 May 1855 – it was no place to go for rest and quiet.
The Freemasons' ball gave a boost to her spirits. Taranaki
Freemasons were of all classes, 'so of course there were both Nobs
and Snobs present'.[20] As a 'frightful extravagance' she bought a
gown for the occasion. The ball was held on 26 and 27 June, breaking
up at eight on the morning of the 27th: 'fancy thirteen mortal
hours of dancing, varied by only an hour's interval for supper!!'[21]
Fortunately for Arthur there was a chess competition and he
established himself as the Taranaki champion. Emily Richmond,
whom many people considered 'the belle of the evening', described
Maria as 'looking very aristocratic and handsome as she always
does'.[22]

One thing which Maria never doubted was her complete
compatability with Arthur. She was capable, so she told her friend,
of taking an unbiased even disinterested view of him.

He is such an odd fish that he is quite indescribable & I believe
only two or three people in the world have even a dim glimmering
notion of what he really is. Don't imagine that I consider him
above & better than all the world . . . but he is different.[23]

Possibly because of the age difference they were able to be mutually
supportive whilst also preserving a healthy independence of spirit.
Arthur was not above teasing 'old wifey', as he often refers to
Maria in his diary, and Lely observed that he could be 'facetiously
aggravating'. But when Maria was ill, and especially during her
first difficult confinement, Arthur nursed her with devoted care.
Reading aloud to each other was a shared pleasure, and during
the winter of 1855 they read Shakespeare together in bed – 'there
is so little time during the day'. On reading *Hamlet*, Arthur was

struck by the many ways in which Hamlet resembled James; Maria
had always thought this, though had never said so for fear of being
laughed at. Arthur enjoyed listening to Maria playing the piano
but in music, as Maria informed Margaret, 'he had the bad taste
not to enjoy Mozart properly', preferring the 'modern German
school' of Wagner, Brahms, and Liszt. Farming at Merton did not
provide him with enough stimulation. Maria was aware of his
restless, probing nature – 'Weary of myself and sick of asking
what I am and what I ought to be,' he once wrote in his diary
– and she realised that the cosiness of Merton would never extend
his capabilities. 'Bird's heart is in the bush land [Hurworth],' she
wrote to James, 'his heart is not here.'[24]

As a means of whiling away the winter months Arthur and Maria
edited, and others of the mob contributed to, the *Aspective Review*.
It established their reputation in the settlement as 'the literary
bushmen'. Compared with the interest and pertinence of the letters
they wrote, their sally into the classic pastoral mode of the *Review*
is contrived and dull. Several issues appeared during the winter
months of 1855–57. The venture did have one totally unexpected
consequence: it was the precipitating cause of Charlie Wilson's
derangement.

Maria's young cousin Charlie had seemed perfectly contented
as a bushman working mainly at the Hurworth clearings and living
with Henry. He was also pursuing a satisfactory affair with Mary
Hinde. The appearance of the *Aspective Review*, however, caused
him to be afflicted with a 'writing mania'. He produced his own
weekly, the *Axeman*, in which he acclaimed himself a literary genius.
Dr Neild gave him sedatives which temporarily calmed his excited
state, but soon there were more eruptions of his 'egotistical ravings'.
It was a disaster for which the family group was totally unprepared.
'Our great trouble now is about Charlie's state,' Maria wrote to
James; 'he is downright crazy,' wrote William. One of the most
distressing things for the perplexed relatives was that they did not
know from one week to the next what form his mania would
take. He abandoned Mary Hinde and declared passionately for
Blanche Hursthouse and then for Nellie; one week he gave up
work completely, the next he rose at dawn. Tobacco, for which
he had an insatiable desire, seemed to be a stimulant, and Maria
wondered whether the New Plymouth stores should be asked not
to supply him. He was also using Lely's credit to chalk up hotel
meals and beds. It was all most embarrassing. His decision to return
to a state of nature and sleep naked in the bush, even in the pouring

rain, followed by an obsession that death was only a fancy – he
wanted Arthur to poison and then bury him – convinced the others
that he was moving beyond their ability to look after him. There
was no asylum in New Plymouth. The only institutional alternative
for relatives was the gaol. Various schemes were considered: perhaps
the Hursthouses might be paid for looking after him? Perhaps a
Maori might act as his keeper? Ati Awa had already brought him
back after finding him wandering in the Waitara district. The
problem dragged on over the next two years. To an extent, as
his frenzies were replaced by lethargy, the family allowed Charlie
to do as he wished. In his saner moments he spoke of returning
to England, and in August 1857 the Richmonds finally sent him
there at their expense. 'I am afraid he is very mad,' William wrote
to his uncle, 'but so quiet . . . that a stranger would not be likely
to find it out.'[25]

W.S. (Bill) Atkinson was also 'rather a weight upon our minds',
Maria wrote. He had taken a great fancy to Helen (Nellie)
Hursthouse and, as Henry commented to James, 'her kind little
heart is easily got at'. For once John Hursthouse and his wife were
of one mind and strongly opposed the match, especially when it
became known that during his more dissolute sailing days he had
fathered children in Mauritius. James suggested that he should bring
out the mother and children to join the mob in Taranaki; this
was not followed up. Meanwhile the other problem member of
the kin group, John Hursthouse, continued as ever. He talked of
leaving New Plymouth and starting up again at Auckland which
would have bereft his family of the Richmond–Atkinson support
group. There was hope for a time that he might follow the example
of Arthur Standish, a New Plymouth lawyer considered 'worse
than Papa', and give up alcohol entirely, but the arrival of the
troops made his drinking even more excessive. Lely considered
him 'stultified by spirits'. His eldest son, Wilson, was learning to
be a surveyor under F.A. Carrington, and in July 1856 Helen began
a small school in New Plymouth township (where it would not
rival the Kings' school), walking to and from the town each day.
None of the children held any affection or respect for their father
but, confided Nellie, 'if only he would give up his bad habits . . .
poor Mamma might have a chance of being happy'.[26]

All family problems were passed on to James on the Isle of Arran,
where he had gone at the suggestion of his English friend, Basil
Holmes, to satisfy his yearning for wild natural beauty of the
'romantic' sort. He was particularly missed during the trouble with

Charlie. James's own volatile nature, his family reasoned, would have made him more able to cope with Charlie's. To a separated and isolated James it must all have made depressing reading, and in one of his replies he questioned the mob's ability to stay together. He was reproved by Maria:

> I think you greatly exaggerate to yourself the want of smoothness & union amongst us of late; we are all very often sadly faulty in our dealings with each other, but still there is a real need of each other & love for each other to be found but rarely in families.[27]

Margaret Taylor had met James when he first arrived in England and she had been impressed:

> dear James looked anything but a satisfactory specimen of a colonist . . . he overturned all the theories people are fond of propounding as to colonial life making men rougher and dragging them downward into mere tree felling working animals. I think he is grown more refined, more gentle, more charming.[28]

Margaret's view of James alarmed Maria. She wrote to her brother that as neither he nor Margie seemed to need each other 'in the absolute way that would alone give you happiness in marriage . . . I should be better pleased to know that you had *entirely* given up all thought of meeting your fate with M.'[29] Maria missed James badly – 'the one empty space spoils the whole group'; equally she dreaded the thought of his coming back still a bachelor and 'vainly striving to settle down to colonial life without a partner or any home of your own'.[30] She was confident of his eventual return, for she doubted whether painting would be sufficiently lucrative to keep him in England. 'Perhaps', she wrote, 'you will meet some Highland lassie who will suit you & the colonies & *then* you will feel you can – must – settle in Taranaki.'[31] During the summer tourist season on Arran there were plenty of young ladies about, botanising, sketching or reading, but James 'in great loneliness and trying humbly to take up this art',[32] was not attracted. He was already bespoken.

The Smith family of Newark, cousins of the Atkinsons, were known to the Richmonds and well liked by them. Both Mary and Annie Smith had been bridesmaids at William and Emily's wedding, and it was hoped that their brother, Sam, would soon join the mob in Taranaki. James renewed his acquaintance with Mary shortly after his arrival in London. By the end of March 1855 she was writing to him: 'Yes Jas dear I do trust & rest in you fully and would not do anything to make you grave or sad for the world.'[33] Mary Smith taught women's classes at F.D. Maurice's Working

Men's College, London. From a religious family (Church of England
with evangelical leanings), she was herself exceedingly so, although,
as often happens, she admitted herself 'stricken with doubts' and
'seeking & seeking without rest'. A devotee of Maurice (she also
taught in his Sunday school) and of Charles Kingsley, she was as
intense as James but steadier. She was also very much in love although
with James on the Isle of Arran for four months during 1855 and
then in Namur working for a Belgian railway company[34] for three
months during 1856, she saw little enough of him before marriage.
They wrote long letters to each other at least twice weekly, full
of affection, theological discussion, and self-analysis.

News of James and Mary's engagement gave much satisfaction
in Taranaki. While Maria had been fantasising about 'Highland
lassies', Lely, quartering the field with a more practised eye, had
already written to her son: 'a dream some of us have had about
one of those sweet sisters of Sams might not be so difficult of
realization. James dear, your position in N.Z. will not be a bad
one . . . those Smith girls are very much to our liking.'[35] William
expressed the general feeling when he told James that the
engagement was 'the very thing we had been wishing for although
scarcely dared to hope';[36] and Maria wrote to Mary welcoming
her (entwining her, one might hazard) to her new new kin group:

> It seems as though I could never find words to tell you the deep
> delight with which I learnt you were to be my sister . . . my
> knowledge of James . . . made me believe that he would think
> himself too unworthy of your regard ever to try to win it . . .
> I suppose & earnestly trust this will find you man & wife, you
> dear creatures.[37]

James, at thirty-four, was twelve years older than Mary, but
when it was the man – the protector and provider – who was
the elder there was not the slightest affront to convention. They
were married on 21 August 1856 at Flamstead, near Hemel
Hempstead in Hertfordshire, and spent the following week in the
Welsh mountains. A little later, on 30 August 1856, Mary's brother
Sam Smith married Kate Atkinson of Frindsbury and there were
high hopes among the mob that both couples would come to
Taranaki, possibly bringing Mary's mother and her younger sister,
Annie, as well. The stumbling blocks were Sam's business commitments, Mrs Smith's horror of emigrating, and Annie's refusal to
leave her mother. Even James and Mary were undecided. His
employment with the Belgian railway company could be extended
indefinitely and he saw the advantage of alternating money-making

spells with periods off for painting and study. Mary rather favoured living in Belgium where she would be closer to her beloved sister, but James had forebodings about the all-pervading Roman Catholicism of that country and, although married, found it hard to contemplate living permanently apart from his family. By June 1856 James was so far settled on returning to Taranaki that he was busy reckoning the expense necessary to establish them there in comfort.

The road to Hurworth had been completed by the middle of 1855 – 'a pattern to other roads in the province' – and the mob's bachelors were living in rough whare on the Hurworth land. Harry and Bill Atkinson, with Frank Adams and Teddo Patten, were at 'Fern Post Lodge'; Henry Richmond shared his whare, called either 'Kohekohe Lodge' or 'Slab Cottage', with Charles Wilson until the latter returned to England; Calvert Wilson was mostly at Merton. Harry was the first to build a permanent sawn-timber house at Hurworth. The previous year he had informed his Aunt Coster in England that he was thinking of getting married as soon as he could get up a decent house. Jane Skinner of Rochester, a frequent caller at Frindsbury, was his intended. No correspondence between them survives but there must have been a firm understanding. In July 1854 Maria had written to Mary Hutton, 'If you hear from James that a certain Miss Jane Skinner of Rochester is likely to come out you can let her have the hints [to emigrants] to copy.'[38] Anxious to make more money, Harry had apprenticed himself to Broadmore as a sawyer's mate. He was expecting to make a 'good thing out of it'. When the troops arrived at New Plymouth, Harry purchased a bullock train to cart firewood and stockade posts at twelve shillings a load. However, working long hours and living in the damp bush was proving too much for his health. Like Lely and William, he suffered from recurrent bouts of asthma, and that winter of 1855 he was also plagued with boils and bronchitis: 'I trust . . . Mrs Hal will leave England this year. Harry has been very delicate all this winter tho' it has been a fine one & he needs a wife's care greatly.'[39]

Jane Skinner and Decimus Atkinson (the tenth living child of John and Elizabeth) arrived from the *Cashmere* on 22 November 1855. Nineteen-year-old Des or Decie, as he was known, fell into place at once. He was immediately taken in charge by Arthur to help with the latter's clearing at Hurworth. Jane, twenty-four, seemed equally adaptable. She was surprised at the domestic comforts of New Plymouth and at the attractiveness of its young women. After meeting Nellie Hursthouse she remarked 'in her simple way' to Emily Richmond, 'I wondered Hal remembered me.'[40] Shortly after she arrived, Harry took his bullock cart and all the mob journeyed to Hurworth to introduce Jane to the bush. It was agreed that in the meantime she should stay with William and Emily at Beach Cottage so that she might see from a slight distance her mode of life and become inured to it before marriage. Henry wrote to James, 'One cannot help wishing for something rather higher for Harry',[41] but Maria was satisfied:

> Jane takes to the life very well. She is a capital nurse & makes unexceptionable pies & puddings. Hal has been giving her some lessons in ironing shirt collars. [She] was certainly born to a bullock cart & submits to being driven up & down the steepest hills & through ruts where one wheel is about a foot below the level of the other with the greatest calmness. She seems glad to be the possessor of so substantial a conveyance.[42]

Over the next few months various members of the mob worked with Harry to finish his house;[43] even the 'great Broadmore' helped with laying the floor, hanging windows and doors, and 'directing' the others. The day before Harry and Jane's wedding, Maria came over 'to put things to rights a little in the house' while the bushmen cleared up outside. They then adjourned to Fern Post Lodge, drank punch, and sang before going on at about midnight to Merton, where they were all to stay. It seemed to Lely that they were 'afloat' all through the remainder of the night. The wedding was celebrated at St Mary's on 25 March 1856 at 8.30 in the morning. William Richmond gave Jane away; Bill Atkinson was groomsman, and Blanche and Nellie Hursthouse, Bessie Crompton, and Julia Horne were bridesmaids. Twenty-two, mostly family, sat down to the wedding breakfast at Merton which, apart from the cake and two pork pies, had all been prepared by Maria – 'all our best china, crockery, glass & plate, the latter in a state of great brilliancy, set off with flowers, made [the table] quite superb'.[44] Later in the day Jane and Harry, both on horseback, with Cassy the cat in a kit slung over Harry's shoulder, set off at a canter for Hurworth. That same evening there was a 'spirited' dance at Merton to which about forty were invited. 'We did not subside,' Arthur wrote in his diary, 'until nearly 2 a.m., most of the guests then walking home through a beautiful moonlit night.'[45]

Henry Richmond too had been successful in love, although the signs had not always been propitious. His Hurworth clearing of ten acres was a fine piece of land with a splendid view of the mountain and of the kohekohe on C.W. Richmond's land. Much of it was planted in grass, with parts fenced off for crops and orchard. The earthquake had rekindled his interest in science and he had posted off his observations and theories about it. Lely later wrote, '[Henry] is so atrociously wicked . . . as to crave after earthquakes, and feels disappointed we are visited so rarely by them.'[46] He was also collecting botanical specimens for his naturalist friend in England, Dr Arthur Henfrey. He seemed, so Emily Richmond thought, 'just the same grave hard-working creature as always'.[47] But he was given to periods of depression which he tried to hide from his family. He badly needed a suitable companion. From the time of his arrival at Taranaki, he had been attracted to the quiet, homely, sensible Blanche Hursthouse. It was difficult for friendship, so much taken for granted between cousins, to deepen into love. Blanche, about sixteen at the time, seemed to accept all Henry's advances (he was ten years her senior) and showed no apparent unwillingness to be wooed, but she gave no discernible answering signals. In despair he wrote to James: 'someone [is] sitting near me to whom I am now neither a cousin or a lover'.[48] Perhaps competition quickened Blanche's interest. Mrs Mary King noted a 'violent flirtation between Henry and Miss Curtis in which the lady was not the aggressor.'[49] By Christmas 1855 an understanding must have been reached, for Nellie Hursthouse wrote to James that Henry was completely changed: 'He is not like the same person; he is always in very high spirits and as lively & merry as can be. I did not think any one could alter so much for the better.'[50] During the Christmas and New Year festivities Henry and Blanche's names were linked together in Arthur's diary, and on 12 March 1856 Emily wrote in hers: 'Henry and Blanche are now said by the NP gossips to be engaged.' Maria wrote that the 'cousinship has of course been an objection in all our minds, but it is impossible not to rejoice in seeing the new creature the prospect . . . has made him'.[51]

Maria and Arthur were now as anxious as any of the mob to make a beginning at Hurworth, but Arthur had his cows as well as other farm duties to attend to at Merton and could scarcely spare the time or the energy for an eight-mile walk every day. He advertised for a strong quiet mare, free from vices, and in foal. The investment – £65 for the horse and £4 more for saddle and bridle – seemed a 'fearful sum' to Maria, but she agreed with Arthur that only by going to and fro on horseback could he begin clearing his Hurworth land. 'Nancy Bell' could also carry a lady, though until they could afford a side-saddle Maria thought she would not be able to mount very often. In August 1855 they both went to Hurworth to choose the site for their house. From then on Arthur spent much of his time there cutting underbrush and boundary lines. On 15 September he wrote in his diary: 'began to fell for the first time on my own land'.

Money – 'so much has been going out & so little coming in' – was a perpetual worry. Nearly all available funds had been invested in Hurworth without showing any return, even though the completion of the road had seen the land double in value. Running stock in the bush at Hurworth proved a poor speculation: 'We have not only lost much time in hunting the things, but have also lost several animals.'[52] The arrival of troops during 1855 pushed up the cost of living, 'making bread two shillings the quarter loaf and everything else to match': 'As this place [Merton] continues halfway house & free quarters for the bush men – good accommodation for man & beast, ordinary at 12 o'clock, charge £0-0-0 – you may imagine the money runs out to a pretty good tune.'[53]

In sending her list of things to James to bring from England, Maria stressed that she and Arthur would have to do without luxuries; striped or checked tablecloths, for example, would have to replace damask. Arthur and Harry had small family allowances, and money from English investments came regularly to Lely, but the latter's expenses at Merton had been considerable and she had made numerous advances to others of the kin group. Lely had experienced straightened circumstances in England. She had not expected to suffer them again in Taranaki: 'This running into debt is to me the most unpleasant fact of NZ life & what I certainly did not calculate upon when I left England. [It] weighs upon me.'[54]

The one member of the mob relatively free of money worries was C.W. Richmond. Initially he had been as keen to become a bush farmer as any of the others and had invested in Hurworth land, but the reality of the Taranaki situation was that he had more financial security working in his legal profession. Writing to the father of Charlie and Calvert Wilson, who was himself thinking of emigrating, William stated:

> Men of middle age . . . are glad to fall back on their old employments as their surest if not their only means of subsistence . . . Your mainstay I should think would be some kind of clerkly or quill driving labour – as it has proved in my case. Clerks, doctors, pastrycooks I have known to take to the bush with a delight at

their escape from the old hated mill round, but in a twelve month we have them back in the town again.[55]

In addition to his paid official position as provincial secretary and attorney, William had a small private practice in New Plymouth. He did not describe this as lucrative, for his legal rival, Frederic Norris, had got 'firm hold of the moneyed men'. Nevertheless, with his regular salary augmented by what he earned from his private practice, he, Emily, and their growing family were comfortably settled in Beach Cottage. Henry described him as 'very busy & happy & strong'.

Early in 1855 William had turned down a request to represent the town of New Plymouth in the General Assembly at Auckland. However, greater pressure was applied later in the year as the calibre of some of the other candidates became known, and Emily came to accept that it was necessary for her husband to accept nomination: 'his saying no appears to be of no use'. In November he was duly elected. Arthur commented: 'I am sorry we hadn't the chance of returning him instead of the townspeople. There is no doubt they have got the best man in the place.'[56] Maria told James that William 'groans a good deal & longs for retirement', but she believed he could have satisfaction only in finding his real usefulness acknowledged.

William, Emily and Anna – Mary was to stay with Aunt Maria – left for Auckland on 12 April 1856. They were effectively leaving Taranaki for good. 'Stafford', William wrote, 'has taken a sort of fancy to me and has almost from the beginning of the session been trying to hook me into the Cabinet.'[57] 'C.W.R. is Prime Minister!!! of New Zealand,'[58] Maria exalted at the beginning of June. In fact E.W. Stafford had taken office, with C.W. Richmond as colonial secretary entrusted also with native affairs. Maria was naturally proud of her brother, even if it was a blow to lose him and Emily from their midst. One of the firm intentions of the mob, as Maria expressed it, had been 'to pass our lives near each other, and know each other's children from their birth'.[59] For Lely the 'loss' of her two elder sons after coming all the way to New Zealand in order to keep the family together seemed particularly hard. She wrote to Emily in Auckland:

Does it not seem strange to you that Maria who was once so nearly becoming the spouse of a man standing every chance of rising to great legal eminence [Lely probably had Henry Hutton in mind] should have become the partner of an obscure bushman, whilst you share the fortunes of a man raised to high public office . . .

I try to look on you as only separated from 'The Mob' for two
or three years.[60]

For a Christmas present in 1855, Bill, Decimus, and Harry Atkinson
had combined to give Maria a side-saddle. In January Arthur bought
her the mare, Lallah Rookh. To have a horse 'of my very own'
was a sheer delight. Cream coloured with black points, Lallah Rookh
was so gentle that Maria could catch her and go anywhere on
her alone. She told Margaret: 'When I canter along the beach
at sunset, when sea, earth & sky look most glorious & peaceful
. . . I am happier I think than I have ever been in my life.'[61]

There were now five horses among the mob: Arthur and Maria
had two; Harry had two, and Henry one. 'The Hurworth people
seem to be mad about horses,' Nellie Hursthouse wrote to James.
'William Richmond has not one yet, I think he considers it rather
foolish of them to buy while they are so high.'[62] In spite of the
price and William's disapproval Maria considered the convenience
and enjoyment so immense that 'we all wonder how we endured
life without'. Riding excursions, going to the races – horse racing
vied with cricket as the mob's pastime – and the Tradesmen's ball
provided the highlights of the late summer of 1855:

Ar & I rode down [to the ball] carrying my finery in a huge kit
[and] after tea dressed at the Beach Cottage . . . [The ball] was
altogether a much more spirited affair than the Governor's Ball
(at which NB his Excellency was not present) in opposition to
which it was started, as that was conducted on such painfully selected
principles so as to enrage a large proportion of the population of
the Province . . . Among the tradespeople & their relatives a good
deal of originality both of costume & deportment is to be found
but they know really quite as well how to conduct themselves as
many of the 'haut ton'. The Miss Murrays, the insufferable daughters
of the commanding officer, were as supercilious & boring as usual
& a good many officers got quite tipsy after we left which wa
about ½ past 2. None of our young bushmen except W.S.A. were
asked.[63]

At the time of the Tradesmen's ball Maria was pregnant, and
she did not go to the Freemason's ball in June 'not on accoun
of health or my own feelings so much as out of respect to th
feelings of friends who may feel distressed at my personal appearanc
which is certainly . . . far from elegant.'[64] Maria now had househol
help, as Blanche Hursthouse, to both Maria and Henry's satisfactior
was living at Merton. 'How agreeable,' Lely wrote, 'to have th

society of so fresh & sensible a young creature.'[65] Maria was well and strong for the greater part of her pregnancy and in letters to James and Margaret confidently expected that her confinement would be a very rapid affair – 'if I imitate the majority of NZ mothers'. But she was also well aware that at thirty-two she was older than the majority of women expecting a first confinement, and she wrote in a rather different tone to William and Emily when she asked them to take care of 'poor old Lely if it should please God to take me away in August':

> You must not imagine that I am in the least cast down; in feeling I am full of life, health & hope but my *reason* tells me there is a considerable risk both for the child & myself at the actual time . . . I can't help wishing sometimes that Sept. had come.[66]

Throughout her pregnancy Maria had been practising the 'active muscular exercise system' and possibly took it a shade too far; the day before her confinement she was hanging curtains. Her baby daughter, Margaret, arrived prematurely and stillborn on 27 July 1856. Dr Neild had twice turned the foetus to get it into a better birth position and at his third attempt Maria requested chloroform. The result was spectacular. From agonies of pain Maria passed into a state of ecstacy. She was conscious of the others in the room, talking to them mostly in German, and, although convinced she was dying, was serenely happy. She wrote later of the experience: 'Whatever life may bring me, and whatever death I may die, it *has* been granted to me to taste the infinite bliss of a death full of triumphant faith and happiness.'[67] Maria was also convinced during this experience that William was in heaven waiting to receive her. Such was her certainty of this that Lely, writing immediately afterwards to William, said, 'I shall rejoice to hear you are in life . . . so clear was her vision of you in heaven.'[68]

For the others present it had been a day of 'shuddering terror'. This day I will not write about', is the entry in Arthur's diary. Maria refused to credit that any drug could so affect her, and his belief was probably therapeutic. She wrote to Emily:

> You dear Em with your Mother's heart will be thinking sadly how I grieve for the little one, yes I do, at moments I yearn for it, but . . . it is as great a privilege to feel the pains and sorrows of motherhood as the joys. I had rather be as I am, than never have borne a child.[69]

Arthur sent away Mrs Bishop, the nurse, and insisted on caring for Maria himself – 'he is such a dear old clever fidgety nurse as you never saw'.[70] She hoped that if she died Arthur *might* come

out of his shell to be 'both daughter and son' to Lely, but feared
that her death would just as easily 'shut him up entirely in himself'.[71]
Their shared bereavement and Arthur's devoted care brought them
to an even closer understanding. Within a few days Maria seemed
perfectly recovered, if still a little weak.

> Physically I am a wonder. I am really of an iron constitution &
> after going through what Aunt [Helen Hursthouse] considers equal
> to three severe natural labours, I am not as uncomfortable as the
> generality of women after a first confinement.[72]

The most pertinent comment came from her brother, Henry:

> On Sunday night when I went for Dr Wilson [also in attendance]
> I thought she was going to be taken from us, & what we should
> all have done here without her I cannot tell. I felt for the first
> time fully what support we all derive from her strong faithful spirit,
> & I felt as if it were almost impossible that our lonely little
> community should continue its existence without her.[73]

While the mob got on with its ever-expanding life in Taranaki,
the sporadic outbursts of fighting from the 'native feud' continued
almost as noises offstage. The unprotected state of the province
led to several resolutions from the provincial government and
petitions to central government at Auckland. The settlers felt that
a body of troops should be stationed at New Plymouth to protect
them and maintain government neutrality. The latter argument
was a little specious. It was not strict neutrality which was sought.
A military presence, it was thought, would encourage the minority
Maori faction which wished to sell land and would offer protection
if the 'friendlies', as C.W. Richmond called them, had to retreat
to the town. The colonial secretary's reply at the beginning of
1855 was cautious: central government doubted the expediency of
making New Plymouth a military post, for this would be likely
to increase the danger of hostilities, would deter immigrants, and
thus further impede the progress of the province. A measure of
self-help was suggested. On 21 April 1855 Superintendent Charles
Brown called for volunteers to form a Rifle Corps, with companies
at New Plymouth township, Omata, and the Grey and Bell district.
Each company was to elect its own officers and frame its own
regulations. Volunteers would also be excused from militia duty.
Arthur Atkinson attended the Grey meeting at which there were
about fifty present, but only twenty-six signed up as volunteers.
None of the mob was alarmed about the local situation, and indeed
showed more interest in the Crimean War: 'I think they would

volunteer in a body if we were nearer England, so delightful it would seem to be cut in two by a cannon ball in the Crimea.'[74]

The Puketapu feud flared again in July 1855. Arthur recorded in his diary:

4 July 1855. Yesterday the combined forces of Katatore and Wiremu Kingi taking advantage of the absence of some of Adam Clark's [Arama Karaka's] men made an attack on the Ninia pa (the new pa that Adam Clark built on the spot where Rawiri Waiaua was shot) but were repulsed . . . today Adam Clark made a return attack. July 14. We heard the Maoris firing away at each other – no harm was done which is their usual practice.[75]

On 5 July the *Alexander* from Melbourne put in to New Plymouth and off-loaded sixty tons of iron barracks. An order countermanding the delivery – the barracks were intended for the Bay of Islands – arrived after the ship had sailed. So, inadvertently, New Plymouth had acquired barracks but had no troops to put in them. Many of the local settlers were reluctant to shoulder arms in their own defence, maintaining that 'they did not come out here to fight, that is the business of Government; it is paid to take care of us.'[76]

At the beginning of August 1855 a powerful party of Ngati Ruanui reinforced Katatore and, according to C.W. Richmond (who at this time was still at Beach Cottage), threatened to annihilate Arama Karaka and his people at Ninia pa. A public meeting at New Plymouth, 'very discreditable in its behaviour' Richmond thought, decided to take matters into its own hands: special constables were to be sworn in, arms were to be issued, the barracks were to be erected as a place of refuge for women and children, and a permanent committee of public safety was to be appointed. While William was at this meeting, Emily was alone at Beach Cottage:

. . . the panels in the gable cracked terribly and I thought I heard the Maories howling on the Beach, so I found I was *very short of tea* & was obliged to borrow a cupful of Mrs Lewthwaite. I knocked at her door but Lewthwaite being out at the meeting, Mrs L. very naturally took me for a Maori & would not let me in. At last having reconnoitered she opened the door & was so kind as to put on her bonnet & came accompanied by her small servant to help me carry back the tea.[77]

This example of prudence and propriety overcoming fear was in sharp contrast to the bellicose attitude of the men:

There has been a great deal of casting bullets, grinding cutlass, sword, bayonet, fitting guns & pistols & going to town. The Maories have been firing at each other a great part of the day and even the sleepy townspeople are at last getting a little excited. By the steamer yesterday there came 200 lbs of powder which Charles Brown had ordered from Wellington. This is very welcome . . . I believe there was not a pound to be had of any of the storekeepers.[78]

A fortnight later the *Duke of Portland* came in with 250 troops, part of the 58th Regiment from Auckland, and a military camp was set up on Mt Eliot. On 8 September a similar force from the 65th Regiment arrived from Wellington. Full of confidence in the situation, Maria wrote to Margaret:

I must dismiss the subject of Maoris (who by the bye have not occasioned me a minute's fear or uneasiness so far) . . . now that the people are prepared to defend themselves there seems no particular cause for alarm. The arrival of the new Governor, Colonel Gore Browne, is expected this month. If he only proves a *man* and not a red tape phantasm or military clothes horse we shall do very well.[79]

Also visiting Taranaki in August and not nearly so welcomed by the settlers was Bishop Selwyn. He called on Wiremu Kingi Te Rangitake at Waitara and found no signs of hostility towards the Pakeha; in fact most of his people had gone to tow an English schooner off the river bar. At St Mary's Selwyn preached on covetousness, illustrating his sermon from the Old Testament story of Naboth's vineyard. It did not go down well. 'It seems that Wiremu Kingi & Katatore[80] are churchmen and therefore in the right, though there are heretics in Taranaki who do not think so,'[81] complained Arthur.

The arrival of troops caused a temporary lull in fighting and both Maori parties looked to future trading advantages. Arama Karaka's people sent cartloads of potatoes and an immense pig to Mt Eliot. Their adversaries also sent potatoes, but their carts were stopped by Karaka's men who told the drivers, 'we sent for the soldiers, and we shall feed the soldiers. You sent for Ngati Ruanui and you may feed them.'[82] The redcoat invasion also caused a certain upset in Pakeha society:

Many of the Taranaki young ladies showed symptoms of scarlet fever the day after the redcoats landed, and the disease is making steady progress . . . talk of the dear officers starts up all the bristles of all the youths within hearing, bushmen and fernmen, they make common cause against the enemy . . . The young girls will I hope recover but Miss Edmonds is past praying for except by a good Catholic like me who can pray as far as Purgatory.[83]

Rivalry spilt over into cricket as well. The 65th were renowned cricketers and had always beaten the civilians at Wellington. With odds of four to one against them, 'the bush', largely composed of Hurworthians, took them on. Arthur's bowling and Harry's fielding rattled the military and 'the bush' won this first encounter with a wicket to spare.

Arthur, like most of the Hurworth bushmen, now drilled regularly twice a week with the volunteers under the direction of Major Lloyd. He was working hard at Hurworth, fencing, planting an orchard, and digging a vegetable garden, as well as tending his cows at Merton. He and Maria had drawn up plans for their house, and in August 1856 Arthur engaged with a New Plymouth builder, Purnell, to put up the frame and cladding. He intended to shingle the roof and do the interior carpentry himself.

On 11 October 1856, Marion (Polly) and Eliza Ronalds arrived from the *Gipsy* to join their brothers at Denby Farm adjacent to Hurworth. Like their brothers they initially thought the Richmonds, including 'Mrs Arthur Atkinson', 'rather stuck up', but soon found how genuinely friendly their neighbours were. Maria thought them 'extremely agreeable unaffected girls' and had them to stay for a week at Merton, which was less crowded and more easily managed with the continued assistance of Blanche Hursthouse. Maria was now leading a comparatively 'fine lady life'. Suffering and loss had drawn Arthur and her more closely together: 'I have a sweet though sad feeling in looking at our little daughter's grave, and in fancying what she would have grown like . . . I can now never feel childless.'[84]

The Christmas season of 1856 began with a large party and dance for fifty at Merton. Christmas Day was celebrated at Harry and Jane's house at Hurworth. The repast was dominated by a huge plum pudding and by the first Hurworth cheese, produced by the Ronalds. It was cut and pronounced very good: Lely prophesised that Hurworth would prove to be the Stilton of New Zealand. For Maria and Arthur, however, the climax of the year came on 30 December: 'Last night, dearest Maggie, we slept for the first time in our new home at Hurworth.'[85]

CHAPTER
SIX

The Hurworth Community

New Plymouth, Jan. 1857–March 1860

They do not go to make a fortune but to found a home where they can have abundant employment & where we may all live in health & at ease.[1]
So Maria had written to Margaret Taylor at the time of James and Henry's departure for Taranaki. Now, after years of preparation, the end of the journey was at hand, with the kin group settled close together at Hurworth. Even C.W. Richmond had his clearing and contemplated living there when he could rid himself of politics. Lely may have complained that 'Christian Socialism does not work well for the Richmond pocket', but their close-knit communal life, however impecunious, seemed to prove Maria's contention that among the mob was a 'real need of each other & love for each other to be found but rarely in families'.[2]

From the beginning of 1857 Maria and Arthur regarded Hurworth as home. There was still a good deal of travelling along the Carrington Road between their partly finished house and Merton, where Lely remained. Maria was uneasy at having her mother living 'at a distance', and 'Ar', she wrote, 'won't' be easy in *his* mind if I turn highway woman & take to the roads.' The future of Merton posed a problem. Lely could go to Auckland and live with William and Emily, who had now moved to a pleasant house set in seven acres at Parnell. But would Auckland's climate suit her? Henry, with marriage in mind, was busy putting up a permanent house at Hurworth and would be ready, so he estimated at the beginning of the year, to receive Lely in about four to five months. Merton could easily be let, though with Mary and James's arrival imminent it was clear that they would need somewhere to live until their Hurworth home was ready. It was decided to retain Merton in the meantime for family use.

In January Arthur paid Purnell £37.13.9 for putting up the frame, cladding, and chimney of their house. By the end of the month Arthur had finished shingling the roof and glazing the windows, the latter to the accompaniment of *Two Gentlemen of Verona*, which Maria read aloud. An addition to the original house was the du Moulin's[3] prefabricated kauri cottage, 28 feet by 14 feet, for which Maria paid £92 from her capital. Cheese making was to be their occupation at Hurworth, with Maria putting into practice all she had learnt from her lessons in the Cheshire farmhouse. She wrote to Emily in Auckland:

> . . . we may yet get our du Moulin house up before the timber is all spoilt. At present our one room serves as kitchen, scullery, workshop, cheese room, storeroom-laundry, dining & drawing room so that my elegant papers would hardly be in keeping . . . I find cheese making attended with great anxiety; crocks, flies etc haunt our dreams but such is life! At least such is life except at Paris, Auckland[4] & places of the kind.[5]

The Hurworth cheese factory was soon in full production. Harry Atkinson supplied the milk at sixpence halfpenny a gallon – the rate depending on the price gained – to the Ronalds, Henry Richmond, Maria and Arthur, all parties making up to 25 pounds weight per day.

In February Arthur attended a meeting of the 'men of Hurworth' to consider the prospect of selling cheese on the Sydney and Melbourne markets, and farm produce such as vegetables, pork, bacon, ham, cheese, butter, eggs, and fowls from a shop in New Plymouth which Hugh Ronalds would manage. The Atkinsons and Richmonds advanced the capital and were the chief shareholders. Hugh Ronalds, who made splendid sausages, was full of schemes for trading with Auckland and the Nelson goldfields but these markets proved as unreliable as the coastal shipping. The Australian market was also illusory. After a promising start, the fortunes of Hurworth's 'Country Produce Store' waned, and after little more than a year the store closed. Lely attributed some of the blame for the failure to Hugh Ronalds' erratic management. Ronalds himself was sanguine: 'It is one blessing in this country you may do anything without being considered disgraced and need never fear not being able to earn bread and cheese.'[6] Maria commented, 'Virtue *may* be its own reward but cheese making is not.'[7]

Nor was mail carrying. In February 1858 Hurworthians successfully tendered for the weekly conveyance of mail overland between New Plymouth and Wellington. Carrying the mail offered splendid

opportunities for horse riding, and the Hurworth riders, mostly
Decimus Atkinson and Frank Ronalds, provided an efficient service.
But Harry, the chief promoter, had not sufficiently considered the
cost of maintaining the horses, especially as the supplementary Maori
riders used them for their own purposes as well. The tender of
£600 per year did not cover expenses; each of the five contractors
had to part with an additional £25, and the contract was not renewed.

Of the two money-making schemes which had failed, Maria wrote
in 1859: 'if any of the set but Henry & Hal had made money in
the last four years it must have fallen into their mouths . . . Hal
when experience sobers him *will* get on.'[8]

More successful was the Hurworth venture into local politics.
The mob had hitherto supported Charles Brown, though with
decreasing enthusiasm. In the election of 1857 for the office of
superintendent of the Taranaki Provincial Council, Charles Brown
was defeated by George Cutfield, of whom, said Maria,

> I say nothing for I know nothing of him except that he would
> like a tax on carts & that he seems to have been consistent in
> this desire for some years – a very natural one, seeing he has no
> cart I believe . . . but he now appears as the puppet of a set of
> knaves & fools.[9]

The chief 'knave' was Richard Brown, the town's principal
merchant, who was a 'malignant' opponent of Charles Brown and
equally detested by the mob.

An enlarged provincial council allowed seven members for the
Grey and Bell district. Harry Atkinson was an obvious choice and
his election was assured. The other Hurworth candidate, 'poked
forward into public life a good deal against the grain', was Henry
Richmond. He was fully occupied in building his house but,
according to Maria, both he and Harry felt it 'quite a duty to
go into the Council to speak for the bush which but for them
& one other member [Thomas King] would be quite unrepre-
sented'.[10] Henry had been made a JP in 1856, and his success in
the provincial council elections 'added greatly to the dignity of
his demeanour'. At the beginning of July 1857 Henry was appointed
provincial treasurer, though, as he told Blanche, 'If I should feel
in the course of a few months that my influence is still very small
I shall get out . . . as I have not the slightest idea of going or
long taking £100 a year for formal attendance at [Executive] Council
meetings.'[11]

The first second-generation Hurworthian, Harry Dunstan
Atkinson (known as Dunstan), was born to Harry and Jane on

8 February 1857. Of all the mob, Harry was the one who looked most likely to become a successful farmer. To supply the cheese makers with milk he had, in partnership with Robert Pitcairn, increased his dairy herd to seventeen. He was also the Hurworth carter, reared calves, pigs, turkeys, ducks, and fowls, and employed two men and two boys. Clear of all expenses he reckoned that his dairy returned him 25 per cent on invested capital. Dunstan seemed a suitable heir. At the age of two he was completely unafraid of the farm animals and shaped well to become a competent bullock driver.

Hard on the heels of Dunstan came William and Emily's third daughter, Margaret. Before she was born, Maria had written to Emily on the subject of girls' names, 'such a difficulty I think . . . I freely give you up Margaret as I don't think we shall now ever want names'.[12]

Of all the arrivals during 1857, none gave more satisfaction than that of James Richmond accompanied by Mary. The *Kenilworth* arrived at Auckland on 4 May and James and Mary stayed for some weeks with William and Emily. As soon as news of their arrival reached New Plymouth, Maria busied herself in putting Bird's Nest in order for their use. On 8 July the *Kenilworth* was sighted in the roadstead and James and Mary came ashore in the early evening.

> They are come at last! and I am in that state of bewildered enjoyment consequent on such an event . . . It seemed more than I could believe or take in to see James again, with a wife, and such a wife, and to know that they had come to live amongst us. The night was moonlight though showery, and the procession soon started for Merton . . . [Mary] must have felt it a wild strange scene, for the light was dim and uncertain, and before we reached home a pelting shower came on. Lely had nearly made up her mind that no passengers could land that night, and was therefore properly surprised . . . We find James to be James and nothing else . . . Mary is grown taller and thinner, and she is even more delightful than we expected. She will be a blessing.[13]

The weather had not introduced Mary kindly to Taranaki: the road to Merton was a sea of mud, 'worse than I expected and I expected a good deal'. And when, the following week, James and Mary visited Hurworth, the sight of the small clearings – James's among them – hemmed in by primeval forest must have shocked her with its strangeness, reinforcing the homesickness which even her new family's warm welcome could not allay.

> To think that your dearest ones may be in sorrow or danger, lying seriously ill, perhaps dying & yet that for months one can know nothing of it – do nothing to help or comfort them . . . Year after year . . . to go on trusting that all is well is almost beyond one's power.[14]

James was healthier and happier than in England and, for his sake, Mary felt that they had done the right thing in coming out. But James, as Maria had pointed out, was still James and before he had even seen Hurworth he was talking of going sheep farming in Hawkes Bay. The pull of family, however, remained strong and eventually he decided to stay in Taranaki. Both he and Mary had money to hand and they had brought with them 'everything to make their house comfortable . . . even elegant', including heaps of books, many of them recently published. 'We have just come out of Polar seas with McClure [an English Arctic explorer] and are plunging into Central Africa with Livingstone,'[15] remarked Maria, who was also 'luxuriating' in their collection.

Among the books was *Aurora Leigh* by Elizabeth Barrett Browning, published in 1856. A novel in blank verse, it centred around a young woman 'of good family' who chose to live by herself in London, preserving her reputation and establishing herself as a writer. At a time when more and more educated, articulate women were becoming writers, social critics, and reformers, *Aurora Leigh* was an immediate success; the second edition was published within a fortnight and the third a few months later. In spite of this, Maria did not care for it: 'I am sorry to say I have read 'Aurora Leigh' and *cannot endure her* or Mrs Browning. She is just the sort of woman that makes me ashamed of my "sect" [?] and wish that there were no such thing as authoresses and poetesses.'[16]

Maria's attitude is interesting. It is now all too easy to interpret her forthright independent opinions, her disgust with the inferiority of girls' education, her scorn for the fripperies which encumbered women in society, and her delight in the freedom of her pioneering life, as evidence that she was also a pioneer feminist. Maria would have hated the term 'feminist' and spurned the accolade. Her later Nelson letters, in particular, show that Maria was convinced that a 'great change' was needed to the status of women. She saw the ordinary life of women in New Zealand as either 'constant drudgery or complete frivolity'; she believed in 'women's rights', although she wished 'some of its advocates had more common sense and tact, for they seem to retard the cause', and she was positive that 'whether we like or not the next century will see an enormous change in the position of women'. Her strong dislike of Aurora Leigh is entirely consistent with her detestation of Shirley in Charlotte Brontë's novel. Both characters questioned the role of women; both asked whether marriage was necessarily a good thing for a woman with a vocation, and Aurora Leigh proclaimed that a woman had the right to determine her own career. In Maria's English letters to Margaret Taylor she had frequently referred to their likely state as 'old maids', accepting the prospect with good humour and determining to be a favourite maiden aunt to her future nieces and nephews. Yet Maria accepted without question that the supreme lot for a woman was to be found in marriage and within her family. In reply to a remonstrance from Margaret, Maria acknowledged she was 'a heretic' about *Aurora Leigh* and she was not prepared to recant.

At Hurworth, Arthur was employing carpenters to join the house which Purnell had built to the one Maria had bought from du Moulin. On 17 July the job was completed, with Arthur helping to cut a doorway from the old house into the new. Later, in 1858, Lely described the house to Emily:

> You enter by a half glass door into a small passage, on the right hand at the extremity of the passage, a door leads into a small kitchen with a French window, through the kitchen is a bedroom of similar dimensions with a fire place – this is Arthur & Maria's room – it is lined & papered with Mr du Moulin's papers & is very comfortable. This is the old part of the house. On the left a door leads into a very cheerful light bedroom, the paper like that in the Bird's nest . . . this is to be appropriated to me. It has no fire place but the sun is seldom off it. Another door from the passage, also on the left, opens into the sitting room, about 24 ft long . . . & 13 ft 4 inches wide – very lofty with open ceiling roof. Two French windows [are] opposite the fire place & door & a bow or bay window at the end. It is as yet unpapered & carpetless & contains a heterogeneous collection of goods.[17]

The money problems which always bedevilled Hurworthians eased a little for the Atkinsons during 1857, when they inherited from their parents' estates.[18]

> Now our fortunes have arrived we are getting on fast. Hal has ordered a chaise-cart, and is going to have his mare broken in to harness. The cart is to have broad wheels and he expects to be able to use it during six months of the year or more. It will

save sending in the bullock cart about small affairs and enable Jane
and Dunstan to see more of the world.[19]
Arthur invested in more land and, with Harry, leased one of John
Hursthouse's paddocks in which to grow potatoes. He also had
W.S. Atkinson's gang of Maori labourers fell about ten acres which
lay between the house and Te Henui river. When cleared and
planted, it opened up a view of the opposite river bank so that
from the east windows of their house they could see 'the forest
in its untouched freshness' overhanging the river, instead of the
usual edge-of-clearing bush 'left ragged and scathed by fire and
axe'. The house – Arthur added a verandah right around it – settled
snugly under a little hill planted in fruit trees, and a small stream,
the Awanui, flowed through the property.[20] The farm fitted well
into Hurworth self-sufficiency.

> Having no rent and our garden beginning to produce, our household
> expenses are a mere trifle. I can't make out that we spend nine
> shillings a week in living, but a great deal of our business is done
> by barter (we exchange cheese for milk, butter and eggs with Hal
> and Dec) . . . We have bacon and hams of our own curing. The
> mares, besides their usefulness, give fair interest in their foals . . .
> Arthur and I with our land, house, horses and £50 a year feel I
> think quite as rich as we should in England with four or five hundred
> a year; we are quite at ease. At any time by working for others
> . . . Ar could greatly increase our money income if we felt the
> necessity.[21]

It was an over-sanguine view of their situation, for ready money
was always hard to come by, but Maria was satisfied. On sunny
days, basking on top of the little hill 'having a good talk or reading
an exciting book' took the place of Sunday excursions to the Te
Henui from Merton.

A report that gold had been discovered in the Huatoki raised
excitement in New Plymouth in August 1857 and caused Arthur
to go prospecting, without luck, in the Te Henui. More promising
were the Aorere diggings, and at the beginning of September Calvert
Wilson and Teddo Patten left Hurworth for Nelson, where wages
were higher and there was the prospect of making money faster
than they could at Taranaki. Maria was cautious about their chances:
'Calvert seemed very jolly at starting but Teddo's heart seemed
a little faint at last and he said he wanted the day of return already
. . . I am not much afraid they will wish to leave us entirely.'[22]

There was a lull in the 'native feud' during 1857 but skirmishing
continued between 'some of the very wild officers here[23] and the

young civilians who don't like to be insulted by the redcoats'.[24]
The chief culprit was a certain Captain Marsh, whose influential
connections in England apparently deterred his commanding officer
from taking action against him. Maria, as usual, did not mince
words: 'It was a dreadful thing for the uneducated young men
of this place to have such abominable officers as examples amongst
them.'[25] Marsh was, however, decisively defeated by Hurworthians.
'Tremendous rows' blew up after the annual Freemasons ball at
which a drunken Marsh, backed by an equally drunk 'moustachioed
Adams – a very disreputable young man with 11 inches of moustache'
– insulted Robert Pitcairn, James Ronalds, and Decimus Atkinson.
Arthur recorded what happened later in his diary:

> 4 July. Rode to Merton with Maria then to town. Among other
> things I saw Pitcairn whip Moustachioed Adams as he refused to
> apologise . . . There are three summonses to come off on Tuesday
> next.
>
> 7 July. Started off about 8 a.m. – was overtaken by Harry, Bill,
> Deccy, Pitty, J. Ronalds – rode with them to town. The case of
> Marsh v Pitcairn was withdrawn and also Adams v Pitcairn. Pitcairn
> v Marsh was postponed. If it had been proceeded with he would
> have lost his commission. So after several consultations (in some
> of which we had *Dicky Brown* before us as his advocate) we decided
> on the following conditions, which Marsh agreed to, 1) that he
> should exchange into another regt. as soon as possible, 2) in the
> meantime behave decently in public.[26]

More acceptable to civilians was the 'Military Theatre', which
entertained weekly with a repertoire of melodrama and farce, and
the military orchestra which provided music for public balls. The
mob participated in all New Plymouth social events. Maria, always
fond of dancing, enjoyed the balls, and Arthur, like other male
Hurworthians, seldom missed an opportunity of going into town:

> Saturday is the great day for transacting business. There is no market
> day so called, but sales of cattle and goods of all sorts go on at
> the different auctioneers . . . and most men have something or think
> they have something, to take them to New Plymouth on that day.
> More than half the people find half their business to consist in
> talking politics or gossiping in knots about the inns and stores.[27]

In November 1857 Henry resigned the treasuryship and his seat
on the provincial council. He had gone to Auckland on council
business, and on his return found his seventy-acre clearing covered
in thistles, his house (still only a shell) wet throughout, and his
garden full of weeds. He followed up his resignation by postponing

his marriage, and set to work without distraction on his house
and land. James who had declined a seat in the Legislative Council
in August that year – a 'nominee assembly' did not appeal to the
mob – now agreed to stand for the provincial council in Henry's
place. There was only a week between the latter's resignation and
the by-election, but though Harry and Arthur did what they could
to canvass support for James, there seemed little interest: 'Spent
half an hour trying to induce the Frenchs to come in to vote –
they were hacking for turnips. They had wit enough to understand
the virtue of turnips – what good voting would do them they
could not see.'[28] James, as he thought he would be, was defeated.
Undismayed, he settled back to his desultory farming and to
designing an iron bridge over the Waiwakaiho River. At the end
of October 1858 he was again persuaded to stand for a vacancy
on the provincial council. This time he was elected with ease,
after the other candidate withdrew. The following year he became
provincial secretary. His official salary of £75 per year scarcely
answered in money terms, as he had to employ a man at Hurworth
for £50, but involvement in public affairs was more to his liking
than bush farming.

Mary was a source of anxiety to Maria, who valued her
enormously: 'She is one of those rare women who are quite
independent in mind and think for themselves on all important
subjects without a tinge of strong mindedness.'[29] This remark says
as much about Maria as Mary. Concern arose because Mary was
'inclined to be morbid in some of her notions . . . She has a too
compassionate heart.' She was a vegetarian who held the view
that the sacrifice of animal life by humans or other animals for
their own sustenance was inconsistent with the existence of a
benevolent creator. On a farm where pigs, chickens, sheep, and
cattle were raised for consumption as much as for anything else,
she found things to jar and upset her at every turn. The mob,
as far as possible, tried to be accommodating:

> Harry has bought all James's pigs, so these 'mysteries of creation'
> are off Mary's mind . . . How a butter or cheese-making dairy
> farm is to pay without pigs I am at a loss to imagine. If James
> keeps cows he must take to raising calves, as they are used for
> milch cows and working bullocks *before* finding their way to the
> butchers (that goal of all farm stock). Mary can I suppose shut
> her eyes to their being 'part of the system'. I have been advising
> James to let his cows to Harry for a time, for I foresee in the
> present state of matters that no Waiwakaiho bridge plans,[30] no house

improvements here [at the time of writing James and Mary were still living at Merton] or superintendence of Hurworth clearings can go on.[31]

Mary's susceptibilities did not interfere with the usual family feast at Christmas. With Maria's help she provided a sixteen-pound plum pudding and mincemeat; Harry provided turkey, ham, almonds, and raisins; Arthur and Maria, beef and gooseberry pies, and the Ronalds, five fowls. Rain prevented an outdoor meal so the Hurworthians, eighteen in number, dined in Maria and Arthur's 'long room' where kauri boards made an excellent table. 'We missed our absentees very much, no Lely, no Nellie,[32] no Teddo, no Cal on a festive occasion like this seemed strangely unnatural.' Everybody adjourned to Hal's for tea.

Just as Maria had once been convinced that she would remain a spinster, so she was now certain, after the death of her first daughter Margaret, that she and Arthur would remain childless. However, in 1858 she was again pregnant. Mary Richmond was also expecting and she and James came to stay with Maria and Arthur at Hurworth so that James could more readily supervise the building of his own house there and Mary could have Maria's company now that Lely was in Auckland. Mary was still missing her English family. Arthur described her as sitting in a corner everlastingly writing letters – this is possibly an exaggerated view, as his diary also notes, 'Maria and Mary gadding about as usual.' Mary was not as competent a horsewoman as Maria, but provided her mount went slowly she felt safe enough. Merton, where Hugh Ronalds and his sister, Marion, were now living, was once again a useful resting place on their journeys to and from town. Various English friends of Mary, including R.H. Hutton, Dr Joseph Kidd, Rev. F.D. Maurice, and Annie, her sister, had all tried in letters to induce Mary to abandon vegetarianism. It was Maria's 'kind urgency', for Mary was looking painfully thin, which finally induced her to eat a little meat. The sitting room at Hurworth was as yet without wallpaper or curtains but 'huge back logs and blazing fires' made the room comfortable over the winter months. James and Mary provided music in the evenings, the *Aspective Review* was revived, and the Hurworth Debating Society began meeting weekly in Bill Atkinson's house. On 30 July Mary's baby, Ann Elizabeth (Anneliz, later shortened to Alla), was born. The night before, at 2.30 am, Arthur had gone for the doctor and nurse:

Routed out Dr Neild. He appeared with a flannel nightcap on &

shawl. 'You don't mean to say you have come to fetch me for
Mrs James?' 'Yes I have Dr. It's a fine night.' 'Oh, goodness me
& I've got such a *shocking cold.*' Fetched Mrs Wakefield from
Mangorei.
30 July. At 12–30 pm heard first cry of a new voice.[33]
Maria had been apprehensive as to whether her own baby would
be born alive. After Mary's successful confinement and with spring
that year producing perfect weather, she found it impossible not
to feel cheerful and optimistic. There were to be no more energetic
pursuits or last-minute hanging of curtains. She now employed a
young servant girl.

> I have been quite a fine lady again for weeks past, sitting in the
> parlour at needlework, or on sunny days on the hill, reading. My
> hands are growing quite smooth and genteel, but I shall not be
> at all sorry when the time for active work comes again, as apart
> from the satisfaction of the suspense being ended, my housemaid
> soul chafes at being so long kept from congenial occupations and
> I am forced to shut my eyes to many household disorders to keep
> myself out of mischief. . . . You need have no uneasiness for me;
> I am made of good tough material.[34]

Because of her inactivity, Maria's 'housekeeper's heart' was
particularly pleased with Arthur's present for her thirty-fourth
birthday: 'it is a solid smooth box made of handsomely veined
red pine, calculated to contain a hundred pounds of flour; the lid
fits in without hinges and when taken off forms an excellent pastry
board'.[35]
Lely[36] reported to Emily at the end of September that Maria
was sunburnt and in 'buxom health'. On 21 October, just a quarter
of an hour before Arthur's birthday was officially over and a quarter
of an hour before Dr Neild arrived, Maria gave birth to an eight-
pound daughter. There were no complications, Arthur administered
the chloroform, Maria was splendid, and the following day it was
only Arthur who seemed a little seedy. The baby's name was Edith
Emily: as neither Maria nor Arthur could make up their minds
about which name should come first, it was left to their friend
Mary King to decide. A few weeks later Emily, who had come
to stay, wrote to William, 'I found them all very well here, Mary
and Maria with two of the dearest little babies you can think of.'
For her part, Maria wrote to Margaret:

> I have come to the conclusion that after all those are best off who
> suffer at first from hope deferred, and the prospect of a childless
> life . . . all the deprivation of liberty to go about, which the care

of a young child here involves, seems a treat; whilst we hear young
mothers who have begun early and go on briskly increasing their
families groan and moan on their sufferings and slavery . . . I wish
I could show you Edith, dearest Margie, or express to you properly
the hourly joy she is to me.[37]

And so Edith continued throughout her early childhood: forward
for her age, walking before ten months ('trotting about all over
the house as strong as a little elephant',) 'interesting & intelligent
looking rather than pretty'.[38]

Emily had come to Hurworth to await the arrival of her
fourth child, as William was now frequently absent from Auckland.
There was also another reason for William's wishing his wife to
spend a little time with her 'bush' family. He wrote to Harry
Atkinson:

I hope you will occasionally help me to rub off the worldliness
which is fast crusting over her who was once emphatically the
child of nature. It is a sad sight to see her sailing about in the
saloons of Auckland the complete creature of convention.[39]

James, Mary, and Anneliz moved into their own house at
Hurworth at the beginning of October 1858. It was in a very
unfinished state, little more than a lean-to, but James wanted to
be on the spot to supervise his builders. Henry was hard at work
on the joinery of his house, called 'Damper Hall' by the mob –
'I think he is careless of his diet & lives too constantly on damper
& cheese,'[40] Maria wrote. Lely worried about his 'poverty' and
forthcoming 'imprudent' marriage. She thought he had over-
extended himself with his seventy-acre clearing, and he had
borrowed heavily from William. Henry himself was confident that
he and Blanche could live in the bush for less than £60 a year
(the amount of his allowance from Lely), and Maria was adamant
that his marriage should no longer be postponed:

I will not be a party in any way to deferring young Henry's marriage
much beyond December. I am so *clear* that in every way including
his worldly prospects it is wisest & best for him to be married.
Of course I am a romantic mad woman but I should not fear with
Hy's industry, good head & clever hands seeing them married
tomorrow. Henry's grand error he feels to have been felling faster
than his means allowed of his fencing effectually . . . But let him
be married, be quiet & settled . . . & see in a few years whether
his fortune is so very deplorable. Of course as Mr Stafford justly
remarked to Ar's great delight 2 years ago, 'N.Plymouth is not
fit for the *residence* of a *gentleman*,' but some of us 'thank the gods

we are not gentlemanly' & for plain yeomen it is a happy home.[41]

Henry and Blanche were married on 18 December 1858. John Hursthouse had, to begin with, created a difficulty. He would consent to give his daughter away only if the Rev. Joseph Long, a Primitive Methodist minister known for his affability, married the couple, and if the ceremony took place in his carpenter's shed which he was prepared to set up as a chapel. Otherwise his brother-in-law, John Stephenson Smith, would have to act in his place. It was not John Hursthouse's defection as such which caused indignation at Hurworth, but rather the fact that it opened the way for Hannah Stephenson Smith to be mistress of ceremonies: 'She intends to have it as near like *the last royal marriage* as circumstances will permit,' Emily reported to William.[42] In the event the marriage was solemnised in St Mary's, Mr Lally (Govett's locum) officiating. John Hursthouse came to Merton for the wedding breakfast and the festivities afterwards '& conducted himself in his usual absurd way.' It was to be the last formal occasion on which their first home was used by the mob. The following January Emily described it as 'dreary in the extreme'; a goat was wandering about inside, there were beetles on the floor, and outside gates and fences were broken. Like Beach Cottage it was to be let as soon as possible.[43] Lely was critical of the mob's improvident attitude to their former home:

> It was not for nothing I hesitated to leave [Merton]. There has been a great waste of property for want of someone interested to care for things – it was impossible for those living at Hurworth to keep a vigilant eye upon Merton.[44]

Meanwhile, the Hurworth community flourished. Emily took a gloomy view of its future and wrote of the 'incessant toil . . . which can bring no result'. Maria replied:

> With the exception of the first year & a half here, I should say that *most* of the energy has been expended in riding about & enjoying themselves, & that the incessant toil has been consistent with a larger amount of whole & half holidays than absolute health rendered necessary.[45]

Cricket and horse racing were taken seriously by the male Hurworthians. A pitch had been early laid down, and when riding into New Plymouth on business, there seemed always time for a few circuits of the race track on the way. Maria once chided William when he imagined them living in a state of mental stagnation: 'every subject under the sun & I may say *above* the sun [the passing of Donati's comet had caused Arthur to take a

keen interest in astronomy] is discussed with the liveliest interest.'[46]
The debating group met weekly; so too did the singing class
conducted by James. Marion Ronalds held an evening German class
which was studying *Wallenstein's Tod*, the third part of Schiller's
dramatic trilogy. Arthur at first insisted on having it translated
into blank verse but the ladies rebelled, saying they were too busy.
Bill Atkinson led a Maori language class.[47] On Sundays a church
service was held at either Harry's or James's. The *Aspective Review*
made spasmodic appearances and, as the various houses were
completed during 1858 and 1859, there were housewarmings
followed by 'theatrical productions' and dancing. 'There is certainly
no slowness in the life here, for with such a wide family connection,
something exciting or amusing or interesting is always going
forward.'[48]

Lely, however, interposed a cautionary note: 'I wish we had
some more people, I mean right sort of people, amongst us. We
ring the changes too much upon each other & run great risk of
becoming *squaddish*.'[49]

The variety offered by Hurworth suited Arthur's temperament,
for it was in many ways a continuation of his eclectic upbringing
at Frindsbury. He eventually sold his cows to Harry, on whom
the cheese-making reputation of Hurworth finally rested,[50] and
concentrated on raising, training, and racing horses, becoming a
steward of the Taranaki Racing Club and, according to William,
'one of the most turfy characters in N.P.'. He was devoted to
Edith. 'If only Edith were a boy,' Maria noted, 'his joy would
be complete.' Like other Hurworth husbands he took his share
of the housework, making bread, baking, and brewing a kind of
sugar beer. 'It is surprising how the life here develops talent of
this sort among the men,' Lely informed Margaret.

> As to James, he is a perfect *fid-fad* in a house, so over & above
> thorough & particular. I do believe his soul delights in scouring
> & brightening saucepans . . . William, before his rise in life, used
> to go about the Beach Cottage routing out & sweeping like a
> whirlwind . . . Henry is just now hanging out the clothes in the
> garden.[51]

With a view to a possible job with the Native Office sometime
in the future, Arthur consulted Maria as to 'whether it would be
well to go among the Negroes for six months to learn Maori'.[52]
Maria must have said 'no', but each week he went to one of the
local pa to sit among the people and absorb the language. He had
a Maori named Mohi working for him, and together they indulged

in bird watching – Arthur noting down Maori names and bird lore – and collected plant and insect specimens for Dr Ferdinand von Hochstetter.[53] He read French with Maria before breakfast and was an enthusiastic member of Marion Ronald's German class and Bill Atkinson's Maori one. Apart from his horses, and military duties with the volunteers which became more demanding as the debacle of the Waitara purchase approached, his interests lay where his active mind took him. Fortunately Maria understood him and made allowances which might have been beyond the tolerance of a younger wife.

> For one who has had no strict or methodical training in early life, Ar is remarkably concentrative. I believe if he should go to college now he would work hard & enjoy doing so & would pass in a high class for he has a real relish for mental work.[54]

Arthur enjoyed Hurworth but was not entirely satisfied or extended by it. He wrote to William in September 1859 to see whether the latter would be willing, if he escaped from politics, to take him on as an articled clerk. William replied that such were his political commitments he would not be able to accede to this request 'for a long time'. So Arthur contented himself (although with an eye to the law he began Latin with James) with his life of 'supreme potterings' – 'my highest ambition being to win cricket matches, shoot straight with a rifle and, best of all, sometimes win a race.'[55]

Christmas 1858 was 'a marked day to be remembered always.' It seemed in its passing to bring to fruition all the hopes vested in Hurworth.

> The weather was perfect and we all assembled to dine on a ridge commanding a splendid view . . . Every household contributed something towards the feast . . . In all twenty nine people [members of the Hursthouse family were also present] dined together. I wish I could make a sketch of the group as we sat dining – children, babies, dogs & all. The glorious summer day set off the bush to great advantage, backed by the grand old Mountain, now fast parting with his snows. After dinner the party broke up adjourning to Henry's house to admire his cheerful sitting room & freshly papered bedroom . . .
> We all adjourned to James & Mary's for tea. I was perfectly astonished at the beauty of the room . . . The roof is open, with cross-tied beams with ornamented ends and pendants. The paper is a sort of gold arabesque pattern on a cream coloured ground

and a velvety looking dark green border runs round the room . . .
James had ornamented each side of the window in the gable end
where bookshelves are to be fixed hereafter with a beautiful group
of the leaves of nikau and the effect was considered Moorish in
style . . . Everybody was arrayed in their best and looked their
gayest & happiest; altogether it was the jolliest evening I ever spent
in New Zealand and I have had many pleasant ones.

We were all so grand that I must tell you some of the dresses.
Lely in a splendid black moire antique in which she figured off
at Government House when in Auckland. Mary, who looks sweeter
than ever I think since she was a mother, in a bronze silk with
white muslin jacket. Nellie looked most bewitching in a scarlet
lama made low, showing her fair fat shoulders and neck to great
advantage. I was elderly, but of *course* distinguished, in black satin
with black lace jacket.[56]

The golden weather of Christmas day continued all that summer,
'the longest and finest we have known,' and, with prescience, Maria
seemed almost reluctant to pass the threshold of 1859, when 'some
unknown trial may be awaiting us.'[57]

There were several additions to the mob during 1859. The event
of March was the birth of Lely's first grandson, Christopher Francis
Richmond, to William and Emily.

We are all glad to have the Richmond name kept up though William,
who might be expected to care most for a son, is very good and
grateful whatever comes; he is so thankful to have living and healthy
children.[58]

Not all the additions were 'of the right sort'. Jane Atkinson's brother,
Henry Skinner, came to Hurworth at the beginning of 1859. He
had already abandoned the navy and thrown up a good job;
emigration seemed the only prospect left, although his father was
doubtful whether his son would ever 'alter very much for the better'.
He did not. Then there was Arthur Wilson,[59] an eight-year-old
whom James and Mary considered adopting and who arrived from
Sydney in March. It was difficult to see how he would fit into
the 'Palace of Art' (the mob's name for James and Mary's house),
as Emily described him as a 'horrid vulgar little Sydney boy'. Mary
and James scarcely mention him, but it would appear they came
to share Emily's opinion. October saw the return of Charlie Wilson;
a legacy from his Aunt Wright had enabled him to pay his passage
back to Taranaki, which he now considered he had made a grave
mistake in ever leaving. He took a sawing job with Frank Adams
and seemed to work steadily, although Arthur considered he was

not any better in his mind. Alfred Charles Atkinson ('Ninety'),[60]
the youngest of the Atkinson family from Frindsbury, was also
to have come out during the year. Arthur, who was very much
attached to his young brother, had been encouraging him by letter
to practise bowling as the Hurworth cricket team badly needed
a bowler. In October Arthur received 'the saddest news I ever
had yet': Ninety, aged thirteen, had died of diphtheria.

A more welcome guest during 1859 was Bessie Domett, the
fifteen-year-old stepdaughter of William's friend and colleague.[61]
Domett, uneasy about Bessie's education 'which seems to have been
. . . too much filled up with frippery & crinolines',[62] agreed with
William's suggestion that she spend some time at Hurworth. She
arrived in June and was, as Maria reported to William, very well
received:

> We like Bessie Domett very much, & Lely is going to ask Mr
> Domett to let her remain till Xmas with us. One can easily see
> what the improvements are he wishes to have effected in her . . .
> She wants her ideas on 'the true object of life' raising a little but
> as the various members in the Ngati-Richmond & Ngati-Atkinson
> are far from agreed on the matter, her mind may be only confused
> by her visit. At present she has a clear conception of the vital
> importance of balls, ball dresses & starched petticoats. How is one
> to undeceive her?[63]

As a practical beginning, Lely began to teach Bessie to spell.

Adjacent to Hurworth was Denby Farm, owned by the Ronalds.
They had always considered themselves honorary members of the
mob and in 1859 the connection was made secure by marriage.
During the year Bill Atkinson and his younger brother, Decimus,
became engaged to Eliza and Marion (Polly) Ronalds respectively.
Decimus was an agreeable, light-hearted fellow who worked as
a sawyer with Hugh Ronalds. They had plans to erect a sawmill
designed by James Richmond on Deccy's land. Hugh Ronalds was
dubious about Bill Atkinson's ability to provide for Eliza; his early
reputation for 'knocking about' still clung to him. Eliza was,
however, completely under her fiancé's influence – he was thirty-
seven – and as the year progressed Hugh came to accept their
forthcoming marriage. He was even looking forward to freeing
his house from 'two smitten sisters':

> You can have no idea of the comfort it will be to me when they
> are married. Fancy two great soft spoonies [he was including
> Decimus] coming as regular as clockwork every night and stopping
> until bedtime, carrying on muttered conversation or else using paper

and pencil to express very deep tender speech . . . It is enough
to make one forswear ever being in love oneself.[64]

Then, quite suddenly, Marion broke off her engagement to
Decimus[65] and 'out of health & out of spirits' went for a change
of scene to Nelson. On 26 November Bill Atkinson and Eliza Ronalds
were married in St Mary's. It was to be the last celebration of
the Hurworth community.

> The wedding was altogether original, being an equestrian one. The
> bridegroom and his man preceded the main body by half an hour
> or more. We of the main body, sixteen in number all riding in-
> cluding the bride and her brother Frank (who acted as Father).
> These two heading the procession, arrived in town . . . looking
> more dusty than was correct, for we had to ride quickly . . . owing
> to the bride's horse whose toilette [all the horses had their manes
> plaited with white satin] took longer than any of the bridesmaids
> did.
>
> After the ceremony . . . we rode from town to a very lovely
> spot on the Waiwakaiho river where it is joined by the Mangore
> . . . which we call 'The Meeting of the Waters'.[66]

On the way the wedding party was joined by a horse and cart
bringing older and younger Hurworthians and by Harry's bullock
cart with 'ample provisions'.

> Under the trees at the water's edge the wedding breakfast was
> spread, and we grouped irregularly about, the horses being tethered
> a little way off. After breakfast the bride and bridegroom rode
> home. Soon after the party broke up, some going straight home
> and the rest, chiefly the young unmarried people, escorted by Jane
> and me in the character of dragons, prolonged their ride to the
> Upper Mangore district (which runs parallel with our Hurworth
> district on the opposite, northern bank of the Henui river) before
> proceeding home. In the evening the party assembled at our house
> and danced and acted charades till half past twelve.[67]

After a visit to Taranaki in 1859, C.W. Richmond wrote to English
relatives about the mob's situation at Hurworth:

> I find Hurworth much improved since my last visit: the clearings
> extend considerably above a mile along the road . . . The houses
> of the various members of the two families rise in all directions.
> All seem more than contented. They are attached, even with a
> kind of Taranaki fanaticism, to the life.[68]

Attached with an equal determination to the Waitara, the anvil
on which Maori–Pakeha relations were hammered out in Taranaki,
was Wiremu Kingi Te Rangitake:

Waitara is in my hands. I will not give it up; ekore, ekore, ekore'
(I will not, I will not, I will not). I have spoken.[69]
Taranaki settlers, factious in most matters, were united in feeling
that from the beginning of settlement there, they had been badly
served by various agents of government over land buying: 'The
want of land – open, available, accessible land – when hundreds
of thousands of acres lie waste and unprofitable around, is the
great misfortune under which we labour.'[70] C.W. Richmond,[71] who
had had the management of Native Affairs since he joined the
Stafford ministry, shared Taranaki settler chagrin:

> It is impossible to conceive of any European feeling anything but
> shame and indignation at such a state of things as we have had
> in New Plymouth since 1854. I feel a passionate desire to terminate
> it, but we must cut our coat according to our cloth.[72]

The constraints which he saw were: the need to keep land-
purchase policy firmly under the control of central government
and clear of dictation by reckless provincial ambition; the limited
capability of the country's military forces, and, following from
that, the danger, by an injudicious move, of involving the country
in a full-scale war between Maori and settler. Hurworthians never
fully appreciated these constraints. The pressure which they put
on William for decisive action during the years which led to the
Waitara purchase was considerable; even Emily must have come
to dread the arrival of yet another letter from Maria full of 'disgust'
at the government's handling of the 'native feud'. William's replies
to the mob were, on the whole, calmly reasoned. He attributed
some of its criticism to 'the well known overdose of cayenne in
the Atkinson blood', and in another letter referred to 'the whole
angry tribe of Hurworth'. But the battering to which he was
subjected by his impatient kinfolk, bearing in mind that in essence
he shared the same determination to extend European settlement,
took a toll. Tempering passion with judgement and ends with means
left him, as he described it, 'in a very delicate position', about
which he received very little sympathy from Hurworth. 'I have
ceased, with great regret,' he wrote to Emily, 'to expect any support
from them.'[73] His health suffered, and his asthma attacks increased.
'I hate them [politics]', he wrote, 'though I can scarcely talk or
think of anything else.'[74]

Te Ati Awa opinion over the possible sale of their land was
divided, although not as divided as both government and settlers
wished to believe. The uncompromising stand of Wiremu Kingi
Te Rangitake over Waitara, regarded by settlers as the promised

land, was well known, but neither the effectiveness of his chieftainship nor the strength of his mana was fully appreciated. C.W. Richmond saw him as 'a rascal' and 'the bad genius of Taranaki'; Gore Browne saw him as an 'infamous character'. Josiah Flight, resident magistrate at New Plymouth, described him in one of the affrays of the 'native feud' as 'screaming and screeching like a woman'. Even Grace Hirst, pious and practical, thought of the Ati Awa chief as 'a nasty old wretch . . . who lays about in a blanket without even a shirt'. The remarks were always disparaging, and his real weight was never taken. Elements of Te Ati Awa were still dispersed,[75] but the fact remained that Wiremu Kingi was the tribe's effective leader at the Waitara. As a corollary to this underestimation of him, both government and settlers ascribed more strength and cohesion to the Maori 'selling party' than it ever really had; the very words 'selling party' could be accounted a European interpretation of motives, and open to question.

Naturally C.W. Richmond's understanding was limited by the paradigm of nineteenth-century imperialism – 'the necessities of colonisation', as he later expressed it – and he chose to interpret the dispute in the terms and in the manner of thinking he was accustomed to. Writing to Henry Sewell, absent in England, Richmond said of the Maori King movement: 'I hear in it the voice of a people crying out to be governed – a people weary of anarchy and desiring guidance in the right way.'[76] One of the 'right ways' was to individualise Maori land ownership. In this, Richmond simply expressed a basic conviction held alike by European settlers, administrators, and the majority of missionaries.[77] He was also aware that, however much he desired it, there was no such thing in Maori lore as an individual title to land. When Robert Parris was appointed land purchase commissioner in Taranaki, C.W. Richmond's advice was to act on the established principle of not buying a disputed title: 'The Government will not have anything to do with land which it would require an armed force to keep possesion of.'[78] Yet, revealing the ambivalence of the administrative position, he added in the same letter: 'a site for a town on the Waitera [sic] must be secured'. In a letter to a member of the Taranaki Provincial Council, Richmond wrote: 'I do not believe a man in New Zealand wants to see the Waitera (or at least one bank of it) in the hands of Government [more] than I do. You may rely on the cash being found if the native demands are anything in reason.'[79]

In May 1857 the *Taranaki Herald* responded in typical settler fashion

to another offer of land at Waitara by the Ati Awa chief, Ihaia
Te Kirikumara; it was land which Wiremu Kingi had already
asserted belonged to the 'whole people': 'We do not know what
degree of chieftainship he [Ihaia] holds among the Natives, and,
moreover care not. Sufficient for us is that he is at the head of
the "Progress Party" and the open friend of the Pakeha.'[80] The
Reverend John Whiteley held that Ihaia's claim was good but
suggested caution lest, in this prolonged Ikamoana land dispute,
the more eminent chief, Katatore, take offence and refuse to part
with land. The latter, thought Whiteley, was likely to come forward
as a seller. So Ihaia's offer was again left in limbo.

This did not please the mob at Hurworth, who maintained that
government (which it tended to equate with William) was
continually turning a deaf ear to the 'selling party'. Its most fiery
advocate wrote to Emily:

> The position we are in with respect to land purchasing can hardly
> be made worse . . . the only hope is that one day the Maoris may
> get so impudent in Auckland province or some *important* place that
> they will drive the Governor into a more dignified position, when
> I believe it will turn out that had the British Lion had the heart
> to say 'bo' to a goose a little sooner a good deal of bother might
> have been saved & the Maoris themselves really more advanced
> in civilization than they can become under the lollypop system . . .
> I really believe that instead of being a misfortune it might do lots
> of us a good deal of good to have our houses burnt over our heads
> & be deprived of our usual comforts. I fear the 19th century is
> spoiling the race with ease & safety.[81]

If Maria had studied previous clashes between military and Maori
she would have discovered that the British lion's 'bo' had not been
overwhelmingly successful.

Another twist to events leading to war was the killing of Katatore
and his brother on 11 January 1858 by Tamati Tiraurau, brother
of Ihaia, with some of Ihaia's men.[82] Ironically, the previous August,
Katatore had offered land at Waitara. C.W. Richmond's comment
on the killing was: 'It is merely the latest scene in a play (call
it a tragedy if you please) in which the British government has
elected to take the part of a spectator only.'[83] In the wake of this
act, fighting again broke out between the opposed parties in the
'native feud'. This time there were incidents within Bell block
itself. The Taranaki Provincial Council sent a memorial to central
government and in reply the executive council issued a proclamation
which stated that Maori fighting in areas owned by settlers would

be treated 'as if they were in arms against the Queen'; if the order not to fight on settlers' land was disobeyed, the commanding officer in New Plymouth would have the authority to call out the militia and to order settlers to come into town. In a memorandum to C.W. Richmond, Governor Gore Browne stated that although he had 'profound sympathy' for the settlers, he had the military capability neither 'to follow the natives into the bush' nor to defend outlying farmers in their homes; 'to shew our teeth without biting would be imbecile'.[84]

Fortunately for both settlers and government, Ihaia[85] moved with his people from his pa, Ikamoana, near Bell block which had been destroyed either at his own command or by Katatore's followers, to another pa, Karaka, a few miles beyond the Waitara. This pa was immediately besieged by Wiremu Kingi. With the battlefield moved to the Waitara, the settlers' situation eased and C.W. Richmond wrote to his brother, 'there is no present danger of their fighting on our land which was what the proclamation was issued to prevent'.[86] At New Plymouth a notice signed by Resident Magistrate J. Flight and Major G.F. Murray, officer commanding the troops stationed there, warned the settlers against going to the Waitara 'or in any way interfering with the present Native disturbance'. This state of affairs may have satisfied the 'peaceable quiet part of the community here', as Flight wrote to Richmond, but it did not appease Hurworth. Maria wrote to Emily:

> We learnt with positive dismay that the Government meant to do nothing more for the peace of the settlement than Ihaia had kindly anticipated them in effecting by his removal with his party beyond the Waitara simply to prevent murders at our very doors. The Natives continue to parade the settlement fully armed at all times.[87]

William did nothing to mollify Hurworth opinion by suggesting that the bands of armed Maori were no more dangerous to the settlement than the guards on London bridge were to Londoners.

One can deplore Maria's readiness to confront 'Maori anarchy with British law & British bayonets',[88] but when she wrote, 'We (or some of us do) love the place with a sort of family affection which will make us cling on to the last',[89] she strikes a sympathetic chord which echoes still. Nevertheless, the question remains: what would have happened if the Taranaki settlers had pursued peace as energetically as they now prepared for war? Conflict over land probably was inevitable given the momentum of nineteenth-century colonisation, although events in Wanganui during the brief campaign of 1847 showed that Maori then drew a clear distinction between settlers and soldiers; Maori resentment against the former arose only when they became identified with government policy.[90] One Taranaki settler, a former Baptist minister in England who farmed at Omata, firmly believed his countrymen brought destruction on themselves.

> Had it not been for the dragging of the settlers into the quarrel, to this day I believe they might have remained on their farms and in their quiet homes. There was something more than mere suspicion of the intention of Government in the minds of the more intelligent natives, when they saw the encouragement given to the formation of the Volunteer Rifle Corps, and the constant rifle practice at a target; and a full realization was arrived at, on the very day that the militia was called out for active service, guns served out, and stockades commenced. This was their frequent enquiry – 'Why all this preparation? Why should every settler be made to bear arms, except it be to exterminate the Maoris?[91]

At the beginning of March 1858, 300 Taranaki settlers were sworn in as militiamen.[92] The Hurworth members had for some time been drilling regularly as volunteers and practising rifle and pistol shooting. Harry Atkinson was all for the militia being engaged in any actual fighting which might ensue while the British troops were used merely to defend the town. None of the mob felt any apprehension and were not thinking of abandoning Hurworth to take refuge in New Plymouth: 'if the worst comes to the worst,' Harry wrote rather pretentiously, 'we will fall with our houses.'[93] Henry Richmond was offered a lieutenant's commission in the Grey section of the Taranaki militia, and Hurworth was largely satisfied with its settler officers. Other militiamen were less pleased and a public meeting was held to protest. Major J.Y. Lloyd, the regular forces' officer in charge of militia appointments, was regarded as too much a soldier 'of the oldest or most absolute school', as James explained to his brother:

> The people quite rebel at absolute government. Major Lloyd hardly sees the full mischief, I think. We shall have men assembled with a determination to be indocile . . . The corps will be a byeword and results even worse may follow.[94]

Arthur wrote in his diary, 'The old Major is obstinate & the people pigheaded', and Maria wrote to Lely in Auckland: 'There has been such fussing & talking & meeting about the militia & Major Lloyd's appointment of officers that the Maoris have sunk into insignificance.'[95] The governor, Colonel Thomas Gore Browne, also a soldier of the 'absolute school', stated firmly that to recognise the opinion of the men would be to establish a 'democratic precedent' to which he would never consent. On the other hand, he thought it would be prudent for Major Lloyd to make a choice of officers which would not be 'unacceptable to the *sovereign people* of New Plymouth'. The first 'general muster' of the Taranaki militia was also its last for some time:

> We got on very well . . . especially when the Major told us 'to take up the British cheer when we charged'. We did this so well that we didn't hear the order to halt. After we had finished we got £1 and we were told we were not wanted any more just now.[96]

The *Taranaki Herald* expressed surprise and dissatisfaction at this decision: 'If [the militia was] necessary for public safety, the disbandment of the force is inexpedient and hazardous,' it complained.[97] Arthur Atkinson immediately put his name down for the volunteer company which was being formed in its place. Most male Hurworthians eventually became members of the Taranaki Volunteer Rifle Corps which, as Maria later informed Margaret, was 'in existence long before the Volunteer movement in England was heard of, so don't suppose we can't originate things out here'.[98]

Another difference between C.W. Richmond and the mob surfaced in 1858 over the choice of candidate to fill the vacant Grey and Bell seat in the General Assembly caused by the resignation of J. Lewthwaite. Hurworth, who had been doubtful of Lewthwaite's mental agility, supported the nomination of Francis Dillon Bell,[99] largely because he took a stronger line on the 'native question'. William disapproved. The man he wanted was Thomas Hirst who, like Lewthwaite, was a Taranaki settler – although William had no belief in Hirst's ability. In the Assembly, party lines were scarcely discernible, but William, an advocate of strong central government, was coming under increasing pressure from 'provincialists':

> the inferiority of Hirst in many points is signal . . . [but] the individual qualifications of a member have become in most cases a matter entirely secondary to the question of which side of the house he will vote with. I count on Hirst as a sure vote – on Bell as a very doubtful one.[100]

Hurworth was far from satisfied: 'Hirst is a pompous impracticable blockhead who may be expected wherever there is a wrong view of any question to take it and adhere doggedly.'[101] In another letter, James advised his brother 'not to seek to be our wet nurse so much'.

Hirst withdrew his nomination, Hurworth confidently expected Bell to win and then, at the last possible moment, Charles Brown came forward and won the election.

These differences between William and Hurworth weighed particularly heavily on Emily and Lely. While staying at Hurworth from the end of 1858 through to early 1859, Emily wrote to her husband:

> I made a great goose of myself and cried half of last night because they would discuss the Native policy. I have always hitherto gone out of the room when I thought the dangerous subject likely to be brought forward, but last night I stayed too long. I hope you will be able to talk it all out . . . I have heard enough.[102]

William replied: 'It was indeed a most exceedingly foolish thing to cry about the Native Policy. What, my pussy, have you got to do with the Native policy. Never mind it. Don't cry about it till I do.'[103] No doubt comforted and soothed by being cast in the accepted feminine role, Emily wrote back: 'I am going to eschew the native question altogether but I do wish with all my heart that you would take the Treasury and give Mr Sewell the Natives to manage.'[104] Lely was also in a 'lugubrious state of mind' about the differences 'the boys' were having with William. 'Lely', wrote Maria in a private letter to Emily while her mother was in Auckland, 'seems to feel it some reflexion on C.W.R's personal character that he is not thought to be taking the right course in Maori affairs.'[105] Maria thought it absurd that her mother should take the difference of opinion so much to heart:

> Does Lely suppose that the strongest affection and respect blind people to mistakes in judgement or defects of character in those they love? I know I love & esteem Arthur not a little, but should I like to see him in a position where rapid decisions & prompt actions were needed? Of course I am not such a goose, but can this be casting a slur on his moral or intellectual nature? I hope not, but Lely's letters seem to show that brother may not criticise brother without cruelty as a wife can freely criticise her husband.[106]

From the end of May 1858 until March 1859, when negotiations began for the purchase of Teira's claim at the Waitara, 'native disturbances' receded. The volunteers continued to drill regularly, but otherwise the mob continued with its own affairs, and letters to William became less barbed. Concern over William's heavy work load caused Maria to write to him in her usual forthright fashion and demand that he visit Hurworth for rest and recreation.

Various individuals here are, or rather have been, looking forward
with much pleasure to going up old Taranaki with you this summer;
but owing to your Spartan or Brutus like temperament I suppose
their hopes will be blighted. Why *you* have not a fair right to
a decent length of vacation when all the rest of the Ministry rush
about the world to races or in search of wives,[107] or what not
. . . I can't see . . No doubt you are, as I may say, the Atlas
of New Zealand, but the social fabric will not topple into universal
smash if you take three or four weeks more than you originally
intended after being more than two years absent from your proper
home.[108]

William came 'home' on 27 February and stayed a month, enabling
him to be present for the birth of his son.

In March 1859 Governor Gore Browne and C.W. Richmond
attended a large Maori gathering in Taranaki at which Te Teira
and Te Retimana offered to sell a small block of land at Waitara
– the Pekapeka block. Among those present was Wiremu Kingi,
who declared his intention of never allowing a land sale at Waitara
– he was actually living and had cultivations on part of the land
Teira offered[109] – and with his supporters withdrew from the meeting.
At a public meeting of settlers in New Plymouth four days later,
Gore Browne declared his intention 'of not allowing any native to
interfere in the sale of land but such as have a claim in the land
in question, i.e. not to allow the rights of chieftainship'.[110] Gore
Browne was now prepared to sanction the buying of a disputed
title, even when the prospect of peaceable possession was in doubt,
if the sellers (irrespective of their chiefly status) at Waitara were,
in government opinion, the owners. On 25 April 1859 Wiremu Kingi
wrote to Gore Browne: 'Your letter has reached me about Te Teira's
and Te Retimana's thoughts. I will not agree to our bedroom being
sold (I mean Waitara here) for this land belongs to the whole of
us; and do not you be in haste to give the money.'[111] Wiremu Kingi
did not put forward a formal claim of his own to the land which
belonged 'to the whole of us', nor was he willing to delineate the
areas he had under cultivation on the land Teira offered. C.W.
Richmond and Gore Browne chose to interpret this as conceding
ownership. They attached little weight to the mana of his chieftainship.
In their opinion it was his 'usurpation' of sovereignty, his refusal
to recognise let alone participate in the Pakeha ritual now determining
land ownership, which gave government the right to acknowledge
and accept Teira and Retimana's offer. To the governor it was also
becoming a matter of principle:

I have insisted upon this comparatively valueless purchase, because
had I admitted the right of a chief to interfere between me and
the lawful proprietors of the soil, I should soon have found further
acquisition of territory impossible in any part of New Zealand.[112]

Te Teira's offer was, however, kept in abeyance until November
1859. In June, Robert Parris, land purchase commissioner in
Taranaki, wrote to C.W. Richmond that Teira was becoming very
anxious about his offer, which 'is regarded as the turning point
of the land question in this Province'.[113] From England, Stafford
warned Richmond of an 'unusually large emigration to New
Zealand' and claimed that 'unless land in sufficient quantity and
quality awaits this immigration . . . disappointment will ensue to
an extent which will be widely circulated in this country . . . No
blow to the progress of New Zd whh. it has yet encountered will
equal what will follow from such an omission.'[114] He urged
Richmond to buy as much land as 'the Natives will in any way
consent to part with'. In September a public meeting in New
Plymouth chaired by J.C. Richmond expressed complete
dissatisfaction with the 'apathy of Colonial Government' over its
negotiations with Teira. The mob's doctor, J.C. Neild, stated that
he had expected to live in a 'progressive settlement of a British
Colony – not to be cooped up in some ten square miles of territory'.[115]
On 27 August, two memoranda from Gore Browne reached
Richmond, the first recommending the purchase of Teira's land
'*when* it can be done without danger of causing other troubles',
the second that 'Instructions should be sent to Taranaki to close
the purchase of Teira's land . . . without delay *if possible*'.[116] The
same day Richmond wrote to Parris, 'The Governor feels he is
pledged to effect the purchase.' And still the purchase hung fire
Parris was obviously delaying payment in the hope that 'the people
might be led to see the inconsistency of their opposition to Teira',[11]
whose claim to ownership he was more than ever convinced was
just.

The first instalment of £100 for the purchase of the Pekapeka
block was paid to Teira on 29 November 1859. The balance was
to follow, at the discretion of Parris, either before the land was
surveyed or afterwards. By January 1860 Teira and his followers
had taken refuge in New Plymouth. On 20 February Octavius
Carrington, accompanied by Parris, went to survey the land. As
soon as Carrington set up his tripod, a party of 'old Maori women'
seized the legs of it and, when he tried to reclaim it, seized the
chain. No violence was offered by any of Wiremu Kingi's followers

who were present and no weapon was seen. Octavius Hadfield, commenting later on Wiremu Kingi's action, stated that it was not the latter's intention to 'break the peace, but to act legally, that is, to remove trespassers, but to do so without violence. He wished merely to assert his ownership to the land.'[118] Back in New Plymouth, Major Murray declared martial law on 22 February, in spite of the fact that no Maori act of aggression had been carried out except the unarmed obstruction of a survey party by the people who were living on the land in question.

C.W. Richmond did not expect war.[119] The day before the survey Maria wrote to Margaret Taylor that William's information had led him to believe that no active opposition would be made and that when the government showed a firm hand all would end peaceably. 'At present, however,' she added, 'matters wear a warlike aspect . . . everybody is flocking into town, bag & baggage.'[120] Hurworthians were among those who more correctly estimated the likelihood of war, even cancelling a cricket match with Wanganui in case they were called into action. They would have preferred the advantage of a 'first strike'. James Richmond, convinced that collision must come, wrote to his brother on 9 February, before the attempted survey, 'I want to effect something by fighting.' Realising that war would be disastrous to the settlers if protracted – £5,000 worth of property at Hurworth could be destroyed in an hour – he advocated going in 'at full strength to make the conclusion rapid'. This attitude was also shared by Arthur and Harry Atkinson. The latter wrote to William, again before the attempted survey, urging that Wiremu Kingi's pa be taken by stealth and that if there was any resistance, Wiremu Kingi and other leading men should be hung and the rest deported: 'My great fear is that things will be only *half done at first* . . . The great thing to be avoided is to begin a war with the Maoris by driving them into the bush.'[121]

Further military reinforcements, the governor, C.W. Richmond, HMS *Niger*, and Colonel C.E. Gold to take command, arrived at New Plymouth at the beginning of March. Maria assured Margaret Taylor that none of the mob was alarmed by events or apprehensive of personal safety except Aunt Helen who seemed at times 'to expect we shall all be murdered'. The relatively few casualties of the 'native feud' were cited as evidence that the Maori were cautious fighters and seldom came within gunshot of each other: 'don't believe any of us would have felt afraid to remain at Hurworth if all our men folk had been at home & at liberty to organise a system of defence.'[122] The mob's earlier determination of, if necessary, falling with their houses was prevented by the volunteers being required to serve as directed by the officer in command at New Plymouth. His orders, in the event of hostilities, were to defend the town, hold the land in question at Waitara, and maintain communications between Waitara and New Plymouth.

Although most Taranaki settlers, even those less bellicose than the mob, supported Charles Brown's statement that 'we had better have a row once & for all, & be in peace afterwards than to be always expecting a bobbery',[123] there was some criticism of the timing of the survey. The growing season had been a very good one, but much of the grain had not been harvested and secured in the town. John Hursthouse beseeched Richmond to try to put the war off 'for another month or so . . . None of my crops are fit to cut at present.'[124] James Richmond, however, reported to William that the temper of the settlers was excellent, even in the face of possible property loss: 'There is but one word among us, "To be thus is nothing! but to be safely thus!" or rather to be thus in an orderly place and under real government is worth every sacrifice we can make.'[125] 'We are strictly in the right,' wrote Thomas Hirst, a settler with whom the mob did not often agree,

> I have not heard a single settler condemn the decision of the Governor – and that is a great thing to say when we are all likely to be severe sufferers, some in life, all in property. We are . . . in good spirits and determined to grapple with the Rebels . . . I never saw a community (I mean those immediately around us), so cordial so united so determined.[126]

The word 'rebel' was useful. It reinforced settlers' feeling of being 'in the right'; it put Queen Victoria and the panoply of Empire firmly on their side. The aggrandisement of land was, perhaps, a less seemly cause; rebellion, even if only the first seeds of it, could be put down in all good conscience. There were probably other settlers like the Rev. Thomas Gilbert of Omata who sensed provocation in government action, and other women like Helen Hursthouse who were sensibly fearful of the consequences of warfare, and there was one man, an obscure Taranaki settler who in the midst of the excitement of 'battle stations', spoke out – or rather, addressed a petition to Gore Browne – at what he called 'this eleventh hour'. William Turner was educated, conversant with the intricacy of the Puketapu feud, a believer in Christian principles and shortsighted (this last piece of information is the only definite thing he says about himself: it would have disqualified him from

joining the militia, had he wanted to do so). His petition asked
for a 'thorough and impartial investigation' of the Waitara purchase.
He understood the principle of chieftainship, that Teira had the
support of an 'inconsiderable fraction' backed as he (Teira) believed
by 'British bayonets', and that ranged against him was 'the great
Majority [of Ati Awa] with the principal Chief at their head'.
Turner also understood the basic thinking of his fellow settlers:
'A good Native, here, means one who offers his own or other
men's lands for sale – a bad Native, one who declines to sell his
own land, and does not think he has any right to sell the interests
of others.'[127] Turner called the war which was likely to eventuate
from government response to Teira 'unjust', and saw in it a violation
of the Treaty of Waitangi. But the 'eleventh hour' was too late.
The justice of his assessment of the situation in 1860 has been upheld
by a later generation. At the time, his petition was acknowledged
but excited no action.

Lely, early in January 1860, was already thinking of temporary
quarters in New Plymouth to accommodate some of Hurworth's
women and children. At the end of that month, as if in confirmation
of C.W. Richmond's belief that Wiremu Kingi was bluffing and
that in the face of a determined Pakeha stand war would be unlikely,
William and Emily's three young daughters arrived at New
Plymouth. During Auckland's hot, drought-stricken summer, typhus
had become widespread, with mortality high among children.
Taranaki must have seemed safer. They arrived unheralded and
were met, by chance, by Mary Hursthouse: 'Your three *unprotected*
children arrived,' she wrote to Emily. Their protector was in fact
Mary Richmond, the eldest, not yet seven, who knew exactly where
their luggage was stowed and how many packets and kegs there
should be. Pale, but in high spirits when they came ashore, the
three sisters soon improved in health. Their arrival determined
Lely to rent the S.P. Kings' stone cottage in New Plymouth.

Caught up in the general excitement, Maria seems to have left
Hurworth without a backward glance. Setting the Kings' cottage
to rights' now absorbed her energy. She wrote to Margaret on
9 February 1860:

> I have spent a very busy week in packing our goods at Hurworth
> and moving down here. There seems little chance of my writing
> a very intelligible or coherent account . . . for the hubbub and
> noise is generally considerable in this small mansion which now
> accommodates six adults and five children,[128] besides occasional
> visitors from Hurworth who pop in for a meal or 'shake down'

at night . . . This cottage is admirably adapted for the purpose as it is only a few yards from the houses occupied by Mr & Mrs S.P. King and the Miss Kings. The four buildings (one is Mr S.K.'s office, he is Registrar to the Province) stand in one garden and form a group we have always called Kingston . . . Lely has taken it for a year, and its first use to us is as a refuge in the expected war. You would hardly suppose we were in town if you could take a peep at us but we shall be within the lines of sentries and have a special guard close at hand as all the important papers of the Province will be in Mr King's office.[129]

Maria's greatest fear was that 'some peace in the Villa Franca style[130] should be patched up leaving us no better off than before . . . but all will be money well invested if this period is indeed the turning point, and the crisis ends in our gaining new blocks of land and thus allows scope for the increase of the place.'[131] Jane and Eliza Atkinson (wives of Harry and William respectively), together with Jane's two young boys, were in the storeshed at Beach Cottage – the cottage itself was still let – which had been enlarged to accommodate them. Blanche (Henry's wife) with her newborn baby came to stay with her mother. The Hursthouse farm was on the very outskirts of New Plymouth proper, and the family was prepared to move further into town if necessary. Male Hurworthians were all with their units and ready for action, although James, a marksman in the volunteers, was, as provincial secretary, excused from military duties. Harry was a sergeant in the volunteers. Henry had 'his own fortress'; he was captain of the militia company defending the recently completed Bell Blockhouse where William Atkinson was 'Native Interpreter'[132]. Hugh, James and Frank Ronalds, and Decimus Atkinson were in the volunteers, along with Arthur, 'steadily improving himself as a rifleman' and the best long-distance shot among them. 'I really think he enjoys the whole affair,' Maria wrote, 'he was evidently meant for less peaceable days than those he has fallen among.'[133]

Excited rather than despondent, the Hurworthians failed to appreciate the nature of the coming conflict. Eliza Atkinson wrote later: 'We just rode away on our horses one summer evening, the 4th March (1860) & thought it was only a precaution & we should be back soon: but I never saw it [her house] again for the Maoris burnt it down.'[134] On 8 March 1860 C.W. Richmond, who had come to New Plymouth with the governor, made one last visit to Hurworth. He wrote to Emily: 'I have been up to deserted Hurworth. I went last Sunday and felt quite peace sick and home sick. There is a good site for [our] house on one clearing, but God knows when we shall be allowed to build it.'[135] Arthur, who had ridden with him, brought away a small black clock.

Dispersal

March 1860–Aug. 1860

> Please on no account forget to send me a piece of each of the
> boys' hair . . . every night I dread something dreadful happening
> at N.P.[1]

In Auckland Emily Richmond was fearful of the consequences of
war, but in Taranaki, during the first few months of 1860, the
majority of the settlers were not. They had great expectations.
At last something was to be effected, land was to be obtained
freely, mastery was to be demonstrated and established, all shilly-
shallying with the natives was to cease. Captain Cracroft of the
Niger, who later wrote of this 'iniquitous war' and whose men
took possession of the first of Wiremu Kingi's abandoned pa at
the Waitara (5 March 1860), described New Plymouth as 'like a
fair'. C.W. Richmond's letter from New Plymouth, written to
reassure Emily, spoke of 'the boys' as being in 'great spirits' and
the town generally as participating fully in its new wartime status:

> At every corner you see some acquaintance with musket on shoulder
> parading up and down as sentry. People are generally addressed
> by their style as officers – Harry is always 'Sergeant Atkinson'.
> 'Captain Watt', 'Captain Brown' etc. etc. are household words.
> Henry has risen far above all in the services. He is now Captain
> of the Bell Co.[2]

Harry soon caught up with Henry. He was elected captain of No.
2 company of the Taranaki volunteers, in which most of the
Hurworth men served, on 16 March.[3] His warrant of appointment
came through three days later. The S.P. Kings' stone cottage which
held Maria, Lely, eighteen-month-old Edith, Arthur, and C.W
Richmond's three daughters was described by Lely as 'a very helter-
skelter household' with 'armed men coming in at all hours
diplomatists pacing the garden . . . children vociferating, parent
and guardians alternately scolding and coaxing'.[4] In the evening
there was often 'music and Shakespeare' at the S.P. Kings' house
and during the daytime there were occasionally 'sand picnics' fo

all the children on the beach. At the end of the month William and his three girls returned to Auckland.

The early months of the war brought temporary prosperity to the Ronalds, whose Denby Farm adjoining Hurworth had never been particularly successful. Hugh Ronalds was given leave from the volunteers so that he could drive his cows to the Waitara to supply the military camp there with milk at twopence a quart. For as long as the fighting lasted, Hurworthians had employment, rations, and pay – a shilling a day for privates. Harry Atkinson eventually rose to the rank of major, and later in the sixties secured a meat contract for supplying the military at New Plymouth. J.C. Richmond remained a civilian. Harry insisted that he stay out of the early fighting because of Mary's condition; he was also provincial secretary and from mid-April represented the Omata district in the General Assembly.

The euphoric mood of the Taranaki settlers did not last beyond the end of March 1860, by which time several facts were becoming obvious. The most important was that the war would not be won quickly. British troops, used to moving with cumbersome baggage trains and untrained in the skirmishing skills necessary to engage Maori, had the added disavantage of being commanded by an incompetent colonel who was unable or unwilling to alter military tactics to suit changed circumstances. In a letter written three years later, Eliza Atkinson still despaired about the redcoats' ability to defeat Maori:

> I am afraid it will take a long time before trained soldiers will be able to fight Maoris. The Maoris are like eels and can curl and slip themselves in and out of holes and behind flax bushes and the poor soldiers can do nothing but stand bolt upright where they are ordered to be shot at. It is such a different kind of warfare to fighting a civilized enemy on a regular battlefield.[5]

The troops succeeded in capturing abandoned pa but did not inflict decisive defeats. Ngati Ruanui and Taranaki to the south made common cause with Ati Awa, and Waikato tribes, especially those of the Maori King movement, made it obvious where their sympathies lay. Settlers and government now spoke of the necessity of subduing 'rebel natives', but their Maori opponents had no doubt that land was the basis of the argument. A large meeting of Waikato tribes was held at Waiuku on 13 March 1860 to consider letters addressed to King Potatau requesting support from the runanga of Waitara and Waitaha. At this meeting Te Tuhi Wiremu Patara of Ngati Mahuta, one of the founders of the King movement and now editor of *Te Hokioi*, the King newspaper, read a document which set out a Maori interpretation both of what was at stake and of Pakeha motives. The translator was T.H. Smith of the Native Secretary's Office. The asterisked notes are also his.

> The Pakehas say, that this vesting of authority in a King will not stand because the 'Mana'* of this island has passed to the Queen in virtue of: discovery by Capt. Cook; the Treaty of Waitangi; the Treaty of Waikato; the right of the Crown to the gold of New Zealand.
>
> The Pakehas say, that our island has passed to them. This assertion is wrong: it implies theft; it is like the flitting evening moth, or a summer cloud,* and that we, friends, are but as mere parasites, whereas we are really the true offspring of the soil.*
>
> The Pakehas say, that Potatau was chosen to be a King for the purpose of making war. It is not so; for his word is, that the Maoris and Pakehas should dwell in peace and mutual goodwill, observing the precepts of Christianity and love, obeying the Law also. If evil befall, while adhering to these principles, the Law must deal with the wrong and with the right.*

Notes: 'Sovereignty'
'Unsubstantial – having no solid basis'
'have a natural and not a merely acquired, right'.
'condemn the one and justify the other'.[6]

Alongside the British and colonial forces encamped at Waitara were about 300 kupapa or 'friendlies' – Ati Awa belonging mostly to Teira's party. They now have their place among the hatchments which line the walls of St Mary's church at New Plymouth, but during the first part of the Taranaki War their association was not so felicitous. One of W.S. Atkinson's jobs as interpreter at the Bell blockhouse was to ameliorate the conditions of the kupapa. It was not easy. British officers with recent experience of the Indian mutiny suspected all dark faces of treachery, and colonial troops in skirmishing situations were never entirely sure on which side the 'friendlies' were. The term 'nigger' became common usage. At the very beginning of the campaign, troops occupying the disputed Waitara block were told not to fire unless fired upon, but the settler/soldiers 'all said they would fire as soon as they saw a chance of killing a nigger'.[7] Nor was it only soldiers in battle situations who were determined to distrust; Grace Hirst told her sisters in England, 'there are a good many that are called friendly natives but I do not believe in them at all as it seems to me race against race'.[8] As might have been expected, relations between Maori and settler worsened even in areas outside the actual fighting. William Swainson's Auckland of 1852 had for all practical purposes been sustained by the good will and trade of Waikato and Thames Maori. In March 1860 Rev. Robert Maunsell, a Church Missionary Society (CMS) missionary in Waikato, wrote to C.W. Richmond about the insults and abuses Maori now suffered when they visited Auckland. In a letter to Maria of 19 April 1860, Emily mentioned the arrival of two large canoes with about fifty armed Maori from Thames – 'They looked disagreeable.'

On 18 March Te Kohia pa, built on the disputed land at Waitara, was captured and found to be empty; even the dead had been carried away. Arthur Atkinson was extremely dejected: 'instead of smothering the wasps in their nests we have just irritated them and let them fly, making a war of indefinite extent.'[9]

The tedium of night picket duty and early morning parades was broken by the battle of Waireka on 28 March. The previous day three men and two boys from Omata had been ambushed and killed,[10] and the volunteers were called out to rescue those families remaining on their farms in the vicinity. When the volunteers came under heavy fire they received no support from troops under the command of Colonel Murray of the 65th; Murray withdrew his men and returned to New Plymouth, leaving the volunteers besieged in an abandoned farm building with little ammunition and no food. Sailors from the *Niger* under Captain Cracroft created a diversion by storming the main pa at Waireka. But even so, as Arthur wrote later to William, 'Very few of us expected to see the town again . . . I remember, as I lay in the straw, looking up at Orion just visible between the clouds and wondering whether I should soon be up there among the unvoyageable stars and speculating as to which of them I should be in.'[11]

Confusion in the field was matched by confusion in town. The alarm guns were fired when it was believed that Ngati Ruanui and Taranaki intended to attack. Women and children moved up to either the Marsland Hill barracks or the sanctuary of St Mary's church and dissenting chapels. Thomas Gilbert's wife later described the scene to her husband:

> She saw the smoke of the cannon, and heard the dreadful booming of the report, and immediately a stream of women were to be seen hurrying up the steep path into the barracks . . . some women with a child under each arm, without either hat, bonnet or shawl – some with a bundle hastily thrown together, and many seemed

utterly bewildered amidst the confusion and noise of women crying, children screaming, and the eager, anxious questions to know what it was all about.[12]

The expedition had set off without sufficient ammunition, and Robert Pitcairn and some others volunteered to carry additional supplies on horseback. When, after no little danger, they reached the troops, they discovered that they had been loaded with ammunition for muskets rather than for rifles: it was, in short, useless. Neither had the commissariat, whose job it was to see that the troops were fed, made any provision for feeding the volunteers, who had survived the whole day on the hunk of bread which Harry Atkinson had had the foresight to give each one before they set out. At this point Maria became a combatant:

> I was really the first person in town who thought of bread and brandy for them . . . I attacked Black who thought something should be done but had no orders . . . the red tape boobies hummed and hawed and made difficulties about complicating the accounts and so would have sent nothing because they could not tell whether the food and the brandy would be used by troops or volunteers.[13]

James solved the impasse by suggesting that bread for the volunteers might be put down to his account – there is no further mention of the brandy. To 'deafening cheers and mad excitement' from the townspeople, the volunteers eventually came marching back after midnight, shouting 'Rule Britannia' till hoarse. The excitement of battle had a dramatic effect on the usually taciturn Arthur: 'it worked the miracle of making him talkative', Mrs King wrote to Emily, 'at least he talked ever so much the only twice I have seen him since'.[14]

In appreciation of the sailors' action, Maria got up a testimonial from 'the Mothers, Wives, Daughters and Sisters . . . to tender their grateful thanks to Captain Cracroft his Officers and Men, for their prompt and gallant attack and capture of the "Waireka Pah", by which a diversion was effected in favour of the Militia and Volunteers . . .'[15] Almost immediately after the battle of Waireka the *Niger* was recalled to Auckland, as Gore Browne feared that the Waikato supporters of the Maori King might attack the capital. 'We almost went into mourning on the departure of Capt Cracroft and the Niger,' Maria wrote to Margaret Taylor, 'he was such a beau ideal British naval officer; had he been at the head of affairs the war might be over now.'[16] And in a letter to Emily she wrote, 'We had rather you took all the redcoats.'

Britannia's rule was not exemplified by Colonel C.E. Gold, the commanding officer at New Plymouth. His military incapacity, together with his reluctance to engage the 'enemy', at least kept casualties to a minimum on both sides, but he exasperated the mob. Maria complained to William of the 'daily, hourly mismanagement of Gold', of his 'wearing out the men's strength in absolutely useless works', and of his 'having ridiculous parades at early hours when many are worn out with the night's watch, and feel that crops are wasting and a hundred things being neglected while the old fool is keeping them kicking their heels being inspected'.[17] In spite of the presence in New Plymouth of 1,200 armed men, she described the surrounding countryside as 'conquered' – 'the Maoris can go where they like and do as they like and no one dreams that they can be interfered with'.[18] A letter in the *Taranaki Herald*, signed 'A Volunteer', incensed the military but delighted the mob by voicing dissatisfaction publicly:

> What are the authorities dreaming of? Here are some thousand or twelve hundred men huddled together in half a square mile, protecting the town, whilst the country districts on which we are dependent for supplies are virtually abandoned to the enemy.[19]

The writer suggested that the imperial troops take over guard duties in New Plymouth and free militia and volunteers to secure the potato crop. 'As it is now ordered we are actually feeding the enemy.' And Arthur, in his usual vein of light sarcasm, wrote to his brother-in-law:

> There is a problem engaging the attention of the authorities here which they cannot answer, can the wise men of Auckland help us? If it takes a 1,000 men a fortnight to do nothing, how long will it take how many men to capture William King? It is a question I know will please you because it is on the metaphysical side of mathematics.[20]

Naturally the mob turned to William – native minister and chief adviser to Governor Gore Browne – to vent its indignation and mortification. William was sympathetic; his letter to Arthur asking for details about the battle of Waireka is as excited as a schoolboy's, but he did add a postscript: 'For Heaven's sake don't fall out with the Red Coats.' He feared that complaints and divisions would weaken the settlers and that any criticism of the British commanders in the press would be dangerous. The mob, as interpreted by Maria, felt that strongly voiced criticism was the only way to restrain Gold's folly. Emily, under constraint from William not to pass on privileged information to her Taranaki relatives, felt pulled two ways: 'I never felt such a desire to disobey William's commands as I do now . . . and tell you all I know from time to time.'[21]

On 20 April Colonel Gold, in command of a large force and accompanied by fifty carts pulled by 200 bullocks (these cost £50 per day; 200 volunteers could have been had for approximately £25), left New Plymouth to catch Ngati Ruanui and Taranaki to the south of the town. The 'Golden calf expedition', as Maria called it, got as far as Tataraimaka, where Gold halted. No Maori had been encountered but Gold ordered his men to thrash the wheat stacks still standing in the fields, leaving the grain scattered and trampled. Maria commented that the poor Tataraimaka settlers had never grown such expensive wheat and that Gold's visit had been as destructive as a Maori raid. After firing a few shots into the pa at Warea, the expedition returned to New Plymouth.

Bishop Selwyn and missionary clergymen associated with him were also targets for the mob. Selwyn's pastoral letter of April 1860 repeated the censure of his sermon preached at St Mary's some years earlier: 'You are very comfortable,' he wrote, 'your houses good, your pastures green, your crops heavy. Why covet your neighbour's property?'[22] Maria expressed the opinion that if the governor was completely converted to the missionary view and if Government House was, as rumoured, 'swarming with black coats and white chokers' and a 'most ignominious peace' seemed likely, then 'a large body of us hold ourselves in readiness to leave for New Caledonia'.[23] This remark seems to have been made more to firm up Emily's resolution than to show a definite intent. Emily was partial to the bishop (although not to his views on the war) and particularly enjoyed the company of the Selwyns' close friends, Sir William and Lady Martin. In fact, far from influencing him, Gore Browne complained that clergy such as Selwyn, Hadfield, Abraham, Patteson, and laymen of like opinion such as Swainson and Martin had seemingly withheld advice during the year leading up to the Waitara purchase. He now saw their stand as disloyalty to the Queen.[24] In New Plymouth, Archdeacon Govett, vicar of St Mary's, walked a fine line between offending the settlers and revealing his true feelings, which were closer to those of Selwyn and his friends than to those of, for example, John Morgan, a CMS Waikato missionary.[25] Arthur Atkinson wrote in his diary, 25 May 1860, without comment: 'It is interesting to know that the Rev. Govett thinks it would be as much murder for us to go and kill W. King and his men as it was for the Taranaki to kill Ford and the others at Omata.'[26]

The Treaty of Waitangi was also brought into the dispute and

a new twist given to its meaning to suit settler interests. J.C.
Richmond probably wrote the following extract from an article
in the *Taranaki Herald*.

> Treason [i.e. fighting against the British forces] has since cancelled
> what was otherwise little known, and where known, ignored . . .
> English rule must extend through the length and breadth of the
> land. Our holdings must be secured to us; confidence must be
> established on the basis of power.[27]

It was asserted that the relationship between the British government
and the Maori at the time of the signing of the Treaty was 'not
that of contracting parties but of guardian and ward'.[28]

Another, more probing view of the likely effects of the fighting
came in a letter from Mary King to Lely in Nelson:

> You have heard of all our excitement, despair and exultation, you
> might also hear of our bloody mindedness; truly I think a few months
> of this warfare would make savages of us. The evening before Mrs
> James Richmond went to Nelson, she sat a little while here and
> all our talk was of killing.[29]

A public notice posted at New Plymouth on 28 March 1860 advised
that free passage to Nelson would be given to a limited number
of women and children. There, as refugees, they would also receive
rations provided by the Taranaki provincial government. Alfred
Domett had already written to Lely offering hospitality to 'as many
daughters, goddaughters etc. as our house will hold *roughing* it',[30]
and with Mary Richmond ('Mrs James') seven months pregnant,
the Hurworth women were anxious for her to escape the excitement
– and tension – of Taranaki. So, on 31 March, Lely, Mary, and
her daughter, together with Blanche Richmond ('Mrs Henry'), her
baby daughter, Helen Hursthouse and her unmarried daughters,
Helen (Nelly) and Kate, sailed for Nelson aboard the *Airedale*. Marion
Ronalds was already there, having broken off her engagement to
Decimus Atkinson; Harry's wife, Jane, and her two boys left for
Nelson on 5 April.

If war was the ostensible reason for flight, there were some
other, perhaps unforeseen, advantages in the Nelson sojourn. It
enabled Mary Richmond to rid herself and James of their erstwhile
adopted son', Arthur Wilson, who had never fitted into even junior
Hurworth society. He was returned to his mother in Sydney. 'Is
it not a great weight off your mind?' Emily wrote to her sister-
in-law, while Arthur commented, 'He goes unregretted and without
regret.'[31] Nelson also provided a haven of refuge for Helen

Hursthouse. Her husband, John Hursthouse, wrote Lely, had sunk
into a state of 'utter degradation'. Kate Hursthouse feared that
if he were to come to Nelson her mother would let him live with
them again, 'just as though he were a proper husband or father',
but emboldened by the physical distance now between them, Helen
wrote: 'Before I left you, I told you that I would forgive you
John, but I said then, and I repeat it now, that *I never will live
with you again, unless you give up all spirituous liquors.'*[32] At the beginning
of May Lely was able to report that Aunt Helen was looking much
better 'since she escaped from her husband'. The Nelson climate
was agreeable; the people kind and hospitable, and although living
space was cramped – most of the Hurworth women and children
were living in a 'perfect nutshell of an abode' – Maria informed
Margaret Taylor that 'our people seem as comfortable as one can
expect *refugees* to be'.

Maria had decided to remain at New Plymouth. She felt perfectly
safe and two-year-old Edith seemed untroubled by the fires and
noise of Marsland Hill. She was joined at the Kings' stone cottage
by Eliza Atkinson, whom Maria described as 'a dear good creature;
what a lucky dog W.S.A. is to have got such a wife!'[33] The cottage
became the headquarters of the Hurworth cabal where the men,
when not on duty, held 'incessant cabinet councils': 'I am sure
if Eliza and I were not here everything must get into a frightful
muddle.'[34]

Arthur, always in the company of other volunteers, continued
to make occasional visits to Hurworth, which throughout 1860 was
untouched, even by the military: 'All the houses within reach are
robbed by the soldiers, and there won't be a fowl, duck or turkey
alive in the place in another few weeks except in the remote bush
regions.'[35] Hurworth cattle and horses were as fat as butter and
'seemed glad to see a human face'. The horses Arthur drove into
a stockade at Merton and three of them, including Maria's Lallah
Rookh, he took back to New Plymouth. On another visit he dug
his carrots and sowed his twenty-acre clearing. By May the fences
at his place still held, but cattle and pigs had broken into the other
gardens, destroying fruit trees and eating potatoes; Arthur cheered
himself by thinking that whatever happened to the houses and fences
the site itself could not be destroyed.

After the action at Waitara and Waireka during March, the
Taranaki War seemed to be puttering to a close. It was over
according to Gold, who at the beginning of May advised settler
living in 'open land' – that is, not on bush farms – that they wer

free to return. In Nelson, Mary's baby, Maurice Wilson Richmond, was born three weeks prematurely, on 26 April. He was the smallest baby Lely had ever seen and 'very pretty'. James had just visited Mary and arrived back at New Plymouth the very day his son was born. Subsequent stormy weather prevented the Nelson steamer from anchoring in the roadstead and news of the birth did not reach James until nearly three weeks later; Maurice was three months old before his father saw him. A sense of duty kept James at New Plymouth. He, as provincial secretary, and Thomas King, provincial treasurer, felt themselves to be the effective civilian government at Taranaki. Neither had any confidence in Superintendent George Cutfield who, Lely wrote, 'requires to be in leading strings'. King had the larger family and James gave most of the opportunities for family visits to him. On 16 April 1860 James had, moreover, been elected member of the House of Representatives for Omata. Apart from the time he and Mary were together at Auckland during the General Assembly session later in 1860, this year marked the beginning of their virtual separation, which continued until Mary's death. James's attachment to his wife did not weaken; he wrote frequently, and thought of her often: 'The dear wistful anxious eyes come before me at night and I long to be with you.'[36] But James's thoughts were not enough to prevent Mary from fretting, and she pined for him.

Meanwhile Maria fidgeted about 'this wretched pretence of a war'. She badly wanted to visit Nelson but doubted whether it was right to leave the men or to spend money on a 'visit of enjoyment' which did not merit a free passage. She rather wished that Arthur had received a 'nice *mild* wound at Waireka' which would have relieved him of aimless parades, sentry duty, and equally useless expeditions to cut supplejack with shingle hammers and little axes. The lull in fighting, however, enabled Eliza, Maria, and Edith to picnic on the Henui beach, and on 10 May, 'a most lovely day', Maria and Eliza, with Arthur, Henry, Harry, Isaac Watt, and Robert Pitcairn as escort, rode down to view the Waireka battlefield. Maria was mounted on Vixen and Eliza on Lallah Rookh; it was the first time either of them had been on horseback for nearly three months. In the evenings, when Arthur was not on sentry duty and Frank and Hugh Ronalds could join them, they began again the singing class under James's tuition, 'reviving in pleasantly melancholy manner our Hurworth meetings in Jas and Mary's nice room'.[37]

The question that had agitated C. W. Richmond and his colleagues from the very beginning of fighting in Taranaki was: What would Waikato do? Richmond had before him the views of Waikato missionaries John Morgan and Robert Maunsell, and of Land Commissioner Donald McLean. Morgan pointed out that the tribes were divided on the question of active support for Wiremu Kingi, but there was definitely a pro-war party among them. Maunsell[38] was more non-committal. McLean's advice, given at the Queen's birthday meeting at Ngaruawahia on 24 May, was that nothing should be done at Waitara with the present force of armed settlers and British troops for fear of bringing Waikato down on the settlements at Auckland. Arthur Atkinson, who could be said to represent the views of the war party among the Taranaki settlers, welcomed the possibility that a great part of Waikato would join in the war. 'The more the merrier,' he wrote in his diary; and to William: 'The sum of my wishes is that we may have Waikato and all other anarchical Maoris in arms against us now – that we may settle the question absolutely for all time to come.'[39]

On 5 May it was rumoured that a force of about 1,000 Waikato were assembled at Kawhia and expected down at any time. The news caused little consternation in the Kings' stone cottage where Arthur cast revolver bullets, Maria and Eliza continued with their needlework, and James, after he had finished writing articles for the *Herald*, read Molière aloud to them. On 15 May news came from the Bell blockhouse that Waikato taua had been seen by telescope joining Wiremu Kingi's people at the Kaipakopako pa. On 20 May the kupapa brought in reports that the town was to be attacked either that night or the following morning. The Kings were very alarmed, but their tenants frankly did not believe the reports. It was a beautiful day and Maria and Arthur spent a good part of it out of doors enjoying Molière and Tennyson. 'Nervous old ladies have been suffering great alarm for two nights,' Maria wrote to Emily,

> some people sat up on Sunday night, and last night half the troops were under arms all night. Neither Eliza [who was now pregnant] or I can get up a twinge of alarm . . . The guards round town are doubled tonight, we have Ar on sentry go round about this house which is very agreeable except that he pops his head in at my bedroom window in an alarming manner at all sorts of odd hours which I think quite as terrific as hearing a Maori war whoop.[40]

Nothing happened. The next report from Bell blockhouse stated that the Maori had disappeared into the bush. Life in the town resumed more of an even tenor.

'A 'dimly mysterious consolation' in a letter from Emily during
May hinted to Maria that nothing of an aggressive nature was
to be undertaken at Taranaki until more reinforcements arrived
from Britain and another military leader took over from 'old Gold'.
Maria saw no hope for the province except in vigorous military
action and she considered that impossible until Gold was dispensed
with. She told Emily:

> You must not imagine we feel a personal bitterness towards Gold,
> there is something so touchingly dense in his stupidity that you
> can view him as a gigantic baby . . . I do feel savage at a system
> which can allow such fools the power of doing so much harm.[41]

One of the many rumours circulating in New Plymouth was that
General Pratt, who was to be Gold's replacement, had given orders
for the latter's arrest if matters were not better conducted than
at the beginning of the war. Not everybody, however, shared the
mob's view. According to Maria, 'the snobs' thought Gold 'a wary
and sagacious leader using laudable caution in his movements'.[42]
She defined 'snobs' (and included a relative, John Stephenson Smith,
among them) as those whose livelihoods were not affected by the
present state of affairs. With this remark Maria dismisses in too
cavalier a fashion those who were opposed to or frightened by
the fighting. Thomas Gilbert's description of the townspeople on
the day of Waireka shows that there was a genuine apprehension
which might easily have turned to panic. Women 'crying and
wringing their hands, children screaming and clinging in fear to
their mothers, men running to and fro'[43] is scarcely a description
of 'snobs'.

In spite of the apparent moratorium on the use of British forces,
fighting broke out again in June. Bell blockhouses were plundered
and on 23 June a fierce conflict took place in front of Puketakawhere
pa, just outside the land claimed by Teira at Waitara. Harry Atkinson
tried to get the volunteers included in the attack on the pa; Gold
would not allow this 'on account of their families'.[44] The British
forces failed to capture the pa and eventually retreated, leaving
twenty-nine dead or wounded on the field. Maori casualties were
estimated at 200. It was nominally a defeat for the British, but
Arthur regarded it as a 'splendid affair – if only to show that
all English officers are not fools or cowards and that English soldiers
can fight, when they get the chance, even against Maoris'.[45] Gold
showed no further inclination to fight. Meanwhile Ngati Ruanui
and Taranaki fired the Tataraimaka houses and considered the
settlers' farms theirs by conquest. It seemed Omata houses would

soon follow suit. James wrote desperately to William:

> Soon we shall see smoke at Hurworth. We do not quite understand
> what the good fruit of delay is supposed to be. We see nothing
> but destruction, demoralization and doubled bloodshed . . . We are
> absolutely in the dark as to your views and plans . . . Hal and
> and I have even tried to persuade Herbert[46] to put him [Gold]
> under arrest, he listened at all events which shows what he thinks
> of the case.[47]

As winter wore on with bitterly cold weather and gales from
the south, Maria thought the state of the settlement infinitely worse
than could have been imagined during the heady days at the
beginning of the year. She felt keenly for the military settlers from
the Australian colonies, among whom there was much illness and
discontent. They were living in tents which offered little protection
against the south-west winds and rain; their blankets were wet
for a week at a time, and yet there were empty houses near their
camp outside the picket lines. Many townspeople were also ill with
feverish colds, and typhus fever made its first appearance. As always,
it was the children who were the most vulnerable. Rumours were
constantly flying about the town, 'the most active scandal mongers
living within a stone's throw of each other'. The settlement was
crowded and, denied opportunities to trade, it was also stagnating.
It was impossible to keep all the cattle and pigs in the town so
they broke fences and destroyed crops and gardens in the outlying
districts; there had been a fine crop of potatoes on the surrounding
farms, but with insufficient storage space in New Plymouth they
were left for pigs, cattle, and Maori foraging parties; there was
at least six months' supply of wheat at one of the town's stores
alone. James Richmond pleaded with his brother to allow these
surplus commodities and livestock to be exported; Gold, who had
absolute jurisdiction over the town while it was under martial law,
refused to grant this request. 'This little population is sorely tried,'[48]
James wrote to Mary, although he was agreeably astonished at
the patience shown by the people in general. Lely, participating
vicariously in the settlement's sufferings, wrote to Emily from
Nelson: 'Murder and sudden death are minor evils compared with
mischief produced at NP by utter mismanagement. All is
uncertain.'[49] Frank Ronalds wrote to his father that the province
was completely laid waste: farms were deserted, cattle were running
wild, and no crops were being put in for the future:

> meanwhile we have wearily to keep watch night after night round
> the town wet or fine . . . It is sad to think of all the energy and

downright hard work that has been expended, and find out in the end you are worse off than when you commenced, it leaves a chap so little pluck to commence again.[50]

Maori too were suffering severely from influenza and many were reported to have died. The Taranaki Colonial Hospital, which had once been widely used by them, was now under the guns of the Melbourne military settlers camped nearby. Rev. John Whiteley, of the Wesleyan Missionary Society at the Wesleyan Institute, New Plymouth, who continued to hold services at Puketakawhere on Sundays, reported the inhabitants as being in a dejected frame of mind.

Waikato's involvement in the war at Taranaki now made Arthur uncertain whether Maria and Edith should remain at New Plymouth. Maria herself wished to stay until the last possible moment. With illness widespread and morale deteriorating through inaction, she felt that the departure of the women would not improve matters for the husbands and brothers left behind. Nor did she want 'to die by inches from anxiety, for I know when at a distance I shall probably magnify the dangers Arthur is exposed to'.[51] Arthur had made shutters for the windows of the stone cottage and Maria believed they should be safe inside, even if the Maori did invade the town. 'I can't believe they will remain in it for long, for I suppose in such a case as that the troops will be permitted to attack them.'[52] On the other hand, James and Harry were 'rabid' about sending off all the women and children, and in Nelson Mary was feeling dismal without James, and Lely, approaching seventy, was missing her beloved daughter. To both of them Maria felt some obligation, particularly as it seemed James's sense of duty would tie him to New Plymouth. There was also Eliza's approaching confinement to think about: she might be more comfortable in Nelson, although without her husband. Mrs Blackett, the Richmonds' former Mangorei friend, had offered to board her, and her sister, Marion Ronalds, would also be at hand. Emily, however, was most anxious that Maria, Edith, and Eliza too, if she felt so disposed, should come to Auckland, which the governor had just said was 'as safe as London'.

By mid-June the impasse was ended. James had arranged for Mary and the two children to go to Auckland to be with him while the Assembly was in session, and Maria had come to the conclusion that 'if I *must* leave *here*' Auckland would be preferable to Nelson. She wrote to Emily:

I really think we should all be jollier in Auckland near you and

the children . . . If . . . you could find out what a small box of
a place in your neighbourhood [Parnell] would cost. A sitting room,
2 bedrooms and kitchen or use of kitchen if any part of a house
could be had, would be what Lely, Mary, Jas and I would want,
as Lely does not mind sleeping with me, and I could bring Edith's
cot.[53]

Emily replied that Maria, Lely, and Edith might stay with her
until suited, and that the place they thought of taking for James
and Mary was a comfortable and clean lodging, with two bedrooms
and a sitting room, and only ten minutes' walk away. The elderly
landlady seemed to Emily 'slightly mad' and 'given to tippling',
but William was in favour of taking it on a weekly basis. The
terms of £3 a week for 'lady and gentleman, a servant and 2 children'
were considered reasonable.

Before Maria could begin packing, all her plans were upset by
Edith's alarming illness. Doctors Neild and Rawson considered it
to be gastro-enteritis. Dr Neild at first prescribed calomel; then,
when that did not produce any benefit, jalap and castor oil. Both
purgatives and sweat-producing drugs made her worse; she was
wracked by violent paroxysms of pain, which were relieved only
by wrapping her in hot wet blankets. It was probably Edith's
essentially sound constitution which pulled her through rather than
the doctors' ministrations. By the end of June, although weak and
torpid, she was thought to have weathered the worst.

At the beginning of July the atrocious winter weather gave way
to clear days and calm seas. With the uncertainty of a combined
Maori attack still hanging over the town, Eliza Atkinson resolved
on Nelson and the Miss Kings on Auckland. It was pain and grief
for the latter to leave their beautiful garden, and Maria remarked
that she believed 'it would please Miss Martha better to be
tomahawked in her own bed than sleep out of it'.[54] On 3 July
Eliza went to Nelson on the tiny paddlesteamer *Tasmanian Maid*.
Maria sat on Mt Eliot watching the small vessel out of sight and
saw the disconsolate William Atkinson ride his horse as far out
to sea as possible to wave a last farewell. The same day the Miss
Kings went to Auckland by the *Airedale*. After watching the
departure of her friends, Maria returned home to English letters
and news of another parting. Dr Joseph Hutton had died.

How little I dreamt as I returned to this lonely house after seeing
all our dear people embark . . . that our dear Derby friends . . .
had to return to a darker sadder house than mine. Coming in the
midst of all these changes and partings this sad news made me

sadder, but did me great good. There seems a support and comfort
in the thought of his peaceful holy death.[55]
He had died on 28 March, the day of the battle of Waireka. James,
writing to Mary, mused: 'I wonder what the kind peaceful creature
would have thought of us all that day.'[56]

Once Edith was better, Maria began packing in earnest.

> By this day week we may be off. I feel very queer at the thought
> of leaving Ar in such times . . . However, it is Ar's wish that
> I should go with the child, and tho' I am still incredulous as to
> the Maoris making an attack on the town, I see that with such
> mismanagement as we are subject to, the very faintest possibility
> of such an event makes it perhaps wiser to leave home.[57]

The town had been supposedly strengthened by a ditch dug around
it. The Kings' cottage was now some way outside this defensive
ring which, as Maria pointed out, would not do much to keep
out Maori unless sentries were placed along its bank at night. A
further inducement to quit New Plymouth was a proclamation issued
by Colonel Gold advising women and 'helpless persons' to volunteer
to leave, otherwise they were likely to be sent.

Henry had decided to move into the stone cottage. Unfortunately
he came down with a cold which turned into influenza which James,
Arthur, and Maria all caught. James and Arthur made their illness
worse by insisting on going with a volunteer force to Hurworth
to bring away more of James's possessions and Harry's cowshed,
which was to become the guard house at Fort Herbert. Heavy
rain set in; the men arrived back wet through with three cartloads
of drenched goods. Everything was now 'in a fearful confusion'
– the verandah choked with bundles, boxes, and drums. The
household reached the 'acme of discomfort'. Everybody, apart from
little Edith who was eating one long breakfast, was ill. The weather
again turned cold and stormy, and Maria had the additional worry
about the safety of the Nelson party – Lely, Mary, Blanche, and
three young children – who had already embarked for Auckland
via New Plymouth. In fact conditions off the Taranaki coast were
so bad that the captain of the *Airedale* put back to Nelson. At last,
on 24 July the ship arrived in calm weather at New Plymouth.
Arthur seemed a little better and Maria much worse. It was her
deteriorating condition and the thought that if she became really
ill there would be no one to look after Edith which precipitated
her departure:

> I felt I was going to give way or I should never have resolved
> to leave a house full of sick helpless men, who had not when ill

much notion of making themselves comfortable. I certainly hoped
and believed Arthur had got over the worst when I left him.[58]
Just before Maria left the cottage, Blanche Richmond appeared,
confused and worried because Henry had not been on the beach
to meet her, and with a 'strange gentleman' carrying her baby.
In her 'bewilderment', as Maria put it, 'she never introduced him,
but instinct made me say "Mr Domett".'[59] Blanche could not bring
herself to leave Henry again so stayed behind at the stone cottage.
Maria, Edith, James, and Alfred Domett joined Lely, Mary, and
their children on board the *Airedale*. Arthur walked slowly down
to the beach with them – 'My day of grief', he wrote that night
in his diary.

The strain of packing up when ill had given Maria such a violent
headache that she actually wished for seasickness to relieve it. On
arriving at Auckland she went immediately to William and Emily's
house where for a fortnight she was very ill, her symptoms
aggravated by delirium and an inability to sleep until early in the
morning. 'I was seized with a great longing to get to a quieter
house than Em's and Wm's [there were five young children in
it] fancying the excitement there kept me from sleeping.'[60] Edith
stayed with her aunt and uncle while Maria shifted to the lodgings,
Athol House, which Emily had taken for Mary and James. There
she gradually improved. On 7 August, to everyone's astonishment,
a tired and wan Arthur appeared – 'quite skin and bone'. He had
continued so weak and good-for-nothing after his bout of influenza
that he had been given sick leave from the volunteers and had
determined to join Maria in Auckland. 'What a pretty pair of broken
down Taranakians we looked.'[61]

Auckland Interlude

Sept. 1860–July 1862

I sleep well again and eat like a ploughboy and I shall soon revive my former dimensions.[1]

It was now the beginning of September 1860; Maria had been seriously ill for over a month. She remembered the onset of her illness as a time of 'utter misery': of nights and days of anxiety over Edith, followed immediately by the sickness of the rest of her household; of packing up to leave amid the sodden clutter of James's possessions from Hurworth; the trauma of leaving Arthur, and then finding at last that she, the indefatigable workhorse, was on the verge of collapse. It seemed, in retrospect, like an accelerating nightmare.

It is also likely that at some time during her illness Maria suffered a miscarriage. Four years later, when Mary and her six-month-old baby, Richard, were staying at Beach Cottage, Maria wrote of the baby's fondness for Arthur and herself: 'we think he must be the little boy we missed having in 1860 . . . Mary has some idea of leaving him with us as a changeling.'[2]

The unexpected boon of Arthur's company, the quietness of Mary and James's lodgings, and Auckland itself, removed as it was from the fighting, gradually brought about her recovery. Maria had earlier rather disparaged Auckland, describing it as 'something like an English watering place where people do little but dress and visit',[3] and had frequently teased Emily about her fondness for its 'high society'. Now Maria herself, back with William and Emily, was living 'a complete fine lady life' in which all her wants were met by servants.[4] She had all the time she wanted for books (Maria and Arthur were currently reading Froude's *History of England, Adam Bede*, and J.S. Mill *On Liberty*), needlework, 'calling', and other 'pleasures' – mostly musical *soirées* and *conversazione* at Government House, and 'poetical evenings' at William and Emily's, where Alfred Domett read from Wordsworth, Shelley, and Tennyson. But Maria did confess to Margaret Taylor that she often longed for her 'own quiet home and more domestic occupations'.

In a footnote to his diary entry of 7 August 1860, Arthur had written: 'I have applied for my discharge from the volunteers that I may come up here and turn lawyer.' The remark underlines how disillusioned and wretched he must have felt when he left Taranaki, because although to his surprise and annoyance – 'I could say nothing but "damn" when I opened the letter'[5] – his discharge was granted, it was Taranaki and the war rather than Auckland and the law which remained at the forefront of his mind. Shortly after Arthur's arrival at Auckland, Gore Browne requested an interview with him in order to 'gossip' about New Plymouth affairs. Arthur was more circumspect than usual but left the governor in no doubt about his opinion of the military leadership. Gore Browne raised the question of a 'bush corps' – a band of volunteers relieved of other duties and free 'to roam about the country routing out Maoris'.[6] In July Arthur had already persuaded Harry Atkinson to see if the latter could get Gold's permission to set up such a body. Gold was not enthusiastic. Arthur had two further interviews with Gore Browne about the 'Bushrangers'. The governor liked the idea, but General T.S. Pratt,[7] who had assumed command of all British forces in New Zealand, doubted both their usefulness and their military propriety.

News from Taranaki further increased Arthur's mortification at leaving. 'I am ashamed to be sneaking away now there is danger.'[8] Henry had written that things were looking blacker than ever. Pratt, although 'a gentleman and very courteous', was thought no improvement on Gold as a tactician against the Maori. Houses only a mile from the town were being burnt every night. Militiamen (in Henry's command) were tired of exposing themselves to danger when in many cases it seemed that the regular soldiers were not accepting their fair share of risk, and the settler-soldiers, having seen their own property destroyed, had lost heart in trying to save that of others. 'Altogether', Henry wrote, 'we are in a more disorganised and disheartened state just now than we have ever been.'[9] A letter from Josiah Flight to C.W. Richmond confirmed the gloomy news: 'The events of the past five months have brought down the spirit of our Taranaki people from enthusiastic action to dogged endurance bordering on despair.'[10]

During his convalescence Arthur, sometimes accompanied by Maria, went to the House of Representatives and listened to debates. He acknowledged but scarcely appreciated the opportunity to hear reasoned argument on the other side of the principal topic, the

Taranaki War. 'The worst of those who oppose the bill [Native Offenders Bill] because the most able are Sewell, Fox and Featherston.'[11] Politicking, aimed at turning out the Stafford ministry rather than supporting Wiremu Kingi's stand at Waitara, was at the heart of the parliamentary opposition. C.W. Richmond, leading off the debate on the Native Offenders Bill, took refuge in the sophistry of arguing that now Wiremu Kingi stood condemned as a rebel chief, his title to the Waitara land, even 'if he had the best in the world', was merged in his rebellion.[12] Dr Isaac Featherston queried the ministry's policy of individualising the native title and suggested that a tribal right to land had been guaranteed by the Treaty of Waitangi. At this time Wellington's '3 Fs' – Featherston, Fox, and Fitzherbert – were anathema to Taranaki settlers. Sewell's vacillation on native policy – in 1857 he had advocated the systematic extinguishing of the native title – was also roundly condemned by Maria: 'What a blow that Mr Sewell should be a mere political adventurer after all, there will be a pretty pair of them when he and Mr Fox get together.'[13] A handful of churchmen and churchwomen[14] had also spoken up against 'the selfish set at Taranaki'. Admittedly none of them had seen their livelihood destroyed nor suffered directly from the war, although enduring hardship with long periods of separation from their families was the common lot. Wiremu Kingi's chief European protagonist was Octavius Hadfield. In his *One of England's Little Wars*, written in May 1860 and published in England the same year, Hadfield called the purchase of the Waitara land, its survey, and occupation a 'flagrant act of injustice'. He described Teira correctly as a 'man of no rank', and wrote of the 'forcible expulsion of William King', whom he had previously described as a 'loyal chief', from land inherited by him 'from a long line of ancestors'.[15] Maria and Arthur were still convalescing in Parnell when, on 14 August 1860, Hadfield stood for four hours at the Bar of the House answering written questions presented to him about the history and legality of the Waitara purchase.[16]

Nothing heard by members of the Richmond–Atkinson family, then in Auckland, made them in any way question either the advice William had given the governor or the justice of the latter's decision to go ahead with the purchase and survey at Waitara. They were, however, reconciled to the Stafford ministry's probable defeat over its native policy. Emily Richmond in a letter to her brother summed up the mob's attitude:

The ministry will have a hard fight for life . . . The Wellington men are taking part with the Bishop, they call the war unjust, and unholy. One of them had the wickedness to propose the examination of Native witnesses in support of Archdeacon Hadfield. The wretched Auckland members are almost to a man for peace at any price. The missionaries say that if it were not for their unceasing efforts two thirds of the Natives would be in arms against us. Mr Sewell talks in the house of conciliation and . . . is behaving very ill.[17]

With William's political position looking anything but secure it seemed as if Auckland would provide only a temporary haven. Yet Nelson was so associated with refugee status that none of the mob then thought of settling there permanently. Taranaki remained the promised land, in spite of the war, which Arthur despondently believed was so ill conducted by the military that it would end only when the Maori forces became tired of fighting: 'O joy for New Zealand when she has enough riflemen of her own to do without the help(?) of soldiers.'[18] Military reversals filled Arthur with a 'desperate longing to be back at the old place'. William, was thinking of Otago, where he already had an interest in the 'ministerial run' in the Ida Valley,[19] and of practising law in Dunedin. Others of the mob did not react enthusiastically to the notion of following him to the deep south. Maria wrote: 'Arthur elegantly remarks "he'll be blowed if he does" and James agrees with him that migration to an entirely "nigger" settlement would be preferable to living amongst those Scotchmen.'[20]

Arthur, whose diary for the remainder of 1860 frequently carries the phrase 'pottered about', was particularly troubled in mind as to what he should do. It seemed to him that he had three options: first, 'volunteering again', after getting the volunteers, with the governor's help, put on an independent footing; second, 'going to the Bay of Islands or somewhere to the North' and secluding himself among the Maori to learn the language and customs 'as a means to other things'; or third, 'turning lawyer' by articling himself to an Auckland attorney. Maria favoured the law but was careful not to impose her wishes. She recognised Arthur's facility with languages and his immediate wish for acquiring a fluency in Maori.

In October Arthur followed up his earlier 'gossip' to Gore Browne about military affairs in Taranaki by presenting a number of propositions to the governor about the reconstruction of the Taranaki Volunteer Rifles. They were favourably received. 'There is no doubt about it, his blood is up now, and he is very anxious for success.'[21] The governor, somewhat to Arthur's surprise, expressed himself freely 'sub rosa' about General Pratt's inability to capture anything but empty pa. Gore Browne had advised Pratt 'in a friendly way' to convert a large number of his men into a kind of guerrilla force. The general was dismayed by the suggestion, believing it 'impossible to surprise Maories', and that the plan, if carried out, would end in the defeat and loss of his men. Arthur then asked the governor whether if the general refused to establish the corps, he could not force his hand by threatening to disband the militia. The governor doubted his power to do so. 'If the aged Genl.[22] *does* refuse I don't know what we are to do; and the war will end when the Maories are tired,'[23] lamented Arthur.

Whenever he heard of some engagement at Taranaki, Arthur berated himself as 'a poor coward' for not being there. It was not a view shared by Henry Richmond or Harry Atkinson who were both completely opposed to his returning to Taranaki as a volunteer. Henry wrote,

> I suppose it is no use saying anything to you about your own course as you are too pig headed to take good advice. I will only say that if you come back to the Volunteers in their present condition treated as they now are in every respect rather worse than common soldiers, you will be doing no good to yourself or any one else.[24]

Carrying on with his Maori studies was more successfully accomplished. Arthur made the acquaintance of John White, then interpreter to the Native Office, and frequently walked into Auckland with him, 'gently absorbing Maori' the while. Later in 1860 he was able to take up another of his options. On 18 December he left on an expedition to the Kaipara with John Rogan, a land purchase officer, and Maria's young kinsman, S. Percy Smith, a government surveyor. The Maori boat crew were amazed at Arthur's 'folly' in drinking water when he could have tea, and said they would like to go on a journey with him because there would be no raruraru (fuss) about the form of refreshment.

James Richmond was also undecided as to what he should do. At this time he and Mary were living in Parnell while James attended the General Assembly as member for Omata. Stafford offered him the job of editing a proposed government newspaper in Auckland, and Mary, who was at a loss during her husband's frequent absences and more inclined to become agitated over his future than was Maria over Arthur's, favoured his accepting. But, like other Hurworthians, James was loath to abandon Taranaki. He also fancied there was a strong possibility he would be elected superintendent of the province. He returned to New Plymouth after the House was prorogued on 5 November 1860, leaving Mary and the two children behind. Once there, he determined not to accept Stafford's offer of the paper, and admonished Mary not to chide him for his decision. James had no difficulty in being re-elected for Omata and William, though not present, was returned unopposed for the town. But grievances about rations and prospects aired by the Taranaki refugees in Nelson had made James and Thomas King most unpopular among some sections of the New Plymouth townspeople, and James wrote to Mary that he might as well give up the idea of becoming superintendent. G.W. Woon was anxious for him to take over the management of the *Taranaki Herald*, to which he agreed, believing, too, that he could further augment his income by becoming the Taranaki correspondent of the *Nelson Examiner*. He slept with Mary's portrait under his pillow and thanked God 'for letting me have you at intervals'.

Reports from Harry and James showed that the Hurworth houses were still standing, although windows were broken and fires had burnt holes in the floors of two of them. The Hurworth horses had been driven off or killed, and the remains of dead animals poisoned the wells. Scotch thistles rampaged over gardens and clearings. News of the fighting, however, seemed more cheering. In the wake of the dejection caused by Pratt's action against empty Waitara pa – Wiremu Kingi and his defenders must have seen the mile-long column of 1,500 men, artillery, and bullock carts heading towards them all day, and simply retired at an appropriate time – there was on 6 November an encounter at Mahoetahi, north of New Plymouth, near Bell block. 'We have done a glorious day's work,' Harry Atkinson wrote of the volunteers, for whose dash and fighting qualities they were 'honoured' with the name 'Taranaki Devils' by one of the British officers. After the battle, Wetini Taiporutu, a chief of Ati Awa fighting against the colonial forces, his son, and four others were buried in the grounds of St Mary's vicarage by order of General Pratt. Archdeacon Govett read the service in Maori. The same afternoon he buried two volunteers in the churchyard. In his dying speech, translated by Alexander King and printed in the *Taranaki Herald*, Taiporutu urged Maori and Pakeha to live together peacefully for 'the best blood of Waikato flows for your murdered men'.[25]

News of the battle reached Auckland as Arthur and Domett were having their photographs taken. 'But it is cruelly exciting. And it is to be noted that I was having my portrait taken for a hero, while these fellows were fighting,' Arthur noted.[26] To which

Harry replied, 'Three of us [Harry, William and Decimus Atkinson] are quite enough to be risked in any fight.'[27]

In the aftermath of the 'glorious day's work', Harry Atkinson nearly lost his commission[28] and, in spite of his popularity among the settlers, was sick of being separated from his family (at Nelson) and 'tired of doing nothing'. Maria, in a letter to Jane, had mentioned a chance of employment for Harry as manager of the Ida Valley sheep run. 'Is there still any chance?' Harry replied, 'I am disgusted with everything except Taranaki and the more I think of going away the more I seem to like it.'[29] Maria, meanwhile, pursued her relatively tranquil life in Auckland, enjoying plenty of music, walking or picnicking in the domain with Arthur and Edith, going regularly to Government House and to Emily's, even attending church with some regularity while Arthur looked after Edith.

At the beginning of October 1860, they shifted from William and Emily's into lodgings at a Mrs Taylor's house between St Mary's and Newmarket. Maria's letters are sparse for this period – two of her regulars, Mary and Emily, were living close at hand – but in a letter to Margaret Taylor she left a valuable impression of Harriet Gore Browne and her Government House 'At Homes'.

Mrs Gore Browne (the Governess as James calls her) is a woman after your own heart; she is remarkably energetic and clever, without being in the least strong minded, but on the contrary very feminine and ladylike. She really governs the country as much as the Governor, for he does nothing and writes nothing without consulting her first. The weekly 'At Homes' at Government House during the sitting of the Assembly are very pleasant. You meet everyone worth knowing, and have excellent music in one room whilst there is dancing in another. Mrs Gore Browne has weekly meetings in her drawing room for the practice of glees, madrigals and masses. There are many people here with real musical taste; the performances are excellent. Some beautiful quartettes for four men's voices were sung last Monday, and one of Haydn's symphonies well played.

It is amazing the work Mrs Gore Brown gets through. She has four children, the eldest, her only girl, she educates herself. She seems to know and *remember* everybody, having something to say suited to the person and adapted to draw out his or her peculiar gift; perhaps this tact is her most remarkable quality and fits her for the post so well. She is an admirable hostess, but you can see by her special and intimate friends that though agreeable to the public at large, she has judgement and discrimination in selecting for intimacy.

I have seldom seen a woman I could more respect and admire; one could soon love her too I have no doubt. It will be a heavy

loss to the colony if the Home Government foolishly recalls this
Governor because of the war. They had better recall their military
leaders than Colonel and Mrs Gore Browne.[30]

In all the comings and goings of 1860 there was an important
arrival, a final departure, and, happily, a celebration. Mary
Richmond's mother (known to the rest of the family as Aunt Smith),
who in 1857 was appalled by the prospect of losing Mary to New
Zealand and was not prepared to accompany her, now decided
to brave the long sea journey, war in Taranaki, and temporary
accommodation in Auckland, in order to pay a visit. She brought
with her Mary's younger sister, Annie,[31] and her twenty-year-old
niece, Alice, the youngest Atkinson daughter from Frindsbury. They
arrived at Auckland on the *Lord Worsley* on 26 November 1860.
'Poor little Alice looks delicate,' Arthur commented on seeing her;
as yet undiagnosed, she was already showing symptoms of rheumatic
fever.

A week earlier, 17 November 1860, John Hursthouse had died
at New Plymouth of a 'cataleptic seizure' induced by alcoholism.
James was in New Plymouth at the time and attended his funeral.
He was buried in a small graveyard near the Stephenson Smiths
where his father, 'old Mr Hursthouse', also lay.

> It was very very dreary to think that a man who had been so
> very popular and had so much practical ability should pass away
> leaving so little regret behind. At the service there was little said
> on the subject of the man that was gone. Evidently it must be
> a relief that a career of such hopeless degradation is closed.[32]

The next Hursthouse occasion was a more joyous one. Helen
(Nellie) Hursthouse, who had come up to Auckland from Nelson
in July, married A.C.P. Macdonald on 6 December, with the
reception held at William and Emily's. Maria often worried about
Nellie's mother, Helen Hursthouse, in Nelson. She had not been
able to afford the fare to Auckland to see her daughter married
and her prospects in the school she conducted with Marion Ronalds'
help were not encouraging. According to her youngest daughter,
Kate, Helen looked 'dreadfully fagged'.

The end of 1860 saw the mob dispersed into three groups. At
New Plymouth were Henry and Blanche Richmond with their infant
daughter; Harry, William, and Decimus Atkinson; Frank and James
Ronalds, and Wilson Hursthouse (Helen's son) who lived with Henry
and Blanche. At Nelson were Helen Hursthouse and her three
younger children; Marion Ronalds and Eliza Atkinson (William's
wife) with her young son, and Jane Atkinson (Harry's wife) and

her two boys. At Auckland were William and Emily with four children; Lely; Mary and James (who was briefly at Auckland for Christmas) with their two children; Helen Macdonald (née Hursthouse), and Maria and Edith (Arthur was at Kaipara). The Auckland group was augmented by Aunt Smith, Annie Smith, and Alice Atkinson. Although scattered, Taranaki still held them. Edith's bedtime stories were all about Nancy Belle, Lallah Rookh, Platterfoot, Vixen, Supplejack, and 'other Hurworth worthies'. 'Poor dear old Taranaki,' Kate Hursthouse wrote to Lely, 'I cannot tell you how I sometimes long to be there again. I cannot bear to think of the peach trees (that are left) and all the other flowers coming into blossom.'[33]

Christmas in Auckland with Arthur away seemed unreal and melancholy to Maria. She was also concerned for William's health now that the lengthening shadow of the Waitara purchase was falling across him. In November he had handed over native affairs to F.A. Weld, who had joined the Stafford ministry in July. Now far from well, he was working on an answer to Sir William Martin's pamphlet, *The Taranaki Question*, which had appeared in mid-December. On the last day of 1860 Maria wrote to Margaret:

> It is just midnight dearest Margie, and I have written 1860 for the last time. I do not know that I have ever felt the death of an old year so deeply. How little I dreamt when it came in of all the change and utter dispersion of our little community which would be effected before its close.[34]

Arthur returned to Auckland briefly on New Year's day. On 18 January he was off to Kaipara once more with Rogan and, to give him a complete change of scene and release from politics, with C.W. Richmond as well. Again, Arthur the enthusiastic volunteer, now the keen student, observed Maori ways of doing things, talked, listened, and recorded in his diary. He noted that his party were 'very civilly entertained' and that his hosts were as interested in discussing battlefield tactics – even those used at Taranaki – as was Arthur himself. The only irritants were the fleas and mosquitoes. Rogan returned to Auckland from Kaipara, and William and Arthur, with two Maori guides, went on to Hokianga by horseback. William had been very wheezy with asthma when he left Auckland, but once away he managed better than expected with the aid of a few pipes of stramonium, by taking the hills at a gentle pace, and by sleeping outdoors on new fern. He and Arthur returned to Auckland (and William to his own battlefield) on 15 February.

William's war was fought with pen and ink, and in the long term was as damaging to his reputation as if he had exchanged pen for the sword of one of the British generals whose military prowess he so despised. His reply to Sir William Martin's pamphlet immediately brought forth another stinging attack from Octavius Hadfield, written in February 1861 and published later that year as *The Second Year of One of England's Little Wars*. Hadfield wanted Gore Browne recalled immediately, an investigation conducted into the Waitara purchase and, if injustice was proven, adequate compensation paid. 'Natives', he wrote, 'regard themselves as fighting in support of law and order, in opposition to the illegal conduct of Governor Browne.'[35]

It was not a popular view. The Duke of Newcastle (Secretary of State for the Colonies) concluded that the bishops of New Zealand (Selwyn and Abraham) and Archdeacon Hadfield had 'done much mischief'. Hadfield seemed little short of a traitor to most settlers, and he saw himself as probably the most unpopular man in the colony. At least Maria, in her condemnation of the Featherston–Fox faction, criticised the church and missionary view as wrong-headed but nonetheless sincere and consistent:

> The wretched men who for interested motives took up the honestly meant Bishop and Church Missionary cry of an 'unholy war' in order to get into office themselves, have all explained away their own words; those who could not have lost their seats.[36]

The January elections had returned to the General Assembly a number of new men who were considered to be unfavourable to the Stafford ministry. Even so, Maria was positive, and correctly so, that 'no Ministry advocating the "peace at any price" principles of the last sessions opposition can come in'.[37] What she would have liked, if William's health could stand it and if he could have the support of 'working' colleagues (both Sewell and Stafford had spent a considerable portion of their parliamentary term in England), was for a Richmond ministry to replace that of Stafford.

News from Taranaki was once more gloomy. 'The Natives are swarming around and have complete command of the bush,' James wrote.[38] Townspeople had been fired on as close to New Plymouth as the Waiwakaiho bridge. General Pratt's strategy at Waitara was to construct 'a long sap' which would give cover to his men and artillery as they progressed slowly towards Wiremu Kingi's palisaded stronghold of Te Arei. Harry Atkinson did not think highly of this technique: 'The General at Waitara is continuing the sap and will . . . get to where the Natives are in from te to fourteen days. And almost as a matter of course when he gets there the Natives will be as far off.'[39] With skirmishing virtually at an end, volunteer morale was low, 'nothing but "sentry go" and bullying', one of them told Arthur.

Summer dust made it impossible for people to keep their crowded houses clean; fleas were a pest. James had returned to the town towards the end of January and was living in temporary quarters while having a small two-storey cottage put up for him close to Mt Eliot. The cottage would have a spare room to which Henry could bring Blanche and her infant in case of alarms. 'It will be quite a bachelor's house,' he told Mary, 'but I can't help thinking of you in it.'[40] He had carefully packed away all his painting materials before leaving Hurworth and now could not remember which box held them. Editing the *Taranaki Herald* and attending to local issues – he thought that the Nelson criticism was abating – kept him occupied, but he easily became depressed.

> I was sorely tempted to go on board the Ld. Ashley the other day, with nothing but the clothes I had on. It was a beautiful quiet day and I stayed on the beach watching her steaming off to the delightful north. After she was gone I fell into a torpid state from which I only got free after finishing the little newspaper.[41]

He wrote often to Mary; his letters possibly brought cold comfort to a not very resilient and lonely wife, for although he thanked her for her 'dear company' which 'had been a gift beyond all price', his recurrent theme was death and insecurity. He also frequently told her to stop worrying.

In March 1861, rumours of truce negotiations at Waitara induced Arthur to make a reconnaissance trip to Taranaki. It was a 'great treat to see the old mountain again', but also to be seen was the smoke from burning houses in the outlying districts. It was not a hopeful augury of peace. However, once reunited with Henry and Blanche, Harry and Jane (she had returned from Nelson in January), he wrote, 'Taranaki is the right place and Taranaki fellows the right people.'[42]

On 24 March, Harry and Arthur obtained permission from the military authorities to take what was supposed to be an unarmed party of ten to Hurworth.[43]

> The first place we called at was Hursthouse's. The house is standing but very few peaches left. Dick Lethbridges's burnt, Broadmore's burnt. Just before we came to Merton we passed the scattered and whitening bones of a little horse once called Sylvia. At Merton the house, Bird's Nest and gallery are burnt, the shed and cowshed

standing. [There follows a list of other Carrington Road houses
which had been burnt.] At Ratanui the house and sawmill burnt.
After this came a mile or so of bush with nothing to show a state
of war but the thistles flourishing luxuriantly . . . When we got
to the last little hill this side of Hurworth there was Harry's house
right before us looking just the same as ever. This cheered us and
we went on. The dormitorium[44] standing. Just beyond this we got
sight of a rounded little hill standing on the left of the road against
the bush – but alas no house at its foot.[45]

James's house was still standing but doors and windows had been
broken, crockery dug up and smashed, paper torn from the walls,
furniture chopped up. On the walls an inscription in Maori stated,
'Men of taua don't burn this house but leave it as a sleeping place
for people going to Waitara. (Signed) Te Tapihana (a chief of
Ngatihikairo, Kawhia)'.[46] Henry's house had gone, Harry's house
had its windows broken, and a fire lit on the kitchen floor had
burnt a large hole. His dairy was also burnt. Both William Atkinson's
and the Ronalds' houses were destroyed. Decimus Atkinson's small
one was still standing, as were the early makeshift raupo and ponga
dwellings, Kohikohi Lodge and Fernpost House. All that was left
of Maria and Arthur's house were charred piles, chimneys, a door
('so we have got something towards another house'), and the flour
box Arthur had made for Maria's thirty-fourth birthday. 'The
universal feeling was expressed in the wish that we had been present
to assist at the burning of our homesteads.'[47]

Nevertheless, a flag of truce was flying at Waitara; Wiremu
Kingi had withdrawn from Te Arei into the bush and eventually
into the King Country to live with Ngati Maniapoto; McLean was
negotiating with the Ati Awa chief, Te Hapurona, and Waikato
were going home. It seemed as if the war-torn province was about
to enjoy a little peace, although a sceptic might well have pointed
out that a truce in Taranaki was considered vital to the defence
of Auckland, and to an attack on Waikato.[48] To Arthur a more
favourable omen than a truce flag was the surprise arrival at New
Plymouth on 30 March of a new general straight from Engand.
The following day Arthur travelled back to Auckland in the *Airedale*
with Major General Duncan Cameron. He debated whether, instead
of sitting on his portmanteau on deck as was his custom, he should
spend the extra money for a chief cabin fare in the hope of
'insinuating some correct notions about the bush and fighting in
it'. Reluctantly he decided that he could not afford the expense.

The truce terms negotiated by early April 1861 gave little

satisfaction to Taranaki settlers and effected a stalemate rather
than an end to the fighting. Te Ati Awa was to submit to the
Queen's authority and return plunder. In return, and to the chagrin
of the settlers,[49] Teira's title to the disputed Waitara land, which
was what had triggered the fighting in the first place, was to be
once more investigated. Waikato taua returned home, but neither
acknowledged the Queen's authority nor made restitution. Ngati
Ruanui and Taranaki remained defiant and in arms. The former
warned settlers not to go on land south of Waireka as it was theirs
by right of conquest – perhaps a tit-for-tat reprisal, as all the land
belonging to 'rebel' Ati Awa at Waitara which troops had occupied
during the fighting was to be retained. Maria saw the issue simply
in terms of a paternalistic government versus recalcitrant natives
who ought to have been punished more severely: 'In fact,' she
wrote to Margaret Taylor, 'the terms granted them [Ati Awa]
however they may sound to English ears at a distance, consist in
greatly enhancing the value of all their possessions at Waitara,
inflicting no penalty but that of in future governing them by British
law.' Of Waikato she observed, correctly,

> These, the most powerful tribe we have to contend with, continue
> quite unbroken in spirit. They are just now tired of fighting, and
> being in need of ammunition and stores, have abandoned the
> Ngatiawa's quarrel, but they do not feel us to be their masters,
> and have no idea of giving up their King, or their own way of
> managing their affairs.[50]

Maria conceded that if the King (Matutaera Tawhaio, Potatau II)
was acknowledged by all Maori (which was not the case), and
if he and his council provided a genuine authority to which 'our
Government' could apply for redress when aggressions were made
on Europeans (she apparently did not envisage that 'aggressions'
could be the other way round), then such a separation of power
might be the easiest way for the two races to live together. She
was scathing about the 'mistake' made by Selwyn and the missionary
party in treating 'Natives' as 'weak parents treat their children
– they are not to be asked to obey unless they understand the
reason for obeying and acquiesce willingly'.[51] And in the full flush
of righteous indignation that the sanctity of private property should
be brought into question, she wrote,

> You would hardly believe it possible that men of sense and thought
> could be found to talk the stuff that is talked about the injustice
> of governing the Maoris, until they help to frame our laws. They
> can obtain the franchise just as any other man in N.Z. can, by

having possession of land under Crown grants, by renting land or
houses to a certain amount. Holding their own wide uncultivated
wastes as they do in communistic style, it would be impossible
to ground their right to vote on this sort of ownership.[52]

A few days after Maria's letter to Margaret, a family tragedy
took precedence over public affairs. Nellie Richmond, the infant
daughter of Blanche and Henry Richmond, left on her own for
no more than a few minutes, fell into the pond at the bottom
of Martha King's garden at New Plymouth and drowned.[53] The
distraught Blanche, who was pregnant, told Henry she feared going
mad if she remained at the Kings' stone cottage, where they had
lived from the time Arthur and Maria left. Henry obtained a month's
leave from the militia and they came to Auckland. Maria, also
pregnant, was deeply affected:

> I cannot look at any of the little flock here without thinking of
> the lost lamb . . . Until children are given us, it seems as tho'
> half the possibilities in human life for bringing joy or sorrow remain
> unrevealed, at least with me it has been so. My happiness in possessing
> Edith is always tempered by the thought of what I may be called
> on to suffer in losing her, or, far worse, in seeing her become
> very different in character from what I wish and hope she may
> become.[54]

In the middle of April, Maria and Arthur moved from Mrs Taylor's
lodgings to Athol House, Parnell, where they were to live *en famille*
with Mary and James (when the latter was at the General Assembly),
Aunt Smith, Annie Smith, and Alice Atkinson until they returned
to New Plymouth. Henry and Blanche were there as well. It was
a large household of nine adults, three children, and two servants.

Discussing plans for the future once again occupied the family
during the winter of 1861. Henry was thinking of becoming a brewer,
a very profitable occupation in New Zealand. James, whose
popularity in New Plymouth waxed and waned according to public
reaction to his leading articles in the *Herald*, was again hopeful
of the superintendency.[55] William, fairly certain that his political
career was ending, had, during April, gone on an exploratory trip
to Dunedin and sounded out T.B. Gillies, a parliamentary colleague,
as to the possibility of entering into a legal practice with him.
Gillies, William reported to Emily, was anxious to have him as
a partner and could assure William of £1,000 a year to begin with.
'You must keep this strictly to yourself and Lely,' he warned. As
refugees were beginning to return to Taranaki, Maria and Arthur
toyed with the idea of going back and putting up a little hut near

the beach. Beach Cottage itself was let, and even Arthur felt there was insufficient security in the district for them to make another start at Hurworth. Maria's baby was due in September and the public health situation in New Plymouth was alarming. Temporary houses had sprung up within the sentry lines; diphtheria was rife and carrying off many adults as well as children. Helen Hursthouse, who returned in June, described the town as dirty, squalid, and muddy. The only accommodation she and Kate and her younger sons could find was in a Devon Street shop – Helen would not think of returning to her former home – for which Wilson Hursthouse and Henry Richmond paid the 'exorbitant' rent of one pound per week. There was not an unoccupied cottage or house in the town or immediate suburbs; even local 'friendly' Maori had been evicted from their pa inside the town, and the authorities, both military and civil, would permit further families to return only if they could prove they had sufficient accommodation to secure health. All this made Maria decide to remain in Auckland at least until spring. She expected that Arthur would wish to return sooner.

Arthur's indecision – 'the Law or the Bush' as he put it – ended temporarily in May when, in order to improve his knowledge of Maori and to give himself the satisfaction of regular employment, he joined the Native Office in Auckland as 'Supernumerary Translator without Salary'. At the end of August he was appointed to the paid staff as 'Extra Clerical Assistant' at eight shillings per day, and by the end of 1861 was drawing a salary of £180 per annum. During the evenings at Athol House, working in the loft out of reach of flies and visitors, he was compiling a Maori–English dictionary. Each morning as he walked to work with John White, Arthur discussed his latest entries. A friend once came across two boys shaking their heads after this oddly conversing couple had passed by: ' "Them two coves is always talking Maori" to which the other answered, "What bl--y fools they must be." '[56]

He also received help from Bishop Selwyn who gave him some books on the different languages of Polynesia. By chance in the Auckland Domain, Arthur encountered Mohi, his bird-watching, mountain-climbing Maori tutor from Hurworth days, and more recently a 'rebel' Ati Awa warrior at Mahoetahi. Arthur was delighted to see him and his companion, Haiminia, but when in the evening he went to the hostelry where they had been staying, they had gone. 'I suppose they were afraid I should turn informer, which is a pity.'[57] Another chance meeting with two Ati Awa was more fruitful. The three of them decided to hold a weekly 'Maori and English mutual instruction class' at Athol House. 'The members of it are 1st President & Profesor of English – the present editor. [A.S.A.] 2nd. Professors of Maori – Wirihana Matene & Rawiri Taiwhanga.'[58]

The expected defeat of the Stafford ministry occurred on 5 July 1861 when it failed by one vote to survive a no-confidence motion. Had the division been delayed by even one hour, the result, on this occasion, could have been different, as Harry Atkinson, who on 20 June had been overwhelmingly returned in a by-election for the Grey and Bell seat, would have been present and voted with the government. The previous week, when Harry should have taken his passage to Auckland, bad weather had prevented the *Airedale* from calling at New Plymouth. At the time Arthur noted in his diary, 'alas no Harry . . . Affairs have come to a point at which one vote may make a great difference in the future of the country.'[59] Harry eventually arrived at Onehunga the very afternoon of the debate. A horse was waiting and he rode straight to the Assembly, only to find that the division bell had already rung. The Stafford ministry tendered its resignation half an hour after the rising of the House.

During the debate Dr Isaac Featherston had charged C.W. Richmond with having 'exerted improper influence in regard to the purchase of Maori lands in Taranaki' – in other words, he claimed that Richmond was seeking the aggrandisement of the Taranaki province for his own personal benefit. William immediately demanded a select committee investigation which, when adopted by the House on 6 September 1861, completely vindicated him. (History has since severely criticised his judgement over the acceptance of Teira's offer at Waitara but has not impugned his integrity.) Maria, who had spent a great deal of time in the House listening to the debate, described the ministerial crisis to Margaret Taylor:

> We have been living in the greatest political excitement for a fortnight . . . and I have felt it almost impossible to sit down to letter writing . . .
>
> However we all feel that it is much better as it is. It would have been unsatisfactory to retain office with half the House voting against them, but it is glorious to fall by a majority of one after five years of office. To judge from the speeches the best brains were on our side. It is very doubtful whether Mr Fox, the Leader of the Opposition, who was called on yesterday to form a cabinet,

will be able to do so . . . I hope in any case William will not
be recalled to office, in fact I am almost afraid his life might fall
a sacrifice to a continuance of such wear and tear as he has gone
through of late.[60]

Emily had earlier expressed her own concern: 'I cannot help feeling
this five years has told upon you more than I could have believed.'[61]
Signficantly, the Stafford government finally vacated office on 12
July 1861, the day of William's fortieth birthday. His involvement
with political office, which he had always found distasteful, was
over; his more successful, but still to him unsatisfactory, legal career
about to begin.

I . . . am out of New Zealand politics, I believe, for ever. I have
been praised and censured beyond my deserts. Latterly I have
received really quite a nauseating amount of laudation . . . I feel
neither capacity nor disposition for public affairs.[62]

For a brief period, until William resigned from parliament altogether
on 20 January 1862, Taranaki representation in the House was
entirely in the hands of the mob. William was member for New
Plymouth, James for Omata, and Harry for Grey and Bell.

Hard on the defeat of the Stafford ministry came the recall of
Governor Gore Browne.[63] There was immediate settler sympathy
for him. Taranaki settlers almost to a man signed a farewell address,
which was presented at Government House by Charles Brown,
James Richmond, and Arthur Atkinson. The governor was ill, so
his wife received the deputation, describing Taranaki people as
'true steel'. Maria particularly regretted the loss of Harriet Gore
Browne:

There will be a complete breaking up of Auckland society in the
course of the next two or three months. Mrs Gore Browne's going
will be an immense loss socially . . . she has made Government
House a centre where all ranks have met sociably and with enjoyment
and benefit.[64]

There was little likelihood of Auckland society forming around
the new governor's wife, for she and Sir George Grey had separated.

Nobody was quite sure what to expect from Grey. Maria was
certain that 'the Bishop's party' would conclude that the British
government had endorsed its censure of Gore Browne, yet all
despatches had seemed to support the latter's policy and that of
his advisers. It was generally assumed that it would be in character
for Grey to represent his predecessor's acts in as unfavourable a
light as possible in order to enhance his own credit if he restored
peace. Arthur reported Auckland's reception to Grey on 26

September 1861 as 'friendly but not enthusiastic perhaps'. Grey, however, could be charming. Harriet Gore Browne was among the first to be made conscious of his spell, although there is a vein of Scottish canniness in her appreciation:

> Sir George is the most wonderfully agreeable man I ever met – his conversation is charming and he evidently prides himself upon his power of using it to *raryfy* [sic] those with whom he talks . . .
> Sir George *appears* to agree perfectly with Col. Brownes's views.[65]

By November, from Sydney where she still closely followed New Zealand politics, she wrote to J.C. Richmond warning him that 'Sir George and Mr Fox are one'. Later, totally disillusioned, she wrote to C.W. Richmond:

> I did not believe in any man being *such* a profound humbug. I heard him with my own ears tell Col Browne he hoped the natives would not submit as it would be better for both races that they should be conquered.[66]

British government policy required a man as equivocal as Grey. He was to pursue peace initially, but if that seemed unobtainable, then it was to be war quickly won. Of his early plans little was known. Arthur wrote, 'Being a Maori scholar he does his own correspondence & the N.O. [Native Office] knows nothing of it.'[67]

Maria's establishment in Parnell – the 'Athol club', Harriet Gore Browne called it – broke up towards the end of 1861. The two servants had been unsatisfactory and Maria feared Aunt Smith would send home gloomy reports of colonial housekeeping because she could never get used to the servants' harum-scarum ways. In every other respect the large household had worked capitally, 'in spite of varying tastes and tempers'. Although Maria deplored the communal Maori lifestyle, there was something tribal in the mob's ability to live together at close quarters, either from choice or necessity. It has been an enduring characteristic and proves Maria's claim that in this respect, if in no other, they were a remarkable family.

James and Mary's third child, Dorothy Kate (Dolla), was born alive and well at Athol House on 12 September 1861. It was a great relief. The last few weeks of Mary's pregnancy had been overshadowed by tragedy which had once again struck Henry and Blanche. Their son, born on 19 August, died within a fortnight of an organic heart disease which Dr Rawson attributed to the shock Blanche received when her little girl drowned. She had been unable to feed him and he had been kept on cow's milk mixed with a few drops of wine. Blanche, who was very ill after the birth, became demented when told of her son's death. Helen Hursthouse wrote to Lely that such was Blanche's agony of mind for her lost ones that both she and Henry 'almost prayed that God would take her too as there seemed no hope of happiness for her on this earth'.[68] After three weeks of critical illness, during which Henry, also suffering from ill health, was constantly at her bedside, Blanche's strength began to return and her grief of mind to abate.

The following month James took his family to a small house he had rented at Onehunga, about seven miles from Auckland, where the air was considered more bracing. At the beginning of November, James returned to Taranaki, along with Alice Atkinson and Annie Smith. Alice was to stay with Harry and Jane, and Annie and James were to spy out the land for a possible home for Mary and her family. This latter move did not entirely please Mary, left behind at Onehunga. There was talk of James being offered the editorship of the *Nelson Examiner* which Mary found gratifying insofar as James would earn more money, though it would mean living apart from the others. This latest separation from James she found more distasteful than ever. She and her sister had a strong affection for each other yet, reading between the lines, there is no doubt that tucked into Mary's sweet and long-suffering nature was a little jealousy, not simply because James and Annie were together, but because their situation seemed designed always to keep James in a place where Mary was not. James was totally unaware of Mary's sensitivity on this point, and kept up a flow of letters describing how he and Annie were 'gadding about' on foot or on horseback – though 'we do not see any beautiful thing without thinking of you'. His letters contained their customary mix of balm and irritation: '. . . dear Annie, her kindness and thoughtfulness for me are too much, far far too much . . . My heart smote me at having suggested her coming down here and leaving you.'[69] Annie dismissed James's little house near Mt Eliot as 'utterly unsuitable' (James managed to lease it to the Bank of New Zealand for a year) and was generally pessimistic about house hunting and house keeping in New Plymouth. Rents were high, servants were bad. Annie also told Mary not to fidget because James was away. 'One must be philosophical and rise above little things or there is no peace for us in this life.'[70]

One expedition James and Annie made was to Hurworth. It was William and Eliza Atkinson's wedding anniversary and they wished to celebrate it with members of the mob at their former home. The sight of Hurworth, and the urging of Harry and Henry that he stay at Taranaki, shook James and inclined him to abandon Nelson and the *Examiner* for New Plymouth and the *Herald*. A soft green turf relieved by English trees had crept over the garden. There were no horses or sheep, but lots of fine sleek cattle. The thistles were less advanced than he expected. Hurworth, however, needed money and peace before it could be lived in, and neither of these seemed assured. Annie thought James and Mary's house – the shell had survived – 'very pretty', but found the intense quiet and 'uninhabitedness' of the place most oppressive. She firmed up James's resolution to abide by the Nelson plan and decided to go there with him. Mary was most displeased at her so doing. By mid-December they were living in a Nelson boarding house and looking for a house for Mary and the children. 'My own darling Polly,' James wrote to Mary,

> I don't know how to begin writing to you seeing that your wishes about dear Annie have not been complied with . . . I felt a little hurt at the extreme anxiety you showed for it assumed that I should be selfish enough to urge Annie . . .[71]

And Annie too wrote to Mary, 'James and I have been longing for you all day as we do every day dearest . . . I am so very sorry that you and dear James cannot be together.'[72]

A few years later it was Maria's turn to be left with the children for a lengthy period, and a similar miasma of loneliness and depression threatened to envelop her. But not quite. Maria was resolutely practical; was never inclined, as was Mary, to clasp thorns to her bosom. She possessed a healthy scepticism and an ability to stand back from her predicament and view it objectively. This gives Maria's letters an incisive edge and a contemporary quality which Mary's entirely lack. Both had unconventional, unpredictable husbands. Both relied on a strong faith; Mary's was based on religious belief, Maria's on her own heart and will.

Maria's pregnancy had been uneventful. She was confined on 19 October 1861 without complication, alarm, or benefit of doctor's attendance: Arthur went looking for him but could not find him in time. He did manage to procure some chloroform – 'one of the most blessed discoveries ever made', Lely thought – and under its soothing influence Ruth was born. Of course there had been expectations that the child would be a boy:

> If I could have chosen I should have had a son, for Arthur's sake, he seems to think so much of having a boy as his constant companion in a way a daughter can hardly be. But when you hear the child

is living and healthy your hearts seem so overjoyed there is no room for a regret left.[73]

Ruth was not quite so pretty as Edith (now three) had been, but she was equally fat, contented, and flourishing. 'How excellently I go through my confinements now,' wrote Maria, now thirty-seven, and what an excellent nursing mother she was, feeding both Ruth and the infant son of John and Mary Gorst whom she wet-nursed to health. She occasionally obliged in the same way for Helen Macdonald who was having trouble feeding her baby daughter, Flora.

On 9 November, Maria and Arthur left Athol House for Onehunga – a move that meant Arthur had a seven-mile walk to and from the Native Office, as he begrudged the shilling it cost to take the horse-drawn van. (From a salary of approximately £3 per week, a deduction of ten to twelve shillings was a high expenditure.) Onehunga's sea breezes tempered the heat and humidity of Auckland's summer. It was also the point of departure for all west coast sea traffic and, in that respect, represented the jumping off place for Taranaki. They rented a comfortable small cottage with garden and fine prospect, conveniently near Mary Richmond's house where she had been joined by her mother, 'Aunt Smith'. Here Maria enjoyed the luxury of having a 'jewel of a maid'. Ann was a Northcountry woman from near Stockton-on-Tees. Maria engaged her on the spot for old time's sake and never regretted it. The 'jewel' was always up by five o'clock – on washing days she was up at four – and kept the cottage in apple-pie order. On Sundays she took Edith to the Sunday school at the Methodist chapel where her brother, Joseph, was the preacher.

Lely, now seventy, was once again living with Maria and Arthur. Her sight was failing and she regretted the 'gradual decay of my powers of usefulness'. She had borne all the anxieties, changes, and suspense brought about by war wonderfully well, but she grieved about the further, possibly more permanent, dispersal of her family. William and Emily's likely move to Dunedin was a great blow to her, and to James and Mary as well. They had hoped William would begin his legal practice at Nelson: 'We might as well be in England for what we shall see of you and what intercourse we shall have.'[74]

William's family was increasing rapidly – Emily was expecting their fifth child – and his priority was to make some money: to become 'a worshipper of the golden calf of Tuapeka', as he told his mother. To which report Harriet Gore Browne replied, 'I should

like to see what effect riches would have upon that thin earnest
face.'[75] Lely needed to be reassured about Dunedin society. Because
of the gold rush she imagined it full of opportunists, highwaymen,
and, of course, Scotsmen. William replied:

> The effects of the gold diggings on society here I think has stirred
> up the good as well as the bad. There are excellent elements among
> the old Scotch population. Many minds are, I think aroused to a
> sense of the duties to which this enormous and sudden accession
> of wealth and influence has brought along with it. For my own
> part I hold that it is a man's own fault if he does not find worthy
> people and make good friends wherever he goes. In many ways
> I am disposed to prefer society in Dunedin to what it is in Auckland
> – understand that by society I do not mean evening parties.[76]

He was not sure how the Dunedin climate would affect his health
and he regretted his isolation from the family, but in mid-January
1862 he determined to accept T.B. Gillies' offer of a partnership
and £1,500 a year.

In the middle of January 1862 there was a partial exodus of
the clan from Auckland. James came up from Nelson to take Mary
and their three children, together with Aunt Smith, Emily, and
two of her children, back to Nelson via New Plymouth. Emily,
who was six months pregnant, intended to break her journey at
Nelson before joining William at Dunedin. She left two of her
daughters, Mary (9) and Margaret (5), with Maria. Arthur and
Maria had thought of returning to Taranaki at the same time, but
Henry Richmond, whose advice had been sought, did not think
that Arthur could yet get back on his Hurworth land; nor did
he see any other available work which would return the salary
he drew from the Native Office. Maria and Arthur decided to
stay on for a few more months, and to have Lely with them.
Onehunga now seemed desolate:

> I see now what it must feel like to be in a colony to people who
> emigrate alone, not in a body as we did. There is no house near
> one wishes to call at, no creature to drop in at unceremonious
> hours, no children for these to go out walks with; it is a complete
> isolation.[77]

Compensation for losses they had suffered in the war had come
through. 'Fancy having £104-6-8 in lieu of all we have lost,'[78] Maria
wrote to Margaret with a mixture of indignation and resignation.
Their claim had been for approximately £800. She realised that
their plight was easy compared with that of older settlers who
had invested all they had in their farms. In addition to Arthur's

salary, they received £100 a year from money held on mortgage in Canterbury.

Arthur's last few weeks in the Native Office were clouded by a falling out with John White. White had earlier lent him some of his manuscripts on Maoritanga which Arthur considered 'as full of matter as an egg is full of meat but not very well arranged. It is a pity that the little man has little literary ability.'[79] At the end of the previous November, White had told Arthur that Governor Grey was thinking of setting in train a Maori dictionary to which White was to contribute all he knew. He asked Arthur to put his (White's) contributions into shape – 'his notions of English being somewhat vague' – and also took Arthur's dictionary to show to the governor. Grey was impressed and asked Native Minister F.D. Bell to appoint Arthur 'assistant lexicographer' and increase his salary by £50 as a bonus. At the end of January, Bell, in some embarrassment, wrote to Arthur: 'There is evidently some great misapprehension about the dictionary.'[80] White had claimed that he was the compiler and Arthur merely the copier. White also asserted that the arrangement between Grey, Arthur, and himself was that he, not Arthur, was to be the governor's assistant. 'Little White has behaved very shabbily,' Arthur wrote in his diary on receipt of Bell's letter, 'making it look of course rather as if Bell and I were trying to get £50 on false pretences.'[81] Bell was still anxious to keep Arthur in the Auckland Native Office until an opportunity arose for him to become a resident magistrate. Arthur informed him that he really 'belonged to Taranaki' and that, 'unless our "mob" were broken up and the place made uninhabitable', it was most unlikely that he would remain permanently in the native service. The question for Maria and Arthur was when to leave Auckland. Early in February Arthur decided to go to New Plymouth and consult his brothers.

He landed at New Plymouth on 10 February, in time to see the volunteers and militia parade on 'Poverty Square'[82] preparatory to their being dismissed. They were offered work on the roads at four shillings a day. Arthur found that none of his brothers was certain of his own future, let alone in a position to advise. He wrote to Maria:

> Things are in a muddle. Henry's intention is to stick to the place as long as he can . . . Harry is wavering as to the sheep run . . . As is his custom he wants to see what will turn up. In the meantime he gets 10/- a day as sub-commissioner of the Relief Fund . . . If we come we shall have a little more society than we get at

Onehunga . . . Our income will be reduced £50 or £100 and some important sources of knowledge will be cut off.[83]

Arthur thought he could get the sub-editorship of the *Taranaki Herald* and, with that to keep the pot boiling, could devote the rest of his time to restoring his Hurworth farm. There were two more considerations: 'If we come here we shall probably rear our children which is doubtful in Auckland. On the other hand if we come it will be putting you to domestic slavery.'[84] Still undecided, Arthur returned to Auckland on 1 March. The debate over 'the bush or the law' went on. William had spoken to Gillies about taking Arthur into the firm, and the latter was willing to do so for an initial £50 a year and his articles of apprenticeship. William, however, did not press the move. Already Dunedin's weather was aggravating his asthma and he was not sure that he would be able to survive the winter there. He tipped the argument towards the bush:

The New Plymouth Aphrodite (as Maria calls it) has for me as for you the greatest charm, and were I a bachelor I would not hesitate in my preference. Looking on my string of little ones[85] it has not seemed to me right to follow my natural inclination . . . My present life contradicts every taste and feeling of my nature and I adopt it only as a hard duty. But if you and Maria see your way to a livelihood and public usefulness in Taranaki it may very likely be right for you to stick to the dear old place.[86]

Further news from Taranaki seemed to indicate that the remnants of the mob were settling down more firmly. Henry was likely to become provincial treasurer; the manager's job on the Ida Valley run had been filled, so Harry's future seemed fixed in Taranaki; Decimus Atkinson was establishing himself as a blacksmith and had married Marion Ronalds[87] on what Helen Hursthouse considered 'absolutely nothing – but it is rather in the family I think'. As a final inducement, Henry offered Arthur a half share in editing the *Herald*. The exiles decided to return. Maria wrote to Mary Richmond in Nelson, 'I am very thankful to think of being near some of our own people again, the last 4 months has not been real living to me.'[88]

Arthur went to the Native Office for the last time on 3 May. He had found his days there pleasant enough, and the translating work not arduous; it had allowed him ample opportunity for improving his linguistic knowledge of Maori. Since his disagreement with John White, he had walked to work with and developed a 'genuine affection' for Wirihana Matene, who had also been a member of the Maori–English instruction class at Athol House.

As a conciliatory farewell gesture, Arthur called on White and left his dictionary with him. 'I am going to let him have what I have got. I don't want to be at enmity with the foolish little man.'[89]

Lely, Mary and Margaret (Emily's daughters), Edith, Ruth, Arthur, and Maria – but unfortunately not the 'jewel' – embarked on the *Airedale* for Taranaki on 9 May. Their passage was smooth and quick, yet Arthur, as usual, was seasick, and on arrival Lely found it difficult to get from the steamer into the open surfboat. Moreover, Lely's travelling chest of drawers was left aboard and continued the voyage southwards, to be returned only when the *Airedale* came north again. Its loss would have been severely felt, for in addition to Lely's clothes it contained many little extras bought in Auckland to get them through the Taranaki winter. Maria immediately noticed how much New Plymouth township had grown, and was pleasantly surprised that the houses were not as 'villainously ugly' as she had expected. Many of the outsettlers had built their town cottages with the intention of eventually dragging them back to their farms by bullock train. Major Matthews was renting Beach Cottage so Maria, Arthur, and their party were temporarily accommodated with Henry and Blanche. Again it was a crowded household – Helen Hursthouse, Kate, and Flinders were living there as well – but 'we fit in better than could be expected', Maria wrote. Their numerous goods and chattels were an embarrassment and most were left unpacked, awaiting the move to Beach Cottage.

The second evening of their homecoming was given over to a meeting of Hurworthians in Blanche's sitting room. Maria thought that Henry, who was now provincial treasurer and editor of the *Herald*, looked much older, with deep lines of sorrow etched on his face: 'Blanche and he are quietly cheerful but there seems no spring or life in them.'[90] Henry thought Arthur more vigorous and mentally active than ever. Harry and Jane seemed the same as always, 'hospitable, cheerful and active'. Their third child, Fanny, was a fine fat baby now eleven months old. She had been born on 30 June 1861, so the bad weather that had delayed Harry's departure for the Assembly in Auckland and consequently brought down the government had meant that Harry had been able to be with Jane for the birth. Harry had been re-appointed captain in the volunteers and was drawing military pay as well as his civil salary as a relief commissioner. His Hurworth house had been sufficiently repaired to be lived in, and he had also bought a town house. He and Jane were living, so Maria concluded, 'in apparent affluent abundance'. William and Eliza Atkinson – Eliza 'prettier than ever' – had a nice-looking son, Willie.[91] William still held his post as a native interpreter but was likely soon to lose it and had no further prospects other than working on the roads. Neither he nor Eliza wished to leave Taranaki.

Of all the Hurworthians gathered together that evening, it was Decimus and Marion Atkinson whom Maria thought to be in a 'fair way to greater and sounder worldly prosperity than any Atkinson has yet attained'.[92]

> One of the most cheerful sights here is the establishment of Mr and Mrs Decimus Atkinson . . . Decie has turned blacksmith! and yet Marion has taken him in spite of a tinge of gentility pervading her views such as few of us possess. He is getting an excellent business and works very hard indeed . . . The house is all newly papered and with bright curtains and fresh furniture looks quite an elegant little place. It would be a novel sight for most English people to take tea with them, and see Deccie come in with his blacksmith's apron on, and greasy hands and face. He takes his bed candle, disappears and returns looking quite a fashionable young fellow, to sit down to a very prettily set out tea table . . . I believe they will soon be comfortably off in the world, certainly they promise to be as happy in marriage as any of the set.[93]

Maria's children seemed well pleased by the move. Edith, three and a half, was delighted to be surrounded by so many relatives, and Ruth, seven months, objected only to Jane Atkinson whose voice she found 'startlingly different'. Both children adored Arthur: 'I hope I shall have a son some day,' Maria wrote, 'who will give *me* a little filial affection. These despised girls are all taken up by the parent who professes to look down upon them.'[94]

Arthur quickly settled into the routine of newspaper work. 'Slew my mataika [first person taken or killed in a fight],' he wrote in his diary for 15 May, a reference to his first editorial for the *Herald*. Unlike Henry who found it irksome, and James, who ground out the *Examiner* in Nelson, Arthur thoroughly enjoyed the regular writing. Before breakfast he read Latin (useful for his legal option), then did a session with the *Herald*, followed by shingle splitting as a preferable way of earning extra money to working on the roads. With £50 from the *Herald*, £100 from their Canterbury mortgage, and what little extra Arthur might earn, Maria was confident they would keep clear of debt.

Maria had to restrain her housekeeping urges until her family was settled in Beach Cottage, whose situation, overlooking the open roadstead, she much preferred to any other in town. 'It is so pleasant to be able to walk on the sands without passing through the muddy town and so especially convenient with young children to have a dry place for walking close at hand.'[95] Lely, who was to continue living with Blanche and Henry until Beach Cottage was enlarged, also liked the idea of living there. And there was particular satisfaction in spending a little money on improvements when the cottage at least belonged to one of the family.[96] Maria and Arthur intended to build extra bedrooms 'on moveable principles' so that they could be taken to Hurworth when it became possible to live there again – 'a consummation devoutly to be wished and firmly believed in as coming by Ar'.

And so once more my dearest Margie, I date from the only place in New Zealand that feels like home. It is a year and ten months since I left it, little imagining then that I should be absent so long.[97]

Thus began Maria's long homecoming letter to Margaret Taylor. On 14 July 1862, Maria, Arthur, Edith, and Ruth (Mary and Margaret Richmond had gone on to Dunedin) took possession of Beach Cottage, their last Taranaki home.

'Otago & the law or Taranaki & joy'

New Plymouth, July 1862–Dec. 1863

Maria once said that although Arthur was 'the best of men', she would never be foolish enough to trust his judgement in a situation which required an instant decision. His tendency to vacillate is nowhere seen more clearly than in the debate which waxed and waned during the next eight years over whether he should leave Taranaki and the war for Dunedin (later Nelson) and the law. It might be truer to say that in spite of his critical self-analysis about drifting 'like a log in the tide', Arthur really preferred the untrammelled life of adventuring with the volunteers, writing for the *Herald*, and pursuing his various scientific and linguistic predilections to settling down within the more restricted orbit of legal studies. He was still a young man – twenty-nine when he returned to Taranaki – whereas Maria was approaching the more sedate age of forty. From the beginning of their relationship, however, when Arthur, to quote Maria, did not have the 'sense to see the error of his ways in preferring old age to youth', she *chose* to allow him to come to his own decisions.

She could have done otherwise. Nineteenth-century women were not often the 'choosers of their own path', although they were not without some skill in determining its direction. Emily Richmond fussed and became inadequate; Mary Richmond fretted, uncomplaining but pale; Marion Atkinson could become genteel; Annie Atkinson (Harry's second wife) planned and presented. Earlier in the century even that intrepid band of missionary wives, or some of them, were 'taken poorly' or pleaded delicate health when moves to the south of the Bay of Islands were mooted. Maria employed no such artifice. She wanted Arthur to be a lawyer; she said so; the subject was frequently aired, with Maria stressing constantly that the final decision was to be his. Again she could have done otherwise.

Maria possessed a strong personality as well as an informed mind and a natural bent towards practicality. In photographs of the maturing Maria, when she was on the way to becoming 'Aunt Maria' and even 'Great Aunt Maria', there is purpose in her otherwise serene face. She had been the one who had held together that numerous and diverse early household at Merton. 'What should we all have done without her,' Henry wondered when her life was endangered by her first pregnancy. She also had a good sense of her own worth: 'I, of course, was dignified in black' was not entirely a humorous comment about her appearance at balls or parties. Other people frequently remarked on her handsomeness. Arthur, a natural tease, was not averse to chancing his arm with that dignity. His appalling nickname, 'old wifey', meant affectionately, Maria apparently accepted with equanimity. In fact she seems at times to go out of her way to emphasise the age difference as though it allowed Arthur even more licence to do as he wished. Towards the end of their stay at Beach Cottage, when Arthur was a member of parliament, of the provincial government, of the Bushrangers, and proprietor as well as editor of the *Taranaki Herald*, Maria did wonder whether his general usefulness to Taranaki was such that he ought not to be spared. But for the greater part she hoped that 'the law' would prevail, convinced as she was that Arthur's largely self-taught and eclectic mind would find no difficulty – indeed, would probably delight – in exploring the labyrinthine ways of due legal process. A professional career, moreover, would give financial security and ballast to both their lives. She had long doubted whether he would ever be a successful bush farmer, even if that life were to be resumed. Apart from raising race horses, and that was a risky venture, nothing in farming had engaged his attention for long. Social status was not an issue. Maria was not vain or puffed-up, but she never doubted her own position in society. Arthur, apart from his newspaper involvement, seldom bothered with society; in fact, he rather rejoiced in being an apparent misfit.

At times Maria did not possess her soul in patience when her husband produced yet another excuse to prevent his taking up the legal option. However, resilience, fortitude, and a practical capacity to make the best of the moment were part of her make-up. She was able to draw a line between independence of mind and what she called 'strong mindedness'. The former trait she particularly admired in women, the latter she abhorred. It is a distinction which, for better or for worse, present-day feminists, and their critics, have obscured.

Major Matthews of the 57th, the last tenant of Beach Cottage, had left the place 'in a frightful mess', and Arthur hired two soldiers to clean it up. Matthews had also converted the front entrance into a pantry, forcing visitors to come and go through the French window. Lely provided the money for the bedrooms to be repapered; large-scale alterations such as making a new entrance and enlarging the cottage generally were left in abeyance until Arthur's plans became more definite. For, in spite of Major Matthews, Beach Cottage had worn wonderfully well. Lely, who moved back shortly after Maria and Arthur had taken possession, wrote to Mary:

> I never appreciated the situation of the cottage as I do now – the little bit of greenery in front, though the garden has run wild, between you & the sea, is a great relief to the eye . . . I hope it will never go out of the family again . . . unless we are all permanently driven from Taranaki.[1]

Edith, and Ruth as she grew older, revelled in the cottage's situation, with beach and sandhills for a playground, and Mt Eliot sheltering it from the chill mountain wind. The sea itself must always have been treated as a dangerous, forbidden element. In all the years that Arthur, Maria, and their children remained in New Plymouth, there is no reference to anyone so much as paddling in it.

Maria, without a servant when she first moved in, but 'as cheerful and energetic as ever', found Beach Cottage all that her fancy had depicted. But it seemed as if they might not be staying long. William had written renewing his offer to Arthur on even more favourable terms. He would give Arthur his articles, guarantee a salary of £100 a year which he felt Gillies would increase to £150 once he saw how useful Arthur could be, and even if ill health forced William to leave Dunedin, Gillies would continue as Arthur's mentor. In characteristic fashion Arthur recorded in his diary after receiving William's letter, 'Otago & the law or Taranaki & joy'.[2]

At the end of July, Henry and Blanche (who was pregnant and poorly) joined Maria, Arthur, and Lely in Beach Cottage. As likely future occupier, Henry wished to put the garden in order and plant seeds. Within a few days of their arrival Alice Atkinson, who had been living with Harry and Jane, also came to stay. She was suffering badly from rheumatism and had found the 'noisy mismanagement' of Jane Atkinson's household too much for her peace of mind. It was hoped that the sea air and Arthur's lively company would restore his young sister's flagging body and spirit. Once again Maria was in the midst of what she called a 'close packed' household of six adults and two children.

The change brought no improvement to Alice. She was soon bedridden. Lely gave up her bedroom to her and moved back to live with Helen Hursthouse. Arthur helped out with nursing, and it was he who always rose early, lit the fire, and got breakfast, but the main burden of the household, including the never-ending chore of washing, fell on Maria. Servants were hard to come by. Townspeople complained of being badly off, yet nobody was anxious to let their daughters go into service. Lely expostulated to Emily, 'all the people send their children to school with their relief money'.[3] Considering the high illiteracy rate, among children especially, one would have thought this use of the money might have appealed to Lely. But Beach Cottage needs were urgent. When at last Maria employed Ann Foreman at the end of July, she reported, 'I have just got a new maid & Ar is suffering a good deal in consequence' – his miscellany of books, papers, and insects was endangered by too-efficient tidying. Maria found Ann Foreman's work more useful than that of most colonial servants. She bore a good character for honesty and steadiness, but, as was so often the case, was soon to have a child.

Arthur was currently engaged in editing the *Herald* with Henry Richmond, each producing the paper on alternate weeks. On 10 August he wrote to William that he had finally decided to go to Dunedin. He followed up his decision with a resigned prognostication in his diary: 'Die Zukunft decket/Schmerzen und Glücke/Schrittweis dem Blicke.' ('The future is covered up. Sorrow and happiness wait on each footstep.') What made it all seem worse was that a few days after coming to this decision he went with Maria, the children, Henry, and Blanche to Hurworth, Maria's first visit since the war.

> It was one of the finest days we have had since we have been here, 'the heavens laughed with us in our jubilee'. We went to our place, drank to our next merry meeting in the Awatuna & had dinner on the little hill. After that I dug to find buried crockery until we started to go back but did not hit on the right place.[4] The notion of leaving is worse than ever . . . A glorious day. The Mountain & Bush looking as they only can under a Taranaki sky.[5]

It was not only Arthur who was affected. Lely records, 'it set them all longing to return to the peaceful and primitive life of the bush'.[6] At the end of the month Arthur visited Hurworth by himself to dig, again unsuccessfully, for crockery. The visit was profoundly disturbing: 'The place is as lovely, and perhaps even more quiet and peaceful than in the old days: "over all things

brooding slept the quiet sense of something lost".'⁷ 'Here am I,'
he wrote to Mary Richmond, 'leaving this and a life of joy, and
of work as a part of it, in a mad chase after superior usefulness.'⁸
Nevertheless, plans went ahead for their removal to Dunedin,
possibly with Lely and Alice as well. Arthur took what comfort
he could from thinking that if he stayed at New Plymouth he
would probably fritter his life away, while by going to Dunedin
he would be made to work with some consistency. It was the
mental stimulus of legal studies that he saw as their only value.
He wrote to Harry Atkinson, away at the General Assembly, 'We
have settled that I shall go down to the South Pole next month,
i.e. 25 Sept.'⁹ He would go first to secure a house, and the others
– although there was now some doubt about Lely and Alice –
would follow in two to three months' time.

If Maria had long wished to see Arthur become a lawyer under
William's tutorship, she had hitherto pictured it as happening in
Taranaki, with the mob unbroken and the Hurworth community
flourishing. The move to Dunedin seemed something of a leap in
the dark. There were advantages in leaping. Arthur would have
a profession worthy of his mental agility and precocity. He would
also be able to leave volunteering behind. For all her apparent
sang-froid when Arthur was absent, whether with the volunteers,
travelling among Northland Maori, or, in former days, carrying
the mail, Maria confessed to Mary, who was feeling badly about
being left in Nelson whilst James was away sketching on the West
Coast, that she too often felt lonely and fearful. 'Every night I
used to picture him as either killed, or maimed for life by a fall
from his horse. [Interpolated in Arthur's handwriting] "He hasn't
got a horse to fall from, worse luck".'¹⁰ She foresaw that fighting
must break out again in Taranaki and, as the 'slow-and-do-nothing'
style had been universally condemned, she feared that the next
series of mistakes would be of the 'rash-and-hasty' character. Of
one thing she was certain: if volunteers were called for a bushranging company, Arthur, if still in Taranaki, would be one of
them.

In Dunedin she hoped they would live well on £200 to £250
a year. Arthur's salary, as William had informed them, would most
likely be £150 a year; the Canterbury investment brought in another
£100, and they had already received some money in compensation
for damage to their Hurworth property.¹¹ With that and another
£100 left from Aunt Wright's legacy, they would be able to put
up a 'little box of a house' on land which William had bought

for his own house. Because they were 'Taranakians at heart', she hoped that when Arthur had qualified he would set up in legal practice at New Plymouth and they would return as 'independent gentle folks to improve & beautify our property for our pleasure, not our profit'.[12] The stumbling block to moving south, for Maria, was her concern for Lely. Would her mother's asthmatic condition deteriorate in Dunedin's winter climate? Lely could have remained at Beach Cottage with Henry and Blanche but, as Maria confided to Mary, much as Lely loved Henry, she felt 'so little at home & so little intimate with Blanche & necessary to Blanche that I know she would not be happy left long without your household or ours or Wm's near her'.[13]

In the event, 25 September, Arthur's date for the 'South Pole', came and went with the *Airedale* sailing without him. Two unrelated events had provided him with an excuse for a longer sojourn in his beloved Taranaki. Alice Atkinson's illness had progressed to an alarming stage. Dr Rawson was called in and he pronounced that her heart was now seriously affected and that there was no hope of recovery. All he could do was to provide palliatives. Arthur declared that he would stay both to give his sister the comfort she took in his presence, and to give Maria help with nursing. The other change of circumstance came when Domett, who on 6 August 1862 replaced Fox as leader of government, offered a judgeship to C.W. Richmond. The law practice of Gillies and Richmond was prospering, but William's asthma attacks were much worse. Mrs Bell had reported earlier in the year that he looked 'quite ghastly'. 'Is it not shocking & what is it all for?' Maria wrote in distress to Mary:

> I am quite oppressed by the thought of Wm's killing himself that his family may have wealth. Cannot people learn to live on £100 a year or less if necessary? Surely it is better to be poor than fatherless. I do wish we could stop him before it is too late.[14]

William saw his new office as a judge as a 'harbour or refuge' from the turmoil of private practice. It looked at first as if he might be able to live at Nelson. James wrote to his brother that Judge A.J. Johnston would be willing to exchange the 'Cook's Strait Station' for Dunedin, and that William could then have the option of living either at Nelson or Wellington. It had, however, become established practice for the judge of the 'Middle District' to reside in the latter and William decided against entering into any exchange – much to James and Mary's disgust. Emily predicted that living in Wellington among the supporters of William's recent political opponents – the 'three F's' – would be worse than living in exile in Dunedin, 'for here all the people like us'.[15]

Arthur seized upon William's altered circumstances as a valid reason for postponing his entry to the law. He wrote to his brother-in-law saying that it made all the difference to him whether William, who would spend part of the year on circuit, was to be permanently in Dunedin during the time of his 'servitude':

> Coming to Otago & the law and leaving the tilling of my Happy Valley has appeared to me a rather painful and not always a clear duty. So that if you consent to adorn the Bench with your many virtues, I shall accept it as the decision of Fate, cheerfully.[16]

Arthur's diary reveals that he really regarded fate as an ally: 'It has seemed to lift a burden from my head & leave me freer.' That same afternoon he and Maria walked to the top of the highest hill near the town. 'The furze hedges were delicious & the country looking as it always does, & the thought that I may not have to leave after all made my eye happier & more easily pleased.'[17] As a gesture to the law he continued to improve his Latin by reading Cicero, Ovid, or Virgil before getting breakfast.

Other job opportunities were forthcoming. F.D. Bell was anxious to have Arthur back in the Native Office. Messages to this effect were sent to him by Harry Atkinson and James Richmond, who both thought Bell was about to offer Arthur the editorship, recently relinquished by Walter Buller, of the *Maori Messenger*. It seemed appropriate. Arthur had a real interest in the Maori language and, as Maria told Margaret Taylor, 'has now got a character as almost a *learned* Maori scholar having only been much occupied about the language for two years'.[18] James considered that although the *Messenger* had at the moment a 'wretched reputation' it could under Arthur's guidance become 'a means of acting on the natives equal to anything in our power, and far more efficient than any political organisation that has yet been proposed'.[19] F.D. Bell eventually wrote a vague letter offering Arthur 'dictionary work or something of that sort at Auckland. If I "could come up things should be made pleasant".'[20] Arthur did not see anything at all pleasant in working with Grey, whose reputation was fast sinking among Richmonds and Atkinsons. Furthermore, living in Auckland would involve another sort of exile and 'work among aliens'.

Another proposition, for Arthur and Harry jointly to consider, was a history of the Taranaki War. In the course of the parliamentary session, J.E. FitzGerald asked Harry Atkinson if he would write a history of the war to be published first as a series of articles in the Christchurch *Press* and then as a pamphlet which FitzGerald undertook to have reviewed in *The Times*. Presumably it was intended, in spite of FitzGerald's philo-Maori sentiment, to be a counterblast to the critical, missionary-oriented view of Hadfield and the Auckland coterie of Selwyns, Abrahams, and Martins. Harry discussed it with Arthur who would have been his co-author. The latter was of the opinion that what was wanted was 'another war, not an account of the old one'. If they did go ahead, Arthur considered they would need William's advice on the law of libel. Would strong accusations against the professional competence of Gold and Pratt, even if dressed in 'grave historical language', be libellous or fair criticism? William was no doubt relieved when the project was quietly dropped.

What finally did appeal to Arthur was Henry Richmond's suggestion that he take sole responsibility for editing the *Taranaki Herald*, at least for a period. Henry was heavily engaged in his work as treasurer of the provincial council and in his experiments into the commercial viability of Taranaki's iron sands and 'petroleum springs'. 'Editing and thistling take up all Arthur's time,' Lely wrote to William,

> I suppose it is useless regretting, but it does seem a pity his time and talents should not be devoted to a fixed pursuit. It seems to me that literature is his vocation . . . he writes off a leading article with astonishing facility and with none of the groans of spirit with which James's and Henry's offspring are brought forth.[21]

And later, when Henry had totally made over his involvement with the paper to Arthur, she wrote: 'The editorship seems to sit wonderfully light on Arthur – it gives him a chance of venting his sarcasm upon his less gifted mortals, but I hope and believe he will restrain his propensity within proper limits.'[22]

So there was Arthur varying *The Origin of Species*, Latin authors, and writing for the *Herald* with walks to Hurworth to cut thistles – 'on the whole enjoying myself amazingly'. And there was Maria, attributing her good health to leading such a 'toilsome life', constantly in attendance upon Alice, and snatching what time she could to write scraps of letters before the gun sounded and the mail closed. William and Eliza Atkinson's house, built to the rear and slightly above Beach Cottage, was now finished so that Maria could enjoy something of Eliza's company. The whole household revolved around the sick and dying invalid. A young 'nurse girl', little more than a child herself, and now the only servant at Beach Cottage, minded Edith and Ruth in the daytime,

a situation which was not entirely to their grandmother's
satisfaction:

> I don't think it good for Edith . . . she ought to associate with
> her equals & superiors. It is astonishing how soon she learns to
> look down upon domestics as her inferiors . . . I should think it
> is not inherited from either father or mother.[23]

Lely worried about Maria who in spite of her cheerfulness looked
much thinner and more worn than in Auckland. She was also
expecting another baby.

A passing interlude which caused a brief flutter of excitement
was Annie Smith's engagement to Reginald Broughton, recently
appointed headmaster of Nelson College. Relief mingled with the
customary joy of such tidings, for it seemed that Annie would
not now be lost to New Zealand or to her sister. Broughton was
a classical scholar and a master of Hindustani. Arthur, probably
foreseeing pleasant erudite evenings with the mob's newest member,
wrote to Mary that it was 'most creditable to her to have introduced
so good a scholar into the set . . . We have had plenty of Lawyers,
Judges, Statesmen, Senators, Blacksmiths, Editors, Bushmen and
even professors of modern languages – but a first rate classical
scholar was exactly what we wanted.'[24]

Unfortunately, perhaps fortunately, the engagement lasted for
only ten days. The suitor was described as quiet and gentle,
somewhat nervous, but a thoroughly good and refined young man.
The engagement gave satisfaction to Nelson at large, but Annie's
immediate family, and even Annie herself, were not so sure. James
thought him 'hardly powerful enough for dear Annie'; Aunt Smith,
staying at Nelson with James and Mary, wrote in a 'subdued tone'
of the event, and Annie, who was surprised by Broughton's proposal,
was, once engaged, 'thoroughly wretched'. An obstacle in the way
of future happiness was his formidable aunt, Miss Briggs, who had
long enjoyed the management of the Broughton family and was
not prepared to give up the reins. Mary described her as a 'terribly
active, energetic & wilful person to whom . . . [Broughton] feels
it his duty to give way'.[25] In ten days Annie had been quite unable
'to wean him'. By the end of the year Miss Briggs had succeeded
in removing both Annie and Nelson College from her nephew.
She was determined to spite the governors for 'their unpardonable
offence in shutting her out of the college'. Both aunt and nephew
departed to Canterbury, where Broughton was for a similarly brief
period headmaster of Christ's College before returning to the
seclusion of holy orders in England and a fellowship at an Oxford

college. If Annie and Reginald had prevailed over Miss Briggs, it would have been interesting to follow the mob's endeavour to absorb a tyrant as well as a scholar.

The mob continued to find it difficult to absorb Charlie Wilson, whose passage back to England C.W. Richmond and Lely had paid in 1857. His Yorkshire family were equally at a loss, and when Charlie indicated that he had made a mistake in leaving Taranaki, they sent him back. When war threatened he went to live with his brother, Calvert, a surveyor in Christchurch. At the end of 1861 he threw over the job Calvert had found for him and returned to Taranaki. As most of the mob were then living elsewhere, it was Helen Hursthouse to whom he turned. In a letter to her sister she described him as 'dirty and deplorable'. By the time Maria and her family had returned to Beach Cottage, Charlie had obtained employment as a day labourer. Yet again he was unsettled and went back to Christchurch. This offered no solution. Calvert Wilson was thinking of marriage, and his fiancée's parents found Charlie's presence disturbing. It seems likely that his changes of mood, withdrawal, and abnormal behaviour were indications of schizophrenia. Such a diagnosis, even if possible, would not have helped the situation. To his relatives he was a 'terrible nuisance'. C.W. Richmond again provided temporary relief by paying his passage back to England, reasoning that if he had to be maintained it could be done more cheaply there.

Something that weighed on Maria's mind during Alice's illness was that no one felt equal to the responsibility of telling the young girl of twenty-two who clung so pathetically, so tenaciously, to life that she was dying. Alice had set her mind on visiting James, Mary, and Annie at Nelson, and local doctors said that the voyage would not worsen her condition and might raise her spirits. So Arthur made for her a small bed, which was slung in the ladies' cabin of the *Airedale*, and she, Maria, and infant Ruth went to Nelson for Christmas. Lely returned to Beach Cottage from her sister's place to be a surrogate mother to Edith. Their arrival at Nelson on Christmas Day gave little cause for festivity. The Nelson relatives were shocked by Alice's appearance, and once installed in James and Mary's house she seemed to die by inches. Her death on 4 February 1863 offered the only possible relief from suffering, and this thought softened the final blow to those watching.

Alice's lingering illness and death had pressed upon Maria's spirits. Like so many people who have felt helpless and hopeless in such situations, she wanted some assurance that pain and grief were not purposeless, and longed for 'one glimpse behind the dark veil'. She took comfort in the time-honoured way: 'If our little one arrives safely in August & is as I expect a daughter we shall name it Alice, for I feel sure the dear lost Alice would like Arthur's child to bear her name.'[26] To lighten the gloom in Nelson, excellent news arrived from Taranaki. Blanche, Eliza, and Marion had all survived confinement and their babies too were safe.[27] Mary Richmond decided it was time to revisit her relatives and returned to New Plymouth with Maria, taking Anneliz (Alla) with her as a companion for Edith. Aunt Smith and Annie were still at Nelson to look after James, Maurice, and Dolla.[28] Besides being reunited with Arthur and Edith on 17 February, Maria felt it a great blessing to see 'old Henry's face looking on his little son'.

Mary too was in need of the solace provided by her extended family. When she and James had gone to Nelson at the beginning of 1862, they were still hoping that William's legal practice would be in Nelson and that Arthur might be prevailed upon to come there as well. Their hopes had been raised yet again when it seemed that William might exchange with Judge Johnston, and they were upset when he refused. James, as he told his elder brother, was often 'oppressed with his own difficulties and cares', and he found the work of editing the *Examiner* 'thoroughly distasteful'. He made occasional sketching sorties to the West Coast, leaving Mary worrying about his welfare and overburdening him with reminders to eat sufficiently, not to sleep in wet clothes, and to wear his swimming belt when crossing rivers. In his eagerness to persuade Alfred Domett to become head of the new ministry, which in July 1862 replaced that of William Fox, James had agreed to take on his friend's jobs in Nelson. Domett promptly wished to offload the commissionership of Crown lands, which James then became unwilling to accept, disapproving the political morality of a member of parliament – James still represented Omata – holding a government appointment. He left the decision to Mary, who persuaded him to accept Domett's offer, if only for financial reasons – which pleased James even less. He became commissioner of Crown lands, Nelson, in December 1862. James's unavoidable absences during parliamentary sessions, which he himself found tedious,[29] were sorely regretted by Mary. She had the company of her mother and sister but, like James, yearned for the close kinship of the Hurworth days. The words she wrote to Maria shortly after arriving at Nelson were still apposite at the end of the year:

I cannot get over our being all separated – though there are plenty

of acquaintances & people about, we feel very lonely & cut off
. . . It is a strange & painful thing not to have any second house
to enter where we can see familiar faces & feel ourselves at home.[30]
Mary stayed seven weeks at Beach Cottage. The open country,
the sea, the mountain, horse rides, and excursions all had a most
invigorating effect upon her. There was a ritual expedition by
Arthur, Maria, Mary, Edie, Ruth, Alla, Henry, Blanche, Marion,
Eliza, and all three new-born babies, to Hurworth, where Mary
saw for the first time the wreck of a house which she and James
had left 'so bright and pleasant looking'.

As expected, Edie and Alla, both nearly five, got on well together.
Maria thought Edie had grown in her absence at Nelson and was
now looking 'very handsome' – not so much her face, 'tho that
is not plain or inexpressive but she is so well made & moves so
gracefully. I hope she will be skilful with her hands.'[31] Ruth was
growing satisfactorily fatter and chattered incessantly in a baby-
talk which was unintelligible to anyone but her parents. Beach
Cottage remained crowded; Blanche had not regained her strength
and she and Henry and infant son were still living there, as was
Lely. 'Our house got sorely to sixes and sevens during Blanche's
confinement,' Lely wrote to Emily, '& a good deal lies before
Maria to get it all to rights.'[32] Lely had managed to acquire a
servant in addition to the young nurse girl, but there was still
plenty to do, even for an ageing grandmother:

We are kept pretty busy with children, young people, callers,
washings, cookings, scrubbings, etc – there is little chance that
'my weary age will find the peaceful hermitage' & if discovered
I certainly should not like it . . . I am better situated & more
contented with my lot than the Miss Kings who have quiet to their
hearts' content.[33]

Keeping all to rights was more difficult when, shortly after her
return, Maria went down with influenza. Mary came into her own.

We are still basking in the heavenly atmosphere which surrounds
our blessed Mary – what a paradise would this world be if such
women as she abounded. Now that Maria is poorly, Mary glides
amongst us as a ministering angel.[34]

Mary and Alla returned to Nelson at the beginning of April.
After fourteen weeks of her company, the days seemed flat to
Maria – and even flatter to Arthur. Something happened between
Mary and Arthur towards the end of her stay at New Plymouth.
Before coming to Beach Cottage, Mary had been inclined to see
him simply as a tease – 'another mad letter from Arthur' – but

he and she were cousins, were within a year of each other i
age, and he probably fulfilled a brotherly role which at Nev
Plymouth expanded into that of a confidant. On 26 March, as i
is recorded in Arthur's diary, he, Maria, Mary, and Robert Pitcair
rode to Burton's hill, and on the way, 'Poor Mary talked to m
of her trouble – a ride to be remembered.'[35] The day before sh
went home, Arthur addressed a letter to her at Nelson in whic
he acknowledged that she had entrusted him with her 'innermos
secret'. Arthur recommended that 'with God's help she makes tha
portion of her life as if it had never been'. He quoted Mary a
saying, 'I know my remorse would be incurable if I were to spen
all my life as I have the last few years. It must be dark and wicke
to throw away such love as I have had given me.'[36] Had she bee
once in love with Arthur? Was she out of love with James, jealous
perhaps, of the relationship between him and Annie? James, a
his sister, mother, and brothers well knew, could be difficult t
live with. He was twelve years older than Mary, and when on
recollects some of his advice to his young wife – 'don't fidget'
'don't fuss', 'I do wish you could get stout and tranquil darling
– and the regularity with which he dwelt on the fact that they
would be able to enjoy each other's company only at intervals
one wonders if he was ever fully in sympathy with her. Whateve
transpired on that ride to Burton's hill, the bond between Arthu
and Mary became very much stronger, and also included Maria
If nineteenth-century marriages were seldom probed to the bar
bone, were often fudged with conventional morality, they did or
the whole preserve a constancy which may, of course, have simply
reflected the limitations of a woman's freedom. But the historian's
plumbline is always inadequate; one must simply record. The
friendship between Mary, Arthur, and Maria prospered, and there
was a steady flow of letters from Arthur to Mary in which the
bantering tone seems to conceal a mild flirtation. Genuine affection
between all three was not at risk, and Maria on occasion inveigled
Mary's aid as 'the only person I know who can get Arthur to
change his mind' – once it was made up.

Arthur was fond of repeating Jeremiah's warning to the people
of Judah who had foolishly cried Peace, Peace, when there was
no peace. In Taranaki in 1862 few among either Maori or Pakeha
would have so described the uneasy stalemate which followed the
truce of April 1861. William Halse, Crown land commissioner at
New Plymouth, reported to Harry Atkinson in a series of letters

about the state of the province. 'Our native news is darkening,' he wrote in June; the following month he wrote that Taranaki and Ngati Ruanui, who had had the better of the early fighting, were 'most hostile'. To the south of New Plymouth, Tataraimaka was held forfeit for Waitara, and there supporters of the Maori King set up a toll gate, beyond which no Pakeha, or Maori employed by Pakeha, could go without paying. Taranaki would not allow improvements to be made on the road to Waireka and were prepared to resist any road-building south of it. It was rumoured that they were also about to cut a line from Mangaone through the bush to Waireka beyond which Pakeha were not go to. This, if carried out, would effectively cut off most of the bush settlements, including Hurworth. On the other hand, Grey's stated intention of building roads in preparation for Pakeha settlement and, in particular, a military road south of Auckland into the Waikato, was interpreted as preparation for a renewal of fighting and cast doubt on the genuineness of his peacemaking and his fostering of local self-government through tribal runanga. Halse reported that conditions among the settlers were 'deplorable'. Many people who had been too independent to ask favours of government were feeling the pressure of the continued expense involved in living in New Plymouth away from their farms. 'Our most substantial and thrifty men [are] coming in, as the shoe pinches, for rations.'[37] There was an angry reaction at New Plymouth when the governor, at the opening of parliament, failed to express any sympathy for the plight of the Taranaki settlers in his speech.

Neither Arthur nor Maria put any trust in Grey's attempt to pacify Maori. They saw him as two-faced, intent on making cat's paws of his advisers.[38] Maria could not understand William's current advice to hold aloof from politics; she saw his detachment as 'just the way to make a mess of everything [by counselling] our best men to leave public affairs to the fools & knaves'.[39] She judged Grey's early peace-seeking overtures to be 'mollycoddling natives':

> Arthur compares Sir George Grey's present style . . . to the attempt to induce a spoilt child to take rhubarb by *first* administering a spoonful of sugar & then saying, 'Now do take the rhubarb because it is good for you.' . . . Plenty of blackmail *may* keep the peace for Sir George Grey's time, but woe to his unlucky successor who may not be allowed to put his hand so far into John Bull's pocket.[40]

Before her return to Taranaki from Auckland, Maria was of the opinion that 'really clever, honest men' working as lay missionaries could educate the Maori people. 'It needs a peculiar talent & an intimate knowledge of the character & language to influence the Maoris.'[41]

Not one shot had been fired in anger since the truce negotiations, and one shot, it was believed, would restart the war. 'The beginning of the end' was foreseen when the steamer *Lord Worsley* was wrecked a few miles south of Cape Egmont on 1 September 1862. When news reached New Plymouth, a small unarmed reconnaissance party led by Robert Parris and including Colonel Warre set off for the wreck but was turned back at 'the gate'. This rebuff caused 'much excitement & great hope' in the town that the rescue mission planned by Warre for the following day 'would see something done at last'. There was considerable anxiety about the shipwrecked passengers who had already been cut off from New Plymouth for five days and who, wrote Arthur in the *Herald*, were 'entirely at the mercy of the natives in a British colony fifty miles from a garrison town'.[42] There was thus both surprise and mortification when it was learned that the 'disaffected natives' themselves were bringing up the remaining passengers (women and children had already been taken to Tataraimaka to be brought up from there by surfboat) to New Plymouth. Arthur Atkinson was on hand when the bullock train came into town.

> Settling accounts was going on & distribution of food. It was curious to see these fellows whom we have been trying to knock on the head industriously, for two years, & who have tried with equal industry to knock us on the head, here in the midst of us. They have constantly defied our authority (i.e. of the law) & show no signs of any intention to abandon their old custom, & before long we shall possibly be at each others throats again, but there was nothing like ill feeling shown & everything was settled quietly.[43]

Three days later, Arthur and Robert Parris rode out to Mataitawa, Waitara, to see the Maori King's flag raised there on the anniversary of the accession of Te Wherowhero (King Potatau I). Given the flash point of Maori–Pakeha relations – Halse had written that 'a spark may kindle' them – it could have been a risky venture. Instead, Parris and Atkinson were treated as honoured guests. 'We went into a whare & sat in state receiving men of the place who came in one at a time to shake hands. A great many of them hongi'd with Parris & seemed very glad to see him.'[44] All the Maori leaders spoke temperately and there was not the least incivility shown the Pakeha visitors. But there was no mistaking the message they received: 'Heoi ano te kupu ko te kingi te oneone – All that is to be said is, the king & the land.'[45]

Coming back Parris said what I think to a great extent is true, that the Natives as a whole are happier than we are. There is no doubt their minds are more equable than ours . . . Their contentment with a little is a lesson to us . . . Going among [them] commonly makes me want to help in saving them, but it is not possible.[46]

At the end of December 1862, Arthur was again sworn in as a volunteer, 'No. 2 Company of course'. The following March, Grey landed with General Cameron at New Plymouth, where the disgruntled settlers, assembled on the beach, received him in total silence. Grey looked ill, Arthur thought, and Lely, who later met him, described him as a 'sadly shattered man'.[47]

Alfred Domett, who arrived later with Native Minister Bell, was proving a sorry disappointment to the mob. He had long held a high regard for C.W. Richmond's family, especially for Lely, and that regard had been reciprocated. Maria and Arthur had enjoyed Domett's frequent visits to William and Emily's house at Parnell, and had listened to him reading from his favourite poets. Maria had often attended the General Assembly at Auckland and had been captivated by Domett's speeches: 'It was impossible to see him stand up like an old lion in the House, & hear his voice ring out so richly on the right side, & imagine that he could do otherwise when he acted than take the upward & straightforward course.'[48] When Domett replaced Fox, Arthur expressed the consensus of the mob when he wrote, 'we shall have again a Ministry that will not disgrace our country'. The only doubt was his wife's ability to measure up to the social eminence of her husband's position. Domett, however, had not been keen to become leader – he was 'dragged to his duty at last,' wrote Lely – and J.C. Richmond told William that from the very beginning of Domett's acceptance of office, he had had a hard job in keeping him up to the mark: 'He has been on the point of resigning ever since he was in. He cordially hates his job and I cordially pity him.'[49]

Domett sympathised with the plight of the Taranaki settlers and wished to see them re-established on their farms if this could be done 'without producing a general commotion or *war*'.[50] This was altogether too indecisive and quiescent for the mob. Maria, who came to doubt whether Domett had, in politics, ever been more than a figure of sentiment, wrote to Margaret Taylor:

Unfortunately Mr Domett in spite of his fine intellect seems quite unfit to be helmsman in times of difficulties like these . . . a limp will, love of ease & a quiet life overbalance Mr D's other fine qualities & his Ministry will fall to pieces.[51]

While he was at New Plymouth, Domett occasionally called at Beach Cottage. Lely found him 'just as winning as ever' and failed to see why he now caused so much disappointment when his 'lotus eating propensities were no secret'. But she too deplored his lack of political motivation: 'He never actually reads a newspaper from sheer idleness and has come down here comparatively ignorant of the state of affairs.'[52]

Domett slid quietly out of political leadership at the end of October 1863. James, who had earlier 'bullied' his friend into taking office, commented on his departure: 'His was always an incoherent ministry, he had not purpose or belief enough in what he was about to hold others together, and the others with him are not large-minded men.'[53] An interim ministry of five, led by Whitaker as 'first minister' and, surprisingly, including William Fox as colonial secretary, took over. The uniting factor, apart from executive experience, was that all of them, Fox included, now detested Grey's double dealing. Harry Atkinson expressed his satisfaction to Arthur about the strength of will in the new ministry. Harry himself was a rising star in the House, winning renown through his clear and decisive manner. Domett had wished to have him in command of a colonial defence force of mounted men, each hand-picked for character, physique, and daring, which would spearhead any future government force engaged in subduing 'rebel' Maori. Grey, however, refused to countenance such a strong-willed, non-establishment military leader who, according to Maria, was the governor's 'peculiar aversion'.[54] Maria had thought at the time of the ministerial reshuffle that Harry might become 'War Minister', not so much for his military prowess as for his 'sanguine temperament': 'He is so much less anxious by nature than my own brothers.'[55] By the same token she did not wish James to accept any ministerial responsibility:

> I . . . should be sorry to see James in the harassing position of a Minister in these times unless he had a much finer constitution & stronger digestion; besides a constant contact with Grey would permanently depress his spirits, not at any time too high.[56]

The Richmond–Atkinson influence was not without effect at provincial level. Even Charles Brown, many times superintendent of Taranaki, was now 'behaving very sensibly': 'He almost always takes advice with our "mob" before committing any important public act and Henry composes or at all events, revises most of his written acts.'[57]

The arrival of Governor Grey, Cameron, Domett, and Bell at New Plymouth in March had signified a firming up of government resolve to pursue a policy of simultaneously preparing for war and making overtures of peace. Men of the 57th began repairing the road to, and the stockade at, Omata. On 19 March the *Harrier* brought 200 of the 70th from Auckland, and later in the month the *Airedale* arrived with artillery and horses. The volunteers were called out and marched off to the Waiwakaiho bridge with their guns unloaded. Arthur put a paragraph about this in the *Herald* and the volunteers were immediately struck off duty. Towards the end of March news came from the Waikato that Wiremu Kingi Te Rangitake, Rewi, and a party of Maniapoto had dismantled John Gorst's printing press at Otawhao (Te Awamutu). Grey had sent Gorst there as civil commissioner and he had begun printing a paper in opposition to that of the Maori King. This incident presaged the first drops of the coming storm.

On 4 April troops from New Plymouth took unopposed possession of Tataraimaka, deserted by settlers for three years and claimed by southern Maori by right of conquest. It was known but scarcely acknowledged by Taranaki settlers that the mediation of Wiremu Tamihana, which was crucial to the truce of April 1861, had been secured on the promise of an official investigation into the legality of the uncompleted Waitara purchase. It was also known to Grey, although Parris thought it could be done safely, that any attempt to reoccupy Tataraimaka without investigating and probably conceding the disputed Waitara block would be interpreted by the more extreme elements of the King movement, both in Waikato and Taranaki, as a just cause for the renewal of fighting.

The next two events happened within days of each other. On 4 May, two officers and six men of the 57th were ambushed and killed by a party of Taranaki at the mouth of the Wairau stream as they made their way back from Tataraimaka. On 12 May, a proclamation was issued at New Plymouth announcing that the purchase of the Waitara block was abandoned and all claim to it renounced henceforth by the government. The following day the garrison stationed there came away. Arthur Atkinson had been aware that, as he put it, 'underhand work' was going on over Waitara. Te Teira[58] had been asked by Grey whether he had not been bribed to offer the block of land. Grey was also convinced that C.W. Richmond's support for Te Teira's offer was because he (Richmond) had somehow acquired land at Waitara.[59] It was clear from Grey's cursory investigation that he had made up his

mind that the disputed Waitara block was to be returned to Te
Ati Awa, and this decision he forced on his ministers. Most bitter
pill for the mob was the fact that Domett's name was affixed
to the proclamation after Grey's. With sarcasm concealing the anger
he felt at this 'monstrous act', Arthur wrote in the *Herald*:

> Sir George Grey has not been very successful hitherto in his efforts
> .. for the reinstatement of Taranaki, but he has at last succeeded
> in reinstating a portion of the inhabitants; and we suppose he has
> chosen the most deserving to begin with – the leaders in the late
> rebellion – William King's people of Mataitawa, whom he has just
> put back upon land they occupied before the war . . . *Waitara has*
> *been given up, and without investigation.*
>
> It was said of one of the greatest of oriental chess players that
> no one could ever foresee his coming move or discern the object
> of it when it was made. And this is partly true of Sir G. Grey.[60]

The general settler reaction was that the surrender of Waitara,
coming just a week after the 'brutal massacre' of the soldiers, would
be understood by Te Ati Awa, Taranaki, and Ngati Ruanui as
'abject fear' on the part of the Pakeha. An entry in Arthur's diary
supports this view:

> 16 May 1863. I had a most important conversation with Paora of
> Mataitawa this morng. I asked him whether now that Waitara was
> given up the trouble was ended, as that was said to be the root
> of it all?
>
> He hesitated a little at first & then said,
>
> 'No, it isn't over yet.'
>
> I asked him what was the cause (take) of the murders last week?
>
> He said 'Waitara'.
>
> 'Well', I said, 'if the Govr. goes down to seek payment for his
> dead (from Taranaki) what shall you do?' *'We shall go & help them*
> *(Taranaki) because we are one.'* He said: 'We asked the Govr. to give
> us Waitara & he would not . . . But when he heard of these murders
> he said (here he gasped once or twice to show the Govr's state
> of mind) 'Ah! I must give up Waitara.'[61]

The Taranaki Militia and Volunteer Rifles were now back on
active service; this time with guns loaded. Arthur's long-cherished
dream of a highly motivated, mobile band of bushrangers was
favoured by General Cameron. This guerrilla force ('gorillas' was
the preferred spelling) was drawn from the Rifle Volunteers. Most
of those who came forward were from Captain Harry Atkinson's
No. 2 company, and he became the commanding officer of one
band of fifty men. The second group of forty was made up of
volunteers from the other Rifle companies, and was under the

command of Captain F.L. Webster. The Bushrangers, as they came
to be called, made expeditions into the surrounding countryside
three or four times a week in search of 'rebel' Maori, who proved
elusive. Maria dreaded the risk and Arthur enjoyed himself, even
if it sometimes meant marching from six to eight hours with rifle,
revolver, sixty rounds of ammunition, and greatcoat. On most
occasions his sixty rounds were carried back unused: the only shots
fired were from two or three of his companions who 'wanted to
make sure their guns would go off'. This prudence contrasted with
the more profligate attitude of the regular soliders who 'fired a
great deal on the principle that it is enough to carry the ammunition
out without carrying it back again'.[62]

On 12 July 1863 General Cameron, with a large force of British
regulars and colonial irregulars, crossed the Mangatawhiri and
invaded Waikato. While the main thrust of the fighting continued
in that region, British troops, apart from the 57th, were withdrawn
from Taranaki. At the end of June, Tataramaika was again
abandoned and the soldiers there were brought closer to New
Plymouth. Arthur had no objection to the departure of the troops,[63]
but he heard 'with sorrow' that they had taken all four Armstrong
guns. For the 'ruinous price' of £14, he bought his own Schneider
rifle in case the breech-loading carbines with which the Bushrangers
had been issued were taken for the Auckland cavalry.

The defence of the settlement now rested upon the 57th Regiment
under Colonel Warre, who was commander-in-chief at Taranaki,
and upon the militia and volunteers, with the Bushrangers serving
as an advance scouting party. Warre, a regular army officer, could
be testy about the often casual appearance of the Bushrangers.
On one occasion, as they were about to set off on one of their
'search and destroy' missions,[64] he abused them for forty minutes,
calling them, among other things, 'a rabble, not to be trusted in
any post of honour'. He later apologised but, as was the way of
British commanding officers, gave little satisfaction to the settler-
soldiers. On another occasion he asked Arthur the purpose of the
Bushrangers' rifle practice:

> I said to teach the men the use of their weapons. 'But you don't
> mean to say you aim at a Maori when you shoot?'
>
> I told him that I had not often shot at a Maori but I had never
> shot at one without aiming & aiming well too & I should not think
> myself fit to go out if I did not.[65]

On 26 August the *Geelong* arrived from the Australian colonies
with 120 military settlers, attracted by the promise of land grants,

to take over the confiscated Oakura block. The following month, fifty Otago men were put with Harry Atkinson's Bushrangers and a similar number with the other company. 'Some of them we walked off their legs,' Arthur wrote of their first expedition with them; 'No. 1 [Company] abandoned some of theirs.' Grace Hirst was one who found little comfort or security in this increased military presence at New Plymouth: 'everything seems to have a military flash that I do not like,' she wrote. Young men lounged about; young ladies reacted to them 'with so much levity', and, all in all, New Plymouth was so filled up with 'indifferent characters – the overpluss of the diggings that we seem to be more afraid of the white man than the Maorie'.[66]

Arthur was only twice involved in actual fighting during 1863. He wrote of one engagement that after he had built his breastwork of gorse and clods, 'I lay basking in the sun thinking what a curious state of things it was, getting up to have a shot when I heard of anything attractive.'[67] Although he was esteemed in the settler community as a Maori scholar, as 'one of the best lawyers in N.P.', and for his journalism,[68] and although he was an enthusiastic Bushranger, he was never more than a private. Arthur commented on this himself: 'I am in no way a leader of men as witness the fact that after 8 or 9 years service I do not even hold a corporal's commission.'[69] The volunteers chose their own officers and NCOs. It is very likely that his companions never understood and were somewhat in awe of him. He did not tolerate fools either gladly or patiently; his remarks were often too oblique for his listeners – as he wrote once to William, 'The substance of what I say is serious though the surface of it looks only absurd.'[70] He was often wholly wrapped in his own thoughts, preferred walking by himself when out with the Bushrangers, and was not given to making quick decisions. He also had a stammer which was later to cause him some embarrassment in the provincial council and General Assembly. In November, Charles Brown was looking for someone to take over the superintendency; Arthur reported the conversation: 'Harry [Atkinson, deputy superintendent] would not do because he is a military man as well as I am; (speaking to me) your wife might do, but you wouldn't because you say such nasty things to people.'[71]

The second stage of the war in Taranaki posed no real threat to New Plymouth itself, although this was not apparent to the women whose husbands were out with the Bushrangers or stationed at one of the military outposts. Many would have felt as lonely and fearful as Eliza Atkinson did when William was at the Omata camp.

I have to endure my alarms the best way I can. It is very lonely having Will away at the camp . . . It is fearful to think of the mischief they [Maori] might do if they came on a blowy night & set one's house on fire. It would blaze through the town & the confusion would be awful. I have made up my mind to rush down to the Beach Stone Cottage in case of an attack, as that is bullet & fireproof & only a few steps off.[72]

Her sister, Marion Atkinson, with her servant, Elizabeth, decided to sleep in the same room and get under the bed in case of alarm. 'It makes me feel sick and ill when I think of the anxiety before us,'[73] Eliza wrote on seeing the men in the settlement once again in arms. As people crowded back within the entrenched area, the main danger to the town came from epidemics of scarlet fever, diphtheria, and typhus. Every available building was made use of; in some dwellings only canvas partitions separated family from family. Maria was glad of her own pleasant house with its open space all around. Now that Arthur had at least temporarily shelved 'the law', and it was likely that he and Maria would stay in Taranaki, improvements were made to Beach Cottage so that it could more adequately accommodate the two families – Henry, Blanche, and infant son as well as Arthur, Maria, and daughters. A lean-to was added to the kitchen, the existing kitchen became the dining room and playroom, and a new bedroom for Henry and Blanche was added to the dining–playroom area. The cost of £100 was partly paid by Henry out of compensation money. When the additions were completed, Lely (who had been living with Helen Hursthouse since Maria's return from Nelson) moved in and, in August 1863, bought Beach Cottage from William for £500. It was to be her permanent home – so long as Maria and Arthur stayed in Taranaki.

Maria's pregnancy was proceeding smoothly and her domestic arrangements were improving. She acquired a servant who was strong and bore a good character for cleanliness and honesty, but she was not blessed with an even temper. 'However we must put up with her if possible for Maria's sake,' Lely wrote to Emily, I have long been uneasy at the laborious life she is leading.'[74] Maria now had more time for her own amusements – reading, writing, embroidery, and playing the piano. She particularly enjoyed Beethoven's waltzes. Edith was also fond of music and Maria wanted her to be taught by Mrs S.P. (Mary) King, in her opinion the best music teacher in the colony.[75] Mary King's sister-in-law, Martha, had given up her school at the end of 1862 in favour of keeping fowls and pigs, leaving displaced pupils, such as Edith was about to become, with nowhere else suitable to go. Fortunately Edith and her grandmother had a strong affection for each other, and Edie had no difficulty in accepting Lely as her teacher as well as her 'best friend'.

Maria was certain that in August she would have her fourth daughter (the stillborn Margaret was always counted as the first) and had warned Arthur accordingly. The births of Henry and Blanche's son and of James and Mary's fourth, Richard Hutton Richmond, on 1 July, seemed to lengthen the odds for a son. Henry's boy, Francis, 'always knows himself to be a son & heir,' wrote Maria, '& like other babies of his valuable sex takes three times the attention insignificant girls require.'[76]

On 5 August 1863, after midday dinner, Arthur went for Mrs Wakefield, the midwife, and Dr Rawson. He left with some foreboding; as had happened at her first confinement, Maria was a fortnight early, and her waters had broken twenty-four hours before birth took place. However, his diary entry for the day contains the simple understatement: 'at ¼ to 5 my son was born.' The pronoun was totally possessive – not Maria's, not ours, but 'my', and carrying the triumph further, he wrote to William and Emily: 'Think of my having achieved a son at last.' With some wry amusement Mary Richmond also wrote to Emily: '. . . a son at last. Fancy Arthur's exultation. I trust now that he possesses the coveted treasure he will not so exaggerate its value as he has done in past days.'[77] To Maria also the child was a great joy. She had gone into labour thinking that a loss like the one she had suffered in July 1856 awaited her at the end of pain. Instead, lying asleep beside her, was a living healthy boy. Arthur wanted to call him Alfred, but here Maria prevailed: 'I thought I must have a young Arthur in case the horrid war should take away my old Arthur', so Arthur Richmond Atkinson he became – a name soon shortened, with the customary penchant for diminutives, to 'Arfie'.

As usual Maria had plenty of milk and, as usual, after three weeks she was going about 'as strong as ever I was in my life'. She wrote to Margaret, 'No one who is happy enough to do as well as I do [Maria was thirty-nine], need look forward with dread to a confinement.'[78] One voice of tragi-comedy comes through. Edie, inclined to stand on her dignity, did not approve of the pillar-to-post treatment meted out to the eldest, following the precipitate arrival of her youngest sibling: '"This is a hollow day indeed!"', she said to Lely, "One day I dined dinner with Aunt Helen, one day I dined dinner with Aunt Eliza & now I sleep with Granny".'[79]

In addition to a son, Maria had also gained, a little before the former's arrival, 'a really good, active, clever, methodical servant; if only we can retain her services'. She was a 'very pretty' (which was ominous) young widow, married at fifteen and widowed at twenty. The household also included a 'strong young girl' to help Blanche, who was still poorly, and to assist with the general housework. Maria thought it 'rather extravagant to have so many helps' and looked on the arrangement as temporary. It meant that she was no longer so tied to the house and could enjoy a 'good walk along the beach'.

The birth of a son caused 'the law', never entirely quiescent in Arthur's mind, to press its claims more assiduously. 'If Maria . . . bears me only girls,' he had previously told William, 'I have only half a motive for pursuing an intricate and costly study.'[80] Once again plans-for-the-future became the engrossing topic at Beach Cottage. In spite of the arrival of a son and heir, of Maria's wish for Arthur to become a lawyer, and of Arthur's own feeling that he ought to be settled into a career, the scale was still tipped towards 'Taranaki & joy'. Maria had to admit that as yet Arthur's health and spirits had only been improved by his three or four expeditions a week with the guerrilla band. Furthermore, 'joy' was now compounded with duty. As editor of the *Herald* and as correspondent to the Nelson *Examiner* and Auckland *Southern Cross*, Arthur was considered valuable to the Taranaki settlers' cause. Lely wrote to Emily after Arthur's leader on the loss of Waitara: 'It would be a public loss for Arthur to leave Taranaki now, there is no one here capable of writing such forcible yet temperate & clear articles.'[81] Harry, for the same reason, did not wish his brother to leave, and even Maria had conceded, in May, that as Arthur 'takes such an active & *I* think useful part in all public matters, I think he ought to be here'. She wondered if he could be articled to a lawyer in New Plymouth rather than Dunedin and, in so doing, avoid the further difficulty entailed in uprooting Lely from her newly acquired Beach Cottage. William and Emily kept urging removal. It seemed to them imprudent for so many married men of the mob[82] to be engaged in guerrilla fighting. They also thought New Plymouth, with its crowded quarters and dubious military settlers, not a fit place for Lely.

At the end of August 1863, yet another factor entered the argument. Richard Pheney, editor and proprietor of the *Herald*'s rival, the *Taranaki News*, wished to sell the paper, and Harry Atkinson

was prepared to buy it in order to put Arthur in as editor. At
the same time, G.W. Woon, proprietor and printer of the *Herald*,
was thinking of taking a partner, and Arthur as his editor was
the obvious choice. 'Horrible perplexity' now descended on the
Beach Cottage household. Even Edie threw in her small spanner.
Urging her father not to go to Dunedin, she reasoned, 'I know
you will be a judge & not a talker to me any more.' Nevertheless,
while Arthur remained undecided about what he *ought* to do for
the future, there was no doubt that, for the present, he was attached
to his Taranaki life and would seek, as in 1862, any excuse to
stay. Maria, although acknowledging Arthur's 'usefulness' to
Taranaki, still thought legal studies was the right course for him,
and was prepared for Arthur to go to Dunedin alone. September
was fixed upon as the time of decision.

The excuse Arthur seized upon was twofold. He feared, and
Henry backed him up, that the preliminary general knowledge
examination was beyond his present capacity and that, although
a bachelor might qualify as a lawyer in three years, a married
man in a small house with children would find study very difficult
– 'they did not *say* with an elderly wife', Maria commented, 'but
perhaps they thought it'.[83] William rightly called Arthur's excuse
a nonsense. The entrance exam was well within the capabilities
of any candidate with a 'liberal education': 'Have you any reason
to think your capacity is below the average? If I might judge from
the tone of the editorials in the T.H. I should say the writer . . .
does not so judge of himself, nor has any reason so to judge.'[84]

Arthur, however, appeared to have made up his mind to stay
in Taranaki. Maria was greatly disappointed. She felt that he had
given up the opportunity for a 'settled, useful, & honourable career
in which he would have been sure of a livelihood and in all
probability would have become much more serviceable to his fellow
colonists' than he was ever likely to be as a Bushranger-cum-
journalist, or as a bush farmer.

> It would be a great satisfaction to me to feel sure that Ar's grounds
> for abandoning the attempt to qualify himself in three years were
> *sound*. I cannot say anything against his decision because *he* will
> have the work to do . . . I feel tolerably certain that he makes
> too much of the domestic difficulties in the way of studying hard
> . . . How much love of bush-ranging & of his breech-loading carbine,
> & a strong & natural interest in closely watching the course of
> the struggle now going on in this Island, may have to do with
> his decision it would probably be hard for him, & is hard for me

to say. All I can do is to try & reconcile myself & believe it may eventually prove the best course for us all.[85]

Maria may have been disappointed that she had had to give up, as she facetiously put it, 'her ambitions & worldly schemes' for 1863, but she was still confident and hopeful. The year had also seemed to augur well for Helen Hursthouse. In April her niece, Nora Stephenson Smith, was married to Captain Gorton of the 57th. Aunt Helen lent her home to the newly weds for their honeymoon and spent the week after the wedding at Beach Cottage. Then, later in April, Helen's youngest daughter, twenty-year-old Kate, who was staying at the home of Mrs Charles Taylor, formerly Lely's protegée Bessie Domett[86] in Auckland, was suddenly struck down with typhus fever and died on 1 June 1863. Maria could scarcely believe the news when it reached New Plymouth. Kate had been so strong, able to lift Alice out of bed with ease; she was so pretty and lively, so fond of gaiety and the attentions of the young officers, and, most poignant to Maria, so young. Maria feared that for all her aunt's fortitude and stoicism she would not be able to rise from this blow. Kate had been her pride and joy. What made it even harder for Helen was that the road between her home in Poverty Square and Beach Cottage was so clogged with mud as to be impassable for elderly pedestrians, and Lely was unable to visit her.

Towards the end of July, Helen and her two sons, Charles Wilson and Flinders, left Poverty Square and moved into a pleasant house close to Beach Cottage. Here, wrote Lely, her sister was once more 'industriously fulfilling her duties' while awaiting news from Auckland of the arrival of her third grandchild. On 27 July, Nellie Macdonald gave birth to her second child, Norman. Just over six weeks later, news reached New Plymouth that Nellie was dead.[87] Since her son's birth she had suffered from abscessed breasts; the infection spread, and she died after a respiratory collapse. This time her mother appeared to be resigned to the news. From the time of her marriage Helen Hursthouse's life had never been easy and, with some justification, she was inclined to view the future with foreboding. After losing Kate she had had a premonition of another death, but her fears were for her two sons, out with the Bushrangers. To neither Helen Hursthouse nor Maria did orthodox religion give much consolation; indeed, it only increased the perplexity. If only faith were compatible with mental integrity; if only one knew for sure that a young person's death would lead him or her to a happier fulfilment. Helen wrote:

it is very strange – everyone says to you, death is a benefit to the departed, yet everyone grieves when it occurs in his own circle . . . Oh that I could be *certain* of knowing all my dear ones again . . . but I cannot feel certainty – and I suppose this is very wicked to add to my troubles.[88]

Maria took a more sceptical view: 'I fear I am very earthy & materialistic in my affections, for the thought of the decay & entire loss of the *form* of those I have loved is very painful.'[89] Nellie's husband agreed to let Helen Hursthouse look after her grandson until he was one year old; then, as it transpired, he reclaimed him, leaving Helen – and Norman – once more bereft.

A salutary observation can be made at this point. Not one of the Hurworth men who, as members of the militia and volunteers, are commemorated along with the imperial troops and kupapa on hatchments in St Mary's church, New Plymouth, was killed or even wounded during the wars of the sixties in Taranaki. But death frequently came, unhonoured and unsung, to the Hurworth women and their young children through the hazards of childbirth and disease. The hazards were accepted as a normal part of a woman's lot; Adam and Eve have cast a long shadow.[90] When Emily, who was again pregnant in 1863 with her sixth child, complained of pains in her back and legs, Lely admonished her:

I cannot understand your constitution being exhausted by child bearing & raising. There has always been a reasonable space between the births of your children [about a two-year gap] & none of them have depended for any long period *wholly* upon you for sustenance, and child bearing & raising being the *natural occupation* of women, ought not, one would think, to wear them out prematurely.[91]

Emily and William's fourth daughter, Alice, was born in Dunedin on 10 September. Her parents had just moved into their new house, 'Highlawn', built 'in the Italian style' and sanded outside to look like stone. It stood on two acres, and land and house had cost the 'fearful sum' of £4,000. William was finding his workload easier but he did not care either for being 'judged' everywhere, or for sitting with 'horsehair' on his head, 'cautioning and chastizing and reprehending'. It was too easy, he felt, to lose his identity amidst all the pomp and circumstance which surrounded him.

At the end of November, Lely, at Emily's pressing invitation, left Beach Cottage to spend some months in the 'beautiful and commodious' house in Dunedin. She took Edie with her. Arthur was reluctant to part with his lively, intelligent little daughter,

with whom he had a very close bond, but Maria wanted her six-
year-old to get to know her cousins and, in their presence, to
become a little more subdued.

> She is very wild & shouts habitually & is a tremendous manager,
> but I hope having three cousins older can improve her in this respect.
> She is a curious little puss, with immense fondness for dress, &
> a good deal of innate coquetry & much inclined to haughtiness
> – but also affectionate & helpful.[92]

Maria once admitted to Mary Richmond that she had not a grain
of confidence in her own powers of dealing 'rightly' with her child.
It is possible that the very strong companionship between Arthur
and Edith, which made a mockery of the former's affirmations
that boys were the desirable sex, resulted partly from a certain
diffidence on Maria's part towards her eldest daughter as she grew
older.

Meanwhile it appeared that Arthur was prepared to negotiate
a partnership with Woon in the *Herald*, Pheney having declined
Harry Atkinson's offer for the *News*. On 8 October he went to
Nelson to consult with Charles Elliott, proprietor of the *Examiner*.
Elliott considered that a half share of the *Herald* would be worth
between £200 and £250. While at Nelson, Arthur also talked with
William Adams of the legal firm, Adams and Kingdon. Adams
was willing to take him on for three years without premium, but
also without salary for the first year and for £75 for the second.
Arthur decided to confer with Maria. Mary Richmond was reluctant
to let him go, feeling, as was the case, that he would 'escape'
altogether.

Arthur came back from Nelson with a scheme which involved
his going into Adams' office for two years, and then going to
Dunedin for a finishing year. There is no specific comment from
Maria; by now she must have become inured to plans and changes
of plan. Harry was still opposed to his brother's leaving Taranaki
and, after resuming his expeditions with the Bushrangers, Arthur
himself was again caught up in that province.

Christmas 1863 was sombre, as it seemed to have been since
the Hurworth days. Alice, Kate, and Nellie were gone for ever,
and Lely and 'noisy little Edie' were absent. Arthur resumed his
negotiations with Woon and he was fairly confident that in the
new year they would be partners in the *Herald*. His continuing
determination to go out with the Bushrangers, however, was a
nagging worry to Maria. Gone were the days when she confidently
imagined that the 'British lion' would quickly and easily subdue

rebellious natives with British steel. One prefers the realism with
which she now regarded the conflict:

> I sometimes feel that I must be made of stone to take as calmly
> as I do the perpetual risks Arthur is running. I am quite alive to
> them, & as each new risk begins I wonder whether it will find
> me a widow at its close. Still I am not miserable with anxiety.
> I have tried my best to get Arthur away to Dunedin to study the
> law . . . [but] I see Arthur's whole heart is in this business of getting
> the North Island pacified . . . He feels it such a clear and simple
> duty to do his best by sharing the risks, and doing the work necessary
> to bring the war to a close. I am afraid my patriotism takes the
> cowardly form of the most earnest desire to prolong his life for
> the good of the country and his fellow colonists including myself
> and our family.[93]

.C. Richmond's sister, Maria, is the 'Seated Girl' of his pencil drawing, dated 841. She would have been seventeen. *Parliamentary Library, Wellington*

Maria and her mother, Lely Richmond, on the eve of their departure for New Zealand, 1852. *Alexander Turnbull Library (79220½)*

'. . . that thin earnest face . . .' Harriet Gore Browne's description of C.W. (William) Richmond. *Alexander Turnbull Library (C6553)*

J.C. (James) Richmond at the time of his marriage to Mary Smith, August 1856. From *The Richmond–Atkinson Papers, Vol. 1*

Henry Richmond who, of all the original members of the mob, felt he had not realised his full potential in New Zealand. *Taranaki Museum Collection*

Mary Richmond, James's wife and Maria's dearest New Zealand friend. 'A pearl above price', but the pearl was too easily shattered. *Jinny Atkinson Collection*

Emily Richmond (née Atkinson), who married William in 1852. From *The Richmond–Atkinson Papers, Vol. 1*

Helen Hursthouse, Lely Richmond's sister, in later life. For Helen New Zealand was a hard, demanding and perhaps always alien land. *Taranaki Museum Collection*

Maria's confidante, Margaret Taylor. *Jinny Atkinson Collection*

'French's house as it appeared when H.[enry] & I took possession May 1851.' This cottage, enlarged and improved, became New Merton, the Richmonds' first home on the outskirts of New Plymouth. 'Bird's Nest', Maria and Arthur's one-roomed cottage, was adjacent to it. *Alexander Turnbull Library*

'Mt Egmont from off Warea' (close to Cape Egmont), a J.C. Richmond pencil drawing. *Atkinson Family Collection*

New Plymouth in wartime, *c*. 1860. A lithograph after a painting by John Gully shows the town centred on the mouth of the Huatoki with the Pouakai Range leading up to Mt Taranaki in the background. Blockhouses are sited on vantage points around the settlement; the Marsland Hill barracks are above the houses (centre), with the steeply pitched roof of the garrison church of St Mary below. *Alexander Turnbull Library*

'Landing at New Plymouth', a pencil sketch from the Col. H.J. Warre
Album. New Plymouth had no natural harbour, but the surfboat service was
so skilfully managed that vessels in the roadstead were frequently unloaded
and despatched without the delay experienced in Auckland. *Alexander Turnbull
Library*

'Cricket on Poverty Flat, New Plymouth', a pencil sketch from the H.J.
Warre Album. The monotony of wartime within the cramped quarters of
New Plymouth was relieved, for the men, by cricket fixtures between the
regular soldiers and those of the militia or volunteers. *Alexander Turnbull
Library*

The original stone cottage built for William and Emily without the later wooden additions put up while Maria and Arthur lived there. 'I grow fonder of this place as time goes on . . . in time of sickness or trouble it is a priceless blessing to be able to breathe the pure air on the verandah or terrace walk.' A J.C. Richmond pencil drawing. *Taranaki Museum Collection*

Maria and Arthur's house at Hurworth at the foot of the 'little hill'. A J.C. Richmond pencil drawing, *c.* 1858. *Taranaki Museum Collection*

Arthur in his study at Fairfield. It was a 'chaos of bottles, dusty books, cobwebs & wood ashes' which he defied anyone to tidy. *Alexander Turnbull Library (C6555)*

Edie's wedding, 1881. Bride and groom (left front), with Ruth (seated right), Mabel (standing) and Charlie Fell's four daughters as Edie's attendants. The photo also shows the original Fairfield cottage (centre) and the first two-storeyed addition. *Nelson Provincial Museum (C2774)*

Dorothy K. (Dolla) Richmond, Dresden 1876. 'Dolla's face is beautiful . . . She looks so splendid when she comes home from . . . her drawing lesson, she glows out of every pore.' *Jinny Atkinson Collection*

Ann Elizabeth (Alla) Atkinson (née Richmond), *c.* 1896. It was her niece rather than her daughters who inherited Maria's joy of living and of writing. *Jinny Atkinson Collection*

Members of the mob's second and third generation in statuesque pose at Totaranui in 1886. *Jinny Atkinson Collection*

'Cousins dancing on the beach', Totaranui. *Jinny Atkinson Collection*

Teetotal – or 'Learn to say No!' Ruth Atkinson offers herself a glass of beer in one of Charlie Fell's staged photographs. *Jinny Atkinson Collection*

C. and C.W. Richmond in the garden of St James's, *c.* late 1880s. *C.Y. Fell lbum, Alexander Turnbull Library (C6465)*

Alla (standing) and Dolla, *c.* 1887. 'Dearer sister Dolla,' Tudor Atkinson wrote, '. . . if I had been you I shouldn't have let anyone love Alla who wasn't noble & great & strong but then I love you all so that perhaps you will forgive me.' *Jinny Atkinson Collection*

Family group, Fairfield, 1886. Left to right, front row: Arthur Atkinson holding granddaughter Phyllis Fell, Ruth, Richmond (Boy) Fell, and his mother Edie Fell. Back row: Maria with her youngest daughter Mabel, Annie and her husband Harry Atkinson. *Jinny Atkinson Collection*

...ames and Dorothy K. Richmond (Dolla) in their studio at St James's, Nelson. *Nelson Provincial Museum*

Fairfield, Christmas Day, 1887. The structure above the balcony was built to provide a platform for Arthur Atkinson's telescope but, instead, came to be used by the mob's younger members as a vantage point in Charlie Fell's ritual Christmas day photography. *C.Y. Fell Album II, Alexander Turnbull Library*

Maria, Arthur and family, Fairfield, October 1899. From left: Mabel (sitting on grass), Ruth (left facing), Maria, Arf, Arthur and Edie. *Jinny Atkinson Collection*

A gathering of some of the mob's first, second and third generations at
Fairfield, c. 1889. *Jinny Atkinson Collection*

1   Arthur Atkinson
2   Maria Atkinson
3   William (Billa) Atkinson
4   Arf Atkinson
5   Ruth Atkinson
6   James Wilson Richmond
7   Dick Richmond
8   Edie Fell
9   Helen Hursthouse
10 Harry Atkinson
11 Eliza Atkinson
12 Esther (Ettie) Atkinson
13 Annie Atkinson
14 Alfred Richmond
15 Mabel Atkinson
16 James Richmond
17 Alla Atkinson
18 Tudor Atkinson
19 Dolla Richmond
20 Arnold Atkinson
21 Harry Temple Atkinson
22 Hugh Atkinson

An elderly Maria writing at her desk. 'I am not a bit conscious of drying up with age. Every year I feel *more* interested in both my own circle & the whole world.' *Jinny Atkinson Collection*

CHAPTER
TEN

'We must go on bravely'

New Plymouth, Jan. 1864–Nov. 1865

The year 1864 began in a practical and positive manner with Arthur agreeing to pay William Woon £700 for a half share in the *Taranaki Herald*.¹ The paper, published weekly, had a circulation of approximately 500 which Arthur was certain of increasing as the population grew. The venture seemed to promise well, although as Maria wrote to Margaret, it was 'absurd' to think that such a pair as Arthur and she could ever grow rich. Indeed, Maria had consented to the 'printing business' only because she still felt there was a prospect of James and Mary's eventual return to Taranaki.

> Oh we do want them back so very much & when I hear from
> Richie [Hursthouse] how fagged James looks, & how much more
> delicate the children look than ours, & *all* Nelson children than
> Taranaki ones, I feel it would be for their benefit to return.²

James and Mary cried Amen to this. James had been appointed provincial secretary in March 1863 and was as unhappily employed in his office work for the Nelson Provincial Council as he had been in pumping out editorials for the *Examiner*. (He temporarily gave up writing for the paper in June.) 'Public service', he pronounced to William, 'is very disgusting to me in a miserable little dog kennel of snarling curs.'³ He enjoyed more his trips as Crown lands commissioner into the Nelson back country, where at least he had opportunities for sketching. Still, he was financially secure in Nelson, whereas all Taranaki could offer, in spite of Arthur's confidence that 'openings & salaries will be as plenty as blackberries for James when the war is over', was the possibility of his becoming chief government engineering surveyor at New Plymouth, or a job on the *Herald*, or an opening as master of a much needed boys' school. Requiring more urgent attention was James's Omata electorate which both Arthur and Maria thought he would lose if he did not once again reside in Taranaki, 'for the Taranaki moles do not like men that "have not stuck the place" '.[4] James reluctantly concluded that his best financial prospect, for the time being, was in Nelson, and he went ahead with building a new house on Wrey's hill, overlooking Nelson and the Maitai Valley. Four children, a resident sister-in-law and a servant made their Bridge Street house overcrowded. Mary was missing her mother (who had returned to England at the end of 1863), was continuing to worry about James's health because he looked so pale and thin when he was at his provincial secretary's office, and worrying even more when he was journeying in the back country. She had no confidence in his capacity to take care of himself. In fact James returned from these trips into that 'boiling pot of mountains' looking bronzed and fit, just as Arthur's health only benefited from his expeditions with the Bushrangers – 'camping out with a fine view & with plenty of smoked eels to eat'.

The set-piece engagements of the first part of the Taranaki War had, by 1864, been largely replaced by forays of waeromene Pakeha in search of wareomene Maori,[5] both parties travelling kei kitea (crouched down) through the bush. Actual engagements were few but Maria was always conscious of the risk Arthur ran. The attack on Kaitake pa[6] in the lower foothills of the mountain range involved the Bushrangers being away for several days and nights and caused Maria more anxiety than she had ever felt before: 'The 25th March might be the anniversary of the blackest day in my life,' she wrote to Lely in Dunedin; Mary Richmond, who was staying at Beach Cottage, wrote to James, 'we womenfolk feel very anxious and oppressed'. In the engagement only one life was lost on 'our side', and an immense quantity of potatoes was seized. Arthur's main contribution, along with that of other Bushrangers, was to pull up row after row of carefully tended taro, kumara, corn, tobacco, and potato: 'This was perhaps a little painful – or should have been to a well constituted mind – but necessary.'[7]

Any complacency which the Taranaki settlers may have felt after the taking of Kaitake pa was shattered when news reached New Plymouth on 6 April of a surprise attack the day before on a party of soldiers gathering firewood at Te Ahuahu in the foothills inland from Oakura. The men, newcomers to the 57th and military settlers from Melbourne, were all unused to fighting Maori, as was their commanding officer, Captain T.W.J. Lloyd, who had seen little active service anywhere and had spent fewer than three months in New Zealand. The hidden Maori attackers charged; Captain

Lloyd was shot in the first volley, and his men panicked and fled.
Arthur reported the incident in the *Herald* as the first 'real defeat'
of the Taranaki War. Seven soldiers were killed, twelve wounded,
and five of the dead, including Captain Lloyd, had their heads
cut off. This beheading was the first indication to the settlers that
a new religious cult, Pai Marire, founded by the prophet Te Ua
Tuwhakararo Haumene of Ngati Ruanui, was now part of the Maori
opposition to Pakeha domination. Followers of Pai Marire became
known as Hauhau. Maria felt for Captain Lloyd's widow who lived
next to Helen Hursthouse, and who had been miserable since her
husband's posting to the camp at Oakura. The couple had never
before been separated during their seven or eight years of married
life. With her two children she intended to return to Ireland after
she had seen the spot where her husband was buried. The fact
that the body was headless was kept from her. Anxious as Maria
was to avenge 'our people', she wrote to Lely, 'It is curious how
my desire that our people should have an encounter with the Natives
& inflict a severe loss on them is always at war with my dread
that I may be called on to pay a price for it which would make
life of little value.'[8] Arthur stated that the Bushrangers would have
'given anything' for such an encounter with Maori on open land.
They had to wait until reinforcements for the 57th arrived before
a punitive expedition of 500 troops could set out for Te Ahuahu.
The Bushrangers burned whare – Arthur's plunder was a kit load
of Bibles and prayer books – and made a better job of destroying
crops than the soldiers had done.[9]

What with editing, study (Arthur still kept up his practice of Latin
and Greek before breakfast), bushranging, rifle practice, cricket
with the 57th on Poverty Square, and committee meetings of the
Taranaki Institute of which Henry was president, Maria complained
to Lely that she 'hardly ever had a word with Arthur'. And although
Arthur wrote to Mary that 'the life we lead [is] the healthiest
imaginable', there is no doubt that Maria was occasionally fearful,
often bored, and finding the absence of Lely 'an hourly blank'.
At the beginning of 1864 she still had the company of Blanche
and Henry but, like Lely, she found it difficult to be on intimate
terms with Blanche, and Henry, when he was not engaged in
provincial council business, was invariably in the garden shed, which
he had transformed into a chemistry laboratory, absorbed in
experiments with Taranaki petroleum and iron sand – 'alas! he
can find no titanium' – and in evolving a new theory about the

nature of matter. In February Henry bought a small cottage with
two vacant sections on the 'Devon line', a short distance beyond
the Kings' stone cottage. Blanche was 'expecting' in November,
and when she and Henry left Beach Cottage they spent much of
their time establishing a new garden on their land which was not
swept by the sea wind.

Maria found that the 'unquestioning enjoying nature' of the
children was a constant antidote to morbid thoughts. Arfie was
well and high spirited, without a tooth until he was over a year
and then the recipient of ten at once; Ruth (Oofie as she called
herself), 'an odd child, she promises to be like her father in having
strong affections for a few friends'.[10] Young children, however,
scarcely satisfied Maria's wondering and inquiring mind 'for the
why of all around'. In a revealing phrase about the enervating
effect of women's work, she wrote about Blanche and herself 'baby
tending in far corners of the house'. Sharing her thoughts with
Lely, Mary Richmond, or Margaret Taylor nevertheless helped
relieve the tedium of her mother's absence and Arthur's involvement. The first anniversary of Alice Atkinson's death found her
wondering again about the uncertainty of the hereafter in face
of the reality of death.

> For a long time after my illness[11] in '56 I used to feel happy at
> the thought of death fancying it would be passing from darkness
> to light, but now I suppose the children bind me so closely to
> this world that in thinking of death I dread the separation from
> them too much not to shrink from it.[12]

Unitarianism provided Maria with a faith which had never been
propped up by ritual evolved out of past occurrences, but instead
welcomed and sought to encompass the discoveries of contemporary
biblical criticism and scientific thought. It was thus the more able
to withstand the buffeting from 'geology, philology and all the
other ologies' which, as C.W. Richmond told Harriet Gore Browne,
was beginning to expose cracks in the seemingly solid masonry
of the evangelical creed. Even so, when death hovered so close
by those she loved, whether through the dangers of childbirth and
disease or through the ill fortune of battle, Maria turned, still
hopefully, towards Tennyson's lines from the prologue to *In
Memoriam* and shared the thought that she and they were 'not made
to die'. Thus there was a constant interplay in her mind between
a growing scepticism and a very human desire to believe in some
continuum beyond death. She wondered whether she would be
'permitted' to recognise Alice hereafter, and came to the conclusion:

'How paralysed reason & imagination too seem in the attempt to prefigure even vaguely what lies beyond the tomb.'[13]

Eternity may have appeared obscure, but in resolute and typical fashion Maria was determined to defy old age – in spirit – for as long as possible. With her usual sensitivity to her own age as opposed to Arthur's, she was prepared to accept that in her fortieth year old age was already laying hold of the 'outward woman'. (An interesting inversion of this theme comes from Mary King who described 'Mrs Arthur' in 1864 as looking 'so well and young that one wonders how she came to marry such an old man as Mr Arthur'.[14]) Maria reasoned that if the soul was to live for ever, why should the few extra years of old age be deemed so to corrode the personality?

> There is no objective to our thinking more widely and judging more soundly than of old; but why we should feel less keenly and perceive more dimly I cannot tell, if we are doing our best with heart and spirit . . . Are you inclined to the belief that there is a hereafter *only* for such as keep the soul within them alive?[15]

This intriguing idea, Maria thought, was probably not original, but she assured Margaret Taylor that 'she did not get it out of a book'. Following this line of thinking Maria, in an explosive statement which encapsulates the very essence of her own nature, condemned 'torpor not sin as *the* crime against the soul', seeing in it the 'dead level of indifference which seems to characterise so many who never commit crimes and indeed are pointed out as highly moral people'.[16]

Restricted as she was by domesticity, Maria's mind, as always, took flight in letters: 'I feel the truth of your remark dearest Lely, that the female heart needs letters by every mail so keenly that I cannot let the Airedale go without a few lines.'[17] There was also music – occasional Beethoven evenings at Mary King's – and reading. She particularly enjoyed the *Spectator* during this period of close confinement. It was edited by the Richmonds' London friend, Richard Holt Hutton, and was Maria's 'monthly informant of all that goes on in Europe and the civilised world generally, and I feel much disgusted if want of leisure obliges me to miss any article'.[18] She found it 'so much more solid' than the *Saturday Review* which, founded in 1855, saw itself as the 'mouthpiece of . . . thoughtful and educated society'.[19] It did not see women with Maria's eyes, and indeed ignored colonial women altogether. 'Women', one article expostulated, 'being intellectually inferior to men, existed to furnish the elegant graces of Victorian domesticity

and to be admired for their "fine gloss of innocency and delicacy".'[20]
Such an assumption drew the full force of Maria's wrath:

> When I don't agree with the 'Spectator' I feel interested to find
> out why . . . When I differ from the 'Saturday' I am indignant
> or disgusted . . . Its tone about women is enough to make me sick.
> I should fancy the writers have never seen or conversed with any
> *respectable* woman though they may have seen plenty of Mayfair
> ladies in full dress.[21]

Servants were again hard to come by. The continuing stream
into the province of hundreds of military settlers had greatly
increased the demand for female labour. Wages rose 'alarmingly';
ten or even twelve shillings a week was now given for a good
servant, and the 'merest scrap of a girl' could count on four shillings.
Washerwomen were at the end of the scale. James, in Auckland,
came across Mrs Purday who had washed for them when Mary
and Maria were living there: 'Poor woman she has had a hard
time of it. Washing at 2/6 per dozen with bread at 1/- and meat
7d & 8d and rent 12/- per week. She looks pretty well but subdued
and sad.'[22] Marion Atkinson's servant, aged fourteen, 'was obliging
and of good character', but was quite without the skill required
for cooking. Marion paid her eight shillings and then suffered the
mortification of having her 'lured' away by Mrs Halse, who was
prepared to pay the 'outrageous' sum of twelve shillings. Eliza
Atkinson's maid, fresh from Ireland where she had left her baby
to be cared for by her mother, did not look more than twenty-
one and was very quiet and 'simple minded'. Her great advantage
was that she had been in service before and knew the 'ways of
a gentleman's household much better than the colonial girls'. One
cannot be sure whether Maria had managed to retain her 'jewel'
– the 'very pretty young widow' who had been taken on at the
time of Arfie's birth. A comment to Mary Richmond hoping that
her 'good servant' was either 'very ugly or averse to matrimony'
implies that she had not. Letters from early 1864 mention a Mrs
Daley who did the washing and scrubbing, and a young girl, Laura
Cox, who was so happy in Maria's household that she gave up
her schooling for a time. Maria, however, regarded her as 'too
young and giddy' to accompany the children beyond the garden
gate.

In February Maria was tempted to accept Arthur's advice and
Mary's invitation to go to Nelson for a holiday; anxiety about
Marion Atkinson's health and about Arthur's probably sleepless
nights coping with Ruth – a 'perfect little vixen at nights' –

prevented her. The following month Mary came to Beach Cottage with six-month-old Richard. Mary had been ill with a fever and Richard had suffered diarrhoea for three weeks; he improved rapidly in the sea air. Mary once again confided in Arthur '& to no other', writing on her return to Nelson at the end of April, 'God bless you dearest Birdie you are a great comfort to me', and exhorting him to 'Burn this'.[23] Mary was at Beach Cottage during the anxious days while the Bushrangers and other military forces were mounting the attack on Kaitake, and later when the same force set off to avenge the attack on Captain Lloyd's party. She had already tried to persuade Arthur to leave the Bushrangers now that he had a regular business to attend to, and she took umbrage at the flippancy and obstinacy of his refusal: 'It cannot be any pleasure to you though you often talk as if it were in a way that I very much dislike and disapprove.'[24] In spite of the affectionate bond between the two and the closeness of their ages, there is no doubt that as a married couple they would not have worn well together. While at Beach Cottage Mary learned of a 'domestic tragedy' in her Nelson household. Her excellent servant had turned out to be a thief. Mary received the news with dismay and perturbation. Annie, at the scene of the crime, discovered that the drama had done wonders for her headaches.

Maria was very lonely after Mary's departure. She wondered if, by chance, they returned to New Plymouth to live, Mary and Annie would find sufficient 'social satisfaction' to compensate for the orderly 'calling' pattern of Nelson. For example, close to Beach Cottage was Beach House where the Fred Carringtons lived. Maria could not make up her mind whether 'to call': 'We have a speaking acquaintance but the girls are odious & worse than odious too, to my mind.'[25] A contributing factor impeding social intercourse could have been that Fred Carrington had been reappointed to the job of chief government surveyor, which Arthur and Maria thought would have suited James, and worse, he and his family were living in the house that Maria wanted for Mary and her family. Mary thought the women of 'our set' very well in their way, but, she protested, 'they are always having babies'.

Marion Atkinson had continued poorly since her confinement in January. In April Decimus brought her to Beach Cottage for 'some of Mrs Arthur's kind nurse tending'.[26] Maria diagnosed Marion's lassitude as nervous depression exacerbated by her inability to feed her baby adequately. Maria suckled young Frank at nights, and once he was established on a bottle his mother began to improve.

At the same time as Maria was caring for Marion, both Ruth and Arfie developed bad colds which threatened to turn into croup. May and June that year were the coldest months Maria could remember in New Zealand. Scarlet fever was rampant in the town, and Dr Rawson, who was 'nearly run off his legs', attributed the epidemic to overcrowding. People who had once been farming in New Plymouth's backblocks were still living in the town and took in lodgers to make a little money. Several children had already died of the fever, 'the richest as well as the poorest' among them. The William Halses had lost first a daughter, then their only son, and now Mrs Halse was despaired of. Because of the bitterly cold weather, many children, including Fanny Atkinson, Harry and Jane's daughter, suffered relapses. Maria, in this instance, was not surprised:

> Harry & Jane's children are allowed so completely to follow the notions of their own wills & these incline them to wander from home so frequently that I doubted Janes having power to keep Fanny indoors as long as was deemed prudent.[27]

Meanwhile Arthur was still out with the Bushrangers, often spending several days and nights away from home. Harry Atkinson, who had been promoted major in command of the guerrilla force, recommended his brother to give up bushranging, but Arthur could not 'quite make up my mind to it'. In mid-May, while out with No. 2 company, he received a message 'to come in' and relieve a beleaguered Maria. At Dunedin Lely could only hope that Maria would not be too fatigued by the 'extra labour which is continually falling to her share'. She would have been even more concerned if she had known that her daughter was pregnant. Maria had not told her earlier, for until mid-April she was still breastfeeding Arfie and was uncertain herself.

A further cause for concern during the winter of 1864 was Edie's whereabouts. She had been expected home from Dunedin long before winter set in. Now with gales howling outside Beach Cottage, with a schooner already wrecked on the Taranaki coast, and with letters scarce between Dunedin and New Plymouth, Maria's mind was full of misgivings. Arthur did not help matters by saying it was a 'mad scheme' of Maria's to let her go in the first place. '[He] *never never* will let a child leave home again I believe.'[28] Maria remained convinced that Edie would have

> made more progress intellectually by going to Otago . . . & if we are to remain scattered north & south as at present, the only way to keep alive the feeling of relationship amongst the younger branches will be to allow long visits from time to time.[29]

A letter from Emily suggested that Lely and Edie would be on the *Auckland*, leaving Port Chalmers towards the end of June. Maria and Arthur waited with increasing anxiety for the steamer to appear.

> The weather has been off & on very stormy during the last ten days or more, blowing some times a north easterly direction, sometimes a north westerly gale, & not knowing where our dear child was I have been uneasy whichever way the wind came.[30]

They learned later that the *Auckland* had been blown past New Plymouth and became even more concerned about where Edie was. In fact she was still at Dunedin, in bed with croup. Once contact had been re-established between the two families, it was decided that Edie had better remain and recover her strength rather than risk catching scarlet fever in New Plymouth.

Another of the set 'always having babies' was Eliza Atkinson. In July her third was born. The day before birth, William Atkinson borrowed 'Bull's Hints'[31] from Arthur, which, Maria wrote, 'I thought suspicious.' Infant Janet had already joined her elder brother, Willie, in spending most of the day playing at Beach Cottage; when Eliza was confined, they simply spent their nights there as well. Eliza's husband during the first part of the war was a 'native interpreter' with the militia at Bell blockhouse. More recently he had been employed in the Native Office, but had been dismissed because he could not get along with Robert Parris. Finding it difficult to get another job (which did not surprise Maria, who had no high opinion of his ability), he set up as a land and insurance agent. Esther Atkinson was born 'in health and safety' on 17 July. For Eliza it had been a difficult labour. She failed to recover sufficiently to feed her baby, and Esther failed initially to progress on a bottle. The situation worsened when William Atkinson went down with scarlet fever. This time Maria could not 'take on' Esther but, as she told Margaret Taylor (unmarried, surrounded by servants, and living in a castle in Syrgenstein on the Bavarian border, to whom accounts of life and death in Taranaki must have seemed strangely unrelated), 'I shall never again despair.' Marion Atkinson's second, who at birth had been a 'poor, thin unhappy looking baby', was now a 'jolly, plump little fellow on little but bottle food . . . It is wonderful what difficulties babies do struggle thro' in this climate; Mrs Warre[32] evidently thinks it one of the wonders of NZ that ailing artificially fed infants persist in growing up & getting stronger.'[33]

As Esther progressed and William recoverd, Eliza 'became herself' again. Then suddenly Janet, ill for no more than a day, died from croup,[34] aged twenty-one months. She had always been so full of life and had seemed to possess a much stronger constitution than either Ronald Atkinson or Francis Richmond, her two contemporaries. Maria, who had recently dreaded that Eliza would lose her baby, now felt that the latter event would have been a far lighter trial, especially as Esther, though sleeping and eating well, remained thin and constantly had 'spots' which developed into boils. Maria's own family remained well but 'one looks at the children with fear & trembling after such a blow. The step from full health to death seems as nothing.'[35] Like the Richmonds, the Ronalds (Eliza's surname before marriage) were Unitarians, and Janet had not been baptised. For this reason the Rev. H.H. Brown of the Church of England, who had spiritual charge of military camps and outposts during the sixties, refused to bury her. Arthur, who was handling the funeral arrangements for his brother, wrote of his encounter with Brown:

> He asked, 'Is she baptised?' & when I answered 'no' he answered 'that he had no choice in the matter as the rubric of his church strictly forbade such a thing'. And this is the most liberal representative of our national church. Afterwards I went to Mr Whiteley at the Institution[36] who readily undertook it. I went up with Decy & chose a family burying ground among the Independents as the Churchmen will not have us.[37]

By the spring of 1864 Lely and Edie had progressed as far as Nelson. Mary reported that Edie was 'blooming'. Lely was to remain with Mary in Nelson, leaving Annie free to go to Maria for her confinement. Maria thought Arthur 'would be crazy' if Edie did not come back before then. The problem was no longer associated with tempestuous gales but with the six-year-old's safety if she travelled from Nelson to New Plymouth without a lady escort. Mary was certain she could not possibly allow this, Maria was prepared to disagree:

> I have such perfect faith like my little German protegee of 1851, 'Über all man findet gute Menschen' (Everywhere one finds kind people) that I cannot feel the absolute necessity of escorts.[38] I might say without vanity that the names of Atkinson & Richmond are in themselves a recommendation to the politeness & civility of a majority of our fellow colonists.[39]

One recollects that neither Emily nor William had thought it too onerous a responsibility to put their three daughters under the care of the eldest, aged seven, when they despatched them from Auckland to New Plymouth in the summer of 1860. Mary, however, decided to keep Edie until Annie should go to New Plymouth.

Maria celebrated her fortieth birthday on 15 September, Arthur giving her a present of an inkstand. Both she and Blanche Richmond were expecting their babies in November. Maria approached this event with her usual good sense which took a dispassionate account of the possibility that she might not survive it. For this reason too she wanted Edie back.

I fancy if anything *should* go wrong with me, as it has done with others who seemed as strong & healthy as I am now, it would seem sadder not to have her to say goodbye to, & that coming back when it was too late would give Arthur an extra pang. You must not think I have any gloomy forebodings for I am quite cheerful & see no reason to believe I shall do otherwise than well, but one can never forget how many poor women have been full of hope & reasonable expectations of happiness whilst the Angel of death was waiting for them close at hand.[40]

Harriet Gore Browne, daily expecting the birth 'of my 4th son' earlier in 1864, had written in the same quiet, pellucid manner to Emily Richmond from Government House, Hobart. Hers is a classic statement.

I daily expect the birth of my 4th son, & I always have a feeling (perhaps it is only a habit) that it is well to put the house in order, & do what is well to do, before the time comes when it may be too late.

Why do men make such a marvel of people being cheerful & brave in the face of the guillotine when so often as a soul is born into the world we poor women meet a greater pain & almost as great a danger with a pleasant unconcern, and up to the last moment finish up our small affairs and wind up the several threads of our lives as methodically as if we were preparing for an expected entertainment.[41]

Maria's preparation for her own confinement went steadily ahead. She again had a satisfactory servant, Elizabeth, who although already engaged to be married, spiritedly declared that her wedding 'will *not* take place till after my [Maria's] confinement'. Elizabeth also suggested, from an advantageous bargaining position, that if Maria increased her wages to twelve shillings per week, she would remain another six months at least.

She seems determined to try her betrothed's patience, but perhaps he has it better now he can spend so many of his evenings here . . . We told E. to have him in to see her when she liked. He comes about 3 times a week I think but always leaves before 10 o'clock.[42]

Colonial circumstances were very different from those which

had pertained at Springholm, Wimbledon, where a servant had
been dismissed for receiving 'callers' even from as far away as
the gate. Nurses[43] were also in short supply. Maria thought Mrs
Wakefield, who had attended most of the Richmond–Atkinson
births, a poor nurse, but she was honest and Maria knew of no
better one. With Blanche expecting her baby at much the same
time, Maria decided to leave Mrs Wakefield free for her and instead
to rely on 'Arthur's talents' assisted by those of Dr Rawson, for
whom she had little regard. Mrs Henderson, who lived nearby,
was prepared to assist 'in any capacity'. Elizabeth was to take
the children out in the afternoons, even if it meant abandoning
her 'works of supererogation', as Maria called them – '*extra* thorough
cleaning of her kitchen in the middle of the week etc etc. Still
I cannot complain, she has every place so clean & neat, I know
I shall be miserable at first when she goes & we have to relapse.'[44]

About this time Arthur concluded that Maria, as an 'independent
woman', should have her own will. Before their marriage he had
abrogated his right to a marriage settlement, and had agreed with
William that Maria should continue to exercise the same full power
over her inherited Richmond income as she then enjoyed. He now
asked his brother-in-law whether it would do 'mutates mutandis
if I copy mine which you drew up & leave everything to her or
must reference be made to the reason for her being independent?'[45]
The British 1857 Act to reform marriage and divorce laws, passed
since their marriage, now stipulated that a woman might inherit
and bequeath property.

Arthur had quickly responded to Maria's call in mid-May to
'come in'. Bushranging had become most unexciting and consisted
mainly of providing cover for military settlers engaged in building
blockhouses at places where Arthur thought Maori were most
unlikely to attack. He was temporarily struck off duty and rather
begrudged losing his private's pay of thirty-five shillings per week
plus rations. It was a sacrifice Maria felt they could well afford.
To while away the extra hours at home he employed himself in
adding shorthand to his other skills.

At the beginning of August, a rumour that 200 Waikato had
arrived at Mokau and were likely to be joined by another 100
under Wiremu Kingi caused Colonel Warre to take out a combined
force of about 500. No engagement ensued, but Maria had her
own skirmish with Arthur who 'of course wished to go as he scented
fighting'. She wrote to Lely:

I do wish he would agree to remain quiet till Xmas. It seems to me only a reasonable request of mine that he should, & I consider no wife was ever more *unrequiring* than I have been. I have let him bush range for months uncomplainingly when I believe all other wives of our set would have stood out against their husbands' indulgence in such pursuits or amusements, but Ar seems to deem me the most unreasonable of women if ever I endeavour to interfere with his *violent propensity for fighting* (NB Strong sense of duty he calls it, but I say humbug to this.) I don't mean to say I would have him keep out of all the fighting in this cause but just now it would be particularly trying to have his life endangered for private & public reasons . . . The feeling that everything will be wasted & thrown away worse than useless when the Colony is so betrayed by the [Colonial] Office & Sir G. Grey makes it maddening to be asked to risk one's greatest treasures. I sadly want Mary here to back me up for Arthur does not pay heed to any other woman's opinion.[46]

Arthur, in his usual style, added an 'appendix' to Maria's letter:

The author in common fairness should . . . have stated that I have agreed to keep out of danger for the next four months, taking only a course of slight skirmishes which the doctors recommend as an excellent tonic for bracing nerves and fibres relaxed by distilling sixpenny wisdom [a reference to the *Herald*] to the multitude.

Harry Atkinson refused to take Arthur back on active duty and went so far as to say that he would not dream of going out if he had any regular profession by which to earn his bread. By this stage Henry Richmond, Decimus, and William Atkinson had all been discharged. Unable to plead patriotic duty any longer, Arthur fell back on the excuse that as the *Herald* had no other competent person to report on bushranging excursions, he needed to be his 'Own Correspondent' for the paper. At the end of August he heard that No. 2 company was going out and 'as it was a lovely day for a skirmish' he went with them. He was out again early in October when Warre launched an attack on the almost deserted Te Arei pa at Mataitawa. Arthur considered himself well rewarded when he managed to acquire two new Pai Marire prayers as 'plunder'. Later in the month, when Maria was heavily pregnant, he deferred to her wish for him to stay home – or rather, did not go because Maria would not give a 'cheerful assent'. That evening he wrote in his diary: 'Much disturbed in mind because the Bushrangers started for Sentry Hill & are to explore behind Mataitawa tomorrow & Maria does not want me to go being too precious – so at last gave up.'[47]

Although Maria was pleased to have Arthur out of the Bush-rangers, her general attitude to the war was that the colonists should take the 'whole cost of the Native Difficulty' on themselves: 'When we do that we shall be allowed to say what we think even of such a piece of perfection as Sir G. Grey.'[48] She was disenchanted with the British government's attitude, attributing much of the criticism in the British press about a 'war of aggression' being waged in New Zealand on behalf of land-hungry colonists to reports sent 'home' by regular army officers who were 'so sick of [the war] & so savage at being in N.Z.'.[49] The British government, she felt, ought to be better informed about the Taranaki settlers in particular:

> A quieter, less blood-thirsty set of men, or one more inclined to live peaceably with all men, including Maoris, there could not be before the war; and since, they have shown a wonderfully patient endurance under the most trying circumstances . . . Now they are firmly and cheerfully encountering danger and hardship not in defence of property, for few have anything left to defend, but in the hope of bringing about a solid peace which will allow of their returning to their wasted homes and recommencing life.[50]

Like her contemporary, Grace Hirst, she was not impressed with the calibre of the military settlers from Victoria. The 450 arrivals from Melbourne in February had spent their first few days in New Plymouth drunk and disorderly. 'What a pity,' she wrote to Lely, 'the Maoris won't give in without compelling us to settle the country thickly with men of this description.'[51] She concluded that, from the look of them, 'once they get on the [confiscated] land, no number of Maoris will ever get them off again'. Her opinion of the value of the imperial troops, now widely shared by exasperated Taranaki settlers, was such as to wish they would all be immediately recalled, leaving the men in the civilian forces to finish the war 'in their own way'. 'But whilst Governors, Generals & Ministers wrangle or hesitate, the natives plant crops, collect ammunition & make ready at their ease for a fresh campaign.'[52]

Early in September the *Alexandra* arrived from Auckland with bullocks, horses, and troops, and with General Cameron expected to follow to begin his reluctant southern campaign against Ngati Ruanui and Taranaki. T.B. Gillies, C.W. Richmond's former legal partner, now secretary for land in the Fox–Whitaker ministry, had earlier reported to Harry Atkinson: 'We are hard at work trying to get the Genl. to move to Taranaki; but a winter campaign in N.Z. seems to carry with it an idea of all the horrors of a march to Moscow.'[53] Maria as usual was more emphatic:

I am almost sure that the military from the General downwards
mean to do no more fighting . . . You may drive a General to
the wars but you can't make him fight! . . . Mrs Warre said the
other day that 'it was expected that the military would walk thro'
to Wanganui & not see a Native'. I felt inclined to say I thought
there was no doubt of it as they did not mean to look for them.[54]

On 21 October the Taranaki Militia and Rifle Volunteers, apart
from one company of Bushrangers, were discharged and struck
off pay. Grace Hirst wrote that 'the order came upon the people
like an electric shock, many families where there are two or three
young men were entirely depending upon their pay for a
subsistence'.[55] Her son James, recently appointed a captain, did not
get so much as a single month's pay. The following evening there
was a protest meeting. For four and a half years, it was claimed,
the settlers had been called to serve in the militia, and had abandoned
houses and property in order to do so. Since that time they had
been 'alternately used and discarded as suited the convenience of
government'. The province remained in a state of confusion, it
was still unsafe to reoccupy farms, adequate compensation had not
yet been paid, and now military pay and rations were to be
discontinued. Yet apart from working on the roads, no provision
had been made for farmers and labourers to support themselves.[56]
Once again the little province felt sorely tried.

The *Airedale* brought Edith and Annie Smith from Nelson on 3
November. Arthur thought Annie 'rather collapsed' from seasickness, but Edie, to her overjoyed father, looked 'brilliant' and
'improved in all ways'. They were just in time for Maria's
confinement. She got up from bed to greet them, returned to it
at dusk, and at half-past eleven her third live daughter was born
– 'a plump little creature'. The previous week Arthur and Maria
had discussed names, the difficulty being, especially with a girl's
name, 'to avoid the commonplace & undistinguished without falling
into the fancy & romantic'. They agreed ('for a wonder') on Edward
Alfred or Alice Mabel. 'To avoid confusion [William and Emily
had an Alice] we shall use Mabel tho' we cannot put it first, "Mabel
Alice" sounds so awkward.'[57] This time it took Maria longer to
get her strength back,

tho' I dare say many people would laugh at my calling myself
weak, as I have been walking about the house for some days &
was some time in the garden this morning, in fact compared with

all my relatives & connections except Jane [Atkinson] I am of Herculean strength, but compared with myself on former occasions I find my nerves so weak & shaken that . . . it is only by painful self-restraint I can keep from crying at ridiculous little worries.[58]

Arthur would have hoped for Edward Alfred, and Maria, as was the custom, would have felt inwardly downcast at not 'giving him' another son. What made it worse for Maria was that Arthur was again going away as the *Herald*'s 'Own Correspondent', this time with MPs to Auckland for what was to be the last meeting there of the General Assembly. Maria wrote to her mother (still in Nelson), 'I dread Arthur's going away more than I can tell, tho' I would not on any account keep him, or let him know I shall feel it.'[59] She wrote later that she was ashamed of herself for letting Arthur's departure and 'a great many small worries depress me as they did'. All this seems to have had a flow-on effect to Mabel, who was not the contented baby her brother had been. She was 'windy & fidgety from tea time till 9 o'clock by which time I am pretty tired & unfit for writing'.[60] It is significant that Maria's handwriting also shows signs of stress at this time.

Maria had plenty of assistance in the house. Mrs Henderson washed 'mountains of clothes' and did a great deal of work that an 'ordinary nurse' would not normally have done; Harriet Foreman looked after the children. Annie was proving something of a broken reed: the voyage had been upsetting, the sea air of Beach Cottage was 'too exhausting', and her headaches returned. She was no substitute for Lely. Maria had hoped that William, who had recently visited Nelson, would have spared the time to escort his mother to New Plymouth. And then James failed to make more than a brief call at Beach Cottage on his way to Auckland and the General Assembly: 'My brothers never seem public servants but public slaves, & tho' noble devotion to public duty etc reads beautifully in history . . . I should prefer a little "private interest" in my own near relations,'[61] Maria somewhat caustically noted. James had also failed, except by way of a letter in the *Herald*, to address his Omata electors, which omission Maria correctly judged would tell against him. She made a perceptive observation about the current relationship of MPs to their electors:

> It is greatly to be regretted that James did not feel it a *duty* to come here last Sunday . . . It seems to me the grand mistake of most of our NZ politicians that they give no time or thought to the populace – all speeches & writings are directed to the educated public of NZ & to defend the cause & explain our case at home.

Meanwhile the vulgar herd, not understanding half that goes on, will drift away, so that by the time the Native question is settled I expect a very inferior class of men will form the House of Representatives.[62]

The last General Assembly at Auckland was a significant one, and Arthur, although uneasy at leaving Maria, did not regret his attendance as a correspondent. The Whitaker–Fox ministry, unable to make headway or even physical contact with Grey – 'It is now nearly two months, perhaps more, that neither Fox nor I have seen him on business[63] – resigned in November. The day before Arthur left New Plymouth aboard the *Phoebe* he had attended a public meeting in the town which had carried the following 'excellent' resolutions on public policy:

1) That we [colonists generally] must have entire charge of our own affairs.
2) That if necessary to get this we must send all the soldiers home.
3) That we must have a 'governor' in whose wisdom, integrity & firmness we can confide.
4) That we still regret Gov. Browne's having been sent away.[64]

Arthur showed the New Plymouth resolutions to Frederick Weld, who was among the forty members of the Assembly on board, and then, as was his unfortunate custom, was seasick all the rest of the way. When Weld arrived at Auckland, Grey appealed to him to form a new ministry. Weld laid down certain conditions for the governor's assent before he agreed. The imperial government was to be requested to withdraw its troops and to instruct the governor that he should be guided entirely by the recommendations of his constitutional advisers, except on such matters as were reserved under Crown prerogative. Sufficient land was to be confiscated from 'rebel' Maori tribes to fulfil the colony's engagement to its imported military settlers, and the seat of government was to be removed to Wellington[65] after the current session. The New Plymouth resolutions may have strengthened Weld's hand, although in the provinces which were not confused by schemes for separation, there was now a consensus that reliance should be placed on the resources of the colony itself. Another issue which had alarmed Arthur was that the agitation, led by Otago, for the South Island's separation from the North had been brought to crisis point by an Auckland demand for that province to become a separate colony. There was little unity among those with 'suicidal intent',[66] and Arthur was able to report that the Weld ministry, which included Harry Atkinson as defence minister,

was for the time being safe. It also seemed to Arthur that Grey
had been brought to heel. 'Grey seems inclined to suspend his
treacherous practices . . . It is something like poetical justice on
him to have Harry for a Minister, whom he cordially hates – indeed
I think very few Taranaki men are favourites.'[67] Maria was not
pleased to have 'our Harry' in the ministry because 'prompt, decided
and energetic as he is, I feel afraid he has not a wide enough
experience'. She had no such doubt about Weld.

> In Mr Weld lies we feel the only hope for extricating the Colony
> from the Slough of Despond . . . Mr Weld is a real English gentleman
> of the best type, but whether even he can set poor New Zealand
> to rights I don't know . . . A sense of public duty alone induces
> him to take office.[68]

Blanche Richmond expected to have her baby about the same time
as Maria. Her previous confinements had been difficult and had
left her unwell; nevertheless, as she 'tidied up the threads of her
life', she too would have been 'full of hope & reasonable
expectations'. Her daughter was born on 17 November. Maria wrote
to Lely:

> There has been a frightful nurse crisis of course, but as Aunt [Helen
> Hursthouse] is with Blanche & the little maid takes good care of
> Francis in the day & Henry at night, I hope Blanche may not feel
> much worried . . .
>   Blanche is not quite so well . . . & for a week we shall not
> feel *sure*.[69]

Dr Rawson was not alarmed, describing Blanche's condition simply
as a nervous fever incidental to childbirth. She seemed to be
recovering, and then there came a sudden change; her fever increased
alarmingly and she was in great pain. Henry Richmond and Helen
Hursthouse looked on helplessly.

> About an hour before her death[70] she seemed to be aware for the
> first time that she was to die. She could just dimly articulate the
> words mother & husband. She turned her poor weary head and
> parched lips many times first to Aunt and then to kiss me.[71]

'Plain, rough-mannered, awkward Blanche with her large beautiful
eyes and her industrious useful habits'[72] had kept house for James
and Henry when they first arrived at New Plymouth, though only
a child herself. She had been her mother's mainstay when John
Hursthouse was alive and dissolute. She was also Helen Hursthouse's
last daughter. Maria and Lely had found it difficult to establish
really friendly relations with Blanche who, after the tragic death

of her first child, kept herself to herself. Maria had even wondered if she was truly a companion to Henry. After Blanche's death, Maria begged Henry to let her care for the baby, who was given her mother's name.[73] Both he and Helen Hursthouse, however, wished to keep the infant, surviving on goat's milk, close to them. 'One can never see poor Aunt with her careworn face & grey hair minding one or other of her three little motherless grandchildren without wondering at the strange sad loss she is doomed to in surviving her three beloved daughters.'[74]

Recently Helen Hursthouse had heard that Nellie's husband, A.C.P. Macdonald, was engaged to be married. Maria thought her aunt took the news very quietly. She had always expected that he would marry again, but it did seem 'painfully quick' for Nellie's place to be filled by a stranger. 'Of course Mr M. thinks Miss W. [Williams] will make a good mother [to Flora and Norman], men in these cases I suppose always think so, but whether their opinion is of much value seems doubtful.'[75]

Arthur returned from Auckland on 11 December to the pleased surprise of Ruth, who had linked his and her aunt's departure together. A week later, Maria was making plans to visit Nelson and Dunedin in January. Like Mary in Nelson who was 'stunned by these repeated & heart-rendering separations', Maria felt that the 'merest peep at those we love would be worth a great deal'. She had not seen William for three years, and in spite of his judgeship, good social position, and fine new house, was still uncertain whether his move to Dunedin had been wise. His asthma was worse, and, as Maria told Margaret Taylor,

the idea that his life is to be shortened by a residence there is most painful. What will be the worth of any money he may leave his poor children as compared with his presence & guidance: Poor Emily is the least fitted of all our set to be left a widow with a family to bring up.[76]

Maria intended to take Mabel with her to Dunedin. Elizabeth was prepared to look after the three older children, and to postpone her marriage yet again. Arthur was uneasy about even a temporary separation, but agreed that Maria should do as she thought best. 'Expect me only when you see me,' she wrote to Emily, 'at present we are all well but death comes like a thief in the night.'[77]

Not death but Ruth covered in the red blotches of scarlet fever prevented Maria from getting to Dunedin. Ruth ran a high fever for several days:

At night with the little creature beside me tossing in burning fire

& wandering in mind, & the painful feeling that nothing could be done for her, I lost all heart. After the first two days it was impossible to get a drop of medicine forced down . . . If we had lost the darling we should have known that no foolish medical treatment had hastened her end, as it is a good constitution & plenty of pure air . . . carried her through.[78]

Then Edie, then Arthur came down with it – though less severely – and both Elizabeth and the younger maid had milder symptoms. All that summer Maria was preoccupied with the fever, and was 'so shut up that I can think of nothing but our small household cares'. She felt certain that it was Beach Cottage itself which was a major factor in her household's recovery: 'This is a most blessed house for sickness, opening the windows here is equal to taking a walk.'[79]

Scarlet fever ran its course in the town. As the long hot summer wore on, more children and elderly people went down with stomach upsets, diarrhoea, and dysentry. New Plymouth had no drainage system; there were few pure wells, and during the drought which persisted through January and February there was little rain to wash away surface impurities. Marion and Decimus Atkinson's small cottage next to his blacksmith's shop was poorly ventilated and plagued with dust. Both their young sons became ill; Ronald, the eldest, although having no specific illness, wasted to skin and bone; baby Frank suffered diarrhoea for eight weeks. Dr Rawson attributed this to teething. Frank's condition worsened and the whole family moved to Whiteley's Native Institute set on a hill at Ngamotu, where it was airier and cooler. For Frank it was too late. He died there, aged ten months, on 12 February 1865. As sickness continued to cut a swathe through the town's children, Maria commented, 'I have less & less faith in medical science & feel sometimes it is all chance work. But then I am a sceptic to the very backbone. I am not sure that I *do* thoroughly believe anything but my own existence.'[80]

Henry returned from Dunedin, where he had gone to be with William and Emily for a few weeks, to find both his children ill and Helen Hursthouse overwhelmed with domestic difficulties. An over-indulgent use of goat's milk had given baby Blanche a serious digestive upset. Maria insisted that the baby should come to her. Once more Maria was feeding two babies – and Blanche improved almost immediately. Henry instructed Arthur to let him know if it was all too much for his sister, but Arthur was concerned only that the amount of milk Maria was drinking might make her

ill, and that with two babies and three young children in the house
there was too little quiet time in which he and Maria could read
to each other. Arthur still managed to absorb Horace before
breakfast. By mid-February 1865 Maria was able to tell Lely,
suffering from asthma in Nelson, that the pleasantly cool parlours
of Beach Cottage held a flourishing household including 'dear little
Blanche our newest comer'. Edie, however, was missing her grannie:
'She wants your *soft* knee & hand under her chin when she says
her prayers. My crinoline comes up higher than yours & is offensive,
marring her piety.'[81]

That summer seemed to Maria the longest she could remember.
There was constant movement amongst the members of the mob
with steamers taking some away or bringing others back at every
call. Maria was one of the few who 'sat still'. She no longer had
any hard physical work to do, and to relieve Margaret Taylor,
who still envisaged her as the mob's general factotum, wrote,

> I am growing a good, stout, middle-aged woman of the land-lady
> build. Don't imagine me worn in any way. For three years I have
> done no hard work. I am *now* a complete fine lady with two grown-
> up servants at twelve shillings a week each.[82]

She was still subject to an unrelenting daily timetable. The wet
nurse she had engaged at fourteen shillings a week to feed Blanche
twice a day left when her husband objected to milk due to his
son being squandered on another, so Maria continued to suckle
both Blanche and Mabel until the former was six months old. 'The
days are so cut up that reading & writing are almost out of the
question till all the young ones are asleep, & that does not happen
till just upon 8 o'clock; by 9 I am usually half asleep myself.'[83]

As she tended her young ones, Maria worried about Henry's
future. He was bearing his 'bitter trial' without complaint, but
his health was poor. Since his wife's death he had been twice to
the South Island to visit James and William and had left his son,
Francis, temporarily with James and Mary. The problem, as Maria
saw it, was how to bring Henry and Aunt Helen Hursthouse closer
to Arthur and herself without actually having them all under the
one roof. Henry wanted Arthur and Maria to sell Beach Cottage
and build on the two vacant sections adjoining his house. This
did not appeal to Maria. Would there be a temporary solution,
she wondered, if Marion and Decimus, who since their son's death
were unwilling to return to their house next to the blacksmith's
yard, moved into Henry's house, so that a house for Henry could

be put up in the Beach Cottage kitchen garden? Maria, who as usual was prepared to take the responsibility of 'fixing up' the mob on her own shoulders, was perplexed and frustrated. Yet again she longed for her mother's presence: 'I feel the want of you more than ever because I am so shut up in the house & garden that I need a sympathizing *resident*.'[84] As it turned out Henry, while not giving up his own house, spent most of his leisure time at Beach Cottage where he and Arthur studied Latin and Greek and revived their knowledge of German by reading Schiller and Goethe to each other in the evenings.

Another perplexity was Edith's education. During the time she had been with William and Emily at Dunedin she had joined her cousins in the lessons given them by a private tutor. Maria told Mary that she would do her best 'to make Arthur keep up an education agitation & he is willing enough to do it',[85] but there is no evidence in the *Taranaki Herald* that he in fact did so. Maria thought it important that the 'rising generation should be well & *solidly* educated', which for girls, especially, meant that they should go beyond the bit of French, the bit of history and geography, arithmetic and drawing which were generally accepted as sufficient. In New Plymouth there were a number of primary schools of indifferent merit and, in Maria's opinion, 'so many ignorant parents, who tho' they could afford good pay think one school as good as another, & so choose the *cheapest*'.[86] Older boys from Taranaki did well at Nelson College, to which Harry Atkinson had recently taken Dunstan, and, as was usual for the time, the better schools at New Plymouth were all for boys. Even at this early stage Maria fully intended, without having any idea where the money would come from, to compensate for colonial deficiencies in education by sending her daughters to Margaret Taylor in Germany when they were old enough. Edith, now in her seventh year, Maria considered a 'good child but not passionately fond of learning like her father'; she added, in a revealing aside about Arthur, 'her social powers are greater'.[87] For the present she determined to do the best she could with what was available. Arthur, after his early morning Greek and Latin, heard Edie's tables before breakfast. Maria thought her own life was 'too scrambly' to ensure continuity or regularity in teaching. She also wanted Edie to have the companionship of children her own age, so she began a school at Beach Cottage with Bessie Crompton as the paid teacher. The latter's reputation was still in question because of an earlier over-eager liaison with the garrison officers, but Maria doubted he

ability 'to corrupt such young ones'. By mid-March Bessie Crompton
was coming for two hours every weekday to teach Edie, Jessie
Carrington (in view of Maria's earlier opinion of the Carrington
girls, she must have decided to exert a missionary influence), and
Willie Atkinson.

Maria continued with her two twelve-shillings-a-week servants:
the faithful Elizabeth, and Ann Loveridge who was thirty, clean
and industrious, although her 'antecedents' were quite unknown.
One night in March, Maria and Arthur were awakened by an agitated Elizabeth bearing the news that 'Ann had gone mad & said
she had murdered the priest'. Arthur spent the rest of the night
on guard in the sitting room and went at first light to fetch the
Catholic priest to prove to the demented woman he was still alive.
During the day Ann seemed calmer, but that night she rampaged
through the house, threatening to set it alight. There was still no
provision at New Plymouth for the mentally disturbed; the local
priest found a lodging for her until a passage to Auckland was
procured. There she was placed in the charge of Bishop Pompallier.

The same vessel which 'shipped our poor demented lunatic for
Auckland' brought Lely home from Nelson. With courage and good
humour belying her age of seventy-four, she again suffered the
danger and indignity of being lowered from the *Wellington* into
an open surfboat while a gale was blowing:

> I had a very rough landing here . . . Imagine me seated not precisely
> on the top step of the ladder, but even with it, told to let my
> legs hang over the side for the men to take me down. In the midst
> of my fright a thought came over me that the sailors could not
> complain as they once did to Mary, 'you never let us even see
> your legs', for I could not by any possibility adjust my dress with
> a view to propriety.[88]

Lely thought Maria looked remarkably well and that 'poor dear
Aunt Helen was keeping up wonderfully'. Maria found that her
mother's deafness had increased to the extent that she missed all
general conversation. Lely's lively mind was unimpaired, however,
and her letters, no longer so frequent, are still witty and pertinent.
One of her special joys was reading poetry to her grandchildren.
Maria was relieved and thankful to have her 'resident sympathiser'
back at Beach Cottage. She was to need her mother's strong support
in the various crises that broke over the family in the middle of
1865 and made politics and even the war seem of lesser importance.

Jane Atkinson, always shy and retiring in contrast to her husband's

ebullient, confident nature, celebrated her elevated position in
society as a minister's wife by 'bursting out' in an astounding number
of new gowns and bonnets – 'but somehow either from want of
taste or some other cause, her attire does not become her so well'.[89]
Lely was not usually given to such remarks. As had been the case
with Blanche Richmond, neither Maria nor her mother was on
completely intimate terms with Jane, although they unquestioningly
accepted her as a *bona fide* member of the mob. Maria had admired
Jane's ability, when she first arrived at New Plymouth, to accept
the pioneering life, but, favouring good order in a household, she
was often dismayed at the lack of it in Jane's when Harry was
away. It was also feared among the mob's inner circle that once
Jane became socially assured she would veer towards the genteel
– and gentility was anathema to the Richmond family. Jane's brother,
Henry, who now worked as a hospital orderly, did nothing to
improve the Skinner image. His father's fear that he would turn
out to be a ne'er-do-well was only confirmed in Taranaki. Maria
hoped his wife, Kate Dunbar, whom he married in 1864, would
be able to make something of him.

Jane was a productive wife in the mode of Harry Atkinson's
own mother and sister; at two-yearly intervals between 1857 and
1863 she bore him, with apparent ease, three sons and a daughter.
In 1865 she was again pregnant, seemed in excellent spirits, and
expected her fifth baby to be born in their New Plymouth house
in July. Lely and Helen Hursthouse were the first to feel uneasy
about her difficulty in breathing. She had what was popularly called
a 'Derbyshire throat',[90] and though Maria and her mother both
noticed that it had been increasing in size, 'as it was a disfigurement
one did not like to say much about it'. Jane made light of the
goitre and did not persevere with the medicine Dr Rawson had
prescribed. Speaking of her confinements, she said to Maria, 'I
have always done so well.' These were the last words Maria heard
her speak. She choked and died suddenly on 22 June 1865. After
the post mortem Dr Rawson stated that she could not possibly
have lived through her approaching confinement, as the goitre
pressed so heavily on her windpipe that there was scarcely room
for respiration. At the time of her death she had a cold, and an
accumulation of phlegm had been enough to block the windpipe
completely.

Maria blamed Dr Rawson for giving Harry no word of warning
– in fact for reassuring him – about the likely effect of the growing
goitre on another pregnancy. Rawson was certainly aware of the

danger, for he told Arthur that if her labour when Alfred was born had been protracted, she would have died then. As it was, Harry Atkinson was totally unprepared for the news brought to him during the parliamentary session. One now marvels at this. Dr Rawson's examination of Jane's throat revealed that her air passage was so restricted that her breathing would have been laboured for weeks, if not months prior to her death. The two older women were worried but apparently not Harry who, without any misgiving, had left his wife to resume his duties as defence minister. Maria noted later, 'Jane must have been of a singularly uncomplaining nature to make so light of a difficulty in breathing . . . which must have been terribly oppressive'.[91] Childbirth was the lot of wives, and the Genesis guideline was understood and accepted without fuss. 'I have always done so well' was Jane's uncomplaining and proud epitaph.

Harry Atkinson, not a man to brood, felt he had no right to throw up his office and return to Hurworth as was his inclination; 'there is too much work to allow of it,' wrote his parliamentary colleague, J.C. Richmond, 'and this will soften the blow to him.'[92] Thinking over the event and the relationship of Harry and Jane, Maria wrote later to her confidante:

> It often pains me to think how small a blank poor Jane leaves, poor Harry alone suffering . . . he was evidently most deeply attached to her . . . It always seemed to me unfortunate for Harry that his boyish offer was accepted, a different wife would have made him a much finer character, & his children had degenerated from the Atkinson type by the Skinner admixture but of course I would not say this to anyone but you.[93]

Jane's death had a devastating effect on Mary Richmond. Already apprehensive about her own confinement in June, she had written to Arthur in January:

> I never entered upon [a New Year] with so grave a heart. The thought of death and separation clings to me . . . I may before very long have to leave you all [but] one's duty lies straight before us . . . we must go on bravely whatever happens.[94]

James's long absences at the Assembly had depressed her spirits. She had also overtaxed her strength in moving house to Wrey's (they called it Richmond) hill, and had 'taken to the sofa'. James Wilson Richmond was born on 7 June, with 'very little trouble' according to his father; Mary recalled the birth 'as a plunge into the dark during which I doubted whether I would see light again'.[95] Shocked by the news of Jane's death which followed shortly after, she wrote to James:

I can hardly believe it, and yet I think of scarcely anything else.
It seemed to me when I heard of it as if the world were coming
to an end – so strangely unnatural is it that so many wives &
mothers should be taken one after another.[96]
Mary bitterly regretted her inability to dissuade James from joining
the Weld ministry, in which he had accepted the post of colonial
secretary. It was not that she lacked ambition for him; rather,
the 'perpetual blank of separation' which had dogged them for
most of their married life had simply not been filled either by
her mother, when she was in New Zealand, or by Annie who
lived with them. 'I feel James's going away & so soon very much,'
she again wrote to Arthur, 'we had reckoned on a little time
together.'

The nursery at Beach Cottage, now without little Blanche, who
had returned to Henry and her grandmother, was requisitioned
for Harry's motherless children – Tudor, Fanny, and Alfred. Dunstan
was at Nelson College. It so happened that Marion Atkinson was
free to become Harry's housekeeper, Decimus having accepted a
commission as second in command of the 'native militia' at the
military settlement of Urenui, north of Waitara. Once established
with her surviving son, Ronnie, in Harry's town house, she took
charge of Tudor and Alfred while Fanny, for the time being, stayed
with Maria and Arthur.

No sooner had Beach Cottage settled down again than Mabel,
at eight months, became alarmingly ill; for a time she was 'quite
given up'. Dr Rawson thought the initial disorder was caused by
teething and lanced Mabel's gums. He then prescribed morphia.
Maria gave her baby less than half the dose, but it was still too
strong and Mabel's fever was replaced by extreme lassitude. Arthur
called in Dr Webber for a second opinion, and he and Rawson
advised Maria to give Mabel a spoonful of ipecacuanha wine every
quarter of an hour. This purgative only made the baby weaker
and Maria, 'very wisely', according to Arthur, stopped giving it.
She substituted small does of brandy and water. That evening Mabel
revived a little, and the following morning Maria dismissed Dr
Rawson. 'The doctors', wrote Arthur to Mary, 'have through
ignorance converted an indisposition into a severe illness.'[97] Mabel
continued weak, and Arthur called in Dr Tomlinson of the 57th
who thought her recovery was doubtful but who was nevertheless
more attentive than his colleagues. Maria continued with brandy
and water. By mid-July, after a fortnight of severe illness, Mabel
was decidedly stronger and on the way to complete recovery. Arthur

wrote in his diary, 'Maria will hardly believe it.' Within eight months the mob's six households in New Plymouth had experienced four deaths – two children, Eliza's Janet and Marion's Frank, and two mothers, Blanche and Jane. Within eighteen months Helen Hursthouse had lost all three of her daughters. Beach Cottage was the only one untouched, and the nagging thought which had increased Maria's anxiety during Mabel's illness was that it must be their turn next. 'I aged ten years when Mabel was so ill, but as soon as she was out of danger I was a new creature.'[98]

One of the advantages of the mob's close-knit structure was that the children moved comfortably within their extended families. When tragedy struck a particular household, its members were not left isolated. The kin group also rallied when financial disaster threatened to overwhelm Decimus and Marion Atkinson. Maria had been most impressed by Decie's blacksmith establishment on her return to New Plymouth in 1862. She had thought them closer to achieving 'worldly prosperity' than any other members of the set. Marion soon found that living next to her husband's workplace was thoroughly unpleasant – the noise, smell, and dust permeated to every corner of her house. Then came illness and baby Frank's death. Her older boy was also ill, and Marion herself, suffering from violent headaches, looked 'thin and worn'. She continued to live at the Wesleyan mission until her son improved, and was not looking forward to returning to her former house. Decimus, meanwhile, decided to remove his smithy and to build another house on the rising ground near the mission. Without seeing whether his business would survive the change, he rushed into building a large, unattractive house. Neither his assistants nor his customers wished to travel so far out of town. At the same time, to pay for the house, he made 'many wild & foolish investments' which Marion, with an 'unbounded confidence in her husband's business talents', made no attempt to restrain. In retrospect Maria felt that his elders had been remiss about the 'silly laissez faire way in which D. has been allowed to go on . . . Common sense told us he was getting into a mess tho' no one ever guessed how deeply.'[99] When he was proclaimed bankrupt, his debts were found to amount to £4,000. Marion, to whom social position was of some importance, was shattered; Decie's spirits were 'a little flat'. Harry, Arthur, and William Atkinson, together with Henry Richmond who had just lent Decie an ill-spared £300, held a runanga and decided they would pay his creditors eleven shillings in the pound. His house and forge were put up for sale. The main financial burden was borne by Harry and Arthur, possibly with some assistance from C.W. Richmond, who very often quietly responded to any family financial crisis.

Perfectly timed to restore Decie's 'elastic spirits' came Harry Atkinson's offer of a lieutenant's position in the newly formed 'native militia', made up from the kupapa. With his commission and regular pay went 250 acres of land at Urenui. William Atkinson, still struggling to build up his land agency and insurance business, was offered the captain's post but turned it down. Lely was relieved: 'One cannot help being glad that two of the family are not provided for by the present ministry.'[100] It was still a lonely prospect for Marion, who would not be able to rejoin her husband until the following summer at the earliest. Living in a small cottage at the other end of town, she was beyond reach of the 'sociable popping in & out' which her sister, Eliza, and Maria enjoyed. She would have been utterly bowed down, Maria thought, but for the timely necessity of exerting herself for Harry and his children.

Maria continued to attribute her own health and strength during the trials of 1865 to the location of Beach Cottage. Another room and a long verandah were added to it during the autumn to ensure that 'the children have plenty of elbow room without disturbing their Grannie's peace'. From the verandah they could view such exciting events on the beach below as the landing of wild cattle – when this happened, Ruth was very insistent that nobody wore red socks or scarves – or the 'weekly shipwreck': 'One cannot tell what infatuation seizes the little vessels here but come on shore some of them will whatever the weather may be. Even in gales no one is ever drowned & we look on quite calmly at a wreck occurring just under our windows.'[101] After these alterations Beach Cottage became in fact two cottages, one of stone and one of wood, joined together. In the wooden part, from which no sound escaped to the stone, were the kitchen, dining room, nursery, and Arthur and Maria's bedroom; in the stone were Lely's bedroom, two sitting rooms with folding doors opening from the smaller to the larger, and Arthur's study. In the good-sized attic were the servants' rooms.

> I grow fonder of this place as time goes on. The sea never tires one; in its change there seems always a fresh interest, & in time of sickness or trouble it is a priceless blessing to be able to breathe the pure air on the verandah or terrace walk . . . I feel quite cooped up in pretty gardens that have high hedges or palings for privacy & shelter, & for all their rare shrubs & flowers would not exchange our breezy terrace & boundless view.[102]

'Our war is nearly at a standstill,' Arthur wrote in some exasperation to William near the beginning of 1865. A band of fifty Bushrangers drawn from the two former companies still made occasional sorties, but what little fighting there was in Taranaki was mainly between parties of kupapa and 'rebel' Maori. In Arthur's opinion, General Cameron, who had replaced Grey as the mob's *bête noire*, was 'selling out Taranaki': 'He will not fight and will not agree to confiscation down here to any extent and thinks the war unjust. The reason is he is sick of being here.'[103] Defence Minister Harry Atkinson kept up a regular correspondence with his brother so that Arthur was privy to a great deal of the Weld ministry's thinking on the conduct of the war. Shortly after the Taranaki Militia and Rifle Volunteers had been discharged, Grey issued a proclamation, 26 October 1864, offering a free pardon to all 'rebel' Maori who would swear allegiance before 10 December 1864, surrender their arms, and cede such land as governor and government would demand. Taranaki and Ngati Ruanui were interested in peace, but were opposed to the conditions, 'Kei nukarautea e te Kanawa', as Arthur translated it: 'lest they be humbugged (treated treacherously) by the white people'.[104] Grey seemed very willing to go ahead with confiscation and was adamant that there should be a Taranaki campaign – 'the punishment of Natives there must be very severe'.[105] Harry presented him with a confiscation proclamation over 'the whole of the land between here [New Plymouth] & Whanganui & a good slice to the northward'.[106] The kupapa were to have their land back and 'rebels' who submitted were 'to get enough to live on', but because of Cameron's objections to confiscation and his dilatoriness in campaigning (he maintained that it would take him two years to secure the area from Patea to New Plymouth and he was not prepared to march without reinforcements), Taranaki seemed to Arthur to be in its usual stalemated position. To make matters worse – for the settlers – New Plymouth banks refused to cash Taranaki compensation cheques.

On the other hand, the Pai Marire movement was gaining more followers and spreading from Taranaki to the Wanganui region and across the island to the East Coast. On 1 February 1865 250 troops from the 70th left New Plymouth by sea to strengthen the garrison at Wanganui. They were followed on 18 March by 200 military settlers who were to establish posts up the Wanganui River, and fifty Bushrangers bound for Patea. Three days earlier, news had reached New Plymouth of the 'ritual execution' of Reverend C.S. Volkner, CMS missionary at Opotiki. Denied by his 'rascally paper' from rejoining the company of Bushrangers kept on sporadic service about New Plymouth, Arthur turned his attention to a study of Pai Marire. He made contact with a small group of adherents whom he questioned about the origin and meaning of their faith. During April and May Arthur wrote several articles on the subject in the *Taranaki Herald*, making such observations as 'Maoris took up Christianity lightly and lightly put it aside', which is questionable, and 'Before Te Ua and his doctrines were heard . . . natives of other districts had begun to mingle their old heathen incantations with the church service.'[107] He earned a reprimand from John Whiteley for referring to the spiritual food supplied by missionaries as 'husky'.

In March Arthur began a political career, which was briefly to take him to the House of Representatives, by becoming a member of the Taranaki Provincial Council for the district of Grey and Bell. At first glance it seems surprising that it took so long for him to be publicly recognised, but then one remembers that in the volunteers, where all officers and non-commissioned officers were elected, Arthur remained a private. In popular estimation neither his bravery nor his intelligence was in question, nor was he considered a misanthropist, but his teasing wit, which he seldom took the trouble to subdue, always tended to offset recognition of his undoubted ability. Only four electors turned up to vote him in, to whom Arthur made a typical A.S.A. reply which did not earn him friends:

> I complimented them & the electors generally on the interest shown in provincial politics. I felt this mark of their confidence all the more flattering as coming unanimously from so large a body of electors & I should never despair of New Zealand politics while I saw a mere provincial election draw together such a gathering as the present one.[108]

Skirmishing with the provincial councillors Arthur found almost as 'invigorating' as skirmishing with Maori – and certainly more entertaining:

> As everybody knows everybody & there are no parties & therefore no party feeling & as moreover our Speaker [William Crompton] can be resisted or set aside or argued into a confused state of mind when anything is possible, we get along like a 'happy family', at least with great cheerfulness if without much to show for our trouble.[109]

Arthur very nearly became a member of the General Assembly in July when James Richmond, member of Omata, was 'obliged', in Maria's words, 'to be elevated to the peerage' in order to represent the Weld ministry in the Legislative Council.

> James was considered best suited for dealing with the old respectables (or buffers or codgers, as I have heard them disrespectfully called) so had to consent to the dull honour of becoming a peer. The House of Representatives is an infinitely more lively & exciting arena.[110]

Maria was an enthusiastic supporter of her husband's candidature:

> Arthur really is an experienced politician. He has been present [as an observer or reporter] at every session of the General Assembly but one during the last 5 years & is known to most of the leading men. His thorough knowledge of Maori & much better acquaintance with Maoris & their ways would make him really a useful member & I dare say *you will believe even a wife's testimony* that he is intellectually a good deal above average. When one remembers that he only had about a year & ½ of regular schooling & that at a very second rate school, he really is a wonder. He has entirely educated himself & will go on educating himself, I have no doubt, till his dying day even should he live another 50 years.[111]

The element of farce seldom distant from Taranaki politics was again present on polling day. Strictly speaking it was illegal for progress reports to be released during the poll but, as Arthur's diary makes clear, strict adherence to rules would have spoilt the fun:

> The polling was very even at first 10 each, 15 each, till 1 o'clock when I was 5 ahead. This however did not last long & Gledhill[112] led by 3 or 4 at 3.30. I was *one* ahead when Looney brought down Goodwin who had signed my requisition & promised to vote for me & Howell who had promised not to vote at all – & these two gave Gledhill a majority of 1. This made up the whole of their available resources & for half an hour the election was in suspense depending on the arrival or non arrival of two of my men from Tikorangi (Terrill & Gray) who had started with Free in the morning but whom he had left to come on by themselves when he got a horse – sent Free & then Pitcairn on horseback out to meet them & just *4 minutes* after the poll had closed in came Terrill leisurely trotting along. So Gledhill got in by one.[113]

In the event of a tie the returning officer had told Arthur that he would give him his vote. 'It was all rather exciting,' Arthur commented. He went down to Wellington anyway to report the opening session for the *Herald*.

A member of the mob who had never sought public office was Henry Richmond, although as captain of the militia, president of the Taranaki Institute, treasurer, and lately a Crown land commissioner and deputy superintendent of the provincial council, he enjoyed a greater measure of public confidence than his erudite brother-in-law. Henry was not enthusiastic when Arthur first talked to him about standing for the superintendency – Charles Brown had spoken of resigning – and stated that he would consider it only to keep a seriously unfit man out. 'The quiet retiring Henry is coming forward as a candidate,' Maria informed Margaret Taylor. True to past performance, Charles Brown once again offered himself at the last moment. Maria considered it doubtful whether all the people who had signed Brown's requisition would in fact vote for him. The only thing brought against Henry was that he was a member of too influential a family:

> It is quite amusing to see the alarm or jealousy part of the public here feel towards our set, aggravating too because ungrateful, as without our set where would Taranaki be now, for everything written, said or done of any importance during the last four years on behalf of this province has emanated from an A or R's pen or tongue or sword – rifle I should say tho' many bullets have been fired by less influential people![114]

To Henry's surprise, and presumably to that of Charles Brown – it was his first recent defeat – Henry was elected superintendent 'by a good majority'. Shortly afterwards, John Stephenson Smith asked Arthur to speak for him when applications for Henry's former job as a commissioner of Crown lands came down to a decision between two. Arthur thought Stephenson Smith, who was appointed, the better man, but took no part in the selection: 'I did not want it to be said that "the family" began their reign by appointing a connection.'[115] In order to give the quiet serious Henry's superintendency more decorum, Arthur also decided not to stand again for election during Henry's term of office. The reason he gave to the council was 'that they may get on more peacefully without me'.

In Wellington as correspondent for the *Herald*, Arthur made full use of the amenities and opportunities which the capital provided: a secondhand bookshop, 'the first of these admirable institutions I have met with in New Zealand', at which he bought a 'Kaffir grammar' (probably Bantu) and Cromwell's *Letters and Speeches* for Lely to give him on his birthday; geology lectures from Dr James Hector; discussions with Harry and James and other members of the ministry; a visit to Pai Marire prisoners taken at Te Weraroa and kept on board a prison hulk in the harbour, with whom he conversed and 'got names of two fish new to me'. He also enjoyed walking over Wellington's hills and, in the early evening, strolling with James alongside the harbour, 'discussing the moon and the unvoyageable sky to our heart's content'.

In New Plymouth Maria was missing Arthur and disappointed by the paucity of his letters. She complained to Emily:

> I am sorry to say I am not enjoying the session as I hoped to do when Arthur went, his accounts both private & public of what goes on at Wellington are most niggardly, at least so it seems to me, but then I know my appetite is large. We hear of good speeches being made, but get no reports, or very inadequate ones. What does William think of Mr Fitz[Gerald] as Native Minister? I am delighted with the notion. With the most Utopian theorizing on native matters to manage the Maoris there can be no fear in England of our using our army of 1500 men to tyranize over them. Have you read the correspondence between the Gov & the Gen? You will find it very amusing. I could write a whole letter on public matters but it would not be of any value.[116]

Arthur shared Maria's opinion of FitzGerald, thinking him 'a visionary, if not a quack'. James Richmond conceded that he had great ability but rash judgement: 'My chief difference with him is that he will be for ever insisting on applying constitutional maxims and asserting constitutional rights when they don't apply.'[117] FitzGerald was, however, one of the few politicians of the time to make a reasonable and (as far as this was possible for a colonist) disinterested assessment of Maori disaffection. In a letter to J.C. Richmond he wrote:

> Two rules are deeply fixed in my mind.
> 1) To expect men to respect law who don't enjoy it is absurd.
> 2) To try and govern a folk by our courts and at the same time to say that our courts shall take no cognizance of *their property* is amazing folly. Two thirds of the Northern Island is held under a tenure which is ignored by our law. Is it *possible* to govern any people by a law which does not recognise their estate in land?[118]

The alliance of expediency between Grey and the Weld ministry – with Harry Atkinson in particular – against General Cameron gave wry amusement to the mob. 'We must support Grey against the General or we shall be done,' Harry wrote to Arthur. James Richmond's attitude remained cautious:

> Grey is a curious being. He seems much happier in his present company and his present warfare than when he was fighting his late ministers . . . His manner is gentle and amiable to a marvellous degree but one remembers the claws under the velvet.[119]

Weld had earlier written to Harry Atkinson: 'If the General would only go away we might do something.'[120] He did at the beginning of August, but by that time Weld's 'self-reliant' ministry was under severe financial stress and its leader so ill that he could not attend the House with any regularity. 'We shall yet be crushed by finance unless there is great patriotism hidden away in Otago and Auckland,'[121] James wrote to Mary at the end of July. With the country nearly bankrupt, the members for those two provinces joined forces in presenting a resolution to the House which called for a separation at Cook Strait into two separate colonies. Otago, reluctant to spend its goldfields revenue on a North Island war, had pressed for separation for some years. To Maria, its attitude was understandable, if regrettable; it was the Auckland members, who should have known better, on whom she poured her contempt: 'Can a more pitiful part be imagined than that which the Aucklanders have played of late? I wonder any man of mere ordinary manliness can cast in his lot with them except driven to it by pecuniary necessity.'[122] The North Island 'colony' was to be divided into two provinces – Wellington and Hawkes Bay, Auckland and Taranaki. 'A pleasant notion,' Arthur commented, 'being made an outlying district of Auckland.'[123] The motion was lost by a considerable majority, but the position of the Weld ministry remained precarious. James told Mary that the House was 'more anarchical and distracted than ever', and that the only thing working in the ministry's favour was the opposition's distrust of each other. He thought he and his colleagues might hold on for the next nine months.

Maria had intended to visit Mary at Nelson in January 1865 – scarlet fever had intervened. Now she felt that if she did not leave before Arthur returned from Wellington, she would probably not go at all. Elizabeth was still with her, Ann had been replaced, and Lely was a more than satisfactory mother substitute for Edie and Ruth.[124] Fanny rejoined her brothers under Marion's care, and Maria took Arfie and Mabel with her. The weather for the crossing was rough enough to make Maria seasick, but to compensate she and the children had the ladies' cabin to themselves, apart from 'one quiet young Maori woman'. They arrived at Nelson on 22 September.

The month before Maria's arrival three of Mary's children developed scarlet fever. On Dr Cusack's orders Mary turned the living room of their new house into an infirmary for herself and all five children: the carpets and soft furnishings were removed, the cracks of the window frames were stopped up, and a fire was kept burning night and day. All the nursing had fallen on Mary, who wrote to James: 'I am often very very weary, for I have not had a good night for a long time & often very bad ones and am on my feet nearly all day.'125 Thanking James for his 'sweet kind letter', she said, 'I cannot tell you how much it has refreshed and comforted me – and I much needed comfort.'126

It would appear that James was 'sending letters by every mail' but, as had always been the case, it was his presence Mary pined for. She shrank from the idea of another year separated from him, except during spasmodic visits, yet having just settled into their comfortable new house with delightful views over Nelson Haven and across the bay to the distant mountains, she was unhappy at the prospect of a move to Wellington. She also fretted over James's political future: 'I know I should be extremely sorry if I heard the ministry were out, and yet I do not enjoy your being in.'127 In an attempt to make Wellington seem more attractive, Harriet Gore Browne wrote a cheerful letter about the agreeable company she remembered from her Government House days in Auckland, and which Mary would keep in the new capital:

> I do not think there has been any ministry with so many pleasant and popular wives, Mrs Sewell is a host in herself . . . and then Mrs FitzGerald is clever and agreeable and Mrs Weld loveable and pretty so that when you and Miss Smith [Annie] go over you will make a charming society.128

Mary, still extremely fatigued, possibly anaemic, wanted no part of the public life she and James would be forced to lead in the 'strange land of Wellington'; she desired only the quietness she might share with him in this 'sweet place'. If move they must, then 'Taranaki with all of you', she wrote to Maria, was where she wished to be.

Nearly all the letters Mary wrote to James, especially those in 1865, are tinged by an underlying sadness, and give the impression that without her husband by her side the fullness of life simply receded from her. James's letters were full of interesting political gossip which he willingly shared with Mary, but when he wrote of their relationship he tended to reinforce her feelings of deprivation and loneliness: 'I can form no image of heaven or any better life without you, and the days spent away from you are almost lost.'129 Mary would willingly have agreed with this sentiment: her sigh is audible. One does not doubt James's loving appreciation of his wife, yet his days spent away from her were not 'lost'. He was leading a stimulating political life, enjoying the company of 'pleasant highly educated people', and enjoying too the 'very healthy climate' and the beauty of Wellington 'as a piece of landscape'.

When James's letter announcing the near defeat and subsequent resignation of the Weld ministry reached Nelson on 19 October, Mary seemed to Maria to be 'mildly indiposed with a cold'. There was no reason to believe it anything more than influenza, she assured Lely and Arthur (who had returned to New Plymouth at the beginning of the month), and in customary fashion she began to nurse Mary's baby, 'for Mabel is so well & eats & drinks so nicely now that she will not mind being weaned in the day'.[130] 'Little James Wilson', who was to become as her own, 'looks up & laughs in my face when I feed him'. James, out of office, wrote 'most decidedly' of moving off at once to Taranaki. He acknowledged that they had lost money by their various moves in the last few years and that he had been possibly premature in building a house, but begged Mary, who always fretted about finances, not to be anxious about worldly matters. He assured her he would not take 'careless sanguine views in future' – and then proceeded to take one:

> I believe a very little will serve us in a rustic way of life . . . We must keep a cow if possible, and I must try to earn something by painting. Another opening may be in the way of surveys . . . In any case I see no reason for us to be despondent about the means of living. You will not mind Alla quitting silks for the flour bag, and you will let me take to blue serge shirts and canvas trousers.[131]

A return to Taranaki and somehow to the Hurworth idyll had always been Mary's fond wish. Nelson too had become home. In an earlier letter to James she had written of the view from Long Look Out:

> The long mountain range, topped with snow, has that transcendental look that charmed me so much when I was staying at the Port. The whole view looks as if it might melt away. I sigh to think of leaving this sweet place. Its loveliness is very soothing to me.[132]

The thought of moving yet again, financial worries over their recent house building, and the fatigue from her lone battle against scarlet fever following closely upon childbirth all seemed to press heavily on Mary. It is possible too that separation, which had been the theme of so many of her letters, had become, even at thirty-one, an *idée fixe*. One recalls her New Year letter to Arthur, 'The thought of death and separation clings to me', and wonders whether she now chose to accept rather than fight the final separation of death.

What had seemed to be a mild indisposition turned to a fever; she became stone deaf and then delirious; she died at Long Look Out on 29 October, within ten days of the onset of illness.

Maria believed that Mary did not suffer during the last few hours; for herself and Annie it was a 'long protracted, dreadful nightmare' which brought Maria 'greater mental suffering than I ever before passed thro'.[133] The real shock was to James. He left Wellington for Nelson not even aware Mary was ill: 'Think of that poor husband coming home,' Lely wrote to William and Emily, 'anticipating a joyful meeting with his sweet wife and finding her in her coffin.'[134]

Arthur suffered a shock only a little less severe. Impatiently awaiting Maria's return – three birthday celebrations had been held over – he received news in her letter of 23 October that Mary was poorly. Maria was not unduly anxious and the main part of the letter dealt with the likelihood of James and Mary returning to Taranaki. 'Most satisfactory,' Arthur wrote in his diary. On the morning of 3 November, the day Maria had given for her return, he watched

> rather anxiously for the Auckland as the wind was on shore & the sea getting up . . . she came in at 3 – & I went off in the mail boat expecting to find Maria, Harry & some of Mary's children but instead only found Harry & little Arfie & they told me the worst news that ever I heard – that the dear Mary was *dead* but I could not understand it.[135]

In her Christmas letter to Margaret Taylor, Maria wrote of Mary:

> It seems to me impossible to conceive of a nobler, purer, sweeter woman . . . her very mistakes were from the excess of goodness in her nature . . . No effort is needed to imagine her as moving in a world of spirits . . . No trace of selfish thought or unworthy aim did I ever see in her.[136]

In similar fashion Lely described her as a 'pearl above all price'. But the pearl was too easily shattered; the virtues of purity, nobility, unselfishness, and sweetness needed a compensatory spiritual robustness and mental resilience. Yet Maria, that 'energetic scrambler', claimed Mary as her dearest New Zealand friend. She was not to be replaced.

'Tied by the leg'

New Plymouth, Nov. 1865–Feb. 1868.

Maria, James and three of his children – Alla, Dick, and 'little Wilsie' – returned to New Plymouth on 13 November. Ten days later the *Phoebe* arrived from Nelson and Arthur walked down the beach to see whether Annie and the other two children, Dolla and Maurice, had arrived. To his surprise, 'to everybodys surprise and pleasure', not Annie but the head of the family, C.W. Richmond, stepped ashore from the surf boat. He had especially come to be with James for a few days and, as Maria wrote to Emily, 'he roused us all'. Though they had frequently corresponded, it was over four years since Maria and Arthur had seen William. Since leaving Auckland in 1861 both families had added three more children.[1] William looked thin and gaunt, which was usual, and he suffered several asthmatic attacks during his short stay at Beach Cottage. But such was his vitality and energy, romping with the children between fits of gasping for breath, that his visit was seen as 'an unspeakable blessing' which helped to 'turn the current of our thoughts from the sad losses of the last twelve months'. During his visit a family party walked or rode on horseback to Hurworth where Harry Atkinson had sequestered himself. Lely described Harry as 'wonderfully improved' since he had returned to the bush: 'his beloved place seems to have a special healing influence over him'.[2] Dunstan and Tudor (the latter was about to attend the Bishop's School at Nelson) were with him for the holidays. 'The country is a far more fitting dwelling place than the sandhills,' Arthur observed.[3]

After six days William returned to Dunedin. Before leaving he promised Lely that, if it were offered to him, he would accept the Nelson judgeship so as to establish himself within reach of the family.

Annie Smith accompanied by Dolla, Maurice, and a servant arrived by the *Wellington* on 13 December, bringing Beach Cottage to bursting point. Eight adults (including three servants) and ten children (among them Willie Atkinson, whose mother, Eliza, was recovering from the birth of her second son, John, on 5 December), now lived there. Willie distressed his mother by always calling her 'aunty' as his cousins did. Lely eased the strain on the 'elastic cottage' by moving into Henry's house (he was now living with his mother-in-law, Helen Hursthouse, in Cutfield Road), and her room became Annie's. The children, whose ages ranged downwards from nearly eight to six months, divided themselves into amicable or warring couples. Maurice and Willie got on well together, as did Alla and Edie, but Dick and Arfie fought constantly; Ruth and Dolla, while not physically clashing, were standoffish and uncooperative, and it was not long before Mabel became jealous of the attention her mother was giving 'little Wilsie'. After breakfast Arthur, who had given up his study to James, generally went thistling on his Hurworth property.[4]

'Maria is well,' Lely wrote to Emily at the end of 1865, 'but she is so surrounded by little ones'; 'whenever I see her she seems on the point of falling asleep.'[5] Annie, as Lely anticipated – 'I fear she has a very poor constitution' – was not of any great assistance. Since her arrival from Nelson she had been 'quite laid up' with severe headaches and a skin irritation. James seemed to be recovering, was quiet and resigned, even cheerful at times; then would come another bout of depression. 'Both Henry and Harry seem to me to have been raised and expanded by sorrow or by the struggle to bear sorrow nobly,' Maria wrote to Emily, 'but poor James seems harassed and broken – I sometimes fear beyond hope of cure.'[6] A letter which James wrote to William at the end of the year again reveals the tinge of fatalism which had always coloured his relationship with Mary:

> The great change that has come upon me shadows every thought and steeps everything . . . I fancied that because I was constantly aware of the frailty of my tenure of the blessing, that therefore I was nerved to bear its loss, but it is not so . . . My dear brother, I felt all along that she was most unequally mated and that I had no right to her, and now my term is at an end . . . I am forlorn beyond what I can describe.[7]

It seems to have caused neither consternation nor dismay when James and Mary's 'Palace of the Arts' at Hurworth, which had survived the war without structural damage, was accidentally burnt down on 19 December. Perhaps it was seen as an appropriate, even an heroic consummation. Christmas 1865 passed without the usual communal festivity: 'we did not take much notice of its being

Christmastide, we could not do much to keep it,' Arthur wrote in his diary.

Maria found the children an 'antidote to morbidity' and Wilsie 'a perfect baby, more like his dear mother than any of them'. She continued to grieve for Mary: 'Until our dear Mary was taken away I had not had any loss by death coming home at once to my daily life and heart.'[8] In an age when a deeply affectionate relationship for women could be relied on only between bosom friends, it was not surprising that Maria told Margaret that the loss of Mabel, however grievous, would nevertheless have been a lighter load to bear. The survival of infants was always chancy; the death of a confidante was an irreparable loss, not to be tempered by thoughts of heavenly bliss. More of a sceptic than was Margaret, Maria wrote to her friend,

> I do not know that I have the *same* sort of faith in immortality that you seem to possess . . . I do not know that I acknowledge any to myself but the feeling that the holiness and goodness in God's creatures must be as eternal as His own attributes and that real love is of its essence immortal.[9]

Just before Mary's fatal illness Maria had been reading J.E. Renan's *Vie de Jesus* (1863). It had bolstered her growing disbelief in the supernatural, although she could never entirely rid herself of hope in a hereafter, not so much on her own account or even for her friends, but for those 'myriads of human beings . . . born only to suffer . . . It seems as tho' to doubt immortality were indeed to doubt the Justice and Mercy of our Heavenly Father.'[10] Renan's book had created an immediate sensation in Europe and a storm of ecclesiastical disapproval. It repudiated the miraculous element in Christ's life, ignored its moral aspect, and portrayed him as a 'charming and amiable Galilean preacher'. Maria liked a great deal of *Vie de Jesus* 'tho' there is always something in these hypothetical histories eminently unsatisfying to one of my hard sceptical turn of mind'.[11] What she and Mary did find amusing was that it had travelled to New Zealand amongst a heap of evangelical and Calvinistic tracts sent by Smith relatives in England. 'Amongst such "compagnons de voyage",' Mary had said, 'it seemed wonderful that it had succeeded in arriving whole.'[12] More to Maria's taste was John Seeley's *Ecce Homo* (1865) which portrayed Jesus as a moral reformer. It was challenged by the orthodoxy because it laid no emphasis on the supernatural as an integral part of the Christian faith, but Maria could more easily identify with the author's 'Anglo-Saxon imagination' and found it 'such a blessing to get the essence of Xtianity free of dogmatic theology'.[13] She had also been reading Theodore Parker, the American Unitarian preacher and writer (1810–60), who maintained that what was important in Christianity was the *influence* of Jesus. He too had been attacked for his claim that belief in miracles was unnecessary. The Richmonds' Unitarian friend and teacher, James Martineau, was one of his followers. Parker had also been an ardent moral reformer, the leader of the anti-slavery crusade in Boston and advocate of such other causes as temperance, prison reform, and education for women. 'I am not anxious to assume any sectarian name,' Maria told Margaret, 'but I am perhaps nearer being a Parkerite than anything else.'[14]

Maria also found nostalgia to be the companion of grief. She wrote to Margaret of her memories of the English countryside, of walks with Margaret along Devonshire lanes and out on the moorlands,

the smell of the woods and the primroses and violets, the sounds of rooks and larks, what intense joy they gave me after London life and then the quaint old sitting room at Harpford [where she and Margaret had once stayed], your Schubert songs, the readings – Tennyson and Martineau together. Can I ever forget the enjoyment?[15]

But the press of life was ever onward, and public and private events once more engaged her. A mammoth excursion to Hurworth during January saw all the families who had once lived there picnicking at Harry's place. Joining them was Calvert Wilson, who had returned to New Plymouth with his wife.[16] Adults, children, and babies numbered twenty-five. As the summer progressed smaller parties of cousins made their way to Hurworth for a few days of change. The practice was to put the children in a bullock cart under the charge of the driver and give them a bag of biscuits to share on their journey.

In January 1866 the war which had seemed to be at an unsatisfactory standstill in Taranaki received what the settlers considered a welcome boost, with Major General Trevor Chute's[17] ten-day forced march through the bush from Patea to New Plymouth on the eastern side of the mountain. 'Good news', Arthur wrote in his diary, on learning that Chute's mixed force of regulars, Bushrangers, and kupapa had begun such a venture, 'following the natives about in or out of the bush is a thing never before heard of in a British General.'[18] A triumphal arch at the Huatoki bridge and Henry, as superintendent, mounted on a box with a congratulatory address of welcome, surrounded by cheering citizens, greeted Chute and his men[19] when they arrived at New Plymouth. A musical treat equally enjoyable to Maria and Arthur occurred on the same evening. Mr and Mrs Heine, he a blind violinist, she a pianist, who had been 'delighting audiences in the Australian colonies as well as in New Zealand', were giving a series of seven concerts in the Freemasons' Hall. Maria attended them all and was thrilled by the 'delicacy and feeling' of the violinist and the 'brilliant execution' of the pianist. The programme ranged from Beethoven sonatas to such popular favourites as 'Ye Banks and Braes' and 'Home Sweet Home'.

There was further excitement at Beach Cottage when, immediately after the Heine concerts ended, a German piano despatched the previous year by Margaret Taylor finally arrived, having been mis-shipped to Nelson and then carried on to Auckland. Once safely deposited in the Beach Cottage sitting room it was pronounced a very fine instrument by Mary King who came that same evening to try it with Beethoven sonatas. It was in perfect tune, without spot or blemish upon it. Maria, who had earlier wished she had asked Margaret to send out a sewing machine instead, was delighted as soon as she touched it; Lely's worry was how to preserve this 'really elegant and beautiful piece of furniture which puts everything else in the room to shame, from little feet and fingers'.[20] When James's possessions arrived from Nelson, Mary's piano came too. James could not bear to part with something that was so associated with 'dear Mary', but two pianos were rather an encumbrance. Maria took the sensible course: she sold their 'beautiful piano' to Annie. 'I hardly dare confess to you what I have done,' she wrote to Margaret. Annie was fully appreciative.

The other summer 'attraction', General Chute's campaign, which had seemed to augur so well for settler interests, was not progressing so sweetly. On their return march around the Taranaki coast, Chute's men looted and ill treated 'friendly' Maori; in particular, two small hapu of the Taranaki tribe under Wiremu Kingi Matakatea who, although living near Opunake in the midst of Pai Marire followers, had never joined. These people were so roughly handled and intimidated that many of them threw in their lot with the waeromene. The news dismayed both Arthur and Robert Parris. The latter, recently appointed civil commissioner for Taranaki, had the onerous job of pacifying Taranaki and Ngati Ruanui to the south, and General Chute had refused him permission to accompany the troops even through his own district. 'Poor Parris is a good deal cut up about it,' Arthur commented. He wrote a strongly worded leader in the *Herald* condemning Chute's action: 'It will be remembered that the greatest difficulty we have had all along in dealing with the disaffected natives has been their distrust of our sincerity and good faith'.[21]

A month later, when the full extent of Maori alienation was known, he wrote:

> General Chute's march up from Whanganui was about the best thing that has been done in the war but we do not hesitate to say that it would have been better for Taranaki if his march had ended in this town and he had gone back to Whanganui by steamer – for he has left us with more enemies than he found here when he came.[22]

Doubtless Chute's coastal march would have added recruits to the forces of the Ngatai Ruanui fighting chief and master of guerrilla warfare, Titokowaru, who was soon to challenge Pakeha supremacy in south Taranaki. Lely did not share Arthur's concern over Chute's behaviour. When Mrs Warre (who had left New Zealand with her husband in March 1866) wrote to Lely from England that General Chute was not in good repute there because 'he is on too good terms with the settlers and has killed some Maoris', Lely commented, 'Why are soldiers sent here if not to fight, and if they do fight are they not expected to kill? The onesided fanaticism of Exeter Hall I suppose.'[23]

In March Arthur had a long talk with a Maori friend, Hone Pihama, a Ngati Ruanui chief who had fought against the Pakeha. Arthur recorded the substance of the discussion in his diary:

> I asked him why they had come up to join in the war. He said, 'because of Waitara', but when I came to talk to him about it I was surprised to find he knew very little of the main facts . . . I talked to him about Taiporohenui which was built to include (porohe) all the tribes that there might be none left outside to sell land to the pakehas. He admitted that the fear of having the land overspread by the pakehas as the tide overspreads the sandbank was the real cause of the war.[24]

Beach Cottage became less crowded when James obtained a year's lease on nearby Beach House, formerly occupied by the Fred Carringtons. Beach Cottage remained the focal point for the children's activities as Annie, *in loco parentis*, was unable to cope by herself: 'I don't believe her strength and spirits are equal to the management of house and children,' Lely confided to Emily.[25]

Annie, however, was soon to find succour in another quarter.

Both James Richmond and Harry Atkinson had decided to quit politics after the resignation of the Weld ministry and to devote themselves to bush farming. In one of James's last letters to Mary he had told her to prepare herself for resuming life in the bush of either Merton or Hurworth. But a blue serge shirt and canvas trousers had never suited James in spite of his romantic fancies about the pastoral life and his frequent comments about the stultifying nature of politics. After meeting with electors at New Plymouth on 24 February he decided to offer himself for the Grey and Bell seat which Harry had vacated. He was elected to represent that district in the General Assembly on 2 March. Within a week of his election, James took his eldest son, six-year-old Maurice, for a sojourn with William and Emily at Dunedin. He also intended to make a painting expedition into Central Otago.

The candidate for James's former Omata electorate was Arthur Atkinson. F.U. Gledhill, who had successfully opposed Arthur at the time of James's temporary 'elevation to the peerage', now busied himself in drawing up a requisition for his former rival. Arthur was ready for a new commitment. His newspaper relationship with G.W. Woon had never been entirely satisfactory, and in February he had begun negotiating (Arthur called it 'skirmishing') with his partner over control of the paper. Arthur prepared himself for the election by 'taking a ramble on the beach to exercise my oratory a little & actually succeeded in talking consecutively if not intelligibly for five minutes at a time'.[26] On 9 March he was proposed for Omata by William Crompton ('old Crumpty would have liked to have gone himself'),[27] seconded by Gledhill, and elected without opposition. In thanking the electors Arthur referred to his difficulty in speaking coherently – 'the "divine faculty of speech" which was granted so liberally to a few happy souls had been scantily doled out to him'[28] – and then proceeded to give what, in print, appears to be a lucid explanation of his political views. He was a firm believer in the former Weld ministry's twin principles of unity within the colony and 'self-dependence' in defence.

At the time when Arthur was elected to the Assembly, the colony was still threatened by some form of 'separation'. Stafford, according to a letter he wrote C.W. Richmond, was a most reluctant leader: 'I never was in my life – and trust never to be again – in so painful a position as a public man . . . in being compelled to oppose Weld . . . But I felt certain from the first . . . that his propositions were financially impossible.'[29] He was prepared to offer Richmond any office – colonial secretary, native minister, treasurer – if only he would return to politics and shore up a ministry 'bound to maintain the unity of the colony':

> No proposition was ever made from one man to another with more urgent sincerity than that I now make to you, nor with a deeper consciousness of what depends on your decision. I shall await it anxiously – I wish I could say without fear and trembling.[30]

William's reply was an emphatic 'no'. He thought 'separation' was inevitable but stated 'unhesitatingly' that he felt no call of duty to return to politics. Family and health considerations weighed on him, as did the impropriety of leaving the judicial bench to re-enter the political arena and then returning to the bench if defeated:

> You know that I always disliked the plan of making politics a stepping stone to the bench and that I only accepted a judgeship when I had firmly established myself in private business and it was known that I was surrendering great emoluments.[31]

The current political ferment intrigued Arthur, who judged correctly that although the 'separationists' or 'disintegrators', as he called them, might have a majority in the Assembly, 'our chance [he classed himself with the 'centralists' or 'colonial party'] is in the rogues falling out over the division of the spoils'.[32]

Harry Atkinson did not at all like giving up politics, but his private affairs demanded his full-time attention. He had announced that he was not going to stand again at the February meeting of electors. Maria told Emily that Harry and his partner, Robert Pitcairn, had so many irons in the fire that the latter, whose health was not good, could not manage on his own. Harry and he had recently taken over the contract to supply meat to both the troops still stationed in New Plymouth and to the military outposts – 'in fact they are turning butchers or speaking genteelly, "meat contractors" '.[33]

Another of Harry's private affairs, thought scandalous by some of his relatives because Jane was not yet a year in her grave, was his engagement, announced in early April, to Mary's younger sister, Annie Smith. Even Maria, who was able to rationalise the attachment better than others of the kin group, wrote that the 'rapidity of the affair has been a blow to us all'.[34] Annie's own justification was that whereas second marriages were not to be sanctioned if a new love extinguished the old, in their case both the old and the new were to exist side by side, and therefore time had nothing to do with the matter. Maria could not follow this line of reasoning although, leaving the time factor aside, could see many ways in which Annie suited Harry. Seeking to mollify Emily, Maria wrote:

> I quite feel in this case that tho' a more affectionate & devoted wife than poor Jane was could not be found, she was no companion to Harry & that it was natural that he should at once attach himself to a woman who was his equal when he found her so ready both to give & receive sympathy & affection . . . I think Hal in many respects better suited in character to be happy with Annie, her very great delicacy alone would be a constant weight & anxiety on any but a buoyant hopeful nature like Harry's.[35]

It had been thought that, allowing for a more seemly interval, the obvious match would have been between James and Annie. Writing this time to Margaret Taylor, Maria stated,

> It would take a volume to explain in how many ways Harry suited her whilst James did not. You could hardly imagine two great men differing more widely in excellencies & failings, but really her best excuse for marrying so quickly is that she did not believe she added to Jas's happiness . . . Annie is very socially communicative & a great planner. James plans nothing & detests planning at least in all women but dear Mary, who did everything with a tact & charm all her own. I have even seen her planning chafe him a little, but Annie's was too elaborate & her manner of enunciating them too emphatic . . . [James] thought the house & children would have done much better on the laissez faire principle. I mention this point as one amongst various minor ones that made it seem natural & inevitable that what looked such a suitable & right arrangement at a distance, should come quickly to an end.[36]

Maria, with a perception which usually, though not always, cut through social convention, saw that the real sticking point regarding matrimony for Annie was her ability to cope with its inevitable consequence: child bearing and raising. Unless she became stronger and more resilient, both she and Lely thought Annie would be quite unfit to bear the 'ailments & labour of maternity – a broken night knocks her quite up & a couple bring on a terrible headache. Fancy this with teething babies to look forward to.'[37] Annie, as Maria also perceived, was completely dependent 'on the support of daily, even *hourly* sympathy for I never saw her without it.'[38] Mary, who 'felt & showed sympathy for every living creature', never begrudged it to her young sister; for her 'it flowed without measure so that really Annie depended on it as on her daily bread. It was truly her staff in life.'[39] After Mary's death Annie had seemed 'strung up' to work and care for James and his children for Mary's sake, but in the daily wear of life she got no help from James.

'Her spirit pined for *constant* sympathy & she turned where it flowed at all readily for her.'[40] Maria admitted to Margaret that she had been to a certain extent 'mistaken & therefore disappointed' in Annie. She had fancied her a 'more self supporting character' than life had proved her to be. She nevertheless hoped Annie's many good qualities and breeding – both she and Harry were cousins, descended from grandfather Smith – would make her a 'blessing indeed to Harry & his children'.

The wedding at St Mary's on 13 June was to be the quietest affair possible. Annie wore a black riding habit and a black hat with black and white feathers. James, who was uncommunicative, gave the bride away; four or five of the mob's little girls were bridesmaids, and Emily, who had let her brother know something of her disquiet, was now, at Maria's urging, reconciled enough to send a small cruet as a wedding present, reassuring both Harry and Maria that 'Em had survived the shock.' Straight after the church service Annie (28) and Harry (35) rode away to Hurworth. The rather gloomy and short-lived festivities – Edie told her father it was a 'sorrowful wedding' – were not lightened by most of the guests being ill with influenza. Maria, indeed, had not been well for some weeks. 'I am always in a fidget if she has the least ailment,' Lely had written to Emily, 'her health & life are so important to all – on Wednesday afternoon she fairly gave in & betook herself to the sofa, a sure sign that she felt really ill.'[41]

The winter of 1866 looked set to be a long one for Maria. Arthur and James were to leave for the General Assembly in June. She had been delighted with James's sketches of Central Otago and had longed to join him 'to see the glories of the land', but, as she told Emily, 'at present I am tied by the leg'.[42] Not all of James's five were with her; Annie wished to have Dolla and Dick until James was settled, and Maurice continued to stay with his aunt and uncle in Dunedin.

Maria dreaded illness during the winter with Arthur and James away. The only doctor she could send for in an emergency was 'old Dr Rawson': 'At the best of times he is not too valuable in my opinion & now is always overworked & having just got married again will be crosser than ever no doubt if he is called from home at unseasonable hours.'[43] 'But then', as she wrote to Margaret, 'I am the veriest sceptic in all matters of medicine, believing that as a science it is still in its earliest infancy & that it oftener kills than cures.'[44] She did believe that people sometimes benefited from the 'outrageous new schemes of modern doctors', possibly a reference to Annie's English medical friend, Dr Joseph Kidd, who although a qualified surgeon carried on an extensive homeopathic practice. 'Variety when accompanied by hope', Maria added, 'must help many invalids to bear the burden of existence & often thro' the mind benefits the body.'[45]

Neither tragedy nor serious illness made any more visitations to Beach Cottage, and the 'shoal of little ones' were 'as well and happy and troublesome too as heart could desire'. Of James and Mary's children, Maria wrote, Alla (eight) was very motherly towards the younger ones and could be given no greater treat than to be entrusted with Wilsie or Mabel in the garden for a whole afternoon: 'she is very clever and will I think make a fine sensible woman'.[46] Dolla (five) was self-contained, pretty, very quick at lessons and full of quaint, roguish ways; she had spoken clearly from eighteen months. 'Now I come to Dick [three] the rogue, the indescribable naughty, mischievous, troublesome, passionate, attractive little rascal. There is something so winning and droll in his naughtiness that those he bothers most love him best.'[47] Maurice (six) she thought had the deepest affection for his father. He was less sociable than the others, kept himself very clean and compact, was handy with his play tools, and was never dishevelled.

Meanwhile Arthur, James, and Major J.L.C. Richardson[48] had found themselves comfortable quarters in Wellington for the forthcoming session of the Assembly. They were later joined for a few weeks by Henry Richmond. The House was still divided into centralists and those who favoured some measure of separation, with provincial control over native policy and loose federal ties. Both J.C. Richmond and A.S. Atkinson, like C.W. Richmond and Harry Atkinson before them, saw a strong central government as the best means of ensuring some sort of prosperity for Taranaki. There were no Westminster type political parties. Richmonds and Atkinsons thought of themselves as 'conservatives' in so far as they were opposed to rampant provincialism at the expense of central government, but they used the term without any 'Tory' overtones. James wrote to Emily that dark as the clouds were on the issue of separation and self-reliance,

> we shall weather the storm yet and see before long the revival
> or rather constitution of a real colonial government. The cliques
> are so numerous and their selfish ends so mutually hostile that the
> little compact Colonial Party will be able to act effectively.[49]

During the debate on the motion of F.H. Whitaker (Parnell) for the 'better government of the Province of Auckland' which envisaged it as a virtually independent state,[50] Arthur made a quarter-of-an-hour speech attacking the motion. He was the fortieth speaker and, as he wrote in his diary, his speech 'would have been very impressive if anyone had listened'. The parliamentary reporter must also have become weary, for Arthur's speech rates only an eight-line summary in *Hansard*. He had a 'small fight' in committee over the Military and Volunteers Pensions Bill 'trying to get it a little more liberal towards privates',[51] and a harder one, also in committee, against the 'villainous Vagrancy Bill – begging or having no visible means of support punished by 12 months imprisonment – fought hard against it & got it reduced a little but not enough.'[52] He raised the question of compensation for the looting of cattle, horses, and other property belonging to Wiremu Kingi Matakatea and other 'friendlies' by General Chute's men, and was instrumental in persuading government to award £200 compensation to the Taranaki chief. He also moved, successfully, that the relevant correspondence and enclosures to and from Robert Parris on this issue be published.

'The assault on Stafford' was the theme of most of the out-of-House discussion amongst the 'conspirators' – Arthur's name for the group which included the three Taranaki men plus Fitzherbert and FitzGerald – who planned to force Stafford to replace some of his ministers (A.H. Russell, James Paterson, and Francis Jollie) with leading members of the Weld party. 'They could not join Stafford but he must join them.'[53] Stafford resigned, briefly, on 16 August. His restructured ministry included J.C. Richmond as commissioner of customs and stamp duties, Major Richardson as minister without portfolio, and Fitzherbert as minister of lands. There was no native minister as such, Stafford informing the House that the

> state of Native affairs had so much improved that there would appear to be no longer any speciality in dealing with them. As long as there was a line of demarcation between the management of European and Native affairs, so long would there be causes of dissatisfaction and irritation between different parts of the colony. It appeared, therefore, a step in the right direction to do away with the office of Native Minister. Native affairs could, like other affairs, be conducted by the Colonial Secretary or by some other Minister.[54]

Such may have been Stafford's sanguine expectations. The eruption of Titokowaru in south Taranaki and Te Kooti on the East Coast in the late sixties kept 'some other minister' – J.C. Richmond – fully engaged in native affairs. He also became the Stafford government troubleshooter at Dunedin and on the Otago goldfields. It would appear that neither customs nor stamp duties occupied much of his time.

Arthur's letters and his and James's articles to the *Herald* and *Examiner* kept Maria up with the political play. James was also writing leaders for the *Wellington Independent*, 'but you need not tell anyone this,' she cautioned Emily, 'it is probably more beneficial if kept secret.'[55] She was pleased that the 'Conservatives had decidedly the upper hand':

> I suppose whether Mr Stafford stays in or out will be as they choose. Of course *he* will do anything that he sees will keep him in office. Our members hold Councils of War with the two Fitzs. What a curious combination to be on one side of the House.[56]

Lely, on the other hand, was mystified when James joined Stafford's ministry; to her it seemed 'inexplicable'. Harry Atkinson, more used to the shifting factions in this male club, assured her it was 'all right'.

European politics seemed just as confusing. On 18 June Prussia had declared war on Austria, and a few days later Italy, intent on wresting Venice from her traditional enemy, did the same. Maria wrote to Margaret of this 'mighty & horrible European strife' and asked her friend 'with whom ought one to sympathise?':

> I am deeply interested in politics all the world over, & generally take up the cudgels decidedly on one side or the other, but in this case what with a strong desire to see Italy free & united at the same time that I should dearly love to see Prussia get her deserts, I am fairly puzzled. I have such a dread of that horrid long-headed Louis Napoleon that I rather expect after all the misery is gone thro' all the blood & treasure spent, it will turn out that France alone is the gainer . . .
>
> I should like to know if there is any hope that this war will dissipate the political torpor in which Germans must live? How can an intelligent people submit in such a slavish way to the dominance of Count Bismarck & the King?[57]

She conceded that a Prussian victory would be a great gain for the German people generally and hoped that it would then be easier for the German nation to become a 'free people in the English sense of that word, *if they choose*, but what I cannot make out i whether they do as a people care for constitutional government'.[58]

By the beginning of October, with Arthur's absence entering

ts fourth month and one or other of the Beach Cottage children
falling not seriously but messily ill, politics lost all attraction. She
felt a 'faint glow of satisfaction' at 'separation' being defeated by
such a clear majority, but all she now wanted was for the session
– 'a weary tedious affair' – to end and for Arthur to return. He
did so on 12 October.

A religious revival, particularly among Primitive Methodists and
Plymouth Brethren, was taking place in New Plymouth and 'many
reckless men' were becoming steady. A 'gift of prayer' developed
in Richmond Hursthouse though, as Lely dryly commented 'at
present it is kept within the bounds of moderation'.[59] Revivalism
ensured that the question of whether the Taranaki Institute, of
which Henry Richmond was president, should open on a Sunday
became an emotively charged, four-hour debate. At the annual
meeting Henry had advocated Sunday opening mainly on the grounds
that it would give young military settlers at a loose end somewhere
profitable to go. A Bible would be prominently displayed. Henry
felt called upon to explain that he himself did not go to church;
the modes of worship adopted by the different Protestant sects
were so entirely opposed to his ideas that it would jar his feelings
to enter any place of public worship. He gave this explanation,
he said, because as superintendent he might be looked upon as
setting a bad example to young men. The resulting debate a few
weeks later, which Arthur, who also espoused Henry's view,
described as a 'picturesque discussion', resulted narrowly in favour
of Sunday opening.

Henry, as he told William, regarded his last four years as a
valuable period of education during which I have been developing
my eye teeth all the time.'[60] He returned from his few weeks in
Wellington much stimulated by the congenial company and
determined to buy the *Taranaki News*, being 'driven to it' after
attacks made on him for his anti-church stance by the 'pious editor'
(not Arthur, but William Woon) of the *Herald*. He hoped to make
the *News* the leading paper in New Zealand. He was also agitated
about the immediate likelihood of a serious earthquake at or near
the next change of the moon, the earth's surface being then in
a special state of tension' ('please let none of our people sleep
near dangerous chimneys'), and extremely excited about his recently
discovered 'dynamic and metaphysical theory of matter'. He had
sent copies of his thesis to J.F.W. Herschell, the British astronomer,
and to his old teacher, Michael Faraday. Henry claimed that his
theory[61] would 'unlock all the chambers of physical science besides

connecting [science] indissolubly with Metaphysics and Theology'.[62]
Maria thought Henry was in the same 'brilliant' state as he had
been during 1849, conducting electricity experiments in the stables
at Springholm and being unable to sleep or eat from excitement.
Lely wished that he was more interested in things connected with
his and his family's welfare, opining that 'men of science' were
not always gifted with much prudence or common sense. James,
witness to Henry's excitability in Wellington, thought that his
brother's mental state verged on brain fever. Richard Holt Hutton,
to whom Henry had also sent a copy of his pamphlet, replied
encouragingly and wished to involve Henry in an on-going discussion
in the *Spectator* about the reconciliation of science with faith. It
was scarcely the response Henry was hoping for. Of the European
scientists to whom he had written, only one replied. 'A Settler
in New Zealand' was a long way from the fulcrum of scientific
discussion and discovery.

James had returned to New Plymouth, briefly, for Annie's
wedding. Lely described how the children clustered around him
and clung to him, so that he resembled 'a queen bee'. Maria thought
he looked worn and old, though only forty-four. While at the
Assembly he had written to his mother that his 'youth and elasticity'
had gone and that he was 'perfectly indifferent' to the fate of
the government to which he belonged.[63] This 'sense of desolation'
is not, however, reflected in his lively and combative speeches
during parliamentary debates; nor does Arthur remark that James
was a figure of gloom at Miss Vaughan's lodgings. In personal
letters James was always prone to let his thoughts follow his mood
of the moment. Lely would have been long used to this. He wished
to have his children, or some of them, with him and had written
to Mrs Manby, a widow whom the family knew, to ask whether
she would housekeep for him at Wellington. By December he was
living in a 'beautifully clean neat little house' which had once
belonged to Dr Hector. Mrs Manby who had recently been keeping
a boarding house in Nelson seemed pleased with her new position.
James described her as 'not much educated in the common sense
but essentially a lady: her quiet ways are excellent training for
my wild excitable little ones'.[64] It was not long before rumours
of a liaison between James and his housekeeper reached and upset
Emily Richmond at Dunedin. Lely thought it 'incredible that James
should thus replace his loss' and in her reply to Emily discounted
the rumour in her dry manner: 'I think he has been too much
engaged in public affairs & too little at home to have improved

on his acquaintance.'[65] Both she and Maria thought Mrs Manby 'a great treasure'.

A former member of the mob whom the family still paid to keep at a distance was Charlie Wilson. At the end of 1865 he had been reported as being destitute in Melbourne. Calvert, his brother, was now married and working successfully as a surveyor in New Plymouth and Wanganui. The family decided that for Calvert's welfare, Charlie should be kept in ignorance of his brother's whereabouts. 'It was proposed we should subscribe amongst us to do something for Charlie': Calvert was to send him two pounds each month, and another two pounds would be raised from the others to keep Charlie in Melbourne and out of destitution (he managed to make a little money himself by cutting firewood and selling sketches). Another original mob fringe member was Edward (Teddo) Patten, for whom Maria retained a special affection. He had left Hurworth in 1857 for the Aorere diggings in Nelson province and had not made his fortune. In 1866 he secured a berth in the Customshouse at Hokitika, which he then nearly lost through marrying 'in a tipsy frolic a girl of bad character beneath him in every way'.[66] Since his marriage, Maria heard, he had conducted himself very soberly.

The end of 1866 saw Arthur close with Woon's offer of £1,000 for his share of the *Taranaki Herald*; on 28 December he wrote his last leading article. Attendance at the General Assembly for 102 days had yielded an honorarium of £102. That in itself was scarcely enough to support his family nor, once the newspaper was removed, was the four-month parliamentary session sufficiently stimulating to engage Arthur's full attention. During the year he had again increased his holding at Hurworth,[67] and now had just under a mile of frontage along the Carrington Road. Arthur's affection for Hurworth was as tenacious as ever but the land was without a dwelling, and to build a comfortable house would cost at least £500. Moreover, there were no schools in the vicinity. In her New Year letter to Margaret Taylor, Maria wrote, 'It is quite uncertain what Ar will do next.'

January 1867 passed in the usual way with picnics to Hurworth, where Arthur had engaged a Maori gang to fence and clear thistles. He was again thinking of the law and had gone so far as to ask Henry Halse of New Plymouth whether he wanted an articled pupil of thirty-three. 'Halse did not jump at the offer.' Surprisingly, Maria was at this time less enthusiastic about Arthur taking up legal studies if they meant bending him down to a sedentary pursuit. Since his return from Wellington he had, she thought, not been quite as vigorous as he was when leading a more out-of-door life. She was therefore probably not too dismayed when on 20 February Arthur took the opportunity of joining Robert Parris and William Messenger on a journey around the Taranaki coast to Patea, largely to test whether it was now safe to do so, and also to investigate the reasons why Ngati Ruanui in the vicinity of Patea had pulled up surveyors' pegs.

At Tataraimaka the party was joined by 'native friends' – Hone Pihama, Wiremu Kingi Matakatea, Te Teira, and several others. Both Parris and Arthur wanted to go on to Opunake in daylight, 'not liking the rat-like system of sneaking through in the night' as other Pakeha travelling south were accustomed to do. Their Maori friends advised them to wait until sunset to allow the waeromene, who may have been shellfishing, time to leave the coast. At Harriet Beach,[68] south-east of Cape Egmont, they came across tracks of waeromene, and a little further on some of them, unarmed and on horseback, were seen winding their way inland: 'Thereupon Hakaria was sent forward to speak with & see if they would speak with Parris but they would not, "they did not wish to see the face of a pakeha".'[69]

That night Parris and his party slept at Opunake, and the following night at Oeo, where Hone Pihama had been granted 500 acres for 'personal services' to the government. Arthur found that some of Pihama's people had helped fell the first clearing at Hurworth. Once across the Waimate Plains, the road they were on was regarded as being in the possession of waeromene. Pakeha were allowed to pass along it, but if they attempted to follow Maori into the bush, 'mischief' would happen. At Whararoa, near to present-day Hawera, Arthur saw the remains of the great house Taiporohenui, built in 1853. At Turuturu (on the outskirts of Hawera), Arthur learnt further details of Major Thomas McDonnell's 'rascally attack' on the Hauhau stronghold of Pokaikai (inland from Hawera) on 2 August 1866, in which 'rebel' Maori of Ngati Ruanui and Tangahoe, while treating for peace, suffered a surprise attack. As Arthur feared, it confirmed Maori belief in Pakeha treachery. Yet in spite of this, Parris's party was hospitably received. At Turuturu also Arthur happened to come across the Maori who had burnt his house at Hurworth: 'He & Patohe (a brother of Hone Pihama's now at Oeo) went there for pigs etc; they slept in the large room & in the morng. lighted it.'[70] At Manutahi (between Hawera and Patea the party attended a meeting of Maori opposed to the survey. Apart from one old man who told Parris that the surveyors were like cattle 'eating up the herbage of the land as they went' and who then left the meeting to join the 'rebels', the other leading men were 'quiet and reasonable'.[71] The following day Arthur and Parris rode down to the mouth of the Patea, where a small cluster of military buildings and a 'dismal inn' marked the beginnings of a township. In his usual disinterested fashion Arthur discussed battle tactics with Maori who had fought against government forces in the Patea–Wanganui district.

When the party arrived back in New Plymouth they heard that a military settler named Brady, formerly of the 65th, had been shot near Warea, and that they would have passed within a few feet of his body. Arthur and Robert Parris were in favour of getting up an expedition to punish the 'waeros'. Military action always held an almost irresistible appeal for Arthur, and in this case he was intrigued by the fact that the townspeople, or some of them, were thinking of 'engaging in a small war of our own'. Fortunately caution prevailed on both sides. Arthur subsequently learned that Taranaki did not approve of Brady's killing for fear it might be thought that they had recommenced the war; both the men who had taken part in the attack were expelled from the tribe. Henry Richmond, as superintendent, was not willing to call out the militia and, even more to the point, 'Harry [Atkinson] for a wonder was strongly against it.'[72] The shooting had been committed well away from the township, and to send out a punitive force would look to the other provinces as if Taranaki was willing to begin another war.

While Arthur was away, Christopher (Kit) Richmond, William and Emily's eldest son, aged eight, came to stay at Beach Cottage. For his birthday Maria arranged a children's party at Hurworth, where Harry and Annie had gone for the summer. The weather in New Plymouth did not on the day seem propitious for such a venture but, as the bullock cart arrived from Hurworth, Maria assumed that the weather there must be better. She and ten children climbed into the waggon and set off. On the way the wind increased to a gale, blowing dust as well as smoke and ashes from the summer burn-offs into their faces and on to their clothes. Ten crying, dishevelled, sooty children and an equally dishevelled and sooty Maria finally arrived at Hurworth, to the great surprise of Harry and the dismay of Annie who was suffering 'one of her headaches'.

Harry and Maria coped with the birthday party, which restored
everyone's spirits, and Harry escorted the bullock cart on its slow
journey back into town. A more enjoyable outing was with Arthur
to visit Marion and Decimus Atkinson at Urenui: this time the
children were left under Lely's supervision. It was one of the few
occasions on which Maria had been on horseback since leaving
Hurworth. At Urenui they found Marion, Decimus, and their two
sons living in a three-roomed fernpost and raupo whare with
additional accommodation for Maori retainers and visitors provided
by two tents. The Maori, three or four men and a varying number
of 'girls', worked for their keep only, 'which is a convenient
arrangement', Arthur noted, 'as a principal part of their food is
wild pig & fish which they catch themselves'.[73] Before winter set
in, Maria made what was possibly her last sortie into the bush
of her beloved mountain. Arthur records:

> 10 April. The weather looking bad Maria started on an expedition
> to the Lower Range as chaperone to a party of young ladies –
> Miss Browns & Humphries, one of the former being fiancee to
> Arthur Standish who is dragoman of the party.

> 11 April. In the evg. Maria came back having led her party of
> girls up the Ranges. It rained steadily last night.[74]

Unfortunately, as with her other memorable expedition to the
summit, she has left no account.

Maria's servants were now a continuing problem. Mary, like
Elizabeth, had married and left. Unable to find a suitable replacement, Maria had what Lely described as 'an amusing succession
of domestic helps or hindrances': a 'wild Irish woman' followed
by a 'raw Scotch girl' followed by the eldest daughter of a woman
with a large family and a drunken husband. 'It might have been
a pleasure to try & make something of her,' Lely thought, 'if Maria's
hands had not been so filled with children and the girl not quite
so apathetic and slatternly.'[75] She left within the week. Lely was
then living in Henry Richmond's more sedate and quiet household
which he shared with his mother-in-law and in which his two
children were outnumbered by adults. One Sunday in March, Arthur
and Maria 'with their whole flock' and their latest servant came
to visit. The servant was the widow of a military settler shot about
a year previously, and her drawback was that she would obviously
not remain single for very much longer. Helen Hursthouse had
earlier brought such an account of the hectic state of Beach Cottage
that Lely was surprised to see no trace of tension on her daughter's
face. All the children stuck so closely to Maria, whether she was

mother or aunt, that Lely thought she would never be able to detach herself.

In February, Emily and William's eighth child, Edward Thomas, was born. Maria wrote to her brother:

My dear William, Am I to congratulate you or condole with you? There have been eight children domiciled here today & really such a number almost feels like 'an embarrassment of riches', but in my case the fact of having only one small maid to assist may have had something to do with raising the doubt that there may be too much of a good thing.[76]

And Lely wrote to Mary, her granddaughter, 'What a life of usefulness you may look forward to, the eldest of such a family.'[77] Such a remark, if made at all today, would smack of cynicism; then, within the family structure, obligations and duties, for the female members in particular, were generally accepted as the natural corollary of affection and protection.[78]

A sense of duty and obligation towards the children in her care sat rather heavily on Maria at times. She was ready 'to undergo anything' to ensure that they grew into 'noble human beings' – one senses that the role model was the Carlyle 'hero' figure – but doubted her ability to achieve this. She expressed herself to Margaret as uncertain and ignorant of the best way of dealing with children as they grew out of infancy. The question which was to obsess another generation of parents and educationalists – whether heredity was more or less important than environment – also puzzled her. 'Elevating influences' seemed often to have no effect on characters which were in essence 'weak, coarse or ignoble'; yet 'one is amazed at the breadth, warmth & purity displayed by those whose early surroundings were far from auspicious'. 'Is there any law in these things,' she wondered, 'how much of what is right or wrong is born in us, how much is put there by circumstances?'[79] This was the sort of question she would have loved to discuss with Mary Richmond; Margaret, in these circumstances, was too detached a listener. Whatever her doubts as the children grew older, Maria has nevertheless left a delightful account of the Beach Cottage 'shoal of little ones'. Arthur, in Wellington, had written of James's children as 'too much "nerved up" & expected to be always in a fit state to receive visitors' under Mrs Manby's care. Maria told Margaret:

No doubt there are refining influences on the manners in such a system & my young roughs here will contrast painfully after a while. Still physically I am sure J.C.R.'s children benefit by my system or absence of system & always grow more robust looking after a residence at Liberty Hall as Beach Cottage may fairly be called. [She then instanced the healthy state of 'little Wilsie'] owing to his outdoor life & his being allowed to do just as he likes as regards sticks, stones, dirt pies & sand from morning till night. Twice in the twenty four hours they are all made clean, but we let them alone at other times. If they only remained little children I should be well pleased with my own management.[80]

In Stafford's reconstructed ministry, Major Richardson, who represented the town of New Plymouth, was selected as the government member in the Legislative Council. This left a vacancy in the House which the town's electors filled on 29 April 1867 by unanimously choosing Harry Atkinson. The only other candidate, Thomas Hirst, 'prudently retired' before the election. There is no doubt that Harry enjoyed politics and that Annie, far more than 'poor Jane' could ever have done, was of a mind to enjoy the Wellington session of the Assembly. It seemed certain that before long Harry, a popular member of the House when he was not 'special pleading' for Taranaki, would once again become a minister. The mob had now reached a pinnacle of political eminence: Henry was superintendent of the province, and its three elected members to the General Assembly were Harry, James, and Arthur. C.W. Richmond, although he had turned his back on politics, still held the mana of an elder statesman. Taranaki settlers were apparently becoming used to, even proud of the kin group they had once disparagingly called the 'literary bushmen': 'The family question was spoken of [at the election] but rather complimentary than otherwise, Charles Brown stating it as his opinion that no settlement owed so much to any family as Taranaki owed to the Richmonds & Atkinsons.'[81]

Arthur was frequently on his feet during the 1867 sesssion which began on 9 July. He made, for him, a longish speech criticising several aspects of General Chute's campaign, particularly the way in which it had strengthened Maori conviction that Pakeha could not be trusted. Drawing on information he had been given on his recent journey in south Taranaki, he told the House that he 'believed there was a great deal more of show than real effect in that campaign' and that the number of Maori said to have been killed on Chute's march had been exaggerated 'as was generally the case'.[82] Other debates in which he took a brief but pertinent part included the Divorce and Matrimonial Causes Bill, in which he advocated, without success, that desertion for a certain number of years should be grounds for divorce, and the Protection of Animals Bill, in which, among other clauses, it was proposed that all persons killing game, even on their own land, would be fined or imprisoned if caught doing so without the requisite game licence. He stated that if the Bill was enacted as it stood, it would possibly take less than three months before the whole population of New Zealand was in gaol. He attempted, but failed, to have the Bill translated into Maori so that a Maori snaring a pigeon in a district where the measure was to be enforced might at least be aware that he was liable to a fine. Harry, James, and he all supported the Native Representation Bill, enacted in 1867, which divided New Zealand into four Maori districts and extended the suffrage, within the very limited frame of one member for each district, to male aboriginal natives, including half castes, twenty-one years and over. Arthur said, 'He had been a good deal amongst the Natives, but had never found them so keenly desirous of political privileges as it had been said they were,'[83] and, in his usual style, made the point that Maori members might be even more baffled by parliamentary procedure than were some 'gentlemen of that House'. The most significant argument in favour of the measure, he considered, was its educational effect, presumably through enabling Maori to become acquainted with Westminster-style parliamentary procedures.[84]

Arthur gained the reputation of being a conscientious member of the House – he did not miss a day – and a careful reader of Bills. It is interesting to note how other members of the House were now becoming weary of the woes of Taranaki: 'It was too much, Fitzherbert said, to listen to all these tirades [a reference to forthright Harry] if there was any one Province which had been maintained at the expense of the rest of the Colony it was the Province of Taranaki.'[85] Since 1856 it had received 'enormous relief grants', and been relieved both of provincial charges 'to the very utmost' and of its share of the allocated debt. 'Taranaki', he continued, 'must learn to feed herself.'

In spite of this exhortation, or remonstrance, Taranaki province too had high expectations now that the war seemed to be dribbling to a close. But cash in the hands of its settlers, many of whom were now returning to begin again on their farms, was still scarce. The finances of the mob bore this out. Decie's affairs had absorbed most of Arthur's spare cash. Henry had lost nearly £1,000 to him and was also finding that his association with Richard Pheney in

the *Taranaki News* was neither agreeable nor profitable. Decimus
now seemed to be more soundly based at Urenui and he offered
to pay his family creditors by allocating them sections in the new
township he proposed to lay out on his land there.[86] Most of the
troops which were stationed in New Plymouth left in July 1867;
this the *Taranaki Herald* prophesied would be an excellent thing
for the community insofar as it would remove tradesmen from
their chronic dependence. In the short run, however, it meant that
a military supplier like Harry, whose land was also heavily
mortgaged, was faced with financial catastrophe. Maria doubted
whether 'even with Annie's income', added to what he might make
from Hurworth or from his land at Bell block, he would be able
to pay mortgage interest let alone keep the family 'in its accustomed
style'.[87] William Atkinson's land and insurance agency had not
succeeded and he was again working, somewhat insecurely, in the
Native Office. Oil was seen as providing for Taranaki's future
wellbeing, but the Taranaki Petroleum Company which had
capitalised on the early exploration of Carter and Company was,
like its predecessor, short of ready cash. In May 1867 its shareholders
were told that the company would have to suspend operations.
Grace Hirst, whose husband had been a successful entrepreneur
as well as farmer, wrote of the depressed state of the economy
in the absence of war, soldiers, and petroleum, and with many
empty houses in the town, 'we never felt in such trouble since
we left England'.[88] Henry and Arthur saw where the real and future
wealth of the province would lie, but neither had any money to
back Thomas King's proposal to form a company and open the
bush land at the back of the mountain. King intended to ask for
a 50,000-acre Crown grant, stock the clearings with dairy cows,
and, in the course of two or three years, start 'a proper cheese
factory'.

When Arthur left New Plymouth early in July 1867 to attend
the Assembly, he went first to Nelson to meet with William. The
latter had promised Lely after Mary's death that if the opportunity
arose he would shift from Dunedin to be closer to the rest of
the kin group. In January 1867 he accepted Stafford's proposal 'to
conduct the judicial business of the Supreme Court on the West
Coast & at Nelson', determining to fix his residence at Nelson.
Proximity to the family was not his only reason. His asthmatic
condition was now critical. James, who had stayed with him in
1866, wrote to Lely that William was so constantly suffering 'as
to have scarcely any enjoyment in life; he hardly recovers strength

from one fit when another comes on.' Shifting to Nelson would mean leaving the handsome house, grounds, and garden of Highlawn, which he had designed himself and to which Emily had grown accustomed. 'William does indeed seem to have built himself a "lordly pleasure house",' Maria had written to Lely when her mother was staying there during 1864, '& but for such stones as servants, their high wages, the price of milk etc [one] might say almost . . . "make merry & carouse, dear Em, for all is well".'[89]

William left Dunedin in March for a few weeks' rest and recuperation at Idaburn, returned in April to give his farewell charge to the Grand Jury, and by June was boarding at Nelson College until he found suitable accommodation for his family. He wrote to Emily in July that he had leased a house and acquired a cook. On her way from Dunedin in July with seven of her children (Kit was still at Beach Cottage), Emily called first at Wellington to see Annie, who wrote to Lely:

> Emily seems bewildered and overpowered by her family without in truth doing much or anything for them – she has two servants with her, in which she has no confidence, but to whom the care of all the small ones is given up. I am afraid this sounds very ill natured but you know her way – she seems free for any amount of visiting and yet talks with groans of the utter carelessness of the servants.[90]

Her family came together again in Nelson towards the end of August. William was there on his own when Arthur paid his visit, the object of which was to reopen the possibility of studying law under his brother-in-law's guidance.

The law, living goodness knows how, in Nelson, or the outdoor life, doing goodness knows what, in Taranaki, became the focal point of the correspondence[91] between Maria and Arthur while he was at the General Assembly. Neither of them saw the life of a politician as providing long-term satisfaction or even as a long-term option. In the fickle political climate 'a Gledhill or a Lewthwaite might be preferred' by Arthur's electorate. As had been her intention all along, Maria was firm about leaving the final decision to Arthur, but she was not averse to nudging him towards the law. How to live in Nelson while Arthur was in the 'pupa state' presented a problem. Maria thought that if with Lely's help – they were determined not to take money from William – Arthur could be sure of £350 a year, and if they could find a house to hold them all at no more than £40 a year, then 'without imprudence' the venture might be made. She refrained from giving too decided advice for fear of hearing thereafter, 'Now if you had only taken my advice etc', and went on:

This naturally leads me to remark that had you taken my very decided advice in 1860 & Emily's too . . . the most dispassionate male observers here are convinced that at this moment *you would be making with ease* on the *lowest computation £1000 per annum.* Rash reckoners declare Mr Halse to be making £5000; sober ones say his business brings in over £2000.[92]

From a 'worldly point of view', therefore, Maria still saw the legal profession as providing Arthur with the most suitable path in life. She continued,

I also know well enough that wise worldly steps are not the *best* always to take & highly as I value the great advantage I know money would obtain for the children, I feel that by a sacrifice of your health or your freedom & peace of mind they would be too dearly bought, & as you are the only person who can at all judge what the sacrifice would be, you alone can decide for or against becoming a lawyer.[93]

Maria had never been at all concerned about Arthur's lack of formal education; in fact, she was proud of his ability to educate himself. She did not think legal studies would prove too difficult a hurdle but did ask him, 'am I perhaps taking for granted that you would like to study?' Maria was ambitious for Arthur and it would have been impossible, given the age in which she lived, not to have linked her position in society with his. Nevertheless there was probably a twitch to her lips as she wrote, 'I should like the world at large to know you for as clever a fellow as I believe you to be. I should like the position which as wife of a man of note would be mine.'[94] Of far more importance was her ambition to have their children's formal education completed in Europe. The income which Arthur might make as a lawyer seemed a possible way to achieve this.

I am in the position of a gambler. I should be willing to stake a great deal of present comfort & ease for the *chance* offered by this line of life but on no account would I stake your peace & enjoyment of life *for any possible gain whatsoever.*[95]

Lely had always thought that Arthur, with his 'decided devotion to study', should long before this have entered upon a professional career. Now it seemed that Maria's concern for Lely's welfare might place a stumbling block in the way. Lely was comfortably settled in New Plymouth and, at seventy-six, was averse to further change. Maria wondered whether she had the right to uproot her once more. She was certain her mother would be quite happy once she had landed at Nelson – and at least Nelson Haven provided a wharf on to which one stepped rather than a surf boat into which one was lowered. It meant removing her from the company of Henry and her sister; the gain would be William, Emily, and their tribe. At this stage both Arthur and Maria assumed that once Arthur had qualified they would return to Taranaki, but the bond between Lely and Maria was such that neither would contemplate three years of separation from each other.

Maria herself had mixed feelings about leaving Beach Cottage and living for even three years in Nelson. It held two painful associations: she had taken Alice Atkinson there only to see her waste away and die, and she had even more recently witnessed there the death of Mary. However, as Lely wrote to William, 'these feelings would not hinder her from pursuing whatever course appeared most to the advantage of her family'.[96] Maria was always anxious for the young cousins to get to know each other so that the second generation of the mob would be as knit together as the first. Edie would lose Mary King as her music teacher and that would be a definite loss; otherwise, schools in Nelson were considered superior, and Edie, lacking a peer group and inclined to be dominating at Beach Cottage, would benefit from the society of her older cousins.

By the end of the winter it seemed as if Nelson would be their destination and that Arthur would become a lawyer. To that extent, it might be said, Maria had prevailed, yet she became increasingly despondent – more so (from her letters) than at any other time in her life. Children pressed about her; 'much as I love children, at times, I feel more lonely amongst them than I can express, perhaps because one's inner life is so far removed from all they can understand.'[97] She felt that she had 'got into a wrong groove' with Edie, and was likely to do so with the others as they grew older. Arthur's continuing absence meant there was no one 'to laugh at my forbodings'. To Margaret she wrote, 'I never felt much flatter or more hopelessly stupid than just now', and 'I believe I am quite ten years older than I was at this time two years ago.'[98]

Recent studies of nineteenth-century women of Maria's sort – capable, active, intelligent, independently minded, and interested in what was happening in the world – show that many of them felt confined and trapped within the institution of the family. For Maria it was a frustratingly ambivalent situation. Her extended family was all important to her, yet there were Arthur, William,

James, Henry, Harry, all free to move about, to be involved in debating and discussing, in considering and deciding upon matters of moment in which she was just as interested but could not be engaged except in the subordinate role of wife, mother, housekeeper. Once when Annie was staying at Beach Cottage she had written to her sister that she and Maria had been considering 'what a wonderfully blessed thing submissiveness is', for a woman;[99] how trust and resignation were the antidote for fretting and fidgeting about. The perfect example was 'poor dear Aunt Helen' accepting with equanimity all that fate and her husband had chosen to bestow. Yet finally even she had turned and opted for independence when tried beyond patience by her husband's drinking. Arthur and Maria had, more than most of their contemporaries, a marriage of equal partners, but the choices available to the one were not open to the other. At most, Maria could exercise some preference as to whether she was to be the wife of a bush farmer, a bushranger, a politician, a newspaper editor, or a lawyer. Henry's remark when his sister had nearly died during her first confinement – 'what should we all have done without her' – was still apt. Her 'strong faithful spirit' still sustained the kin group. She had again and again been the surrogate mother, feeding, rearing, loving, and nourishing her extended family with her own resilience and strength. Since Mary's death, however, things had worn a greyer, more wintry aspect, and the fluctuating numbers and constant company of small children[100] were more wearying to the mind than to the body.

As despondency increased, self-esteem fell away. The absence of solid teaching for her girls, especially, bothered her, and she was too ready to disparage her own considerable learning and that of her sex in general:

> It is too late for me to have a sound education, but there is nothing I so desire for the children . . . & I want you [A.S.A.] to take the subject up & not despair of the girls because they *are* girls, but see what can be made of even second rate material. I feel certain that . . . one woman in a thousand has a chance of being other than empty-headed & frivolous. After all as a great many wise men are just finding out, women form one half of the human race so that raising them from their degradation ought to be a wide & interesting subject for humane legislation.[101]

The tone of this letter is interesting. Was Maria deliberately copying Arthur's tongue-in-cheek mode of writing in order to engage his attention more readily, or was she attempting to disguise her own belief in women – her whole character is an affirmation of her sex, within its historical context – by such blatant overstatement of their supposed inferiority? One of the 'wise men' would almost certainly have been J.S. Mill[102] whose amendment (defeated) to the Reform Bill on the subject of the franchise proposed that the word 'man' be omitted and the word 'person' inserted. In August 1867 when the House of Commons was debating the final stages of the Bill which was markedly to increase urban male suffrage, and when the General Assembly was studying the Native Representation Bill, the *Taranaki Herald* published an article from the *Spectator* which considered, as Mill had advocated, extending the suffrage to women householders. The article was naturally condescending and paternalistic, but recognised that it was 'far from unfeminine for women to take an interest in politics'. As a class, though, it held that women had little political knowledge and less political capacity. It would scarcely have provided balm for Maria's flagging spirits.

Maria had always been sensitive to the difference in age between herself and Arthur, and now seemed more so than ever. Arthur's life, so full of opportunities, was beginning; hers, she felt, was nearing its end. Given the high mortality rate among the younger women of the set, this was not, of course, an unnatural assumption. When for her birthday that year Arthur sent a copy of Browning's poems (he was reading J.S. Mill), Maria apparently chose to forget that they had earlier read *On Liberty* aloud to each other:

I am very much pleased with your choice of gift. I shall only understand a quarter of it but still it pleases me to puzzle over Browning whereas I should never attempt the other two books you named. For a youth like you I can readily understand Mill is encouraging, you have the brain, the will & the time to accomplish something yet, but I who 'feel the fog in my throat the mist in my face',[103] as your book says, it is too late. Certainly if the language & the work in the next place we get to is to be solely intellectual, we women shall be mostly out of place.[104]

Because of her beleaguered situation, Maria could not rouse herself to take any great interest in the politics of the 1867 session. It is also likely that the steady advance of male suffrage in Britain and, within a limited representation, the enfranchisement of even 'rebel' Maori in New Zealand, made a woman's lot seem more invidious by comparison. In some of her letters to Arthur there is an evident impatience, even exasperation with what seemed to her simply captious politicising. She found the 'incessant bickering & fidgeting' of the parliamentary club 'really aggravating', and

though Arthur's 'colonial party' was in the ascendant and her brother
a minister, she confessed to

> sharing our Editor's [Henry in the *Taranaki News*] ignorance as to
> what Govt is at! Oh the talkee talkee! You may maintain that
> the subjects are nobler than the selection of a carpet or Miss G's
> intentions as to calling . . . the waste of words must be quite equal.
> I should think about 99 out of every 100 could be spared with
> little loss to anyone. But perhaps it keeps you 'poor harmless men'
> out of real mischief & we ought not to grudge you innocent
> amusement; only how you can assume so lofty a tone about motes
> in sisters' eyes being so full of beams yourselves, I don't know.[105]

She was also disappointed in James. He seemed determined simply
to placate his colleagues about the state of the country:

> there is something startling in the effect of office on the human
> mind. I fancied James sure to retain his individuality, but it seems
> official instructions are too strong for him & like the rest he would
> cry 'Peace Peace' where there is no peace. As Member of the Ministry
> it might be all right to say & think as he did, but as member
> for Taranaki it is damaging.[106]

In her view a politician should be a man for the hour, larger minded,
more noble hearted than those around him, and she was sickened
by the pusillanimous attitude of the House towards 'Harry's bill'
(the Public Officers Disqualification Bill) which sought to keep
from the public office of superintendent or member of parliament
anybody found guilty of using public money for private purposes,
as had James Macandrew. He was now sitting in the House as
member for Clutha. She considered, from newspaper reports, that
members were much too 'timid, apologetic and deprecatory' in
their comments. 'I should be unable to express my views were
I in the House,' she told Arthur,[107] and proceeded to write him
three pages of 'views' which she then meticulously overwrote so
as to make them illegible in case Arthur thought her an 'enragée'.

The House may have been weary of hearing about the plight
of Taranaki, but the local settlers still felt themselves unjustly treated
when government decided to withhold the £2,200 the province
received annually in lieu of land revenue, and to take back the
£32,000 allowed for land purchase which had remained unspent
because of war and confiscation. Maria wrote to Arthur:

> You will hear that there has been an indignation meeting[108] & that
> you are all to be requested to resign your seats . . . As far as I
> understand the case it seems that Taranaki is well treated looking
> only at her case, but unjustly treated as compared to Wellington

& Auckland, but then I have only heard one side – the odd part is that you & Harry seem to care so little for how people feel & think.[109]

Even the books she was reading, Mozart's and Beethoven's letters, served only to increase Maria's heaviness of spirit: tragedy and waste and stupidity were as evident in the old world as in the new.

> It makes one hate ordinary human beings to think they are such cold blooded wretches or such thick skulled dolts as to allow their greatest benefactors to be starved or worried out of this world. I thought better of Germans. I could hardly credit it that they had thrown Mozart (after killing him) into a hole, as we would not do to a dog we loved, & then forget where he was laid. It seems indeed a mercy to think of all those petty courts being done away with as they failed in cherishing & protecting genius – (Weimar excepted).[110]

And then there were misadventures at home. Aunt Helen, who had broken her leg and was hobbling about on crutches, slipped and fractured her other leg. Henry, in his excited state of the year before, had formed an attachment to a young Dunedin girl (referred to as 'Miss A.B.' in Maria's letters). Maria considered herself 'pledged' to invite the girl to stay at Beach Cottage; now Henry appeared to dread her coming, wished to abandon his suit, but feared the gossip the girl might suffer if he did so. Mabel fell and broke her collarbone.

In the middle of October Arthur returned. He had reached an agreement with William to serve his three years as the latter's secretary, or 'judge's associate' as the official appointment was called. 'I am very glad you have come to the determination you have,' William wrote to him, 'I believe it will turn out to be an important step in the right direction for both of us.'[111] After an unrecorded six weeks in New Plymouth, Arthur left for Nelson to take up his duties. He was to lodge with Emily and William, who had leased a house, made much larger by additions, in which Arthur occupied a small bedroom crammed with books, desk, and his 'wonderful arm chair'. Emily told Lely that since his arrival he had received four invitations to tea parties, all of which he had refused, saying 'it was not becoming to apprentices to be going to parties'.[112]

Once the decision was made, Maria's hands were full with sorting out and packing up. The whole burden of moving now fell on her, although her end-of-year letter to Margaret reads as if she had laid aside despondency and become again her energetic self.

> I am up to my ears in most earthly cares, such as what furniture, books, pots, pans, kettles etc to take away to Nelson, for thither we actually propose going in about a month's time. Arthur has already gone & become a bondsman to the law . . .
>
> A removal where one takes everything or sells everything is painful enough, but to have to consider the advantages of taking or leaving every article [taxes] the mind more than the body. I heartily wish I was thro' the business & had dear old Lely & the children safely landed at Nelson.[113]

Wedding anniversary and Christmas passed without comment – Maria seldom found anything to celebrate when Arthur was away from home – but the end of the year saw one last family occasion: Wilson Hursthouse's marriage to Ellen Humphries on 29 December. 'Everybody went,' Maria wrote to Arthur. Edie and Ruth were two of the flower girls and they threw their flowers 'most prettily', although their much-practised tableau was lost in the throng. The New Year 'earthquake weather', oppressive and gloomy, firmed up Maria's wish to leave: 'When I thought of how you would feel if an earthquake swept us all away, I agreed with Emily in thinking it wicked for husband & wife to separate.'[114]

The difficult task of choosing an inexpensive but roomy house had to be left to Arthur. To prevent him and Lely from being overwhelmed with noise, especially if they had to house some of James's children as well, Maria favoured a solution similar to that of Beach Cottage – a smaller cottage close to a larger one which would allow 'quietness for you & Granny during the day & some tête à tête for you & I'.[115] The one thing she was emphatic about was that Arthur must avoid any house built on one of Nelson's potential landslides: 'if it were a palace & liable to be overwhelmed some rainy night, or itself go sliding downhill I should never rest well in it'.[116] Arthur sent her a plan of a house which Maria thought would exactly suit, provided that the number of resident children was not doubled. Whether this was the house he finally decided upon is uncertain. His diary for 23 and 24 January 1868 records:

> 23 Jan. Went with William & Emily to look over 'Bleak House' next St Katherines [where William and Emily lived[117]] which may perhaps do for us. It is big enough & high up but wretchedly built & forlorn looking.
> 24 Jan. Saw Moore [?] about taking Bleak House.[118]

Maria was prepared, if necessary, to accomplish the move of the children and Lely singlehanded. However, in mid-February Arthur returned to help with the final packing and despatch of boxes and crates and, presumably, to arrange for the lease of Beach Cottage during his and Maria's absence. The Nelson *Examiner* recorded the arrival of the steamer *Phoebe* from Taranaki on 20 January with 'Mr and Mrs Atkinson, six children [Wilsie and another of James's included with their own] and Mrs Richmond as saloon passengers'. It would seem that, like her departure from Hurworth, Maria went without a backward glance, not realising that, apart from occasional visits, she was leaving the bush of Hurworth, the fern-clad banks of the Te Henui, the wide sea view from Beach Cottage, the sandhills in which the children had played, that mountain, that home, for ever. The only intimation we have of her feelings as she was about to depart comes from a letter to Arthur earlier in the New Year. William's health made it likely that he would resign from the bench before Arthur completed his three years. Maria wrote,

When he is unfortunately obliged to resign we can go into the question of how & where you are to finish. I feel I could not make up my mind to being separated . . . If my ambitious projects end in ruin we can but retire to Urenui & raise potatoes & pigs enough to keep us alive.[119]

CHAPTER
TWELVE

Bleak House to
Fairfield

Nelson, 1868–72

When Maria and her family arrived on 20 February 1868, Nelson was 'fine with a few showers'. The Blacketts,[1] Maria and Arthur's former Taranaki friends, and presumably Emily and William with an assortment of children, were on the wharf to greet them. Seven-year-old Ruth and her cousin Margaret, who was four years older, spent that night in the Blacketts' home. A few weeks later 'Mrs C.W.R. and Mrs Arthur A' called to afternoon tea; later again John Blackett drove 'Mrs Arthur' on an excursion to Waimea West.

Compared with the bulletins which flowed daily from Arthur's pen and only a little less frequently from Maria's or Lely's at Beach Cottage, such details seem insignificant. Their importance lies simply in the fact that they are among the few small details of Maria's daily life at Nelson which were written down. There were now fewer people for Maria to write to: Mary Richmond was dead, and Maria was never so intimate with Annie; Emily Richmond, another to whom Maria and Lely wrote regularly, lived close by; Arthur, apart from his circuit trips with William to the West Coast, was seldom from home; Lely no longer ventured abroad and, worst blow of all to the biographer, Arthur's diary stops after May 1868.[2] It seems odd that he, a man of fixed habits, should have ceased to keep one, after having done so conscientiously from the age of fourteen. An obvious explanation would be that, in line with common practice, Ruth and Mabel, the last of the family at Fairfield, destroyed all later journals when they made 'a good clean up' of the house prior to leaving it in 1921. This too seems uncharacteristic. Later generations of the mob have been at pains to preserve even letters which commenced 'Burn this at once'. Further speculation is useless: the fact remains that if subsequent diaries once existed they now appear to have been lost. Fortunately, Margaret Taylor remained in her castle in Syrgenstein, Bavaria, and Maria's letters, written at intervals, remain as informative as ever. But instead of being able to follow Maria's progress closely, as in Taranaki, we now have to take strides.

Nelson from the late 1860s was scarcely an 'undiscovered bourne', though published accounts of the province are rare for the period between 1850 and 1890. The *Examiner, Colonist* and *Evening Mail*, give some of the flavour of Nelson life in many ways markedly different from that of Taranaki. The most obvious difference, evident in newspaper files, is the length of the shipping arrivals-and-departures column. The *Taranaki Herald* featured a small weekly cluster of vessels which may or may not have included those which, from Maria's account, simply threw themselves onto the beach. Shipping movements in the Nelson newspapers occupied at least a column, sometimes two, with ships from England and the Australian colonies arriving and departing to schedule, and with a multitude of coastal vessels, particularly from the West Coast goldfields, constantly in and out. The same sort of all-male lodges which thrived in New Plymouth did so at Nelson, too. There was an active Acclimatisation Society, a well-supported Harmonic Society, a Scientific Association, and a Literary Institute which boasted a museum, a library, and a reading room. There were volunteer rifle companies and even artillery companies, the difference being that Nelson volunteers engaged in friendly competition with each other; they did not track Maori through the bush. The *Examiner* considered Nelson 'as safe from Maori aggression as Westminster Abbey'. Although Nelson settlers had been spared the social upheaval of war, the *Examiner* was just as insistent as the *Taranaki Herald* that the 'real work' of subduing Maori should be left to colonial forces: 'We hope most sincerely the Government will successfully resist the demands for external assistance of every kind; for to ensure peace we must convince the Maori we are able to enforce it.'[3] Cricket and horseracing were as popular in Nelson as in New Plymouth but the former annually celebrated the founding of the settlement with a yachting regatta. There too singers, pianists, violinists, actors, sometimes troupes of child actors and the occasional circus, complete with 'wild animals', passed through at monthly intervals.

The other clear difference between the two towns was that education had achieved far greater recognition in Nelson, where an educational ordinance of 1856 had imposed a school rating of one pound a year on every householder. The ordinance also stipulated that religious instruction, when given, should be without 'controversial character' or compulsory attendance. Reports of the progress at the various primary schools – separate for boys and girls – featured regularly. There were also the Roman Catholic school of St Mary's, the Bishop's School of the Church of England, and various smaller schools run by women to supplement their income. In 1868 Nelson College received a new headmaster who was to become a good friend of the Richmond–Atkinson families and an ally of Maria when she began her efforts to promote a college for girls. From numerous applications which, the *Examiner* reports, had come from both inside and outside the colony, that of the Reverend F.C. Simmons, formerly rector of Otago Boys' High School, was unanimously chosen by the board of governors. Simmons had had enough of Presbyterian interference in the affairs of the high school and had found Dunedin 'utterly intolerable'. He was to find Nelson College, designed by William Beatson as a miniature Eton in wood, less abrasive and Nelson society more accommodating.

Thus, after its shaky start in the 1840s Nelson was by the end of the 1860s comfortably and conveniently settled, rejoicing in peace, prosperity, and 'city' status.[4] Unlike New Plymouth, its houses had gardens and were not built on 'moveable principles'. In place of gutted farmhouses, neglected orchards, broken fences, and paddocks full of thistles, Nelson outdistricts such as Richmond, Stoke, Wakefield, Waimea, Spring Grove, and Appleby had well-tended farms and an ever-growing population. Hemmed in by hills and mountains Nelson had no large tracts of land to draw on, but its smallholding agriculture thrived as both town and outdistricts provided for the steady influx of miners to the diggings which by 1867 had pushed the European population of the province to nearly 24,000. Taranaki's population, excluding Maori, was 4,359. The West Coast goldfields were Nelson's frontier settlements. Nelson was the only port in regular communication with the diggings, and the goldfield towns of Greymouth, Westport, and Hokitika looked to Nelson province rather than across the mountain barrier to Canterbury for trade and sustenance. Strictly speaking Hokitika was the chief settlement of the newly constituted county of Westland but it was still within the orbit of Nelson, and it and Westport were visited regularly by Mr Justice Richmond and his associate as part of the Nelson circuit.

As a judge, William's place in Nelson's social hierarchy was assured: his movements were noted and his speeches to jurors, college boys, or Nelson citizens were printed in full and solemnly received. When the Duke of Edinburgh visited Nelson in April 1869, William and Emily were among the official party. At the ball in the evening the first quadrille was 'opened' by His Royal Highness and Lady Monro (wife of Nelson's most prestigious citizen) while His Excellency (Sir George Bowen) partnered Emily. William took Lady Bowen to supper. Apart from official intercourse which could not be avoided, William distanced himself (and attempted to distance Emily) from the more convivial demands of Nelson society, thinking it improper to risk even the appearance of compromising his judicial position. It would seem his associate followed his example. Arthur neither joined the local volunteers nor wrote newspaper articles and, though it may well have been 'pain and grief' to him, he did not play cricket. Money would have been a constraint, but so too would have been his early decision that it was 'not becoming to apprentices to be going to parties'. There was, however, one concession which his new position allowed or even forced on him. When William and he travelled to the West Coast to attend supreme court sessions, Arthur shared with William the first-class saloon cabin. His days of sitting all night on deck on his portmanteau were finally over. He was probably no less seasick.

Until Arthur qualified, Maria too would have led a comparatively sequestered life. This would not have bothered her, for with her own and often James's family about her, with William, Emily, and all the young nieces and nephews close at hand, and with Arthur finally embarked on a promising career, she would have been well satisfied. One further reconciling factor was that *both* Arthur and she could now be considered middle aged. The gap which at nineteen and twenty-eight seemed to stretch to the limit of propriety had, at thirty-five and forty-four, narrowed considerably. In her surviving letters Maria no longer excuses Arthur or makes an issue out of the age difference. It is even possible that a more mature Arthur dropped the sobriquet of 'old wifey'.

Arthur's Bleak House on the south-western side of Nelson city in the block between Ngatitama and Ngatiawa Streets[5] was designated in the rating roll as 'a five room cottage' built in 1865 for J. Firth, an absentee owner.[6] With the cottage went half an acre of land. St Katherine's, where William and Emily lived, was not quite 'next door' as Arthur had described it, but was set in seventeen acres and was an altogether superior establishment of sixteen rooms.[7] It had been built in 1863 and named by a previous owner. At the beginning of 1868 William had a 'substantial two roomed cottage' built in the grounds so as to secure the services of a married couple.

Approximately every three months Maria lost Arthur for upwards of a month to the West Coast. This was not, she informed Margaret, such a trial as 'those dreadful session partings', during which Arthur might be gone indefinitely, and now the 'electric telegraph' between Nelson and Hokitika meant that 'we could summon them in case of alarming illness & hear from them in an hour or less'.[8] Nevertheless, at nights when he was away she thought anxiously of 'that horrid Hokitika bar because tho' "men must work & women weep", wives need not for their ambitious ends drive husbands on dangerous careers risking their lives & health.'[9] And if Arthur failed to write, it could still seem 'really months since you left'. Towards the end of September 1868 she wrote to him:

> I hope you are not going to Wellington without coming home. I want someone to say something cheerful so much. What with everybody's mismanagement of everything [rumours from the North Island spoke of demoralised and panic stricken volunteers] & last but not least vigorous mismanagement of the children I must take to chloroform or dram drinking soon if you keep away & can't write.[10]

After receipt of this letter Arthur made a practice of sending Maria a telegram when the vessel was safely over the Hokitika bar.

Arthur, still keeping steadily to his diary on his first two trips with William and still maintaining his habit of 'a little Greek before breakfast', was struck by the appearance of the booming goldfields town of Hokitika. Their first arrival followed a heavy flood and he and William discovered that the hotel in which they were to stay had subsided into the river; another, the Steam Packet Hotel, 'was very appropriately preparing to put to sea, its forepart being supported on temporary props washed by the water'.[11] As was to be expected, the houses and shops were of a makeshift character and included a 'startling' number of public houses:

> There are in Revell St as nearly as I could make out 77 public houses. I looked carefully but did not see one man drunk or disorderly . . . There was no fighting nor did I hear any bad language. I only met three policemen in my walk from one end to the other and back again, and I think only one of these was on duty. This is a creditable state of things considering how a digging population is composed and the large amount of money passing through their hands.[12]

Equally surprising, although the diggings attracted all sorts and conditions of men, was the discovery that the commissioner was a Fellow of Trinity College, Cambridge. George Sale, who came to Canterbury in 1860, gave up his job as editor of the *Press* in order to be agent for the Canterbury provincial government and goldfields' commissioner at Hokitika. He left in 1869 to become foundation professor of English and Classics at the University of Otago. Arthur and he read Browning together. Another kindred spirit and classical scholar with whom William and Arthur stayed when at Westport was Dr Joseph Giles, whose career in New Zealand varied between that of army surgeon and journalist. He became editor of the *Examiner* for a time in the late 1860s and in that capacity was a strong supporter of higher education for women and of women's rights generally. The Bishop of Nelson, Andrew Suter, was also in the habit of staying at the Giles household when on circuit, so that when all visits coincided there was a deal of 'friendly discussion' on metaphysics and humanity's place in creation: this the bishop preferred to be set in Genesis rather than in *Origin of Species*.

In May 1868 C.W. Richmond presided at the trial of seven West Coast Fenians who were charged with 'libel, sedition and treasonable practices'. Their leader was an Irish priest, Father W.J. Larkin. A series of incidents which began with an orderly procession of 600 to 700 Irish miners through the streets of Charleston to the Roman Catholic church where Father Larkin prayed for three Fenians recently executed at Manchester culminated in a 'riot' at Addisons Flat, a tent town some short distance south of Westport. The whole affair was exacerbated when news reached Nelson on 24 March of the attempted assassination by a Fenian of the Duke of Edinburgh at Sydney. On 3 April a party of miners returning from Westport, where they had gone 'to rejoice' at the escape of the Duke, entered Addisons Flat shouting 'Ireland is conquered for ever', which earned them a hail of stones from several hundred 'impulsive' Irish. No great damage was done but the attempted assassination followed by the 'riot' caused passions on the Coast and in Nelson to rise to fever pitch. For a time the 'menace of Fenianism' dominated 'Hauhau outrages' in the columns of the Nelson newspapers. At M. and Mme Simonsen's concert in Nelson an extra verse added to the National Anthem, sung *'con amore'* by the audience, beseeched God to save 'our widow'd Queen' and ended, 'Preserve and soon restore Her noble boy'. Fenians were 'discovered' at Marlborough and Otago; troops were sent to Hokitika, and at Addisons Flat, Irish mustered and Westport 'loyalists' prepared to march against them. Owing to the moderating influence of the Westport warden the opposing forces did not meet, but tempers were still charged and patriotism high when C.W. Richmond came to preside at the trial of Father Larkin and six fellow defendants. Richmond 'under fire' and in a not too dissimilar situation at Waitara had not weighed evidence and had acted precipitately, but as a judge in a court of law which he understood, he kept a cool head and delivered an enlightened judgement which had a calming effect on the prisoners and on the populace. In Arthur's words,

> C.W.R., after a little fatherly advice [he said, 'the Court abstains from all moral comment . . . it leaves you to the admonitions of your own conscience'][13] fined them £20 a piece for the procession business and gave them a month's imprisonment for the libels. This I think has pretty well satisfied everybody – prisoners included.[14]

Maria's paramount interest at Nelson was in the education of the mob's second generation, and of its girls in particular. William and Emily's family ranged downwards in age from Mary, fifteen in 1868, to one-year-old Edward. Kit (Christopher Francis), their eldest boy, had gone to Bishop's School when he first arrived at Nelson and, from a letter William wrote to his uncle in 1867,[15] his school-age daughters were at the Miss Greenwoods. Apart from Wilsie (James Wilson) who was brought up by Maria, James's children shuttled between Wellington, where James remained until 1870, and Emily or Maria at Nelson. As the boys of the extended family grew older, they passed from either Bishop's School or one of the other private schools into the prestigious embrace of nearby Nelson College; there was not the same orderly progression for girls. Nelson boasted a publicly funded primary school system, which concentrated particularly on the 'three Rs'. The Richmond–Atkinson girls went to a variety of private schools where they moved early into French, German and Classics as favoured by their parents. Another perceived advantage may well have been the private schools' encouragement of proper elocution – a concern not noted in public schools. In this, the family was not assiduously mindful of the virtue of egalitarianism. 'Anna, Margie, Edie & Ruth went to hear recitations & songs & see a magic lantern at the Temperance Hall,' Maria wrote to Arthur at Hokitika. 'All the speakers, reciters & singers dropped their hs & some had highly oiled black hair to Margie's disgust.'[16]

Towards the end of 1868, Maria began a morning school at Bleak

House for the older girls (the younger ones continued at their private establishments) and this was still functioning in 1870 when her pupils were Mary, Margaret, Anna, Alla, Edie, who at twelve was old enough to join in many lessons, and Annie Hill, a friend of the St Katherine's girls. Alla's presence 'increased the amount of work done by the others. Margie is more especially improved. She is clever but idle to a degree unless under the influence of emulation. Emily considers Margie rather a genius . . . which is most unfortunate as it has confirmed Margie's careless ways, making her fancy work *unnecessary*.'[17] Maria held out little hope for the scholastic achievement of her own daughters, none of whom showed 'any great avidity for knowledge', though this did not dim her appreciation of them: 'Mabel is a delightful little dunce, but sparkling with life & happiness. She is called "Squirrel" by her Granny from the colour of her hair & her animated movements.'[18] It was the boys, Kit – 'a wonderful command of language', Maurice (James's son) – 'an amazing memory' and dextrous at all manual skills, and her own Arfie – 'he is far from forward but he has the gift of spelling & of language too I think & is wonderfully quick with figures', whom she thought would 'bid fair to sustain the honour of the Richmond name'. All were doing well at Nelson College including 'our hop-o-my-thumb little Arfie' who became a collegian at seven.[19]

'Oh for a girls' college!', Maria exclaimed to Margaret Taylor, 'the paltry three hours with me is curtailed at one or both ends two or three times a week.'[20] She envied Dunedin its Otago Girls' High School, attributing its foundation in 1869 to 'the Scotch, as usual foremost in educational matters', who were willing to use their endowments for both sexes.[21] In another letter written to Margaret in 1870 Maria made a strong plea for equal educational opportunities for boys and girls. It is a letter which brings together Maria's convictions about the value of higher education for women and her forthright opinions on women's rights.

Whatever influence I might have in the world I should wish to use in the cause of education. I want my girls to have a boy's education because it is a better education than what is called a girl's, since it better exercises the faculties God has given girls as well as boys. I certainly approve of any woman studying medicine or anything else she selects provided she does it earnestly. I only wish I had studied medicine myself; the mental training would have made me an infinitely more valuable member of society, to say nothing of the advantages special knowledge of the kind would

have given me. I don't see how any study which strengthens the
mental powers can do otherwise than make women fitter for *their
own special work* [F.P. italics], sick nursing included & I believe that
Nature has so provided that their own desires & affections will
always lead them to discharge those duties first, except in cases
where luxury, idleness & frivolity destroy Nature's promptings.
My experience in the Colony shows me that the most *solidly* educated
women are the most useful in every department of life, & that
so called 'feminine refinement' is fatal to female usefulness. I dare
say we should agree at bottom, only that you imagine (as the
Confederates used to do about the Negroes) that Liberty would
lead our sex into all sorts of wild vagaries & to the neglect of
our own work, & I have more confidence in us. I believe the more
we are educated, the higher we aim intellectually, the better we
shall discharge our own special functions in the world. Just take
my own imaginary case. Had I studied medicine till I was 28 when
I left England, would it have prevented my marrying? I believe
not, but it would have made me a ten times better wife & mother
& a more respectable human being altogether.[22]

On the engrossing topic of women's rights Maria followed her
own consistent line, although this put her out of step with her
more advanced sisters in America. She had long maintained that
female education in England produced a 'complete distortion of
a human being', and in the same letter to Margaret continued:

Something in England needs reforming, even your conservative mind
must admit, or girls would not be the objectionable creatures you
& common report depict them. You can hardly attribute 'the girl
of the Period' to the agitation for Women's Rights as it is called.
She is rather what the *old* system in its latest development has brought
us to, when the increase of wealth for large classes, enables woman
to fulfil the *ornamental* end of her being! I have not a grain of sympathy
with the American aspect of the Women's Rights question. In fact
our worthy brethren & sisters there have a knack of dressing up
the most important truths so nauseously that they turn the strongest
stomachs. There was something so 'creepy' about much of the
Abolitionists' talk & writing that one needed to be very clear in
one's conviction of the sin of slavery to stand it.

Whether we like it or not I feel certain the next century will
see an enormous change in the position of women. It is a part
of Democracy. I am not sure I *like* Democracy. Power coming
without, or long before, wisdom must always be bad.[23]

From the time when as a young woman she had enjoyed *Jane
Eyre* and been irritated by *Shirley*, Maria had maintained that a

woman's true workplace was within the family. Marriage therefore was not only 'an honourable estate', it was, for a woman, a proper one, not to be cast aside for professional employment. In *Aurora Leigh* Elizabeth Browning had explored other possibilities and Maria had not cared for it. Contemporary American feminists, including Elizabeth Cady Stanton (1815–1902) who with Lucretia Mott organised the first women's rights convention in 1848, at Seneca Falls; Emma Hart Willard (1787–1870) who began the Troy Female Seminary in 1814 where 'higher subjects' such as mathematics, history, and languages were added to the 'ornamental' subjects deemed suitable for women, and the Grimké sisters, Sarah Moore (1792–1873) and Angelina Emily (1805–1879), who called women to civil disobedience to defeat slavery, all argued in varying degrees that women had no particular or 'limited' sphere and that they had no fewer rights than men because they were 'moral beings'. Elizabeth Stanton, in particular, who chose to stay home to raise her children, nevertheless saw childbearing as a 'grievous interruption' of her plans. In a letter to be read at the Seventh National Women's Rights Convention of 1858, she condemned marriage for putting women in a 'false position':

> Oh how I long for a few hours of blessed leisure each day. How rebellious it makes me feel when I see Henry [her husband] going about where and how he pleases. He can walk at will through the whole wide world or shut himself up alone, if he pleases, within four walls. As I contrast his freedom with my bondage, and feel that, because of the false position of women, I have been compelled to hold all my noblest aspirations in abeyance in order to be a wife, a mother, a nurse, a cook, a household drudge, I am fired anew and long to pour forth from my own experience the whole long story of women's wrongs.[24]

Maria would have regarded such views as neither 'tactful' nor 'commonsense'. However, if one refers back to the period at Beach Cottage when Maria, beleagered by little ones, described herself as 'tied by the leg' and with insufficient leisure to read, write, or even be stimulated by adult company, and when, in her despondency (which she admitted), she must have contrasted Arthur's freedom with her own lack of it, the distance between Elizabeth Stanton's experience and her own seems to narrow.

The emancipation of American slaves and the emancipation of women were not seen as a single issue but there was a logical connection between them. Campaigns for the enfranchisement and higher education of women, the various temperance and prohibition

alliances in which many women found their political teeth for the
first time, as well as Darwin's theory of evolution and the 'Higher
Criticism' of the Bible which together shook the authoritarian stance
of the church, were all part of the forward movement which excited
crusading zeal, passion, bigotry, and commitment. Maria too was
caught up: 'I rejoice in living in such exciting times, when all
science and philosophy seem to be bent on searching to the root
of things.'[25]

The waves of this disturbance reached and occasionally ruffled
the calm of Nelson. The *Nelson Examiner*, an influential paper which
began its life in March 1842, was owned by Charles Elliott, himself
a supporter of women's rights. Towards the end of its life – it
ceased publication in 1874 – the *Examiner* employed such liberal
editors as Dr Joseph Giles, Rev. Frank Simmons (headmaster of
Nelson College), J.C. Richmond, and Dr F.W. Irvine, the mob's
doctor and an advocate of a college for girls in Nelson. A provocative
article, reprinted 7 July 1868 from the *Saturday Review*, stated that
female suffrage would 'disturb all domestic economy'. It drew a
measured reply from Mary Anne Muller of Nelson, writing under
the pseudonym 'Femina' so as not to disturb her more conservatively
minded husband. The *Examiner* published in full C.W. Richmond's
winter lecture in the provincial assembly rooms on 'Man's Place
in Creation' in which he stated that 'it is not possible in the present
state of Science to establish any anatomical or physiological
distinction between Anthropoid Apes and Man'. William's
exposition drew 'Letters to the Editor' and a courteous protest
from Archdeacon Harper: 'Is there not a physical indicium, which
God in Nature has assigned to the structure of Man – and Ape?
. . . if you take the hand of a monkey, and contrast it with the
hand of a man . . . Isn't one a hand, the other a paw?'[26] William's
lecture was followed by Dr Giles's 'Women's Place in Creation'.
It created less controversy, women being more accepted than
monkeys. Giles began: 'There is a tide in the affairs of women/
Which taken at the flood leads Heaven knows where.' He went
on to list the restrictions imposed on women in property laws,
the franchise, admission to the professions, and in higher education.
'The only way to find out woman's place in creation,' he argued,
'is to give her the fullest use of her powers and let her find her
place for herself.' He drew laughter and applause when he stated
that the 'sentiment "I cannot understand – I love", put by the
laureate [Tennyson] into the mouth of a wife, is more fitted for
a Newfoundland dog.'[27] Giles concluded by recommending to the

people of Nelson – 'called by Sir G. Grey "the Athens of New Zealand" ' – that they should actively support higher, including university, education for women.

In April 1871 the *Examiner* again focused attention on higher education for the girls of this 'Athens':

> one invidious defect exists in our educational machinery . . . The endowments for higher education are confined to one school, and that for boys alone. The Governors of Nelson College recognize the equal claim of the other sex to share the funds, but it would be folly to cripple a school . . . in order to establish a second at the risk that both may languish . . . We ask . . . all persons interested in the question, without waiting for the growth of funds, to set on foot at once, and by private effort, a school which shall be as far as possible for the girls of Nelson – and elsewhere what Nelson College is for boys.[28]

It suggested that the English proprietory school provided the model, whereby capital expended principally on buildings and plant would be subscribed by shareholders. As for the quality of teaching, it was to be 'substantially what is good teaching for boys'. A month later the *Examiner* noted 'with much pleasure that the purpose of a recent article in this paper on the education of girls, is being practically taken up by a number of gentlemen'.[29] It was being practically taken up by two gentlewomen as well. Maria and Emily sought the advice of Rev. F.C. Simmons of Nelson College on the best way to begin. 'He advises seeing all the people who have daughters, to see if they are willing to combine for such an object, and how many children are to be had.'[30] Dr F.W. Irvine from the college board of governors called on Maria and spoke 'hopefully of the willingness and the ability of the governors to help in starting such an institution'.[31] He mentioned a sum of £400 a year as being available. All seemed propitious and Maria and Emily made out a list of about forty potential pupils. The scheme then appears to have been dropped. Gas and waterworks[32] claimed public attention and its purse; higher education for girls slipped away.

By the end of the year the *Examiner*, while still supporting the theory, doubted its practicality:

> We have not, in Nelson, the means . . . of initiating any such movement as that now ripening in England . . . We have to do what lies in us as a community to impart more of earnestness and interest to the lives of the girls growing up in easy classes; to substitute serious work for the butterfly indiscipline to which they are for the most part condemned.[33]

The board of governors, Dr Irvine in the chair, received a deputation of 'ladies and gentlemen' – Emily and James Richmond among them – on 28 December 1871, who submitted a draft proposition and the promise of £200. A sub-committee was set up to report on feasibility; it reported back in January 1872 that no funds were available. The annual report of 20 February 1872 stated: 'The promotion of a LADIES' COLLEGE or HIGH SCHOOL FOR GIRLS has again been carefully considered. So far only moral support has been possible.'[34]

Some small practical benefits accrued to the Richmond–Atkinson girls from the abortive attempt to found a girls' college. Joseph Mackay, assistant master of Nelson College, agreed that if Maria and Emily could gather together a class of at least twelve girls, he would come one evening a week to teach arithmetic and physical geography. Miss Mackay, proprietor of one of the private girls' schools, 'got Uncle James to take a drawing and French class, and Mr Smith of the government school is going to teach arithmetic and Latin if Miss Mackay likes'.[35] Ruth, Mabel, and Anna Richmond attended Miss Mackay's school which Maria thought better than most colonial schools, and Edie and some of her friends were allowed to participate in Miss Mackay's 'Hullah class'.[36] Hullah's system of 'sight-singing' used a tonic sol-fa in which 'do' was fixed to the key of C. It relied on pupils having perfect pitch. 'When other keys were introduced,' wrote the contributor to the *New Grove Dictionary of Music and Musicians*, 'pupils became baffled and abandoned the pursuit.' Baffled, Miss Mackay's class often was, but they persevered. Mary Richmond declared that the 'howls' from the Hullah class during 'music exercises' so alarmed the neighbourhood that police had been sent up to the school to investigate. 'Nevertheless they greatly enjoy it,' Maria wrote, '& the various evening practices at *friendly* houses . . . I let Edie join in hopes that she might improve in her notions of time. She inherits my deficiency of that important bump.'[37]

Living in Nelson had not cut Maria off from the Taranaki section of the mob. 'Our poor relatives at Taranaki are all rather flat,' she wrote to Margaret in 1868, 'W.S.A., Harry and Dec are all suffering from empty purses.'[38] The *Taranaki News* was not filling Henry's pocket either but 1868 had a brighter prospect in store for him:

> Henry . . . has matrimonial views & is living in sunshine, but a
> the young lady (16 years his junior I think)[39] is a conscientiou
> church woman & is really thoughtful, has moreover never fel

matrimonially inclined so far in life, I feel doubtful whether a widower of his age with a free Christian creed, or absence of creed, can be very attractive. The father has a high opinion of Hy & approves his suit.[40]

Maria also approved of Emma Jane Parris, daughter of Robert Parris, the Taranaki land commissioner. 'I feel so far guilty of match making,' she continued, 'that hearing some good things of the lady I repeated them before him.' She admired Emma's musical and literary tastes, too. She was the only one of Mary King's New Plymouth pupils who had learned to appreciate Beethoven, and she had read Matthew Arnold's *Essays* 'with real interest'.

At the end of May, Henry and Emma were engaged, and on 15 July 1868 they were married at St Mary's, New Plymouth. By this time Maria had discovered that Emma's 'orthodoxy' was of the Broad Church type.[41] 'If, as I believe, they grant that it is a duty to search for truth,' she wrote to Arthur, '& that all truth must be divine, I should feel in sympathy with them . . . as one can never be with the cowardly believers.'[42] Maria had a greater problem in reconciling Emily Richmond to the match:

Em & I have had a few brisk encounters on the *lowness* of the connexion . . . From what I can patch together Em's view is that no Richmond should marry anyone whose parents & I might add near relatives are not highly moral, highly educated, superlatively clean, tolerably good looking & whose father could be guilty of putting on the wrong trousers on Sunday![43]

There is no doubt about it, Emily, the one-time 'child of nature', had become a snob. William had seen the seeds of it some years before, but his natural as well as professional aloofness would not have made it easy for Emily, who was not nearly so much her own person as was Maria. To Emily social position mattered. Maria and Arthur were used to Em, and their underlying affection for her was never jeopardised by her and Maria's occasional exchanges of fire. As the children of the various families grew up, there was often a good-natured shrug, as it were, in their letters to Maria: 'Of course Aunt Em would insist . . .' or 'You can imagine what Aunt Em said . . .' Emily for her part held Maria, Arthur, and Lely in the highest possible esteem.

As she came to know Emma, Maria (and presumably Emily) liked her more and more. 'She is very quiet & undemonstrative but I can see a devoted wife to Hy, & a kind judicious mother. She is quite a lady in feelings, manners & language, tho' Taranaki born & bred.'[44] The person Maria felt sorry for was Aunt Helen

Hursthouse who decided to leave Henry's house and her two grandchildren now that her son-in-law had a young wife. She hoped to make her home in Patea where her married son, Wilson, worked as a surveyor. Maria promptly wrote to her aunt begging her to visit them directly after the wedding. Lely was very willing to share her bedroom with her younger sister and looked forward to having her company.

Another change took place among the Taranaki set in 1868 when Annie and Harry Atkinson decided to visit England and Dr Kidd. Marriage had not improved Annie's headaches and there was some hint of gynaecological impediment, which from a remark made by Harry in a letter to Arthur – 'I am very low and wretched at times on her account and my wounded pride'[45] – may indicate that at thirty Annie had a too-well-preserved virginity. They paid a last visit to Maria and Arthur, bringing Helen Hursthouse with them, before sailing for England in the *Ruahine*, along with their children, Dunstan, Fanny, and Alfred. Tudor stayed at St Katherine's and attended Nelson College.

Harry Atkinson's temporary departure left J.C. Richmond as the only member of the mob in parliament. As *de facto* native minister he conscientiously travelled from one trouble spot to another; he had no solution to offer except that wrested by attrition and subjugation. In May 1868 he had accompanied the new governor, Sir George Bowen, on a series of visits to the principal North Island Maori settlements. Bowen was not an army man but a classical scholar, and he had a fondness for ease, comfort, and his day's shooting. James found the vice-regal progress very boring. He noticed, without too much dismay, how depopulated were the Maori districts: 'not from war alone, for the dying off of Ngapuhi is as rapid as that of Waikato'. His exception was Te Arawa, 'the liveliest most energetic, democratic, noisy tribe in N. Zealand', groups of whom fought for the Crown either alongside other colonial forces or on their own. 'If some lay missionary with a good income and genial ways would settle there and organise them into a few joint stock companies they might be made something of yet,'[46] he told William.

James thought that the 'native difficulty in its alarming phase [was] at an end . . . I think the trouble will resolve itself into a little cattle lifting here and there, and the murder of an outsettler . . . Is it not curious how we are broken in to take a dozen or so kohurus [killings by stealth] in the course of the year with philosophic calmness?'[47] On 4 July government affairs in the North

Island took a decided turn for the worse with the escape of Te Kooti Te Turuki Rikirangi and his fellow prisoners from the Chatham Islands. Six days after they landed at Whareongaonga, both Maori and Pakeha settlements in Poverty Bay were once again attacked before Te Kooti fell back into the Urewera wilderness from which he continued to mount successful raids on colonial forces. These, together with Titokowaru's victories at Te Ngutu o te Manu and Moturoa in September and November, shattered any notion of philosophic calm.

In June 1869 Maria went to Wellington to visit James and to bring back his children who had been staying at Nelson. With Arthur away on the Coast, Aunt Helen was left in charge of Bleak House. 'I hope you only feel mildly desolate at my cruel desertion & not implacably indignant. I feel quite sure it is good for them to be without me for a while,'[48] Maria wrote to him. She accompanied James to the opening of the session and attended proceedings from the Ladies' Gallery. Provincialists and centralists were still at loggerheads. One scheme, which Maria attributed to Julius Vogel (of whom she did not approve), had the South Island 'buying itself off from its responsibility in Maori wars by paying the Nth Island a million pounds'. 'I should be inclined to accept the million,' Maria wrote to Arthur. 'Invested at 5 per cent, it might be enough to pension the King & the greatest chiefs; pension to stop when war began.'[49] She drew the line at Te Kooti and Titokowaru whom she felt inclined to shoot if possible, but still marvelled how the experience of the last ten years had changed her views on 'Native Management'.[50] She listened to and was not impressed by Nathaniel Edwards, member for Nelson city, who made the 'lamest of speeches' for which the only excuse could be that he was 'dreadfully nervous'. She could have 'hurled things' at C.B. Borlase, one of the Wellington members, 'a dreadful d-g & aggravating, so glib & pleased with himself'. She was there when the Stafford ministry resigned on 24 June 1869 and was relieved, even though Fox was sent for, that James's political character would no longer be compromised. James was 'gladder every day to be out of the mess,' he wrote to Arthur. 'Happily more than half the discussion of events humanly speaking is with Te Kooti and Co!'[51]

James was out of office, but he still represented the Grey and Bell district. Initially undecided whether to make his home in New Plymouth or Nelson, he eventually resolved on the latter, for the sake of his children's education, and asked Arthur to take a house for him with as low rent as possible. Until the 1870 session began, James stayed in Nelson 'busy with his little tribe to whom he is mother & father in one'. The experiment of having Helen Hursthouse living there as well did not work out. 'Aunt Helen's presence provided a lady at the head of the house' but the restraints she had seen fit to impose irked the children, particularly Alla. Alla puzzled her father, who thought her 'a fine young lady but rough and wild to an extraordinary degree', and delighted Maria.

> Anneliz [Alla] will exert herself & learn to be more tidy & industrious in household matters when left to herself than when directed & talked *at*. She is full of energy & character & is clever & has such an excellent memory that she *will* find an education wherever she goes.[52]

Maria, careful to avoid favouritism in her extended family, had a special empathy with her niece, seeing in her shy, 'uncouth' manner a creative originality. She wrote to Margaret:

> I often wish you could have Edie & Alla for a few years. Alla is more harum scarum & uncouth but I know you would end in liking her best. She has more 'go' & 'pluck' for work than Edie besides being quicker & cleverer by far. Edie's powers of observation are sharp enough but they turn on people's externals as with so many girls.[53]

The three Nelson households mustered eighteen children, and the number was often augmented by visiting cousins from Taranaki. The Highlawn acrobatic team, modelled on a juvenile troupe attached to Foley's circus, practised on trapeze and horizontal bars and kept Dr Irvine busy when they were too enthusiastic. Plays written by James, charades, and outings were all part of the holidays – 'they are all capital walkers right down to Wilson & Mabel so that we make tolerably long excursions without the expense of carriage hire'.[54] Now, too, the children's letters to each other begin to assume a significant part of the family correspondence. A particular responsibility was borne by Mary Richmond, the eldest of the second generation, on whom Emily, her mother, came more and more to lean. Maria, middle aged and looking back at all that happened since war destroyed the mob's home at Hurworth, wrote, 'Some of the changes would have seemed unbearable could we have anticipated them but the inevitable has to be borne . . . Children are the reconcilers here keeping mind, heart & fingers always busy.'[55] In the same letter she told Margaret of the presumed death of Calvert Wilson, his wife, and their two children, who on 18 May 1869 had sailed from Lyttelton to England on the *Matoaka*. The ship, not heard of again, was believed to have struck an iceberg while rounding Cape Horn.

Maria fully expected that James would be 'snapped up . . . & put into harness again somewhere for the public service'. In fact although he several times later offered himself as a candidate, 1870 was to be his last year in the House and his last, in any paid capacity, as a public servant. It was unlikely that the Fox ministry would survive, Maria informed Margaret: James 'dreads the thought of the session rapidly approaching & would like to resign his seat, but dare not lest his example should offer an excuse to two or three of our best members who long to cut politics, for resigning likewise.'[56] Again Maria was responding over-readily to one of James's passing moods. He was often dejected about politics and, as he wrote to Harry, the care of his young family weighed on him: 'Disturbed by double duties, I do nothing efficiently and often get into great depression.'[57] But he seems to have been in no real hurry to give a politician's life away. He returned from Wellington in mid-September 1870 and the following month was off to New Plymouth to see if his former constituencies (Omata, 1860–65; Grey and Bell, 1866–70) would have him. Maria was not confident. She thought they would choose a 'narrower & more provincial member' and that James could easily get into the Assembly for one of the Nelson seats. She was right about Taranaki, and wrong about Nelson. F.A. Carrington was elected for Grey and Bell; W. Gisborne for the newly constituted Egmont seat, and nothing in Nelson was forthcoming. At the end of 1870 James received and accepted a 'very influentially signed requisition from Wellington city' which, 'as it has hitherto been the very citadel of his enemies . . . is very flattering'.[58] James reported from Wellington in January that he was holding well-attended meetings and was confident of success. The *Wanganui Chronicle* quoted in the *Examiner* saw his 'bold stand against the financial proposals of Mr Vogel' as conclusive proof of 'how much more he cares for the public welfare than for party ties or personal interests. Mr Richmond, moreover is a gentleman of education and high culture.'[59] But time and tide were turning against prudence and the *laissez faire* economy which James advocated;[60] nor was 'high culture' what the increasing male electorate necessarily wanted in its political representatives. Wellington city turned from James – 'the *Independent* cannot stomach him at all,' William had warned Emily – and elected two local men, George Hunter and Edward Pearce, both supporters of Fox and Vogel. James returned to Nelson to edit the *Examiner*, join William in giving winter lectures in the provincial council assembly rooms, pursue his interest in education via the Nelson Schools Committee, think about visiting England with his family, and paint. His paintings were beginning to attract attention. Arthur Eccles, a prominent Dunedin surgeon, art collector, and promoter of the 1865 New Zealand Exhibition, wished to take with him on a visit to England 'some good specimens of New Zealand work and scenes'. The artists whose work he sought were John Gully, Charles Heaphy, and James Richmond.

While still in the House, James had 'earned the applause of the advanced liberals'[61] by introducing a Bill to amend the law regarding married women's property. To show that it was a non-party issue, Fox seconded the measure. James's object, he told the House, was not to 'unsex women' (a phrase apparently common at the time) but to place a married woman at no greater disadvantage in respect to her property than if she had been single. In the absence of specific details drawn up in a marriage settlement, the law as it stood left a woman, separated from her husband, without any right to property. Apart from a scanty alimony allowance if the husband could be found – and the 'nomadic habits of the labouring classes' often meant that he could not – wife and children were left destitute. 'The principle of the Bill was not to protect, but to place married women in a position to protect themselves.'[62] The Bill encountered little opposition in the House but was 'burked', as Maria put it, 'for this session by some old "duffers" of lawyers in our House of Lords, alias Legislative Council'. She was confident it would be passed during the next session 'as it is not a party question & [has] the best men of both sides in its favour'.[63] James's Bill, however, was pulled about so much that the Married Women's Property Protection Act, 1870 which emerged in its place still left a married woman in the position of being her husband's chattel.[64] Until 1884 the legal status of married women was summarised in the saying that 'husband and wife are one person and that person is the husband'.

Maria was becoming more and more disenchanted with New Zealand politics. They were attracting, she considered, 'a lower set of men'. In international affairs her German enthusiasm had 'cooled down a good deal, perhaps because I have an unreasonable hatred of Bismarck & can't endure all the credit of success [in the Franco-Prussian war], which must be due to the wonderful spirit of the people, being placed to his wonderful genius.'[65] She looked to Margaret for a 'little political insight'. Religion also posed new possibilities. Maria had no time for 'cowardly believers' – those who sheltered behind credal statements and were unwilling to expose their faith to the probing of intellect or to their own experience. The death of friends and of children had not led her with any conviction to seek solace in the promise of an eventual reunion; in fact she was now prepared to shed this cumbersome piece of theological baggage for 'my favourite doctrine of Eternal Death' and was 'curious' to see that 'Extinction is coming into vogue amongst Critical people'.[66] She was disappointed in Richard Hutton's 'conversion' to orthodox Christianity, seeing it in the influence of F.D. Maurice:

> He [Hutton] always seemed to have a clear & logical intellect, but to be driven back on a form of orthodoxy by the warmth of his affection & spiritual feeling. His intellect seemed to tell him that *unless* the Incarnation was a fact, Christianity could retain no hold on human nature; his heart & spirit clung to Christianity with such power that the Incarnation became therefore a fact to him. Wanting his warmth of nature I used to say to myself, then Christianity must go for me as nothing can ever make the Incarnation conceivable to my mind.[67]

Miracles too failed to pass her sceptical mind. 'I cannot honestly believe in miracles, so called, of any kind & have the greatest interest in hearing how minds infinitely more powerful & more fully informed than my own retain their belief in the face of modern science.'[68] As well as honesty there was a basic humility and curiosity in Maria's nature. She was often forthright but never sought to impose her views or close her mind. She genuinely wanted to know about things, to explore, to risk discovery. In spite of baulking at the incarnation, miracles, and the resurrection, she was prepared to think of Christianity as a 'living organism that can have nothing but a divine origin because it lives & grows'.[69]

Arthur sat the first part of his law exam[70] in the middle of 1870. Maria did not doubt his ability but wondered whether his lack of formal schooling would tell against him in answering examination questions. He passed with 'flying colours', and received a 'highly complimentary private note' from Judge Johnston, one of his examiners. The following January his final exam took place. After the first result Maria was confident of his success: 'he really knows more law now than half the men who have been years in practice here,' she told Margaret Taylor.[71] Neither study nor William's company had changed Arthur's singular nature. He

evolved for himself, as William told Emily, 'a remarkable course
of diet . . . He has found out that neither the middle of the day,
nor from 6 to 7 o'clock is a proper time for dining. He postpones
his eating until 9 or 10 at night. He has procured me a bottle
of square gin, and for himself some sour ale, which he quaffs with
soda from a wine glass.'[72] In his later years Arthur's wine glass
would have held soda water only. Towards the end of January,
Maria received a telegram from Arthur to say he had 'scrambled
through', which, as she explained to Margaret, was his way of
announcing that he had passed well. His next letter was signed
' "Your affectionate Barrister" '. One could say Maria's eleven-
year-old scheme had been realised, except that this would seem
to imply a measure of manipulating and contriving which she had
never really practised. She had always insisted, with an open
countenance, that the choice had to be his. 'You will excuse my
being rather proud of Arthur,' she wrote to her English friend
Ann Shaen, before going on to relate Arthur's untutored and diverse
career. Judge Johnston had let it be known that he had 'passed
"a brilliant examination" '.[73]

Maria and Arthur had assumed that once he qualified they would
return to Beach Cottage. 'I begin to build airy plans for settling
down at the Beach as a sort of double household in one,'[74] she
told Margaret. Living as an extended family was a long-accepted
mob lifestyle, and Maria thought that a 'double household' would
allow James privacy with his children when he chose, while she
acted as 'mother in all matters needing a mother's eye & care'.
Taranaki still held them: '[its] very misfortunes seem to have
endeared the place to us as much as its beauty & fertility'.[75] They
possessed 330 acres at Hurworth but other factors now made the
anticipated return doubtful, and the idea of a 'country house' and
workplace at New Plymouth seemed forever 'a chateau en Espagne'.
Arthur needed to make some money. There were already six 'more
or less learned in the law' at New Plymouth, and in the continuing
straitened circumstances of the province it was doubtful whether
there would be sufficient remuneration for a seventh. Wellington
figured briefly as an option when, as James's political prospects
looked brighter, some of Maria's friends told her that he was sure
to be elected for either a Wellington or a Nelson seat and was,
furthermore, likely to be called on to form the next cabinet. Maria
assumed that Arthur, 'as a secret & unsalaried member of the
Executive . . . would be almost as much in [his] element as when
directing the Bush Rangers when full private'. She continued:

It seems probable that by rushing on Taranaki at once our present impecuniosity may be 'fixed & frozen to permanence' & my lively sense of the desirability of say £500 per annum obliges me to pause 'ere 'I shut your life from happier chance'. Still if *you* choose to take the decision on your own shoulders I am content to abide by it . . . if you give orders for up anchor I shall by no means sing 'naked we go & void of cheer'.[76]

Nelson's climate exercised its customary seductive charm, Nelson College suited Arfie's precocious intellect, and in Nelson they had 'many conveniences and social advantages not obtainable in so small & remote a province as Taranaki'. What finally settled the question was the offer of a partnership with an established Nelson lawyer. Arthur had made a temporary arrangement to work with 'a young solicitor in good position here . . . At the end of the stipulated six months, the two worked so well together & liked each other so much that Mr Fell offered to take Arthur into partnership & the firm has been Fell & Atkinson since the 1st of Nov. last.'[77]

Charles Yates Fell, who was to become Arthur's son-in-law as well as his partner, was born at Nelson on 6 August 1844. His father, Alfred Fell, a Yorkshireman, had landed at Nelson Haven two years previously and opened a general merchant business which developed into Fell and Seymour. Alfred and his wife, Fanny, had eight children, of whom Charles was the last. In 1859, when Alfred had made a 'decent competence', the family left Nelson for England. Charles went to King's College School in London and then to St John's College, Oxford, where, according to his autobiography,[78] he 'worked very hard [at Law and History] but without the least idea of how, and with no one to show me'. His remark, 'What I learned I taught myself', would have struck an immediate chord with Arthur, as also his passion for cricket. Fell married Edith Louise Bainbridge, the daughter of a well-to-do London merchant, in 1869, and the following year returned to Nelson, where C.W. Richmond admitted him as a barrister and solicitor of the Supreme Court. He rapidly became a member of the Nelson synod and of the college board of governors. As his partner, Arthur was guaranteed at least £700 a year.

Harry and Annie Atkinson returned to New Zealand on 23 October 1871. Annie's progress under Dr Kidd had been spasdomic – 'somewhat better and sometimes worse'. She had endured two painful but not life-threatening operations. Dr Kidd was confident that he could see his way to a 'satisfactory end to most of Annie's troubles', but he could not cure her headaches – over-excitement or fatigue immediately brought one on. Annie also suffered a stillbirth; a note from Arthur to Harry in January 1871 said, 'May God help you both to bear your loss.'[79] Margaret Taylor must have met them, briefly, in England for Maria wrote to her expressing regret that she could not have seen more of Annie:

> You could not fail to find much to like & admire; great life & warmth of intellect & heart, which makes her a refreshing companion. On various subjects we think & feel very differently, but since dear Mary was taken there is no one whose society does me more good (of the female sort) here.[80]

It is a testimony worth recording. There is otherwise a tendency, reinforced by the memories of later generations, to see Annie largely as a hypochondriac. Now back at Hurworth, Harry and Annie seemed to be contentedly 'jogging along'; a new room was added to their house; at Christmas children were exchanged. Then came William Gisborne's resignation from the Egmont seat. Harry was elected on 3 October 1872, and his long parliamentary career recommenced.

The fortunes of Henry Richmond also changed around this time. He sold his Hurworth land to Harry in 1868. The following year he lost the superintendency to F.A. Carrington, and with the *Taranaki News* continuing unprofitable he was undecided what to do. His next and more successful venture (1873) was a boys' school at Beach Cottage, to which he shifted towards the end of 1872.

Lely paid the passages of Henry, Emma, and their children, Francis and Blanche, to Nelson so that they would all celebrate Christmas together. It was the first time they had done so since living in New Zealand, and the first time that all twenty of Lely's grandchildren had assembled. (William and Emily's ninth and last, also called Emily, was born on 15 August 1869.) Emma Richmond pleased her mother-in-law by 'her gentle manners & soft voice' and continued to be rather a wonder to Maria:

> she is so solid & well balanced for one so young & having seen nothing beyond the Colony. I never detected in thought, movement or expression anything one would call underbred or common & yet most of her people are what we would call uneducated. Tho' she might be my daughter I could quite look on her as a sister & contemporary. Granny & I do feel thankful Henry has got such a wife.[81]

The families went for picnics and excursions, Maria sporting her 'mushroom' – 'the only hat affording any shade & comfort in this sunny climate. I only wear it for country walks, always thinking a bonnet needful for dignity at my age in town or making calls, tho' why, now they are so hideously insignificant, bonnets should seem less girlish head dresses than hats, I cannot tell.'[82] Climbing the Dun Mountain at the back of Nelson was a favourite expedition. The tramway which had been constructed to bring down chrome and copper ore was almost disused and provided a 'safe bridle path winding round the side of hills, creeping along steep wooded gorges, & almost everywhere affording lovely views'. William had found that staying for a time in a deserted house about half-way up the mountain had eased both his asthma and a nervous disorder brought about by lack of sleep. The absence of five young children, including a baby, would have had a soporific effect.

In July 1871 William was fifty. He was from home at the time and Maria wrote to him:

> There is a great difficulty in understanding that we are really growing old. To me, I suppose my wonderfully good health makes me feel quite as lively & energetic as ever, but it cannot be long before decaying powers bring the fact home, & when I look at James I ought to be reminded as rheumatic twinges are affecting his gait just now. I think too he is getting anxious about money matters.[83]

Thomas Richmond (younger brother of Lely's husband) died in England on 25 April 1870. The interest from his estate, divided equally between his seven nieces and nephews, brought some pecuniary relief to James, Henry, and Maria. The bulk of the property was to go to the grand nephews and nieces of his 'favourite brother', Christopher, when the youngest of them came of age. Here Emma Richmond's youth was a distinct disadvantage, as the fecundity expected of wives could leave the capital intact for another forty years. It would be churlish to suggest that Uncle Thomas's will acted as a constraint on Henry and Emma, although their third and last child was born when Emma was only thirty-three.[84]

Towards the end of 1871 Arthur and Maria, in keeping with Arthur's improved and assured prospects, moved from Bleak House to Fairfield. It was not of course as simple as that, and speculation about how and when the three distinct stages of Fairfield's construction occurred is not helped by the lack of written evidence. The first extant letter from Maria at Fairfield is dated 14 July 1872, but a letter to her from Annie of 4 May that year mentions the 'annoyance of carpenters' as a reason for Ruth and Mabel's attendance at Miss Mackay's school. And the 1871 Nelson rating roll, made up towards the end of the year, has the name of the previous owner, J. Blackett, crossed out and that of A.S. Atkinson substituted. What is clear is that the Fairfield which now stands commandingly at the southern end of Trafalgar Street, flanked by mature native and exotic trees, and with an early colonial cemetery near the gates, is not the same building into which Arthur, Maria, Lely, and the children first moved. In the 1871 roll it is described as a 'cottage'; by 1873 it has become a 'house + wing' with eight acres of land. Neither Maria nor Arthur described the appearance of their new house; the clearest evidence comes from a Charles Fell photograph taken at the time of his marriage to Edie in 1881, which shows two stages of Fairfield's development. The main building is a pleasant but somewhat crudely constructed one-storey house with a verandah along the front and two dormer windows in its hip roof. Attached to this, in a manner reminiscent of the 'giraffe' addition at Merton, is a more finely detailed, two-storeyed building with a gable roof. It was the construction of this addition which caused the disruption to Maria's school. Lely's room was on the upper floor.

Nelson's climate had suited Lely, although she preferred the 'perfect Autumn days' to summer heat, which often left her 'dizzy & dazzled'. Towards the end of 1870 she was laid low by bronchitis but rallied after the Christmas visit of her children and grandchildren. Maria worried nevertheless, and wrote to Margaret: 'it makes me tremble to think how likely we are to lose her whenever illness assumes a severe form'.[85] At the beginning of December 1872 Lely, in her eighty-first year, was again seriously ill. Maria was loath to ask the doctor how much longer her mother was likely to live as she feared what the answer would be. She wrote to William, who was holding a court session at Blenheim, to prepare him. On 19 December Lely was carried into her pleasant large room, '*just* that morning completed'. Her sight had gone but she spoke cheerfully. She died shortly afterwards 'without a moan or a struggle'. 'It was just such a departure as she would have chosen for she dreaded long confinement to bed & helplessness.'[86] Her sister, Helen Hursthouse, who had been at Fairfield for the greater part of 1872, helped Maria to close Lely's eyes.

The funeral on 22 December, 'very early on a most perfectly lovely summer morning', was quite private; 'we purposely kept the day & hour secret, for William & James are so widely known & our Mother so respected half the town would have thought it a duty or a kindness to follow'.[87] She was buried at Wakapuaka cemetery alongside Mary Richmond's grave, and the mourners, seeing through the closed eyes of the dead, again took comfort and strength from that magnificent view over the calm waters of the bay to the distant mountains.

European Cultivation

1872–1881

> The only, but *huge*, deficit I find in my new home, is that it can never be familiar to those I love so dearly . . . it seems like madness to dream of revisiting the old places & friends, but yet I *do* dream such mad dreams sometimes; I cannot help it, & I believe they do me good.[1]

It was seventeen years since Maria had written this to her friend Kate Whittle; now there was an increasing likelihood that the 'mad dream' might be realised. She had no thought of returning to England to live; the colony exerted too strong a claim: 'I should only wish to *visit* England, not to settle there.'[2] The reasons which had led the family to emigrate – lack of opportunity, 'overgrown towns with their vice & misery' – were still, she believed, applicable, and after her years in Nelson she added to them the English climate. Arthur had received a letter from Alfred Domett in which the latter quoted Hamlet's exclamation, ' "O horrible, horrible, most horrible" ', as the only apt description of London's grey mist and fog: 'after long sojourn in New Zealand, one seems *always* in the dark'.[3] 'Young folks & sunshine have become such necessaries of life to me,' Maria wrote to Ann Shaen, 'that I would get on badly without them.'[4] There was one thing wanting in this natural paradise – 'higher education for our girls' – and in this respect the pull of the old world was irresistible.

The first of the mob to set off, with some of his family, was James Richmond. Maria doubted whether he could afford the expense, though agreed that it was right to go 'before age creeps on him'. His eldest son, Maurice, was a prizewinner at Nelson College, but Classics was the favoured field there and Maurice had a mathematical and technical bent which his father wished tested in some European institution, in case his son should turn towards applied science or even engineering. As for Alla and Dolla, James had been worried for some years by the inadequacy of their schooling and by the turbulence of their spirits. He thought both

his girls would benefit from disciplined studies and, as he wrote
to Ann Shaen, wanted them 'to have some art or profession by
which she [Alla, but the remark applied equally to Dolla] may
earn a living and at all times feel as much independence as mortals
have a right to feel'.[5] Towards the end of April 1873, with Alla,
Maurice, and Dolla in their fifteenth, thirteenth, and twelfth years
respectively, James left Nelson for Melbourne, where he hoped
to sell sufficient paintings to pay their passages to England. As
was usual, his two remaining children were easily accommodated;
Dick went to Uncle Henry's school at Beach Cottage, and Wilsie,
along with Thomas Gray (the cat) and the canary, came to Aunt
Maria's. At about this time, Eliza and William Atkinson also shifted,
leaving Taranaki to live at James's house at Nelson. William was
to become C.W. Richmond's associate, and Eliza was pregnant
yet again. Maria did not approve of babies arriving at yearly
intervals: 'one *every other* year [is] quite sufficient with a narrow
income'.[6]

James's stopover at Melbourne was successful: 'Father has so many
picture orders that he has to have a studio where he spends most
of his time,' Alla wrote to her Aunt Emily.[7] The Melbourne art
dealer, A. Fletcher, 'who never buys except to sell at a profit',
was eager to take what James had in stock or could complete on
the voyage to England. James was also making wood engravings
taken from his sketchbook for a newspaper: 'The pay is very good,
two guineas for a little sketch that I can execute in an hour or
two.'[8] After a profitable fortnight, the family left on the
Northumberland for England, via the Cape of Good Hope, arriving
at Gravesend on 3 August 1873. Waiting to welcome them and
to give them a home at Blackheath was Mary's brother, Tom Smith.
He was a successful manufacturer of confectionery and, like his
brother Sam, had become a Plymouth Brethren. He also had eight
children whom Alla promptly dubbed the 'Black heathens'. Mary's
mother, Aunt Smith, lived nearby. Maria wrote to her niece, 'It
must be delightful to have such numbers of relations of all ages
ready to welcome you & love you in the old world; we are deeply
interested in all you can tell of the young cousins we only know
by name.'[9] James's impression of London was of crowds, bustle,
and a 'wilderness of great houses'. Competition between rival
merchant princes had produced the most successful architecture:
'money without stint had done wonders'. With more dismay than
wonder he gazed at the new and 'sumptuous' Albert Memorial,
'a sort of crucial proof of the attainments of Great Britain in

architecture and sculpture – and in taste generally . . . One of Michael Angelo's great sepulchral statues is worth ten such things – or rather is incommensurably more precious.'[10] He renewed his friendship with Alfred Domett, then living quietly with his wife and son near Kensington Gardens; with the Shaens, also at Kensington; the Hutton brothers, Richard and Joseph; the Martineaus, and with his painting colleague, Basil Holmes. Ann Shaen, the 'bright pretty self-possessed girl' who had so tormented James in his youth, was now in his eyes a 'vigorous thoughtful looking woman'.

The children's schooling was not progressing quite as James wished. Maurice, nicknamed 'little Maori', was at the Hove school at Brighton where his father, uncle, and cousin Dunstan had been before him. There were now only eighteen boys (Joseph Hutton's change to orthodoxy had repelled the former Unitarian connection) and James was uncertain of the school's future. Shortly after his arrival, James made the acquaintance of Frances Mary Buss at the North London Collegiate School for Girls, whose pioneer work to put girls' education on a proper intellectual footing was now recognised. He wished to enrol Alla in the more recently established Camden School for Girls,[11] also under the aegis of Fanny Buss, but found that his was the seventy-seventh application for only fourteen vacancies. So Alla and Dolla went with other Blackheathens to Miss Cranch's day school for girls where they learnt 'deportment and dancing' along with history, English, French, and drawing. If it was Miss Cranch's ambition 'to breed up little butterflies' she must have thought the two colonial girls a deviant strain. She found Alla's ability 'puzzling'; neither of the sisters would have anything to do with the drawing master, whose ability they despised. Their Grandmother Smith was also finding them difficult to manage. She attempted the same bit-and-bridle method as Helen Hursthouse had done and was no more successful. Alla was generally 'good and dutiful', only now and again bursting out with impatience, but Dolla was 'dogged and to the last degree provoking'. When the Christmas holidays came, James found the Blackheath establishment much too noisy, and removed himself to a studio in Kensington where he could paint without interruption. He also consulted Ann Shaen about schools in Europe. 'The reputation of the Zurich schools is of the highest,' he wrote to Maria, 'but Swiss manners are not agreeable and Swiss girls in particular are thought undesirable company.'[12] Nevertheless, one advantage of a Zurich school would be its proximity to Syrgenstein and Margaret Taylor.

In March 1874, James, Maurice, Alla, and Dolla set off to
investigate Swiss schools and to visit Syrgenstein. James's preference
was for a public school, but admittance was dependent upon passing
a preliminary examination for which German was essential. At
Zurich, James heard of a promising girls' private school conducted
by 'Frau Professor Schulz-Bodmer'. James was pleased with Frau
Bodmer, and particularly by a requirement in her prospectus for
six large white aprons: all girls were taught housekeeping. Her
school was settled upon, but first the party journeyed to Syrgenstein:

> The road to Syrgenstein runs in Bavaria and is pushed out into
> Wurtemberg where it continues by the precipitous bank of the
> Argen (the boundary stream) upon which Syrgenstein stands . . .
> Margaret saw us as we came up the steep road and met us and
> Mr Whittle was at the gate way.[13]

One hopes that something more than is recorded was made of
this initial meeting. Here were the first of the mob's offspring
returning not to the country but to the culture which had nurtured
them from birth. Here was the woman who was to fulfil Maria's
own role as the person to whom the children would naturally turn.
At this time James was simply glad to be away from London, and
his children were probably shy at meeting the 'Miss Taylor' who
lived, surrounded by servants, in a castle with her invalid sister
and husband. The castle was begun in the ninth century and parts
of the present structure dated back to the sixteenth. (It still stands,
and may be visited on a 'castles tour' of the Federal Republic of
Germany.) The Whittles and Margaret had lived in it for just over
twenty years. There were Whittle family portraits on the walls
alongside spears, battle axes, and daggers from its warlike past;
there were two suits of armour, numerous rooms, staircases and
articles of furniture (on a later visit C.W. Richmond counted
twenty-eight wardrobes and escritoires), and an immensely high
ceiling supported by a maze of timbers. The fact that the Schloss
was a difficult and costly place to keep warm would not have
detracted from its romance. 'Miss Taylor' soon became 'Aunt
Margie'. 'Such a delightful creature,' Alla wrote to her cousin
Edie, 'she reminds me very much of Aunt Maria and she is so
unselfish and good.'[14]

Returning to Zurich, Alla and Dolla found Frau Bodmer's school
well regulated, but not nearly so proper or stultified as an English
boarding school:

> It is more like a large family and Madame the mother . . . At
> Miss Cranch's at meals no one speaks a word and they eat as if

they thought the Queen was looking at them, while here everybody talks to who ever they like to – we certainly don't eat too elegantly.[15] Alla's sociable and frank ways made her popular. She learnt easily and delighted in her music lessons: 'I am now playing Mozart's concertos. They are perfectly beautiful.'[16] The practical white aprons must have been used to good effect, too, for Alla told Edie that her 'great desire' was to be a 'good housekeeper and learn to cook well'. Dolla was not so settled. She was in a different classroom and often did not agree with her teacher. Alla was able to persuade Frau Bodmer to allow Dolla, whose German was almost equal to her sister's, to be in the same class. 'It is much pleasanter now.'

Maurice was placed at Hofwyl School near Berne. The school, founded in 1799 by Philipp Emanuel von Fellenberg, a colleague of the Swiss educationist Pestalozzi, attracted pupils from all over Europe; English boys in particular who had been expelled from their public schools had often been sent there as a last resort. To counteract this tendency Dr Muller, the present headmaster, refused to accept boys over fourteen. James liked both Dr Muller and his English wife. He also approved of the 'high moral', as well as practical training the school provided – Maurice even built a boat in one of the school's several carpentry shops. Like Frau Bodmer's, Hofwyl was different from an English boarding school. 'When a new boy comes they don't tease him at all, but they bring him books to read and lots of things to amuse him with, and ask him to play with them.'[17]

From Fairfield, Maria maintained a steady correspondence with her mob abroad, ensuring that New Zealand was not forgotten.

> Here all is beauty & a lovely mixture of the tenderest greens, apple blossoms & snowthy hawthorne. We can't enjoy the beauty enough tho' we are all downstairs before seven o'clock. The sunshine is glorious & the larks sing as tho' they might burst with joy. If the crop of cherries equals the show of blossom it will exceed last years.[18]

Shortly after Lely's death Maria paid a visit to Taranaki, her first for five years. She was there when Henry and Emma's daughter, Beatrice Jane, was born (February 1873), and rejoiced with Henry that both Emma and her baby were well and strong and continued so. Such was Beatrice Jane's health, good temper, and energy that she became known in the family as 'Busy Bee'. Marion Atkinson's prospects, however, were depressing. In the five years Maria had been away, Marion had produced another three babies, all sons; she was to have another during 1873. Apart from fathering sons, Decimus, according to Maria, 'did nothing',[19] and Marion provided for the family by conducting a small school. The future of Marion's sister, Eliza, seemed more assured. As C.W. Richmond's associate, her husband, William, had a secure job and, in his late forties, could look forward to a legal career. Their home, situated between St Katherine's and Fairfield, allowed for regular contact with the kin group. Then, as so frequently happened to both Eliza and Marion, tragedy struck. In August 1874, William Atkinson was found to have cancer. Morphia kept pain under control, but nothing else could be done. He died, aged forty-eight, at Bleak House on 3 September 1874. Showing its usual solidarity the mob closed about his widow: C.W. Richmond instructed Emily to see that all Eliza's immediate financial wants were met; Maria was prepared to have a cottage built for her in Fairfield's orchard, and, more usefully, James contacted Eliza's affluent relatives and friends in England. He wrote to Maria:

> I think Eliza may dismiss all anxiety or sense of being burden-
> some from her mind. I have been able to speak confidently to all
> of them that if her health continues fair she will not be wanting
> herself or capable of living indolently on others, however wealthy.[20]

English friends and relatives responded by providing an income of £200 a year. Eliza was able to stay on at Bleak House and afford a 'cheerful immigrant maid' to help with the children.

Harry Atkinson had come from Wellington to be with his brother when he died. In the House, Harry was moving towards an accommodation with Vogel. 'The fact being', he wrote to Arthur, 'that the House has quite made up its mind that the country desires Vogel to hold office until it can see his scheme bearing fruit either in taxation or income . . . I think the right thing is to give the Government what they ask as necessary to their policy.'[21] The following year, not without some hesitation and misgiving, he joined Vogel's ministry and gradually assumed a leadership role within it. In provincial politics Harry, to his surprise, was defeated in his 1873 bid for the superintendency of Taranaki by F.A. Carrington. He later acceded to Carrington's request to become provincial secretary. It was not a task which concerned him for long. In the 1875 parliamentary session, Atkinson introduced a Bill to abolish provincial governments, which was passed on condition that it was not acted upon until after the 1876 parliamentary session. By November 1876 provincial councils ceased to exist.

It was concern for their daughter Margaret's further education which prompted William and Emily to be the next of the mob to embark for Europe. Emily, Maria, and Arthur had long felt that Margaret's sharp intellect had never been sufficiently engaged by the spasmodic education she had received in New Zealand. She lacked application; she was often bored and irritable. James advised that she might be placed in a college for girls in either England or Germany or, even better, might spend time with Margaret Taylor 'whose measured, industrious, sternly methodical way with herself would be splendid example, and who manages nevertheless to attach young people to her'.[22] Another factor which helped William and Emily in their decision was William's re-appointment (in November 1874) to the Dunedin circuit. 'We are very vexed,' Maria wrote to Alla, 'as there seems little chance of Dunedin suiting uncle's asthma.'[23] She wrote more vehemently to James:

> It is a comfortless life for him never able to stay in his own home for any time. If I were Emily I had a hundred times rather he took a small [sheep] run & settled in any corner of N.Z. where he could breathe & keep with his family & have him throw up his judgeship, but she does not feel so at all I can see, except for a day or two when really frightened for his life.[24]

Having been granted leave of absence from government it was, ironically, the £4,500 William received from F.D. Bell for his fourth part of the Ida Valley run which made it financially possible to take, at Emily's insistence, all nine of his children abroad. It was a formidable, even a foolhardy exercise which William came to regret, and it placed a strain on his marriage. The children's ages ranged downwards from twenty-two to six. James was dismayed, thinking that neither William's nor Emily's health would benefit from looking after 'such a party of helpless ones', and with the fate of the Calvert Wilson family in mind, thought it was 'too much risk for the whole good breed to be exposed in one bottom'.[25]

The mob's second generation was not 'helpless'; its members were as resolute and capable of looking after themselves as their parents. They were also used to living in various combinations. James's description of the Richmonds and Atkinsons abroad (Maria and Arthur's lot joined the others in 1877) as a 'corps d'armée' was apt. Detachments set out from various points, regrouped, and returned unscathed. Nobody got lost, although James and William were often out of sight for weeks at a time. William took every opportunity of slipping away by himself to go on a walking tour, and James seldom bothered with plans or timetables. Very often, until she too set forth, it was only Maria in Nelson, writing and receiving letters, who knew whether James was painting in the Pyrenees or constructing railway lines in Algeria. 'My dear Father,' Anna Richmond once wrote, 'We very much want to know how and where you are.'[26]

Maria wondered whether Edie should have gone with her cousins: after all, if nine went, why not ten? Arthur, who still remembered the anxiety of not knowing Edie's whereabouts during the winter of 1864, was opposed to her going without Maria. At seventeen, Edie was moving beyond ordinary schooling in which she, although above average in intelligence, had never shown much interest. Ruth and Mabel were at Mrs Pickett's school. Mabel, eleven in 1875, showed 'more interest & willingness with lessons than either E or R', and Maria considered sending her to the Miss Greenwoods' school in Wellington, now attended by her cousin Fanny Atkinson, although she had some misgivings about Wellington society. 'The drawback is that the gossipy low tone of the society does affect even the young girls . . . so that deep interest in dress & other people's flirtations begins with their teens.'[27] Arthur, too, protested. He would often point to the book-lined walls of his study and suggest that if the tools of knowledge were really required they were close at hand.

A college for girls in Nelson seemed as far away as ever. The *Colonist*, taking over the crusade from the *Examiner*,[28] attempted to shame Nelson into action by recalling Maria and Emily's earlier efforts to find potential scholars and to arouse support from the Nelson College board: 'to the shame of the men of Nelson . . . they were allowed to labour and plead in vain'.[29] The previous year Canterbury Provincial Council had passed an ordinance setting up a university college. 'How that Canterbury Province seems rolling in wealth,' Maria wrote to James. 'They are giving something to education (not a word or shilling that I know of for the girls of the upper class) & there are to be three more professors at £600 per annum appointed.'[30] Nelson College prizegivings always rekindled passing interest in a similar institution for girls. The headmaster, F.C. Simmons, writing under the pseudonym, H. Spelaeus, posed the significant question that if the position were reversed and a girls' college had been endowed, would not the fathers and leading men speedily have made provision for their boys? The editor responded by again advocating the proprietary school model, this time with an interesting cautionary note: 'unless some such outline is adopted, the girls trained in the humble and unpretending public [primary] schools will be found thrusting from their stools the expensively educated daughters of the higher and middle classes.'[31] The simple, if temporary, expedient of opening Nelson College to girls as well as boys was not favoured: 'in America the experiment of educating girls and young women, pari passu with boys and young men produces the worst physical results.[32] Henry Richmond, who was living in Nelson in 1875, also entered the lists. His letter, signed 'Colonist', criticised the proprietary school suggestion, and argued that it was the duty of the state to make equal provision for the higher education of both boys and girls. Maria, while praising Henry's willingness to 'stir people up', was doubtful whether anyone would make a practical move. Her prediction was correct. For all that the advocates of a girls' college expostulated with cries of 'shame' or 'injustice' in the newspaper columns (there was seldom an opposing view), the general populace simply read and read on. So Ruth and Mabel continued at Mrs Pickett's, where Mabel won prizes – although there was a clear difference between Mrs Pickett's prizegiving and that of Nelson College. Bishop Suter, who distributed prizes at both schools, put various questions to the girls which 'revealed a good deal of portentous ignorance', Maria wrote to Mary Richmond. The previous year at the college, Arfie, not yet twelve, won the prestigious Newcome Scholarship worth £300. The examiner remarked, 'He is a singularly advanced boy for his age . . . not very far below the highest scholar.'[33]

After the departure of the C.W. Richmond contingent on 13 February 1875, Maria and the girls cleared out a 'strangely empty' St Katherine's. (They found that Kit's puss had had six or seven kittens in the nursery.) 'Anything more depressing than its aspect is impossible to imagine . . . it really needs an effort to persuade oneself you are all alive & enjoying yourselves.'[34] The house was rented to the Foys who assured Maria that there was no other one in Nelson for which they would exchange it. 'I think they are an affectionate & clean family & Mrs F. seems to have some more sensible ideas than many women who drop fewer hs.'[35]

In the middle of the 1875 parliamentary session, Arthur received a telegram from Harry, now colonial treasurer, asking him to come over and, in Arthur's words, 'hold Harry's hat while he delivered a Financial Statement'.[36] Maria and Edie went with him, leaving Aunt Helen Hursthouse nominally in charge at Fairfield. Helen's eyesight was failing and Ruth was the effective housekeeper. 'Ruthie has really been very good & managed nicely in my absence,' Maria wrote to Anna on her return. 'She will have more talent for housekeeping than for any literary or artistic pursuits.'[37] Arthur enjoyed being of use to his brother. Both he and Maria thought that the work of the session which fell upon Harry as leader of the House had taken a toll.[38] He looked considerably older and by the end of the session was 'almost worn out' by the late hours and by his skirmishes with the 'cantankerous minority' led by his old enemy, Sir George Grey.[39] Harry's financial statement was well received, they thought, 'even by his foes'. 'I think it will show that Vogel is not the only politician of ability left in N.Z.', Maria commented.[40]

The give-and-take of political debate stirred Arthur's blood and made him keen once more to re-enter politics. 'As I sit up in the Speaker's Gallery and watch them all wriggling below I feel quite Lucretian, at least I should if it were not for the unphilosophic but keen desire to be down wriggling among them myself.'[41] Harry must have taken seriously Arthur's uncharacteristic and probably facetious request (the letter is lost) for his name to be considered when appointments to the Legislative Council next came under review. Harry, while admitting that his brother would be of great use to the country in either House, thought his chief value would be in the lower one. He did not put his name forward because 'there is a very great disinclination to increase the numbers in the Upper House amongst my colleagues'. Harry asked Arthur to write to him again 'if you feel very strongly about it'.[42] There is nothing to suggest Arthur did.

Maria and Edie stayed on with Harry and Annie until the session ended. Annie now had a child of her own, Samuel Arnold (known as Arnold), born the previous year,[43] but she was still a 'creaking door', especially as Wellington's winds brought on her neuralgia. She and Maria enjoyed each other's company; otherwise Maria was not impressed with the capital's society:

I have just come in from a ladies' luncheon party, & dear me! I am thankful I live in Nelson! Fancy the trouble & expense of getting up a really elegant little dinner for 8 ladies who meet & chat for 3 hours, the conversation never rising above the level of an ordinary morning call.[44]

It seemed likely that William would be stationed at Wellington on his return and Maria warned Emily that they would be 'much pinched' on William's salary of £1,500 a year.

I suppose you *must* live in society, & after all it is paying the price of gold for pinchbeck, the tone of society is apparently so poor intellectually. The old people gossipy, the young ones fast & gossipy too. Edie who has not been in it & only caught the murmurs on the edge, feels slow old Nelson is much more wholesome & satisfactory as a residence.[45]

However, when Anna Richmond requested her aunt to send her the latest Wellington gossip, Maria showed that she had an acute ear for the 'murmurs':

> You will be glad to know that Amy Fitzgerald is safe from her old lover having engaged herself to W. Levien. We had a very pleasant visit from Mrs Fitzg whom I thoroughly like & admire & she spoke her feelings very freely. She is satisfied & believes Amy will be happy but is not at all *elated* nor much pleased at being repeatedly told how charming the match is *because* W.L. is so rich! She says Amy's family & connexions are rich in things no money can buy & that she can't feel it any honour for an F to become a Levien . . . Some of the brothers do not at all admire the connexion nor relish having a Jew for brother in law! Mrs Danniells a young widow of Wanganui (formerly) Mary Imlay of Taranaki has become engaged. When visiting Taranaki last year [she] declared herself quite averse to matrimony having suffered in various ways during her first trial of that state. She seemed to be happy in her freedom, her £700 per annum & two nice little daughters. However time will show whether she has thought not better but *worse* of the matter. Maud Snow has re-engaged herself to Mr Werry & they look very happy! but as he has a homeopathic income & is in debt there does not seem a brilliant prospect for her . . . Did I tell you that Archdeacon Pritt is going to be married to Alice Williams, Mrs A.P.G. Macdonald's sister who is just 19! How ridiculous all the old widowers are here . . . However I hope you won't be deluded by one of them tho' you would make a remarkably nice step-mother I admit. One comfort is that in a year or so you will be quite too old to suit any of these grey or bald headed gentlemen with grown up children.[46]

The first report of the C.W.R. detachment, who had arrived in England in May 1875, came from James who saw them all at Blackheath. William was free from asthma and Emily was 'a new creature'. Since her numerous pregnancies, Emily had suffered pain in her legs, and Maria had advised her to have a course of massage or, as she called it, 'a rubbing': 'Women on the Continent make a profession of it, Kate Whittle or M.T. can hear where good rubbers are to be found.'[47] The excitement of being in English society with relatives, friends, and expatriates such as the Selwyns and Gore Brownes, all offering hospitality, worked wonders with Emily's legs. James wrote of her as 'cheerful and interested in everything around and can walk for ten minutes or a quarter of an hour without a pause . . . She has lost considerably in bulk but still finds it difficult to rise from her seat without help.'[48] Emily was forty-five. 'I like everything except the expense,' she exclaimed to William. 'I wish I had money plenty of money that I might go everywhere.'[49]

William enrolled his eldest son Kit at Magdalen School, Oxford; then, leaving Emily, Mary, and the two youngest children with his cousin Hetty Walduck (née Wilson) at Carnforth in Westmoreland, he set off with the others for Syrgenstein. On the way he dropped off Bob and Alf at Hofwyl where they joined their cousin Maurice, and picked up Alla and Dolla from Frau Bodmer's school. The plan which James had earlier worked out with Margaret Taylor was for the latter to take a house in Dresden from which all five girls – Anna, Margie, Alla, Dolla, and Alice – would attend day schools or classes. By October, with Margaret Taylor as their chaperone, counsellor, and friend, the girls had happily taken up residence in the house of Baron von Seckendorff at Dresden. With the exception of Dolla, who attended a drawing academy, they went to a Lyzeum which was to their liking and where Alla had a good music teacher. Concerts were their chief delight – Mozart, Beethoven, Wagner, Schumann: 'with three more to go this year, it is too splendid to think of'. James wrote to Maria that Margaret Taylor considered herself 'pledged before almost everything to help in the case of Margie'. It was Dolla, however, who had most cause to be thankful for Dresden. In Herr Simonsson she found an art teacher she respected and with whom she had immediate rapport. 'Dolla's face is beautiful and since she came to Dresden she holds herself far better . . . She looks so splendid when she comes home from [the gallery] or her drawing lesson, she glows out of every pore,'[50] Margie reported. Herr Simonsson acknowledged that Dolla had a 'wonderful talent': 'I can't tell you how glad I am,' Alla wrote to her Aunt Maria, 'it is so nice for Father.'

James found that London's lack of sunlight conflicted with his desire to paint. He therefore made several excursions, sometimes collecting Maurice to accompany him, to the Swiss Alps. 'Atmosphere is the thing to aim at wherever you be – atmosphere and sunlight.'[51] While in Paris in October 1874, he became acquainted with 'Mr Harding', a wealthy entrepreneur who held a concession from the French government to construct a branch railway in

Algeria. Harding wanted an English engineer to act as his agent and overseer and asked James to undertake the job. James was at first reluctant, aware that his engineering was 'rusty'. When Harding assured him he would not be responsible for technical matters but for appointing staff, controlling labour, and dealing with officialdom, James consented. 'The fact that . . . I was outrunning the constable [in debt],' he wrote to Maria from Oran, 'decided me to go over and earn a few pounds to help balance accounts.'[52] So by mid-1875 James was in Algeria and thinking of taking Maurice from Hofwyl in order that he might join him and be introduced to the practical side of engineering. William equally out of sight on a sketching–walking tour of Switzerland, Austria, and France, was thinking of Kit 'installed with bell-topper, pot hat and other necessities' at Magdalen School. Emily, staying with her party at Hetty Walduck's, was wishing 'we could all be together again'.

Kit, in his English public school, was far from happy. Hofwyl or even Dresden with Margaret Taylor's band would have suited him better. He was a clever but delicate boy, like his father afflicted with asthma, and was inclined to be stubborn and moody. He also suffered from being the first-born male of the Richmond line: too much was expected from him. He had won prizes at Nelson College but was still outshone there by his brilliant and more industrious younger cousins, Maurice Richmond and Arthur Atkinson. Like many nineteenth-century English public schools, Magdalen indulged in bullying, beating, and covert homosexual practices. From Switzerland, William wrote his son the sort of letter which, though well intended, would not have helped Kit's situation. His advice to his son was 'to dissent from the doings of one's company' and 'to bear the ridicule and unpopularity': 'It is wonderful to see how the bestial mind shrinks abashed before the manifestation of this sort of power.'[53] It was all too much for Kit; in addition to being mauled he was also underfed and cold. He left before Christmas. It would seem that William was disappointed that his son did not tough it out. He wrote to Arthur that he was now 'at a loss what to do with Kit'. Maria was indignant and forthright: 'What a mercy that dear Kit has escaped from that little h--- upon earth! & that he was old enough & well-principled enough to be unhurt by the contamination.'[54] But Kit had been scarred, as his subsequent rather unhappy life was to show.

At the end of 1875 William rejoined Emily and the 'main body' left England for a *pension* at Montreaux, from which William made a brief sortie to the girls at Dresden and Emily wrote to Alice:

> I think of dear old St Katherine's and cannot help wishing all of us back again, and that this day all the Aunts and cousins would have assembled under the willow tree. But perhaps I should not say this, as I believe and think we did right to come, and I hope and think you will all be benefited by coming.[55]

William no longer thought so. He confided to Arthur, 'I hate the thing [being abroad] – & wish (however foolishly) a hundred times a week I had never come.'[56] The well being of both Kit and his wife weighed heavily upon him. After her initial burst of activity, Emily simply sat. William wrote:

> Spring is now fairly begun & the children & I enjoy our walks. But Emily & Mary see nothing but what is to be seen from the windows. Of course Maria will say 'why don't you take them about?' which cannot be answered in carbon.[57]

From Fairfield, Maria tried to jolly Emily along:

> I do grieve that you are not gaining ground, dear Emily, as you seemed to be doing at first . . . You ought not patiently to submit to being an invalid all your days . . . remember you have the duties & pleasures of a grandmother to look forward to & you must try to put yourself in better working order before your return.[58]

Maria had imagined that at least Mary would be out and about 'taking beautiful walks & climbs with William', but her mother's lethargy had affected her as well. On one occasion Emily had roused herself to go from her *pension* in Montreaux to another in Lausanne, leaving Mary with Kit and Ted. Both were ill, Kit with asthma, Ted with congested lungs. As the eldest daughter, Mary had appeared to accept that her place in life was to be the helpmate of her father and mother – not quite the unpaid drudge but 'Miss Richmond', the daughter of the house. In a moment of rare candour, she wrote to her sister Anna at Dresden: 'Words cannot express how much I dislike this lively cage, this enchanting basin in which we dwell. I am as discontented as a cat in water & as blue as the deep sea. I want badly to be free.'[59] 'Father & mother & Kit are the cause of considerable anxiety to me,' she continued, 'this minding of the family is bad for the spirits & the body . . . The only thing I have gained by my trip is experience in nursing inflammation of the lungs.'[60]

Despite his misgivings about Emily, in August 1876 William informed Arthur that 'we seem to be gradually settling down to the plan of leaving Emily with seven children another year in Europe.

Being here it seems advisable they should stop long enough to get a real hold of German and French.'[61] He proposed returning to New Zealand with Margaret and Kit. The news caused consternation at Fairfield; more dismaying was the fact that even by the fast Panama overland mail route it would take at least two months for despatches from Fairfield, suggesting a more sensible deployment, to arrive at Emily's probable winter quarters in Lausanne. Both Maria and Arthur thought it would be a 'fatal mistake' to break into Margie's educational opportunities by too early a return home. She needed some 'placid intellectual atmosphere,' Arthur advised; adding, 'I believe the filial bond wd. be indefinitely strengthened . . . if it were for a time less liable to be strained.'[62] Maria, recalling her recent experience of Wellington's 'fast' and frivolous society, wrote, 'This is my last chance of a protest & I say solemnly & from my heart dear William, beware of bringing Margie back to Wellington life & society until she has ripened some of the good seed which is now quickening within her.'[63] The same day a letter arrived at Fairfield from Ann Shaen, who had taken over at Dresden from Margaret Taylor. Her letter, from which Maria rushed extracts to Lausanne, confirmed Fairfield opinion that Margie should stay. One of Ann's phrases on growth and fulfilment leaps straight into this decade: 'what she must have is space to make her own individuality a real life . . . I think it is beginning to be understood what a moral blight falls on girls whose intellectual hunger is unappeased.'[64]

William would have left for New Zealand before these letters arrived, but Maria had written earlier of her belief that both Kit and Margie should stay. Kit's 'cross grainedness' she attributed to a want of steady occupation, '& I think shows too that he had better for a time be in a less close relationship with his father'.[65] Magdalen School had been a mistake; she suggested Clifton or Marlborough. For Margie, she advised Girton College, Cambridge. Margaret Richmond added her own weight to the argument, writing to her father that she had been very happy in the company of both Margaret Taylor and Ann Shaen and was now 'feeling very miserable at leaving Dresden'. The upshot was that Kit, who appears to have acquiesced in the decision, and Anna sailed with William from Venice on 10 October 1876. Alf and Bob remained at Hofwyl, where they were later joined by Ted; Alice and Margie were at Dresden, where the latter was now to prepare for Cambridge; Mary and Emmie, the youngest, stayed with Emily in Switzerland.

It was not only the future of Kit and Margie which exercised

Maria. 'I feel absolutely desperate when I try to scheme out plans for any of you,' she wrote to Emily. What was to happen to Dolla, Alla, and Maurice if James persisted in supervising railways in Algeria? The question also bothered James. He had completed his line to Sidi bel Abbés by the end of 1875 and Harding,[66] pleased with his work, wished to re-engage him. James had found time and opportunity for painting in Algeria and was excited by the 'glorious masses and glorious intensity of the wild flowers'. Nothing, however, equalled the clear light, and the streams and forests with their 'spice of snowy peaks and lakes' of his adopted country. He longed to be back. Still, the money he made in Algeria paid for Alla and Dolla in Dresden, and would pay for Maurice when he ceased working as a draughtsman for his father and entered either a technical institution or a university. James accepted Harding's new contract and by March 1876 was back in Oran with Maurice. Maria, 'quite taken by surprise', was not pleased.

> Oh dear! it is sad that he should be getting worn out in the service of an uninteresting millionaire & in benefiting an alien land when good, honest, able men are so much needed in the Colony. It should not be allowed for a day if I could stop it.[67]

After three years of 'wandering', she felt he ought to be making a home somewhere. But where was the right home for James? Both he and Maria realised that Dolla would be the greatest obstacle to an early return to New Zealand, where it would be difficult for her to carry on with an art education. James wrote to Ann Shaen, 'I half dread lest a rival should have been introduced into my home whose dwelling is and must be Europe, whilst mine, if I have a few more years of life, must be New Zealand.'[68]

When she was not vicariously in Europe, Maria was busy with her own household at Fairfield. Servants continued to be either scarce – 'some people think scarcer than before free immigration began altho' 6000 single females have been imported'[69] – or a thorn in the flesh to Arthur because of their habit of tidying away his books, papers, and specimens. Maria now sent out her starched washing and employed a weekly woman for mending and sewing. Christmas parties still managed to 'scrape together' upwards of twenty family members at Fairfield. In 1875, Henry Richmond gave up his school at Beach Cottage and came to Nelson to be employed as a clerk at Fell and Atkinson's and to study for the law under Arthur's tutelage. Francis was already at Nelson College, so Emma, Blanche, and Busy Bee accompanied him to Nelson where they rented a house.

Henry, at forty-six, was a reluctant law student, seeking the profession more as a last-ditch means of achieving an even tenor to a life which, he wrote to William, 'has hitherto been so much of a failure that I cannot feel sanguine of success in any new undertaking'.[70] Maria was concerned for his health. The tragedies of his life – one of which was that in coming to New Zealand he had given up his true vocation in science – had given him a stoical acceptance of misfortune. He was not strong, and although a 'mild practice at the present Taranaki speed' would suit him Maria feared that 'sharper practitioners would make the struggle keener before long'.[71] Another child, Rachel Mary, was born in 1876. At the end of that year Henry sat his general knowledge exam and, as might have been expected, passed it well. He also passed his law final with 'considerable credit'. He was sworn in as a barrister and solicitor in December 1877, and returned to practise at New Plymouth – where 'I shall be thankful if at the end of another year I find myself earning a hundred or so'[72] – and to live quietly at Beach Cottage.

Arthur had resumed playing cricket, which Maria began to wish he would give up, as he was always damaging his right thumb. Her own first concession to approaching age was reading glasses.

> On New Year's day I made myself a present of a pair of spectacles which I really need at night either in reading small print or threading needles. My appearance in them excites deep disgust in Arthur & he pretends to think I wear them from pure affectation or a desire to look 'blue'.[73] It is a wonder if his eyes do not soon fail, he is always trying them in the examination of spiders' eyes or old coins etc.[74]

Early in January 1876 Maria received a cry for help from Annie at Elibank[75] in Wellington. Her neuralgia was worse, and a mutual friend, Mrs Wm. Pharazyn, described her as 'completely prostrated'. Taking Ruth and Mabel with her, Maria immediately went to her aid. Annie improved rapidly and Maria had a pleasant three weeks. She made excursions with Mrs Blackett (who had Ruth and Mabel to stay) to the Hutt, Somes Island, and 'Lyell's Bay', but her opinion of Wellington did not alter: 'the town grows sooty, the drainage is unsatisfactory & expenses are heavy'.[76] She advised William, about to reside in Wellington, that he should live out of town and keep a carriage: 'It would be good to strain off part of the society of the place, & people you really liked & wanted would find their way out.'[77]

Maria, probably influenced by Harry, had modified her views

on Sir Julius Vogel. She no longer thought his policies were leading the country to ruin: 'Population flows in, & has not begun to flow out, all the labour seems readily absorbed. The number of Australians visiting N.Z. increases, & its fame too in neighbouring colonies.'[78] With the abolition of the provinces a *fait accompli*, she saw that there would have to be a new disposition of parties in the House but doubted whether they would 'arrange themselves into compact masses marked M[inisterial] & O[pposition]'. She hoped Vogel's return would lighten Harry's load, and longed for the day when, 'laying aside the cares of office, he might retire to his beloved farm'.[79] When Vogel resigned as prime minister to become agent-general in London, and Harry took his place in office (1 September 1876), all her former distrust returned, quite swallowing up pride in Harry's achievement:

> It seems to me Vogel's retirement just as the pinch [debt repayment] is coming, shews him to be . . . a mere carpet-bag politician. His health never has been good, but it appears like a shallow pretext to say he retires on that score when he is undertaking the work of agent General at £1500 per annum, in *addition* to the schemes which are to make his fortune in Europe . . . Unless wool rises again there must be hard times to come before the Colony recovers a healthy tone, but anyway *I* think we are well rid of Vogel.[80]

Another member of the mob was also in the House. Helen's son, Richmond Hursthouse, who had married Mary Fearon of Motueka, was elected to represent that constituency in January 1876. Maria was not pleased with his elevation either. 'I can't think it will be a good thing for himself & his family he should succeed,' she wrote to Mary Richmond before the election, 'as entering on politics before he has made his way in life, or even possesses a home of his own appears to me to be beginning at the wrong end altogether.'[81]

When enthusiastic letters from the nieces at Dresden arrived at Fairfield, Maria regretted that Edie was not with them – and wished, too, that she could be there herself: 'I feel so jealous of all the young creatures seeing so much that is wonderful without being there to hear & see *them* see it.'[82] James's decision to stay at least another two years in Europe was also unsettling: 'It is very depressing to feel how gradually & unconsciously events are drawing our dear Jas to make Europe his home. If I do go I hope I shall be able to do something towards turning his face this way again.'[83] There were also James's two younger sons at Fairfield to consider. James and Maria agreed that thirteen-year-old Dick and twelve-year-

old Wilsie should join him at the beginning of 1877, and Maria
hoped that Arthur would consent to Edie going with them under
escort of a friend. Maria 'worked away' at Arthur and he 'fell
back' on his old answer that if she was so intent on 'European
cultivation' for the children, Maria should take them herself. During
this impasse Maria felt a little let down by the lack of advice
from the family abroad:

> It is curious that whilst M.T. & A. Shaen are writing most strongly
> in favour of our letting E. go at once, none of our own people
> allude to the subject . . . A few words from William would have
> had more weight with Arthur than bushels from women.[84]

The thought of Edie, in particular, missing out on the Dresden
experience, and the need to find 'trades' for the girls – 'unfortunately
none of our three have a special gift' – spurred Maria on. She
secured passages on the *Avalanche* for Edie, Ruth, Mabel, Dick,
Wilsie, and herself, 'the voyage, ship compasses going wrong,
icebergs, collisions, fires, hurricanes, gunpowder etc' notwithstanding'. The compromise reached with Arthur was that if he
subsequently felt that Arfie ought to go to England, then the two
of them would follow in a year or eighteen months. 'But to leave
him alone longer I cannot.'[85]

The returning party of William, Anna, and Kit arrived at
Wellington from the *Ringarooma* on 17 January 1877. Maria had
written to the Bluff, their first New Zealand port of call: 'We
all long to see your dear faces & have no end of talk. You will
find us in a chaotic state but able to give you a warm welcome
so come, come one or all. Your most loving Aunt Maria.'[86] All
three came to Fairfield for a brief reunion. The *Avalanche*, a Shaw
Savill Albion vessel of 1,160 tons, was due to sail from Wellington
at the end of February. It was still in the stream waiting a favourable
wind when William wrote to Emily that, although the ship was
a fine one and the captain and first officer 'bore good characters',
there were 'many uncultivated people' on board. ' "They have
not an H among them," says Edie.'[87] Maria made several excursions
ashore; the last one, so Edie informed her father, was to 'Kororia'.

> Edie's spelling of Karori (Kororia) put rather a new aspect on the
> affair, as the latter is the Maori attempt at 'glory', so that when
> she reported that Mother had gone to Kororia I hardly knew what
> to make of it. Then got a telegram from Harry, 'Sailed this morning
> [16 March]. Good breeze'.[88]

The voyage proved that Maria's fears of hurricanes, icebergs and
the like were not groundless. A hurricane blew up the first day

out from Wellington, and the *Ocean Mail*, sailing the same course, was wrecked on the Chatham Islands. Edie wrote of 'stirring rough days rounding the Horn'. On the return journey to New Zealand the *Avalanche* collided with another vessel in the English channel and sank. There were no survivors. Maria's confidence in the captain and the ship had encouraged Emily to consider returning on her, so news of the loss caused 'a day and night of terrible uncertainty' at Fairfield and Wellington, until James cabled Arthur: 'none ours in Avalanche'.

Maria and her party arrived safely at the London docks on 4 June 1877 and were met by the reliable Tom Smith of Blackheath. Emily was in Switzerland and James was elsewhere. Tom Smith had arranged and paid for a 'delightful lodging' in London from which Maria visited the Shaens, the Martineaus, and the 'dear Blackheathens'. Edie and Ruth, 'sensible enough to think it best they should go at once', went to Octavia Hill's boarding school[89] for the remainder of the term. It had been well recommended as 'not an ordinary school' by Ann Shaen. The problem of what to do with Dick and Wilsie in James's absence was further compounded by Emily's indecision over whether to take her boys from Hofwyl and entrust them to Maria's care. It appeared that although the boys could chatter freely in French and German, their English was now deficient. Marcella Wilkins (née Nugent), who had met the C.W. Richmond family in Brussels, was full of praise for the girls, who had not the 'slightest touch of fastness'; of the boys she wrote: 'my dear Mrs Richmond they speak through their noses'.[90] Marcella was sure she could cure them of their colonial speech but Maria thought London University School would be better. (In the event the boys remained at Hofwyl.) Maria was relieved to find that Margie was now at Newnham College, Cambridge (opened for women students in 1871), and assured Emily that she would be a 'mother to her when you are gone'. Here was the rub. Maria was certain that now she was in England Emily would wish to rejoin William in Wellington. Emily was reluctant to give up European society, and when Maria inquired about a passage for her on the *Avalanche*, she became upset and refused to travel on an 'emigrant ship'. On this occasion Emily's snobbishness probably saved her life.

The Dresden establishment had closed with Margaret Richmond's departure for Newnham. Alice rejoined her mother, and Alla and Dolla went to James and Maurice in Algeria. Oran, 'a horrid little town', was a far cry from Dresden, but riding on James's railway

'in an open truck with chairs to sit on and ladders to climb out
of' was 'great fun'. Otherwise Alla closeted herself with George
Sand, Dumas and, in case these two ran away with her, Macaulay.
James wrote of her at this time: 'Few girls are further from the
orthodox french lines of beauty . . . but her keenness of sympathy
with all that is good and not artificial and her natural liveliness
and good sense make her a great favourite.'⁹¹ Alla was a skilful
pianist, who 'takes a very humble view of her own capacity [and]
works away at the piano out of sheer love of music'.⁹² She was
never envious of Dolla's talent nor resentful of the extent to which
James sought to make provision for her younger sister and brother
while she was largely left to fend for herself. At the end of January
1877 Maurice resumed his academic studies by spending two terms
at Heidelberg University until he was old enough, at seventeen,
to matriculate at London University. He told his Aunt Emily that
at Heidelberg 'a new world opened to him'. Emily passed this
information onto her disgruntled son, Kit; it did not reconcile him
to his situation in New Zealand.

While James continued in Algeria, Alla and Dolla came to Maria.
Dolla obligingly went to Octavia Hill's school with Edie and Ruth.
Maria took Wilsie, Dick, and Mabel, with Alla to teach them
French and German, to visit Hetty Walduck who secured a cottage
for them near her own house in Westmoreland until the term ended.
In August, James completed his final Algerian contract and returned
to England, intending to spend the rest of his time abroad with
his family.⁹³ He took a furnished, semi-detached house at 34
Clarendon Road in the 'less costly part of Notting Hill' which
provided Maurice with a study (he was now working for a BSc
at London University), and James with a studio on which he hoped
to 'eke out' his means by 'making a few potboilers'. 'Tell Gully,'
he wrote to Arthur, '[he] gives me credit for too proud aesthetic
aims.'⁹⁴ Alla and Dolla worked at home for the Cambridge entrance
examination, and Dick and Wilsie attended London University
School. Dolla was still a 'ticklish character'. Separated from her
Dresden art teaching, she was inclined to be despondent and languid.
She had also developed, according to her father, a 'strong taste
for the comforts of rich people's life though despising mere swell
society'.⁹⁵

Maria and James eventually came together at Notting Hill. James
thought his sister looked older though still 'thoroughly vigorous',
surprising all her older friends. The girls were 'hardly so beautiful
as I had expected but are certainly handsome fine creatures. I speak

of E. & R., at present Mabel is not pretty, but straight, healthy & bright.'[96] In the autumn of 1877, Maria and her daughters made their long-awaited visit to Syrgenstein. Again Maria amazed her friends by her enthusiasm for getting about; such verve contrasted with James's habits there: 'the pine woods rejoice me as much as a languid nature can be rejoiced and I could lie down and fade out with a sort of pleasure at Syrgenstein as men die with open veins in a warm bath'.[97] If Dolla's languid nature often bothered her father, in this she simply took after him. In a pencil fragment of a letter, probably not sent,[98] James warned Dolla against the prevalent, almost fashionable, malaise of 'Wertherism'.[99] It was James, however, particularly in his youth, who had worried his friends by precisely this preoccupation. During Maria's visit, death nearly did claim a victim, when Ruth developed diphtheria. 'I tried to create just enough alarm in you, poor M. & Jas,' Maria wrote later to Emily, 'to prevent the *worst*, which for three nights & two days I dreaded, coming with too great a shock.'[100] Ruth's strong constitution enabled her to rally with 'wonderful rapidity', but 'you can pretty well imagine what a dreadful time it was for me when I dreaded the dear childs being choked at any minute & how inexpressibly I longed for dear Arthur's support & sympathy'.[101]

Arthur received Maria's letter telling him of Ruth's illness just after he himself had spent a month helping to nurse his seriously ill partner, Charles Fell, at St John's. Fell had alternated between the delirium of a raging fever and complete prostration, verging on coma, and his wife, who was in the last stages of pregnancy, had asked Arthur to help with the night watches. By mid-January Fell was recovering and able to greet his first son, born that same month. Fairfield was fuller than ever, with a mix of adults, teenagers, and young children. Arthur was philosophical. 'The house doesn't seem too full,' he wrote to Maria, 'the weather is in our favour.' Eliza Atkinson had moved in with her five children and was acting as housekeeper. Kit was also staying, his father hoping that Arthur's company might stimulate him sufficiently to begin legal studies. Eventually Kit was uncomfortably employed at Fell and Atkinson; he left after a blazing row with Arthur, during which he lost all self-control. Arthur's brand of facetious humour, bordering on sarcasm, would not have suited him. Kit next went to live at New Plymouth with his less abrasive Uncle Henry who, with business slow, was glad of the company. Kit, aggrieved at having to leave England with so little to show for it, continued disconsolate:

I have not yet succeeded in quarrelling with my relations here.

If I did I shd quarrel with the whole town as nearly everybody
is a connection or relation of some kind . . . Uncle Henry is
grievously disappointed in me and tells me so every day, which
is trying.[102]

Until he joined Maria in England in May 1878, Arthur resumed
his diary[103] and sent it off at intervals to his wife. He had fixed
a 1½-inch telescope in his garden; on clear nights he looked at
the stars and, when the moon was full, sometimes thought
romantically of Maria doing the same. He also busied himself
planting poplars and sycamores on the slopes of the Grampians
at the back of Fairfield, and put a Wellingtonia (sequoia) by his
front gate:

> It looks straight down Trafalgar St to the Church door. I had some
> difficulty in choosing a suitable place . . . because of the size its
> brothers grow in their native California. I was embarrassing myself
> with thinking how awkward it wd. be when it spread its arms
> out here & there when it suddenly occurred to me that it wd.
> take 500 years to grow as big as that, & I laughed & went off
> in another direction.[104]

He counted thirteen species of birds in Fairfield's garden:

> Tui, Korimakos (bell birds), mirumiru, wheorangi (silver eyes),
> Kingfishers & riroriro & Larks, blackbird, chaffinch, greenfinch,
> sparrow, minah & Californian quail. They will all come oftener
> & stay longer when my trees grow up & they understand who
> is in possession.[105]

Arfie, fifteen in 1878, was head boy, head scholar, and captain
of cricket at Nelson College. His father was increasingly exercised
over his immediate future. F.C. Simmons had died suddenly in
1876 and during the interim,[106] and for the first year of the Rev.
J.C. Andrew's headmastership, it seemed to both Maria and Arthur
that the college had lost its earlier momentum. Furthermore, Arfie
had been there since he was seven and Arthur thought there was
a 'great danger of his being completely asphyxiated' if left much
longer. 'With much reluctance,' he told William, 'I am coming
to the conclusion that . . . it wd. be better he should go now at
once [to England], and I have even thought of taking him.'[107] At
the end of February he and Arfie were on their way by the 'Frisco
route'. Arthur's only comment on the trip, which took them by
train across America to New York, was about the contrast in the
weather and the fact that the Mormons, with whom they stayed
for a day, had in their country the biggest spiders he had seen
in his travels. They arrived at Liverpool on 19 May and were at

Notting Hill by evening. Two days later Arthur, Arfie, and Edie went to Lords and saw the Australian eleven beat the MCC: 'This will make the British Philistines respect the poor Colonists a little more,' Arthur wrote.[108] James thought Arthur looked 'brown, pinched and wrinkled' . . . 'However he is in good spirits and active and I think eats an ounce or so more a day than he used to.' Arfie was 'wonderfully improved in physique'.[109]

Maria and her girls had spent the London summer in Ann Shaen's 'pretty little place' at Camden Hill,

> but we are all too fond of the country ever to enjoy living in town, and unless we had quite 4 times as much money to spend as we have now Europe would not suit me to live in. It is the old story, plenty to see & hear but if you have not the means to travel you are better further removed from temptation. Still I am thankful the girls are here for a time, they are widening & improving & as far as I can yet see will only more thoroughly appreciate the good points of their native land after having seen the Mother country.[110]

When Arthur arrived, both families crammed into James's house. At the beginning of June, Arthur took his son to Clifton College, Bristol, where Arfie was to sit for an entrance scholarship. Maria, according to James, resumed 'her energetic performance of social and sightseeing duty with undiminished vigour'. Edie, Alla, and Dolla were now attending classes at Bedford College (founded in 1843 as a training college for women teachers); Ruth and Mabel were at Octavia Hill's; Maurice, a 'delightfully tranquil student', read mathematics and physics at London University, and Dick and Wilsie continued at London University School. Housework at 34 Clarendon Road largely devolved on Alla, with spasmodic help from the others.

> The young ladies encourage one another in good works such as parties, at homes, but especially operas, plays and concerts . . . I was trotted out yesterday to an 'at home' of the Miss Martineaus. This invention has grown up out of the impossibility of ever finding anyone at home when called upon . . . Alla outshone all else in the brilliancy of an 'art blue' merino with cape and train and Dolla came next in an 'art green' ditto.[111]

Margaret Richmond was twenty-one in 1878. Members of the family from their various abodes sent her letters of congratulation: 'Alla and Dick wrote in German, Maurice in Latin, Wilsie in Maori, Dolla in French, Edie with an eloquent verse and Aunt Maria wrote a sensible one in English.'[112] Margaret was in her element at

Newnham; she told Mary she had never felt so happy or so well in her life. The one question which clouded her outlook was whether William, who was less avid about higher education, and Emily, who was inclined to fuss over her children's health, would allow her to stay long enough to complete the course for a teaching certificate. Her mother had already written to Newnham's principal, Anna Jemina Clough, and Margaret had been mortified:

> Miss Clough was not at all nice to me. She seemed very much to resent all the fuss that had been made & said a good many disagreeable things to me in an agreeable way . . . On no account please write to Miss Clough about my health. It is most unpleasant for me & I am both willing & competent to take care of myself.[113]

She was reading zoology and physiology, and described to her mother how 'the ladies', unseen by and separate from the male students, sat on a backless bridge or gallery above the tiers of benches in the lecture hall. 'After the lecture wh. I liked ever so much, 4 rabbits (deaders) were brought up for us to dissect so I plunged in . . . Yesterday I brought home a rabbit's head surreptitiously in my pocket to look at the nerves of the head.'[114]

In the term holidays, Margaret joined the Notting Hill household. 'She is immensely benefiting by her time at Cambridge,' James wrote to William, 'she is mellowing down into a very delightful companion.'[115] She was also popular:

> [Margie] would be invited by a Newnham friend to an afternoon concert . . . & it would be arranged that she should come home in the evening. Instead a telegram arrives, 'Goodnight they have persuaded me to stay. Best love', and Margie disappears for a week.[116]

This popularity was an aspect of Newnham which troubled her elder sister, Mary, when she and her mother paid a visit to London: 'I am afraid Newnham has not been altogether wholesome for her,' Mary wrote to Anna.

> She seems to have been the general pet & has so many young lady lovers that Mother & I do not know what to do with her or them . . . I feel inclined to be very stern and unsympathetic with them. I don't believe in letting 'the feelings run in soft luxurious flow' . . . But perhaps I am too hard on this new development and behind the century.'[117]

July 1878 brought news that Arfie had gained an entrance scholarship worth £30 a year to Clifton College and Maurice two prizes in physics and mathematics and a first-year student scholarship, also of £30. At Bedford College Alla, who mixed study with housekeeping and music, was to come second in the London

University entrance exam, and Dolla was working (successfully) for a fine art's scholarship to the Slade. 'We feel NZ & the A & R Mob are looking up,' Maria wrote to Emily. During the summer holidays everybody went off to the continent: James, Alla, Dolla, and Dick to Florence; Maurice on a walking tour, and the rest, with Maria, joined Emily's party in a small chalet 'like a doll's house' at Simplon, from which they overflowed into the *pension*. Arthur had been a reluctant traveller. 'You know how men go on at times, seeing endless difficulties [Arthur's concern was that he did not know *all* the languages likely to be met with] where a woman knows there are none.'[118] Maria returned to set up a family base at Bristol, where she could watch over the experiment of entrusting Arfie to an English public school. She had offered to take any of Emily's younger children whom the latter chose to leave behind when she returned to New Zealand.

Emily and William had 'fallen out' over when, or even if, Emily should return. The expense of maintaining his wife and Mary at Swiss *pensions*, the boys at Hofwyl, Alice and possibly Emmie at a Swiss school, Margaret at Newnham, and himself, Anna, and Kit at Wellington, where he had taken a house, had been a considerable burden to William. Anna was poorly, Kit was 'difficult' and poorly, and William himself had suffered a serious bout of inflammation of the lungs. He felt deprived of his family and pessimistic about how its members would now react to New Zealand. 'I am afraid when you come back it will be as Uncle Arthur gloomily says, "this poor country will not be good enough for its own children". I am afraid this going to Europe was a great mistake.'[119] Emily wanted the younger boys to go to an English public school 'to learn English and cricket', William to retire in England, and Kit to go to either Oxford or Cambridge – 'if he dies, through climate or anything else . . . surely it is better than eating his heart out as he is now doing'.[120] William replied, 'You seem to have forgotten that people can get a very fair education in N.Z. – better than I got.'[121] He pointed out that the only benefit of an English public school was a social one – which was very likely what Emily had in mind. He reiterated that expense alone would prohibit him from retiring to England, even if he wished to. This caused Emily to reply: 'I feel some rekindling of the old thoughts & feelings when I read your letter, but it is difficult for me to believe you personally care twopence where I am so long as I am not spending too much.'[122] William telegraphed, 'Come'.

At the end of December 1878, Arthur booked passages, via Suez, for Edie and himself, and for Emily, Mary, Ted, and Emmie. Margaret had obtained her teaching certificate and pleaded with her parents to be allowed to continue with medical studies at Cambridge. She had Maria's support: '[Margie] finds these studies more absorbingly interesting than anything she has yet learnt.' She doubted whether her niece had the 'strength & toughness of constitution & brain to be a doctor', but was sure a knowledge of medicine would be valuable to her as a teacher and as a woman. Margaret was allowed to stay. Maria would have liked Edie to have had another year in England, but considered that she was now 'thoroughly awakened intellectually' and 'if alone with her father need not go to sleep again even in Sleepy Hollow'. Edie was also determined that her father should not go back to Nelson alone. The plan now agreed upon between Maria and Arthur was that if Arfie was happy being a weekly boarder at Clifton, Maria would stay at Bristol until he was ready to go to Oxford in three years' time. 'I of course mean to live simply & as inexpensively as is consistent with health & a good education.'[123] She had found that there was good teaching for girls at Bristol but was reluctant to move Ruth and Mabel from Octavia Hill's London school where they were now joined by Alice Richmond. Maria thought the intellectual atmosphere there 'encouraging'. William, when he learnt that Alice was getting up before six in the morning to study, did not:

> It is foolish for growing girls . . . to exhaust the strength which they will need for the practical duties of life. I think many people in England are quite crazy on the subject of what they call 'education' – which is merely cramming . . . This is not the way to teach people to use their minds.[124]

Arthur had arranged for Bob and Alf to become weekly boarders at the prep school for Clifton at Bristol, so the ten-roomed furnished house Maria had taken near the college for £130 a year (use of piano included), was filled only at weekends and holidays. Maria had the curious experience of being on her own:

> I had to take a lonely walk on the Downes yesterday to enjoy the wonderful clearness of the sky. The sky was real blue, the colours of rocks & foliage brilliant . . . [but] I wanted someone to enjoy it with me.[125]

Neither she nor James shared Emily's wish to remain abroad indefinitely: 'New Zealand, not England nor any part of Europe, is my home,' James declared,[126] and Maria, on hearing of the catalogue of illness afflicting the young cousins at Blackheath, wrote.

'Dear me I seem daily to feel what a great deal the young folk have to be thankful for in being born to a fresh, clean country like N.Z.'[127]

The other family base, James's house at Notting Hill, was also quieter. London's climate and Dick and Wilsie's white faces had impelled James to place them at King Edward School, Retford, in Nottinghamshire, where the headmaster was a friend of R.H. Hutton. Dolla was at the Slade School of Art attached to London University. Her work was well thought of by Professor Alphonse Legros, the French 'realist' painter, and she herself was 'in great request among her lady friends'. Margie was a frequent visitor. 'I find unmixed sunshine in her,' James wrote to Margaret Taylor. 'She is impetuous and eager, never walks into a room but bursts in breathless.'[128] Dolla sent an amusing letter to Emily about a meeting of the 'Ladies' Society' at London University to debate the question, 'Is discontent an advantage?' Most of the evening was spent in a wrangle over choosing a new president.

> Alla if she had been there would have proposed Mrs Langtry, but we think as George Elliot [one of those proposed] is too decidedly connected with literature perhaps Mrs Langtry might be said to be too decidedly connected with the Prince of Wales. Mrs Oliphant was also one proposal, but it was discovered that her reputation was on the wane, so also is that of Mrs Langtry, who is, I hear quite supplanted in the photographers' windows by Mrs Cornwallis West.[129]

Dolla might well have proposed Ellen Terry, the household being 'Hamlet-mad'. 'I wonder if Irving is less in love with her than we are?'[130]

Apart from his satisfaction with the progress of his young, James found little else to cheer him in London. Lack of sunlight, anxiety about his finances, failing eyesight, and what he described as 'feeble health' were all obstacles to painting as he wished. A painting of 'Mt Egmont' had been exhibited at the Royal Academy: 'It has some goods points but is as usual fumbled.'[131] Hoping to compensate for time lost in foggy London, he went to Cornwall, only to find more dull skies and bitter weather. Maria worried about his 'old looks and failing sight'.

William was now based in Wellington which did not please Maria, who thought the town 'anything but healthy in spite of the breezy climate'. 'Mulligan's castle' was a four-storey house (one up, three down) on the high point of Wellington Terrace and William had taken it for three years. The house was commodious but inelegant. Anna, in her mother's absence, had chosen furnishings which reflected her taste, and probably that of William Morris, rather than her father's:

> The yellow-green silk settee *swears* at our present green rep curtains and yellow brown carpet. I don't think it will do to shew people just off steamers into one of these higharty rooms. It might make them bad again. In N.Z. we like bold contrasts of pure colours. Red and yellow is the mixture most in vogue now.[132]

William had visited Taranaki at the beginning of 1878. Harry's ministry had been temporarily defeated in October 1877, and he and Annie had returned to Hurworth. With Dunstan and Tudor's help, he farmed 400 acres at Waitara as well as Hurworth. Here William found the pastoral quiet which had eluded him elsewhere: 'The old times have come back upon me, and I have been sucking melancholy under the greenwood tree as a weasel sucks eggs . . . Shall we clear, plough up, take a crop of wheat, sow down in grass – and build?'[133] The question was largely rhetorical; Emily had no intention of abandoning herself to the countryside, and not all the ways and paths of Taranaki promised pleasantness and peace. The following year Henry from Beach Cottage wrote to his brother: 'The strange shape that the Maori difficulty has assumed oppresses us like a nightmare, as no one can say as yet what the outcome of it will be.'[134]

When Arthur and Edie arrived back at Fairfield towards the end of March 1879, they were met with the news that Edith Louise Fell, wife of Arthur's partner, had died a month earlier at the age of thirty-four, leaving Charles Fell with five young children. A letter from Maria to James indicates that the 'little Fells' were soon in the habit of coming to play at Fairfield. In 1880 Charles took his two elder daughters with him to his wife's affluent parents in England. Within a week of their arrival they were clamouring to return to Nelson, and Fell, without demur, took them straight back again. Perhaps father and children sensed that solace, companionship, and love were closer to hand at Fairfield than in a Victorian mansion in England.

Maria's letters are sparse for the remainder of her time abroad. In 1879 she decided to board Bob and Alf herself and let them attend Clifton College as day pupils. Arf (he finally ceased to be Arfie) continued to excel there. Mabel, Alice, and Ruth, who hoped to make a career as a photographer, were also at Bristol. At the end of 1879, Margaret Richmond visited Syrgenstein and Italy before returning to New Zealand with Alf. They were back at Wellington by October 1880. Bob Richmond, who was to stay on at Clifton with Arf, Maria described as 'happy-go-lucky, growing fast and [has] no appetite for school work'. She thought he would make a successful merchant or surveyor. He came back by himself in December 1881. Alice was the only one of the second generation who, Maria thought, had become quite alienated from New Zealand. Maria did not wish to stay beyond Arf's last year at Clifton and wished to time her departure with James's, but 'as you know', she wrote to William, 'he never *plans* & neither his route nor time of leaving England will be known till the latest moment possible'.[135] For a few weeks in 1879, both families came together at Clovelly. They had intended to go to Brittany where living was particularly cheap but an outbreak of typhoid had diverted them. 'Maria is telling you with lively detail which I cannot equal of our state here,' James wrote to Arthur. Unfortunately, as with other correspondence from this period, her letter is lost.

In October 1880 Maurice passed his final BSc exam 'in the first division'. He had been consistently at the top of his classes, and his physics professor looked on his departure as a 'personal loss'. Both families, James with five, and Maria with her two daughters and Alice, set off on a farewell visit to Syrgenstein and Italy, planning to meet the ship which was to take them back to New Zealand at Suez. The Whittles and Margaret Taylor joined them, and from Syrgenstein they made their way by Florence and Venice to the seaport of Brindisi at the Mediterranean end of the Adriatic. 'The gondolas were heavenly at Venice,' Alla wrote to Annie Atkinson, '& we were always sorry when our glides came to an end.' 'Of course we have to separate a good deal,' she continued, 'as we do not wish to be taken for a Cook's tourist party, & still more we do not wish to feel like one.'[136]

Also returning to New Zealand by the Suez route were the successful Wellington merchant, Walter Turnbull (father of Alexander Horsburgh), and his daughter Isabella. On 26 November, at three in the morning, passengers and mail from Brindisi arrived on board the steamer *Kaiser-i-Hind*; the noise and bustle was considerable and, to Turnbull's annoyance, prevented him from sleeping.

> This morning I made up to and had a long talk with J.C. Richmond tho' he and his family are studiously keeping aloof from the other passengers. His daughters are very plain looking and are dressed

in a most extraordinary fashion quite aesthetic, loose robes with tippets and girdles round the waist, with hair cut short, in other words perfect guys; their cousins the Atkinsons are not quite so outre in their apparel.[137]

It was a portent, if indeed any of the party was aware of his scorn, of how the girls, in particular, might be regarded. New Zealand 'polite society' was unsure of itself and clung to conformity. Differences in dress, manners or outlook tended to be ridiculed as eccentricity. For this reason the returning members of the second generation were to find the fellowship of the mob as necessary to their sense of well being as their parents had done. Maria was sure where her feet were planted, but for some of her nieces the term 'New Zealander' was to carry an overtone of exile.

The Turnbulls changed vessels in Ceylon, while the Richmond–Atkinson party came on to Melbourne and from there, by the *Rotorua*, to Wellington, arriving on 7 January 1881. Arthur was 'too busy to come', but William was there to greet them. 'James is very grey – or rather grey-bearded,' he wrote to Emily at Auckland. 'He would look younger if he shaved more.'[138] Alla and Dolla must have been wearing the same ensemble which had amazed Walter Turnbull: '[they] might have walked out of one of Walter Crane's books. Dolla has certainly a beautiful face – very beautiful – and is most picturesque in appearance altogether.' 'Mabie is so much grown,' William continued, 'and Ruthie a handsome girl with a Roman nose.' He found his sister 'a good deal bent from rheumatism', but otherwise 'she is just the same as ever'.[139]

'Young folks & sunshine'

Nelson 1881–1914

From the late 1880s onwards those who had made up the original nucleus of the mob gradually aged and died so that by the 1900s, following the death of Arthur Atkinson at the end of 1902, only Emily Richmond and Maria Atkinson were left. Aunt Maria and Aunt Emily they had become by then, for the second generation maintained the social cohesion of their elders. This trait has continued. Ann Paterson, a descendant of both Helen Hursthouse and Harry Atkinson, records in *Stories of York Bay* (1983), that when her father was killed in the First World War,

> [the] five sets of aunts and uncles (then living at York Bay) closed ranks about us and were a truly protective shield between us and the world . . . They represented all that was good in the extended family: we could borrow books, ask for knowledge or just sit with them in the sun. When strife broke out at home, peace could be found in a relation's house nearby.[1]

Relationships within the mob were not always unruffled, nor were newcomers instantly accepted or content to find themselves caught in the family's embrace. Emma Richmond, Henry's second wife, had fully satisfied Lely and Maria, but she chose to distance herself from the mob's connections in Taranaki. Henry's son, Francis, was also inclined to hold himself aloof. His sister, Blanche, allied herself more to her grandmother in Nelson than to her New Plymouth family. Liza Gibson, Kit Richmond's fiancée, was thought unsuitable by Emily, and her parents even more so. Kit continued a loner, seldom comfortable with his family and too readily finding grievance. The mob was as alarmed by the prospect of Maurice Richmond's misalliance with Mrs Rogers of Melbourne as it had earlier been by the possibility of accepting the formidable aunt of Annie's one-time suitor, Reginald Broughton. Occasionally there was, as it were, a takeover bid from another family: Alla considered

that the Pikes, whose daughter Georgina married J.C. Richmond's
son Dick, had completely absorbed her brother, and it was only
the sudden death of their daughter which allowed the warmth of
Alla's affection to flow towards them. On the whole, however,
those who married members of the mob's second generation were
accepted and welcomed into family gatherings at Fairfield or at
the summer camp at Totaranui, just inside the western entrance
of Tasman Bay. Occasionally, as happened in large, cohesive
nineteenth-century families, the mob doubled back on itself and
cousins married cousins or second cousins, as did Alla Richmond
and Tudor Atkinson, Flora Macdonald (her mother was a
Hursthouse) and Maurice Richmond, May Hursthouse and Arnold
Atkinson.

Of all the newcomers, perhaps the most significant for the family
as a whole were C.Y. (Charlie) Fell and his younger brother, Walter,
who married Edie Atkinson and Margaret Richmond respectively.
Walter Fell became the family's doctor at Wellington and his
influence rivalled that of Dr Joseph Kidd, the London homeopath
whom ailing members of both generations continued to visit.[2]
Charlie Fell, also Arthur's legal partner, was an excellent amateur
photographer so that although Maria's letters become increasingly
sparse,[3] photos of her amidst family gatherings abound. He was
an enthusiastic, gregarious man who fitted into the mob's communal
lifestyle and delighted in making Totaranui the Christmas holiday
centre. In the Fell albums are amusing photos showing parties –
of the second generation – elegantly poised on rocks, dancing along
the sands, or carefully arranged in tableaux. The younger ones
generally reached Totaranui aboard Charlie Fell's yacht; their elders
arrived more sedately on the Anchor Line paddlesteamer, *Lady
Barkly*. 'Don't let minor difficulties hinder your coming,' Maria
advised Emily on one occasion, 'it is much better for you to let
the main body go first, so as to avoid the first scrimage of settling
down. Don't load yourself with luggage, you need so little in the
way of toilette.'[4]

Money was not considered a prime requisite for marriage,
although Maria and Emily begged to differ on this. Qualities of
mind and heart and 'coming from an interesting stock' were valued
more. In the early 1880s Maria chided Emily for wishing to spurn
a suitor for one of her elder daughters (possibly Mary) because
of his pecuniary circumstances.

> Whatever his income, I should not consider he had inflicted a
> grievous wrong upon her or dream of abusing him for asking

her! . . . Not one of the clan would have married as they did had
he or she thought so in the old days . . . There is more real sterling
worldly wisdom in the parents who desire before all things to be
assured their future son-in-law is pure, honest, sober, industrious
& kindly than in those who demand certainty as to the number
of hundreds per an. he is offering their daughter. I have several
cases in mind, the income was excellent but has departed. The
qualities were never there & never will be!⁵

Except for the Fells, who inherited comfortable means, and C.W.
Richmond's daughter, Alice, who married into an English county
family, making ends meet was still a familiar problem. It did not
affect the mob's social position. Members of the family continued
to be invited to vice-regal functions and their children to parties
at Government House, where Mary Richmond's kindergarten
children sometimes provided an entertainment. Both generations
accepted a structured society in which the 'classes' were separated
from the 'masses' as much by education and a firm grasp of the
elusive 'h' as by anything else. In the 'classes', the 'élite and the
vulgar' were eschewed. Alla, who used the phrase, probably counted
nouveau riche and society swells as belonging to the former group.
No matter how tight the purse strings, however, a servant was
considered essential, except perhaps on holidays when a maid's
inability to adjust to her family's relaxed lifestyle often made her
'uppity' and 'put-upon'. It was not advisable for a servant to bear
a 'light character'; on the other hand one who was a 'lady' had
to be allowed to sit with the family. Amiability, but not 'amiability
gone bad', as Maria once expressed it, was desirable; all the family
found Aunt Annie's 'grenadier' far too uncomfortable and far too
uncomprising to have about.

   With C.W. Richmond a judge (his nephews and nieces often
called him Uncle Judge) and Fell and Atkinson an established law
firm, it was almost too easy for second-generation sons to enter
the legal profession. Eight became lawyers, serving first as William's
secretary or associate and then completing their apprenticeship with
Fell and Atkinson, or occasionally joining Henry's more struggling
practice at New Plymouth. The decision to become a lawyer seems
often to have been made, as it had earlier by William himself,
'because it was expected'. Maurice Richmond, trained in
experimental physics would, like his Uncle Henry, have preferred
a more abstract intellectual pursuit such as that which he later
found as a lecturer in jurisprudence and constitutional law at the
newly established Victoria University College. Arthur Atkinson

(Arf) had a natural flair for journalism and for being a political gadfly. Maria and Arthur did their best to ensure that it was Arf's own decision to turn to law. During 'the Long Depression' (1878–95), however, there were few other obvious openings, apart from teaching, for a well-educated man who wished to remain in New Zealand. Hurworth remained a hallowed place in the mob's affections but it did not hold the active interest of either the first or second generation of the mob for long. The exception was Harry Atkinson, and even he enlivened farming with warfare and politics.

In politics the influence of what the editor of the Nelson *Colonist* sneeringly called the 'governing family'[6] began to wane during the 1880s, although the pragmatic, conscientious Harry Atkinson held office either as colonial treasurer or as prime minister during most of the decade. An advocacy of thrift, industry, and self-reliance, an independent stance and obvious integrity had previously served the family well enough in politics, but these virtues held little appeal and were of little use to the unemployed urban workers, disillusioned immigrants, and struggling small farmers who made increasingly effective use of the ballot box. Harry Atkinson's Compulsory Insurance Bill (1882)[7] was an honest attempt to grapple with poverty and insecurity; it was ridiculed in the House and failed to gain support outside. He struggled on in declining health until his ministry was defeated at the end of 1890. Richmond Hursthouse kept him company in the House until 1887, but apart from the maverick onslaught mounted by Arthur Richmond Atkinson against Seddon in the late 1890s which led him to the House from 1899 to 1902, there were, to Maria's intense disappointment, no further members of the mob in the House of Representatives.[8]

But, if the mob lost its men from direct political influence, it had its women to the fore in the hustings; the Temperance Movement was a natural partner to the agitation for women's suffrage. Again and again women and their families suffered through the excesses of the liquor trade. Husbands could disappear and survive on the goldfields or as itinerant workers, leaving wives and children destitute and dispossessed. 'Temperance and the vote', as Raewyn Dalziel has written, 'were the means of safeguarding the morality of the colony and the sanctity of the family.'[9] Maria Atkinson had long maintained that a woman's place within the family was of paramount importance to that institution and to society, and she had a high regard for the good sense of the majority of her colonial sisters. She was never as militant as her daughter-in-law, Lily

Atkinson (née Kirk), nor, because of age, was she as active in the New Zealand Alliance as her daughter, Ruth, but as a woman with mana she spoke in public for both causes and, in her very old age, accosted Seddon. In Wellington Mary Richmond, Margaret Fell, Alla Atkinson, Dolla Richmond, and Lily Atkinson (as well as her husband, Arthur) were all caught up in the heady excitement of the Forward Movement.

An Oxford friend of Arthur Atkinson once asked him: 'One thing I particularly want is an up-to-date exposition of this mysterious "moral sense" which all the Richmonds and Atkinsons think they know all about.'[10] There is an element of truth in this taunt. Neither Maria nor the inner circle of the mob ever divorced politics from morality. Both were based on the family's own code of values which in turn (for the Richmonds) rested on the Unitarian ethic. 'That thin earnest face', as Harriet Gore Browne described William's appearance on the floor of the House, was the sort of face Maria expected to see in politics. She was not sure about the value of democracy, even after allowing for the advantage which she hoped would accrue from the enfranchisement of women. Her distrust deepened when she and Ar read together W.E.H. Lecky's *Democracy and Liberty*;[11] she found the work 'terribly depressing and pessimistic'. 'The people are so besotted' was a sentence she used with increasing frequency; she saw 'Seddonism' as encouraging bribery, corruption, overseas borrowing, and taxation. That 'the people' hungered and thirsted for something more immediate and substantial than righteousness was something she could accept but did not consider worthy. When the family went to the wall in politics one cannot quite say that morality went with them, but from one generation to another there has been a distinctive aura. John Beaglehole, writing of Maurice Richmond when he was on the teaching staff of Victoria College, described him as: 'Sensitive, serious, refined in face, of a philosophical, even metaphysical cast of mind, with all his family's slavery to the demands of a painful and urgent conscience.'[12] He might well have been describing C.W. Richmond. It is not surprising that it was the same Maurice Richmond who suggested the college's motto *Sapientia magis auro desideranda* which, Alla commented, 'we all liked very much'; that wisdom was more desirable than gold was a family truism. In similar vein, F.A. de la Mare, writing in *Spike* after the death of Margaret Fell (née Richmond) in 1933, stated: 'To make a prejudicial or unfair statement in her circle was to be called before the bar of a mind just, judicial, penetrating.

To have lied to her would have been an outrage, not to a person but to a universe.'[13]

In 1881, however, all this was still in the future, written here simply to provide a setting, a valedictory one, for the lengthy and, as far as family records go, fragmentary period of Maria's life in which she is seen as much through the letters of her 'young folks' as in her own writing. Once she returned from Europe, Maria remained at Fairfield, apart from family visits within the colony, for the rest of her life. Old age inevitably slowed down her physical ability, but the ferment of ideas continued. The photograph of an elderly Maria writing at her book-strewn desk is the strongest image we have of her. 'Every year,' she declared, 'I feel more interested in both my own circle & the whole world.'[14]

Almost as soon as she arrived back in New Zealand, in January 1881, Maria was off to New Plymouth with other Nelson members of the clan to attend Fanny Atkinson's marriage to Clement Govett, son of Archdeacon Henry Govett. Annie Atkinson was in her element; there is no mention of neuralgia. The mob had been summoned and it had responded. 'Here we are, millions of us, standing round to assist Fanny to be married,' Alla wrote to Ann Shaen. 'We alarm the population of New Plymouth very much when a regiment or two of us goes out shopping or arrives at a tea party . . . but they are interested too, for they have known our fathers & mothers years ago.'[15] The wedding went off with élan. There was an afternoon tea and a dance for the fifteen bridesmaids at Beach Cottage – Aunt Emma responded as well – and the following day 'a magnificent excursion' to the lower ranges. Maria stayed a further week at New Plymouth 'to let the relations down more gently', and divided her time between Beach Cottage and Hurworth. Henry she thought looked tired, Emma was 'most hospitable', Decie had 'cement on the brain' and was still much too sanguine about finance, Marion was careworn.

Alla was with Fanny again a year later when her first child was born. The forthright tone of her letter to Maria about the event is reminiscent of Maria's writing at the same age:

Just think Clement had said that he thought Fan had better not have chloroform and so she deliberately was not going to, unless she was particularly bad! I told her she might tell Clement he was an idiot and that she might as well have been born in queen Elizabeth's days; and so Dr Leatham now is to do as he pleases & I suppose he will give chloroform as he is a sensible young man.[16]

Marjorie Govett was born 'safe & fat'. 'It was awful at the time Fan and I thought but the Dr did not, I believe.'[17]

A quieter but more important wedding for Maria and Arthur also took place in 1881. Edie, at twenty-three, married Charles (Charlie) Fell, thirty-seven, and became stepmother to five young children whose ages ranged from three to twelve years. Maria had thought Edie unlikely to marry. Visiting male cousins were used to being snubbed by her: 'She grows no less fastidious,' Maria told Emily when her daughter was eighteen, '& views the male sex especially with such a critical eye that in spite of her good looks she is no favourite with them.'[18] Charlie Fell's age, experience, and success in the world bridged the gap which Edie would probably always have chosen to find between herself and a man of her own age. According to Alla, there was consternation at Fairfield when Charlie proposed, but Maria and Arthur's concern was short-lived, Maria wrote:

> Yes after all I suppose I am thankful that Edie has taken the *one* Nelson man that it would be possible for her to marry as it is a very great blessing to keep her near us. At first I was stunned by the thought of losing her so soon . . . I must say E. is most bare-faced considering all the contempt she has hitherto poured on love & love making.[19]

They were married on 22 July 1881 at Bishopdale Chapel. A photo of the wedding group in front of Fairfield shows a serious-looking Edie and Charlie surrounded by equally serious children. In the background Maria and Arthur look pensive. Obviously no light step had been taken. Charlie's children stayed behind when their father and Edie went on what Alla called their 'wedding journey' and, under her and Dolla's guidance, prepared 'Alfred, a Drama' to entertain the couple on their return. 'Mr Fell I like better every day,' Alla informed Ann Shaen, 'he is so clean and kind and fond of Edie.'[20] The following year Charles Richmond Fell was born – his name within the family was 'Boy' – and his father became mayor of Nelson. Within little more than twelve months, Edie was married, had a family of six,[21] and was Nelson's first lady.

The Fells lived at St John's at one end of Brougham Street; Fairfield was towards the other end, and between the two James Richmond purchased a house[22] which he naturally named St. James.[23] James stated many times in his life that politics sickened him. In fact they intrigued quite as much as sickened and he had to be decisively defeated yet again before deciding finally to quit representation. He contested a by-election for Nelson City in June

1881. 'Most people seem to think Father is safe,' Dolla wrote, but he was not. He had two opponents; H.A. Levestam, who stood against him, and Joseph Shephard, editor of the Nelson *Colonist*.[24] Shephard, a property owner in the Upper Wai-iti, also represented Waimea and was a close associate of Richard Seddon. In a vitriolic attack in the *Colonist*, 2 June 1881, he accused James of being 'one of the most cherished offshoots of the most prominent of the governing families of New Zealand', claiming that he represented 'undoubted wealth and pretended culture' and had been 'foisted into the Weld Ministry by the influence of his family'. The family in question seem to have been bemused rather than infuriated by the attack, to which James did not deign to reply. A more friendly critic in Nelson's other paper, the *Evening Mail*, dismissed the *Colonist*'s charges as 'absurd and abusive' but did concede that James's delivery was 'awkward'.[25] Levestam made a more telling thrust when he stated that in the House 'only one class had been represented'.[26] The mob gave its full support to James; nineteen of them went to his opening address on the parlous economic state of the country, but the 'stupid people', as Dolla described them, chose Levestam by a narrow margin. Maria was convinced that neither abuse nor argument but beer had won the day.

James had a more direct confrontation with Shephard when in December 1881 he contested the Waimea seat in the general election. He had the company of Richmond Hursthouse standing for Motueka. 'Richmond is more suited to this sort of thing than Father,' Dolla commented, 'the men are a most unmannerly and amusing set and Richmond suits them for he addresses them with his hands in his pockets and uses homely illustrations and much slang.'[27] Again the Nelson contingent turned out in support, Dick Richmond in moleskin trousers: 'he says that at the next election he will go in his dirty workmen's clothes onto the platform with Father as the missing link between Father & the people'.[28] This time James, who had spoken out against 'excessive borrowing for public works', was decisively defeated. (Richmond Hursthouse was returned.) James, without rancour, wrote to William that he had now done his share for the 'soberer side' and could sit down with a safe conscience 'convinced that I am not a man for popular favour. So my pictures will move on better in future.'[29] Margaret Taylor wrote: 'I was amused at your coming out in the character of a Conservative Aristocrat! With your views it must have been almost insult enough to drive you back to the side of the world on which your character would *not* lie under that imputation.'[30]

That summer a family party which included James, Maria, and Arthur set off for Totaranui.[31] Dolla writing to Ann Shaen captures something of its beauty and the ease with which members of the mob, young and old, settled in together:

> it was gorgeous, a bay with yellow sand & great forest covered hills behind our little cottage. Our cottage had three bedrooms & there were always from 13 to 15 of us in it. Two of the bedrooms were given over to the ladies, the third to the maid & two children & the rest of us were accommodated on the floor, father on the sofa.
>
> The beach was our common bath & dressing room, some preferred a tub in a lovely little stream which ran through the bush close to the house. We mostly bathed in the sea three times a day . . . Charlie Fell used to bathe with us in the morning to teach the children, he looked horrid in a skin tight vest & a very loose pair of old bathing knickers of Allas, purple with white spots. He swims splendidly . . . [In the afternoons they went fishing and sailing.] What lovely things sailing boats are, they are constantly posing in picturesque attitudes & can't possibly be anything but graceful.[32]

The glorious weather culminated in a glorious gale. Dolla clad in bathing costume and ulster stood out in it all morning. Her enjoyment recalls James and Maria's 'most glorious storm' on the Dawlish coast which exacted a soaking in return for 'our love of the sublime'.

At Nelson, which was at least better than Wellington – 'so full of rules of what you may or may not do and what kind of clothes you must wear'[33] – Alla and Dolla tried to keep themselves occupied so as not to mope too obviously for 'home' which had become England. 'The people of Nelson seldom seem to think much beyond it, which is perhaps a virtue but hard to acquire at my advanced age.'[34] Alla taught French and German to private pupils and found relief in Greek and in slipping off to St John's to play on the new Steinway: 'I am happy there is one in the family.' Dolla painted and conducted a drawing class. They both refurbished St James so that 'now it is high art'. Above the venetian red fireplace Dolla painted, after Kate Greenaway, a fresco of five geese dancing to the moon; they were to be an 'allegorical representation of us five'. The boys seemed to adjust with ease. Maurice was 'well and cheerful' as a clerk in Fell and Atkinson. He had only to complete an apprenticeship and pass a final law exam to become a barrister and solicitor. Dick was a cadet on the Greenwood farm at Motueka and Wilsie an engineering apprentice at the Anchor Foundry. Alla and Dolla also devoted a good deal of their time to Aunt Helen Hursthouse who lived mostly with the Hursthouses in Motueka. Approaching eighty, she was quite blind and very frail: 'she has not had a cheerful life to look back on now when she can see nothing,' said Dolla.[35] Maria suggested to the others that if they provided £30 a year, Aunt could end her days in a small cottage near the family in Nelson. This came about and until her death on 1 April 1895 she appeared regularly in photographs of mob gatherings at Fairfield.

Since the family exodus abroad, the trees in Nelson had grown to such an extent that St James, flaunting 'high art' colours, was discreetly hidden from its neighbours. From the high ground at the backs of St John's, St James and Fairfield, Nelson looked 'more like a small forest than a town'. This gave the family a certain much-relished privacy. Alla described an afternoon in early spring when she, Dolla, Edie, and Maria sat at the top of St James's hill looking across Tasman Bay, the air 'full of breezes & swift clouds & wavy shadows & sunshine':

> We are sitting . . . under a great willow, to the left of us more willows & the afternoon sun is shining through them . . . The town is almost hidden from us by a small hill with gum trees & a few rather ugly houses that will soon be hidden by aspens etc. Dolla is reading letters aloud to Edie who is lying down in some dead willow branches: the kittens have been having their afternoon cream. Aunt Maria has been having afternoon tea up here and we had hysterics once, but now we are better. Edie has just begun to say hurrah because we see a steamer sailing away which is taking from Nelson a little girl who, Edie thinks, was corrupting her little girls, and who has hitherto lived next door.[36]

Other Nelson citizens must have feared that an equally corrupting influence emanated from St James. As it had done on their return to New Zealand, Alla and Dolla's aesthetic appearance caused comment. Once when Alla was returning from Nelson College for Girls, Judge Lowther Broad, a family friend, overtook her and asked 'what particular piece of wickedness' she had been perpetrating lately. 'I was a little surprised and said I could not remember being worse than usual . . . Then he told me that twice lately he had come upon Colonel Wallcott[37] kneeling outside our red gate praying for me.'[38] Bobbed hair, the absence of stays, a red house, a whiff of Oscar Wilde? Whatever it was that brought Colonel Wallcott to his knees, Alla found his action 'horrible'. There is nothing to suggest that Dolla and she were ostracised, although this might have been the case in Wellington. Holidaying with the E.C.J. Stevens in Christchurch, Alla was introduced as 'Mrs Steven's aesthetic young lady'. In Nelson the two sisters clung to one another 'like limpets and drowning straws': 'I tried sleeping in a separate bed for a little while, but I grew so wretched that my nights were a burden to me so we have returned to our one big bed.'[39]

Visiting and local companies did their best to bring something of Dresden and London to the émigrées. The local opera company produced Weber's *Der Freischütz*: 'the fireworks in the incantation scene were a marked success, the fire brigade were in waiting outside the theatre, the hose was prepared, we wished we had brought our umbrellas'.[40] 'A more decent company than usual' produced *Hamlet*. But if the leading actor was allowed some merit, Ellen Terry had left too lasting an impression: 'I can't tell you what Ophelia was like . . . There was a woman who said the words . . . She succeeded in drawing tears of rage from me, but that was all.'[41]

Nelson College for Girls opened quietly[42] in an unfinished building on 2 February 1883. It provided an opportunity for involvement by St James, Fairfield, and St John's, which became the venue for classes for eighteen prospective pupils immediately prior to the school's opening. Charlie Fell was a member of the board of governors which administered both the boys' and girls' colleges. Maria was quick to appreciate and make friends with the young principal, Kate Edgar,[43] and with two of the assistant teachers and the matron, Elizabeth Bruce Bell. Alla held a temporary appointment to teach German and French, and Dolla was appointed to teach art[44] her salary dependent on the number of her pupils.

During 1883 and 1884 the final alterations at Fairfield were completed. These transformed it into the fine-looking house which, restored and cared for, stands today.[45] Ever since Lely's death, Maria had wanted a 'commodious kitchen & pantry. It is quite impossible to keep these old ones decently cleaned & I am sure I wonder any good servant could live in them so long.'[46] The alterations finally carried out under the supervision of A.T. Somerville, a Nelson architect, were more extensive, and resulted in the whole of the original cottage being pulled down or completely reconstructed and the addition of a second storey and verandah. Arising from the second-storey verandah was a two-tiered, ballustraded platform on which Arthur intended to fix his telescope. He later found that his original garden site was just as adequate for observation and probably less threatening to his neighbours. The platform became a useful prop on which to accommodate the middle-age range of the mob in Charlie Fell's photographs of gatherings. Along with reconstruction went refurbishing. Maria asked Emily Richmond in Wellington to choose the drawing-room carpet to go with salmon walls and dark maroon curtains: 'a general kaleidoscope muddle of every colour will be safe'. Later she wrote, 'I grieve to say that I fear it is my painful duty to give up the marble fender & tiles.' Arthur had never cared for them: 'men don't often understand the comfort of things that look well & *save work*'.[47]

In July 1883 'while work all around the house was going on', Arf came home on a visit before going to Oxford. He had continued to gratify his parents by showing the same academic prowess and qualities of leadership at Clifton College as at Nelson. The previous year he had been awarded an exhibition to Corpus Christi College but his housemaster advised that he was expected to become head of school and that this post 'would do more to educate his "political" powers than entering on Oxford at once.'[48] Some of his school holidays had been spent at Syrgenstein, and Margaret added her voice to the paean of praise.

I rejoice all day and every day over Arfie, and it made me full of sunshine to think that he really could like the dull old Aunts. He has such variety in him, he is a perpetual feast, ready for all moods, and brim full of pranks and mischief as he is of sense and ability.[49]

Arf's homecoming was 'dreadfully exciting' for his parents, Dolla wrote: 'he is the apple of their eye'. Where did this leave Ruth and Mabel? Neither was good looking, apart from Ruth's Roman nose, but they seem to have grown accustomed to being 'good sorts', practical, unselfish, energetic – they both trained as nurses. The clear distinction between what men and women did made it quite acceptable for both unmarried daughters to live at home. Letters from either of them are almost non-existent; when Maria, Alla or Dolla write of them they always seem to be too busy. But did the busyness hide something else? Being a 'delightful little dunce', as Maria had once described Mabel, was all very well for a child but, as she grew older, did Mabel (or Ruth) come to enjoy the intimate affection and rapport so obvious between their mother and Alla? Fortunately the nuclear family was generations away and in the mob's extended family Ruth and Mabel had their place. Prohibition and, as a consequence, the affairs of the Baptist church, came to absorb Ruth's energy; being the family's flying angel despatched on the instant from Fairfield to cope with illness or death within the clan became Mabel's accepted role. It would seem too that Ruth from time to time 'adopted' or looked after an unwanted child or one for whom the mother was unable to provide. The term is imprecise because no great issue was made of Ruth's action in family letters; it was simply accepted as something Ruth did. Meantime their clever brother could do intensely impractical things like missing the *British King* which was to take him back to England and having to seize an inferior passage on the San Francisco mail steamer.

'Can't we go to England soon?', Dolla asked her father in September 1884. The time was inopportune; James had recently lost money in an investment in a Waikato coal mine. Dolla's health, however, was precarious and she was often absent from college. The family attributed her malaise to her too rapidly outgrowing her strength, and Alla was at pains to explain to Ann Shaen that the indisposition of her 'ewe lamb sister' had nothing to do with boredom or depression 'because some people can't see that her illness is entirely physical'. (Some people were probably correct.) It was thought that she should see Dr Kidd. Annie Atkinson had set off for this purpose in January; Edie and Charlie Fell, following the difficult birth of their daughter Phyllis, made the pilgrimage in September. Dolla's sudden departure on the *Rimutaka* at the beginning of March 1885 was precipitated because three of her friends – Isabel Blackett who was going to the Slade, Alice Jervois the governor's second daughter 'who we know quite well' and Miss Lysaght 'a lady we all like very much' – were all going by the same vessel. The plan was that once Dr Kidd had restored Dolla to health, she would continue to study and paint either in England or on the continent for another year and at the end of that time, finances permitting, she would be joined by Alla and her father.

Alla's affection for her younger sister, poured out in letters[50] whenever Dolla was abroad, might today seem incestuous. Affection came easily to Alla, she expected to love people. She had from the time of Mary's death assumed her mother's role within the family. Close bonding between women was also part of the ambience of the age. Mary Richmond and her mother had found Margaret's Newnham 'lovers' importunate, even 'maddening', but not immoral. Alla, more fearful for Dolla's health than for her morals, was upset to learn when Dolla was in England, from 1900 to 1903, that she was sharing a bed with Connie, a painting companion who was consumptive, and that Margaret Shaen (niece of Ann), the third member of the trio, was jealous: 'It would solve the difficulty if one of you three would turn into a man.' Alla was better pleased when Dolla left Connie and Margaret Shaen and went off with Frances Hodgkins to paint in France and Italy. Of course in large families neither rooms nor beds were exclusive. Edie had been used to sleeping with her grandmother, Lely with her sister; children frequently slept three together, and none of the aunts so much as raised an eyebrow at Alla and Dolla's preference for sleeping in one large bed.

Dolla arrived safely in England and had the Shaens, the Blackheathens, and Charlie and Edie close to hand. But photos which showed her looking gaunt, and a letter in which she sounded sad and lonely, sent Alla 'into a state of temporary insanity'.

> . . . then I said, 'Idiot, take the letter to somebody, say Aunt Maria . . . and see what a calmer more resourceful mind will evolve.' Of course this was the right thing. Aunt Maria shortly after reading the letter said, 'if Uncle Arthur thinks it a good plan, I see no reason why *I* should not go & be with Dolla . . . until Father has rounded the corner financially . . . and can join her later on' . . . Immediately ten or a dozen tons burden rolled off my soul, and I felt I could stand upright again.[51]

Then a 'gift' from 'dear Aunt Fanny' (most likely a bequest) made James's income 'rather less cramped', and towards the end of 1885 he and Alla set off for Dolla who was now, with Margaret Taylor and James Whittle,[52] impatiently awaiting them at Naples.

> They may be in tomorrow morning. They might have been in ever so often. Our hearts are sick with hope deferred . . . Every morning when I wake up I think 'Perhaps tonight they will be here & Alla & I shall be sleeping under one mosquito net.'[53]

The very next day James and Alla arrived: 'dear old Dolla was fatter than we expected after the fright those horrid photographs gave us.'

Dolla had not absorbed all of her sister's thoughts and affection. In September 1885 Alla became engaged to her second cousin, Tudor Atkinson, who had left Hurworth in 1884 and was now a law clerk with Fell and Atkinson. He appreciated Alla's value and having been raised in the mob knew the tug of its various relationships. He did not presume to claim exclusive possession. 'Dearer sister Dolla,' he wrote, '. . . if I had been you I shouldn't have let anyone love Alla who wasn't noble & great & strong but then I love you all so that perhaps you will forgive me. Your loving cousin brother Tu.'[54]

Maria missed her St James family: 'We feel horrid when we go past your poor deserted home where the garden has been glorious with roses & all kinds of flowers blooming unheeded.'[55] Mabel was out a good deal, often acting as an invigilator at the girls' college. Ruth was 'wrapped up in her baby' (in this case the baby was her niece, Phyllis Fell, left in Ruth's care while her parents were in England), and 'Uncle unless obliged never speaks . . . books at any rate abound'. Maria went on to give Alla the latest news of the girls' college and to describe the 'Olde English Fayre' with which Nelson welcomed the advent of Christmas:

> It is really quite picturesque & much more amusing than I imagined it could be . . . the ladies have their goods displayed in the semblance of old English shops & they are attired in the costume of some distant period of history varying from Henry VI to Sir J. Reynolds . . . Everyone looks better than in the dress of *this* period. Why can't women *always* pick out something becoming or picturesque for themselves & avoid the cruel *monotony* of ugliness to which the modern world seems doomed.[56]

Maria suffered recurring bouts of rheumatism during 1885, and Emily who visited in November found Fairfield lacking its usual good order. 'Nothing was tidy or regular'; Ruth was taken up with baby; Mabel flew about 'always kind & merry' but effecting nothing; the general servant had red hair and was cross; the cooking was not good. For Christmas that year twenty-six were seated at table in the Fairfield drawing room, with Arthur at one and and Charlie Fell (who, with Edie returned towards the end of the year) at the other. The food, augmented by the St John's pudding, was pronounced excellent. Afterwards everybody assembled on the verandah for the ritual photograph and the younger ones went sailing in Charlie Fell's yacht.

Arthur Atkinson, at Harry's request, continued to play an effective role as his brother's ex-parliamentary adviser. 'You are wanted next week so get ready at once to come', was one peremptory summons from Harry in May 1882; 'Why not come over . . . and have a finger in the pie?'[57] he wrote in July 1884. Politics fascinated Arthur more than legal practice in which most of the firm's clients were Charlie Fell's. They remained in amiable partnership and, weather permitting, played tennis together after work with their law clerks of the mid-eighties, Maurice Richmond and Tudor Atkinson. Arthur maintained his interest in philology, studying most of the indigenous South Pacific languages; he contributed to the

Transactions and Proceedings of the New Zealand Institute, was a keen member of the Nelson Philosophical Society, and, after his successful observation (with Maurice's help) of the transit of Venus, 7 December 1882, regarded himself as the 'Astronomer Royal of Nelson'.[58] He was still affronted if any attempt was made to tidy his study.

> Just after getting inside F. [Father] stood still & took a rapid survey of the chaos of bottles, dusty books, cobwebs & wood ashes wh. to the ordinary eye seemed untidy & undisturbed enough. Then fixing his eye on a far corner where stands his escritoire laden with 100s of bottles he said, 'Hm – why should my Fiji spiders be put there?' The secret was out – there had been some tidying.[59]

The family was spared further expensive trips to England to consult Dr Joseph Kidd when in 1886 Margaret Richmond married Walter Fell,[60] Charlie's younger brother, and so acquired its own resident physician and surgeon. 'Margaret's choice gives us thorough satisfaction,' William wrote to him, while Margaret herself marvelled: 'Walter is really a person of superior qualities. I never believed I should come to this, and especially for an *Oxford* man'.[61] Margaret had been a successful and popular teacher at Wellington Girls' High School since its official opening in 1883. Her elder sister Mary, whose time to embark on a career had finally come, was also a member of the staff from 1884 until she left for England in 1890.

Maria, bearing 'two very handsome chinese jars' as a present, came over for the wedding, held in St Paul's on Easter Monday.

> Everybody here [William and Emily were living in Tinakori Rd] I found fairly well . . . Mary has been rather fagged & had to keep quiet in her room several evenings, but last night school work having ended for some days, she revived & was playing the banjo & singing appropriate love ditties outside the drawing room whilst W.F. & Margie had their evening tête à tête inside.[62]

The couple were going to live in a 'very satisfactory town house'. 'The fear is,' Maria continued, 'that WF's ideas in the furnishing line are too colossal & that he will keep adding every handsome looking article he sees . . . until it may be too hard to find room for human beings.' Emily's cup should have been full and running over but she was pained by Margie's wedding dress which she thought 'fitter for a coronation or court dress' and 'gave no feeling of purity and modesty'. Edie and Ruth were bridesmaids and the last-minute change of headdress from veils to straw bonnets was also 'a dreadful blow to Em'. After the wedding Maria stayed on in Wellington; Emily described her to Anna 'reading aloud when she is not writing – she is very serene and delightful, clever and handsome'.[63]

Annie Atkinson's neuralgia prevented her from attending the wedding. Arthur suggested that Maria should go on to New Plymouth: 'if anyone can cheer up Annie, Maria will – though I do not like her going off unattended in such a cockleshell.'[64] Maria had a pleasant passage: 'There was a very decent ladies' cabin & a clean cheerful young stewardess who managed to keep fresh air in the cabin all night.'[65] Until the weather at New Plymouth improved enough for her to go on to Hurworth, Maria stayed with Fanny and Clement Govett. After five years of marriage Fanny had four little girls. 'Dear me,' Maria exclaimed, 'Fanny has her hands full with two that can't walk & the other two but mites.'[66] Maria could no longer pay her customary visit to Marion Atkinson. During 1884 she and Decimus moved to Whangarei where the latter was confident a fortune lay in portland cement. Tragedy again intervened. Decimus was swept away and drowned while attempting to ford a river at Pahi, Kaipara Harbour, 23 October 1884. At the end of 1885 Marion and her youngest son went to visit her English relatives.[67] Maria found Annie much better and 'nearly as well as usual'. Dunstan too had married[68] and left Hurworth to grow oranges at Parua Bay, Whangarei Heads. Harry Atkinson was thinking of selling Hurworth and living permanently in Wellington. 'The poor old place,' Tudor wrote to his brother. 'I'm awfully sentimental about it – I love it – but reason has long admitted that it was right to part.'[69]

James, Alla, and Dolla returned to Nelson in September 1886. Italy had transformed Dolla: 'I am better & quite jolly & old Kiddy says I can be quite strong in a year – in six months I may ride & do gymnastics & use a tricycle.'[70] Dr Kidd considered Dolla's spine was weak and instructed Alla to hose it down each midday. Dolla kept up a succession of piercing shrieks during the five-minute operation but 'she enjoys it and says it makes her feel very vigorous'.

Weddings of the second generation continued during 1887. On 16 February Kit Richmond married Amy Liza Gibson at St Paul's Wellington. As he was William and Emily's eldest son, the wedding might have been expected to rival Margaret's. It did not. There were very few guests present and William and Emily regarded the marriage as a potential disaster. Kit had continued difficult, asthmatical, delicate, and stubborn. After serving as his father's

secretary he and his cousin, Maurice Richmond, had gone into
business together as Richmond and Richmond, Solicitors, Lambton
Quay. They also helped produce a periodical, *Monthly Review*, and
were active members of the 'Winter Evening Debating Society.'[71]
A distressed Emily wrote to Anna:

> Kit should have a serene benign wife more of the nature of a Lysaght,
> not one warped & crippled . . . yet I can understand a person who
> never sees any other woman being interested in Liza – both your
> father and I consider it a serious mistake, but see nothing to be
> done.[72]

Mary, also writing to her sister, doubted whether the couple were
really 'lovers' as they always remained 'as far off each other as
they possibly can'. Kit threatened his mother that if she did not
'gladly receive' Liza he would not remain in Wellington. He also
insisted on, and paid for, an operation to remove a wart on Mrs
Gibson's face which, he said, would spoil the wedding photographs.
Emily had not wanted the engagement talked about. After the
wedding everyone, including Maria, simply hoped that all would
be well.

> How important events seem crowding on the family & how entirely
> it seems out of anyone's power to say what the effect of these
> marriages is going to be. I try to hope Kit will be much better
> in all respects than you dare now to expect. Who knows that some
> grandson of yours springing from it may not leave his mark on
> the 20th century . . . I don't think Kit & Liza will give birth to
> fools or commonplace children, nor give them a conventional
> training so as to stifle all originality, do you? Anyway the thing
> is done, & one must hope for the best.[73]

The double wedding of Alla Richmond and Tudor Atkinson and
of Flora Macdonald and Maurice Richmond was an altogether
happier affair. Maurice had caused alarm by asking a 'Mrs Rogers',
presumably a widow, to marry him after no more than a week's
acquaintance. Alla wrote to Mrs Rogers; so did Maria and 'some
of the others'. Maurice was rescued but 'looked sad'. He was not
enjoying his partnership with Kit and thought of becoming a
journalist. His engagement at the beginning of 1887 to Flora
Macdonald, granddaughter of Helen Hursthouse, was a relief to
everyone and persuaded him to accept the drudgery of the law,
along with its certainty of £200 a year, for a little longer. Maurice
assured his father that he and Flora were both ready 'to make
an attempt at plain living and high thinking' in a cottage at
Wadestown: 'scrubbing and washing of course would be done by

outsiders and I should do the wood chopping, water fetching, fire lighting etc'.[74] Tudor Atkinson wished to postpone marriage until his law partnership in Wellington with R. Clement Kirk had become established, but Arthur urged him not to delay. Alla was twenty-eight; her child-bearing years, free of complications, would be limited. 'I have hitherto when contemplating our prospective marriage thought rather of the sweet companionship,' Tudor replied in a letter marked 'strictly private',

> but now I cannot fail to bear in mind the feature you have pointed to. Your own experience enables you to speak with authority, and I accept your statement regarding the increased difficulties & even danger perhaps which poor suffering woman is called upon to endure in postponing that cruel trial which all mothers have to bear.[75]

Both couples came together at St James during January 1887. 'We are glad and getting gladder every day,' Alla wrote. Flora effectively exorcised Mrs Rogers and was regarded as 'sweet, intelligent, unselfish, very pretty & full of character'.

> Where Tudor & I or Maurice & Flora sit to talk business together is always called the quarantine station & other persons approach very warily . . . Altogether there is a suffocating atmosphere of being engaged all over our house now-a-days, & to think that this should have come to us of all people – why when we arrived in New Zealand six years ago & Fanny Atkinson was to be married we thanked our stars we were not going to do anything so low ourselves.[76]

The double ceremony took place at Bishopdale Chapel on 12 May 1887. The fourteen bridesmaids all in 'apricot pink & veils' stood along the drive to the chapel. 'The bridegrooms not being well off for money did not give us any presents,' Emily's daughter, Emmie, wrote to Anna. Of the forty-three guests who sat down to a breakfast without ceremony, speeches, or champagne, all but Bishop Suter, his wife, and some teachers from the girls' college were family.

With the possible exception of Kit and Liza's, Maria saw no reason to doubt that any of the marriages of the second generation would be 'less happy than ours of the first'. 'Fancy what a different existence mine would have been had my Mother raised obstacles & kept me out of Arthur's way because he was young & poor,' she wrote.[77] She was therefore incensed when the following year the Blacketts, friends of the mob from Taranaki days, refused to countenance Dick Richmond's proposal for their daughter Isabel, Dolla's painting friend. Since farming at Motueka, Dick had widened his experience on a sheep run in Central Otago. Then with his father's help he and Billa[78] Atkinson had bought a property at Stoke where they intended to raise berry fruit. Emily, always inclined to see virtue in an assured income and a profession, must have supported the Blacketts. Maria, taking her stand on the family's good name and on her belief that young people 'of the right sort' should be allowed to make their own decisions, attacked. At sixty-four she had lost none of her style; the Blacketts joined 'rebellious' Maori and hapless British generals:

> It seems to me that the Bs [Blacketts] are quite as insulting to their own prize child as they are to Dick. If she were 16 & without taste, judgement or common sense one could understand its being 'a cruel wrong' to make her an offer, but really at her age when reason must have fully come unto her, if she is ever to have any it strikes me as insulting nonsense to speak in such a way. However I have not an ounce of patience with the Bs, if they had shown moderation & kindliness whilst objecting to D's poverty it would be different. I don't ever wish to see them or hear of their sayings & doings again until they are clothed in decency & in their right minds . . . By the bye if your idea and the Blacketts is correct, and a living is not to be made out of the soil of N.Z. even with a little capital & gt industry, the sooner all the young men pack their portmanteaux & move on the better, for there cannot be work in offices, banks & towns for long if the country is to be left depopulated & unproductive . . . How all the young lawyers are to find bread to say nothing of butter or cheese, is what puzzles me, but perhaps this is because I feel so much less inclined to spend money on going to law than on strawberries, tomatoes & other tempting fruit such as R. & A. of Stoke will shortly be offering.[79]

It seems a pity after such a spirited defence that Dick turned to dentistry and Georgina Pike, and Billa to establishing a preparatory school, Hurworth,[80] at Wanganui.

In 1888 Nelson celebrated Victoria's jubilee and Arf returned from England. For the first occasion 'everybody turned out in their best and all the country folk came to town'. The mayor, Charlie Fell, was up early fixing flagstaff and bunting to the St John's chimneys. In the town he hoisted the royal standard, proclaimed a public holiday, attended a church service, gave dinner to the oldest inhabitants, led the procession and, on its way, jumped over the fence to turn the first sod in the Queen's Garden. Edie presented medals and had, with Dolla, a more sedate day in her carriage. Guns were fired, *feux de joie* rattled out, thousands of buns, cakes, and sweetmeats were distributed. Even Arthur '*processed*', putting himself in charge of a group of college boys who were without a leader. Their headmaster, W.J. Ford, being 'too grand & uncolonial' gained by his 'stupid gentility the character of being disloyal as an Irishman'.[81] The evening illuminations were dimmed when a real fire broke out, only to be quickly quelled by the firemen taking part in a torchlight procession.

Arf returned to Nelson after having eaten his dinners and being called to the bar of Lincoln's Inn. To the surprise of his friends and relations he had not graduated from Oxford with first class honours, which fact Alla attributed to vegetarianism. Maria had also had expectations of her son's friendship with a fellow student, Agnes Cawker, who seemed from his description 'a very sensible, original & fine natural girl'. Arf, however, was indignant at her suspicions, as they seemed 'to imply doubts of the possibility of real friendship between young people of opposite sexes!'[82] Henry Newbolt, a contemporary at Corpus Christi, described him as an expert classicist. 'But his most unusual talent was for irony, parody and subtle argumentative traps.'[83] Right down to vegetarianism and an abhorrence of alcohol (although he ate at accepted times), Arf was his father's son. To a degree the fondness of both Arf and Arthur for 'argumentative traps' was self-defeating. Both were clever, able men who would have enjoyed a longer period in the House if they had not been the despair of friends and supporters.

Following in the footsteps of his cousins, Arf became William Richmond's secretary, but neither 'Uncle Judge' nor his parents were convinced that the law satisfied his interests. 'He takes such a vivid interest in things,' William wrote to Emily. His room was strewn with newspapers, its walls decorated with caricatures of Salisbury, Balfour, and Joseph Chamberlain. 'If the country were only ready for it, or he had independent means, I should say journalism would suit his taste and powers,' Maria wrote.[84] She hoped that William would talk to his nephew about his future: 'It seems to me that sons cannot confide their real feelings & wishes to their parents, or else we are exceptionally unsympathetic in spite of our having no motive or desire in dealing with ours but that he should become a useful & happy man.'[85]

Arf continued to be his uncle's associate and remained undecided about his future for the next four years. He had 'nibbles' from Dunedin and Wellington law firms and considered school teaching. Maria thought him '*very* cool & deliberate about settling himself anywhere, tho' it seems to *me* high time he did so'. Arthur wrote to his sister:

From the time he went to Oxford I have been urging on him that
he must paddle his own canoe . . . I wd. always advise if he wanted
advice but . . . he must steer. He will be 26 in two months, when,
if not now, he ought to be good for something better than football![86]
Maria pointed to the moral of the story: 'never leave a son educating
for 8 years in England, especially when you have only one'.[87] In
January 1892, to his family's relief, Arf entered into partnership
with C.B. Morison of Wellington, adding yet another Richmond–
Atkinson connection to Wellington's legal fraternity.

Family comings and going increased towards the end of the decade.
'Our guests come indeed,' Maria commented, 'but eat even their
Xmas dinner with their carpet bags beside them.' William Shaen,
with either one or both daughters,[88] visited New Zealand in 1885.
His son, Godfrey, and two daughters, Margaret and Lily, came
out in 1890 and took Alice and Mary Richmond back with them
in September. For a brief period Godfrey Shaen and Mary Richmond
were engaged, but then Godfrey became ill and died. Mary, after
spending part of a year at Newnham College, returned to New
Zealand with Margaret and Lily in 1892. Alice Richmond remained
in England. Through the Shaens she had met Edward Jarman Blake,
a solicitor and Unitarian, whom she married at Midhurst, Sussex,
on 5 January 1892. William Richmond replied to his prospective
son-in-law's request for Alice's hand that separation was now
'painful to old people' but 'I own that your ancestral connection
with that small and despised body which through good and evil
report has maintained the possibility of a rational Christianity is
a comfort to me.'[89]

William and Emily had also moved about. In 1880 on a visit
to Fairfield, William walked over the hill to look at St Katherine's
and made the wistful remark, 'I shall not see trees of my planting
in any new spot.' He assumed on returning to New Zealand that
he would be circuit judge in Wellington. Instead, in July 1880,
he was appointed to Auckland where he acquired a house in Remuera
which Emily 'transformed' and where they settled down to enjoy
the 'beauty and salubrity' of its situation. Judge Gillies and William
must have later arranged a swap because by 1882 William was
back in Mulligan's Castle on Wellington Terrace; Emily remained
in Auckland. The following year he moved with Emily to Tinakori
Road, and in January 1888 made yet another move to 54 Brougham
Street, Mount Victoria. F. de J. Clere 'revamped' the house and,
as 'Windhover', it became William and Emily's final home together.

Emily continued to have the occasional falling out with her husband over money: 'I do wish I knew how to make you happy & make myself more to your mind but that is past praying for.'[90] They had nevertheless weathered through together, and William wrote a sonnet for Emily's fifty-second birthday which began, 'Dear partner, climbing with me side by side . . .' A shared commiseration which bothered Emily more than William was that none of their sons showed any promise of achieving distinction in their generation.

For some of the mob the end of the decade was a final departure. Margaret Taylor, the family's long-time confidante, had been in declining health since the mid-1880s. She was reported to be dangerously ill in May 1888 and died in June. James and Dolla determined to go to Europe to be with James Whittle. Maria disapproved: 'I have said my say to Jas & D but it is a sheer impossibility for him to understand the kind of strain there must be on D. alone in a foreign land with two old infirm men.'[91] Alla called it a 'mad expedition . . . One of you is sure to get ill.' But off James and Dolla went to Naples where Whittle now lived. They were unable to persuade him to come to New Zealand and returned alone. He died in 1890. 'I don't think I can ever want to go to Europe again & find it empty of him & Aunt Margie,' Alla wrote to Dolla. 'Dearest we *must* all live closer together.'[92]

At the end of 1890 Henry Richmond, youngest of the three brothers, died. He was on his way to Dunedin to consult with Dr Truby King, a former pupil of his Beach Cottage School, when he collapsed and died in Christchurch on 7 December. Maria thought he had looked tired for some years, and it was thought he may have had a brain tumour. Henry left few worldly goods and Emma[93] returned with her children to live with her parents.

> I hear Uncle William doesn't like his girls to go out in colours & has said Em is to wear black & white & he wishes to have a band on his arm & that the boys should too . . . I was very surprised . . . it doesn't mean anything to me. I think Uncle W. must feel as if he wanted to be extra particular because of dear Uncle Henry's having been uncared for so much when he was alive.[94]

'I am not sure that I feel internally any older,' Maria wrote to Emily on her sixty-fourth birthday,

> tho' I *am* conscious that only six years remain of my allotted span. Unless things happen to make me very miserable within that time I shall not be at all willing to depart, for life seems to get fuller

& fuller of interest each year & I want to see the children's children develop. How numerous they are becoming this year.[95] Her involvement in public affairs actually increased as she grew older. The Nelson Winter Debating Society met fortnightly, and Maria organised a ladies' section whose debates were taken very seriously by its members. Free trade was one subject for which Maria was a protagonist. 'By reading I make myself a much stronger Free Trader but I doubt whether I can convince the hazy minds of female opponents. N.B. I am not at all sure they are as hazy as many of our male politicians on the question.'[96] She also used the debating society to advance the cause of women's suffrage. She stood *in loco parentis* to the staff of Nelson College for Girls – 'Miss Watson is spending part of the holidays with us, & Miss Hamilton & Miss Morgan are coming in turns' – and encouraged her relatives to visit Fairfield: 'the beginning of Dec. will be just perfect for sitting on the hill reading & you can do your mending as well'. Harry Atkinson (he became Sir Harry in 1888) and Annie spent part of their last summer together there: 'They both enjoy the hill & the loveliness of Nelson at this season . . . This is a glorious one for the flowers & the promise of fruit.' She continued to read widely and she wrote copiously: 'I never give up a correspondent.' She also kept up with comment on New Zealand affairs, taking the *Monthly Review*, the *Zealandia* (a Dunedin monthly), and *The Citizen*, journal of the Forward Movement. Sometimes she doubted whether these periodicals were managed in a sufficiently business-like manner: 'I did grudge Ar's £5 towards it [*Monthly Review*] because no watering can keep it alive if it throws out no roots, & I greatly want the money for charity.'[97]

Maria would have greatly preferred Harry Atkinson to quit politics and preserve his health. However, he went into the 1887 election confident of regaining power. Maria hoped that whatever happened Richmond Hursthouse, who had only won narrowly in 1884, would at least defeat the 'loathsome Jack Kerr' at Motueka. But this time he was defeated, as he was again when he stood for Nelson City in 1893. 'It is at present a great disadvantage in NZ to be a gentleman, or to be supposed to be in any way connected with gentlefolk,' William commented.[98] Maria's attitude to the struggle of workers for improved conditions and to the emergent trade union movement was predictable; she separated the two. A group of workers battling in isolation was one thing – she and Arthur were 'longing for the dock labourers to win the day' in the London dock strike of 1889; when that strike gave an impetus to organised international trade union solidarity, she, like other elders of the mob, drew back. She attended a meeting in Nelson to discuss the maritime strike of 1890 and found it all 'very interesting',[99] but saw the dispute as simply adding to 'poor Harry's burden'. Trade unions, she considered, might ameliorate conditions but she would not concede unionists' right to organise in order to challenge government. 'It is a great trial to the working men's friends to see that by grasping at too much power the good the Unions might effect must be greatly delayed if not lost altogether.'[100] Unionists, however misguided, might be tolerated; anarchists could not. 'I cannot abide Anarchists & dynamite.'

Harry Atkinson's party, loosely labelled Conservative, was defeated in the 1890 election, although Harry had retained his Egmont seat. John Ballance, the Liberal Leader, took office and ready in the wings was his lieutenant, Richard John Seddon. Atkinson, now something of an embarrassment to both government and opposition, was sidelined as Speaker of the Legislative Council. He died while attending the council on 28 June 1892, aged sixty-one.[101] Arthur wrote to Emily:

> His end was like his life full of courage and kindliness, no distrust and no shrinking, no perturbation even. We were talking one morning at breakfast about his state [Arthur had visited him in April] and he said 'Of course I don't want to go, but when the Dr told me what it was [heart disease] it did not seem to affect me at all.'[102]

As for William: 'It is strange that an "eggshell" like me should outlast a powerful Highlander like Menzies,' he wrote to his daughter, Alice Blake, on the death of his friend J.A.R. Menzies. Increasingly frail, prey to bouts of asthma and bronchitis, William continued as a circuit judge and as a courteous bystander at Emily's crowded 'at homes'. His letters to Alice reveal his wry detachment from the direction in which New Zealand under 'Seddonism'[103] appeared to be heading.

> We are getting ahead famously in politics. Being, as we are, far ahead of both Europe and America in time we are bound to lead the world. We are going to have *Women's suffrage* (universal like men's), *Compulsory Conciliation* for making employers pay proper wages, *Prohibition* so that we may not let those wicked brewers go on *forcing* us to intoxicate ourselves . . . Militant temperance, recommended by Arfie in 'The Prohibitionist', we have, thank heaven, already. Militant vegetarianism is in the background and coming we hope. It is quite settled that the rich people are to

pay all the taxes and the poor people are to vote all the expenditure. Under this regime things will soon be righted. We have plenty of new statesmen coming into the field – carpenters, boiler-makers, printers etc, who for the salary of £240 per annum (which we hope shortly however to increase a little) will regulate all our affairs . . .

You see I am fast getting rid of my Tory prejudices, and only wish that all these young people of ours had begun sooner with their reforms, as some of us will scarcely live to see the beneficent effects of Social Democracy.[104]

In another letter he described Maria as 'cock-a-hoop' or rather 'hen-a-hoop' about women's suffrage. On the eve of enfranchisement, in September 1893, a 'monster meeting' was held at Nelson: 'The body of the hall filled with ladies – men in the gallery. Aunt Maria in great force.'[105] Maria spoke first; her speech was prudent, conciliatory, even admonitory. Her opening statement drew cheers from both floor and gallery: 'they stood in the proud position of the first women in this world allowed to exercise the franchise'.[106] She then thanked the men in both Houses 'who for 14 years had urged on the movement', citing John Ballance, John Hall, Julius Vogel, Harry Atkinson, Alfred Saunders, Richard Oliver; she was possibly glad that Richard Seddon was not an advocate. There were obviously many women for whom the franchise was a step away from the accepted relationship of helpmeet. To them she said, 'we must encourage each other'.

Many of us . . . are timid, and rightly so too. It was a heavy responsibility placed upon them, rather than a right . . . Not many of them were able to go into questions of policy or finance deeply, but they could all consider morality and honesty. They could ask themselves was a man upright, was he square, was he honourable, did he treat his family properly. Men thought lightly of these things, they only thought of their locality and their purses – they were satisfied if they got a line here or a road there, but, she said, such things would never build up a nation . . . It was not, she thought, they would do better than men, but they would do differently – they might not take the same high intellectual stand, but she thought they would educate.[107]

This was all very worthy, but only towards the end of her speech, on the question of voting being 'too masculine', did something of Maria's spirit with pen in hand come through. 'To record a vote was no more masculine than to send a telegram . . . They must then put aside all squeamishness.' Two of the speakers who followed were more forceful. Mrs Tullock ('a lady from Scotland') claimed 'women had been robbed of rights', and Miss Crump of the Temperance Movement stated that 'no favour had been granted, but rather a right, long withheld and long usurped'. The crux of the matter was that before the meeting only 240 out of approximately 2,300 Nelson women who were eligible had registered. More did so afterwards. The *Colonist*'s view was that 'the great majority of women would vote the same way as their husbands and that therefore the extension of the franchise would be unlikely to lead to ill effects'.[108]

The enfranchisement of women would not have affected the return of Seddon in 1893. It was more apparent in the heavy vote for Prohibition in Wellington, Christchurch, and Dunedin in the 1894 licensing poll. In Wellington A.R. Atkinson had thrown himself into the 1893 election to campaign for three Wellington City candidates who were endorsed by the temperance ticket.[109] His advocacy of Prohibition,[110] however, cost him his partnership and at least a £1,000 a year. Morison and Atkinson could have purchased W.B. Edward's practice when the latter became a judge, but some of Edward's richest clients were brewers and 'men of the Trade . . . who would not have anything to do with a fanatic like Arf'.[111] Morison terminated the partnership. Arf was not dismayed. 'It is often our duty to stand in our own light . . . but the thought of standing in other people's is odious.[112]

The Forward Movement led by the Congregational minister, W.A. Evans, and, in particular, its journal, *The Citizen*, took up much of A.R. Atkinson's time. Evans described the movement as 'the expression in modern terms of the true Evangelical faith', Atkinson as 'the application of a robust and militant Christianity to politics'. *The Citizen*, to which Arf, Maurice Richmond, and Mary Richmond all contributed, carried articles on civic duty, economic policy, social justice, political corruption, and the 'new' woman.

Arthur Atkinson himself stood for Wellington City in 1896. Neither his mother nor his father was optimistic about his chances in the prevailing climate. 'I can't believe Arf will get in because he is far too outspoken & enthusiastic for the classes, & his name & good education brand him as a Tory to the masses,'[113] wrote Maria. Arf was difficult to label. He was against Seddon but not for Opposition leader W.R. Russell or any of the others from the rump of Harry Atkinson's old party; he particularly disliked being called 'the rising hope of the Conservatives'. He was prepared to devote his life to an uphill struggle for political and social causes, yet always found politicking 'great sport'. He knew his chance of success would be better if he stood for Wellington Suburbs but told Maria, 'Of course it would be much better fun fighting in town . . . There would be some fun in slamming Seddon before large and lively meetings.'[114] Ruth and Mabel came from Fairfield to help in their brother's campaign. He was narrowly defeated. 'Arf was well supported by the "toffs" which ought to please you,' Maria wrote to Emily, 'but this did not alienate the Pros [Prohibitionists]. Admiring relatives & friends wrote glowing accounts of his good speeches & the pluck & good temper he showed thro' barracking & interruptions . . . So anyway Arf has made a very successful debut in politics.'[115]

'Clouds of mortality are gathering thickly around us', William wrote to Alice Blake in June 1894. The clouds were gathering about both generations. Anna Richmond had made the pilgrimage to Dr Kidd in 1886 to consult him about a lingering malaise. Like many of William's children she was also an asthmatic. In England she became worse and when she returned to New Zealand Alla described her as 'thinner & prettier & invaly-er, but very cheerful'. The cause of her illness was never diagnosed; she remained an invalid for the rest of her life.[116] Ted Richmond, William and Emily's youngest son, practised as an architect in partnership with F. de J. Clere in Wellington. He contracted tuberculosis and left New Zealand for New South Wales. For Christmas 1894 he returned to his family and spent a last holiday with his father at Paradise, Lake Wakatipu; both were watched over by Mary.

> Mary (dear child) . . . is always looking after us. Even on the hottest days she tries (and fights) to muffle me up in woolly wraps and brings out the black goggles whenever the mountains are looking splendidly bright. I have been trying various sketches but have been able to finish nothing.[117]

Ted died in New South Wales in 1896. In August 1895 William was again laid low by one of his recurring bouts of bronchitis. Maria hoped that his 'elastic constitution' would carry him through, but she had no wish for his life to be preserved in 'suffering & privation when all its joy & usefulness are gone'. He died at Windhover on 5 August 1895. Just a fortnight before his final illness William had been at Fairfield enjoying 'lovely weather' and the company of the Fell children. 'How bright & vigorous his mind was,' Maria wrote to Emily. 'He spoke cheerfully of the end of his life as not far off. I am more thankful than I can say for that sunny bright week he spent here.'[118]

Failing health had caused James Richmond to resign from the Legislative Council in 1892.[119] He spent his last years at St James, looked after devotedly by Dolla who kept a notebook of his increasingly eccentric sayings. He died on 19 January 1898 while visiting Alla and Tudor Atkinson, who were then living at Otaki. At the end of April in the same year his youngest son, James Wilson, who had become a railway engineer in the Public Works Department, died suddenly, probably of peritonitis. 'He was so madly heroic,' Alla wrote, 'yet he seemed to melt away like thin air.'[120]

Old age niggled Maria. Rheumatism in her knees prevented her from going on long walks and 'lawyers' incomes being affected by these very dull times', Arthur and she could afford to hire a pony chaise only occasionally. Maria thought about a tricycle: 'Cycling is quite the rage here giving the younger folk great enjoyment & improving women's health . . . I quite believe I could work a light tricycle with pneumatic tires, but am afraid it would be too expensive a luxury to experiment on.'[121] Maria had seldom in New Zealand been a regular church-goer. But at Nelson in the 1890s a succession of able and thoughtful ministers who spoke always of the 'practical application of Christianity' and were, moreover, ardent protagonists of the temperance cause gave her 'much satisfaction'. In fact, with F.W. Chatterton (Anglican), W.A. Evans (Congregational), F.W. Isitt (Methodist), and G. Gray (Baptist) there was an embarrassment of riches for Sunday services. She was inclined to favour William Evans who in Kate Edger, former headmistress of Nelson College for Girls, had a wife whose good sense equalled his own. When Evans left for Wellington in 1893, Maria turned to R.S. Gray the Baptist minister whose family became close personal friends. 'We shall remain Baptists,' she wrote in 1902, 'unimmersed of course.'

Visits to nieces and nephews took Maria occasionally from Fairfield. In 1896 she was away for ten weeks at Wellington, Taranaki, and Otaki where Alla and Tudor reared their young children in what one of them later described as 'virgin New Zealand teeming with variety and wonder'.[122] Back at Fairfield she wrote to Emily about her young folk:

It would be hard to say that any one of them is not a favourite & worthy to be so. They were all most flatteringly glad to have me, & affectionate, which made my various visits quite a treat. The grand nieces & nephews are most interesting & promising young creatures, & add immensely to the pleasure of living beyond my natural span.[123]

It was now Arthur who was ageing; he was slightly deaf, rheumaticky, and still a faddist about food. 'For fanatical faddism,' Maria once wrote, 'there is no match for a true born Atkinson.'[124] There was as yet nothing the matter with his mind. His ridicule of posturing, whether by a British officer, a politician, or, as in this case, by a Maori 'scholar', could still by devastating. In 1892 he mounted an attack on Edward Tregear's *Maori–Polynesian Comparative Dictionary* (1891). 'The weak point, as it seemed to me, in Mr Tregear's work lay in the fact that the learned author had not waited to learn the Maori language before beginning to write his Maori dictionary.'[125] Arthur criticised Tregear's work in detail in three papers read before the Nelson Philosophical Society, which later published them as *Notes on the Maori–Polynesian Comparative Dictionary of Mr E. Tregear* (1893). When Arthur sent this to the governors of the New Zealand Institute (of whom Tregear was one), the board took refuge in the sophistry that as Atkinson's papers were not in manuscript it would neither print them in the *Transactions* nor comment on them. T.M. Hocken described Arthur's criticism (which was in essence supported by Archdeacon W.L. Williams and John White) as 'severe, cynical [?] and accomplished'.[126] Maria wished that Arthur would leave his office work and live at Fairfield with his trees, spiders, Maori studies, and telescope. 'Dearest Uncle Arthur,' Alla wrote to him, 'do try to stay with us younger ones for many years yet – indeed we cannot spare you – and I am so afraid, if you don't eat & rest enough (I know you are laughing . . .) you may get very ill. It seems such a waste of these precious years that are left us all together.'[127]

Mabel went to England between 1893 and 1895 to train as a midwife. On her return she went to Wellington Hospital for a general training. 'She is learning literally nothing,' Maria wrote, '& spoiling her hands for massage & real nursing by 8 hours hard charwoman's work daily.'[128] The hospital had been quite different when Ruth had earlier learned to nurse victims of typhoid and other complaints in a short four-months' course. Maria persuaded Mabel to leave and to learn from taking Dr Mackie's cases *gratis* in Nelson. He also taught her dispensing.

On 10 June 1897 Maria unveiled the Nelson College honours board; on 27 November 1899 she and Jane Gully opened a retrospective exhibition of J.C. Richmond and John Gully sketches and paintings in the Suter Art Gallery.[129] Mrs Gully wished to decline the offer but was told she need say nothing, only open a door, as Mrs Arthur Atkinson would be the spokeswoman. The

latter, never so confident on her feet as with a pen, wrote in haste
to Dolla: 'I am not in the least artistic, or aesthetic & have no
Ruskin from which to extract some appropriate quotation. Do write
a few sentences & something from Ruskin, or I must run away,
or be taken ill before the 27th.'[130] In the event Jane Gully managed
a few words and Maria spoke without benefit of Ruskin. Next
day the *Colonist* reported that there was a large attendance for
a 'function of this kind'. Maria said that James had been entirely
self-taught and that there was no reason why any young person
in Nelson with the same love of art and real spirit should not
rise to the same level. 'There were many in the Colony who
considered that the want of advantages prevented such a rise . . .
there was more advantage in being forced to go direct to nature.'
In similar vein she wrote to Emily about 'a delightful letter' Edie
had read from her stepdaughter, Lily Fell.

> It quite did my heart good to hear it after all that is said of the
> advantages of art & high civilization & the way some girls consider
> home ties, duties & affection mere dust in the balance when weighed
> against European culture & advantages. I had far rather my children
> & grandchildren grew up loving dunces than have them value
> intellectual gains as the supreme objects to be striven for in life
> . . . I believe that in helping to train the musical talent & taste
> of dwellers in this obscure corner of the world, Lily has a higher
> career before her than in remaining to enjoy the most exquisite
> music Europe can produce, for at the same time she will have
> a home life to keep her heart & sympathies warm.[131]

Arf, she was beginning to fear, was just such a one whose 'intellectual
gains' had been made at the expense of home life.

In 1898 Arf began working closely with 'Miss Kirk' of the
Women's Christian Temperance Union.[132] The following year
letters to 'Miss Kirk' in his letterbook became more frequent, longer,
and full of erudite references to Greek and Latin authors, as well
as to immediate meetings and lectures. One comes to realise that
they are, if not quite love letters, then partnership letters between
a colonial Sidney and Beatrice Webb. Lily's to Arf begin, 'Dear
Sir', his to her 'Dear Madam'; they refer to each other as 'agitators'.
Lily Kirk was proven – efficient, knowledgeable, abreast of politics
(she was often in the gallery of the House), and committed. When
she became 'his betrothed' Arf wrote of her to one of the Shaen
sisters.

> The lady (Miss Kirk) is a prodigy of talent, public & private. She
> spent last year touring for the N.Z. Alliance, and did as good work

as anybody we had . . . She is a beautiful platform speaker & as strong off the platform where so many good platform hands are weak.[133]

Arf was determined to stand for Wellington City in the 1899 elections,[134] 'even if it costs me my last copper'. His letters to Maria are full of the political manoeuvres; she was more inclined to worry about his health. He saw his best chance for success as an independent opposition candidate.

There is absolutely no ground for hope in the official opposition and their Parliamentary incapacity has undoubtedly strengthened Seddon's hold . . . [Russell's forces] make such a miserable display that I feel no regret at the action of the National Ass. wirepullers here in continuing to regard me as an outsider. I shall be safer as well as freer as I am.[135]

His campaign committee was mostly women 'and nearly all of them real workers', Mary, Margie, Dolla (Alla was at Otaki), and the Kirk sisters among them: 'Miss C [Cybyle] Kirk says all Dolla needs to do to capture votes is to smile.' Atkinson was one of the three members elected for Wellington City. Arf and Lily's wedding took place in a friend's house, with Rev. Frank Isitt officiating, on 11 May 1900. Mabel and Ruth prepared the couple's Wadestown house by laying fires and table and 'putting potplants all over the place'. There was no honeymoon or 'wedding journey'. Within a day or two Lily was off campaigning.

In the middle of Arf's election year, Maria was Nelson's delegate to a New Zealand Alliance rally at Wellington. 'We all greatly enjoyed her visit,' Arf wrote to his father, '& thought her younger than ever.' Arthur's health, however, had deteriorated and he suffered a stroke which affected his power of speech. Edie asked Alla to come for a visit. 'I dreaded meeting beloved Uncle Arthur but he was cheerful, recognised me & understood everything but can't give expression to ideas in his mind,' as she later wrote.[136] He was also 'a little stout': for the first time in his life he was eating all that was put before him. Maria had also been ill and was depressed because under doctor's orders she was confined to the Fairfield garden. 'But the thing is,' Alla continued to Dolla, 'Aunt Maria doesn't like giving up gardening & lifting & walking into town & going to meetings & concerts & Edie thinks that if it were not for Uncle Arthur & her great desire to survive him she would go on as usual & some day just die in an instant.'[137]

Alla was appalled at Ruth and Mabel's attitude to their father. Ruth was busy spring cleaning: 'I wonder if she is too busy to ever be anything else.' Mabel tried to manage him in trifles that did not matter, and both treated him far too much as if he were a 'lunatic': 'I feel that Uncle Arthur wants them more than all besides – probably he could understand and appreciate a loving touch.' This was the real tragedy at Fairfield; the pattern was set. Arthur, absorbed in his dictionaries and specimens, had shut himself away too often. Ruth and Mabel probably felt excluded from the intellectual companionship Arthur shared with Maria, and had protected themselves by being 'distracted by many tasks'. Maria understood this: 'Arthur *needs me*,' she told Alla. 'I don't know what would happen if I go'. For the meantime Alla, Maria, and Arthur sat together on the verandah or went with Edie for drives up into the Maitai Valley. It was spring and giant aspens were coming into leaf, hawthorn hedges into white blossom, and 'the sound of the cheerful river was pleasant to one's ears'. 'Uncle is very quiet always when he is driving.' Alla stayed with Edie and Charlie Fell at St John's. 'I felt nearer to her [Edie] than I have ever done, she has become so wonderfully gentle & tolerant. I used to shut up most of my thoughts when we were together years ago.'[138]

'Great news for Aunt Maria,' Alla wrote to Dolla (in England) on her return to Wellington, 'Arf and Lily hope for a baby in May.' Tudor and Alla, who came back from Otaki to Wellington in 1900, had seen little of Arf and Lily, and Alla was a little in awe of Arf's reputable wife: 'I was very grateful to her for not being the fierce prejudicial kind [of Prohibitionist].'[139] Lily wished to have a woman doctor attend her'; Alla, thinking Dr Elizabeth Platts 'nervous and inexperienced', recommended to Arf ('I don't think he regarded it as interference') Walter Fell. The baby arrived early – Lily had been lecturing just before the event – but all seemed well; the doctor (whether Fell or Elizabeth Platts) was highly pleased, the birth weight of twelve pounds was a record for the third generation, and (this for Arthur's sake) the baby was 'the right sort'. 'Sir Robert Stout anticipated that he would have brains,' Arf wrote to Maria, 'but I liked better Lady Stout's rejoicing that another fighter was born into the world.' The most striking of Tom's features were a 'square determined chin' and 'a singularly beautiful and clearly cut nose' inherited from both grandmothers. Tom lived for three days; his death was a mystery. Lily took the news with 'wonderful calmness'. After the funeral Arf heard for the first time, from Emily, how his mother had faced the loss of her first born.

By September 1902 Arthur was gradually taking in less and less of what was happening around him. 'Still he likes being read to & every now & then astonishes me with what he remembers of former events,' Maria wrote. He grew steadily weaker, suffered no pain, was very patient, and died on 10 December 1902. Alla was there and wrote to Dolla: 'How lonely it seems without the precious old people – they don't seem old to me but . . . they stand for so much that no one else can be to us . . . I am glad I knew & loved him & was not afraid of him.'[140] Rev. R.S. Gray, the Baptist minister, took a simple service in the Fairfield drawing room. It was all too simple and extempore for Alla, who wanted 'a Martineau or a F.D. Maurice at least'. After the funeral Arf read 'cheerful things' and 'Aunt Maria's colour returned'; Alla also noted that Maria and her daughter-in-law were very fond of each other. Miss Bremner, a devoted family retainer, insisted on sewing for Maria who, as was customary, would now be in mourning garments. As she had long looked 'dignified in black' these would not have been distasteful, except for the widow's cap which she had always hated. Miss Bremner effected a compromise.

Arthur had died at sixty-nine. Maria lived in reasonable health and interested in what was happening about her until she was ninety. Arf kept her fully informed of the political scene in Wellington, although after the general election of 1902 he was no longer in the House. He had, Alla thought, so demolished his opponent that he created sympathy for him. If only, besides being amusing and clever, he could be 'harmonious'.

> We are all angry because when Arf was invited . . . to take part in the reception [to a returning Seddon] & asked if he wanted tickets for the banquet, instead of politely declining, he has gone out of his way to give [the committee] a slap in the face. Of course his letter was amusing & clever but so terribly impolitic & so unnecessary, not to say undignified. I *wish* he wouldn't do such things, it is heart rending to his friends.[141]

In the style of a 'true born Atkinson' he wrote to his mother: 'I could be Attorney General . . . if I took the right course; or if that sounds too arrogant, let me say that I know which is the way up, and I'm not taking it.'[142]

Maria's private income of £300 a year enabled her to stay at Fairfield, where she had her own garden with her favourite flowers – roses, poppies, and calendula. She continued to take as keen an interest as ever in her mob, now well into its third generation, and her visits to Wellington were greedily devoured. 'Aunt Maria thanks-be-praised is giving us a fortnight of her blessed presence – she is so well & so unsurpassable delightful.'[143] During this visit she went across the harbour on the ferry to Walter and Margaret Fell's holiday cottage at Mahina Bay. Their son, Christopher, collected her at Days Bay and rowed her over to Mahina. On her return, she travelled to Tudor and Alla's house in Gladstone Terrace by the Kelburn tram in which 'Auntie hardly turned a hair'. 'She is rather tired so she is reading a short story in Harper instead of an article in the Nineteenth century & is not writing to anybody for a change.'[144]

During another visit Alla wrote, 'She is splendidly well & very beautiful, an ivory bas-relief ought to be made of her head I often think as I watch her. I like to tell how beautiful she is – she is delightfully scornful about it.'[145] Two months later she was back in Wellington again, this time as the Nelson representative in a delegation led by Rev. F.W. Isitt to meet Seddon and request an amendment to the licensing laws. 'We are all hoping Aunt Maria may have to speak & wishing we could be hidden to hear her – even to see her shaking hands or bowing before the great man would be worth a good deal.'[146] Lily and Arf's daughter, Janet, was born alive and well towards the end of 1904. In a diary in which each new word and development was recorded Lily noted that at four and a half months, 'Janet constantly turned her head to her grannie's portrait laughing & jumping towards it.'

Emily Richmond moved from Windhover in 1905 and took a house in Hobson Street with Mary and Emmie, her youngest daughter. Mary Richmond was now a person of some eminence in Wellington. She had gone to England again in 1896 to study the development of Froebel's kindergarten system. On her return she began a kindergarten school in Wellington. She also wrote nature poetry which was published in the newspapers and her advice on women's affairs was frequently sought. Like Maria she held together a belief in the importance of higher education for women and of its use within the family: 'Girls do not think that the cleverer you are in the halls of the University the stupider you should be in the kitchen.'[147] Emily's last letter to Maria, written a few weeks before her death on 28 November 1906, began: 'My very dear Maria, What a lively person you are', and went on to detail the latest gossip about the family: how Dolla was going to take charge of Annie A. 'which some of us fully believe will kill her'; how Mary was teaching her kindergarten boys to be good fathers, and that

if Maria meant to come over 'do tell me in time as our house
is generally packed but you could have the study & a tin bath
in it'.[148] Kit Richmond, who with his wife and two children now
lived precariously in a Sydney suburb, wrote to Mary about his
mother after her death.

> Poor dear old warrior how I loved her and fought her. What a
> glorious wild nature . . . her waywardness was part of her eternal
> youth. Her strength of hate and scorn was marvellous & her coinage
> of phrase & epithet was the work of a woman of great intellectual
> power . . . Her illiteracy never troubled her for an instant. She
> bravely tackled some of the heaviest reading, and . . . got out of
> it, and could give you much more than the host of professional
> critics and pedants.[149]

Maria must have always realised, because they remained close friends
in spite of tiffs, that under the acquired social veneer there remained
'the child of nature'.

Maria lived for another eight years, surviving every other member
of the first generation except Annie Atkinson. A trickle of letters
remain; it is obvious that rheumatism, arthritis, and failing eyesight
laid hold of her; photographs show her increasingly bent. It is
unnecessary, even if it were possible, to probe further. She would
have greatly enjoyed the notebook diaries[150] which Alla sent back
to New Zealand during a visit to England in 1913. Alla wrote
at length and daily; the diaries intended mainly for her children
were also passed around the family, beginning with Fairfield. If
ever proof was needed that Alla inherited Maria's joy of living
and of writing (although she was seldom as vehement in her
opinions), then it is in these quite delightful diaries. It seems fitting
that Maria's last letter quoted here should be a thank-you one
to Alla. The words are carefully, even laboriously formed, but
the spirit is unchanged.

> Dearest Alla, What a precious gift of God is humour! Your delightful
> letters do me more good than tonics or stimulants. I must send
> you a few lines to thank you most heartily for them & say how
> much they are appreciated. For the first time since I came back
> [from Wellington] I am basking in the sunshine which I believe
> may do me more good than drugs.[151]

Maria died at Fairfield on 29 September 1914. Alla heard the
news when she and Tudor were on their way back from England.
It was Dolla who wrote of the last day.

> . . . darling Aunt Maria [is] slipping quietly away from us. Dr
> Gibbs thinks she can't last more than a day. We all sit in her room

& talk gently to one another – there is a sweet little nurse & Faith [one of Ruth's adopteds] runs in & out & thinks everything is all right.[152]

Outside Fairfield, Nelson was responding to the excitement of war: Ruth was already a member of the Belgian Relief Fund committee; Mabel was to go overseas as a VAD; various members of the mob's second and third generation were to be killed in action. None of this would have impinged on Maria's fleeting moments of consciousness. Instead she might have glimpsed again the blue-green bush of Hurworth, the mountain soaring above, or recognised a figure scrambling down the banks of Te Henui or galloping Lallah Rookh along the New Plymouth foreshore; there might have been a flash of sunlight on calendula, on cherry blossom, on hawthorn, or filtering through the high trees of Fairfield – momentary passing images of her 'bright clear land'.

Sources

Richmond, Atkinson and Related Collections

Other sources are cited in the reference notes for each chapter.

The bulk of the various collections consisting of letters, journals, lectures, speeches, reports, photographs, sketches, drawings, and miscellaneous manuscript and printed material is in the Alexander Turnbull Library, Wellington. The Turnbull also holds papers of the related Hursthouse and Stephenson Smith families. Of these Turnbull collections, the largest and most important is Richmond–Atkinson family ms papers, Acc 77–253. References from this material are cited in italics.

Some explanation of the history of this collection is necessary in order to understand the source references to bound volumes, additional letters, and, in particular, the use of the odd term 'discards'.

Towards the end of last century Maurice W. Richmond (son of J.C. Richmond) and S. Arnold Atkinson (son of H.A. Atkinson) began making notes and collecting material for a biography of Sir Harry Atkinson. The biography was not proceeded with, but papers were gathered together and family reminiscences were written down. This large mass of material was eventually held by Mary and Emily Richmond, C.W. Richmond's two unmarried daughters, who lived until 1949 and 1960 respectively. The two sisters prepared and Emily Richmond edited a two-volume typescript of some of the family letters, including many from Jane Maria Atkinson. These are now Volumes 38 and 39 of the Richmond–Atkinson family ms papers, Acc 77–253. Originals of many but not all of these letters are in the first six bound volumes of this collection. In the late 1940s Mary and Emily Richmond gave the papers they held, 'as a gift to the nation', into the hands of Dr Guy H. Scholefield, then chief librarian of the General Assembly Library. The first batch of papers consisted of letters and a miscellany of other documents as well as bound volumes of family diaries and letterbooks. The General Assembly Library arranged the loose material chronologically and bound it in ten folio volumes. The remaining already-bound volumes, mostly diaries, were numbered 11 to 47. A later deposit by Emily Richmond almost equalled that already received. These 'additional' letters and papers remain unbound; they are cited by the year and serial number given them by Dr Scholefield.

Working from the bound volumes and the additional letters, Dr Scholefield edited *The Richmond–Atkinson Papers*, published in two volumes by the Government Printer in 1960. Letters from the 'additional' deposit which he did not use he called 'discards'. In his introduction he stated that 'Mere gossipy passages' were not considered 'worthy of reproducing'. Frequently these 'discards' contain important social comment, particularly about women. Dr Scholefield defaced the letters and journals he used by crossing out, either in ink or coloured pencil, all sections he did not wish to be published. He also rewrote the date (occasionally incorrectly) and frequently added or appended his own notes to the manuscript. This was also done to a lesser extent by Emily Richmond. These markings, however, have not significantly impaired legibility. The General Assembly Library kept Dr Scholefield's 'discards' with the collection.

In May 1977, as part of a transfer of archival material from the General Assembly (now Parliamentary Library) to the Alexander Turnbull Library, the Richmond–Atkinson family ms papers were lodged with the latter library. This collection, Acc 77–253 (ATL), has not yet been catalogued, nor does it have a preliminary listing, and although freely available to researchers still bears the references bequeathed by Dr Scholefield. The following is a summarised inventory of this collection:

Vols. 1–6. 1827–48, 1848–51, 1852–57, 1858–59, 1860–61, 1862–69: Family letters and letters mainly to C.W. Richmond from other public figures of the day including Gore Browne, Domett, Bell, Stafford, McLean, Sewell, Weld, and from Revs Hadfield, Maunsell, Morgan, and Whiteley.

Vol. 7 Mainly letters from H.A. Atkinson to his brother, A.S. Atkinson.

Vols. 8–10 Miscellaneous papers including drafts of lectures by C.W. Richmond, reports on 'Native' policy, C.W.R. warrants of appointment, and obituary notices. Vol. 9 includes notes on family history.

Vols. 11–12 Typed copies of C.W. Richmond's letter copybooks which also exist in manuscript as Vols. 41 & 42.

Vol. 13 Abridged copies of J.M. Atkinson's first four 'General Letters' and C.W. Richmond's ship journal.

Vols. 14–24 Diaries of C.W. Richmond, Maria (Lely) Richmond, Emily E. Richmond (née Atkinson), and H.A. Atkinson.

Vols. 25–36 A.S. Atkinson diaries covering the years 1847–May 1868.

Vol. 37 Bound with 31A.

Vols. 38–39 'Family Letters of the Richmonds and Atkinsons, 1842–62', edited by Emily Richmond. Many of these letters are from J.M. Atkinson; originals for some are in Vols. 1–6 or in the additional letters. Others survive only in this typescript.

Vol. 40 'The Aspective Review', 1855 & 1857.

Vols. 41–42 C.W. Richmond's ms Letter copybooks, 1854–59, 1859–75.

Vol. 43 H.A. Atkinson's outward (official) correspondence, 1880–82.

Vols. 44, 46–47 Miscellaneous material relating mainly to C.W. Richmond, J.C. Richmond, and H.A. Atkinson.

Vol. 45 C.W. Richmond's sketch book.

Acc 77–253 also includes:

Additional letters, many from J.M. Atkinson (7 boxes)

Discards (2 boxes)

Box of miscellaneous, undated letters, many from J.M. Atkinson. Two A.S. Atkinson diaries are not included in this collection as they were donated separately:

Arthur Samuel Atkinson Diary, 2 April 1865–24 Aug. 1866, MS sequence, ATL;

Arthur Samuel Atkinson Nelson Journal, 16 March 1877–2 Feb. 1878, MS sequence, ATL.

Other Richmond and Atkinson MS collections held by the Alexander Turnbull Library

Richmond Family Papers, Acc 77–173

These are not catalogued but a preliminary listing exists for the 68 boxes of letters. The correspondence is mainly between members of the second generation.

Richmond Family Papers, Acc 84–56

A preliminary listing exists for the 7 boxes of letters and diaries mainly related to Mary and Emily Richmond.

Richmond Family Papers, Acc 85–50

Of marginal relevance; mainly concerned with genealogies. A preliminary listing exists.

Sir Harry Atkinson, MS Papers 91

There is a full inventory for this collection

Arthur Richmond Atkinson, MS Papers 204
    Letterbooks 1896–99, 1899–1902. These include letters to his mother, J.M. Atkinson. Inventory.
Arthur Samuel Atkinson Papers lodged with the Polynesian Society, MS Papers 1187
    Correspondence related to Polynesian linguistics. Inventory.
Arthur Samuel Atkinson Maori Letters, MS Group 31.
    There is an inventory for this group.

Related family papers in the Alexander Turnbull Library

Hursthouse Papers
    Diary of John Hursthouse 1841–43. q MS sequence
    A typescript copy of this was produced in 1983 by Peggy Griffiths and Jinny Atkinson.
Stephenson Percy Smith Papers
    'Reminiscences of a pioneer surveyor from 1840 to 1916'. q MS sequence.
    'Chronicles of the Crompton-Smith family of New Zealand, compiled by S. Percy Smith. New Plymouth, 1902', 2 vols. Acc 88–362.
The Photographic Archive (ATL) holds various Richmond-Atkinson family groups in its two C.Y. Fell albums, as well as daguerreotype copies of family members on the eve of departure for New Zealand.
The Drawings and Prints Collection (ATL) holds C.W. Richmond's sketch book, various J.C. Richmond sketches and drawings, and copies of his work held privately or in other libraries and galleries.

Collections held in other institutions

Dunedin Public Library
    A.H. Reed collection, 32 letters from various Richmonds and Atkinsons
Nelson Provincial Museum
    Charles Yates Fell, 'Autobiography', written from St John's, Nelson, 1 July 1913 (Betts Collection).
    Charles Yates Fell photographic album
Taranaki Museum
    Hursthouse Family Letters 1788–1854 MS 042 (Microfilm held by ATL, Micro MS 449)

Private Collections

Jinny Atkinson Collection

A) Letters by C.W. Richmond 1824–34; letters from J.M. Atkinson, J.C. Richmond, Margaret Taylor, E.T. Atkinson, D.K. Richmond, A.E. Richmond, M.W. Richmond

B) Seventy-two (some missing) Notebook Diaries 1913–14, A.E. Atkinson

C) Ronalds Papers: Letters 1853–60 Ts from Hugh, Frank, and James Ronalds to their father and mother; reminiscences of Eliza and Marion Atkinson (née Ronalds); handwritten copies (1903) of 11 letters together with some notes about Hurworth.

D) Photographic collection: a large holding of family groups, portraits, and original daguereotypes.

E) Drawings, paintings, and sketches by J.C. Richmond and D.K. Richmond. This group forms a part of the Atkinson Family Collection.

Ann Paterson MS Collection

Letters from Helen and Kate Hursthouse 1860–64

Letters from J.C. Richmond 1862–67

Letters from J.M. Atkinson mainly 1867

Letters from Maria Richmond

Elsie Crompton-Smith Collection

Photocopies of the Hursthouse Family Letters 1788–1854 held by the Taranaki Museum.

Notes

References to *Richmond–Atkinson family ms papers, Acc 77–253 (see Sources), are cited in italics.*

Chapter One: A Modest Competence

1. C.W.R.–J.C.R., 12 June 1842, *Richmond–Atkinson family papers, Vol.1 p.67.*
2. Richmond names can be confusing. Maria Richmond (mother) was known within the family as Lely. Her daughter, Jane Maria, and her eldest son, Christopher William, were always referred to by their second names. I have retained this family nomenclature in the narrative although reference citations use the full initials.
3. Marcella Nugent–M.R. 28 June 1842, *Discards.*
4. Battescombe, Georgina and Laski, Marghanita (eds), 'Charlotte Yonge's Ethics: Some Unfashionable Virtues' in *A Chaplet for Charlotte Yonge* (Cresset Press, London, 1965), p. 22.
5. M.R.–Charles Hursthouse, 23 June 1838, Hursthouse Papers.
6. C.W.R.–M.R., 31 July 1841, *Vol.1, p.9.*
7. Helen Hursthouse–M.R., 4 June 1842, *Discards.*
8. Orr, John, *Unitarians in the Present Time* (London, 1863), p.5.
9. M.R.–Charles Hursthouse, 23 June 1838, Hursthouse Papers.
10. J.M.R.–Margaret Taylor, 21 July 1849, *Vol.2, p.14.*
11. Quoted in Mare, M.L. and Percival, A.C., *Victorian Best Seller: The World of Charlotte M. Yonge.* (Harrap, London, 1947) p.67.
12. C.W.R.–M.R., 4 May 1841, *Vol.1, p.4.*
13. *ibid.*, 13 July 1841, *Vol.1, p.8.*
14. N. Clegg–M.R., 20 June 1842, *Addl 1842/7.*
15. C.W.R.–M.R., 13 July 1841, *Vol.1, p.8.*
16. J.M.R.–M.T., 12 Aug. 1848, *Vol.1, p.110.*

17. Marcella Nugent–M.R., 23 Nov. 1841, *Discards.*
18. *ibid.*, 28 June 1842, *Discards.*
19. J.C.R.–C.W.R., Sept. 1841, *Vol.1, p.11.*
20. *idem.*
21. C.W.R.–M.R., 31 July 1841, *Vol.1, p.9.*
22. J.C.R.–M.R., 4 Jan. 1842, *Vol.1, p.15.*
23. Marcella Nugent–M.R., 9 Oct. 1841, *Discards.*
24. *ibid.*, 23 Nov. 1841, *Discards.*
25. Helen Hursthouse–M.R., 4 June 1842, *Discards.*
26. J.C.R.–M.R., 9 Oct. 1841, *Vol.1, p.13.*
27. . M.R.–C.W.R., 14 Feb. 1843, *Vol.1, p.48.*
28. J.M.R.–C.W.R., 18 Apr. 1843, *Vol.1, p.57.*
29. M.R.–C.W.R., 14 Feb. 1843, *Vol.1, p.50.*
30. J.M.R.–C.W.R., 18 Apr. 1843, *Vol.1, p.57.*
31. M.R.–Charles Hursthouse, 15 Apr. 1843, *Vol.38, pp.56–7.*

Chapter Two: 'Uncertainties & scheming'

1. Hannah Hursthouse married John Stephenson Smith, 1 May 1839.
2. William Stanger married Sarah Hursthouse, 27 Sept. 1842.
3. Wakefield, E.G., *A View of the Art of Colonization* (London, 1849), pp.135–6.
4. Dickens, Charles, chapter LVII, 'The Emigrants', *David Copperfield.*
5. Helen Hursthouse–M.R., 4 June 1842, *Discards.*
6. *idem.*
7. Charles Wilson–M.R., 22 Mar. 1842, *Addl 1842/5.*
8. J.C.R.–M.R., 17 Aug. 1842, *Vol.1, p.29.*
9. Catherine Wilson–M.R., 1 Aug. 1842, *Discards.*
10. Griffiths, Peggy and Atkinson, Jinny

(eds), 'Diary of John Hursthouse 1841–43' (privately printed 1983), 9 Jan. 1843.

11. Charles Wilson–M.R., 4 Dec. 1842, *Addl 1842/12.*

12. 'Diary of John Hursthouse', 31 Jan. 1843.

13. J.M.R. general letter no. 4, 13 Nov. 1853, *Vol.13.*

14. Helen Hursthouse–Charles Hursthouse, 18 June 1848, Hursthouse Family Letters.

15. The Hursthouse farm, Tarahua, on the Carrington has now been absorbed within the New Plymouth suburb of Vogeltown.

16. Smith, Stephenson Percy, 'Reminiscences of a pioneer surveyor from 1840 to 1916', p.17.

17. Helen Hursthouse–Catherine Wilson, 28 Sept. 1851, Hursthouse Family Letters.

18. In London post office directories of the 1840s, Carter Lane chapel is sometimes described as Presbyterian. During the nineteenth century English congregations of Presbyterian descent frequently inclined towards Unitarianism. If the minister and the more widely read held Unitarian views and could carry the trustees with them, the meeting often became Unitarian; the remainder of the congregation either accepting or seceding. Apparently Carter Lane was Unitarian by doctrine but Presbyterian by title.

19. J.M.R.–M.T., 3 July 1848, *Vol.1, p.108.*

20. *ibid.*, 4 Sept. 1848, *Vol.1, p.113.*

21. J.C.R.–C.W.R., 12 May 1864, *Addl 1864/30.*

22. J.M.R.–M.T., 17 June 1848 and 10 Aug. 1848, *Vol.1, pp.107 and 110.*

23. *ibid.*, 13 Apr. 1850, *Vol.2, p.34.*

24. *ibid.*, 28 Apr. 1850, *Vol.2, p.36.*

25. M.R.–M.T., 25 Sept. 1850, *Vol.2, p.43.*

26. J.M.R.–M.T., 22 Oct. 1848, *Vol.1, p.116.*

27. *ibid.*, 28 May 1849, *Vol.2, p.7.*

28. *ibid.*, 17 Feb. 1850, *Vol.2, p.30.*

29. Possibly 'Hargrave'. Maria referred to him as Charles or Chas, and Lely only by his initials.

30. J.M.R.–M.T., 4 Oct. 1848, *Vol.38, p.91.*

31. *ibid.*, 10 Aug. 1848, *Vol.1, p.110.*

32. *idem.*

33. *idem.*

34. J.M.R.–M.T., 25 July 1848, *Vol.1, p.109.*

35. J.M.R.–M.T., 25 July 1848, *Vol.1, p.109.*

36. *idem.*

37. J.M.R.–M.T., 3 July 1848, *Vol.1, p.108.*

38. *idem.*

39. J.M.R.–M.T., 10 Aug. 1848, *Vol.1, p.110.*

40. *ibid.*, 28 Sept. 1848, *Vol.38, p.87.*

41. *ibid.*, 24 Mar. 1849 and 10 Aug. 1848, *Vol.2, p.5 and Vol.1, p.110.*

42. *ibid.*, Jan. 1850, *Vol.38, pp.118–9.*

43. *ibid.*, Jan. 1850, *Vol.38, p.119.*

44. *ibid.*, 11 July 1849, *Vol.2, p.12.*

45. *ibid.*, 24 Dec. 1848, *Vol.1, p.120.*

46. *ibid.*, Jan. 1850, *Vol.38, p.119.*

47. *ibid.*, 3 July 1848, *Vol.1, p.108.*

48. *ibid.*, 28 Sept. 1848, *Vol.38, p.88.*

49. *ibid.*, 5 Dec. 1848, *Vol.38, p.94.*

50. *ibid.*, 24 Mar. 1849, *Vol.2, p.5.*

51. *ibid.*, 2 Mar. 1849, *Vol.2, p.3.*

52. *ibid.*, 10 July 1849, *Vol.2, p.12.*

53. *idem.*

54. J.M.R.–M.T., 24 Mar. 1849, *Vol.2, p.5.*

55. *ibid.*, 10 June 1849, *Vol.2, p.9.*

56. *ibid.*, 26 Aug. 1849, *Vol.2, p.16.*

57. *ibid.*, 9 Mar. 1850, *Vol.2, p.32.*

58. *idem.*

59. *idem.* H.D. Hutton practised law in Dublin.

60. J.M.A.–M.T., 3 Aug. 1870, *Addl 1870/9.*

61. J.M.R.–M.T., Jan. 1850, *Vol.38, p.119.*

62. *ibid.*, 10 Apr. 1850, *Vol.2, p.34.*

63. C.F. Hursthouse–Charles Hursthouse, 3 May 1848, Hursthouse Family Letters.

64. Helen Hursthouse–Charles Hursthouse, 18 June 1848, Hursthouse Family Letters.

65. *idem.*

66. J.M.R.–M.T., 26 Aug. 1849, *Vol.2, p.15.*

67. *idem.*

68. *idem.*

69. J.M.R.–M.T., 1 Nov. 1849, *Vol.2, p.26.*

70. *ibid.*, 1 June 1850, *Vol.2, p.38.*

71. *ibid.*, 21 June 1850, *Vol.2, p.40.*

72. *idem.*

73. Wakefield, E.G., *A View of the Art of*

Colonization (London 1849), pp.135–6.
74. Stevens, Joan (ed.), *Mary Taylor, Friend of Charlotte Brontë: Letters from New Zealand* (Auckland University Press, 1972), p.19.
75. J.M.R.–M.T., 25 Sept. 1850, *Vol.2, p.43.*
76. *ibid.*, 21 June 1850, *Vol.2, p.41.*
77. M.R.–M.T., 25 Sept. 1850, *Vol.2, p.43*

Chapter Three: 'Meetings & partings'

1. J.M.R.–M.T., 24 Mar. 1849, *Vol.2, p.6.*
2.. *ibid.*, 17 June 1848, *Vol.1, p.107.*
3. *ibid.*, 26 Aug. 1849, *Vol.1, p.15.*
4. Frindsbury, Strood, Rochester, and Chatham grew together to form a congeries of towns with the Medway River separating the first two from the others. This contiguity explains what would otherwise appear to be the Atkinsons' unusual ability to walk to all three from Frindsbury within a morning and to Gravesend and back during the afternoon.
5. J.M.R.–M.T., 1 June 1850, *Vol.2, p.38.*
6. Scholefield, G.H., *The Richmond–Atkinson Papers* (Government Printer, 1960), *Vol.1, p.25.*
7. J.M.R.–M.T., 6 Sept. 1849, *Vol.2, p.18.*
8. 'Family Notes', *Vol.9.*
9. *idem.*
10. J.M.R.–M.T., 26 Aug. 1849, *Vol.2, p.15.*
11. *ibid.*, 6 Oct. 1850, *Vol.2, p.57.*
12. *idem.*
13. M.R.–J.M.R., 15 Apr. 1851, *Vol.2, p.73.*
14. The palace was totally destroyed in the saturation bombing of Dresden at the end of World War II. East German art authorities have assiduously but unsuccessfully hunted for photographs of this frieze.
15. J.M.R.–M.T, 20 Oct. 1851, *Vol.38, p.142.*
16. *ibid.*, 1 Jan. 1852, *Vol.3, p.5.*
17. *ibid.*, 19 Apr. 1852, *Vol.3, p.11.*
18. M.R.–J.M.R., 11 Mar. 1851, *Vol.38, p.132.*
19. C.W.R. Diary, 23 May 1851, *Vol.14.*
20. J.M.R.–M.T., 20 Oct. 1851, *Vol.2, p.101.*
21. The intermediate passengers were divided into messes and James's job was to ensure that the basic rations were equitably divided.
22. Part of section 62 adjoining 75 on the 1848 'Plan of the Settlement of New Plymouth' (ATL).
23. H.R.R.–M.R., 25 Mar. 1851, *Vol.2, p.68.*
24. H.R.R.–C.W.R., 3 Apr. 1851, *Vol.2, p.71.*
25. *idem.*
26. J.M.R.–M.T., 20 Oct. 1851, *Vol.2, p.101.*
27. *ibid.*, 19 July 1851, *Vol.2, p.89.*
28. M.R.–M.T., 6 Aug. 1851, *Vol.2, p.94.*
29. J.M.R.–M.T., 19 Aug. 1851, *Vol.2, p.96.*
30. *ibid.*, 25 Sept. 1851, *Vol.38, p.141.*
31. *ibid.*, 1 Jan. 1852, *Vol.3, p.4.*
32. H.R.R.–J.M.R., 15 July 1851, *Vol.2, p.88.*
33. The New Plymouth Kings are confusing; there were at least three separate families. The ones referred to here were Samuel Popham King, his wife Mary, and his sisters, Martha and Maria.
34. J.C.R.–M.R., 31 Aug. 1851, *Vol.2, p.98.*
35. J.M.R.–M.T., 23 Aug. 1852, *Vol.3, p.8.*
36. *idem.*
37. J.C.R.–M.R., 2 Nov. 1851, *Vol.2, p.106.*
38. *ibid.*, 1 Dec. 1851, *Vol.38, p.228.*
39. H.R.R.–M.R., 18 May 1851, *Vol.2, p.79.*
40. In William's opinion C.F. Hursthouse, since his return to England, looked more like a semi savage than ever, 'so dirty, so hairy & uncivilized'. (M.R.–J.M.R., 15 Apr. 1851, *Vol.2, p.73.*
41. C.F. Hursthouse–C.W.R., *c.* Oct. 1850, *Addl 1850/1.*
42. C.W.R. Diary, 30 Apr. 1852, *Vol.15.*
43. J.M.R.–M.T., *c.* Apr. 1852, *Vol.3, p.13.*
44. C.W.R. Diary, 27 Apr. 1852, *Vol. 15.*
45. M.R. Diary, 1 May 1852, *Vol.16a.*
46. M.T.–J.M.R., 27 May 1852, *Vol.3, p.16.*
47. J.M.R.–M.T., 17 June 1852, *Vol.3, p.17.*
48. *ibid.*, 19 Aug. [1852], *Vol.2, p.96.*

49. C.W.R. Diary, 12 May 1852, *Vol.15*.
50. William was slightly built. Emily recorded in her diary after they were married that he was only nine stone nine pounds, she was ten, five.
51. J.M.R.–M.T., 17 June 1852, *Vol.3, p.17*.
52. *ibid.*, 11 Nov. 1851, *Vol.2, p.105*.
53. *ibid.*, 17 June 1852, *Vol.3, p.17*.
54. *ibid.*, 17 July 1852, *Vol.3, p.19*.
55. C.W.R. Diary, 2 Aug. 1852, *Vol.15*.
56. C.W.R. Diary, *Vol.15*, A.S.A. Diary, *Vol.29*.
57. C.W.R. Diary, 30 Aug. 1852, *Vol.15*.
58. M.R.–M.T., 8 Sept. 1852, *Vol.3, p.22*.
59. J.H. Hutton–C.W.R., 27 Aug. 1852, *Addl 1852/1*.
60. J.M.R.–M.T., 14 Aug. 1852, *Vol.38, p.151*.
61. J.M.R.–E.E. Atkinson, 27 Aug. 1852, *Addl 1852/10*.
62. J.M.R.–M.T., 28 Nov. [1852], *Vol.3, p.29*.
63. M.R.–M.T., 8 Sept. 1852, *Vol.3, p.22*.
64. J.M.R.–M.T., 12 Sept. 1852, *Vol.3, p.24*.
65. *idem*.
66. Two of the others, Mary Smith and her sister, Annie, were later to become the wives of James Richmond and Harry Atkinson respectively.
67. J.M.R.–M.T., 8 Sept. 1852, *Vol.3, p.21*.
68. *ibid.*, 27 Sept. [1852], *Vol.3, p.25*.
69. *ibid.*, 12 Sept. 1852, *Vol.3, p.24*.
70. *ibid.*, 31 Oct. 1852, *Vol.3, p.28*.
71. C.W.R. Diary, 23 Oct. 1852, *Vol.15*.
72. *idem*.
73. J.M.R.–M.T., 28 Nov. [1852], *Vol.3, p.29*.
74. *ibid.*, 6 Dec. 1852, *Vol.3, p.30*.
75. General Sir James Brind, Indian Army. His son James was the eldest of ten..
76. J.M.R.–M.T., 28 Nov. [1852], *Vol.3, p.29*.
77. *idem*.
78. J.M.R.–M.T., 6 Dec. 1852, *Vol.3, p.30*.
79. Written by Susan Warner under the pseudonym Elizabeth Wetherell, it proved very popular, although one would not have supposed it to the taste of either James Martineau or Maria. A later writer has commented, 'It was full of very interesting information and religion and a little

girl cried on nearly every page.' (Howard, E.J., *The Beautiful Visit*, Harmondsworth, Penguin, 1976, p.83).
80. Talked of but not negotiated between New Zealand, New South Wales and Panama until 1863. The proposed route allowed for the carriage of mail across the isthmus.
81. A composite extract from three sources: J.M.R.–M.T., 28 Nov. and 6 Dec. 1852, *Vol.3, pp.29 and 30*, 1 June 1850, *Vol.2, p.39*.
82. M.T.–J.C.R., 30 Dec. 1881, Jinny Atkinson Col.
83. Brontë, Charlotte, *Shirley*, chapter XVIII.
84. J.M.R.–M.T., 19 Apr. 1852, *Vol.3, p.11*.
85. *ibid*; 27 May 1853, *Discards*
86. J.M.R. general letter no.1, 25 May 1853, *Vol.3, p.41*.
87. There was a weekly overland postal route between Auckland and Wellington; it followed the west coast to New Plymouth.

Chapter Four: Settling In

1. Helen Hursthouse–Catherine Wilson, 28 Sept. 1851, 'Hursthouse Papers'.
2. Settlers even as late as the Richmonds and Atkinsons occasionally called the mountain by its Maori name.
3. J.C.R.–M.R., 15 Apr. 1851, *Vol.2, p.75*.
4. The Plymouth Company formed 25 Jan. 1840 to bring emigrants from the west of England was a subsidiary of the New Zealand Company. Financial difficulties forced it to merge, 17 Feb. 1841, with its parent body.
5. Jupp, George, 'The Diary of a Taranaki Pioneer', Vol.1, p.15 (ATL).
6. Taranaki was often used as the name of the settlement; going to New Plymouth or going to Taranaki, for settlers, meant the same thing. It had always been a Maori tribal name.
7. J.C.R.–M.R., 1 Dec. 1851, *Vol.38, p.229*.
8. J.C.R.–J.M.R., 15 July 1851, *Vol.2, p.95*.
9. Hugh Ronalds–Eliza J. Ronalds, 19 Sept. 1853, Ronalds Papers.
10. A bridge over the Huatoki was one of

New Plymouth's first public works and it became the community centre for the town. Public notices were often attached to it.

11. *Taranaki Herald*, 19 Oct. 1853.
12. H. Ronalds, 4 Oct. 1855, Ronalds Papers.
13. C.F. Hursthouse–C.W.R., *c.* Oct. 1850, *Addl 1850/1*.
14. Thomas Arnold quoted in Earl Grey–Gov. Grey, Despatch No.23, 23 Dec. 1846, G1/17, (National Archives).
15. Earl Grey–Gov. Grey, Despatch No.23, 23 Dec. 1846.
16. 'Report . . . on New Zealand 29 July 1844', *British Parliamentary Papers 556*, p.5.
17. J.C.R.–J.M.R., 13 Aug. 1851, *Vol.2, p.95*.
18. J.M.R. general letter no.4, 24 Sept. 1853, *Vol.13*.
19. Quoted in *Appendices to the Journals of the House of Representatives*, 1861, E–1, Appendix, p.19. The letter is in English only.
20. C.F. Hursthouse–Charles Hursthouse, 3 Apr. 1847, Hursthouse Family Letters.
21. Earl Grey–Gov. Grey, 23 Dec. 1846, Despatch 23, G1/17.
22. Owing to the tribal turbulence associated with its purchase, the Bell block was not opened for sale and settlement until 1853.
23. J.M.A.–E.E.R., Mar. 1858, *Vol. 4, p.14*.
24. C.F. Hursthouse–C.W.R., *c.* Oct 1850, *Addl 1850/1*.
25. H.R.R.–C.W.R., 3 Apr. 1851, *Vol.2, p.71*.
26. J.M.R.–M.T., 1 July 1853, *Vol.38, p.247*.
27. To safeguard it from demolition, Beach Cottage, minus its later wooden additions, was shifted from its original site in 1961 and relocated near the Taranaki Museum. It is preserved as an historic building, owned by the New Plymouth City Council and renamed Richmond Cottage.
28. J.M.R. general letter no.3, 2 Sept. 1853, *Vol.3, p.47*.
29. *idem*.
30. J.M.R. general letter no.4, 24 Sept. 1853, *Vol.13*.
31. J.M.R. general letter no.3, 2 Sept. 1853, *Vol.3, p.47*.
32. J.M.R. general letter no.4, 24 Sept. 1853, *Vol.13*.
33. *idem*.
34. J.M.R. general letter no. 4, 24 Sept. 1853, *Vol. 13*.
35. Hammerton, A.J., *Emigrant Gentlewomen: Genteel Poverty and Emigration 1830–1914* (Croom Helm, London, 1979), p.12.
36. Wright St Clair, R.E. *Thoroughly a Man of the World, a biography of Sir Donald Monro M.D.* (Whitcombe & Tombs, Christchurch, 1971), p.74.
37. Letters of Sarah Greenwood, Aug. 1843, Mar. 1844, Greenwood Family Papers, Folder 14 (ATL).
38. Stevens, Joan (ed.), *Mary Taylor Friend of Charlotte Brontë* (Auckland University Press, 1972), p.94.
39. J.M.R.–M.T., 4 Dec. 1853, *Vol.38, p.262*.
40. J.M.R. general letter no.2, 17 July 1853, *Vol.13*.
41. *idem*.
42. J.M.R. general letter no.4, 24 Sept. 1853, *Vol.13*.
43. John Blackett, an engineer from Newcastle-on-Tyne, came to New Plymouth with his family in 1851.
44. C.W.R.–T. Richmond, 8 Aug. 1854, *Vol.41*.
45. J.M.R.–M.T., 4 Dec. 1853, *Vol.38, p.262*.
46. J.M.R. general letter no.4, 24 Sept. 1853 (entry 13 Nov), *Vol.13*.
47. J.M.R. general letter no.2, 17 July 1853, *Vol.13*.
48. *idem*.
49. J.M.R.–M.T., 30 Oct. 1853, *Vol.3, p.49*.
50. *idem*.
51. J.M.R.–M.T., 12 Mar. 1854, *Vol.3, p.57*.
52. *idem*.
53. J.C.R.–Mary Smith, 13 Feb. 1856, *Addl 1856/23*.
54. M.T.–C.W.R., 23 June 1855, *Vol.3, p.64*.
55. J.M.A.–M.T., 4 Feb. 1855, *Vol.3. p.63*.
56. A.S.A. Diary, 25 Oct. 1853, *Vol.28*.
57. *ibid.*, 18 Dec. 1853, *Vol.28*.
58. J.M.R.–Mary Hutton, 31 July 1854, *Vol.3, p.60*.
59. J.M.R.–M.T, 12 Mar. 1854, *Vol.3, p.57*.

60. M.T.–C.W.R., 23 June 1855, *Vol.3,*
    p.65.
61. *idem.*
62. Hurworth was the village of Durham
    County which besides being Arthur
    Atkinson's birthplace, was where the
    Wilsons and Richmonds had first met.
    It held 'many pleasant associations for
    Lely and her sisters'.
63. J.M.R. general letter no.1, 24 Feb.
    1854, *Vol.3, p.56.*
64. *idem.*
65. J.M.R.–M.T., 24 June 1854, *Vol.3,*
    p.58.
66. J.M.R. general letter no.2, 17 July
    1853, *Vol.13.*
67. J.M.R. general letter no.1, 24 Feb.
    1854, *Vol.3, p.56.*
68. *Taranaki Herald,* 8 Mar. 1854.
69. J.M.R. general letter no.1, 24 Feb.
    1854, *Vol.3, p.56.*
70. *Taranaki Herald,* 22 Mar. 1854.
71. C.W.R.–T. Richmond, 8 Aug. 1854,
    Vol.41.
72. This caused a change in hospital
    routine. Because of the tapu
    surrounding the death of a chief and
    because of fear of retaliation, there
    were few Maori in-patients during
    the remainder of 1854; 392 were
    treated as out-patients.
73. C.W.R.–T. Richmond, 8 Aug. 1854,
    Vol.41.
74. C.W.R.–C. Brown, 28 July 1854,
    Vol.41.
75. *idem.*
76. C.W.R.–T. Richmond, 23 Aug. 1854,
    Vol.41.
77. J.M.R.–Mary Hutton, 31 July 1854,
    Vol.3, p.60.
78. *idem.*
79. C.W.R.–T. Richmond, 20 Nov. 1854,
    Vol.41.
80. Helen, Blanche, and Kate Hursthouse.
81. J.M.A.–M.T., 20 Jan. 1855, *Vol.3,*
    p.62.
82. *ibid.,* 4 Feb. 1855, *Vol.3, p.63.*
83. *ibid.,* 20 Jan. 1855, *Vol.3, p.62.*
84. *idem.*

Chapter Five: 'Bird's Nest' at Merton

1. Emily Richmond (daughter of
   C.W.R.) has interpolated 'Miss
   Martha King' in her typescript of this
   letter. Martha King, one of S.P.
   King's sisters, was New Zealand's
   first resident botanical artist.
2. A day school run by Mrs King and
   her two sisters-in-law.
3. J.M.A.–M.T., 4 Feb. 1855, *Vol.3, p.63.*
4. *idem.*
5. J.M.A.–M.T. journal letter beginning
   20 Jan. 1855, *Vol.3, p.62.*
6. These explosions may have been
   caused by slips along one side of Mt
   Taranaki's cone. C.W. Richmond
   reported that many New Plymouth
   settlers thought the earthquake had
   altered the shape of the mountain.
7. J.M.A.–M.T., 20 Jan. 1855, *Vol.3, p.63.*
8. *idem.*
9. J.M.A.–M.T., 13 June 1855, *Vol.38,*
   p.285.
10. Charlie Wilson included Decimus
    Atkinson in the party but the latter
    did not arrive at New Plymouth until
    22 Nov. 1855. With other
    Hurworthians he climbed the
    mountain the following year.
11. J.M.A.–M.T., 13 June 1855, Vol.38,
    p.285.
12. J.M.A.–J.C.R., 28 Aug. [1855], *Addl*
    1856/12.
13. A.S.A. Diary, 29 June 1855, *Vol.28.*
14. M.J. King–J.C.R., 17 Nov. 1855, *Addl*
    1855/20.
15. M.R. Diary, 24 Aug. 1856, *Vol.17.*
16. J.M.A.–M.T., 5 Dec. 1855 and 13 June
    1855, *Vol.38, pp.298 and 284–5.*
17. J.M.A.–M.T., 12 Aug. 1855, *Vol.38,*
    p.289.
18. *ibid.,* 13 June 1855, *Vol.38, p.286.*
19. M.R.–J.C.R., 30 May 1855, *Addl 1855/*
    10.
20. There was some fluidity in the social
    structure. When Sophy Cuttress
    married Dr White of the 65th Regt
    she improved her status to the extent
    of being 'able to snub all the folk that
    had snubbed her and her sisters . . .
    and I hear she avails herself
    considerably of her privilege'. (Mary
    King–J.C.R. 17 Nov. 1855, *Addl 1855/*
    20.) New Plymouth society did not
    accept intermarriage. When 'Mrs
    Maori Carrington', as Lely referred to
    her, was seriously ill with
    consumption, she was taken at her
    own request to die at her pa.

21. J.M.A.–M.T., 28 June 1855, *Vol.38, p.287.*
22. E.E.R.–J.C.R., 22 Sept 1855, *Addl 1855/15.*
23. J.M.A.–M.T., 4 Feb. 1855, *Vol.3, p.63.*
24. J.M.A.–J.C.R., 8 Aug. 1855, *Addl 1855/12.*
25. C.W.R.–T. Richmond, 27 May 1857, *Vol.41.*
26. Helen M. Hursthouse–J.C.R., 22 Jan. 1856, *Addl 1856/20.*
27. J.M.A.–J.C.R., 8 Aug. 1855, *Addl 1855/12.*
28. M.T.–C.W.R., 23 June 1855, *Vol.3, p.64.*
29. J.M.A.–J.C.R., 8 Aug. 1855, *Addl 1855/12.*
30. *idem.*
31. *idem.*
32. J.C.R.–C.W.R., 1 July 1855, *Vol.38, p.289.*
33. Mary Smith–J.C.R., 28 Mar. 1855, *Addl 1855/7.*
34. The 'Grande Campagnie du Luxembourg' intended to connect Brussels and Luxembourg by rail. James called it the 'Campagnie du Luxe' on account of the light work and high pay.
35. M.R.–J.C.R., 4 Dec. 1855, *Addl 1855/ 22.*
36. C.W.R.–J.C.R., 3 July 1856, *Discards.*
37. J.M.A.–Mary Smith, 25 July 1856, *Addl 1856/7.*
38. J.M.R.–Mary Hutton, 31 July 1854, *Vol.3, p.60.*
39. J.M.A.–J.C.R., 28 Aug. [1855], *Addl 1856/12.*
40. E.E.R.–J.C.R., 25 Nov. 1855, *Addl 1855/26.*
41. H.R.R.–J.C.R., 2 Dec. 1855, *Addl 1855/5.*
42. J.M.A.–Mary Smith, 31 Dec. 1855, *Addl 1855/23.*
43. Hurworth on the Carrington Road is now owned by the New Zealand Historic Places Trust. The Trust restored Hurworth to the simple but elegant cottage it had been when Jane and Harry lived there.
44. J.M.A.–M.T. journal letter beginning 24 Jan. 1856, *Vol.38, p.301.*
45. A.S.A. Diary, 25 Mar. 1856, *Vol.29.*
46. M.R.–M.T., 4 Sept. 1859, *Vol.4, p.98.*
47. E.E.R.–J.C.R., 22 Sept. 1855, *Addl 1855/15.*
48. H.R.R.–J.C.R., 11 Aug. 1855, *Addl 1855/3.*
49. Mary King–J.C.R., 17 Nov. 1855, *Addl 1855/20.*
50. Helen M. Hursthouse–J.C.R., 22 Jan. 1856, *Addl 1856/20.*
51. J.M.A.–Kate Whittle, 5 Dec. 1856, *Vol.38, p.323.*
52. H.R.R.–J.C.R., 2 Dec. 1855, *Addl 1855/5.*
53. J.M.A.–J.C.R., 8 Aug. 1855, *Addl 1855/12.*
54. M.R.–E.E.R., 29 Aug. 1856, *Vol.3, p.72.*
55. C.W.R.–C. Wilson, 23 Dec. 1855, *Vol.41.*
56. A.S.A. Diary, 5 Nov. 1855, *Vol.28.*
57. C.W.R.–R. Pheney, 18 May 1856, *Vol.41.*
58. J.M.A. Diary, 4 June 1856, *Vol.3, p.67.*
59. J.M.A.–M.T., 1 June 1856, *Vol.38, p.313.*
60. M.R.–E.E.R., 6 June 1856, *Addl 1856/ 5.*
61. J.M.A.–M.T., 24 Jan. 1856, *Vol.38, p.300.*
62. Helen M. Hursthouse–J.C.R., 22 Jan. 1856, *Addl 1856/20.*
63. J.M.A. journal letter 30 Mar. 1856, *Vol.3, p.67.*
64. J.M.A.–E.E.R., 24 May [1856], *Addl 1857/11.*
65. M.R.–J.C.R., 15 July 1856, *Discards.*
66. J.M.A.–E.E.R and C.W.R., *c.* July 1856, *Discards.*
67. *ibid.*, 1 Aug. 1856, *Vol.38, p.317.*
68. M.R.–C.W.R., 29 July 1856, *Vol.38, p.315.*
69. J.M.A.–E.E.R. and C.W.R., 1 Aug 1856, *Vol.38, p.317.* Maria always considered Margaret as her first child.
70. E.E.R.–J.C.R., 6 Aug. 1856, *Addl 1856/10.*
71. J.M.A.–E.E.R. and C.W.R., *c.* July 1856, *Discards.*
72. *ibid.*, 1 Aug 1856, *Vol.38, p.317.*
73. H.R.R.–C.W.R., 31 July 1856, *Addl 1856/9.*
74. J.M.A.–M.T., 13 June 1855, *Vol.38, p.285.*
75. A.S.A. Diary, 4 July 1855, *Vol.28.*
76. J.M.A. journal letter, 28 June 1855, *Vol.38, p.288.*
77. E.E.R. Diary, 4 Aug. 1855, *Vol.21.*
78. A.S.A. Diary, 6 Aug. 1855, *Vol.28.*
79. J.M.A.–M.T., 12 Aug. 1855, *Vol.38, p.288.*

80. Actually Selwyn had made a point of accusing Katatore, when he met him at Waitara, of the murder of Rawiri Waiaua.

81. A.S.A. Diary, 24 Aug. 1855, *Vol.28*.

82. C.W.R.-T. Richmond, 27 Aug. 1855, *Vol.41*.

83. Mary King–J.C.R., 17 Nov. 1855, *Addl 1855/20*.

84. J.M.A.–Kate Whittle, 5 Dec. 1856, *Vol.38, p.322*.

85. J.M.A.–M.T., 31 Dec. 1856, *Vol.38, p.325*.

Chapter Six: The Hurworth Community

1. J.M.R.–M.T., 21 June 1850, *Vol.2, p.41*.

2. J.M.A.–J.C.R., 8 Aug. 1855, *Addl 1855/12*.

3. J.P. du Moulin was in charge of the Commissariat at Mt Eliot camp. In Dec. 1856 he rented Beach Cottage from C.W. Richmond.

4. Maria could never resist jibing Emily about her society life in Auckland. William described it as a 'bad imitation of English life'.

5. J.M.A.–.E.E.R., [1857], *Discards*.

6. Hugh Ronalds–Edmund Ronalds, 5 Sept. 1858, Ronalds Papers.

7. J.M.A.–E.E.R, 3 May 1857, *Addl 1857/7*.

8. *ibid.*, [1859], *Addl 1859/1*.

9. J.M.A.–E.E.R. and C.W.R., 12 Jan. 1857, *Vol.3, p.85*.

10. J.M.A.–M.T., 31 Dec. 1856, *Vol.38, p.326*.

11. H.R.R.–Blanche Hursthouse, 12 July 1857, *Vol.3, p.94*.

12. J.M.A.–E.E.R, 27 Sept. 1856, *Discards*.

13. J.M.A.–M.T. journal letter, 10 July 1857, *Vol.38, p.329*.

14. Mary Richmond–E.E.R., 12 July 1857, *Discards*.

15. J.M.A.–M.T., 15 Sept. 1858, *Vol.38, p.379*.

16. *idem*.

17. This description comes from an undated fragment in Lely's handwriting, *c.* July/Aug. 1858, *Discards*.

18. Elizabeth Atkinson died in August

1855; her husband, John, in April, 1856.

19. J.M.A.–E.E.R., 27 Dec. 1857, *Vol.38, p.346*.

20. The 'little hill', perfectly conical, is still known by that name, and there is still an uninterrupted view from it across grassed paddocks to the far bank of the Te Henui. The line of the present Carrington Road, cut in 1865, went 'just by the side of my little hill'. (A.S.A. Diary, 20 June 1865).

21. J.M.A.–M.T., 15 Nov. 1857, *Vol.38, p.343*.

22. J.C.R.–E.E.R., 20 Sept. 1857, *Addl 1857/39*.

23. 'The soldier officers are most of them brave enough, but their whole course of education seems to unfit them for any practical business. They never learn to do any work. They spend their best years in kicking their heels, balls, billiards, flirting, drinking . . . They have to turn out once a week or so on guard or picket and once in three months they go on an expedition. If the British people want to have a stock of competent officers, they must find work for them. It need not be fighting, but topography, explorations, public works . . . Work should be exacted in peace if competency is hoped for in war.' (J.C.R.–M.T., 9 Dec. 1860, *Vol.5, p.43*.)

24. J.M.A.–M.T., 27 June 1857, *Vol.38, p.328*.

25. J.M.A.–E.E.R., 4 Jan. 1857, *Vol.3, p.66*.

26. A.S.A. Diary, 1857, *Vol.30*.

27. J.M.A.–Kate Whittle, 9 Sept. 1857, *Vol.38, p.336*.

28. A.S.A. Diary, 21 Nov. 1857, *Vol.31*.

29. J.M.A.–M.T., 15 July 1858, *Vol.38, p.355*.

30. J.C.R.'s tender for the Waiwakaiho bridge was not accepted.

31. J.M.A.–M.R., 6 Dec. 1857, *Addl 1857/47*.

32. C.W. Richmond paid a one-day visit to Hurworth on 28 Nov. 1857. Lely and Nellie Hursthouse went back to Auckland with him.

33. A.S.A. Diary, 1858, *Vol.31*.

34. J.M.A.-M.T., 15 Sept. 1858, *Vol.38,p.379*.
35. *ibid.*, 15 Sept. 1858, *Vol.38, p.378*.
36. She returned from Auckland in August. 'The descent from the W.Swan was certainly not very agreeable, the boat could not keep alongside. I had to walk along what appeared to me in my nervous fears a ladder laid horizontally supported by Mr Carkeek's strong arm, thence I was seized by a boatman and precipitated into the boat, not without the infliction of some bruises on my shins. I don't suppose there was any real danger but I could not help being frightened and wondering what business people in the decline of life had to be wandering over the face of the earth.' (M.R.–Helen M. Hursthouse, 10 Oct. 1858, *Addl 1858/29*.)
37. J.M.A.-M.T., 24 July 1859, *Vol.38, p.405*.
38. *ibid.*, 28 Aug. 1859, *Vol.4, p.98* and 16 Jan. 1859, *Vol.38, p.381*.
39. C.W.R.-H.A.A., 4 Jan. 1858, *Vol.41*.
40. J.M.A.-M.R., 28 Mar. [1858], *Vol.4, p.24*.
41. J.M.A.-E.E.R., 27 June 1858, *Addl 1858/20*.
42. E.E.R.-C.W.R., 14 Nov. 1858, *Vol.4, p.56*.
43. Before that happened, Maria put Merton sufficiently to rights for Emily to give birth to her fourth child, Christopher Francis, there on 12 Mar. 1859.
44. M.R.-C.W.R., *c.* Jan. 1859, *Vol.4, p.73*.
45. J.M.A.-E.E.R., 27 June 1858, *Addl 1858/20*.
46. *idem.*
47. W.H. Atkinson who later became a 'native interpreter' with the Taranaki militia, appears to have 'picked up' the Maori language rather than more studiously acquiring it. He frequently employed Maori to clear bush.
48. J.M.A.-M.T., 2 Jan. 1859, *Vol.38, p.390*.
49. M.R.-M.T., 2 Sept. 1859, *Vol.4, p.98*.
50. 'Harry's cheese is making quite a talk in this place. Mr Leech has never eaten cheese equal in excellence and thinks that if the cheeses weighed 10 lbs each instead of 50 or 60 they would be quite fit for the Indian market.' (E.E.R.–C.W.R., 30 Jan. 1859, *Vol.4, p.67*).
51. M.R.-M.T., 4 Sept. 1859, *Vol.4, p.98*.
52. A.S.A. Diary, 19 Sept. 1858, *Vol.31*.
53. An advertisement in the *Taranaki Herald*, 22 June 1859, stated that Hochstetter would be 'happy to receive specimens illustrative of *any branch of Natural History from any part of New Zealand*, together with information relative to the location'.
54. J.M.A.-M.T., 15 Nov. 1859, *Vol.38, p.419*.
55. A.S.A.-C.W.R., 27 Jan. 1860, *Addl 1860/8*.
56. J.M.A.-M.T. journal letter, 15 Sept. 1858, entry 26 Dec. 1858, *Vol.38, pp.380–1.*.
57. J.M.A.-[M.T.], 31 Dec. 1858, *Vol.4, p.60*.
58. *ibid.*, 27 Mar. 1859, *Vol.38, p.402*.
59. His father, James Wilson, was a Smith relative who had recently died in Sydney, leaving his widow and large family poorly provided for.
60. He was the ninth Atkinson child born to Elizabeth and John who had lived beyond twelve months.
61. Domett was one of Lely's favourites, but 'scandalous reports', she stated, 'were circulating about his domestic relationships'. He married Mary George, a widow, whom Lely described as 'a quiet amiable woman, inferior to her husband [and] might pass for his housekeeper', on 3 Nov. 1856 at Wellington. Mrs George is reported to have had 'one boy and two half-grown girls' at the time of her marriage to Domett. (H.R.–M.T., 4 Sept. 1859, *Vol. 4, p.98* and *Nelson Evening Mail*, 2 June 1931.
62. M.R.-M.T., 4 Sept. 1869, *Vol.4, p.98*.
63. J.M.A.-C.W.R., 24 July [1859], *Vol.3, p.71*.
64. Hugh Ronalds–Edmund Ronalds, 28 Aug. 1859, Ronalds Papers.
65. 'She doesn't feel that perfect love for me which she thinks she ought,' Decimus wrote to Emily. He added that he was still determined 'to have her', which he did three years later.
66. J.M.A.-M.T., 15 Nov. 1858 (entry 11 Dec. '59) *Vol.38, p.416*.

67. *ibid., Vol.38, p.417.* After the wedding *Bill* Atkinson, probably at Eliza's wish, becomes *William.*

68. C.W.R.–J.S. Atkinson, 23 Mar. 1859, and C.W.R.–T.Richmond, 24 Mar. 1859, *Vol.41.*

69. Quoted in *Taranaki Herald,* 12 Mar. 1859.

70. *ibid,* 26 Feb. 1859.

71. He was formally appointed minister of native affairs in August 1858. In addition he was either colonial secretary or colonial treasurer during the Stafford ministry's term of office, 1856–61. 'The Atlas of New Zealand' was Maria's exasperated description of him when Stafford's departure for England in Jan. 1859 left Richmond as virtual leader of government.

72. C.W.R.–H.R.R., 21 Mar. 1858, *Vol.41.*

73. C.W.R.–E.E.R., 13 Jan. 1859, *Addl 1859/2.*

74. *idem.*

75. Land Commissioner D. McLean believed that by getting absentee Ati Awa living in Queen Charlotte Sound and about Nelson to 'dispose' of their claims to the Waitara, he had weakened the opposition of Wiremu Kingi. (D. McLean–C.W.R., 25 Apr. 1859, *Vol.4, p.72.*

76. C.W.R.–H. Sewell, 16 June 1857, *Vol.42.*

77. Two missionaries who frequently corresponded with C.W. Richmond were John Whiteley of the Wesleyan Missionary Society and John Morgan of the Church Missionary Society. Both advocated that central government should extinguish the 'native title' as soon as practicable.

78. C.W.R.–R. Parris, 6 July 1857, *Vol.41.*

79. C.W.R.–I.N. Watt, 25 May 1857, *Vol.41.*

80. *Taranaki Herald,* 2 May 1857.

81. J.M.A.–E.E.R., 14 June 1857, *Addl 1857/17.*

82. In Aug. 1854 Rawiri Waiaua, an advocate of land sales, had been killed by Katatore and his followers. See Chapter Four pp.70–1.

83. C.W.R.–T. King, 25 Jan. 1858, *Vol.41.*

84. T. Gore Browne–C.W.R., 6 Feb. 1858, *Vol.4, p.7.*

85. Ihaia refused a government offer to have himself and his people deported to the Chatham Islands. He was also unwilling to give himself up to European authority unless those who had killed Rawiri Waiaua were also brought to justice.

86. C.W.R.–H.R.R., 21 Mar. 1858, *Vol.41.*

87. J.M.A.–E.E.R., [Mar. 1858], *Vol.4, p.14.*

88. *ibid.,* 12 May 1858, *Vol.4, p.32.*

89. J.M.A.–E.E.R., [Mar. 1858], *Vol.4, p.14.*

90. See Wards, Ian, *The Shadow of the Land* (Government Printer, 1968), pp.301–5.

91. Gilbert, T., *New Zealand Settlers and Soldiers; or the War in Taranaki* (1861), p.22.

92. The Militia Ordinance of 25 March 1854 provided that all able-bodied European males between 18 and 65 were to hold themselves ready for service which was limited to a radius of 25 miles from the local post office.

93. H.A.A.–C.W.R., 8 Feb. 1858, *Vol.4, p.7.*

94. J.C.R.–C.W.R., 28 Feb 1858, *Vol.4, p.11.*

95. J.M.A.–M.R., 25 Feb, 1858, *Vol.4, p.13.*

96. A.S.A. Diary, 31 Aug. 1858, *Vol.31.*

97. *Taranaki Herald,* 31 Aug. 1858.

98. J.M.A.–M.T., 26 Feb. 1860, *Vol.38, p.430.* The 'volunteers' with whom Arthur and other Hurworthians had previously been training were an unofficial force.

99. Bell lived in Wellington and had been a member of both the Legislative Council and, as member for the Hutt, the General Assembly.

100. C.W.R.–I.N. Watt, 12 Apr. 1858, and C.W.R.–T. King, 12 Apr. 1858, *Vol.41.*

101. J.C.R.–C.W.R., 11 Apr. 1858, *Addl 1858/10.*

102. E.E.R.–C.W.R., 7 Jan. 1859, *Vol.4, p.3.*

103. C.W.R.–E.E.R., 13 Jan. 1859, *Addl 1859/2.*

104. E.E.R.–C.W.R., 28 Jan. 1859, *Vol.4, p.65.*

105. J.M.A.-E.E.R., 12 May 1858, *Vol.4, p.32.*

106. *idem.*

107. A dig at Stafford. His love of horse racing was well known; he also married in England.

108. J.M.A.-C.W.R., 24 Jan. 1859, *Vol.4, p.66.*

109. See Sinclair, Keith, *The Origins of the Maori Wars* (Auckland University Press, reprinted 1984), p.168.

110. A.S.A. Diary, 12 Mar. 1859, *Vol.31a.*

111. *Appendices to the Journals of the House of Representatives*, 1860, E-3, p.6.

112. Gore Browne-Newcastle, 22 May 1860, enclosed in Grey-Newcastle, 24 Apr 1863, *AJHR* 1863, E-2, p.3.

113. R. Parris-C.W.R., 21 June 1859, *Vol.4, p.84.*

114. E.W. Stafford-C.W.R., 17 Aug. 1859, *Vol.4, p.95.*

115. *Taranaki Herald*, 10 Sept. 1859.

116. T. Gore Browne-C.W.R., [27 Aug. 1859], *Vol.5, p.23 and Vol.4, p.97.*

117. R. Parris-C.W.R., 19 Nov. 1859, *Vol.4, p.105.*

118. Hadfield, Octavius, *One of England's Little Wars* (London 1860), p.10.

119. Speaking in a debate over the Waitara purchase in 1861, Richmond told his colleagues, 'we never contemplated war, nor did the Governor, nor anyone in the colony; nor was there any reasonable expectation that the steps then taken would lead to war.' (*New Zealand Parliamentary Debates 1861*, p.156.)

120. J.M.A.-M.T., 19 Feb. 1860, *Vol.38, p.427.*

121. H.A.A.-C.W.R., 10 Feb. 1860, *Vol.5, p.3.*

122. J.M.A.-M.T., 26 Feb. 1860, *Vol.38, p.430.*

123. C. Brown-C.W.R., 19 Feb. 1860, *Vol.5, p.4.*

124. John Hursthouse-C.W.R., 20 Feb. 1860, *Addl 1860/18.*.

125. J.C.R.-C.W.R., 24 Feb. 1860, *Vol.5, p.5.*

126. Thomas Hirst-William Hirst, 24 Feb. 1860, Hirst Family Letters, Vol.3, p.69. (ATL).

127. William Turner-T. Gore Browne, 22 Feb. 1860, Colonial Secretary's Correspondence, IA 61/116 (National Archives).

128. The children were Mary (7), Anna (5), Margaret (3) from Auckland; Maria's Edith (2) and Mary's Alla (2). The adults were Mary and James, with Martha, their maid; Maria, Lely, and Nellie Hursthouse. Lely had engaged the last named as her housekeeper.

129. J.M.A.-M.T., 19 Feb. 1860, *Vol.38, pp.427-8.*

130 In the Italian War of Liberation, about which Maria felt passionately, Cavour's hopes were dashed when, with victory over Austria virtually assured, his ally, Napoleon III, drew back and concluded a peace treaty at Villafranca, July 1859.

131. J.M.A.-M.T., 19 Feb. 1860, *Vol.38, pp.427-8.*

132. His instructions were 'to stop all Maoris from going [freely] into Town, to explain to the friendly Natives that it was out of kindness to them the Governor had issued the order not from any ill feeling towards them, and to those I did not consider well disposed, merely refuse passes.' (W.S. Atkinson-C.W.R., 9 Mar. 1860, *Vol.5, p.8.*

133. J.M.A.-M.T., 26 Feb. 1860, *Vol.38, p.431*

134. Eliza Atkinson, Reminiscences, Ronalds Papers.

135. C.W.R.-E.E.R., 10 Mar. 1960, *Addl 1860/25.*

Chapter Seven: Dispersal

1. E.E.R.-C.W.R., 4 Mar. 1860, *Vol.5, p.6.*

2. C.W.R.-E.E.R., 10 Mar. 1860, *Addl 1860/25.*

3. There were two volunteer companies. No.1 was drawn from the town of New Plymouth and No.2 from country districts. In democratic fashion, of which the governor did not approve, the men elected their own officers. Two were proposed for the rank of captain of No.2 company: 'Sergeant Atkinson, 100 votes; Lieut. Hirst, 15.' (A.S.A. Diary, 16 Mar. 1860, *Vol.31a*).

4. M.R.-E.E.R., 13 Mar. 1860, *Addl 1860/26.*

5. Eliza Atkinson–Ellen Ronalds, May 1863, Reminiscences and Letters from Eliza and Marion Atkinson, Ronalds Papers.

6. T.H. Smith–F. Whitaker (enclosure), 16 Mar. 1860, *Addl 1860/32*.

7. Hugh Ronalds Diary, 13 Mar. 1860, *Addl 1860/24*.

8. Grace Hirst–sisters, 9 Mar. 1860, Hirst Family Letters, Vol.3, p.89.

9. A.S.A. Diary, 19 Mar. 1860, *Vol.31a*.

10. The 30 settlers who were brought into town had, in spite of the killings, been as much 'protected' by friendly and even warring Maori as 'rescued' by the troops.

11. A.S.A.–C.W.R., 9 Apr. 1860, *Addl 1860/41*.

12. Gilbert, T., *New Zealand Settlers and Soldiers*, p.119.

13. J.M.A.–C.W.R. and E.E.R., 6 Apr. 1860, *Addl 1860/39*.

14. Mary King–E.E.R., 3 Apr. 1860, *Box of Misc. Letters*.

15. *Vol.5, p.10*. In fact the pa was virtually empty. 'Edd Messenger who went up into the pa with the storming party . . . "couldn't see anyone to stick or shoot" '. (A.S.A. Diary, 2 June 1860, *Vol.32*.) See also Belich, James, *The New Zealand Wars and the Victorian Interpretation of Racial Conflict* (Auckland University Press, 1986), pp.84–8.

16 J.M.A.–M.T., 22 Apr. 1860, *Vol.5, p.14*.

17 J.M.A.–C.W.R. and E.E.R., 6 Apr. 1860, *Addl 1860/39*.

18. *idem*.

19. *Taranaki Herald*, 31 Mar. 1860.

20. A.S.A.–C.W.R., 9 Apr. 1860, *Addl 1860/41*.

21. E.E.R.–J.M.A., 15 May 1860, *Addl 1860/55*.

22. Quoted in *Taranaki Herald*, 5 May 1860.

23. J.M.A.–E.E.R., 23 Apr. 1860, *Addl 1860/36a*.

24. See J.C. Patteson–J. Patteson, journal letter 10–27 April 1860, in Starke, June, 'The Waitara Purchase' in *The Turnball Library Record*, May 1973, Vol.6, p.19.

25. Morgan firmly believed that peace should not be contemplated until 'the Aborigines have been humbled and really feel themselves beaten'.

(J. Morgan–C.W.R., 5 Mar. 1860, *Vol.5, p.7*).

26. *Vol.32*.

27. *Taranaki Herald*, 12 May 1860.

28. *ibid*, 19 May 1860.

29. Mary King–M.R., 3 Apr. 1860, *Box of Misc. Letters*.

30. A. Domett–C.W.R., 21 Mar. 1860, *Vol.5, p.9*.

31. E.E.R.–Mary Richmond, 30 Apr. 1860, *Addl 1860/47* and A.S.A. Diary, 14 Apr. 1860, *Vol.31a*.

32. Helen Hursthouse–John Hursthouse, 22 May 1860, Letters from Helen and Kate Hursthouse 1860–64.

33. J.M.A.–E.E.R., 3 June 1860, *Addl 1860/61*.

34. *ibid*., 23 Apr. 1860, *Addl 1860/36a*.

35. J.M.A.–E.E.R., 20 May [1860], *Addl 1860/57*.

36. J.C.R.–Mary Richmond, 29 Apr. 1860, *Addl 1860/46*.

37. J.M.A. Journal, 22 May 1860, *Vol.5, p.16*.

38. Archdeacon Kissling from Auckland asked Maunsell to send in a daily report on the state of his district. This Robert Maunsell refused to do, writing that he would never allow himself to be employed as a spy.

39. A.S.A.–C.W.R., 22 May 1860, *Addl 1860/58*.

40. J.M.A.–E.E.R., 20 May [1860], *Addl 1860/57*.

41. *idem*.

42. *idem*.

43. Gilbert, T., *New Zealand Settlers and Soldiers*, p.119.

44. When Gold was leaving New Plymouth he said to Robert Parris: 'I have seen you do a great many imprudent things. You ought to remember you are a family man.' (A.S.A. Diary, 1 Aug. 1861, *Vol.33*.)

45. A.S.A. Diary, 25 June 1860, *Vol.32*.

46. Major Herbert, 58th Regt.

47. J.C.R.–C.W.R., 2 July 1860, *Addl 1860/71*.

48. J.C.R.–Mary Richmond, 17 May 1860, *Addl 1860/56*.

49. M.R.–E.E.R., 22 May 1860, *Addl 1860/59*.

50. Frank Ronalds–Edmund Ronalds, 25 June 1860, Ronalds Papers.

51. J.M.A.–E.E.R., 3 June 1860, *Addl 1860/61*.

52. *idem.*
53. *idem.*
54. J.M.A. Journal, 1 July 1860, *Vol.5, p.17.*
55. *ibid.*, 2 July 1860, *Vol.5, p.17.*
56. J.C.R.–Mary Richmond, 3 July 1860, *Addl 1860/72.*
57. J.M.A. Journal, 14 July 1860, *Vol.5, p.17.*
58. J.M.A.–M.T., 2 Sept.1860, *Addl 1860/80.*
59. J.M.A. Journal, 24 July 1860, *Vol.5, p.17.*
60. *ibid.*, 19 Aug. 1860, *Vol.5, p.17.*
61. J.M.A.–M.T., 2 Sept. 1860, *Addl 1860/80.*

Chapter Eight: Auckland Interlude

1. J.M.A.–M.T., 2 Sept. 1860, *Addl 1860/80.*
2. J.M.A.–M.R., 10 Apr. 1864, *Addl 1864/26.*
3. J.M.A.–C.W.R., 29 Dec. 1856, *Vol.3, p.84.*
4. Maria was about to enter her servant era and its consequent problems-with-servants. Emily's two maids were said 'not to answer', nor were she and William happy with their manservant.
5. A.S.A. Diary, 15 Sept. 1860, *Vol.32.*
6. *ibid.*, 21 Aug. 1860, *Vol.32.*
7. He arrived from Melbourne, 3 Aug. 1860.
8. A.S.A. Diary, 23 Aug. 1860, *Vol.32.*
9. H.R.R.–J.C.R., 18 Aug. 1860, *Addl 1860/73.*
10. Josiah Flight–C.W.R., 6 Aug. 1860, *Vol.5, p.24.*
11. A.S.A. Diary, 11 Sept. 1860, *Vol.32.*
12. *New Zealand Parliamentary Debates*, 3 Aug. 1860, p.178.
13. J.M.A.–E.E.R., 3 June 1860, *Addl 1860/61.*
14. Notably Caroline Abraham, Sarah Selwyn and Mary Martin. The first gave a prophetic warning of the likely consequences of the Waitara purchase in a letter, subsequently published, to friends in England. 'What one chiefly mourns is the thought of our doing wrong to this people, and then supporting it by force and so beginning what may be a long chain

of wrong and misery to both races; like all evil, the beginning seems small.' (Caroline Abraham, 24 Apr. 1860, *Extracts of Letters from New Zealand on the War Question*, privately printed, London 1861.)
15. Hadfield, Octavius, *One of England's Little Wars*, pp.3,6,19.
16. In a note from Gore Browne to C.W.R. about the questioning of Hadfield in the House there is this postscript: 'If William King's letters to Hadfield come under discussion, I do not hesitate to affirm that if they had been shewn to me no war would ever have taken place. I should have asked Hadfield to act as mediator and it is clear that King would have acted on his advice.' (Gore Browne–C.W.R., 14 Aug. 1860, *Vol.5,p.25.*)
17. E.E.R.–H.A.A., 25 Aug. 1860, Sir Harry Atkinson MS Papers 91.
18. A.S.A. Diary, 3 Sept. 1860, *Vol.32.*
19. In 1858 C.W. Richmond, Stafford, Bell, and Steward, the governor's secretary, became partners in a sheep run in Central Otago.
20. J.M.A.–E.E.R., 17 July 1860, *Addl 1860/77.*
21. A.S.A. Diary, 1 Oct. 1860, *Vol.32.*
22. A rhyme in C.W.R's handwriting went:
    General Gold was not very old;
    General Pratt was not very fat;
    But all the motions of General Gold
    Were as slow as if he'd been fat and old,
    And all the motions of General Pratt
    Were as slow as if he'd been old and fat. *Addl 1861/39.*
23. A.S.A. Diary, 2 Oct. 1860, *Vol.32.*
24. H.R.R.–A.S.A., 17 Oct. 1860, *Addl 1860/92.*
25. *Taranaki Herald*, 15 Nov. 1860.
26. A.S.A. Diary, 7 Nov. 1860, *Vol.32.*
27. H.A.A.–A.S.A., 17 Nov. 1860, *Vol.5, p.41.*
28. Harry called 'Purveyor Adams' of the Commissariat ('that mountain of flesh', as Emily described him) a liar. Adams, drunk at the time, accused Harry of disobeying orders when the latter had the body of one of his volunteers removed from a pile of corpses 'lying together like firewood'. Harry told Adams that the body had

not been treated respectfully. When Adams denied this, Harry accused him of lying. On the strength of this Pratt recommended to the governor that Harry's commission be taken away. It was not. (A.S.A. Diary, 23 Nov. 1860, *Vol.32.*

29. H.A.A.–A.S.A., 21 Nov. 1860, *Vol.5, p.42.*

30. J.M.A.–M.T., 3 Oct. 1860, *Vol.38, pp.469–70.*

31. Later to be Harry Atkinson's second wife.

32. J.C.R.–Mary Richmond, 20 Nov. 1860, *Addl 1860/95.*

33. Kate Hursthouse–M.R., 30 Sept. 1860, Letters from Helen and Kate Hursthouse 1860–64.

34. J.M.A.–M.T., 31 Dec. 1860, *Vol.38, p.479.*

35. Hadfield, Octarius, *The Second Year of One of England's Little Wars* (1861), p.6.

36. J.M.A.–M.T., 31 Dec. 1860; entry 20 Jan. 1861, *Vol.38, p.481.* Maria was probably thinking of two Auckland members, Thomas Forsaith and William Dalby.

37. *idem.*

38. J.C.R.–Mary Richmond, 20 Jan. 1861, *Addl 1861/2.*

39. H.A.A.–A.S.A., 27 Feb. 1861, *Vol.5, p.50.*

40. J.C.R.–Mary Richmond, 3 Feb. 1861, *Addl 1861/8.*

41. *idem.*

42. A.S.A. Diary, 19 Mar. 1861, *Vol.32.*

43. A note in Arthur's diary adds, 'There were however some rifles besides double barrelled guns and revolvers among us and the whole party numbered over fifty when we got to Merton, but it did not keep together.' (A.S.A. Diary, 24 Mar. 1861, *Vol.32.*)

44. This is the first mention of such a building. Presumably it had been put up to accommodate the numerous Hurworth bachelors such as Teddo Patten, James Brind, Henry Skinner, Frank Adams, and James Crow who appeared from time to time.

45. A.S.A. Diary, 24 Mar. 1861, *Vol.32.*

46. *idem.*

47. A.S.A. Diary, 24 Mar. 1861, *Vol.32.*

48. During the winter of 1861 Taranaki's military forces were reduced to the 57th Regiment and local militia and

volunteers, all under the command of Col. H.J. Warre.

49. C.W. Richmond, who visited New Plymouth during April, found the settlers 'in a blaze of indignation' at the terms offered Te Ati Awa. (C.W.R.–E.E.R., 12 Apr. 1861, *Addl 1861/16.*)

50. J.M.A.–M.T., 5 Apr. 1861, *Vol.39.*

51. *idem.*

52. *idem.*

53. Helen (Nellie) Richmond died, 10 April 1861.

54. J.M.A.–M.T., 1 May 1861, *Vol.5, p.57.*

55. James Richmond stood but was defeated by Charles Brown.

56. A.S.A. Diary, 11 May 1861, *Vol.32.*

57. *ibid.*, 23 July 1861, *Vol.33.*

58. *ibid.*, 21 Aug. 1861, *Vol.33.*

59. *ibid.*, 29 June 1861, *Vol.33.*

60. J.M.A.–M.T., 7 July 1861, *Vol.38, p.493.*

61. E.E.R.–C.W.R., 2 May 1861, *Vol.5, p.58.*

62. C.W.R.–T. Richmond, 7 Apr. 1861, *Vol.42.*

63. He was later appointed governor of Tasmania.

64. J.M.A.–M.T., 7 July 1861, *Vol.38, pp.497–8.*

65. Harriet Gore Browne–C.W.R., 2 Oct. 1861, *Vol.5, p.77.*

66. *ibid.*, 10 Jan. 1862, *Vol.6, p.2.*

67. A.S.A. Diary, 11 Oct. 1861, *Vol.33.*

68. Helen Hursthouse–M.R., 4 Sept. 1861, Letters from Helen and Kate Hursthouse 1860–64.

69. J.C.R.–Mary Richmond, 26 Nov. 1861, *Addl 1861/29.*

70. Annie Smith–Mary Richmond, 26 Nov. 1861, *Addl 1861/30.*

71. J.C.R.–Mary Richmond, 13 Dec. 1861, *Addl 1861/36.*

72. Annie Smith–Mary Richmond, 13 Dec. 1861, *Discards.*

73. J.M.A.–M.T., 6 Dec. 1861, *Vol.5, p.85.*

74. Mary Richmond–E.E.R., 10 Mar. 1862, *Addl 1862/11.*

75. Harriet Gore Browne–C.W.R., 27 Feb. 1862, *Vol.6, p.5.*

76. C.W.R.–M.R., 15 Dec. 1861, *Addl 1861/37.*

77. J.M.A.–M.T., 2 Feb. 1862, *Vol.38, p.503.*

78. *idem.*

79. A.S.A. Diary, 17 May 1861, *Vol.32.*

80. F.D. Bell–A.S.A., 31 Jan. 1862, *Addl 1862/4.*
81. A.S.A. Diary, 31 Jan. 1862, *Vol.33.*
82. The block bounded by Pendarves, Lemon, Liardet, and Grover Streets.
83. A.S.A.–J.M.A., 14 Feb. 1862, *Vol.6, p.5.*
84. *idem.*
85. Alfred, their fifth child, was born at Dunedin, 12 April 1862.
86. C.W.R.–A.S.A., 21 Mar. 1862, *Addl 1862/13.*
87. They were married 25 March 1862.
88. J.M.A.–Mary Richmond, 6 May 1862, *Addl 1862/21.*
89. A.S.A. Diary, 17 Apr. 1862, *Vol.33.*
90. J.M.A.–Mary Richmond, 1 June 1862, *Addl 1862/25.*
91. Born during Oct. 1860 at Nelson.
92. In retrospect an ironical prophecy. Within a few years his relatives were struggling to accept the burden of his quite enormous debts.
93. J.M.A.–M.T., 28 May 1862, *Vol.38, pp.509–10.*
94. *idem.*
95. *idem.*
96. Beach Cottage was owned by C.W. Richmond.
97. J.M.A.–M.T., 28 May 1862, *Vol. 38, p.505.*

Chapter Nine: 'Otago & the law or Taranaki & joy'

1. M.R.–Mary Richmond, 16 July 1862, *Addl 1862/42.*
2. A.S.A. Diary, 29 July 1862, *Vol.33.*
3. M.R.–E.E.R. 16 July 1862, *Discards.* Money made available by central government to settlers who claimed compensation for losses during the war.
4. The grandfather of the present farmer discovered Maria's china buried for safety in the side of the 'little hill' and returned it to Maria's daughter, Edith, then living in Nelson.
5. A.S.A. Diary, 15 Aug. 1862, *Vol.34.*
6. M.R.–Mary Richmond, 21 Aug. 1862, *Discards.*
7. A.S.A.–Mary Richmond, 24 Aug. 1862, *Discards.*
8. *idem.*
9. A.S.A.–H.A.A., 10 Aug. 1862, *Discards.*
10. J.M.A.–Mary Richmond, 6 May 1862, *Addl 1862/21.*
11. From Sewell's award under the Taranaki Relief Fund Commission, they were to receive £465-5-0, and from the supplementary Beckam award, £87-10-0.
12. J.M.A.–M.T., 3 Aug. 1862, *Addl 1862/54.*
13. J.M.A.–Mary Richmond, 30 July 1862, *Discards.*
14. *ibid.*, 6 May 1862, *Addl 1862/21.*
15. E.E.R.–H.A.A., 3 Oct. 1862, *Discards.*
16. A.S.A.–C.W.R., 7 Sept. 1862, *Addl 1862/71.*
17. A.S.A. Diary, 7 Sept. 1862, *Vol.34.*
18. J.M.A.–M.T., 3 Aug, 1862, *Addl 1862/54.*
19. J.C.R.–Mary Richmond, 1862, Letters from J.C. Richmond 1862–67, Ann Paterson Coll.
20. A.S.A. Diary, 3 Oct. 1862. *Vol.34.*
21. M.R.–C.W.R., 5 Nov. 1862, *Addl 1862/83.*
22. *ibid.*, 19 Nov. 1862, *Addl 1862/88.*
23. M.R.–E.E.R., 6 Dec. 1862, *Addl 1862/96.*
24. A.S.A.–Mary Richmond, 7 Nov. 1862, *Discards.*
25. Mary Richmond–E.E.R., 19 Nov. 1862, *Discards.*
26. A fragment only in Maria's handwriting. *Discards.*
27. Blanche and Henry Richmond, a son, Francis William, born 13 Jan. 1863; Eliza and William Atkinson, a daughter, Janet, born either late Jan. or early Feb.; Marion and Decimus Atkinson, a son, Hugh *Ronald*, born 12 Jan. 1863.
28. 'Dolla' came from Anneliz's attempt to say Dorothy Kate – 'Dollafa Kate'. About this time Anneliz became 'Alla', presumably by the same process. Dolla and Alla remained the two sisters' names within the family.
29. 'I cannot describe to you the difference that William's absence makes to me. The very soul seems to have gone out of the House. I miss hourly his eager eyes and voice and can find nothing to rest upon.' (J.C.R.–Mary Richmond, 18 July 1862, *Addl 1862/45*).

30. Mary Richmond–J.M.A., 27 Mar. 1862, *Addl 1862/16*.

31. J.M.A.–M.T., 9 April. 1863, *Vol.6, p.39*.

32. M.R.–E.E.R., 23 Feb. 1863, *Discards*.

33. *ibid*, 6 Mar. 1863, *Addl 1863/10*.

34. *idem*.

35. A.S.A. Diary, 26 Mar. 1863, *Vol.34*.

36. A.S.A.–Mary Richmond, 30 Apr. 1863, *Discards*.

37. W. Halse–H.A.A., 9 Aug. 1862, *Addl 1862/58*.

38. From Tasmania Harriet Gore Browne continued to vent her indignation to the mob against the man who had supplanted her husband and, to begin with, beguiled her with sweet talking. 'He is absolutely unscrupulous and while he gains one by flattery he will frighten another by threatening, convince a third by his arguments and buy a forth by his favours.' (Harriet Gore Browne–Mary Richmond, 7 Aug. 1862, *Addl 1862/25*).

39. J.M.A.–Mary Richmond, 1 June 1862, *Addl 1862/25*.

40. J.M.A.–M.T., 2 Feb. 1862, *Vol.38, p.502*.

41. *idem*.

42. The *Lord Worsley* had gone aground, without loss of life, in Te Namu Bay, and the 60 passengers, one of whom was the redoubtable Miss Briggs on the way to join her nephew, Reginald Broughton, at Nelson, were being housed by Wiremu Kingi Matakatea and his hapu who had recently come over to the government side. At a hui held there after the shipwreck, the Maori King supporters at Kapoaiaia pa (in his diary A.S.A. calls them the people of Warea) decided that as the disaster had been a 'mate moana', the iwi would assemble to bring the passengers to New Plymouth.

43. A.S.A. Diary, 7 Sept. 1862, *Vol.34*.

44. *ibid.*, 10 Sept. 1862, *Vol.34*.

45. *idem*.

46. *idem*.

47. M.R.–E.E.R., 6 Mar. 1863, *Addl 1863/10*.

48. J.M.A.–E.E.R., 17 May 1863, *Addl 1863/33*.

49. J.C.R.–C.W.R., 13 Sept. 1862, *Addl 1862/74*.

50. A. Domett–H.A.A., 1 Nov. 1862, *Addl 1862/82*.

51. J.M.A.–M.T., 9 Apr. 1863, *Vol.6, p.39*.

52. M.R.–E.E.R., 24 Mar. 1863, *Addl 1863/15*.

53. J.C.R.–M.R., 28 Oct. 1863, Letters from J.C. Richmond 1862–67, Ann Paterson Coll.

54. Grey was furious at the Taranaki settlers' memorial to the Queen, which he put down to Harry Atkinson's instigation, asking that the Taranaki predicament be better known in England.

55. J.M.A.–M.T., 9 Nov. 1863, *Vol.38, p.522*.

56. J.M.A.–E.E.R., 27 Dec. 1863, *Addl 1863/74*.

57. *ibid.*, 17 May 1863, *Addl 1863/33*.

58. Te Teira was to get £600 as compensation for the failure of government to complete the purchase. A.S.A. commented, 'not for the land but for the Govr's love'.

59. In 1878 F.A. Weld (governor of Tasmania) wrote to C.W.R. for his views on Waitara. In his reply Richmond wrote: 'Many calumnies were circulated about myself at the time. Parris told me this story as we were riding together over the ground a few years ago. Sir George Grey and Sir D. Cameron were in a tent together at Tataraimaka in 1863. Parris came in and Sir George said, "By the way Parris whereabouts is Mr Richmond's land at Waitara?" *Parris* – "He never had any Yr Excellency". *Sir Duncan*, "That makes a difference Sir George," '. (C.W.R.–F.A. Weld, [1878], *Vol.7, p.34*).

60. *Taranaki Herald*, 16 May 1863.

61. A.S.A. Diary, *Vol.34*.

62. *ibid.*, 23 Dec. 1863, *Vol.35*.

63. Nor did he object to the departure of the governor for Auckland on 4 June. It was not Grey's native policy or his duplicity which finally sickened Arthur, but his 'immorality' and 'cowardice'. Grey had had his way with a 'harem' of Maori women while at New Plymouth, for which Arthur called him in his diary 'a whited sepulchre'. The cowardice charge arose because Grey insisted that twelve men, whose proper duty was to guard the magazine on Mt Eliot, should leave their post and rush to

Mrs Cudlips, where he lodged, to protect him if the town was attacked. Harry Atkinson had then to rush twelve of his men to guard the magazine. Many houses, Arthur commented, had no men in them at all.

64. 'Rebel' Maori were seldom seen, but deserted whare, kumara plantations, and food caches were always destroyed when found.

65. A.S.A. Diary, 2 Oct. 1863, *Vol.34*.

66. Grace Hirst–sisters, 9 Sept. 1863 and 8 Mar. 1864, Hirst Family Letters, Vol.4, pp.61 and 112.

67. A.S.A. Diary, 2 Oct. 1863, *Vol.34*.

68. In Feb. 1863 he was offered the editorship of the Auckland *Southern Cross* which he declined, but he agreed to be its Taranaki correspondent.

69. A.S.A. Diary, 14 Nov. 1863, *Vol.35*.

70. A.S.A.–C.W.R., 7 Sept. 1862, *Addl 1862/71*.

71. A.S.A. Diary, 14 Nov. 1863, *Vol.35*.

72. Eliza Atkinson–Ellen Ronalds, 26 May 1863, Reminiscences and Letters of Eliza and Marion Atkinson, Jinny Atkinson Coll.

73. *idem*.

74. M.R.–E.E.R., 25 June 1863, *Discards*.

75. D. Saul, reminiscing about 'Old Musical Days in Taranaki', described Mary King as 'the parent of music in New Plymouth'; she 'gave lessons in music to so many people that one can scarcely encounter a lady who has lived in New Plymouth for twenty-five years who was not taught by her. Her execution on the piano was brilliant.' (*The New Zealand Illustrated Magazine*, Vol.3, Oct. 1900–Mar. 1901, pp.40–4).

76. J.M.A.–E.E.R., 17 May 1863, *Addl 1863/33*.

77. Mary Richmond–E.E.R., 26 Aug. 1863, *Discards*.

78. J.M.A.–M.T., 6 Oct. 1863, *Vol.38, p.517*.

79. M.R.–M.T., 7 Aug. 1863, *Addl 1863/49*.

80. A.S.A.–C.W.R., July 1863, *Addl 1863/44*.

81. M.R.–E.E.R., 17 May 1863, *Addl 1863/34*.

82. Harry, Arthur, William, and Decimus Atkinson. The two older (unmarried) Hursthouse boys were also Bushrangers.

83. J.M.A.–E.E.R., 24 June 1863, *Discards*.

84. C.W.R.–A.S.A., 15 Nov. 1863, *Addl 1863/70*.

85. J.M.A.–E.E.R., 26 Sept. 1863, *Addl 1863/63*.

86. Bessie Domett had married C.T. Taylor of Auckland.

87. She died 14 Sept. 1863.

88. Helen Hursthouse–M.R., 23 Dec. 1863, Letters from Helen and Kate Hursthouse, Ann Paterson Coll.

89. J.M.A.–M.T., 6 Oct. 1863, *Vol.6, p.46*.

90. '. . . in sorrow shalt thou bring forth children; and thy desire shall be subject to thy husband and he shall rule over thee.' (Genesis 3:16).

91. M.R.–E.E.R., 17 May 1863, *Addl 1863/34*.

92. J.M.A.–E.E.R., 11 Dec 1863, *Addl 1863/73*.

93. J.M.A.–M.T., *c.* Oct 1863, *Vol.38, pp.518–19*.

Chapter Ten: 'We must go on bravely'

1. The agreement, taking effect from January, was not signed until 18 June 1864.

2. J.M.A.–M.R., 28 Jan. 1864, *Discards*.

3. J.C.R.–C.W.R., 1 Jan. 1864, *Addl 1864/1*.

4. A.S.A.–E.E.R., 23 May 1864, *Discards*.

5. The term 'waeromene', wild men, was sometimes applied to Bushrangers as well as to 'rebel' Maori.

6. A general engagement in which military settlers from Victoria and Otago, regulars from the 57th, and Bushrangers all took part.

7. A.S.A. Diary, 22 Mar. 1864, *Vol.35*.

8. J.M.A.–M.R., 10 Apr. 1864, *Addl 1864/26*.

9. 'With regard to destroying maize we came through a field of it which Cap Woodall & the 57th had destroyed & there it was nearly every plant cut off just *above* the cobs which were thus left to ripen

undisturbed.' (A.S.A. Diary, 21 Apr. 1864, *Vol.35*.)

10 J.M.A.-M.R., 14 July [1864], *Box of Misc. Letters*.

11. A commonly used subterfuge to cover the 'unclean' nature of childbirth was to refer to it as an illness.

12. J.M.A.-Mary Richmond, 4 Feb. 1864, *Addl 1864/8*.

13. *idem*.

14. Mary King-E.E.R., 17 May 1864, *Box of Misc. Letters*.

15. J.M.A.-M.T., 20 Jan. 1864, *Vol.38, p.537*.

16. *idem*.

17. J.M.A.-M.R., 10 Apr. 1864, *Addl 1864/26*.

18. J.M.A.-M.T., 20 Jan. 1864, *Vol.38, p.538*.

19. Sullivan, Alvin (ed.), *British Literary Magazines: The Victorian and Edwardian Age 1837-1913* (1984), p.379.

20. *idem*.

21. J.M.A.-M.T., 20 Jan. 1864, *Vol.39, pp.537-8*.

22. J.C.R.-Mary Richmond, 11 Dec. 1864, *Addl 1864/67*.

23. Mary Richmond-A.S.A., 1 May 1864, *Discards*.

24. Mary Richmond-A.S.A., 14 Feb. 1864, *Addl 1864/14*.

25. J.M.A.-M.R., [July 1864], *Addl 1864/39*.

26. Mary King-E.E.R., 17 May 1864, *Box of Misc. Letters*.

27. J.M.A.-M.T., 7 July 1864, *Discards*.

28. J.M.A.-M.R., 29 June 1864, *Discards*.

29. J.M.A.-M.T., 7 July 1864, *Discards*.

30. J.M.A.-M.R., 29 June 1864, *Discards*.

31. Bull, Thomas MD, *Hints to Mothers, for the management of health during the period of pregnancy, and in the lying-in room; with an exposure of popular errors in connection wth those subjects* (London, 1837). It ran through 13 editions before 1876.

32. Mrs Warre commanded infinitely more respect from New Plymouth's women than did her husband from the settler-soldiers.

33. J.M.A.-M.R., 27 Sept 1864, *Addl 1864/49*.

34. 18 Oct. 1864.

35. J.M.A.-E.E.R., Fragment only [Oct. 1864], *Addl 1864/59*.

36. The Grey Institute at Ngamotu was set up as a Wesleyan Training Centre in 1847. Closed in 1860 on account of the war, it was used by government in 1863 as temporary housing for displaced Maori. Rev. John Whiteley then returned and recommenced teaching.

37. A.S.A. Diary, 19 Oct. 1864, *Vol.35*.

38. A reference to a young 'unprotected' German girl Maria befriended when returning from a visit to Margaret Taylor.

39. J.M.A.-M.R., 27 Sept. [1864], *Addl 1864/49*.

40. *idem*.

41. Harriet Gore Browne-E.E.R., 20 Mar. 1864, *Vol.6, p.49*.

42. J.M.A.-M.R., 18 Aug. [1864], *Box of Misc. Letters*.

43. The term 'nurse' was loosely used and, in appropriate circumstances, interchangeable with 'midwife'.

44. J.M.A.-M.R., 18 Aug [1864], *Box of Misc. Letters*.

45. A.S.A.-C.W.R., 19 Sept. 1864, *Discards*.

46. J.M.A.-M.R., 5 Aug. 1864, *Addl 1864/41*.

47. A.S.A. Diary, 14 Oct. 1864, *Vol.35*.

48. J.M.A.-E.E.R., 24 June 1863, *Discards*.

49. J.M.A.-M.R., 10 Apr. 1864, *Addl 1864/26*.

50. J.M.A.-M.T., [*c*. Oct. 1863], *Vol.38, p.519*.

51. J.M.A.-M.R., 20 Feb. [1864], Richmond Family Papers, Acc 77-173, Box 7.

52. J.M.A.-M.R., 27 Sept [1864], *Addl 1864/49*.

53. T.B. Gillies-H.A.A., 27 Aug. 1864, *Addl 1864/46*

54. J.M.A.-M.R., 4 Oct. 1864, *Addl 1864/46*.

55. Grace Hirst-sister 2 Nov. 1864, Hirst Family Letters, Vol.4, p.160.

56. See *Taranaki Herald*, 22 Oct. 1864.

57. J.M.A.-M.R., 28 Aug. 1864, *Addl 1864/47*.

58. *ibid.*, 18 Nov. 1864, *Discards*.

59. *idem*.

60. *ibid.*, 13 Nov. [1864], *Addl 1864/62*.

61. J.M.A.-E.E.R., 5 Nov. 1864, *Addl 1864/61*.

62. J.M.A.-M.R., 13 Nov [1864], *Addl 1864/62*.

63. F. Whitaker–C.W.R., 17 Oct. 1864, *Addl 1864/58*.
64. A.S.A. Diary, 19 Nov. 1864, *Vol.35*.
65. Commenting on this shift recommended by the 1864 Seat of Government Commission, Lely wrote, 'Dr Featherston has feted & palavered the Commission to some purpose'. (M.R.–E.E.R., 21 Oct. 1864, *Addl 1864/66*).
66. 'Think of the immediate destroying of the colony placed in the hands of Grey & the Auckland men . . . but indeed it is better not to think of it.' (A.S.A. Diary, 6 Dec. 1864, *Vol.35*.)
67. A.S.A.–E.E.R., 18 Dec. 1864, *Addl 1864/69*.
68. J.M.A.–M.T., 3 Dec. 1864, *Vol.38, p.540*.
69. J.M.A.–M.R., 18 Nov. [1864], *Discards*.
70. 26 Nov. 1864.
71. H.R.R.–M.R., 29 Nov. 1864, *Discards*.
72. J.C.R.–Friends in England, 19 May 1851, *Vol.2, p.80*.
73. Her full name was Maria Blanche.
74. J.M.A.–M.R., 18 Dec. 1864, *Box of Misc. Letters*.
75. *ibid.*, 4 Oct. [1864], *Addl 1864/52*.
76. J.M.A.–M.T., 8 Sept. 1864, *Discards*.
77. J.M.A.–E.E.R., [*c.* Dec. 1864], *Discards*.
78. J.M.A.–M.R., 8 Jan. 1865, *Discards*.
79. *ibid.*, 19 Jan. [1865], *Addl 1865/10*.
80. *ibid.*, 8 Feb [1865], *Box of Misc. Letters*, and 8 Jan. 1865, *Addl 1865/2*.
81. *ibid.*, 28 Dec. 1864, *Box of Misc. Letters*.
82. J.M.A.–M.T., 3 Sept. 1865, *Vol.6, p.58*.
83. *ibid.*, 6 Apr. [1865], *Discards*.
84. J.M.A.–M.R., 8 Mar. [1865], *Discards*.
85. J.M.A.–Mary Richmond, 9 Sept. 1864, *Addl 1864/47a*.
86. J.M.A.–M.R., 8 Mar. [1865], *Discards*.
87. *ibid.*, 18 Nov [1864], *Discards*.
88. M.R.–E.E.R., 20 Mar. 1865, Addl 1865/33.
89. M.R.–E.E.R, 18 Apr. 1865, *Addl 1865/33*.
90. 'Simple goitre' was endemic in Derbyshire where its occurrence was attributed to lack of iodine in the water.
91. J.M.A.–Mary Richmond, 28 June 1865, *Addl 1865/48*.
92. J.C.R.–Mary Richmond, 28 June 1865, *Addl 1865/49*.
93. J.M.A.–M.T., 3 Sept. 1865, *Vol.6, p.58*.
94. Mary Richmond–A.S.A., 1 Jan. 1865, *Addl 1865/1*.
95. *ibid.*, 22 June 1865, *Addl 1865/45*.
96. Mary Richmond–J.C.R., 1 July 1865, *Discards*.
97. A.S.A.–Mary Richmond, 8 July 1865, *Discards*.
98. J.M.A.–M.T., 7 Aug. 1865, *Vol.38, p.542*.
99. J.M.A.–Mary Richmond, 28 June 1865, *Addl 1865/48*.
100. M.R.–E.E.R, 28 May 1865, *Addl 1865/36*.
101. J.M.A.–E.E.R., 6 June 1865, *Addl 1865/38*. The following year W.T. Doyne, an Irish engineer who had come to New Zealand to construct the Dun Mountain railway at Nelson, prepared plans for a harbour at New Plymouth which, in essence, by using the protection offered by the Sugar Loaves and by constructing a north-easterly mole, remains the present-day harbour. (See Charles Brown–H.A.A., 23 Dec. 1864, *Addl 1864/72*.)
102. J.M.A.–M.T., 3 Sept. 1865, *Vol.6, p.58*.
103. A.S.A.–C.W.R., 9 Feb. 1865, *Addl 1865/17*.
104. A.S.A. Diary, 17 Nov. 1864, *Vol.35*.
105. H.A.A.–A.S.A, 7 Jan. 1865, *Vol.6, p.52*.
106. A.S.A. Diary, 6 Jan. 1865, *Vol.35*. The governor was to 'take possession of and retain in the country between Wanganui and New Plymouth, and in the Province of Taranaki such land belonging to the rebels as he may think fit'. (*Appendices to the Journals of the House of Representatives*, 1873, C-4B, p.1.) The 1873 report gave this total as 1,144,700 acres, disposed of to military settlers, to 'natives' for 'Military or Special services', with the bulk held as either native or Crown reserves. An adjustment more favourable to Maori interests was made in 1928. (*Appendices to Journals* 1928, G-7, p.7.)

107. *Taranaki Herald*, 8 Apr. 1865.
108. A.S.A. Diary, 17 Mar. 1865, *Vol.35*.
109. Atkinson, Arthur Samuel, Diary 1865–66, 31 Oct. 1865, MS sequence (ATL).
110. J.M.A.–M.T., 3 Sept. 1865, *Vol.6, p.58*.
111. *idem*.
112. F.U. Gledhill.
113. Atkinson, Arthur Samuel, Diary 1865–66, 18 July 1865, MS sequence (ATL).
114. J.M.A.–M.T., 3 Sept. 1865, *Vol.6, p.58*.
115. Atkinson, Arthur Samuel, Diary 1865–66, 12 Oct. 1865, MS sequence (ATL).
116. J.M.A.–E.E.R., 27 Aug. [1865], *Addl 1865/75*.
117. J.C.R.–C.W.R., 14 Aug. [1865], *Addl 1865/70*.
118. J.E. FitzGerald–J.C.R., 25 Aug. 1865, *Addl 1865/45*.
119. J.C.R.–Mary Richmond, 28 June 1865, *Addl 1865/49*.
120. Cameron had offered his resignation to the War Office in Feb. 1865; in June he received permission to leave New Zealand.
121. J.C.R.–Mary Richmond, 24 July 1865, *Addl 1865/59*.
122. J.M.A.–E.E.R., 27 Aug [1865], *Addl 1865/49*.
123. Atkinson, Arthur Samuel, Diary 1865–66, 2 Sept. 1865, MS sequence (ATL).
124. '. . . the little girls are no trouble, better even I think than when their mother is at home, as is the wont of children. I don't think they are in awe of me, yet they certainly take fewer liberties than with their mother.' (M.R.–E.E.R., 8 Oct. 1865, *Addl 1865/94*.
125. Mary Richmond–J.C.R., 21 Aug. 1865, *Addl 1865/73*.
126. *idem*.
127. *ibid.*, 10 Aug. 1865, *Addl 1865/67*.
128. Harriet Gore Browne–Mary Richmond, 3 Sept. 1865, *Addl 1865/80*.
129. J.C.R.–Mary Richmond, 18 Aug. 1865, *Addl 1865/72*.
130. J.M.A.–M.R., 21 Oct. [1865], *Discards*.
131. J.C.R.–Mary Richmond, 19 Oct. 1865, *Addl 1865/96*.

132. Mary Richmond–J.C.R., 8 Aug. 1865, *Addl 1865/66*.
133. J.M.A.–M.R., 1 Nov. [1865], *Discards*.
134. M.R.–C.W.R. and E.E.R., 8 Nov. 1865, *Addl 1865/101*.
135. Atkinson, Arthur Samuel, Diary 1865–66, 3 Nov. 1865, MS sequence (ATL).
136. J.M.A.–M.T., 7 Dec. 1865, *Vol.38, p.546*.

Chapter Eleven: 'Tied by the leg'

1. William and Emily's seventh, Robert Richardson, was born towards the end of October 1865.
2. M.R.–E.E.R. 18 Nov. 1865, *Discards*. Harry had let his town house to Frank Ronalds. Frank's sister, Marion, lived there also and looked after Harry's two younger children.
3. Atkinson, Arthur Samuel, Diary 1865–66, 25 Nov. 1865, MS sequence.
4. In August 1864 Arthur increased his holding by taking over Frank Ronalds' 170 acres to prevent 'a stranger buying in'.
5. M.R.–E.E.R., 23 Dec. 1865, *Addl 1865/108*.
6. J.M.A.–E.E.R., 28 Feb. 1866, *Addl 1866/11*.
7. J.C.R.–C.W.R., 29 Dec. 1865, *Addl 1865/109*.
8. J.M.A.–M.T., 21 Jan. 1866, *Addl 1866/3*.
9. *ibid.*, 7 Feb. 1866, *Discards*.
10. *ibid.*, 21 Jan. 1866, *Addl 1866/3*.
11. *ibid.*, 3 Mar. 1866, *Addl 1866/13*.
12. *idem*.
13. *idem*.
14. *idem*.
15. J.M.A.–M.T., 21 Jan. 1866, *Addl 1866/3*.
16. He was now a trained surveyor. Maria thought his wife 'most suitable'. 'She is simple and unpretending in manner and tho' she has had a hard-working practical life is not at all rough or coarse.' (J.M.A.–M.T., 6 Apr. 1865, *Discards*.)
17. Chute arrived in New Zealand as Cameron's successor, 8 Oct. 1865.
18. Atkinson, Arthur Samuel, Diary 1865–66, 19 Jan. 1866, MS sequence.

19. All except Dr Isaac Featherston, in command of the 'native contingent', who put off his entry into the town till dark, 'being almost in a state of nature, literally without trousers'. He had suffered much from fatigue and hunger, being unable to eat horse flesh. (M.R.–E.E.R., 28 Jan. 1866, *Addl 1866/8*.

20. M.R.–E.E.R., 17 Feb. 1866, *Addl 1866/10*.

21. *Taranaki Herald*, 17 Feb. 1866.

22. *ibid.*, 17 Mar. 1866.

23. M.R.–E.E.R., 30 Oct. 1866, *Addl 1866/39*.

24. Atkinson, Arthur Samuel, Diary 1865–66, 6 Mar. 1866, MS sequence.

25. M.R.–E.E.R., 7 Feb. 1866, *Addl 1866/9*.

26. Atkinson, Arthur Samuel, Diary 1865–66, 28 Feb. 1866, MS sequence.

27. Crompton had represented Omata from 1853–55.

28. *Taranaki Herald*, 10 Mar. 1866.

29. E.W. Stafford–C.W.R., 23 Oct. 1865, *Addl 1865/97*.

30. *idem*.

31. C.W.R.–E.W. Stafford, 4 Nov. 1865, *Vol.42*.

32. Atkinson, Arthur Samuel, Diary 1865–66, 13 Mar. 1866, MS sequence.

33. J.M.A.–E.E.R., 26 Feb [1866], *Addl 1866/11*.

34. *ibid.*, 28 May [1866], *Addl 1866/21*.

35. *idem*..

36. J.M.A.–M.T., 30 Dec. 1866, *Addl 1866/47*.

37. J.M.A.–E.E.R., 28 May [1866], *Addl 1866/21*.

38. J.M.A.–M.T., 30 Dec. 1866, *Addl 1866/47*.

39. Annie's 'staff in life' became, as she evolved from Annie Smith to Lady Atkinson, a rod which she often used to subject other people to her own convenience. One does not doubt the misery of her headaches or the fret of her largely unsuccessful search for a holistic cure, but with the skill of a hypochondriac she was not above manipulating and using those closest to her. She has come down into living memory (she died in 1919 aged 81) as something of a domestic tyrant: 40 bottles of medicine on her bedside table; hot-water bottles rejected if the water was not actually boiled; shawls which had to be classified by weight to suit the weather; maids always leaving, and a daughter who, to the relief of the kin group, finally escaped into matrimony. Alison Atkinson, that thoughtful and wonderfully wise woman who died at York Bay in 1986 at the age of 94, would sometimes threaten her family, twinkle in eye, 'to do a Lady A!'

40. J.M.A.–M.T., 30 Dec. 1866, *Addl 1866/47*.

41. M.R.–E.E.R., 27 Apr. 1866, *Addl 1866/18*.

42. J.M.A.–E.E.R., 3 June 1866, *Addl 1866/22*.

43. J.M.A.–E.E.R., 3 Aug. 1866, Addl 1866/26. The first Mrs Rawson had died 'from a premature confinement of twins'; she had already borne ten children.

44. J.M.A.–M.T., 30 Dec. 1866, *Addl 1866/47*.

45. *idem*.

46. J.M.A.–M.T., 3 Oct. 1866, *Vol.38, p.552*.

47. *idem*.

48. He had formerly represented Dunedin in the General Assembly but was opposed to James Macandrew and separationist politics. When he lost his seat there, owing to the re-emergence of Macandrew in public favour, he stood and was elected for the town of New Plymouth.

49. J.C.R.–E.E.R., 9 July 1866, *Addl 1866/25*.

50. The Bill attracted support mainly from Auckland and Otago; it was well defeated.

51. Atkinson, Arthur Samuel, Diary 1865–66, 1 Aug. 1866, MS sequence.

52. *ibid.*, 2 Aug. 1866.

53. *ibid.*, 20 Aug. 1866.

54. E.W. Stafford, 24 Aug. 1866, *NZPD 1866* p.895.

55. J.M.A.–E.E.R., 3 Aug 1866, *Addl 1866/26*.

56. *idem*.

57. J.M.A.–M.T., 4 Sept. 1866, *Vol.6, p.64*.

58. *idem*.

59. M.R.–E.E.R., 3 Dec. 1866, *Addl 1866/41*.

60. H.R.R.–C.W.R., 14 Oct. 1866, *Addl 1866/35.*

61. Henry Richmond's pamphlet, *Ether is Matter; and Matter is Force, an Essay by a Settler in New Zealand,* was an early precursor of nuclear physics.

62. H.R.R.–John Tyndall, 28 Sept. 1869, *Vol.6, pp.94–7.*

63. J.C.R.–M.R., 27 Aug. and 23 Sept. 1866, Ann Paterson Coll.

64. M.R.–E.E.R., 3 Dec. 1866, *Addl 1866/41.*

65. *ibid.,* 27 April 1867, *Discards.*

66. J.M.A.–M.T., 11 July 1866, *Discards.*

67. At the end of Nov. 1866, Arthur bought Teddo Patten's 50-acre block for £150.

68. Named from the wreck of the brig *Harriet* there, 29 Apr. 1834.

69. A.S.A. Diary, 20 Feb. 1867, *Vol.36.*

70. *ibid.,* 24 Feb. 1867, *Vol.36.*

71. *ibid.,* 9 Mar. 1867, *Vol.36.*

72. Actually Arthur and Robert Parris had received a warning three months earlier that owing to the (Arthur's words) 'military ignorance & stupidity' of Col. Hamley in charge of the garrison at Warea, utu might be exacted from a Pakeha on the Opunake road. In Nov. 1866 two 'rebel' Maori coming to the garrison to treat for peace were taken prisoner on the colonel's orders and subjected to considerable indignity. Hone Pihama told Arthur and Parris at the time of this outrage that the 'Waeros wanting utu will take it out of him perhaps & the Opunake road will be unsafe.' Parris then sent Pihama to tell the 'Waeros' at Waikoukou that he was willing 'to talk of peace'. Arthur was doubtful of success when their two 'ambassadors' were in prison. (A.S.A. Diary, 24,26,28 Nov. 1866, *Vol.36*).

73. A.S.A. Diary, 24 Mar. 1867, *Vol.36.*

74. *ibid.,* 10 April 1867, *Vol.36.*

75. M.R.–E.E.R., 2 Apr. 1867, *Discards.*

76. J.M.A.–C.W.A., 14 Feb. [1867], *Box of Misc. Letters.*

77. M.R.–Mary E. Richmond, 15 Feb. 1867, *Box of Misc. Letters.*

78. When Mary was 12, she and her three-year-old brother went to stay with friends. William wrote to his daughter, 'Be sure to change Alfie's boots when required & not let him eat berries or leaves. *Attend* to him regularly last thing at night and when he awakes. Recollect he is in your charge, and that it is a great responsibility and do not forget your duties in your pleasures.' (C.W.R.–Mary E. Richmond, 24 Oct. [1865], *Discards.*)

79. J.M.A.–M.T., 3 Jan. 1867, *Addl 1867/1.*

80. *ibid.,* 31 Aug. [1867], *Addl 1867/45.*

81. A.S.A. Diary, 29 Apr. 1867, *Vol.36.*

82. *NZPD 1867,* Vol.1, p.381.

83. *ibid.,* 1867, *Vol.1, pp.460–1.*

84. The *Taranaki Herald* opinion of the Act was that it would remain a 'dead letter'. But 'having admitted this we think that the cost of a little paper and printing is a cheap rate at which to get rid of that appearance of injustice towards the Maoris, which is so fruitful a theme to philanthropists, both in the colony and at home.' (*Taranaki Herald,* 31 Aug. 1867.)

85. *NZPD 1867,* p.1279.

86. 'Decie's town sections have sold much better than even his sanguine mind had pictured. He got £162 for those sold, some realising less than £11, the highest selling for £15.' (J.M.A.–A.S.A, 14 July 1867, *Vol.6, p.74.*)

87. J.M.A.–A.S.A., 18 Aug. 1867, Ann Paterson Coll.

88. Grace Hirst–sisters, Dec. 1866, Hirst Family Letters.

89. J.M.A.–M.R., 5 Feb. 1864, *Addl 1864/9.*

90. Annie Atkinson–M.R., 22 July 1867, Ann Paterson Coll.

91. At least this seems so from Maria's letters. None of Arthur's to her, including his diary which he possibly sent also, have survived.

92. J.M.A.–A.S.A., 14 July 1867, *Vol.6, p.74.*

93. *idem.*

94. *ibid.,* 18 Aug. 1867, Ann Paterson Coll.

95. *idem.*

96. M.R.–C.W.R., 17 July 1867, *Box of Misc. Letters.*

97. J.M.A.–M.T., 31 Aug. 1867, *Addl 1867/45.*

Notes

389

98. *idem.*
99. Annie Smith–Mary Richmond, 27 Nov. 1864, *Discards.*
100. 'Ruth enters into the spirit of the household; she wished to know this morning who was coming when Kit went away & when I said nobody till Father comes home, "Oh but may'nt we have Tudor?" ' (J.M.A.–A.S.A., 18 Aug. 1867, Ann Paterson Coll.)
101. J.M.A.–A.S.A., 18 Aug. 1867, Ann Paterson Coll.
102. Mill was briefly (1865–68) a member of the House of Commons. The enfranchisement of women was part of his political philosophy.
103. 'Fear death? – to feel the fog in my throat/ The mist in my face.' (From Browning's *Prospice.*)
104. J.M.A.–A.S.A., 27 Sept. 1867, Ann Paterson Coll.
105. *ibid.*, 18 Aug. 1857, Ann Paterson Coll.
106. J.M.A.–A.S.A., 2 Sept. 1867, Ann Paterson Coll.
107. *ibid.*, 14 Sept. 1867, Ann Paterson Coll.
108. Henry Richmond as superintendent of Taranaki had drawn up a memorial to government which he presented, at the end of August, to a public meeting. The memorial stated that without money in lieu of land revenue it would be impossible to carry on provincial government in Taranaki.
109. J.M.A.–A.S.A., 14 Sept. 1867, Ann Paterson Coll.
110. J.M.A.–M.T., 31 Aug. 1867, *Addl 1867/45.* The duchy of Saxe-Weimar was regarded as a centre of European liberalism and of German art and culture. It was the home of Goethe and Schiller.
111. C.W.R.–A.S.A., 30 Sept. 1867, *Addl 1867/47.*
112. E.E.R.–M.R., 10 Dec. 1867, *Discards.*
113. J.M.A.–M.T., 30 Dec. 1867, *Addl 1867/52.*
114. J.M.A.–A.S.A., 2 Jan. 1868, *Vol.6, p.76.*
115. *ibid.*, 29 Dec. 1867, *Vol.6, p.76.*
116. *idem.*
117. The lease of their first Nelson house expired at the end of December. William and Emily must have moved into St Katherine's, their permanent Nelson home, in January 1868.
118. A.S.A. Diary, *Vol.31a.*
119. J.M.A.–A.S.A., 2 Jan. 1868, *Vol.6, p.76.*

Chapter Twelve: Bleak House to Fairfield

1. John Blackett's private journal contains brief social references, among which visits by Emily and Maria are occasionally noted. 'John Blackett Papers 1851–1892', MS 1704, Vol.3 (ATL).
2. His 1868 Diary continues in normal fashion until 25 Jan., resumes at 10 May and ceases at 20 May.
3. *Nelson Examiner*, 6 Jan. 1869.
4. Because Nelson was a bishop's see, Queen Victoria had already (1858) constituted it a city.
5. Section 1045 on Frederick Tuckett's 'Plan of the Town of Nelson, 28 April 1842', Nelson Museum Library.
6. 'Board of Works Rating Rolls', Nelson Museum Library.
7. St Katherine's would have been near to the present Barnicoat House of Nelson College.
8. J.M.A.–M.T., 10 May 1868, *Addl 1868/3.*
9. J.M.A.–A.S.A., 4 Jan. 1868, A. Paterson Coll.
10. J.M.A.–A.S.A., 22 Sept. [1868] A. Paterson Coll.
11. A.S.A. 'Diary', 7 Jan. 1868, *Vol.37.*
12. *ibid.*, 19 Jan. 1868, *Vol.37.*
13. *Nelson Examiner*, 4 June 1868.
14. A.S.A. 'Diary', 20 May 1868, *Vol.37.*
15. C.W.R.–Thomas Richmond, 14 Oct. 1867, *Vol.42.*
16. J.M.A.–A.S.A., 27 May [1868], A. Paterson Coll.
17. J.M.A.–M.T., 23 Mar [1870], *Addl 1870/2.*
18. *idem.*
19. J.M.A.–M.T., 3 Aug. 1870, *Addl 1870/9.*
20. *idem.*
21. Otago Girls' High School, the first public secondary school for girls in New Zealand, opened in 1869. Its foundation was not due only to Presbyterian advocacy of learning or

to the bonanza provided by the
goldfields but also to the vigorous
agitation of Learmonth Whyte
Dalrymple.

22. J.M.A.–M.T., 23 Mar [1870], *Addl
1870/2.*

23. *idem.*

24. Quoted in *In Her Own Right The Life of
Elizabeth Cady Stanton*, Elizabeth
Griffith, Oxford University Press
(New York) 1984, p.95.

25. J.M.A.–M.T., 23 Mar. [1870], *Addl
1870/2.*

26. H.W. Harper–C.W.R., 16 Aug. 1869,
Addl 1869/10.

27. *Nelson Examiner*, 9 Oct. 1869.

28. *ibid.*, 29 April 1871.

29. *ibid.*, 20 May 1871.

30. E.E.R.–C.W.R., 12 May 1871, *Addl
1871/5.*

31. *idem.*

32. Nelsonians were excited by a proposal
to light their city with gas and at the
same time to extend the city water
supply. The provincial government
raised a loan for the purpose.

33. *Nelson Examiner*, 16 Dec. 1871.

34. 'Minutes of the Nelson College Board
of Governors', Nelson Museum
Library.

35. Anna Richmond–C.W.R., 12 July
1871, *Addl 1879/9.*

36. John Pyke Hullah (1812–1884), an
English composer and teacher of
music.

37. J.M.A.–M.T., 3 Aug. 1870, *Addl 1870/
9.*

38. J.M.A.–M.T., 10 May 1868, *Addl
1868/3.*

39. Emma Parris was 23 when she married.

40. J.M.A.–M.T., 10 May 1868, *Addl
1868/3.*

41. Nineteenth-century Anglicanism
ranged from the 'high church' stance
of the Tractarians to the 'low church'
conviction of the Evangelicals. Being
of the 'broad church' implied that one
sought to interpret doctrine in a
'broad' or liberal sense.

42. J.M.A.–A.S.A., 27 May [1868], Ann
Paterson Coll.

43. *idem.*

44. J.M.A.–M.T., 31 Dec. 1870, *Addl
1870/18.*

45. H.A.A.–A.S.A., 7 Sept. 1868, *Vol.6,
p.83.*

46. J.C.R.–C.W.R., 29 June 1868, *Addl
1868/6.*

47. *ibid.*, 31 May 1868, *Addl 1868/5.*

48. J.M.A.–A.S.A., 1 June 1869, Ann
Paterson Coll.

49. J.M.A.–A.S.A., 9 May 1869, Ann
Paterson Coll.

50. *idem.*

51. J.C.R.–A.S.A., 16 Aug. 1869, *Addl
1869/11.*

52. J.M.A.–M.T., 23 Mar. [1870], *Addl
1870/2.*

53. *ibid.*, 3 Aug. 1870, *Addl 1870/9.*

54. *ibid.*, 24 Oct. 1870, *Addl 1870/13.*

55. *ibid.*, 23 Mar. [1870], *Addl 1870/2.*

56. *idem.*

57. J.C.R.–H.A.A., 4 Oct. 1870, *Addl
1870/11.*

58. J.M.A.–M.T., 31 Dec. 1870, *Addl
1870/18.*

59. *Nelson Examiner*, 12 Jan. 1871.

60. Unlike Vogel he was not in favour of
heavy government expenditure on
public works, arguing that that
activity belonged to commercial
enterprise. To his electors at Grey and
Bell he wrote, 'my cure for our
difficulties is that we should wind up
with the least possible delay all affairs
in which the Government is
concerned beyond the true function of
Government'. Or, as he wrote to
William, 'make the country rely less
on and think less about government'.
(J.C.R.–Electors of Grey and Bell, 15
June 1868, *Vol.6, p.78* and J.C.R.–
C.W.R., 31 May 1868, *Addl 1868/5.*)

61. J.M.A.–M.T., 2 Oct. 1870, *Addl 1870/
10.*

62. *NZPD* 23 June 1870, Vol.1, p.48. For
the details of J.C. Richmond's Bill,
see *Lapsed Bills, 1870*, Parliamentary
Library.

63. J.M.A.–M.T., 3 Aug. 1870, *Addl 1870/
9.*

64. It established that in certain cases
when a husband was living in open
adultery or was habitually drunk, or
habitually failing to provide
maintenance, a magistrate 'may order'
the wife to have custody of the
children and the husband to pay £1
per week for each child under ten
years.

65. J.M.A.–M.T., 4 Feb. 1871, *Addl 1871/
4.*

66. J.M.A.-A.S.A., 15 Jan. [1869], Ann Paterson Coll.
67. J.M.A.-Ann Shaen, 14 July 1872, *Addl 1872/5*.
68. *idem*.
69. *idem*.
70. This preparatory examination consisted of a general knowledge paper set by Judge Johnston, and papers in Greek and Latin.
71. J.M.A.-M.T., 2 Oct. 1870, *Addl 1870/ 10*.
72. C.W.R.-E.E.R., 20 Jan. 1871, *Addl 1871/3*.
73. J.M.A.-Ann Shaen, 14 July 1872, *Addl 1872/5*.
74. J.M.A.-M.T., 23 Mar. [1870], *Addl 1870/2*.
75. J.M.A.-Ann Shaen, 14 July 1872, *Addl 1872/5*.
76. J.M.A.-A.S.A., [Jan. 1871], *Addl 1871/ 2a*.
77. J.M.A.-Ann Shaen, 14 July 1872, *Addl 1872/5*.
78. Fell, Charles Yates, 'Autobiography' (TS.) Bett Collection, Nelson Museum Library.
79. A.S.A.-H.A.A., 4 Jan. 1871, *Addl 1871/1*.
80. J.M.A.-M.T., 2 Oct. 1870, *Addl 1870/. 10*.
81. *ibid.*, 4 Feb. 1871, *Addl 1871/4*.
82. *ibid.*, 30 Apr. 1870, *Addl 1870/3*.
83. J.M.A.-C.W.R., 12 July 1871, *Discards*.
84. When the provisions of the will were being discussed, Maria recollected that there was a Richmond cousin, John Reeves Richmond, the same age as herself, living in Australia. She gave no further details about him.
85. J.M.A.-M.T., 31 Dec. 1870, *Addl 1870/18*.
86. J.M.A.-Ann Shaen, 9 Apr. [1873], *Addl 1873/12*.
87. *idem*.

Chapter Thirteen: European cultivation

The Richmond Family Papers referred to are Acc 77–173, ATL.

1. J.M.A.-Kate Whittle, 5 Dec. 1856, *Vol.38, p.323*.
2. J.M.A.-M.T., 23 Mar. 1870, *Addl 1870/2*.
3. A. Domett-A.S.A., 27 Nov. 1872, *Addl 1872/8*.
4. J.M.A.-Ann Shaen, 14 July 1872, *Addl 1872/5*.
5. J.C.R.-Ann Shaen, 22 Aug. 1873, *Addl 1873/19*.
6. J.M.A.-J.C.R., 25 Dec. 1873, *Addl 1873/32*.
7. Ann E. Richmond-E.E.R., [May 1873], *Discards*.
8. J.C.R.-J.M.A. 8 May 1873, *Addl 1873/17*.
9. J.M.A.-Ann E. Richmond, 22 Oct. [1873], *Addl 1873/27*.
10. J.C.R. circular letter, 3 Sept. 1873, *Addl 1873/20*.
11. The Camden School for Girls, established in 1871, offered an inexpensive grammar school education for the daughters of the middle class. Its fees were only four guineas a year, its leaving age was 16, and scholarships were provided to carry the most promising to the North London.
12. J.C.R.-J.M.A., 9 Mar. 1874, *Addl 1874/5*.
13. J.C.R. circular letter, 31 Mar. 1874, *Addl 1874/6*.
14. Ann E. Richmond-Edith E. Atkinson, 6 Sept. 1874, *Addl 1874/18*.
15. *idem*.
16. *idem*.
17. Maurice W. Richmond-Richard H. Richmond, 5 May 1874, *Addl 1874/9*.
18. J.M.A.-Ann E. Richmond, 22 Oct. [1873], *Addl 1873/22*.
19. He was experimenting with concrete blocks. Some years later he was foreman of a road gang.
20. J.C.R.-J.M.A., 17 Nov. 1874, *Addl 1874/27*.
21. H.A.A.-A.S.A., 6 Sept. 1863, *Vol. 7, p.20*.
22. J.C.R.-C.W.R., 15 May 1874, *Addl 1874/12*.
23. J.M.A.-Ann E. Richmond, 19 Nov. 1874, *Addl 1874/28*.
24. J.M.A.-J.C.R., 8 Mar. 1875, *Addl 1875/7*.
25. J.C.R.-C.W.R., 30 Apr. 1875, *Addl 1875/10*.
26. Anna W. Richmond-C.W.R., 12 Sept. 1875, *Discards*.

27. J.M.A.–Anna W. Richmond, 26 Oct. 1875, *Addl 1875/28*.
28. The *Nelson Examiner* ceased publication in January 1874.
29. *Colonist*, 17 Jan. 1874.
30. J.M.A.–J.C.R., 25 Dec. 1873, *Addl 1873/32*.
31. *Colonist*, 14 Dec. 1875.
32. It was, nevertheless, practised to a degree in Dunedin. The Otago Girls' High School, opened in Feb. 1871, shared for some 15 years the same building which housed the Boys' High School. A fence separated the two playing areas.
33. *Colonist*, 22 Dec. 1874.
34. J.M.A.–E.E.R., 9 Feb. [1875], *Discards*.
35. J.M.A.–Mary E. Richmond, 14 Dec. [1875], *Addl 1875/35*.
36. A.S.A.–C.W.R., 2 Aug. 1875, *Addl 1875/16*.
37. J.M.A.–Anna W. Richmond, 26 Oct. 1875, *Addl 1875/28*.
38. Julius Vogel was absent in England. Dr D. Pollen, who replaced him as prime minister, conducted affairs from the Legislative Council.
39. Grey was elected MP for Auckland City West, 27 March 1875.
40. J.M.A.–C.W.R., 4 Aug. 1875, *Discards*.
41. A.S.A.–C.W.R., 2 Aug. 1875, *Addl 1875/16*.
42. H.A.A.–A.S.A., 26 Jan. 1876, *Vol.7, p.27*.
43. 9 July 1874.
44. J.M.A.–E.E.R., 5 Sept. 1875, *Addl 1875/21*.
45. *idem*.
46. J.M.A.–Anna W. Richmond, 26 Oct. 1875, *Addl 1875/28*.
47. J.M.A.–E.E.R., [5 Sept. 1875], *Addl 1875/21*.
48. J.C.R.–J.M.A., 28 June 1875, *Addl 1875/14*.
49. E.E.R.–C.W.R., 30 Aug. 1875, *Addl 1875/20*.
50. Margaret Richmond–A.S.A., 23 Dec. 1875, *Addl 1875/39*.
51. J.C.R. circular letter, 28 May 1874, *Addl 1874/13*.
52. J.C.R.–J.M.A., 3 Mar. 1875, *Addl 1875/6*. Harding's proposed railway track left the main line about 30 kilometres from Oran and ran south to a 'great plateau' covered in esparto grass which was collected for paper making. The line was 50 kilometres long and ended at the newly developed French town of Sidi bel Abbés.
53. C.W.R.–Christopher F. Richmond, 21 Sept. 1875, *Addl 1875/24*.
54. J.M.A.–E.E.R., 30 May 1876, *Addl 1876/19*.
55. E.E.R.–Alice Richmond, 25 Dec. 1875, *Box of Misc. Letters*.
56. C.W.R.–A.S.A., 21 Aug. 1876, C.W.R. Letterbook in *Box of Misc. Letters*.
57. *ibid.*, 3 April 1876, C.W.R. Letterbook in *Box of Misc. Letters*.
58. J.M.A.–E.E.R., 31 May 1876, *Addl 1876/19*.
59. Mary E. Richmond–Anna W. Richmond, 23 Mar. [1876], *Box of Misc Letters*.
60. *idem*.
61. C.W.R.–A.S.A., 28 Aug. 1876, C.W.R. Letterbook in *Box of Misc. Letters*.
62. A.S.A.–E.E.R., 18 Sept. 1876, *Addl 1876/35*.
63. J.M.A.–C.W.R., 18 Sept. [1876], *Addl 1876/36*.
64. Ann Shaen–J.M.A., quoted in J.M.A.–C.W.R., 19 Sept. 1876, *Addl 1876/36*.
65. J.M.A.–E.E.R., 19 Aug. 1876, *Addl 1876/29*.
66. Harding's latest interest was in provincial tramway systems. He asked J.C.R. 'to take the map of France and suggest lines!! It's almost as inebriating a position as that of Sir J. Vogel with his 10 mill. and the 1500 miles.' (J.C.R.–J.M.A., 8 Nov. 1875, *Addl 1875/32*.)
67. J.M.A.–E.E.R., 15 Nov. 1876, *Addl 1876/41*.
68. J.C.R.–Ann Shaen, 20 Mar. 1876, *Addl 1876/11*.
69. J.M.A.–Mary E. Richmond, 14 Dec. [1875], *Addl 1875/35*.
70. H.R.R.–C.W.R., 17 May 1877, *Addl 1877/5*.
71. J.M.A.–E.E.R., 19 Nov. 1875, *Addl 1875/33*.
72. H.R.R.–C.W.R., 17 May 1877, *Addl 1877/5*.
73. 'A female pedant or learned woman

who tends to neglect "feminine graces" and their accompaniments.' *Brewer's Dictionary of Phrase and Fable*, 1st published in 1870.

74. J.M.A.–C.W.R., 10 Feb. 1876, *Addl 1876/5*.

75. A two-storey house standing in three-quarters of an acre on the corner of Wellington Terrace and what was to become Bowen Street. It was bought by Walter Turnbull as his home in 1869. Later he rented it to government for a ministerial residence.

76. J.M.A.–C.W.R., 10 Feb. 1876, *Addl 1876/5*.

77. *idem.*

78. *idem.*

79. J.M.A.–E.E.R., 31 May 1876, *Addl 1876/19*.

80. J.M.A.–C.W.R., 19 Sept. 1876, *Addl 1876/36*.

81. J.M.A.–Mary E. Richmond, 14 Dec. [1875], *Addl 1875/35*.

82. J.M.A.–C.W.R., 4 Aug. 1875, *Discards*.

83. *ibid.*, 31 Dec. 1876, Richmond Family Papers Box 7.

84. J.M.A.–E.E.R., 15 Nov. 1876, *Addl 1876/41*.

85. *idem.*

86. J.M.A.–Anna W. Richmond, 12 Jan. 1877, *Discards*.

87. C.W.R.–E.E.R., 10 Mar. 1877, C.W.R. Letterbook in *Box of Misc Letters*.

88. A.S. Atkinson Nelson Journal, 16 Mar. 1877, q MS sequence.

89. Octavia Hill (1838–1912), a protégée of F.D. Maurice and John Ruskin, had been secretary of Maurice's Working Men's College during the 1850s and would probably have known Mary and Annie Smith. In 1861 she and her sisters began a school for girls at Nottingham Place, London. William Shaen, brother of Ann, was their legal adviser.

90. Marcella Wilkins–E.E.R., [c.1877], Richmond Family Papers, Box 6.

91. J.C.R.–E.E.R., 27 Apr. 1877, Richmond Family Papers, Box 6.

92. *idem.*

93. At the end of 1876, Harry Atkinson, using the patronage of his office, offered James a senior position in the

civil service which the latter declined: 'My desire is to have a few years of moderate health among you all in the Colony which I may spend in reading, painting and wine growing.' (J.C.R.–A.S.A., 12 Dec. 1876, *Addl 1876/44*.

94. J.C.R.–A.S.A., 18 Oct. 1877, *Addl 1877/18*.

95. J.C.R.–A.S.A., 20 Sept. 1877, *Addl 1877/16*.

96. J.C.R.–E.E.R., 26 June 1877, *Addl 1877/10*.

97. J.C.R.–J.M.A., 3 Aug. 1877, *Addl 1877/15*.

98. J.C.R.–Dorothy K. Richmond, 23 June 1877, *Addl 1877/9*.

99. In Goethe's widely read *Die Leiden des jungen Werther*, the young poet hero, obsessed by love and introspection, and vacillating between joy and despair, takes his own life. The work was a dramatic representation of the *Sturm und Drang* period of Goethe's own life.

100. J.M.A.–E.E.R, 5 Oct. [1877], *Discards*.

101. *idem.*

102. Christopher F. Richmond–Anna W. Richmond, 25 Feb. 1878, *Addl 1878/7*.

103. Atkinson, Arthur Samuel, Nelson Journal, 16 Mar 1877–2 Feb. 1878, MS sequence ATL. (The journal also contains a few entries for 1879).

104. A.S.A. Nelson journal, 10 June 1877.

105. *ibid.*, 8 July 1877.

106. Maria had hoped that their English schoolmaster friend, J.H. Hutton, would apply. 'I suppose J.H.H. is longing for some ideal country living with an ivy covered church & parsonage & a simple believing flock & that the principalship here would have no attractions.' (J.M.A.–C.W.R., 31 May 1876, *Addl 1876/19*.) Hutton applied, but doubted his chances, 'I have never been a critical scholar such as our English colleges would take for their head or principal.' (J.H.H.–C.W.R., 31 July 1876, *Addl 1876/28*.) J.C. Andrew, a former Oxford don turned runholder and member of parliament, was appointed headmaster in Sept. 1876.

107. A.S.A.–C.W.R., 21 Feb. 1878, *Addl 1878/5*.

108. A.S.A.-E.E.R., 22 July 1878, Richmond Family Papers, Box 6.
109. J.C.R.-C.W.R., 22 May 1878, Addl 1878/14.
110. J.M.A.-C.W.R., 3 Jan. 1878, Richmond Family Papers, Box 7.
111. J.C.R.-C.W.R., 9 June 1878, Addl 1878/16.
112. Alice Richmond-E.E.R., 14 Apr. 1878, Richmond Family Papers, Box 7.
113. Margaret Richmond-E.E.R., 18 Oct. 1878, Richmond Family Papers, Box 8.
114. idem.
115. J.C.R.-C.W.R., 3 Jan. 1878, Addl 1878/1.
116. Ann E. Richmond-A.S.A., 31 Jan. 1878, Discards.
117. Mary E. Richmond-Anna W. Richmond, 2 Oct. 1878, Richmond Family Papers, Box 10.
118. J.M.A.-E.E.R., 1 July [1878], Richmond Family Papers, Box 6.
119. C.W.R.-Mary E. Richmond, 2 June 1877, Discards.
120. E.E.R.-Anna W. Richmond, 3 Oct. 1878, Richmond Family Papers, Box 10.
121. C.W.R.-E.E.R., 22 Sept. 1878, Addl 1878/22.
122. E.E.R.-C.W.R., 22 Oct. 1878, Richmond Family Papers, Box 6.
123. J.M.A.-Anna W. Richmond, 3 May 1878, Richmond Family Papers, Box 7.
124. C.W.R.-Alice Richmond, 13 Sept. 1879, Addl 1879/11.
125. J.M.A.-Maurice W. Richmond, 14 Nov. 1879, Discards.
126. J.C.R.-E.E.R., 22 July 1878, Richmond Family Papers, Box 6.
127. J.M.A.-E.E.R., 22 Nov. 1878, Addl 1878/28.
128. J.C.R.-M.T., 20 Dec. 1879, Discards.
129. Dorothy K. Richmond-E.E.R., Richmond Family Papers, Box 7.
130. idem.
131. J.C.R.-C.W.R., 22 May 1878, Addl 1878/14.
132. C.W.R.-E.E.R., 11 Feb. 1879, Addl 1879/1.
133. ibid., 29 Jan. 1878, Addl 1878/3.
134. H.R.R.-C.W.R., 29 July 1879, Addl 1879/8. That year the first party of ploughers, under the leadership of Te

Whiti O Rongomai, were arrested for obstructing the opening up of the Waimate Plains of South Taranaki.
135. J.M.A.-C.W.R., 31 Dec. [1879], Discards.
136. Ann E. Richmond-Annie Atkinson, 10 Nov. 1880, Discards.
137. Turnbull, Walter, 29 Nov. [1880]. Journal . . . 1825-80 ATL. (The journal contains four letters written on the Kaiser-i-Hind en route to NZ, Nov. 1880.)
138. C.W.R.-E.E.R., 14 Jan. 1881, Addl 1881/1.
139. idem.

Chapter Fourteen: 'Young folks & sunshine'

The Richmond Family Papers referred to are Acc 77-173, ATL.

1. Paterson, Ann, Stories of York Bay, (privately printed, 1983), p.81.
2. A drop of aconite was the mob's initial reaction to almost any illness.
3. She obviously continued writing but most of her letters have disappeared. In this last period Maria seldom included a year date.
4. J.M.A.-E.E.R., 29 Dec. [c. 1885], Box of Misc. Letters.
5. ibid. [c. 1888], Discards.
6. see page 332.
7. He recommended 'compulsory co-operative thrift'. Men and women, married or single between the ages of 18 and 65 would receive graduated weekly payments when ill – there was a separate annuity for orphans and the elderly – which would be financed from a fund to which all workers would contribute weekly amounts.
8. J.C. Richmond was a member of the Legislative Council 1883-92.
9. Dalziel, Raewyn, 'The Colonial Helpmeet', in New Zealand Journal of History, Vol.11, No.2 (Oct. 1977), p.120.
10. W.F. Howlett-Arthur R. Atkinson, 13 Aug. 1895, Addl 1895/8.
11. Published in 1896. Lecky considered democracy to be inevitable but,

using the examples of 'ignorant Irish' and of negro voters, concluded that it 'levelled down quite as much as levelled up'. He did not think democracy uniformly favourable to liberty.

12. Beaglehole, J.C., *Victoria University College an essay towards a history* (New Zealand University Press, 1949), p.50.

13. Richmond Family Papers, Box 67.

14. J.M.A.–E.E.R., 23 Sept. [1887], *Addl 1887/8.*

15. Ann E. Richmond–Ann Shaen, 20 Feb. 1881, *Addl 1881/3.*

16. Ann E. Richmond–J.M.A., 8 Jan. 1882, *Discards.*

17. *idem.*

18. J.M.A.–E.E.R., [28 June 1876], *Addl 1876/23.*

19. J.M.A.–Anna W. Richmond, 4 May [1881], Richmond Family Papers, Box 11.

20. Ann E. Richmond–Ann Shaen, [1 Aug. 1881], *Addl 1881/11.*

21. Edie had two more children: Phyllis, 1884; Sylvia, 1888.

22. James inherited about £2,500 from the estate of Aunt Smith (Mary's mother), who died in September 1880.

23. It still stands (19 Richmond Avenue Extension) and looks remarkably unchanged from photos of it in the Fell albums.

24. The *Colonist* regarded itself, in opposition to the *Nelson Examiner* which it outlived, as the organ of the working man. Its political alignment whenever it raised its sights from provincial matters was with the Liberals.

25. In the Legislative Council, Hansard reporters sometimes noted that J.C. Richmond was 'inaudible'.

26. *Colonist*, 4 June 1881.

27. Dorothy K. Richmond–Ann Shaen, 27 Nov. 1881, *Addl 1881/17.*

28. *idem.*

29. J.C.R.–C.W.R., 13 Dec. 1881, *Addl 1881/19.*

30. M.T.–J.C.R., 2 Oct. 1881, *Discards.*

31. Totaranui, protected within the aegis of Tasman National Park, remains in essence as it was when the mob disported there.

32. Dorothy K. Richmond–Ann Shaen, 24 Feb. 1882, *Discards.*

33. Ann E. Richmond–Annie Atkinson, 24 Mar. 1882, *Addl 1882/4.*

34. Ann E. Richmond–Ann Shaen, 4 Oct. [1883], *Addl 1884/15.*

35. Dorothy K. Richmond–Ann Shaen, 20 Mar. 1883, *Addl 1883/2.*

36. Ann E. Richmond–Ann Shaen, 4 Oct. 1883, *Addl 1884/15.*

37. Wallcott was an English army colonel and also a captain in the Salvation Army.

38. Ann E. Richmond–Dorothy K. Richmond, 28 Aug. 1885, *Addl 1885/13.*

39. Ann E. Richmond–Annie Atkinson, 24 Mar. 1882, *Addl 1882/4.*

40. Dorothy K. Richmond–Ann Shaen, 4 June 1881, *Addl 1881/7.*

41. Ann E. Richmond–Ann Shaen, [*c.* Aug. 1881], *Addl 1881/11.*

42. Considering the long struggle to achieve secondary education for girls in Nelson, it is surprising that no particular attention was given in either newspaper to the significance of the event.

43. Only 25 when she was appointed, Kate Edger was already famous as the first woman in the Empire to be granted a BA degree. Both she and her sister were now MAs. They had previously taught at Christchurch Girls' High School.

44. Dolla resigned in 1886; for almost all of 1885 she was in England.

45. Maria's letters about the alterations are without year dates. Internal evidence in the letters makes it certain that the bulk of the alterations were carried out during 1883 and 1884. Fairfield now has a 'B' classification from the New Zealand Historical Places Trust and is well maintained by a voluntary organisation, Friends of Old Fairfield.

46. J.M.A.–Mary E. Richmond, 14 Dec. [1875], *Addl 1875/35.*

47. J.M.A.–E.E.R., 12 Sept. [1884], *Box of Misc. Letters.*

48. *ibid.*, 11 May 1881, *Addl 1881/4.*

49. M.T.–J.C.R., 2 Oct. 1881, *Discards.*

50. Family archives contain more letters from Alla than from Dolla, but the

latter's confirm the deep bond between the two sisters.

51. Ann E. Richmond–Ann Shaen, 30 June 1885, *Addl 1885/7.*

52. Kate Whittle died *circa* 1883 and Syrgenstein was sold. Margaret Taylor and James Whittle took a house in Ziegelhaus, near Heidelberg, which seemed to Dolla only a little less grand: 'There are 10 sitting rooms . . . all very pretty & so many of the things from Syrgenstein in them that the house seems quite familiar to me.' (Dorothy K. Richmond–A. Shaen, 9 Sept. 1885, *Addl 1885/14.*)

53. Dorothy K. Richmond–Ann Shaen, 19 Dec. 1885, *Addl 1885/17.*

54. E. Tudor Atkinson–Dorothy K. Richmond, 12 Sept. 1885, *Discards.*

55. J.M.A.–Ann E. Richmond, 4 Dec. [1885], *Addl 1885/16.*

56. *idem.*

57. After the 1884 general election no combination in the House had an assured majority. Arthur advised his brother against a coalition with Vogel. A Stout–Vogel ministry held office for twelve days; it was replaced for less than a week by an Atkinson-led one. Robert Stout took office again and retained it until the 1887 general election.

58. The Royal Society had sent instructions to several colonial observers of whom 'Mr Atkinson of Nelson' was one. Alla described the preparations. 'A little electric house of zinc has been put up on the knoll & telegraph lines connect it with the telegraph office – so the chronometers of all the observers may be exactly together at the critical moment.' (Ann E. Richmond–Richard H. Richmond, 30 Nov. [1882], Jinny Atkinson Coll.)

59. Arthur R. Atkinson (fragment only), 17 Jan. [1899], *Discards.*

60. Walter Fell was born in Nelson in 1855, grew up in France and was educated at Rugby and Oxford. From the latter he graduated MA and MD. He was also an MRCS and LRCP. He returned to New Zealand in 1884 and joined W.E. Collins in a Wellington practice.

61. Margaret Richmond–Anna W. Richmond, 11 Dec. 1885, Richmond Family Papers, Box 10.

62. J.M.A.–Anna W. Richmond, Good Friday [1886], Richmond Family Papers, Box 10.

63. E.E.R..–Anna W. Richmond, [26 Apr. 1886], Richmond Family Papers, Box 10.

64. A.S.A.–Anna W. Richmond, 8 June 1886, Richmond Family Papers, Box 10.

65. J.M.A.–E.E.R., 4 June [1886], *Discards.*

66. *idem.*

67. Marion returned 'more cheerful' at the end of 1886 and opened a boarding house in Wellington which was of use to the younger members of the mob as a temporary billet.

68. Dunstan married Catherine Ann Adams, 6 June 1885, at New Plymouth.

69. E. Tudor Atkinson–H. Dunstan Atkinson, 1 Sept. 1884, Ann Paterson Coll.

70. Anna W. Richmond–J.C.R., 19 July 1886, *Discards.*

71. 'There is a strong and active Irish element in the Society . . . Feeling runs very high in the family on the Irish question, Uncle William and Aunt Emily are violently opposed to Gladstone, Uncle Harry approves of what he is doing . . . Kit takes after his father and mother, I on the other hand throw the weight of my authority in with Gladstone, though I have not cabled him to that effect.' (Maurice W. Richmond–A.S.A., 29 June 1886, *Addl 1886/8.*)

72. E.E.R.–Anna W. Richmond, 3 Dec. 1885, Richmond Family Papers, Box 10.

73. J.M.A.–E.E.R., 17 Feb. [1887], *Addl 1887/3.*

74. Maurice W. Richmond–J.C.R., 16 Jan. 1887, *Discards.*

75. E. Tudor Atkinson–A.S.A., 23 Oct. 1886, Jinny Atkinson Coll.

76. Ann E. Richmond–Ann Shaen, 27 Jan 1887, *Discards.*

77. J.M.A.–E.E.R., 3 Jan. 1887, *Addl 1887/1.*

78. Family alchemy had transformed Willie into Billa. He was in fact

William Edmund Atkinson, eldest son of William and Eliza.

79. J.M.A.-E.E.R., 4 Nov. 1888, *Addl 1888/8*.

80. Hurworth later amalgamated with a preparatory school in Havelock North and became Hereworth.

81. J.M.A.-E.E.R., 22 June [1888], Richmond Family Papers, Box 10.

82. *ibid.*, 23 Sept. 1887, *Addl 1887/8*.

83. Newbolt, Henry, *My World As In My Time . . . 1862-1932* (Faber and Faber, 1932), p.122.

84. J.M.A.-E.E.R., 13 Nov. 1888, *Addl 1888/9*.

85. *ibid.*, 27 Nov. [1888], *Addl 1888/10*.

86. A.S.A.-E.E.R., 8 June 1889, *Discards*.

87. J.M.A.-E.E.R., 21 May [1890], *Addl 1890/2*.

88. Letters to Ann Shaen, William's sister, disappear from the collections in the early nineties. One presumes she died about this time.

89. C.W.R.-E.J. Blake, 18 Sept. 1891, *Addl 1891/15*.

90. E.E.R.-C.W.R., [*c.* Apr. 1884], *Discards*.

91. J.M.A.-E.E.R., 15 Oct. 1888, *Box of Misc. Letters*.

92. Ann E. Atkinson–Dorothy K. Richmond, 5 May 1890, Jinny Atkinson Coll.

93. Emma Richmond had been elected to the Taranaki Education Board in 1886 where she fought 'so far without success for the prohibition of corporal punishment for girls'. (H.R.R.-J.C.R., 2 Nov. 1886, *Addl 1886/15*.)

94. Ann E. Atkinson–Dorothy K. Richmond, 14 Dec. 1890, Jinny Atkinson Coll.

95. J.M.A.-E.E.R., 15 Sept. 1888, *Addl 1888/6*.

96. *ibid.*, 27 Sept. [1887], *Addl 1887/8*.

97. *ibid.*, 21 May [1890], *Addl 1890/2*.

98. C.W.R.-Alice Blake, 30 Nov. 1893, *Addl 1893/12*.

99. The 1890 maritime strike scarcely touched Nelson. Trains kept on running, the Collingwood coal mine supplied gas; the only sign of industrial dispute was an increase in the price of bread.

100. J.M.A.-E.E.R., 26 Sept. 1890, *Addl 1890/10*.

101. Both sides of the House agreed that a grant of £3,000 be paid to Annie. C.W. Richmond was appointed a trustee.

102. A.S.A.-E.E.R., 7 July 1892, *Addl 1892/4*.

103. Richard Seddon became prime minister in 1893.

104. C.W.R.-Alice Blake, 9 Aug. 1893, *Addl 1893/6*.

105. C.W.R.-Alice Blake, 26 Sept. 1893, *Addl 1893/9*.

106. *Colonist*, 26 Sept. 1893.

107. *idem.*

108. *Colonist*, 11 Sept. 1893.

109. Robert Stout, John Duthie, F.D.H. Bell; all were elected.

110. A.R. Atkinson fought for total prohibition. In an article in the *Citizen*, he castigated 'sober Christian drinkers' 'drink-selling Christian merchants', 'smug teetotallers' – 'those licensed houses where the poor are robbed are yours in so far as you do not endeavour to preach or vote them out'. (Atkinson, Arthur R., 'Christianity and the Liquor Traffic', in the *Citizen*, Vol.1, No.5, Jan. 1896, p.215.)

111. J.M.A.-E.E.R., 5 Aug. 1896, *Addl 1896/1*.

112. Arthur R. Atkinson–A.S.A., 18 July 1896, Arthur Richmond Atkinson Papers MS 204 (ATL), Letterbook 8a, p.7.

113. J.M.A.-E.E.R., 24 Oct. 1896, *Addl 1896/4*.

114. Arthur R. Atkinson–J.M.A., 11 Sept. 1896, Arthur Richmond Atkinson Papers MS 204, Letterbook 8a, p.33.

115. J.M.A.-E.E.R., 20 Dec. 1896, *Addl 1896/6*.

116. Anna Richmond died, 8 July 1912, in her fifty-eighth year.

117. C.W.R.-E.E.R., 19 Jan. 1895, *Addl 1895/1a*.

118. J.M.A.-E.E.R., 2 Aug [1895], Richmond Family Papers, Box 9.

119. J.C. Richmond had had the satisfaction of seeing his Married Women's Property Bill, defeated when he introduced it in 1870, become law in 1884.

120. Ann E. Richmond–A.S.A., 5 May 1898, Jinny Atkinson Coll..

121. J.M.A.-E.E.R., 11 Apr. 1897, *Addl 1897/3*.

122. H.M.W. (Hal), Atkinson, the younger boy of Alla and Tudor's four children, has given a wonderfully evocative description of his and his brother Esmond's childhood at Rangiuru-by-the-sea, near the mouth of the Otaki River. (*Artist and Botanist: The Life and Work of Esmond Atkinson*, Moore, J.L. (ed) (A.H. & A.W. Reed, 1946) pp.10–15.

123. J.M.A.–E.E.R., 27 Sept. 1896, *Addl 1896/2.*

124. *ibid.*, 9 Aug. [1898], Richmond Family Papers, Acc 84–56 (ATL) Box 3.

125. A.S.A.–editor *Evening Post*, 19 Oct. 1894.

126. Hocken, T.M., *A Bibliography of the Literature Relating to New Zealand* (Government Printer, 1909).

127. Ann E. Atkinson–A.S.A., 7 Aug. 1893, *Addl 1893/5.*

128. J.M.A.–E.E.R., 5 Aug. 1896, *Addl 1896/1.*

129. John Gully died 1 Nov. 1888.

130. J.M.A.–Dorothy K. Richmond, 19 Nov. 1899, Jinny Atkinson Coll.

131. J.M.A.–E.E.R., 20 Dec. 1896, *Addl 1896/6.*

132. Lily May Kirk, daughter of the botanist Thomas Kirk and his wife, Sarah, was born 29 March 1866, and raised on Baptist convictions and social service. She joined the WCTU at its inception and was elected recording secretary; she was dominion recording secretary in 1889 and dominion president in 1901. She led the campaign for women's suffrage in the Wellington province. Before and after her marriage she was an organiser and a speaker for the NZ Alliance and for women's causes.

133. Arthur R. Atkinson–Miss Shaen, 24 Feb. 1900, Arthur Richmond Atkinson Papers MS 204, Letterbook 8, p.213.

134. He had fought and lost a by-election for Wellington Suburbs in 1897.

135. Arthur R. Atkinson–J.M.A., 20 Aug. 1898, Arthur Richmond Atkinson Papers MS 204, Letterbook 8a, p.340.

136. Ann E. Atkinson–Dorothy K. Richmond, 14 Oct. 1901, Jinny Atkinson Coll..

137. *idem.*

138. Ann E. Atkinson–Dorothy K. Richmond, 6 Nov. 1901, Jinny Atkinson Coll.

139. *ibid.*, 28 Nov. 1901, Jinny Atkinson Coll.

140. Ann E. Atkinson–Dorothy K. Richmond, 9 Dec. 1902, Jinny Atkinson Coll.

141. *ibid.*, 28 Oct. 1902, Jinny Atkinson Coll.

142. Arthur R. Atkinson–J.M.A. 29 Jan. 1902, Arthur Richmond Atkinson Papers, Letterbook 8, p.416.

143. Ann E. Atkinson–Dorothy K. Richmond, 1 Mar. 1903, Jinny Atkinson Coll.

144. *idem.*

145. *ibid.*, 6 May 1903, Jinny Atkinson Coll.

146. *ibid.*, 5 July 1903, Jinny Atkinson Coll.

147. Mary E. Richmond, quoted in *Evening Post*, 8 Apr. 1911.

148. E.E.R.–J.M.A., 13 Oct. 1906, Richmond Family Papers, Box 6.

149. Christopher F. Richmond–Mary E. Richmond, 30 Nov. 1906, Richmond Family Papers, Box 13.

150. There were 72 notebook diaries; some are now missing. Jinny Atkinson Coll.

151. J.M.A.–Ann E. Atkinson, 24 Aug. [1903], Jinny Atkinson Coll.

152. Dorothy K. Richmond–Mary Atkinson (Alla's daughter), 2 Sept. 1914, Jinny Atkinson Coll.

Index